To Anna,
with warmest regards,
[signature]
Hong Kong
October 2006

LAW IN EAST ASIA SERIES

CHINA'S PSYCHIATRIC INQUISITION

**Dissent, Psychiatry and the Law in
Post-1949 China**

ROBIN MUNRO

Wildy, Simmonds & Hill

Copyright © 2006 by Robin Munro

China's Psychiatric Inquisition

British Library Cataloguing-in-Publication Data:
A catalogue record for this book is available from The British Library

ISBN 1-898029 85 7

All rights reserved. No part of this publication may be reproduced, stored in a retrieval system, or transmitted, in any form or by any means, electronic, mechanical, photocopying, recording, or otherwise, without the consent of the copyright owners, application for which should be addressed to the publisher. Such a written permission must also be obtained before any part of this publication is stored in a retrieval system of any nature.

First published in 2006 by

Wildy, Simmonds & Hill Publishing Ltd.
58 Carey Street, London WC2A 2JB
England

Foreword

Political Abuse of Psychiatry: Reflections on the Soviet and Chinese Experiences
Richard J. Bonnie *

Robin Munro's comprehensive study of political abuse of psychiatry in China, more than ten years in the making, is a remarkable book in many ways. It is first of all a prodigious scholarly achievement, assembling an extraordinary body of written evidence regarding a social practice that is by nature administered in the shadows in a heavily censored political culture. Secondly, it tells a remarkable story, embedding the changing uses of psychiatric coercion in the dizzying chronicle of Chinese political history over the last half century. Thirdly, unlike the vast majority of historical investigations, it has immediate geopolitical relevance, as democratic nations and world psychiatry decide whether the Chinese regime should be called to account for repressive use of psychiatric hospitalization. The purpose of this foreword is to place Munro's research in the larger context of political abuse of psychiatry, particularly its now-undisputed occurrence in the former Soviet Union during the 1970s and 1980s.

Complexities

On first glance, political abuse of psychiatry appears to represent a straightforward and uncomplicated story – the deployment of medicine as an instrument of repression. Psychiatric incarceration of mentally healthy people is uniformly understood to be a particularly pernicious form of repression because it uses the powerful tools of medicine as modalities of punishment, and it compounds an affront to human rights with deception and fraud. Doctors who allow themselves to be used in this way (certainly as collaborators, but even as victims of intimidation) betray the trust of their fellow man and breach their most basic ethical obligations as professionals.

When the story is so straightforward, political abuse of psychiatry is universally condemned. Even regimes that sponsor psychiatric repression find it morally embarrassing to admit that they engage in such a corrupt practice. When the Soviet Union was defending its suppression of political and religious dissent, it steadfastly denied allegations of psychiatric repression – allegations that have now been well-documented[1, 2] and are no longer contested by the psychiatric leadership in Russia and other post-Soviet states.[3]

---

*   This preface has been adapted from RJ Bonnie, Political Abuse of Psychiatry in the Soviet Union and in China: Complexities and Controversies, *Journal of the American Academy of Psychiatry and the Law*, 30: 136-144 (2002). Richard J. Bonnie is the John S. Battle Professor of Law and Director of the University of Virginia Institute of Law, Psychiatry and Public Policy.

1   Report of the U.S. Delegation to Assess Recent Changes in Soviet Psychiatry, July 12, 1989, together with the Soviet response, reprinted in *Schizophrenia Bulletin*, 15 (Supp): 1-216, 1989.
2   Smith T: No *Asylum: State Psychiatric Repression in the Former USSR*. New York: New York University Press, 1996.
3   Bonnie R and Polubinskaya S: Unraveling Soviet Psychiatry. *The Journal of Contemporary Legal Issues* 10: 279-298, 1999.

If this were the whole story, political abuse of psychiatry would take its odious place alongside torture and other abuses of state power and perversions of medical ethics, but it would not be deeply interesting, either morally or sociologically. However, corruption is *not* the whole story, and political abuse of psychiatry is more complicated than it first appears. Most importantly, whether the dissident individuals subjected to psychiatric confinement are (or are not) mentally ill is often contestable, especially when culturally embedded features of psychopathology are taken into account. The mental health of dissidents could be contested even if diagnoses were grounded in a single internationally recognized system of classification, but the problem is all the more complicated when psychiatrists in different societies are trained to understand normality and psychopathology in different ways. Taking into account culturally linked ambiguities in psychiatric diagnosis, it seems likely that at least some cases of alleged abuse represent good faith efforts by psychiatrists to apply prevailing psychiatric knowledge in politically repressive societies. Thus, two explanations compete for attention in cases of political abuse – corruption and culture.

There is also a second complicating factor. In the "uncomplicated story," human rights and medical ethics are perfectly aligned. Intentional misdiagnosis and naked psychiatric punishment amount to simultaneous violations of human rights and breaches of medical ethics. But what is the normative significance of the fact that some people apprehended for dissident conduct are mentally ill? From a human rights perspective, criminal intervention in such cases is still a violation of human rights because the state has no legitimate authority to arrest anyone for political or religious expression; whether or not the person is mentally ill, the conduct itself may not be proscribed or punished. Moreover, under contemporary principles of mental health law, codified in many countries, a person with mental illness is not properly subject to coerced treatment *solely* for non-dangerous political or religious expression; this is because such a person does not represent a sufficiently serious threat to himself or others to justify the use of coercion. However, it is by no means clear that a physician is behaving *unethically* if she treats a mentally ill person involuntarily to ameliorate a serious condition that happens to be manifested by political or religious expression; coerced treatment may be a justified exercise of paternalism in such cases, especially if the patient lacks the capacity to make a rational treatment decision.

These two issues – cross-cultural ambiguities of psychiatric diagnosis, and divergent norms of human rights and medical ethics – explain why recent allegations of political abuse of psychiatry in China – allegations strongly supported by the extensive research reported by Robin Munro in this book and in prior publications[4] – have stirred up so much controversy. In this brief essay, I will reflect on the connection between the Soviet and Chinese experiences and the evolution of mental health law and ethics in the United States.

Soviet Psychiatry

Beginning in the early 1970s reports began to reach the West that political and religious dissidents were being incarcerated in maximum-security psychiatric hospitals in the Soviet Union without any medical justification. In 1977, the World Psychiatric Association condemned the Soviet Union for this practice, and six years later, the All-Union Society of Neuropathologists and Psychiatrists resigned from the WPA rather than face almost certain expulsion. Throughout this period, while reports of continued repression multiplied, Soviet psychiatric officials denied the charges of abuse and refused

---

4   See, for example, Judicial Psychiatry in China and its Political Abuses. *Columbia Journal of Asian Law* 14: 1-128, 2000.

to permit international bodies to see the patients and hospitals in question.[5, 6] In 1989, however, the stonewalling of Soviet psychiatry was overtaken by *glasnost* and *perestroika.* Over the objection of the psychiatric leadership, the Soviet government allowed a delegation of psychiatrists from the United States, representing the U.S. Government, to conduct extensive interviews of suspected victims of abuse.

The 1989 investigation had two major components. Some members of the delegation conducted intensive clinical interviews with 27 patients whose names had been provided to the delegation by various human rights organizations as well as the U.S. Helsinki Commission and the State Department. Three clinical teams administered standardized psychiatric interview instruments incorporating internationally accepted diagnostic criteria and also interviewed each subject on the forensic and human rights aspects of the case. Separate interviews were also conducted with family members. Soviet psychiatrists were permitted to observe the interview if the subject consented. The entire interview protocol usually took one full day. Meanwhile, other delegation members made site visits to hospitals selected by the delegation disclosed to the Soviets only a few days before its arrival.

The investigation by the U.S. delegation provided unequivocal proof that the tools of coercive psychiatry had been used, even in the late 1980s, to hospitalize persons who were not mentally ill and whose only transgression had been the expression of political or religious dissent.[1] Most of the patients interviewed by the delegation had been charged with political crimes such as anti-Soviet agitation and propaganda or defaming the Soviet state. Their offenses involved behavior such as writing and distributing anti-Soviet literature, political organizing, defending the rights of disabled groups and furthering religious ideas.

Under applicable laws of Russia and the other former Soviet Republics, a person charged with crime could be subjected to "custodial measures of a medical nature" if the criminal act was proven and the person was found "non-imputable" due to mental illness.[7] Non-imputable offenders could be placed in maximum security hospitals (the notorious "special hospitals") or in ordinary hospitals depending on their social dangerousness. All of the persons interviewed by the delegation had been found non-imputable and confined in special hospitals after criminal proceedings that deviated substantially from the general requirements specified in Soviet law. Typically, the patients reported that they had been arrested, taken to jail, taken to a hospital for forensic examination, and then taken to another hospital under a compulsory treatment order without ever seeing an attorney or appearing in court.[8]

The delegation found that there was no clinical basis for the judicial finding of non-imputability (or for hospitalization) in 17 of these cases. In fact, the delegation found no evidence of mental disorder of any kind in 14 cases. Not surprisingly, 12 of these "patients" had been discharged between the time the delegation identified the people it wanted to interview and the time it arrived in Moscow, and the others were discharged soon after the delegation's visit. It is likely that these 17 individuals are representative of many hundreds of others who were found non-imputable for crimes of political or religious dissent in the U.S.S.R., mainly between 1970 and 1990. (It turned out that ten of the patients still hospitalized

---

5   Bloch S and Reddaway, P: *Soviet Psychiatric Abuse: Shadow Over World Psychiatry.* London: Victor Gollancz, 1984.
6   Koryagin A: Unwilling Patients. *Lancet* 1981:821-24
7   Baker J: Nonimputability in Soviet Criminal Law: The Soviet Approach to the Insanity Plea, *Law and Psychology Review* 11: 55-102, 1987.
8   Bonnie R: Coercive Psychiatry and Human Rights: An Assessment of Recent Changes in the Soviet Union. *Criminal Law Forum* 1:319-346, 1990.

at the time of the delegation's visit were actually severely ill individuals whose hospitalizations had been clinically appropriate, and whose inclusion on the human rights lists as "dissidents" had been based on incomplete information.)

The delegation also found conditions in the special hospitals to be appallingly primitive and restrictive. Patients were denied basic rights, even to keep a diary or possess writing materials or books, and they were fearful of retaliation if they complained about their treatment, about abusive conduct by the staff, or about restrictive hospital rules or practices. No system existed for resolving patient grievances.

Most disturbingly, the delegation assembled compelling evidence that medication was widely used for punitive purposes. High doses of anti-psychotic drugs were routinely administered by injection over a 10-15 day regimen to punish violations of hospital rules and to treat "delusions of reformism" and "anti-Soviet thoughts." In addition, medical records and patient interviews also showed that Soviet psychiatrists used a highly aversive drug called sulfazine for the ostensible purpose of enhancing treatment responses to neuroleptic medication. In the view of the U.S. psychiatrists, however, the severe pain, immobility, fever, and muscle necrosis produced by this medication, as well as the documented pattern of its use in 10 of the interviewed patients, strongly suggested that it had been used for punitive purposes. Other treatments, including insulin coma, strict physical restraints, and atropine injections, had been used for patients in whom the delegation found no evidence of psychosis or other significant symptomatology.

Although the most punitive cases of Soviet psychiatric abuse involved criminal commitments to the notorious special hospitals, it is likely that many hundreds, if not thousands, of additional abuses were effected through the non-criminal procedure of "urgent hospitalization," a process roughly equivalent to what is called civil commitment in other countries. Although a criminal commitment must be based on a judicial order, urgent hospitalization has traditionally been within the exclusive control of psychiatrists, and until 1988, was regulated only by unpublished administrative guidelines.

In retrospect, repressive use of psychiatric power in the former Soviet Union seems to have been nearly inevitable. The practice of involuntary psychiatric treatment presents an unavoidable risk of mistake and abuse even in a liberal, pluralistic society. This intrinsic risk was greatly magnified in the Soviet Union by the communist regime's intolerance for dissent, including any form of political or religious deviance, and by the corrosive effects of corruption and intimidation in all spheres of social life. Psychiatrists were not immune from these pressures. It therefore seems likely that a subset of Soviet psychiatrists, associated primarily with Moscow's Serbski Institute for General and Forensic Psychiatry, knowingly collaborated with the KGB to subject mentally healthy dissidents to psychiatric punishment, in blatant violation of professional ethics and human rights. In this respect, abuse of psychiatry in the Soviet Union had less to do with psychiatry *per se* than with the repressiveness of the political regime of which the psychiatrists were a part. Fortunately, democratization seems to have brought the most blatant abuses to an end, and reformers are wisely attempting to establish counterforces to prevent renewed collaboration in the event that a repressive regime is reinstated.

In my view, however, corruption does not fully explain Soviet psychiatric abuse. The pattern of abuse that has been revealed was too pervasive to be attributable to a few corrupt doctors. The U.S. delegation declined to speculate about the motivations of the examining psychiatrists: "It is not possible in this type of study to determine whether the [Soviet psychiatrists'] diagnoses were based on idiosyncratic medical considerations alone or if political pressures influenced their judgment, thus resulting in deliberate misuse of psychiatry for purposes of social control."[1] I believe that both of these explanations accounted for the observed pattern of abuse. In some cases, abuse was undoubtedly attributable to intentional misdiagnosis and to knowing complicity by individual psychiatrists in an officially-directed effort to repress dissident behavior. In other cases, the elastic conception of mental disorder used in Soviet psychiatry was probably bent to political purposes, with individual psychiatrists closing their eyes to whatever doubts they may have had about the consequences of their actions. (Depending on the psychiatrists' degree of doubt, of course, the one explanation blurs into the other.)

The roots of the problem lie much deeper in the attitudes and training of Soviet psychiatrists, and in the role of psychiatry in Soviet society. Repression of political and religious dissidents was only the most overt symptom of an authoritarian system of psychiatric care in which an expansive and elastic view of mental disorder encompassed all forms of unorthodox thinking, and in which psychiatric diagnosis was essentially an exercise of social power.

At one time or another, 24 of the 27 patients interviewed by the U.S. delegation had received a diagnosis of schizophrenia. Under the prevailing diagnostic system in the U.S.S.R., usually identified with Sneyzhneyvsky, the concept of schizophrenia includes mild ("sluggish") and moderate forms which are characterized not by active psychotic symptoms but rather by alterations of personality.[9] As the delegation pointed out in its report:

> Some of the symptoms incorporated into Soviet diagnostic criteria for mild ("sluggish") schizophrenia and, in part, for moderate (paranoid) schizophrenia are not accepted as evidence of psychopathology in the U.S. or under international diagnostic criteria. Specific idiosyncratic examples identified in the interviews included diagnosing individuals demonstrating for political causes as having a "delusion of reformism" or "heightened sense of self-esteem" in order to support a diagnosis of schizophrenia.[1]

In the mid-1980s, Soviet psychiatric officials began to acknowledge that a pattern of "hyperdiagnosis" had resulted in inappropriate psychiatric labeling and unnecessary hospitalization in the U.S.S.R.[10] It was therefore noteworthy that Soviet psychiatrists who interviewed the 27 patients concurrently with the U.S. team in 1989 found no current evidence of schizophrenia in the cases of 14 patients who were thought to be without mental disorder by the U.S. psychiatrists. However, it is also noteworthy that the Soviet psychiatrists nonetheless still retained *some* psychiatric diagnosis for most of these patients. In this respect, the U.S. delegation found continuing evidence of "hyperdiagnosis," particularly in the tendency to characterize these patients as having "psychopathy," a term that seems to be roughly equivalent to the general concept of personality disorder. Specific examples of "psychopathic" symptoms identified in the interviews by Soviet psychiatrists included "unitary activity," which related to a high level of commitment to a single cause, such as political reform, and "failure to adapt to society," which was used to describe a dissident patient who was "unable to live in society without being subject to arrest for his behavior."

One of the Soviet psychiatrists was asked whether a patient who had been sent to a special hospital for distributing anti-Soviet leaflets presented a danger to society. "Of course not," he responded, "everything the patient distributed can be read in the newspapers now."[1] As this observation implies, what had changed was the meaning of a socially dangerous act, not the meaning of mental disorder.

---

9 Sneyzhneyvksy AV: The Symptomatology, Clinical Forms and Nosology of Schizophrenia, in *Modern Perspectives in World Psychiatry*. Edited by Howells JG. New York: Brunner/ Mazel, 1971, pp 425-447.
10 Churkin A: Psychiatry and Politics (Interview with Chief Psychiatrist of the U.S.S.R. Ministry of Health). *New Times* 43: 41-43, 1988.

The end of political hospitalization in the Soviet Union was attributable to changes in Soviet politics, not to changes in Soviet psychiatry. Insofar as psychiatry is concerned, the symptoms have receded, but the underlying condition remains untreated, even today. [3]

Impact in the United States

My colleague Lynda Frost and I recently published a book on the development of mental health law over the last three decades of the 20th century.[11] One of the chapters we commissioned for the book was an essay on the reform of mental health law in Russia and other post-Soviet states in the wake of the political abuse of psychiatry in that country.[12] During the peer review process, a number of reviewers observed that the chapter seemed out of place in a book about the evolution of mental health law in the United States. I persuaded our editor that, to the contrary, the chapter belonged in the book for two reasons, both of which are pertinent here: First of all, Soviet political abuse influenced mental health law in the United States at a formative stage of its development. Second, mental health law in the United States has had a profound impact on the development of mental health legislation in other countries, including Russia, and on the shape of international human rights norms pertaining to psychiatric care.

One of the important aims of mental health law reform in the 1960s and 1970s was to bring coercive psychiatry within reach of the rule of law. Even though libertarian and therapeutic approaches to involuntary treatment continue to vie for dominance, everyone recognizes that psychiatric discretion to hospitalize and treat a person over his or her objection should be constrained by socially prescribed criteria and disciplined by independent external review. This is because coercive intervention, however well-intentioned, carries with it an inevitable risk of mistake and abuse. (By "mistake," I mean outright clinical errors or unduly broad applications of clinical or legal criteria; by "abuse," I mean intentional misdiagnosis or misapplication of the governing criteria – a possibility that arises in even the most progressive society because, after all, human beings are corruptible everywhere.). These concerns are greatest when the criteria for involuntary treatment are most vague, and when clinical diagnoses are most elastic and uncertain.

The risks of mistake and abuse are accentuated in authoritarian cultures (even if they are not politically repressive) because pluralism and tolerance for individual differences tend to push psychiatric (and judicial) judgments in the direction of individual freedom in ambiguous cases, while authoritarian tendencies push in the opposite direction. In addition, psychiatrists in authoritarian cultures are more likely to see people as "diagnoses," rather than as individuals, leading to less flexibility in clinical decision-making than in more pluralistic societies. These patterns remain evident in post-totalitarian Russia.[3]

The risks of mistake and abuse are further magnified, of course, in totalitarian societies, where the state has the power and inclination to bend all institutions to its will, and where the counterforces may be weak or non-existent, depending on the country's pre-totalitarian history. In the Soviet Union for example, the inherent tendencies toward mistake (broad applications of elastic diagnoses such as "sluggish" (latent) schizophrenia) and abuse (outright misdiagnosis) were not checked by either the

---

11 Frost L and Bonnie R: *The Evolution of Mental Health Law*. Washington: American Psychological Association, 2001.
12 Polubinskaya S: Law and Psychiatry in Russia: Looking Backward and Forward, in *The Evolution of Mental Health Law*. Edited by Frost L and Bonnie R. Washington: American Psychological Association, 2001, pp 113-25.

professional culture or the legal system. No independent professional institutions and no legal culture had ever developed before the 1917 revolution. As a result, the psychiatric profession (if that is the right word in such a context) had no control over its own training and no ethical autonomy. In fact, the training of psychiatrists was brief, superficial and dehumanized, leading to a well-documented pattern of hyperdiagnosis in all contexts, forensic and non-forensic, political and non-political. As I suggested above, political abuse of psychiatry in the Soviet Union was inevitable; the only question is why it was not more widespread than it appears to have been.

What was the impact of the controversy surrounding Soviet political abuse of psychiatry on the evolution of mental health law in the United States? The Soviet experience was significant because it provided a vivid illustration of the risks associated with unchecked psychiatric power, and the importance of erecting institutional safeguards to minimize these risks in the context of involuntary hospitalization and treatment. It also helped to shape the ethical understanding of the founding leaders of forensic psychiatry as a specialized discipline in the United States. American forensic psychiatry developed its professional identity and ethical autonomy at the very same time as the controversy about Soviet psychiatry was unfolding. (The American Academy of Psychiatry and Law was established in 1971, for example.)

Finally, the Soviet experience has helped to flesh out basic principles of medical ethics in the United States and world-wide. Consider the core principle that psychiatrists should maintain their clinical independence, and should not bend their opinions to the will of the state or another third party.[13, 14, 15] What are the implications of this principle for managed care utilization review and for a variety of non-therapeutic social roles that psychiatrists sometimes serve – e.g. the assessment of execution competence?[16] When are apparently therapeutic interventions illegitimate? Consider coerced treatment of sexually violent offenders[17] or of condemned prisoners on death row when the effect of treatment is to enable an execution to go forward.[18] Injunctions against basing diagnoses on political values or religious beliefs and against using psychiatric interventions for "non-medical" purposes have also been codified in various ethical statements issued by international organizations, including the World Psychiatric Association [14] and the World Medical Association.[19] All of these threads, as well as the principles of external review of psychiatric judgments, are woven together in the Principles for the Protection of Persons with Mental Illness and for the Improvement of Mental Health Care, approved by the United Nations General Assembly in 1991.[20] As Munro points out, what eventually became

---

13   World Psychiatric Association, Statement and Viewpoints on the Rights and Legal Safeguards of the Mentally Ill, as approved by the General Assembly of the World Psychiatric Association in Athens, October 17, 1989.
14   World Psychiatric Association, Declaration of Hawaii, as approved by the General Assembly of the World Psychiatric Association in Vienna, Austria, July 10,1983
15   World Psychiatric Association, Declaration of Madrid, as approved by the General Assembly of the World Psychiatric Association in Madrid, August 25, 1996.
16   Bloche, MG. Clinical Loyalties and the Social Purposes of Medicine. *Journal of the American Medical Association* 281:268-74, 1999.
17   American Psychiatric Association, Task Force Report on Dangerous Sex Offenders. Washington: American Psychiatric Association, 1999.
18   Bonnie, R: The Death Penalty: When Doctors Must Say No. *British Medical Journal* 305:-82, 1992.
19   World Medical Association, Declaration of Tokyo, 1975, reprinted in British Medical Assocation: The Medical Profession and Human Rights. London: British Medical Association, 2001, pp 539-40.
20   United Nations Principles for the Protection of Persons with Mental Illness and the improvement of Mental Health Care, (1991). G.A.Res. 199, U.N. GAOR, 46th Sess., Supp. No. 49, Annex, pp.188-192, U.N.Doc.A/46/49 (1991).

the UN Principles began with a 1986 report focusing heavily on the problem of political abuse, and highlighting the need for legal control over coercive psychiatry.[4]

The story of Soviet psychiatry came full circle in 1992 when the liberty-protecting norms of U.S. mental health law, and the core ethical principles of professional independence, were codified in Russia's new mental health law.[12, 21] Similar laws have also been enacted in a number of other former Soviet republics since 1992.[3] In sum, the abuses of Soviet psychiatry, and the deeper problems raised by unregulated use of coercion in psychiatric care, have been inseparably linked with contemporary developments in mental health law and psychiatric ethics in the United States and in the international arena.

Chinese Psychiatry

Before Robin Munro began to publish the fruits of his research in late 2000, information on political abuse of psychiatry in China was limited to the occasional case report, together with a large reservoir of suspicion. The pool of available information was very shallow, especially in comparison with the steady stream of reports from the USSR in the 1970s and 1980s. Munro's most important contribution is his painstaking and thorough review of the Chinese psychiatric literature and the official data on forensic assessments, which he has integrated with case reports and placed in the context of China's tumultuous political history over the past 50 years. His work presents an informative and persuasive account of the role of psychiatry in the regime's repression of dissent.

In light of the criticisms that have been lodged against Munro's interpretation of the data he has assembled,[22] I want to emphasize several points. First, Munro hews very closely to the historical record and the published data. Whenever he suggests that the data point in the direction of political abuse, he carefully acknowledges the possibility of alternative interpretations. His balanced presentation and interpretation strengthen my own confidence in the accuracy of his research and the power of the inferences he draws. Second, the major portion of Munro's research traces the role of psychiatry in China's political history from the 1949 revolution, through the Cultural Revolution and over the two decades following the Cultural Revolution into the early years of the millennium. The basic story line about political abuse follows this path. This point warrants emphasis because virtually all of Munro's critics have ignored this overall picture while focusing exclusively on his analysis of recent cases involving hospitalization of practitioners of Falun Gong, a practice that only emerged during the latter half of 1999.

Munro's account of the Falun Gong story is limited to case reports, and is presented tentatively. As he points out, the regime's all-out efforts to disrupt the Falun Gong, including apparently pervasive use of psychiatric intervention, reflects a significant departure from the patterns that had been emerging in political cases over the previous decade. In short, Munro's well-formed views about the ebb and flow of political abuse since the Communist takeover is accompanied by tentative and sketchy accounts of the newly-breaking Falun Gong experience. For this reason, the unsettled debate about the mental status of Falun Gong practitioners who have been hospitalized in recent years should not be allowed to obscure Munro's well-documented and important historical contribution on the history of political abuse in China over the past 50 years, especially its connections to the Soviet experience.

---

21 Bonnie, R. Introduction: The Evolution of the 1992 Law of the Russian Federation on Psychiatric Care. *Journal of Russian and European Psychiatry,* 27: 69-96, 1996.
22 See articles by Alan Stone, Frederick Hickling, and Sing Lee and Arthur Kleinman in the March, 2002 issue of the *Journal of the American Academy of Psychiatry and the Law,* 30:107-125 (2002).

Munro's research indicates, convincingly in my view, that the Soviet system of forensic psychiatry was transplanted to China during the 1950s and 60s, thereby placing a small subset of psychiatrists at the intersection of criminal prosecution and psychiatric confinement, and importing a smoothly oiled process by which psychiatrists found most offenders referred for assessment to lack criminal responsibility, and committed them for treatment without any adjudication or judicial oversight. (Lest the point be misunderstood, let me emphasize that this system of secure psychiatric custody was set up for all mentally ill criminal offenders, not specifically for political offenders.) Eventually, in the 1980s, China also established a system of maximum-security forensic hospitals (Ankang), modeled after the Soviet "special hospitals," for confining offenders who present a "social danger." Munro also shows that a substantial proportion of cases referred for forensic assessment in China involved "political" offenses, and that a high portion of these offenders were diagnosed as schizophrenic, found non-responsible and committed to the Ankang facilities. The proportions of "political" cases have varied over the years, in apparent response to changing ideological orientation of the regime, but the basic Soviet-inspired structure has remained intact.

Among Munro's most interesting findings is the high proportion of political cases among those referred for forensic evaluation during the tumultuous period in 20th century Chinese political history known as the Cultural Revolution (1966-76). For example, a survey of forensic assessments at a Shanghai hospital in 1970-71 reported that 73 percent of the cases were political. Even among mentally retarded people referred for forensic assessment in 1960-76, almost a third were being prosecuted for political offenses. A 1987 study of forensic assessments carried out at a Hangzhou hospital reported that the proportion of examinees arrested for "antisocial political speech" reached 54 percent in 1977, falling to 6.7 percent in 1987. Surely there can be little doubt that the prevailing political ideology was shaping forensic practice, as it shaped everything else, during the Cultural Revolution.

Munro's analysis leaves little doubt that the prevailing ideology also shaped forensic practice before and after the Cultural Revolution. He quotes passages from two forensic texts in 1983 and 1994 in which a distinction is drawn between genuine counterrevolutionaries and "political lunatics" (a distinction that became "grotesquely blurred," as Munro puts it, during the Cultural Revolution). Obviously, some mentally disordered people manifest their illness through "political" (or religious) conduct, and their beliefs may be delusional. In Chinese terms, they would be pseudo-counterrevolutionaries, not genuine political offenders. The underlying question, of course, is whether "political lunatics" are "really" mentally ill, and if not, whether the explanation for their diagnoses is corruption or culture.

Based on Munro's exhaustive research, it seems likely that a significant portion of these offenders was not mentally ill according to generally accepted international diagnostic standards. For one thing, it seems highly unlikely that the high proportion of political offenders found among forensic examinees reflects their proportion in the arrestee population. The proportion of political offenders referred for examination and found non-responsible is naturally higher than in the United States (because the conduct is not criminally prosecutable here) but it is also considerably higher than appears to have been the case in the USSR. The point is made even more compelling by the increases and decreases in forensic referrals in response to changes in the policy of the regime. Putting the Cultural Revolution to one side, Munro shows that the proportion of political cases seems to have dropped from 10-15 percent during the Deng era to only a few percent during the latter part of the 1990s.

As for whether the forensic examiners are colluding with the state, Munro also opts for the more complicated story. In addition to the examiners' fear of crossing the authorities, Munro refers to "the professional acculturation process, in which psychiatrists learn from the official medical literature…that certain types of ideologically non-conformist behavior are attributable to severe and dangerous forms of 'mental pathology.'" In addition, he takes note of the strong emphasis in Chinese-style Marxism on "correct thinking" and suggests that deviation from the prescribed line is even more puzzling to authorities and to psychiatrists than it was in the Soviet Union. The dissidents in China are more likely to be viewed as mentally abnormal because they appear to lack "any normal instinct for self-preservation."

To the extent that psychiatric abuse is a chosen form of repression, rather than a reflection of culturally grounded diagnoses of "political lunacy," we must also ask why the regime sometimes chooses psychiatric punishment in lieu of the labor camp, and why the use of psychiatric punishment waxes and wanes. This question has always puzzled me about the Soviet experience. Why, when so many dissidents were sent to labor camps, were some chosen for psychiatric repression? In a 2001 speech[23], Ukrainian psychiatrist Semyon Gluzman, who spent seven years in a labor camp for exposing Soviet abuse of psychiatry, offers this answer:

> Complete totalitarianism does not resort to psychiatric camouflage. Such was the nature of totalitarianism during the time of Stalin. However, Brezhnev's totalitarianism (which I would define as "exhausted or tired" totalitarianism) did not enjoy that absolute power, and for this reason, psychiatric repression was used as a frightening "super weapon" which was far more horrible than the usual prisons and camps.

The Chinese situation is more complicated. The Cultural Revolution brought on a period of "frenzied totalitarianism" including what the Deng regime readily conceded to be "excesses" of all kinds. Munro suggests, in a variation on Gluzman's hypothesis, that the new reformist orientation of the Deng regime would not allow them to "liquidate" their opposition, and that they needed a "more elaborate mechanism of inducing long-term fear" among their ideological enemies.

Another important part of the political equation of psychiatric repression is the lack of legal accountability. As already mentioned, a continuing challenge in all societies is bringing coercive psychiatry within reach of the rule of law. In China, as in the former USSR, purely "civil" hospitalization is an administrative practice outside the jurisdiction of the courts; it is not governed by law in any meaningful sense of the term. However, because criminal charges typically invoke the jurisdiction of the courts, one would expect some sort of judicial oversight of the process of forensic evaluation and commitment, however shallow it might be in a dictatorship. One of the surprising findings of the United States delegation in its 1989 report was that the procuracy and the courts simply ignored the legal requirements in forensic cases, making the entire process invisible and all the more horrifying to inmates and their families. One of Munro's most intriguing conclusions is that the process of forensic assessment and Ankang hospitalization in China, despite its official characterization as "judicial," is actually a form of administrative detention, since it falls within the discretion of the police and is not within the reach of judicial jurisdiction at all. The decisions by public security officials to send offenders to the Ankang, and by the Ankang psychiatrists to keep them there and to subject them to forced treatment, are altogether outside the rule of law.

Political abuse of psychiatry ended in Russia and the other former Soviet states not because psychiatry changed, but because the politics did – the totalitarian regime "tired," changed direction (under Gorbachov) and then finally collapsed. Notwithstanding the 1992 Russian Federation mental health legislation, coercive psychiatry remains largely unregulated and shaped by the same tendencies

---

23 Gluzman, S. Law and psychiatry: The Totalitarian Experience. *Journal of the American Academy of Psychiatry and the Law* 29:330-35, 2001.

toward hyperdiagnosis and overreliance on institutional care that characterized the communist era. There are hopeful signs of professional independence and consumer advocacy, but little has actually changed in the culture or in professional practice. The challenge of mental health reform in Russia and the other former Soviet states is a daunting one.[3]

There is no sign that the Chinese regime is tiring, or that economic reform will be accompanied by democratization in political life, or that its change in direction will lead to collapse. As long as political and religious dissent is punished, some portion of these cases is likely to be processed through the Ankang system. In this context, what is the most promising path of change?

The only plausible course, it seems to me, is to separate the two threads of the problem – human rights and medical ethics. We should assume that respect for human rights in China is not a foreseeable outcome in the short term. In the Soviet case, the Helsinki process gave the United States a powerful source of leverage for insisting on proof that repressive practices had ended and that all political prisoners and prisoners of conscience had been released from prisons and psychiatric hospitals. The 1989 visit of the U.S. State Department delegation "to assess recent changes in Soviet psychiatry" was a direct outgrowth of the Helsinki process, as was the Soviet desire to win readmission to the WPA. In the case of China, the international community does not appear to be willing to press the regime on human rights, so the path toward ending political abuse will not be through political liberalization. Instead, the only available path, in the short term, is through Chinese psychiatry, using the collegial pressure of international psychiatric and medical organizations.

In 2002, after publication of Munro's findings, the WPA General Assembly voted unanimously to investigate the allegations of political abuse. However, after an unsuccessful two-year effort to negotiate the terms of a site visit by a WPA review team, the Chinese side conceded that "some misdiagnosis [had] occurred" with respect to Falun Gong cases, and the WPA leadership decided that this was a sufficient response to the WPA resolution, over vehement objection of many psychiatrists and human rights advocates. In my opinion, the WPA mistakenly allowed the inquiry to focus on the Falun Gong cases rather than the evidence of systematic abuse of the Ankang system. I also think that the emphasis on "investigation" was a mistake. The Chinese side will never allow an "investigation" of the kind allowed by the USSR in 1989 when the regime was already undergoing profound reforms. Instead, the WPA's goal in China should be to induce the regime to change – specifically by declaring its agreement with the basic ideas that mentally normal people should not be subjected to psychiatric custody and treatment and that the Ankang regime should be brought within the rule of law.

It is conceivable that the Chinese regime would find it useful to dispel the cloud of professional embarrassment in the world psychiatric community. It could do this by sending the message to police and prosecutorial agencies that political cases should no longer be put on a forensic path. This would not end violations of human rights, but it would end the practice of psychiatric punishment. The regime could also send the message that psychiatrists in ordinary hospitals are not expected to hospitalize dissidents, or others who have defied the regime, and that such people are misguided and foolhardy, but are not necessarily mentally ill. Of course, I am assuming that the state has other methods of repression at its disposal, and that it could give up the psychiatric threat without abandoning its effort to suppress the movement. Again, this approach would not end violations of human rights, but it would end the practice of psychiatric punishment.

Would this be a victory? It would be a victory for Chinese psychiatrists, whose exposure to intimidation would have been reduced; it would be a victory for world psychiatry, whose professional solidarity would have been invoked and reaffirmed in support of the profession's highest ethical ideals;

and it would be a victory for political and religious dissidents whose willingness to stand up for their beliefs would no longer be devalued by attributions of mental illness. (Of course, some of the people for whom hospitalization is sought are mentally ill, and psychiatrists should not shrink from the ethical duty to treat those in need). The point is that psychiatrists would be emboldened to act independently. That would be a big step in the direction of establishing embryonic safeguards against future abuse. So too would be the enactment of the new mental health legislation that has been undergoing review and revision since 1985, as well as meaningful regulation of forensic psychiatry which would expose this heretofore invisible process to judicial scrutiny. The one bright sign in Munro's account is the fact that several victims of the Ankang system have recently sued the Public Security Bureau and the Ankang psychiatrists for wrongful detention and forced treatment. Although none of these lawsuits has succeeded, they have received extensive press coverage within China itself, as have some highly critical judicial observations. It is possible that the regime is allowing coverage of these lawsuits to signify a willingness to relinquish psychiatric hospitalization as a tool of repression and to accept the need for some measure of legal accountability. Time will tell.

In the meantime, the world psychiatric community must continue to press for changes in the practice of coercive psychiatry in China, and for greater accountability of a system so easily bent by the authorities to repress dissent. The evidence so carefully assembled by Robin Munro must be taken seriously and should lead the world psychiatric community to stand up for the ethical integrity of Chinese psychiatrists and to press the Chinese government to do the same.

Preface

This study examines the role and purposes of forensic psychiatric custody in China since the late 1950s as an adjunct means – alongside the legal authorities' more frequent use of arrest, trial and imprisonment – of punishing and silencing political dissidents, spiritual nonconformists, whistleblowers and other critics of official corruption or malfeasance. The principal questions addressed in the book are: how common have such practices been in China, during the successive main periods in the country's post-1949 history; how have these repressive practices been theorized and handled under the country's evolving criminal justice system; and why have the security authorities resorted to this, at first sight, uncharacteristically sophisticated form of state repression?

Citing a large body of previously unexamined statistical and case material found in China's official legal-psychiatric archives from the past five decades, the author demonstrates that the forensic-psychiatric labelling of certain kinds of dissidents and other critics of government policies and ideology in post-1949 China as "criminally insane," and the practice of detaining such people indefinitely in high security police-run asylums, has been considerably more widespread and common than it was in the Soviet Union during the height of similar abuses in that country from the 1950s to the 1980s.

On the legal procedural side, the book identifies the crucial formative role played by Soviet forensic psychiatry in the 1950s in training China's first generation of police psychiatrists and in establishing the notion that particularly flagrant or uninhibited expressions of ideological dissent could be attributed to severe forms of mental pathology. This view led, in short order, to the legal or judicial handling of such cases under the heading of criminal insanity rather than that of authentic crime. Despite the formal definition of these law enforcement procedures as being "judicial," however, in practice they are conducted entirely within the realm of police work and with no significant element of judicial oversight or accountability. They are thus characterized here as constituting a previously unacknowledged and especially severe form of administrative detention.

The principal reason why the Chinese security authorities have employed legal psychiatry so extensively as a tool against dissent since the late 1950s is traced in this study to the uniquely Maoist practice of placing extreme emphasis on the importance of "correct thinking" in the realm of politics and ideology – a habit which spilled over naturally but insidiously, during the post-1949 period, into the cognitively analogous domain of individual psychiatry. The author argues that the historically close cooperation between police psychiatrists and law-enforcement agencies in China in such cases is ultimately determined by the Criminal Law's insistence on viewing all forms of political dissent as constituting the most serious possible type of crime, and that it is unlikely to end until such activities have been decriminalized.

The principal significance of the book is that it introduces a whole new field of internationally acknowledged human rights concern into our, by now, otherwise quite thorough knowledge and understanding of the wide range of human rights problems that have characterized China's post-1949 history.

Acknowledgements

My sincere thanks go to the following people: my PhD thesis supervisor, Professor Michael Palmer of the SOAS Law Department, for his unfailing support and encouragement throughout the thesis project that led to this book; Professor Stuart R. Schram, for his warm guidance and inspiration while I was working on a previous incarnation of the thesis many years ago; Sir Joseph Hotung, for his generous financial support of the Senior Research Fellowship at SOAS Law Department during 1999-2002 that allowed me to produce the greater part of this study; Dr. Philip Baker and Lau Bing-sum, who kindly recommended me for the SOAS research fellowship; Professor Donald C. Clarke of the George Washington University Law School, who helped in arranging for the publication of my first article on this topic in the Columbia Journal of Asian Law in 2001; Dr. Jim Birley, former president of the Royal College of Psychiatrists; who provided me with generous financial assistance and much friendship during the later stages of the thesis writing; Robert van Voren, Secretary General of the Global Initiative on Psychiatry, and Professor Robin Jacoby of the University of Oxford's Department of Psychiatry, both of whom brought the subject of this book to the direct and active attention of the international psychiatric community; and Robert L. Bernstein, founding chairman of Human Rights Watch, for his consistent support and wise counsel over the years.

I would also like to acknowledge with much gratitude the kind assistance of all those who provided comments on earlier drafts of this book or on previous articles on the same topic: Dr. Jim Birley, currently a board member of the Global Initiative on Psychiatry; Richard J. Bonnie, John S. Battle Professor of Law and Director of the University of Virginia Institute of Law, Psychiatry and Public Policy; Professor Donald C. Clarke; Dr Frank Dikötter, Director of the Contemporary China Institute, SOAS; John Gunn CBE, recently retired Professor of Forensic Psychiatry, Institute of Psychiatry, King's College, London; Professor Michael Palmer; Leonard S. Rubenstein J.D., Executive Director of Physicians for Human Rights, Boston; and Robert van Voren. The responsibility for any errors of fact or interpretation in the book is mine alone.

Several mainland Chinese sources, who must remain anonymous here, gave generously of their time and information. Other colleagues, friends and professional contacts who contributed valuable information, insights or practical assistance of various kinds include Paul Appelbaum, Jasper Becker, Sidney Bloch, Francis Deron, Ray Freebury, Ed Gargan, Abraham Halpern, Sidney Jones, John Kamm, Nancy Li, Liu Binyan, Sunny Lu, Declan Lyons, Ellen Mercer, Jonathan Mirsky, Hadassah Brooks Morgan, Lalagy Pulvertaft, Peter Reddaway, Jim Seymour, Paula Shaw, Mickey Spiegel, Wang Wanxing, Wang Junying and Sophia Woodman. My sincere thanks go to all of them.

This book is dedicated to my father, Alexander F. Munro.

Robin Munro
Hong Kong,
June 2006

CONTENTS

PART I: LEGAL CONTEXT AND OVERVIEW

1. Judicial Psychiatry and Political Dissent in China 3
    I. Introduction and Overview 3
        The Case of Wang Wanxing 6
    II. Outline of Research Contents and Methodology 15
    III. The Smoking Gun: Official Statistics on Political Psychiatry in China 22
        Table 1: Forensic Psychiatric Appraisals at the Yunnan Provincial Mental
        Hospital, 1960-97 28
        Table 2: Forensic Psychiatric Appraisals in 10 Chinese Journals, 1976-95 29

2. China's Legal Reforms and the Concept of Criminal Insanity 35
    I. China's Post-1978 Legal Reforms and Progress towards the Rule of Law 37
        Official Chinese Conceptions of the Rule of Law 43
        "Thin" and "Thick" Rules of Law 47
        Punishment without Crime 51
        Forensic Psychiatric Committal – A Form of Administrative Detention 57
        Better the Devil One Knows? 59
    II. The Legal Handling of Political Crime in China 61
    III. The Concept of Criminal Insanity 67
        A Comparative Overview 67
        Variation on a Theme – The Insanity Prosecution 73
        The Role of Due Process Safeguards 74
    IV. International Legal and Ethical Standards on Psychiatric Custody 79
        The United Nations 80
        The Council of Europe 82
        The World Psychiatric Association 84
        Cruel and Unusual Punishment 86

PART II: POLITICIZED PSYCHIATRY UNDER MAO

3. Law and Psychiatry from 1949 to the Early 1960s 91
    I. Judicial Treatment of Insanity Prior to 1949 91

II. Inauspicious Beginnings: The Early Years of the People's Republic 93
    The Serbski School of Forensic Psychiatry and its Adoption in China 94
    Three Patterns of Legal-Psychiatric Abuse 100
    The Cases of Lu Ling and Hu Feng 101

4. The Cultural Revolution 105
  I. Forensic Psychiatry in Crisis 106
    The Case of Chen Lining: "A Madman for the New Era" 106
    China's Forensic Psychiatric Inquisition 108
    The Case of Yan Weibing 113
    The Case of Mr. C 116
  II. General Psychiatry in Crisis 117
    "All Mental Illness is Political" 118
    China's Mental Patients in the Dock 122
    The Chenzhou Experience 123
    "Lancing the Boil": Thought Reform for the Mentally Ill 128
    Some Preliminary Observations 131
    The Post-Mao Counterattack: Humane Psychiatry Responds 133
    Refuting the "Ideological Defect" Theory 134
    Chinese Psychiatry Awakens from the Nightmare 138
  III. Medical Neglect and Prison Psychosis 149

PART III: POLITICIZED PSYCHIATRY AFTER MAO

5. The Legal Context for the Handling of Mentally Ill Offenders 157
  I. A Nuanced Reversal of Policy 157
    Table 3: Clinical Diagnoses and Types of Crime in 41 Political Cases 161
  II. Legal Norms and Procedures for the Handling of Psychotic Offenders 163
  III. The Psychiatrist and the Dissident: Some Thorny Legal-Medical Issues 173
    The Dangerousness Criterion 173
    "Presumption of Insanity" and "Lack of Instinct for Self-preservation" 177
    Civil-style Psychiatric Appraisals in Political Cases: The Case of Li Mou 182
6. Close Encounters of the Legal Psychiatric Kind 188
  I. Counterrevolutionary Behaviour by the Mentally Ill 188
    The Case of Mr Liu 190
    The Case of Wang Fumian 192

II. How to Distinguish a Paranoiac from a Political Dissident	195
The Case of Mr Zhu	196
III. Authentic and Borderline Cases: "Folie Politique"	200
The Case of Mr L.	203
The Case of Ms. Li	205
IV. A Theory of "Political Insanity" for the New Millennium	206
Workers Rights Activists	210
The Case of Xue Jifeng	210
The Case of Cao Maobing	212
Petitioners and Complainants Persecuted by Corrupt Officials	215
The Case of Zhang Gonglai	216
The Case of Huang Shurong	218

7. The Falun Gong: Chinese Dissent Goes Cosmic 224
    I. The Reappearance of the "Ideological Defect" Theory 225
    II. Legal and Medical Justifications for the Crackdown 231
    III. The Forensic Assessment of Falun Gong Detainees: Four Cases 237

8. The Ankang: China's Special Psychiatric Hospitals 241
    I. Background 241
    II. The Ankang Custody and Treatment System 245
        Involuntary Psychosurgery 249
        Criteria and Procedures for Admission to Ankang Custody 253
        The Case of Wang Chaoru 258
    III. The Victims Go to Court: Case Notes from the Ankang, 2000-2005 259
        The Case of Qiu Jinyou 260
        The Case of Han Zhenxi 263
        The Case of Wang Henglei 268
        The Case of Meng Xiaoxia 270
        Legal Debate on Meng's case 274
        The Case of Wang Fenglai 276
        A Legal Legerdemain 279

9. The International Campaign 281

10. Conclusions 297

Glossary 307

Table of Legislation 315

Bibliography 321

"Without a correct political standpoint,
one has no soul."

Mao Zedong, 1957

PART ONE
LEGAL CONTEXT AND OVERVIEW

CHAPTER 1
Judicial Psychiatry and Political Dissent in China

In the Soviet Union today, whoever takes a proletarian standpoint, upholds Marxism-Leninism and dares to speak out and resist ... is either arrested and imprisoned, or declared "mentally ill" and thrown into "lunatic asylums."
— People's Daily, 1964[1]

In the former Soviet Union during the Khrushchev–Brezhnev era, the KGB used its forensic psychiatric institutions to brand, arbitrarily and for political reasons, large numbers of political dissidents as suffering from "schizophrenia" and "paranoid psychosis" and then incarcerated them for long periods in "special psychiatric hospitals." In 1976, the Soviet Union was severely censured on this account by psychiatrists from all over the world at a conference in Hawaii of the World Psychiatric Association. Only after Gorbachev's rise to power were these errors rectified.

We have now discovered that similar practices have occurred in certain parts of China.[2]
— Jia Yicheng (China's top forensic psychiatrist), 1998

I. Introduction and Overview

Since the earliest years of the People's Republic of China, political dissidents, religious nonconformists, whistleblowers, and other dissenting citizens have consistently been viewed by the Communist Party as posing a major political threat to society. Even in today's economically more open China, such people continue to be arrested and imprisoned as enemies of the state. Until 1997, the criminal charge of choice under the PRC legal system was "counterrevolution," while nowadays the less political-sounding charge of "endangering state security" is most often applied.[3]

---

1   All translations of Chinese documents cited in this book are by the present writer, except where otherwise indicated.

  See "On Khrushchev's Phoney Communism and its World Historical Lessons (Ninth Letter to the Soviets)," *Renmin Ribao (People's Daily)*, July 14, 1964. This important article, a fifty-page "Open Letter" sent by the Chinese Communist Party leadership to the Central Committee of the Communist Party of the USSR, signalled the final stages of the Sino-Soviet split. The passage quoted above is said to have been written by Wang Li and Wu Lengxi, but Mao Zedong almost certainly edited and approved the entire article.

2   Jia Yicheng, "A Discussion of Certain Legal Issues Concerning the Hospitalisation of the Mentally Ill," *Shanghai Archives of Psychiatry*, 1998, No.1, pp.6-10. It should be noted here that the Hawaii World Congress of the WPA took place in 1977, and not in 1976 as stated by Professor Jia. For an explanation of the term "forensic psychiatry," see Note 4 below.

3   For details of the relevant legislative changes, see p.66 below. For further details of China's legislation in this area, see Human Rights Watch/Asia and Human Rights in China "Whose Security?: 'State Security' in China's New Criminal Code," *Human Rights Watch Report*, Vol.9, No.4, April 1997.

In a significant minority of such cases, however, the official psychiatric literature in China unequivocally records that since the late 1950s, detained dissidents of various kinds have additionally been ordered to undergo examination by police psychiatrists – a process known as "forensic psychiatric evaluation" – and have then been labelled as criminally insane and forcibly committed to various types of psychiatric institutions.[4] In essence, the question placed before psychiatric examiners in all such cases has been: are the detainees in question "bad" (in the legal sense), "mad" (in the medical sense), or are they – in certain borderline cases – a combination of both? Whatever the verdict given, in the authorities' view socially dangerous acts have "objectively" been committed, and so society must be protected from any further such threat. Freedom, pursuant to a finding that the forensic examinee is both sane and innocent, has thus rarely been an option for those concerned. Even today, the acquittal rate for people accused of political crimes in China is virtually nil, and if found non-prosecutable or not guilty by reason of insanity, dissidents dealt with under the Chinese legal-psychiatric system are in most cases sent for long-term "custodial care."

During the 1970s and 1980s, reports that the security authorities in the Soviet Union were incarcerating substantial numbers of political and religious dissidents in mental asylums aroused widespread concern in the West. As the quantity and reliability of the documentary evidence and victim testimonies steadily increased, the issue of politically directed psychiatry in the Soviet Union quickly became – along with political imprisonment and the refusal of the authorities to allow Soviet Jews to emigrate – a third principal item of human rights contention in Soviet-Western relations. By January 1983, a protracted campaign by Western psychiatric professional bodies and international human rights organizations to expose these abuses led to a decision by the Soviet All-Union Society of Psychiatrists and Neuropathologists to withdraw from the World Psychiatric Association, in order to avoid almost certain expulsion.[5] It was not readmitted to the body until 1989, after several years of *perestroika* and the preliminary establishment of direct access by Western psychiatric delegations to Soviet forensic-psychiatric institutions and their alleged mentally-ill political and religious inmates.[6]

---

4   The term "forensic psychiatry" refers to the field of professional cooperation between psychiatrists and the police or the judiciary. A typical example of such cooperation would be where police officers suspect that a detainee may be mentally ill, and therefore seek expert psychiatric opinion in order to ascertain the detainee's mental capacity to undergo further legal proceedings. Although forensic psychiatry is commonly applied, in China as elsewhere, within both the civil and the criminal sectors of the legal system, the focus of the present study is on its nature and role within the Chinese criminal justice system. See also Note 158 below.

5   Some historical context:

Twelve years ago, during the World Congress of the World Psychiatric Association (WPA) in Honolulu, the Soviet All-Union Society of Psychiatrists and Neuropathologists was condemned by the General Assembly of the WPA for abusing psychiatry for political purposes. Six years later, at the beginning of 1983, it was almost certain that later that year a majority of the WPA General Assembly would vote in favour of either expulsion from the WPA or suspension of membership of the Soviet All-Union Society. Keeping the honour to themselves, the Soviets withdrew from the WPA.

(Robert van Voren [ed.], *Soviet Psychiatric Abuse in the Gorbachev Era*, Amsterdam: International Association on the Political Use of Psychiatry (IAPUP), 1989, p.10.)

6   For full and detailed accounts of the political abuse of psychiatry in the former Soviet Union see: Sidney Bloch and Peter Reddaway, *Russia's Political Hospitals: The Abuse of Psychiatry in the Soviet Union* (Victor Gollancz, 1977), and *Soviet Psychiatric Abuse: The Shadow Over World Psychiatry* (Victor Gollancz, 1984); Theresa C. Smith and Thomas A. Oleszczuk, *No Asylum: State Psychiatric Repression in the Former USSR* (New York University Press, 1996); and Robert van Voren (ed.), *Soviet Psychiatric Abuse* (IAPUP, 1989). See also:

Why did the Soviet authorities resort to this obscure and, at first sight, rather improbable form of political repression, when they had at their disposal the fearsome resources of the KGB, a panoply of legislation tailor-made to criminalize all forms of open dissent in society, and also a vast nationwide network of prisons and labour camps[7] – all of which had been regularly deployed on a massive scale against dissidents of all kinds since at least the 1930s? The answer to this vexatious question is still far from clear, and it remains similarly elusive in the case of China. Scholars who have studied the Soviet psychiatric system in depth have generally been unable to reach any definitive or clear-cut conclusions on the matter. A useful starting point, however, is to look at how those at the sharp end of the system – the victims themselves – have sought to understand and explain it. In a justly famous *samizdat* article smuggled out of a strict-regime labour camp in 1974, titled "A Manual on Psychiatry for Dissenters,"[8] the leading Soviet dissidents Vladimir Bukovsky and Dr Semyon Gluzman – both of whom had received long prison terms for publicly opposing the political misuse of psychiatry against sane dissenters in the USSR (Gluzman was himself a psychiatrist and Bukovsky had earlier been psychiatrically incarcerated on spurious medical grounds) – offered the following succinct explanation:

> It is well known that in the Soviet Union today large numbers of dissenters are being declared insane, and there is reason to fear that this method will be used on an even greater scale in the future. It is not difficult to find an explanation for this phenomenon. From the point of view of the authorities, it is an extremely convenient method: it enables them to deprive a man of his freedom for an unlimited length of time, keep him in strict isolation, and use psycho-pharmacological means of "re-educating" him; it hinders the campaign for open legal proceedings and for the release of such people, since even the most impartial man will, if he is not personally acquainted with a patient of this sort, always feel a twinge of uncertainty about his mental health; it deprives its victim of what few rights he would enjoy as a prisoner, and it provides an opportunity to discredit the ideas and actions of dissenters, and so on.
>
> There is, however, another, no less important side. Dissenters, as a rule, have enough legal grounding so as not to make mistakes during their investigation and trial, but when confronted by a qualified psychiatrist with a directive from above to have them declared non-responsible, they have found themselves absolutely powerless. All this has, inevitably, engendered renewed fear and dismay in dissenting circles and is a reason for cases of unexpected "repentance" and recantation which have occurred in recent months.
>
> Forensic psychiatry has thus renewed the fear of persecution, which a knowledge of the law and skill in applying it had previously dispelled. A mood of resignation to

---

"Soviet Abuse of Psychiatry for Political Purposes," Helsinki Watch, (New York: Human Rights Watch), January 1988; and "Psychiatric Abuse in the Soviet Union," Helsinki Watch, May 1990. Besides political and religious dissenters, the other main targets of psychiatric detention in the USSR were ethnic nationalists, spiritual sectarians, labour rights activists, and Jewish people seeking emigration to Israel.

7   For a comprehensive account of this topic, see Anne Appelbaum, *Gulag: A History* (Doubleday, 2003.)

8   *Samizdat*, meaning "self-published", was the shorthand term used for any kind of dissident or officially unsanctioned literature in the former Soviet Union.

one's fate, a sense of one's powerlessness to resist this method of persecution, has become widespread.[9]

The subject of legal or forensic psychiatry in China has thus far received little academic attention outside of the PRC itself. A number of very detailed and informative studies of the country's general psychiatric and mental healthcare system have been written,[10] but these have rarely addressed the forensic dimension of the topic in significant depth.[11] In particular, very little documentary or other evidence has hitherto come to light suggesting that abusive medico-legal psychiatric practices similar to those that occurred in the former Soviet Union might also have existed, or might even still be found, in China. The general assumption has therefore been that the Chinese authorities, despite their poor record in many other areas of human rights concern, have at least never engaged in the misuse of legal psychiatry as a means of dealing with dissident thought and activity. The purpose of this book is to challenge and correct that assumption.

The Case of Wang Wanxing

From the early 1990s onwards, scattered reports from China began to indicate that political dissidents and other nonconformist individuals were being subjected to psychiatric appraisal by the police and then committed to psychiatric hospitals on an involuntary and prolonged basis. The most famous such case was that of Wang Wanxing, a worker now in his late fifties who had first been arrested in the mid-1970s for supporting the then officially denounced policies of Deng Xiaoping. Partially rehabilitated after the death of Mao, Wang resumed his political-activist career in the 1980s and became personally acquainted with the student leaders of the spring 1989 pro-democracy movement in Beijing. In June 1992, he unfurled a banner in Tiananmen Square protesting the June 4, 1989 crackdown and

---

9   "A Manual on Psychiatry for Dissenters," Vladimir Bukovsky and Semyon Gluzman, 1974; cited in Bloch and Reddaway, *Russia's Political Hospitals* (op cit), p.419. At the time, Bukovsky was serving a 12-year prison sentence for having sent detailed documentation on the psychiatric incarceration of sane dissidents in the USSR to the World Psychiatric Association at its triennial congress in Mexico City in 1971, and Gluzman was serving a seven-year sentence after becoming the first Soviet psychiatrist to publicly oppose these unethical practices. The two men hand-wrote the manuscript in conditions of great secrecy at Labour Camp No. 35 in the Perm Region, whence it was smuggled out to Moscow and then typed up and distributed by fellow dissidents in *samizdat* form before being sent for publication in the West. Bukovsky now lives in the U.K., and a collection of his documents on Soviet-era political psychiatry can be found on the Internet at: http://psi.ece.jhu.edu/~kaplan/IRUSS/BUK/GBARC/buk.html

10   See Veronica Pearson, *Mental Health Care in China: State Policies, Professional Services and Family Responsibilities*, (Gaskell, 1995); Michael R. Phillips, "The Transformation of China's Mental Health Services," *The China Journal*, No.39 (January 1998), pp.1-36; Arthur Kleinman, M.D., *Social Origins of Distress and Disease: Depression, Neurasthenia and Pain in Modern China* (Yale University Press, 1986); and Michael R. Phillips, Veronica Pearson and Ruiwen Wang (eds.), *Psychiatric Rehabilitation in China: Models for Change in a Changing Society*, Vol.165, Supplement 24 (August 1994). For a disturbing photo-journalistic portrayal of conditions in ordinary mental hospitals in China in the early 1990s, see Jurgen Kremb, "Wie ein Tier am Pfahl," *Der Spiegel*, No.32 (August 1992), pp.140-146. See also *Mental Illness in the People's Republic: An Exploratory Study of Chinese Experience*, Ph.D. thesis by Veronica Pearson, University of York, 1991.

11   For an important exception, see Veronica Pearson, "Law, Rights, and Psychiatry in the People's Republic of China," *International Journal of Law and Psychiatry*, 1992, Vol.15, pp.409-423; and "The Chinese Equation in Mental Health Policy and Practice: Order Plus Control Equal Stability," International Journal of Law and Psychiatry, 1996, Vol.19, pp.437-58

calling for greater human rights and democracy in China, and was immediately arrested.[12] His wife was subsequently informed by the police that if she signed a statement saying that he was mentally disturbed, he would be promptly released. When she did so, however, the police then placed Wang in an institution for the criminally insane (the Beijing Ankang special psychiatric hospital) situated in the outskirts of the capital, where he remained – diagnosed by police psychiatrists as a "paranoid psychotic" – until September 1999. In November of that year, at the end of a three-month parole period, after Wang announced his intention to hold a press conference with foreign journalists to discuss his ordeal, he was again detained and sent back to the same psychiatric detention facility. In August 2002, he was transferred to a ward holding psychotic murderers.[13]

From the early 1990s onward, Wang Wanxing's case and others like it became the subject of several statements of concern to the Chinese authorities by relevant bodies of the United Nations.[14] In January 2003, after no satisfactory response to its official enquiries over Wang's case had been received from Beijing, the U.N. Working Group on Arbitrary Detention reported its concerns to the U.N. Human Rights Commission as follows:

> Whether his detention is arbitrary or not depends on various factors. Against the detailed allegations of the source that the detention of Wang Wanxing was politically motivated (he was detained immediately after attempting to unfurl a banner in Tiananmen Square to commemorate the 1989 repression against the pro-democracy movement; Ankang Hospital is run by the PSB [Public Security Bureau]; his wife has been under pressure from the authorities to admit her husband's intense interest in politics; while he was out of hospital for a probationary period he was prohibited from contacting the press and people involved in the pro-democracy movement and from listening to international radio broadcasts) the [Chinese] Government did not submit any evidence or arguments to the contrary. Moreover, the Government did not provide information concerning

---

12   Several foreign reporters and television crews were present at the scene of Wang's arrest in Tiananmen Square on 3 June 1992. When Todd Carrel, ABC's bureau chief in Beijing, attempted to film the incident he was viciously attacked by a group of plainclothes Chinese security officers; in the course of this beating, Carrel suffered neurological damage to his spine that has left him permanently disabled.
13   Mark O'Neill, "Exile Plea for Threatened Dissident: Wife Fears for Life of Political Prisoner Transferred to Mental Ward Housing Murderers," *South China Morning Post*, 3 August 2002.
14   See, for example, Nigel S. Rodley, United Nations, Economic and Social Council, *Report of the Special Rapporteur on Torture, Submitted Pursuant to Commission on Human Rights Resolution 1992/32*, (New York: United Nations, January 12, 1995), General E/CN.4/1995/34. The report stated:

The Special Rapporteur also transmitted [to the Chinese government] reports he had received of persons detained in a psychiatric hospital for political reasons, where no medical justification was said to exist for their detention. The cases summarized in the following paragraphs concerned persons detained at An Kang Public Security Bureau Hospital[s]…Wang [W]anxing was arrested on 3 June 1992 while attempting to unfurl a banner commemorating the June 1989 demonstrations at Tiananmen Square. He was transferred to An Kang in July 1992, where he was allegedly administered medicine that kept him drowsy and weak. Although he was said to have no psychiatric problems, his wife signed documents confirming that he did, after being pressured to do so and being reassured that this would lead to her husband's early release.

According to the U.N. report, the Chinese government replied as follows:

An Kang hospital's psychological appraisals unit had determined that he was suffering from paranoia, that some of his actions were governed by wishful thinking, that he had lost his normal capacity for recognition and was irresponsible. He was continuing to undergo treatment at the hospital.

the legal provisions governing the admission to and the holding of people with mental disorders in psychiatric hospitals, the system of controlling admissions to and stay in such institutions by an independent body, be it a tribunal or a public authority, in order to prevent abuse, and the remedies available to psychiatric patients and their families to obtain a judicial review of the continued detention.

Since the Government failed to adduce convincing arguments or evidence to refute the allegations of the source, the Working Group cannot but conclude that the detention of Wang Wanxing in a psychiatric hospital for approximately 11 years is motivated by his political convictions which he has frequently manifested in public and to which he continues to give expression. Therefore, on the basis of the information available to it the Working Group concludes that, in the light of the particular circumstances of this case, Wang Wanxing was and continues to be detained for having peacefully exercised his right to freedom of opinion and expression, as guaranteed by article 19 of the Universal Declaration of Human Rights and article 19 of the International Covenant on Civil and Political Rights.[15]

Wang wrote numerous letters and petitions to the Chinese authorities during his incarceration, all of them logically well-ordered and presented, protesting his sanity and asking to be released, but to no avail. According to his wife, his daughter and others who regularly visited him at the Beijing Ankang, Wang at no time showed any sign of having any form of mental illness, far less one that would have justified his confinement in an institution for the criminally insane.[16] Throughout Wang's incarceration, moreover, the Ankang hospital authorities refused to give his wife any form of written diagnosis as to his precise mental condition or state; instead, they verbally informed her on several occasions that he was

---

15 See: "Civil and Political Rights, Including the Question of Torture and Detention. Opinion No. 20/2001 (China): Communication addressed to the [Chinese] Government on 14 June 2001 Concerning Wang Wanxing," 59th Session of the Commission on Human Rights, Item 11 (b) of the provisional agenda, E/CN.4/2003/8/Add.1, pp. 4-7.

16 For a detailed account of Wang Wanxing's case, see: Hou Jie, "*Wang Wanxing de 'Liu Hao Bingfang'*" (Wang Wanxing's "Sick Room No.6"), in *Beijing Zhi Chun* (Beijing Spring), November 2002, No. 14; full text available at: http://bjzc.org/bjs/bc/114/09.

Wang's wife, Ms. Wang Junying, and their daughter, Meixi, now live in exile in Germany. On a visit to Washington DC in June 2004 to publicize the plight of her husband, Ms. Wang issued an appeal statement on his behalf which reads in part as follows:

> My husband did not expect to be committed to a mental institution. If he were put in prison, there would be a definite term, e.g. 3-5 years. In a mental institution, there is no diagnosis. The family is not notified of the terms of confinement. That is, the confinement is indefinite.
>
> Wang Wanxing has already spent 12 long years in the mental institution. He has suffered immensely. His head was injured during a beating, requiring stitches. There are scars on his chest. He was assigned to help an elderly patient and [perform] other most filthy jobs. During these indignities, he upholds his personal dignity and strong beliefs: he does not fight back when beaten; he does not return verbal insults. He does this in an effort to avoid being confirmed as a mental case, as well as out of sympathy for fellow patients. He also saved a suicidal patient.
>
> My husband has told me many times that he sympathizes with his fellow patients. He does not react to beating nor verbal abuse. This is his strength and his greatness, under the most difficult and trying of situations.

(Complete statement available at: http://www.chinasupport.net/topbuzz85.htm.)

suffering from "political paranoia" (*zhengzhi pianzhikuang*.) During his long years of incarceration, Wang received personal visits from other prominent Chinese dissidents, including Wang Dan, Jiang Qisheng, Li Hai, and Xu Yonghai.

On 16 August 2005, shortly before an official visit to Beijing by the U.N. High Commissioner for Human Rights, Louise Arbour, the Chinese government unexpectedly ordered Wang's release from the Beijing Ankang. He was driven under police escort directly from the hospital to Beijing Airport and put on a flight to Frankfurt, Germany, where his wife and daughter had resettled as political refugees several years earlier. According to Wang, the last thing one of the Beijing Ankang officials said to him before he boarded his flight to Germany was, "If you ever speak out about your experiences at our hospital, we'll come and bring you back here again." Some weeks later, Wang was interviewed in Frankfurt over a two-day period by the present writer and gave a detailed account of his 13-year ordeal as an inmate of the Beijing Ankang. Human Rights Watch subsequently summarized this account as follows:

> For the first seven years of his incarceration at the asylum, Wang was held in a general ward containing between 50 and 70 inmates. But during his final five years he was placed in a special ward containing similar numbers of severely psychotically-disturbed inmates, most of whom had committed murder. According to Wang, the extent of patient-on-patient violence in this ward was terrifying. He frequently had to force himself to stay awake all night to avoid sudden and unprovoked inmate attacks….
>
> Although Wang had kind words to say about some of the doctors and nurses at the Beijing Ankang, he described others as being "basically sadistic" in nature. Almost every week, and sometimes several times a week, the staff would punish difficult or stubborn patients by tying them to a bed and administering painfully high levels of electric acupuncture treatment. All the other patients on the ward were ordered to watch the punishments being administered. For those patients who became physically desensitized after frequent punishment of this kind, the staff would rapidly alternate between low and high electric currents. According to Wang this method was as painful as prolonged exposure to a high current, and he once personally witnessed an inmate dying from a heart attack while being punished in this way.
>
> On another occasion, Wang says he witnessed an inmate who had been arrested and admitted to the Ankang for persistent petitioning activities, and who had gone on a hunger strike to protest his incarceration, being tied to a bed on the ward and force-fed by other inmates at the direct orders of the nursing staff. Instead of using a feeding tube inserted through his mouth or nose, the inmates simply poured liquid food straight into the man's mouth. As a result he choked to death on the bed. There was no outside investigation of this clear case of death from unnatural causes. Instead, Wang learned that Ankang doctors and nurses – all serving PSB officers – filed a report stating that the man had suddenly died from a heart attack. No staff member was ever punished for either of the two fatal incidents….
>
> As an internationally-known political detainee, Wang was treated relatively leniently, as the staff apparently feared that any severe ill-treatment would be reported in the international news media. Their anxiety was well justified. In 1993, a British television documentary team arranged for a Chinese woman from a European country to enter the Beijing Ankang on a monthly family visits day. Posing as one

of Wang's relatives but carrying a concealed video recorder, she interviewed Wang on camera in a private meeting room in the asylum. A several-minute segment of the interview appeared on British television shortly before the International Olympic Committee meeting to decide on China's failed bid for the 2000 Olympics. When Wang informed the Ankang staff that the television interview had occurred, they dismissed his claim as providing further clear evidence of his alleged "delusional psychotic fantasies." ….

Diagnosed with "Political Monomania" and Drugged

Since his initial detention in June 1992, Chinese authorities have consistently maintained that Wang suffered from either "paranoid psychosis" or "political monomania" – the later condition is not found in any internationally recognized list of psychiatric illnesses. Officials at the Beijing Ankang asylum repeated the claim in a "Summary Medical Report" which they provided to the German government one week before his release in August.

The medical report states that at the time of his release Wang was still suffering from these allegedly dangerous psychiatric conditions. While suggesting that he was otherwise quite normal, the report notes: "When the topic of conversation turns to politics… his [mental] activities are still characterized by delusions of grandeur, litigation mania, and a conspicuously enhanced pathological will." (The label "litigation mania" is often applied by Chinese police psychiatrists to citizens who persistently lodge petitions or complaints with the authorities about their past experiences of political persecution.)[17]

When interviewed by Human Rights Watch over a two-day period in September in Frankfurt, Wang spoke and acted lucidly and appeared to be in reasonably good

---

17 The full text of the official report was as follows:

Summary Medical Record

Wang Wanxing, male, 56 years old, of Han ethnicity, married, a lower middle-school graduate, of peasant origin, no religious faith. He was admitted to the hospital on 30 June 1992. Diagnosis upon admission: Paranoia.

During his 13 years of hospitalization, the patient has been medicated with drugs of the chlorpromazine group, and also with *niuhuang* to stabilize his overall condition. At present, he interacts fairly well with others, his mood is stable, and he obeys the staff. He enjoys listening to the radio and reading books, shows concern toward his fellow patients, and actively participates in work and recreational activities.

When the topic of conversation turns to politics, he displays impairments of thought association and of mental logic. His systematic delusions have shown no conspicuous improvement since he was first admitted to the hospital, and his [mental] activities are still characterized by delusions of grandeur, litigation mania, and a conspicuously enhanced pathological will.

The patient's physical condition is generally acceptable. Blood pressure 120/80 mm Hg; no discernible rales [gurgling sound] in either lung; heart beat 78/second, heart rhythm normal; abdomen soft, with no pain response when pressure applied or released; limbs and spine movement normal. Inspection of the nervous system indicates no obvious abnormalities; blood tests normal on 20 various counts; electrocardiogram result normal; chest X-ray reveals no conspicuous problems; all biochemical tests more or less normal.

psychological health,[18] despite the appalling experience of being incarcerated for 13 years alongside genuinely mentally-disturbed criminal offenders, well over half of whom had committed murder or other violent acts.

At Wang's request, the Global Initiative on Psychiatry is currently arranging for him to be given an independent psychiatric medical examination in order to evaluate the Chinese authorities' consistent assertion that he was "dangerously psychiatrically disturbed" over the past 13 years.

Throughout his time at the Beijing Ankang, staff forced Wang to take chlorpromazine, a powerful antipsychotic drug, three times daily. The nursing staff would watch closely to ensure that he had swallowed the medication. Unable to cope with the severe mental and physical side effects, however, he developed a method of concealing the pills in his mouth until after the inspection and then secretly disposing of them.... [In order to avoid unprovoked night-time attacks by other patients,] Wang used to take frequent brief catnaps throughout the day, and once a week or so, he would swallow several of the chlorpromazine tablets that he had saved in order to get at least one good night's rest.

The Ankang Regime

All staff at the Beijing Ankang, including medical and nursing personnel, are full-time officers in the Public Security Bureau, and all inmates are persons who have been detained for criminal offences committed while allegedly under the influence of severe psychiatric illness. There are currently around 25 Ankang institutes for the criminally insane in China; the government's eventual plan is to build one Ankang for every city with a population of one million or higher. There are more than 70 cities of this size around the country. The name "Ankang" means "peace and health."[19]

Only a handful of foreigner observers have ever been allowed inside these high-security psychiatric facilities. In 1987, for example, a WHO-led delegation briefly visited the Tianjin Ankang. But the great majority of such facilities are strictly off-limits to outsiders of any kind, including Chinese. The Public Security Bureau acts as sole judge and jury over who is compulsorily admitted to Ankang custody, and inmates have no right of appeal or even of periodic medical review of their cases. According to Chinese authorities, the average length of stay in Ankang custody is five years.

The patient is currently being prescribed a daily dosage of [figure illegible] mg chlorpromazine, taken in the evening, and two tablets of niuhuang per day, taken in the morning. We recommend that this treatment regime be continued, and that the patient be kept under strict guardianship.

[Official Seal:] Beijing Municipal Ankang Hospital - Medical Section

11 August 2005

18   Wang Wanxing impressed the present writer, who conducted the two-day interview with him on HRW's behalf, as being in a remarkably good psychological state, considering the severe and protracted ordeal he had been through. He came across as warm and compassionate, with a good sense of humour, and surprisingly free of bitterness or anger toward his former captors.

19   For a detailed account of the Ankang forensic-psychiatric custodial system, see Chapter 8, below ("The Ankang: China's Special Psychiatric hospitals.")

Many inmates are held for 20 years or more. According to Wang Wanxing, several of his fellow inmates at the Beijing Ankang had been there for 30 or 40 years. Moreover, these police-run institutions are subject to no outside scrutiny or supervision, either by the courts or by any other Chinese government agency. The names and current circumstances of most psychiatrically detained dissidents in China remain unknown....

Considerable international diplomatic pressure has been brought to bear on the issue. Wang Wanxing's name figured prominently on lists of Chinese political and religious prisoners that various Western governments were urging the Chinese authorities to set free or provide current information about. And, in the course of her visit to Beijing in August 2005, Louise Arbour, the U.N. High Commissioner for Human Rights, is believed to have raised the issue of China's increasing misuse of forensic psychiatric diagnosis against dissidents and others.

Over the past decade, the Chinese government has periodically released some of the named political and religious dissidents, but until August, all were sent into exile in the United States. In addition to being the first known political inmate of China's Ankang system ever to have been freed and sent into exile overseas, Wang is believed to be the first Chinese political dissident of any kind whom Beijing has exiled to a European country since June 1989.[20]

---

20   See: "China: Political Prisoner Exposes Brutality in Police-Run Mental Hospital – Eyewitness Testimonies from Notorious Ankang Asylum," Human Rights Watch, November 2, 2005. The two-day interview with Wang Wanxing in Frankfurt on which the HRW press release was based was conducted on September 10-11, 2005.

The news of Wang Wanxing's release from the Beijing Ankang and his enforced exile to Germany was widely reported in the international media. See, for example: Richard Spencer, "Tiananmen Protester's 13 Years of Torment in Psychiatric Prison," *The Telegraph*, November 4, 2005; Luke Harding, "In the Grip of the Ankang," *The Guardian*, December 20, 2005; Mark Magnier, "Chinese Dissident Tells of Abuse in Asylum," *Los Angeles Times*, November 9, 2005; Geoffrey York, "Chinese Dissident Diagnosed with 'Litigation Mania'," *Globe and Mail*, November 3, 2005; Annette Langer, "Psychoknast in China: Irre ist, wer aufbegehrt," *Der Spiegel*, November 21, 2005; Georg Blume, "China: Elektroschocks gegen das Virus Freiheit," *Die Zeit*, No.45, November 3, 2005; Associated Press, "Longtime Chinese Dissident Released," in *Taipei Times*, November 3, 2005; and Mark O'Neill, "Dissidents Tortured at Ankang" and "Psych Retort," *South China Morning Post*, December 5, 2005.

In addition, the Council of the European Union issued the following statement about Wang Wanxing's release:

Declaration by the Presidency on Behalf of the European Union on the Case of Wang Wanxing:

The EU welcomes the release of Wang Wanxing. He was on the EU list of individual cases of concern presented to the Chinese Government as part of the EU China Human Rights Dialogue which took place in Beijing on 24 October. The EU hopes that the Chinese authorities will release further prisoners on this list in the near future.

The Acceding Countries Bulgaria and Romania, the Candidate Countries Turkey and Croatia, the Countries of the Stabilisation and Association Process and potential candidates Albania, Bosnia and Herzegovina, the former Yugoslav Republic of Macedonia, Serbia and Montenegro, EFTA countries Iceland, Liechtenstein and Norway, members of the European Economic Area, as well as Ukraine and the Republic of Moldova align themselves with this declaration.

– Brussels, 10 November 2005; 14190/05 [Presse 292], p.126.

In January 2006, at his own request, Wang Wanxing was independently examined over a two-day period by a Dutch forensic psychiatric team at his new home in Frankfurt; the examination was arranged by the Global Initiative on Psychiatry. In their final report, the expert examiners concluded: "The main results of our examination are clear. There was no reason that Mr. Wang had to be locked up in a special forensic psychiatric hospital or in any other kind of hospital. He was not suffering from any mental disorder that could justify this admission."[21]

In recent years, reports of this type have become steadily more numerous, especially in the cases of lesser-known political dissidents, but also of hitherto quite unknown complainants and petitioners against local-level injustice and corruption. Indeed, cases of the latter kind have increasingly, since early 2003, become the subject of investigative news reports in the official Chinese media itself. (A number of these cases are discussed in detail in Chapters 6 and 8 below.)

In November 2005, the same month as Human Rights Watch published the above report, the German magazine *Die Zeit* presented detailed interviews with two other recent political victims of China's Ankang system – both of whom were complainants or petitioners, rather than political dissidents. Along with Wang Wanxing's personal account, the stories of the terrifying ordeals undergone by Qiu Jinyou and Meng Xiaoxia in Ankang custody were the first eyewitness testimonies of conditions in China's police-run institutes for the criminally insane ever to be published outside of China. According to *Die Zeit*:

> Qiu Jinyou was frequently subjected to electric shock treatment by officials at the Hangzhou Ankang, in an effort to make him reveal the names of fellow petitioners against corruption in his village. As a result of the frequent psychiatric medication he was given, Qiu said that his hair began falling out and he suffered from spasms and tremors, nervous despair, memory loss and forgetfulness, food intolerance, and other such symptoms. "The Communists are cruel. Inside the Ankang, there is nothing but terror and fear," said Mr. Qiu. "Not even the murderers there were treated as harshly as inmates of my category - people who had filed complaints or petitions with the authorities. During my time in the Ankang, I was tortured three to four times a week. I thought I was going to die there." ....
>
> Ms. Meng Xiaoxia detailed for the first time the system of punishment and forced medication in the Xi'an Ankang. She was forcibly held there for altogether 10 years,

---

21 The Dutch examining team consisted of B.C.M. Raes, professor in forensic psychiatry at the Free University of Amsterdam and the State University of Groningen, the Netherlands; and B.B. van der Meer, clinical psychologist with wide experience in long-term treatment of mentally disturbed offenders held in a high security forensic psychiatric hospital. The results of the independent examination, which took place on January 3-4, 2006, were made public in the following press release:

"China: No Medical Reason to Hold Dissident - Expert Team Finds Wang Wanxing Wrongly Sent to Asylum for 13 Years," Global Initiative on Psychiatry and Human Rights Watch, March 17, 2006.

See also: "Sane Chinese Put in Asylum, Doctors Find," Joseph Kahn, New York Times, 17 March 2006; "Dissident Held in Mental Hospital 13 Years is Sane, Rights Group Says," Kristine Kwok, South China Morning Post, 18 March 2006; and "China Accused of Locking Sane Dissidents in Asylums," Clifford Coonan, The Independent, 18 March 2006.

without even once receiving a medical or psychiatric examination. She was given electric shock treatment, with electrodes placed on her forehead, on three occasions, and she was also subjected to insulin coma therapy - a treatment that is elsewhere almost unknown today due to its dangerous side effects. More generally, Ms. Meng described everyday life in the Ankang as being one where inmates endured severe punishments on an almost routine basis, creating an atmosphere of constant fear and anguish among them. "The Ankang is like hell," Ms. Meng says. "I would rather die than go there again."[22]

The authorities' medically heterodox justification for forcibly confining dissidents, complainants, petitioners and others in high-security mental asylums has been that the concept of "psychiatric dangerousness" – the principal criterion used by psychiatrists around the world to decide whether a mental patient requires to be compulsorily hospitalized, and the positive determination of which requires that the person concerned be medically ascertained as posing a direct danger (usually physical) to self or others – must in China be conceptually enlarged to include acts or viewpoints which the security authorities perceive as posing a threat or danger to the established social and political order.

By the late 1990s, it had seemed that these abusive practices were steadily diminishing in frequency and could be expected gradually to disappear from China's law enforcement scene. From the second half of 1999 onwards, however, detailed and credible reports began to emerge from China indicating that practitioners of the banned spiritual sect Falun Gong were also being forcibly sent to mental hospitals by the police authorities. Over the course of the next few years, it became clear that China was undergoing a major new epidemic of the misuse of legal psychiatric detention for politically repressive purposes. In early May 2004, China Mental Health Watch, an overseas-based Falun Gong rights monitoring group, conducted a review of all such cases that it had obtained detailed information on since the start of the government's crackdown on the group in July 1999:

> The results show that in the past five years of persecution, psychiatric abuse of Falun Gong practitioners took place in 23 provinces, cities and autonomic regions. At least 100 provincial, city, county and district mental hospitals took part in this persecution. The persecution is planned, is systematic and permeates all levels of governments. So far, at least 1,000 healthy Falun Gong practitioners were injected with central nervous system damaging drugs and were tortured with ropes and electric batons. At least 15 practitioners were tortured to death.[23]

These disturbing developments highlight the need for a comprehensive re-examination of our previous understanding of the role and purposes of legal psychiatry in China, both historically and

---

22 See: "China: Elektroschocks gegen das Virus Freiheit," *Die Zeit*, No.45, November 3, 2005 complete article available at: www.zeit.de/2005/45/Gulag_HL

23 See: "Falun Gong Practitioners Suffer Mental Trauma and Death As A Result of the Jiang Group's Abuse of Psychiatry," Falun Dafa Clear Wisdom.net, 23 July 2004; available at: www.clearwisdom.net/emh/articles/2004/7/23/50560.html. See also: Minghui Net, "*Jianchi Xiulian Bei Guan Jingshenbingyuan Ji Shiyong Jingshen Yaowu de Anli Huibian*" (A Collection of Cases of Falun Gong Practitioners Sent to Mental Hospitals or Given Psychotropic Drugs for Persisting in Their Practice), 6 October 2003; full text in Chinese available at: http://pkg2.minghui.org/renquan_jilu/jingshen_list/jingshen.html.

See also, *Da Ji Yuan* (Epoch Times), "*Zhongguo Shang Bai Suo Jingshenbingyuan Jieshou Zhengzhi Renwu*" (Over 100 Chinese Mental Hospitals Accepting Political Tasks), 14 June 2004; available at: http://xinsheng.net/xs/articles/gb/2004/6/14/27512.htm.

in the present. All countries have valid and necessary reasons for detaining certain criminally active members of the mentally ill population (especially psychotic murderers, arsonists, and rapists) in secure psychiatric hospitals.[24] This also holds true in China where there are officially said to be around 10 million mentally ill people in the country, of whom some ten to twenty percent are regarded as posing a "serious danger" to society.[25] Under internationally agreed standards of legal and medical ethics, however, peaceful religious or political dissidents are emphatically not considered as belonging to this highly select category of people.

A close and extensive study of the officially published legal-psychiatric professional literature in China from the 1950s to the present day, viewed in conjunction with the growing number of independent case accounts of the kinds mentioned above, has now produced a substantial body of documentary evidence to indicate that the Chinese authorities have, in fact, a longstanding record of the misuse of legal psychiatry for politically repressive purposes, one that resembles in all key respects that of the former Soviet Union. The evidence suggests, moreover, that China's record in this respect over the past four decades or so almost certainly exceeds, in both scale and intensity, the by now thoroughly documented abuses that occurred in the Soviet Union prior to 1990.

Perhaps the most striking aspect of all the official documentary sources consulted is the high frequency with which they refer to "cases of a political nature" (*zhengzhixing anjian*) in describing the day-to-day casework of state-appointed forensic psychiatrists in China. Time and again, even in the most cursory accounts of this type of work, specific mention is made of "political cases" as constituting a distinct category among the various types of criminal defendants routinely referred by various law-enforcement authorities for expert "forensic psychiatric evaluation" (*sifa jingshenbing jianding*) – and even percentage rates for cases of this type are frequently given. Indeed, it was from passages of this nature found in the official psychiatric literature well over a decade ago that the evidentiary paper trail for the present study first began. In the Soviet case, by contrast, no such official mention or statistics were ever found in the relevant literature.

It should also be stressed at the outset that the extent to which China's psychiatric profession as a whole is currently directly involved or complicit in these abuses remains unclear. It seems likely that the misuse of legal psychiatry in the suppression of dissent in China is nowadays confined mainly to those working within the sub-specialist domain of police psychiatry – a small and still secretive field of which most regular Chinese psychiatrists appear to have little direct professional knowledge or experience. Despite the worrying numbers of Falun Gong practitioners who have been sent to mental hospitals since 1999, it would probably be doing contemporary Chinese psychiatry an injustice to suggest that more than a small minority of its practitioners are nowadays misusing their professional skills in this way. Over the past two decades or so, the wider field of general psychiatry in China has been moving into steadily greater conformity, in most areas of practice, with internationally accepted standards of mental healthcare diagnosis and treatment.

---

24 According to one source, for example, mental illness was the chief cause of crime in 20.7 percent of all cases of murder, injury, arson, poisoning and explosions committed in a certain area of China in 1982. (See Li Tianfu et. al., *Fanzui Tongjixue* [Criminal Statistics], Qunzhong Chubanshe, 1988, p.45). More recent reports indicate that mental illness-related crime remains a serious national problem.
25 See, e.g., Li Congpei (ed.), *Sifa Jingshenbingxue (Forensic Psychiatry)*, (Renmin Weisheng Chubanshe, February 1992), p.381. According to the author, out of three million mentally ill people in six central Chinese provinces, approximately 400,000 posed a direct danger to society.

II. Outline of Research Contents and Methodology

This study is primarily an attempt to reconstruct the shadowy history of the misuse of legal or forensic psychiatry by state officials in China as a tool of political repression – its antecedents, influences and general nature – and also to assess the degree to which the practices in question remain a problem in China today. In a nutshell, it is about Chinese citizens who have been sent to mental asylums by government officials for political reasons – either to punish or to silence them – rather than on valid medical or legal grounds. It also vividly depicts how a country's legal system, when allowed to become heavily over-politicized, can all too easily become an impediment to the protection of individual rights, rather than serving to guarantee them. The book is divided into three main parts or sections.

Part One provides an overarching introduction to the topic and describes the domestic and international legal frameworks within which it can best be analyzed and understood. In Chapter 1, we have thus far presented a brief account of the main ways in which legal psychiatry in China has been misused, as it was in the former Soviet Union, by police and other officials as a means of political repression, and the remainder of this chapter contains a detailed analysis of the official statistical data that forms the core of the evidence in this regard. The focus is on officially published statistics from China showing the surprisingly high proportion of so-called "political cases" among those brought for criminal psychiatric examination throughout China, and on documentary passages describing the various diagnostic theories and perspectives that are commonly applied in such cases. The chapter concludes with an estimation of the total number of people who have been unjustifiably sent to mental hospitals in China on the basis of these procedures over the past twenty-five years or so.

In Chapter 2, we examine China's post-Mao legal reforms and assess the degree of progress that has been achieved in establishing the rule of law. Among the key issues considered are: the degree to which the residual Marxism of the country's rulers has posed obstacles, insuperable or not, to the emergence of a fair and impartial legal system; the limits of the Communist Party's willingness to take a hands off approach to the courts and to allow law to acquire supremacy over Party policy; and the extent to which law and legality are officially seen as instruments or modalities of rule and control, rather than as goals to be pursued on account of their intrinsic worth or value, especially in encouraging a more individually rights-based society. Two primary systemic obstacles to the latter's emergence are discussed in some detail – the legal authorities' continuing proscription of peaceful and non-violent political opposition of all kinds as constituting serious political crimes; and the maintenance in the post-Mao era of an expansive system of extrajudicial, and thus arbitrary, administrative punishment and detention. Moreover, China's current system of criminal-forensic psychiatric custody is identified as being a previously unacknowledged, and from a human rights point of view the most severe and abusive, form of ad hoc administrative detention found in the country today. We then take a comparative look at how the concept of criminal insanity and the custodial treatment of mentally ill offenders is generally understood internationally, with the judiciary retaining decision-making power in all key areas, and at how these issues are dealt with in China, where the judiciary is accorded virtually no role in the assessment and committals process. The chapter ends with a discussion of the main international ethical standards currently applicable in the field of psychiatry and the law.

Part Two presents a detailed historical account and analysis of the complex interrelationship between psychiatry, law and politics in China during the Mao Zedong era. In Chapter 3, we provide an overview of the origins and development of Chinese forensic psychiatry during the 1950s and early 1960s – the period when Soviet influences predominated and China absorbed and adopted the main doctrines and practices of the Serbski School of legal psychiatry, notably the tendency to identify politically unorthodox views as being indicative of severe mental pathology; and we examine several of the earliest known cases of politically-motivated diagnosis and treatment of "criminal insanity" in the People's Republic. Also discussed are the three main forms of political psychiatric abuse found under the Chinese legal system since 1949: "hyperdiagnosis," or seeing mental illness in the case of dissidents where none existed; "hypodiagnosis," or ignoring clear signs of mental illness so that political enemies could be punished under the law; and straightforward medical neglect, as found most often in the cases of detainees who developed "prison psychosis" or of citizens who were driven mad in the course of China's seemingly endless post-1949 political campaigns.

In Chapter 4 we focus on the Cultural Revolution decade, looking first at the realm of legal or forensic psychiatry, where, despite the breakdown of the country's mental health system as a whole, large numbers of political nonconformists continued to be diagnosed as criminally insane and sent either to secure mental hospitals or to regular prisons; and second, at the wider realm of general psychiatry, where the consequences of Maoist fanaticism were to prove still more disastrous, with the emergence of an insidious new medico-political orthodoxy which sought to depict the mentally ill as being victims not of illness, but rather of their own "backward" or "reactionary" ideology. Previously unknown about in the West, this particular dire episode of Cultural Revolution history, representing the absurd apogee of political psychiatry in China, also provides a key to understanding the persistence of illegitimate forensic psychiatric practices in China during the post-1978 period. The chapter concludes with an account of how ethically-minded psychiatrists in China rallied and fought back in the late 1970s, eventually overturning the pernicious doctrines that had inflicted such damage upon the cause of mental healthcare in China during Mao's last years.

Turning to the post-Mao period, Part Three provides, firstly, a detailed account of the extent to which the Chinese legal authorities have continued, over the past two decades and more, to use involuntary psychiatric detention as a means of removing certain types of dissidents and other nonconformist individuals from the public sphere; and secondly, an exploration of the possible reasons as to why such practices are still to be found in China. In Chapter 5, we discuss how the official rejection of Cultural Revolution ideas and practices in the post-Mao period led not to the abandonment of legal psychiatry as a weapon of state repression, but rather to its re-emergence in a subtly different form. This chapter also provides a comprehensive account of the judicial and legislative framework governing the practice of forensic psychiatry in China: the criminal and civil law contexts, legislation on mental health and forensic-psychiatric assessment, the levels of determination of criminal "non-imputability" by reason of insanity that can be made, the kinds of offenders falling within the system's purview, and the extent to which the rights and interests of the latter are (if at all) taken into account and afforded legal protection. Also considered is the question of China's expansive definition of the key legal determinant of involuntary psychiatric committal, namely "social dangerousness." Whereas under international standards of psychiatry and the law, the applicable scope of the "dangerousness" criterion is restricted to situations where mentally ill people pose a direct physical danger either to themselves or to others, in China it is applied also to those, such as certain types of dissidents, whom the government regards as posing a political threat to "social order."

In Chapter 6, we present a series of detailed case studies of actual individuals who, for reasons solely or mainly to do with their peaceful exercise of the right to freedom of expression, have been diagnosed by police psychiatrists as being "dangerously mentally ill" and then incarcerated in mental asylums over the past quarter century in China. Also discussed are the several main categories of political and religious nonconformists who are especially liable to fall prey to these police-dominated diagnostic and judicial procedures: so-called "political maniacs," whistleblowers and exposers of official corruption, persistent complainants and petitioners, and also unconventional religious sectarians. These case studies also afford an opportunity to evaluate whether or not the individuals concerned may indeed, as claimed by the authorities, have been mentally disordered to any significant degree. While this is clearly a relevant issue, it should also be noted that those in question were in most cases arrested on criminal charges – and moreover for activities not held to be crimes under international legal standards – prior to being committed for forensic psychiatric evaluation. If truly mentally disturbed, they should have been removed from the purview of the psychiatric-criminal justice system and been given appropriate and humane treatment through the regular mental healthcare system. In addition, we examine a number of key texts, drawn from China's official legal and psychiatric literature, that seek to explain and justify the authorities' continued resort to these politically persecutory practices. These passages depict the close and longstanding cooperation between forensic psychiatrists and the security authorities in China in effecting the simultaneous criminalization and medicalization of certain forms of dissenting activity.

Chapter 7 describes and assesses the most recent phase in the Chinese legal authorities' misuse of forensic psychiatry for political ends: the crackdown against the Falun Gong spiritual sect, in which hundreds of practitioners have been summarily diagnosed as suffering from a previously unknown and allegedly "highly dangerous" form of mental illness, one known variously as "dysphrenia" or "evil cult-induced mental disorder." A particularly disturbing feature of this latest round in what had seemed to be a type of human rights abuse in sharp historical decline is that, in most of the reported cases of Falun Gong psychiatric incarceration since mid-1999, the police have made no attempt to follow even the minimum legal procedure for forensic psychiatric appraisal and compulsory committal that has been in place in China for more than a decade. Instead, in an apparent reversion to Cultural Revolution-era practices, the police have simply rounded up Falun Gong practitioners and delivered them directly to mental asylums, without any prior medical examinations being conducted; the psychiatrists and nurses at the mental hospitals concerned have then been ordered by the police to "treat" these Falun Gong detainees, irrespective of whether or not they show symptoms of mental illness. The result has been a legal and medical charade whereby mentally healthy Falun Gong practitioners have been coerced, through the administration of psychotropic drugs and other forms of involuntary psychiatric treatment, into signing police-provided statements in which they renounce their spiritual beliefs as a precondition for being declared "cured" of their alleged mental illnesses and allowed to return home.

Chapter 8 provides an introductory account of China's little-known network of special custodial centres for the criminally insane. Although several such institutions have existed in China since at least the 1960s, in 1987 the Chinese government for the first time decided to establish a nationwide system of high-security facilities for "dangerously mentally ill offenders." These, the equivalent of the USSR's Special Psychiatric Hospitals run by the Interior Ministry, were to be uniformly designated as "Ankang" (Peace and Health) institutions, and were to be directly administered and run by the Ministry of Public Security and its subordinate provincial-level departments. Arrested political dissidents and others in similar categories brought for assessment by the State's forensic psychiatrists are often officially treated as ranking among the most "serious and dangerous" of all alleged mentally ill offenders, and are thus prime candidates for compulsory committal in such institutions. To date, around 25 Ankang facilities have been built and brought into service around the country. These highly secretive institutions deserve to become more widely known as perhaps the last unexplored corner, and possibly the most sinister one, of China's extensive *laogai* system of judicial incarceration. A series of detailed case studies, published in the official media in China only in 2004-05, of persistent complainants and petitioners wrongfully held in Ankang asylums over the past few years serves to bring the account right up to the present. Also discussed is the growing use of psychosurgery within the Ankang system.

Chapter 9 describes the emergence and rapid development over the past few years of an international pressure campaign aimed at ending the political misuse of psychiatry in China. Since early 2001, professional psychiatric bodies and human rights groups around the world have begun calling upon the Chinese government to allow international medical experts to carry out an independent inspection of the country's Ankang facilities and other places of psychiatric custody, and to allow known political activists and others who have been subjected to forced psychiatric treatment to be given an independent medical assessment. In August 2002, the national member societies of the World Psychiatric Association voted unanimously to instruct the organization's leadership to organize and carry out such a mission of inspection, but more than three years later, as a result of the Chinese government's continued refusal to cooperate with the WPA, this initiative had still failed to materialize. But by then, the high level of international media attention given to the issue had succeeded in placing it firmly on the international public agenda. In comparison with the earlier campaign to end political psychiatry in the Soviet Union, which lasted for more than ten years before any breakthrough was achieved, progress in the China case by mid-2005 had been quite rapid and significant.

In Chapter 10, we summarize the main findings of this research study and also hazard some tentative answers to the far from easy question of why China's psychiatric community became drawn, from the late 1950s onwards, into collaborating so closely and extensively with the country's security forces in their implacable war against all forms of ideological heterodoxy and dissent. If one had to single out one factor among all others, it would be that Chinese Marxism, more than any other variant of the faith, has always placed an inordinate emphasis on the importance of "correct thinking and ideology" – or in other words, what goes on inside each individual citizen's mind.

A brief outline of the research methodology used in what follows may also be useful. In a book published in 1989, Dr. Semyon Gluzman, the Soviet psychiatrist who famously broke ranks with his colleagues in the early 1970s to speak out against the political abuses within his profession and then spent several years in prison as a consequence, proposed three different ways to approach the study of the political misuse of psychiatry.[26] Gluzman's "three methods of collecting evidence and analysing the situation" have direct methodological relevance for our present topic.

> The first approach is to personally and objectively examine those who were found non-imputable by reason of insanity after being charged with political and religious crimes… During such an examination, at least the following should be established. 1) Was the victim in fact persecuted for political or religious crimes? 2) Did the victim show any signs or symptoms of psychiatric illness? … 5) What is the internationally accepted standard of psychiatric practice in such cases (including the finding of "diminished capacity" in countries where it is in use?)

In Gluzman's view, this approach to establishing and proving abuse of psychiatry was both procedurally very difficult and also "not in itself effective."[27] However, he argued, "This work must be done: real people, victims of abuse, need protection and help, not academic discussion about humanism and justice." He continued:

---

26 See Semyon Gluzman, *On Soviet Totalitarian Psychiatry*, p.33-35.
27 "First of all, every instance of unjustifiable exculpation indicates only professional incompetence and the responsibility of a particular psychiatrist does not reveal an institutional phenomenon. Secondly, it is difficult to collect such information and therefore the proof cannot be complete. The many difficulties in obtaining all legal psychiatric documentation for an objective study make this approach very difficult" (Ibid, p.34).

The second approach should combine a systematic study of the precepts of Soviet psychiatric theory, consideration of the differences among different school[s] of thought, and serious discussions in which specific disagreements can be focused on, and expert statisticians can be consulted. In my view, this is a very effective approach. But I doubt that such a discussion is feasible because it would require commitment and patience on both sides."

Gluzman's other proposed methodology was as follows:

The third approach is very complex and laborious. It is necessary to examine an enormous number of Soviet psychiatric publications that are available in open libraries, administrative norms, regulations, professional guidelines, monographs, collections of articles, scientific journals, dissertations, etc. As far as I know, nobody in the USSR or abroad has ever undertaken such a study. The advantages of such an approach are self-evident; no "discovery" can be disputed and such "content analysis" will inevitably show who abused their profession and when. It will also reveal their theoretical justifications.

In the case of the Soviet Union, in practice, it was largely by means of the first of these methods – the individual case-based approach – that the problem of political psychiatry first became known in the West,[28] and this remained largely true throughout the subsequent campaign to end psychiatric abuse in the Soviet Union.[29] In China, the practical difficulties associated with this approach are at least as great, and probably much greater, than was the case even in the former Soviet context. In particular, the task of carrying out objective and independent psychiatric assessments of Chinese individuals who have been placed in forensic psychiatric custody solely, apparently, on account of their political or religious views is something that may only become feasible at some point in the future, if and when the Chinese government begins to allow direct outside scrutiny of its practices in this field. At present, in most cases, we do not know even the names of the individuals discussed in the official documents excerpted below. (The Falun Gong cases are important exceptions, though by no means the only ones.)

Similarly, in the case of China, Gluzman's second approach, that of initiating a direct and sustained theoretical dialogue between Chinese psychiatrists and their Western counterparts over allegations of politically-directed psychiatric practice, represents a highly desirable aim but one that is unlikely to be practically attainable in the immediate to near future. While all appropriate efforts should certainly be made toward establishing this kind of intra-professional dialogue, the key determinant to the success of any such efforts, and more importantly, to ending the abusive psychiatric practices at issue, will undoubtedly remain the political will and attitude of the Chinese government.[30]

---

28 That is to say, significant numbers of Soviet dissidents and others still managed, despite the politically repressive environment, to collect substantial numbers of individual case details on people placed in mental asylums on account of their political or religious views, and to transmit these to international human rights groups and the foreign news media. This has only recently begun to happen in China's case.

29 Gluzman's misgivings about the effectiveness of the method seemingly relate more to the subsequent, "post-mortem" phase of investigations into the Soviet case.

30 At present, the general signs in this area are far from being good: in recent years, despite the continuing economic reforms, the Chinese security authorities have redoubled their efforts to suppress all forms of perceived political or religious dissonance in society; and notwithstanding China's current participation in bilateral "human rights dialogue" sessions with Western countries and the European Union, Beijing continues to view human rights issues in general as representing a major "battle front" in its relations with the West.

Since the relatively closed nature of official Chinese society renders, for the meantime, alternative avenues of investigation largely impracticable, the principal methodology used in compiling the evidence of psychiatric abuse in China presented below has conformed, in the main, to the third approach advocated by Gluzman. The principal source of information relied upon has been the wide range of professional legal and psychiatric publications issued officially by the Chinese government since the early 1980s. These include a series of major textbooks and manuals on forensic medicine and psychiatry, legal studies dealing with the psychological dimensions of crime, journals and periodicals dealing with all aspects of law and jurisprudence, various national, provincial and municipal-level laws and regulations on the handling of mentally ill offenders, including rules for the involuntary committal of those viewed as especially "dangerous" to society, and several specialized medical periodicals, notably the *Chinese Journal of Psychiatry* and the *Chinese Journal of Nervous and Mental Diseases*.[31] In addition, a number of first-hand accounts written by former inmates of the Ankang system and other Chinese psychiatric detention facilities have been examined. To a considerable extent, therefore, the present study is a work of legal and medical archaeology.

Although the officially published sources contain, by comparison with the Soviet case, relatively little in the way of detailed individual case material and offer scant insight into the prevailing conditions of treatment and incarceration in China's police-run secure psychiatric facilities, they manifest in full measure the advantages referred to by Gluzman above. First, unlike victim or refugee accounts for example, they are, by virtue of their provenance, not amenable to disputation or refutation by the authorities. Second, they provide a productive source of information for a content analysis-based examination of the issues. Third, they afford major insight into the various theoretical justifications used by Chinese psychiatrists, in their collaborative endeavour with the security authorities to medically criminalize certain forms of dissent.

It should be emphasized that an agnostic position is adopted in what follows on the question of whether some, or perhaps even many, of the victims of China's "political-psychiatric dangerousness" policy are in reality suffering from some form of mental illness or impairment. The truth of this matter can be established conclusively only by the Chinese government agreeing to allow qualified outside observers full access to places of psychiatric detention, so that their alleged mentally-ill political, religious and labour activist inmates can be given an independent medical evaluation. It is entirely possible that at least some of those concerned will prove to be suffering, or to have suffered in the past, from conditions ranging from minor personality quirks or abnormalities all the way through to full-blown mental illness. We will return to this issue at various points in our discussion.

The bottom line, however, is that most of these people should not have been arrested or brought for forensic psychiatric evaluation (formal or otherwise) in the first place, since in the overwhelming majority of recorded cases their only "offence" was to have expressed views or beliefs which served to offend the political sensitivities of the Chinese Communist Party. Any of them who were indeed mentally ill should have been offered suitable medical care and treatment, on an outpatient or in-patient basis as appropriate. Involuntary confinement in mental hospitals (whether civilian or police-run) should be contemplated only in the case of those meeting the internationally agreed minimum criteria for mentally ill persons who pose a direct danger to themselves or others. The Chinese authorities'

---

31 *Zhonghua Jingshenke Zazhi* and *Zhongguo Shenjing Jingshen Jibing Zazhi* (formerly known as *Zhongguo Shenjing Jingshenke Zazhi*; for purposes of consistency, the latter two titles are both referred to in the present article by the journal's current English name, the *Chinese Journal of Nervous and Mental Diseases*). Each journal appears four times a year.

frequent imposition of this extreme measure on individuals (mentally normal or otherwise) whom they regard as posing only a "political threat" to society stands in clear and direct violation both of the World Psychiatric Association's 1996 Declaration of Madrid and of the U.N.'s 1991 Principles for the Protection of Persons with Mental Illness and for the Improvement of Mental Health Care.[32]

The real cause of the misuse of legal psychiatry as a tool of state repression in China today is to be found in the more intractable problem of the Chinese authorities' longstanding insistence upon viewing the peaceful expression of dissident or nonconformist viewpoints as constituting "political crimes" that must be sternly punished by law. Until this fundamental impediment to the observance of internationally recognized human rights in China can be removed, a small but significant proportion of those arrested on such charges will no doubt continue to be diagnosed as having committed their "heinous offences" as a result of mental illness rather than from any politically "hostile" intent. Any genuinely mentally disturbed dissidents and religious believers – and also any non-dissident individuals who happen to express their mental disturbances in the form of politically-coloured thought, speech and action – should be given the benefit of humane and appropriate medical care in a non-forensic, regular psychiatric care setting. Many Chinese psychiatrists now publicly acknowledge that most of those in the latter categories – a quixotic but seemingly quite large group that might best be described as "pseudo-counterrevolutionaries" – became mentally disturbed or were driven insane as a direct result of the incessantly persecutory political campaigns of China's recent past. For the legal and medical authorities to treat such people also as being "dangerously mentally ill criminals" is an affront to human dignity.

III. The Smoking Gun: Official Statistics on Political Psychiatry

The frequency with which "cases of a political nature" are referred to in China's official legal-psychiatric literature has already been noted, and we shall now consider the relevant figures and statistics in greater detail. The fact that these quantitative data exist at all is remarkable; as was noted earlier, no equivalent statistical evidence of this kind was ever found in the Soviet case. Since they have provided the solid and dependable foundation upon which this research study has been gradually developed over the years, it is appropriate that we should examine and evaluate these data thoroughly at the outset of our discussion.

Again, it should be noted that not all of the "political cases" cited in these official publications necessarily involved persons who were of entirely sound mind when detained by the security authorities for exercising their right to free expression. Some of them may indeed have been suffering from various mental quirks, disorders or abnormalities at the time in question, and a certain proportion may even have been in urgent need of psychiatric attention. Two key questions arise in all such cases, however. First, why were the numerous individuals who actually make up these statistics arrested by the police in the first place, since their only real offence seems to have been to voice opinions and viewpoints which, for a wide range of questionable reasons, the Chinese authorities viewed as politically unacceptable? The fact that these dissident, or pseudo-dissident, viewpoints were apparently directed, in a high number of reported cases, against the Communist Party of China neither represents a legally acceptable grounds for arrest, nor – still less – can it be regarded as a medically sound or valid reason for questioning the basic sanity of those involved. And second, why were so many of these individuals, sane or otherwise, seen by the authorities as posing such a serious "danger" or "threat" to society that, upon being arrested,

---

32   For further information on these important documents, see p.80 and p.85 below.

they had to be labelled by forensic psychiatrists as "not legally responsible" for their dissident or pseudo-dissident activities, and then promptly divested, as a result, of most of their civil and litigious rights – notably the right to be tried in court – and finally, sent for indeterminate periods of time to police-run institutes for the criminally insane?

According to the various sources, the incidence of forensic psychiatric "political cases" in China has declined steadily over the past two decades, falling from a level of around seven to fifteen percent in the 1980s to as low as 1 or a few percent in the late 1990s; the general trend thus appears to parallel the sharp decline seen in the numbers of "genuine" counterrevolutionary cases dealt with by the authorities over the same period.[33] The following passages provide a typical cross-section of the numerous statistical references to such cases that have appeared in China's professional literature during the post-Mao era. During the 1980s, the overall statistical profile for political-style forensic psychiatric appraisals was broadly as follows. According to Shen Zheng, a leading authority in the field,

> In a 1986 research study of 83 criminal cases where diagnoses of schizophrenia were made, Zhang Junxian and others found that cases of murder and injury accounted for 55.4 percent, political cases accounted for 13.3 percent, and hooliganism and sexual crime accounted for 10.8 percent.[34]

More specifically,

> Of the eleven cases of antisocial acts or statements carried out by schizophrenics, six involved the writing of slogan-banners in public places, three involved the shouting of slogans amidst crowds of people, and two involved the sending of openly-signed letters by post.[35]

According to Zhang Xinzhi, an elderly forensic medical expert who had worked in the Chinese police force since 1954 (most recently as deputy-head of the Wuhan Municipal Public Security Bureau's department of forensic medicine),

> In criminal cases, mentally ill people, as a result of their pathological thoughts and hallucinatory delusions, may exhibit abnormal behaviour in the form of anti-social acts and statements; for example: murder, arson, rape, theft, injury, disrupting traffic, and writing reactionary letters and posters or shouting reactionary slogans.

Out of a sample group of 50 criminal cases studied by Zhang in which the defendants were examined by police-appointed psychiatrists,

> Altogether six cases, or 12 percent of the total, involved the writing of reactionary letters; and another two cases, or 4 percent of the total, involved the shouting of reactionary slogans."[36]

---

33   For a unique and comprehensive study of the numbers of counterrevolutionary cases dealt with by the Chinese legal authorities in various parts of the country over the past couple of decades, see: "Statistics on Political Crime in the People's Republic of China" (Volumes 1 and 2), The Dui Hua Foundation, San Francisco, April 2001 and May 2004.
34   Shen Zheng, *Falü Jingshenbingxue*, p.302. For the study referred to by Shen, see Zhang Junxian, "An Analysis of the Forensic Evaluation of 83 Cases of Schizophrenia," *Fayixue Zazhi* (*Journal of Forensic Medicine*), 1986, Vol.1, No.2, pp.33-36.
35   Ibid, p.305.
36   Zhang Xinzhi, "A Preliminary Analysis of 50 Cases of Crime by the Mentally Ill," in Zhou Yingde (ed.), *Fanzui Zhenchaxue Gailun: Cankao Ziliao* (*General Theory of Criminal Investigation: Reference Materials*),

The combined incidence of 16 percent in this sample is broadly consistent with the 13.3 percent figure given for "political cases" by Shen Zheng. Moreover, out of an expanded group of 111 cases examined by Zhang from the period 1982-89 in which criminal defendants underwent forensic psychiatric evaluation,

> There were 40 cases of murder, accounting for 39 percent of the total; fifteen cases of rape, or 13 percent of the total; fourteen cases of theft, also 13 percent; six arson cases, or 6 percent; sixteen cases of injury, or 14 percent; twelve cases of writing reactionary letters, or 8 percent; four cases involving the shouting of reactionary slogans, or 4 percent; and four suicide cases, another 4 percent.[37]

The combined incidence for the two types of "political case" noted by Zhang in his expanded study was thus 12 percent, again broadly consistent with the figure of 13.3 percent officially recorded elsewhere in China during the mid- to late-1980s.

The official statistical record from China on "cases of a political nature" in the forensic psychiatric field goes on and on. Here are just a few more typical examples:

- In a disturbing article that reviewed 1,600 cases of forensic psychiatric appraisal of ethnic-minority criminal detainees carried out at the Yunnan Provincial Mental Hospital from the late 1950s to December 1987, Lu Shulian and Liu Keli revealed that "during the 1970s, *the majority* were political cases ('actual speech and expression,' etc.)."[38] [emphasis added]

- A study by Xu Chengxun of 195 cases of forensic psychiatric appraisal carried out at the Qingdao Municipal Mental Hospital between 1982 and 1986 yielded ten "political case" detainees and 6 cases of detained "petitioners who had disrupted Party and government offices," accounting together for 8.2 percent of the total case group.[39]

- In 1987, Huo Kediao et al reported that out of 173 criminal-forensic psychiatric appraisals conducted at the West China Medical University between November 1981 and December 1986, twelve – or 6.9 percent – were "cases of

---

(Beijing 1987), pp.417-422 (volume marked: "Internal teaching materials: keep confidential").
37 Zhang Xinzhi, "A Preliminary Analysis of 111 Cases of Crimes by the Mentally Ill," in Zhai Jian'an (ed.), *Zhongguo Fayi Shijian* (*Forensic Medical Practice in China*), (Beijing: Police Officers' Educational Publishing House, August 1993), pp.556–561. No fewer than 85 percent of the 111 criminal cases reportedly involved schizophrenics. (NB: This sample group of 111 cases appears to have included the fifty cases cited in the 1987 study by Zhang – see preceding Note.)
38 See: Lu Shulian and Liu Keli, "*Sifa Jingshen Jianding Zhong Shaoshu Minzu Huanzhe Xiongsha An 84 Li Fenxi*" (An Analysis of 84 Forensic Psychiatric Appraisals in Cases Involving Violent Crimes by Members of Minority Nationalities), *Shanghai Jingshen Yixue* (Shanghai Archives of Psychiatry), 1988, Vol.6, No.3, pp.124-6.
39 See: Xu Chengxun, "*Sifa Jingshenbingxue Jianding 195 Li Fenxi*" (An Analysis of 195 Cases of Forensic Psychiatric Appraisal), *Shandong Jingshen Yixue* (Shandong Psychiatric Medicine), 1989, No.1, pp.50-54. The author noted that he had "referred to Soviet textbooks on forensic psychiatry" in preparing the article. Unusually, he also gave a breakdown of the cases by medical diagnosis: Among the ten "political cases," five of the detainees were schizophrenic, two had paranoid psychosis, one was a psychopath, another was an epileptic, and one had no mental illness. Among the "disruptive petitioner" cases, three were schizophrenics, two were psychopaths, and one was not mentally ill.

counterrevolution." Moreover, these cases formed the second largest category of offence after murder.[40] In 1999, the same author reported that out of a total of 1,755 cases of forensic psychiatric appraisal carried out at the same university over the entire period 1981-98, altogether 31 (or 2.2 percent) had been "counterrevolutionary cases." Viewed in conjunction with the earlier report, this meant that nineteen cases of counterrevolution by alleged mentally ill people had been dealt with between 1987 and 1998, or around half the average annual rate of the preceding period.[41]

- A study by Yuan Shangxian of 105 forensic psychiatric evaluations conducted at the Tongji Medical University prior to 1988 identified eight separate cases of "anti-social behaviour," accounting for 7.6 percent of the total sample group. The acts in question were described as follows: "one case involved the sending of a counterrevolutionary letter; in another [the detainee] carried out liaison activities and set up a counterrevolutionary organization; and six cases involved the writing of reactionary posters."[42]

- In a retrospective examination of 376 forensic psychiatric appraisals conducted at the Zhejiang Provincial Mental Health Research Institute between 1984 and 1989, Xu Sisun and Xie Liya performed fresh appraisals in 27 of the cases – 17 percent of which were again "counterrevolutionary cases." If representative of the overall sample group, this would mean that a total of 64 cases of counterrevolution

---

40 In a vivid indication of the kind of company that the twelve political and petitioner cases in this sample group had been in, the article added that in one of the murder cases, a schizophrenic had disembowelled his victim (a beggar) and hacked the body into twelve pieces, and had then fried the kidneys, liver and heart in garlic and eaten them. See: Huo Kediao, Liu Xiehe, Hu Zeqing and Zhang Wei, "210 *Li Sifa Jingshenbingxue Jianding Anli Fenxi*" (An Analysis of 210 Cases of Forensic Psychiatric Appraisal), *Zhongguo Fayixue Zazhi* (China Journal of Forensic Medicine), 1987, Vol.2, No.4, pp.198-202.

Out of the 210 cases examined, 37 (or 16.7 percent) were victims and not defendants. According to the article, 41.6 percent of all the detainees had been referred for forensic psychiatric appraisal at the police investigation or custody stage; 26.6 percent had been so referred after relatives, friends or colleagues of the detainees told the police that the latter had been behaving abnormally; 10.9 percent were referred for forensic evaluation because they were found to have a previous history of mental illness; 8.7 of the cases were re-appraisal cases following disagreement over the diagnosis among the original forensic evaluators; in 5.2 percent of the cases, the detainees themselves had requested to be psychiatrically assessed; and one case (0.6 percent of the total) concerned a prisoner convicted of murder (he had also attempted suicide) who was on death row awaiting execution, and about whose mental state at the time of the crime certain doubts had arisen (he was eventually found to be legally responsible.) It is also noteworthy that 14 of the 173 detainees concerned were eventually either sentenced to death or were given suspended death sentences. In addition, two of the 12 counterrevolutionary detainees had been found to bear "partial legal responsibility" for their actions.

41 See: Huo Kediao and Liu Xiehe, "*Sifa Jingshenbing Jianding 1755 Li Fenxi*" (An Analysis of 1,755 Cases of Forensic Psychiatric Appraisal), in *Fayixue Jinzhan Yu Shijian* (Advances and Practices in Forensic Medicine), Hou Yiping and Liu Shicang (eds.), *Chengdu Keji Daxue Chubanshe* (Chengdu Science and Technology University Press), October 1999, pp.337-41.

42 See: Yuan Shangxian, "*105 Li Fayi Jingshenbingxue Jianding Baogao*" (A Report on 105 Cases of Legal-Medical Psychiatric Appraisal), *Zhongguo Fayixue Zazhi* (China Journal of Forensic Medicine), 1988, Vol.3, No.1, pp.44-5.

were dealt with during the five-year period in question – an average of one case per month at a single hospital.⁴³

- A study carried out by Xin Ruimin and presented to the Second National Conference on Forensic Psychiatry in Yichang in October 1989 found that out of 114 cases of forensic psychiatric appraisal conducted in one locality between January 1984 and March 1989, 7 percent were political cases.⁴⁴ Another study presented at the same conference by Chen Fuyin found that 7.56 percent of a sample group of 119 forensic psychiatric appraisals at another hospital had also been political cases.⁴⁵

Similarly, a study by Shen Muci, Jin Wei and other psychiatrists from the Hangzhou No.7 People's Hospital published in the *Chinese Journal of Nervous and Mental Diseases* in 1988, found that out of 654 people subjected to forensic-psychiatric evaluation at the hospital between 1973 and 1986 in connection with alleged criminal acts,

> Altogether 103 cases were of a political nature; of these, 40 cases involved the making of political statements, 25 involved [the display or distribution of] political slogan-banners or leaflets, 21 cases involved acts of political propaganda; and seventeen cases involved [the writing and sending of] letters.⁴⁶

Once again, the aggregate figure for "political-style" criminal psychiatric cases in this particular sample group comes, coincidentally or otherwise, to almost 16 percent – a figure surpassed only, moreover, by the 21.9 percent of those in the same forensic sample group who had allegedly committed murder or serious injury.⁴⁷

In addition, the same study noted that a further one hundred of the 654 cases concerned acts that allegedly "disturbed social order," including 29 cases of "unreasonably making trouble" (*wuli qunao*) – a code-phrase generally reserved by the authorities to denote the legions of "petitioners" (*shangfangzhe*) who regularly besiege the government offices around the country responsible for dealing with citizens' complaints about official malfeasance or corruption, and which are also supposed to handle citizens' applications for official redress of the countless past acts of political persecution and injustice committed by Chinese government agencies.⁴⁸ As mentioned above, many of those falling

---

43   See: Xu Sisun and Xie Liya, "*27 Li Sifa Jingshenbing Chongxin Jianding Anli de Fenxi*" (An Analysis of 27 Forensic Psychiatric Reappraisal Cases), *Shanghai Jingshen Yixue* (Shanghai Archives of Psychiatry), 1991, Vol.3, No.4, pp.194-6.
44   See: Zheng Zhanpei, "*Zhanwang Woguo Sifa Jingshen Yixue*" (Prospects for China's Judicial Psychiatric Medicine), *Shanghai Jingshen Yixue* (Shanghai Archives of Psychiatry), 1990, Vol.2, No.3, pp.53-6.
45   Ibid.
46   Shen Muci, Jin Wei, Cai Jianhua, and Han Baojin, "*Sifa Jingshen Yixue Jianding 654 Li Fenxi* (An Analysis of 654 Cases of Forensic-Psychiatric Medical Evaluation)," *Chinese Journal of Nervous and Mental Diseases*, 1988, Vol.21, No.3, pp.166-168.
47   According to the article, 80 percent of the political cases in this particular study were ones dating back from before 1980, a situation about which the authors comment: "This shows that [the incidence of forensic-psychiatric] cases of a political nature is closely related to [the question of] political movements and social stability" (Ibid, p.168).
48   Usefully, Shen and his colleagues also provide a break-down of the specific medical diagnoses made by state forensic psychiatrists in respect of the various criminal categories included within this large sample group. Notably, of the 103 "political cases," 55 (or more than half) were attributed to schizophrenia; mental retardation was said to account for five of the cases; eight were attributed to mania; seven were described as being due to

in this general category should also properly be seen as "political cases."[49] Out of the one hundred persons accused of "disturbing social order," 48 were diagnosed as suffering from schizophrenia, eight were said to have various personality disorders, thirteen were found to be not mentally ill (and so were "legally responsible" for their actions), while an additional five were diagnosed as being "paranoid psychotics." If cases of this secondary category are added into the various statistics for those primarily defined by the authorities as being "political" in nature, then the overall incidence rates for political psychiatry in China in the 1980s rises to somewhere in the region of 15-20 percent of the criminal psychiatric caseload.

Finally, it should be noted that of the 103 "political cases" in the group, only sixteen, or approximately 15 percent, were determined to be "not suffering from mental illness" and so were liable to criminal prosecution; the majority of the group was found to be mentally ill and thus liable for psychiatric custody. Similarly, of the 100 cases of "disturbing social order," only thirteen were determined to be not mentally ill, while all the rest were found to be not legally responsible and were also therefore candidates for involuntary psychiatric committal.[50]

Turning now to the present era, two recently published studies from China have provided detailed statistical breakdowns of the relative incidence of "political cases" in forensic psychiatric appraisals work during successive decades from 1960 to as recently as the late 1990s. The first of these, published in January 2000, examines the situation in one particular institution in the south-western city of Kunming,

---

anti-social or sociopathic personality disorders; nine were said to be due to reactive psychosis; three more were attributed, respectively, to prison psychosis, "other mental illness" and organic brain disease sequella; and in only sixteen (or 15 percent) of the numerous "political cases" were the defendants found to be "not mentally ill" – and therefore liable to criminal prosecution for their "anti-social" or "counterrevolutionary" acts. (It should be stressed, of course, that the majority of those in the "political" subcategory were not set free by the authorities after being found "not legally responsible" by reason of mental illness; rather, the legal issue then became: in what particular form of "non-penal" state custody would it be most appropriate to place such people in order that society could be afforded maximum protection from their "pathologically dangerous" political behaviour.)

49 For further information on the authorities' application of abusive detention policies to mentally ill persons alleged to have "disturbed social order," see Human Rights in China, *Not Welcome at the Party: Behind the "Clean-Up" of China's Cities — A Report on Administrative Detention under "Custody and Repatriation*," September 1999). In the late 1980s, even orphans and abandoned children, residents of the Shanghai Children's Welfare Institute, were sometimes forcibly sent to psychiatric institutions by the orphanage authorities; this was done to them as a punishment for daring to cooperate with an independent investigation then being carried out by the Shanghai municipal legislature into phenomenally high death rates among infants and young children at the orphanage. For details of two of these cases, see Human Rights Watch/Asia, *Death by Default*, pp.272-275.

50 The authors of the study also offered a statistical break-down of the subjective "motives" (*zuo'an dongji*) underlying the "criminal acts" carried out by the individuals in question. Of the 103 "political cases," 31 were attributed (oddly enough, given the ostensible topic of discussion) to "pathological behaviour" on the defendant's part, thirteen were attributed to "delusions of persecution," fifteen were attributed to "impairments of mental logic," nine were attributed to "auditory delusions," eight to "personality disorders," while a total of twenty were attributed to "non-pathological" motives (note that this figure exceeds by four, for some reason, the overall number who were determined to be "not suffering from mental illness"); the remaining seven cases were attributed, variously, to "delusions of jealousy" (one case), "relational delusions" (five cases), and "impairment of consciousness" (one case). Of the one hundred cases of "disturbing social order," altogether twenty-eight were attributed to "pathological behaviour" on the defendant's part, sixteen to "delusions of persecution," and twelve to "personality disorders"; eighteen cases were deemed to be "non-pathological" in motive; and the remaining twenty-six to various other motivating factors.

the Yunnan Provincial Mental Hospital.[51] The authors of the study offer few specific observations on their various findings, but they provide a very useful set of data, as shown in Table 1.

Table 1: Forensic Psychiatric Appraisals at the Yunnan Provincial Mental Hospital, 1960-97

Period		1960-1979	1980-1989	1990-1997
Total cases		575	1274	936
Violent cases	No.	236	734	437
	%	41.04	57.61	46.69
Economic cases	No.	13	92	131
	%	2.26	7.22	14.00
Sexual assault cases	No.	23	79	60
	%	4.00	6.20	6.41
Political cases	No.	288	54	9
	%	50.09	4.24	0.96
Divorce cases	No.	0	40	52
	%	0	3.14	5.56
Sexual victim cases	No.	1	87	98
	%	0.17	6.83	10.47
Mental injury cases	No.	1	28	61
	%	0.17	2.20	6.52
Appraisals of sentenced prisoners[52]	No.	13	160	88
	%	2.26	12.56	9.40

According to the data, the reported incidence of political cases at this one hospital fell from a high point of no fewer than 50 percent in the 1960s and 1970s,[53] to just over 4 percent during the 1980s, and ended at an average level of just under 1 percent in the 1990s. The total number of political cases dealt with at the hospital between 1960 and 1997 was 351; this represented 12.6 percent of the total of 2,785 cases of all types examined during the whole period. It should be noted, however, that this

---

51 See Yao Zuhua et al., "*Jin 40 Nian Sifa Jingshenbingxue Jianding Anli de Bijiao* (A Comparative Study on the Case Expertise of Forensic Psychiatrics Over the Past 40 Years)," *Chinese Journal of Psychiatry*, Vol.33, No.1 (2000), pp.47-49.
52 This category probably refers to psychiatric appraisals of prisoners who developed various forms of "prison psychosis" while serving their sentences. For more information on this topic, see p.149 below.
53 Interestingly, regarding the figure of 50.09 percent for the 1960s and 1970s, the authors comment: "At that time, when applying for appraisals to be carried out, the judicial organs almost never requested that an appropriate determination of legal responsibility be rendered in respect of the person being examined; in the overwhelming majority of cases, therefore, only a medical diagnosis was made in the appraisal conclusion." This was probably because the police and procuratorial system was in tatters for much of this period: especially during the Cultural Revolution, all such work was subsumed under the activities of ad hoc "security committees" (*baowei weiyuanhui*) set up in all the localities of China.

hospital appears to have dealt with a comparatively low incidence rate of political cases (4.24 percent) during the 1980s; as we have seen, the average level reported for that period elsewhere in China was around 10 percent. Moreover, while the actual number of cases reported for the 1990s was only nine, this was merely the figure for one hospital. If typical for the rest of the country, this low figure would translate into a total for the country as a whole during the 1990s of several hundred "political cases," and possibly thousands.

The second recent study, published in January 1999, surveyed a total of 9,925 cases of forensic psychiatric appraisal that had been reported in 231 separate articles published in ten psychiatric legal-medical journals in China between 1976 and 1995. During the period in question, the authors found a total of 375 "political cases," representing an average incidence rate of 3.78 percent. The overall data from this considerably more representative survey was tabulated in the article as shown in Table 2.[54]

Table 2: Forensic Psychiatric Appraisals Listed in 10 Chinese Journals, 1976-95

Period	1976-1990		1991-1995		Total (1976-95)	
Cases	No.	%	No.	%	No.	%
Murder and injury	2,016	40.90	1,841	36.85	3,857	38.86
Theft	617	12.52	605	12.11	1,222	12.31
Arson	129	2.62	172	3.44	301	3.03
Sexual crime	465	9.43	612	12.25	1,077	10.85
Sexual victims	373	7.57	1,178	23.58	1,551	15.63
Obstructing social order	591	11.99	331	6.63	922	9.29
Politics (zhengzhi)	272	5.52	103	2.06	375	3.78
Hooliganism	81	1.64	88	1.76	169	1.70
Other	385	7.81	66	1.32	451	4.54
Total	4,929	100.00	4,996	100.00	9,925	100.00

Although the time periods used in this survey are not strictly comparable with those in Table 1, what is clear is that among the sample data used, the total number of "political cases" for the five-year period 1991-95 was more than one third of that reported for the entire fifteen-year preceding period. In other words, viewed chronologically, rather than as a percentage of the total cases for each individual period, the absolute per-year numbers of political cases had hardly changed at all between 1976 and 1995. Moreover, even when viewed as a percentage of the total cases for each period, the incidence rate for "political cases" was still, apparently, proceeding along at the quite considerable level of 2.06 percent during the first half of the 1990s, or more than half the average rate for the entire period since 1976. Also important to note is the fact that the figure of 103 such cases for this period was by no means the total number that actually arose around the country. Rather, it was simply the number that happened

---

54 See Zhao Jiancong et al., "*Woguo Sifa Jingshenbingxue Xianzhuang de Yanjiu* (A Study on the Current Data of Judicial Psychiatry in China)," *Chinese Journal of Psychiatry*, 1999, No.1, pp.53-54.

to emerge in a rather large group of separately published local studies. The true figure for China as a whole at that time was undoubtedly far higher than this.[55]

Finally, many of those included under the heading of "obstructing social order" in the above table were probably also "political cases" in the wider Chinese forensic-psychiatric sense of the term, since this is often the police's criminal charge of choice in cases of "litigation mania," whistle-blowing, persistent complaint against authority, and "false accusation" (*wugao*.)[56] If we include these latter cases in the calculation, then the total incidence of political cases rises to 17.5 percent for the period 1976-90, and to 8.7 percent for the period 1991-95, resulting in an average level of 13.1 percent over the entire period 1976-95. Moreover, the total number of political cases for the entire period rises from 375 to 1,297.[57]

Taken together, the above array of statistical data constitutes what is commonly termed, under international legal standards, a clear and consistent pattern of systematic human rights violations. In fact, it is hard to see how the pattern could be any clearer. The data are drawn from all over China, they are remarkably consistent and they all emanate from official sources.

Armed with these various figures, we can now attempt to make a rough "ballpark" estimation of altogether how many political dissidents and people in other similar categories may have been branded as criminally insane and confined to forensic custodial facilities in China over the past two decades or so. It should be stressed that, given the incomplete nature of the currently available statistical evidence,

---

55 Another study published in April 2000, for example, noted that at a single psychiatric hospital, the Zigong Mental Health Centre, altogether 956 cases of forensic psychiatric evaluation were performed over the period 1981-88. If this was roughly typical for the rest of the country, the total number of such evaluations conducted across China as a whole during the same period would certainly have run into the tens of thousands, and possibly even the hundreds of thousands. (See Wei Qingping et al., "An Analysis of Expert Psychiatric Testimony on Epileptic Patients' Illegal Actions," *Chinese Journal of Nervous and Mental Diseases*, 2000, Vol.26, No.2, pp.65-67).

56 For a detailed account of the forensic-psychiatric handling of cases of "false accusation" in China, see *Zhongguo Gong'an Baike Quanshu* (*China Encyclopaedia of Public Security*), p.1965. Chinese citizens who try to expose corruption or malfeasance by local officials often end up being detained and charged under this heading. As this book explains, those found guilty of false accusation are subject to the disturbing judicial principle of "reverse criminal culpability" (*shixing fan zuo zui*), whereby the offender is sentenced to whatever term of imprisonment would have been applied to the person accused in the event that the accusation had proved to be well founded. Whilst mentally ill offenders of this type are supposed be exempted from criminal judgment, they may nonetheless still be subject to the "commensurability principle" (see p.166 below) and so have to spend similarly long periods in psychiatric custody.

57 A third recent study, published in November 2000, also gave separate figures for "political cases" and "cases of obstructing social order," and the results were broadly comparable to those presented in Table 2. (See Lin Hong et al, "*1979-1998 Nian Sifa Jingshenbing Jianding Anli de Fenxi* (An Analysis of Cases of Forensic Psychiatric Evaluation, 1979-98)," *Chinese Journal of Psychiatry*, 2000, Vol.33 No. 4, pp.243-245.) The article provided a statistical breakdown of altogether 1,894 cases of forensic psychiatric appraisal that had been performed over two distinct periods at the Affiliated Brain Hospital of Nanjing Medical University between 1979 and 1998. First, during the period 1979-88, nineteen "political cases" were dealt with at the hospital, or 4.8 percent of the total of 400 cases of all types examined; and there were nine cases of "obstructing social order," or 2.2 percent of the total. The combined figure for both types of offence was thus 7 percent. Second, during the period 1989-98, nine "political cases" were dealt with at the hospital, or 1.2 percent of the total of 757 cases of all types examined; and there were 11 cases of "obstructing social order," or 1.4 percent of the total. The combined total for both types of offence for this second period was thus 2.6 percent.

this is an inherently hazardous undertaking and one that can yield, at best, only a very approximate indication of the actual extent of the problem. As we have seen, "political cases" accounted, according to the official statistics, for around 10 percent of all forensic psychiatric appraisals carried out during the 1980s, and, during the 1990s, for somewhere in the region of 1 to a few percent. The largest statistical indicator on this general topic thus far found in China's legal-medical literature appeared in a volume published in 1988 and was as follows:

> According to statistical materials presented at the First National Conference on Forensic Psychiatry, held at Hangzhou in June 1987, the total number of forensic psychiatric appraisals cases (most of which dated from 1980 and later) handled by a certain number of mental hospitals in China had already reached more than 10,000.[58]

According to the same source, altogether twelve mental hospitals accounted for no fewer than 7,862 of the above-mentioned cases; findings of mental illness were made in 87.51 percent of these cases. In addition, the same source notes that three mental hospitals in Shanghai conducted a total of almost 1,000 cases of forensic psychiatric appraisal over the five-year period between August 1982 and August 1987; again, findings of mental illness were made in approximately 80 percent of these cases. However, another source states that between 1982 and 1989, a single hospital in the Shanghai area – the Shanghai Municipal Centre for Mental Health – carried out as many as 1,034 forensic psychiatric appraisals.[59] Similarly, between 1983 and 1987 a total of 931 cases of forensic psychiatric appraisal were conducted at the Beijing Anding Hospital alone. And the Affiliated Brain Hospital of Nanjing Medical University is reported to have carried out 1,894 forensic psychiatric appraisals during the two-decade period 1979-98.[60] While figures for the total numbers of such appraisals carried out during the 1990s in China are as yet relatively scarce, it is clear from numerous officially published sources that the recent general trend here has been rapidly upwards.

To summarize briefly the above data, during the period 1980-87, twelve hospitals in China performed almost 8,000 forensic psychiatric appraisals, or an average number of 670 per hospital. Applying, conservatively, an average "political case" rate of 10 percent for this general period to the former figure, one obtains a total figure of 800 "political cases," of whom approximately 90 percent (or 720) would have been found legally non-imputable by reason of insanity for their alleged crimes and hence (in most or all cases) sent to forensic custody (the remainder would almost certainly have been sent to prison as counterrevolutionaries.) This works out at around 60 criminally insane "political case" patients per hospital. In addition, we see that the total numbers of forensic psychiatric appraisals that were individually conducted by other mental hospitals in China reached, during the same general period, high triple figures. And finally, we know that the total number of such evaluations being conducted across China nowadays is rapidly rising each year.

In order to estimate, on the basis of these partial figures, the approximate sum total of forensic psychiatric "cases of a political nature" in China since the early 1980s, we also need to know how many mental hospitals there are throughout the country and how many of those were engaged in forensic appraisals work during the period in question. The former figure, at least, is known; according to a recently published article in the Chinese press, "575 hospitals and 77,000 doctors and nurses are

---

58 Jia Yicheng, *Shiyong Sifa Jingshenbingxue* (op cit), pp.1-2.
59 See Lin Huai, *Jingshen Jibing Huanzhe Xingshi Zeren Nengli He Yiliao Jianhu Cuoshi*, p.133. (No rate for findings of mental illness in this group was given.)
60 See above, Note 57.

dealing with mental diseases in China."[61] It is not known how many of these hospitals were qualified or officially authorized to perform forensic psychiatric evaluations during the 1980s. However, we do know that as of January 2003, a total of 143 mental hospitals in China had been officially accredited and authorized to perform such work.[62] Since this has been a growth area in Chinese psychiatry since the early 1990s, the number of mental hospitals engaged in forensic evaluations work in the 1980s would have been substantially fewer than 143.

Let us assume, however, that only one quarter of that number – that is, around 35 institutions – was so authorized; this is likely to be a considerable underestimate of the actual situation. If so, one could reasonably estimate, on the basis of the average number of cases examined by each of the twelve hospitals referred to above, that those 35 institutions performed somewhere in the region of 23,000 forensic psychiatric appraisals during the first seven years of the 1980s alone, and that approximately 2,300 of these were probably political cases. (It should also be remembered that many other cases appraised during the same period, involving "crimes of disturbing public order," did not fall within the authorities' own definition of "political cases" but would nonetheless qualify as such from the international standards point of view.) If this figure is then adjusted to include the remaining three years of the decade in question, during which the incidence rate for political cases continued at a level of around 10 percent, one obtains a total figure for the 1980s as a whole of approximately 3,000 political cases.[63]

If we then apply an average annual incidence rate of only 1 percent to the subsequent 10-year period, and furthermore assume that the annual number of forensic psychiatric evaluation cases of all types did not increase at all over this second period,[64] then we derive the additional number of 300 cases for the country as a whole during the 1990s, making a total of 3,300 political cases for the entire period from 1980 to the present. To this must be added, however, the Falun Gong psychiatric detention caseload. According to the spiritual group's own reported figures, more than 1,000 such cases were recorded during the period from July 1999 until October 2003. Since no systematic independent verification of this figure has been possible as yet, let us assume, for the sake of caution, a 50 percent margin of reporting error for the Falun Gong cases; this would produce a more reliable figure of 500 such cases. Finally, although the official statistics on the number of forensic psychiatric appraisals carried out on those arrested for "disturbing public order" – the persistent complainants, petitioners and whistleblowers – are as yet highly incomplete and therefore non-representative, there is a steadily growing amount of anecdotal and case-based evidence to suggest that this may nowadays be the single largest category of people being sent to mental hospitals without medical justification and for political reasons.

Even allowing for the officially reported decrease in "cases of a political nature" from the early 1990s onwards, therefore, it is reasonable to conclude that somewhere in excess of 4,000 political

---

61   See "Nation's Mentally Ill Need More Care," *China Daily*, November 27, 2000.
62   See: "*Quanguo Sifa Jingshenbing Jianding Danwei Mingce*" (National Register of Judicial Psychiatric Appraisal Units), issued on 21 January 2003 by the Judicial Psychiatric Appraisals Specialist Committee of the Chinese Society of Psychiatry; available from *Zhonghua Jingshen Weisheng Wang* (China Mental Health Network) at: www.21jk.com.cn/p/.
63   Unlike "normal" crimes of counterrevolution, where a single case often involved several or more individual defendants, a "case" here refers to a single individual only. There are no known or reported instances of group-based "political cases" involving forensic psychiatric committal in China.
64   In fact, the annual number increased greatly from around 1990 onwards, but by precisely how much is not currently known.

cases (broadly defined to include all three of the above categories) have been processed by Chinese forensic psychiatric examiners countrywide over the past two and a half decades, and moreover that the great majority of the individuals concerned were subjected, as a result, to some form and duration of forced psychiatric custody and treatment.[65] (Some dissidents arrested in the early 1990s are still being held in mental asylums today, more than a decade later.)[66] This conjectural "ballpark" figure is almost certainly inaccurate, but it probably errs on the conservative side; and it provides, at least, a reasonable indication of the general order of magnitude involved for China's political-psychiatric custody cases in the post-Mao era.

Finally, the figure of 4,000 political cases does not include any of the reportedly very numerous dissident individuals who were subjected to forced psychiatric treatment and custody during the period from the late 1950s to the late 1970s. While absolute numbers for this period are extremely rare, several official documentary sources have been found which state that the percentage rate for political cases in China's criminal psychiatric appraisals work during this 20-year period was in the region of 50 percent or even higher. One very specific figure has come to light, however. In September 1987, Jia Yicheng, one of China's top forensic psychiatrists, reported that out of one composite survey group of 5,680 criminal detainees psychiatrically appraised during the period beginning in the late 1950s and ending in 1976, a total of 1,562 persons (or 27.5 percent) had been detained for engaging in "counterrevolutionary speech and action."[67] But that was only the figure from one rather large survey group.

By comparison, in the case of the Soviet Union, existing scholarly studies indicate that the total confirmed number of political dissidents and others in similar categories who were wrongfully branded as mentally ill and sent to forensic custodial facilities during the entire period from the late 1920s to 1991 was 674, with unconfirmed estimates also extending into the several thousands.[68]

In what follows, we will examine from various perspectives – legal, political and medical, and through numerous individual case studies – the precise nature and content of China's so-called political

---

65 In a previous publication by the present author, a somewhat different method was used to estimate the total number of people in China who were subjected to psychiatric detention and treatment on political rather than medical grounds during the 1980s and 1990s. In that calculation, the figure arrived at was "somewhere in excess of 3,000." (See: Robin Munro: "Judicial Psychiatry in China and its Political Abuses," *Columbia Journal of Asian Law*, 2000, Vol. 14, No.1, pp.1-128. The cover date notwithstanding, this article was completed in November 2000 and the journal issue was published in January 2001.) The present method of calculation is more accurate and reliable because it is based on a quantity that was not known at the time when the earlier calculation was carried out, namely the total number of institutions in China that are authorized to perform forensic psychiatric evaluations.

66 See, for example, the account of political dissidents at the Shanghai Ankang given on p.244 below.

67 "Summary and Analysis of Papers Submitted to the First National Academic Conference on Forensic Psychiatry," by Jia Yicheng (Psychiatric Teaching and Research Group of the Shanghai Railways Medical College), September 1987, *Shanghai Archives of Psychiatry* (*Shanghai Jingshen Yixue*), 1987, No.3, pp.118-24.

68 In 1996, Smith and Oleszczuk summarized as follows the various databases on Soviet dissidents and others in similar categories who had been sent to psychiatric detention facilities: "[A]ll records for individuals against whom definite measures of administrative or court-ordered psychiatric detention or hospitalization can be documented yields a sample of 410 individuals from 1960 to 1981, when records are most complete, and 674 from the late 1920s to 1991 when our earliest observations are included and the Koppers and Mercer data are integrated.... Partial records led to allegations of at least 700, (Reich, 1978:31), though some estimates attributed as many as 1000 to a single psychiatrist (ed. Van Voren, 1989:16, attributable to Serbsky director Daniil Romanovich Lunts." (See: Smith and Olezcszuk [op cit], p.48 and p.54.

psychiatric cases, and we shall see how they have been dealt with in practice by the country's criminal justice authorities over the past few decades.

CHAPTER 2
China's Legal Reforms and the Concept of Criminal Insanity

In order to evaluate China's legal handling of certain types of political dissidents and outspoken social critics as "dangerously mentally ill," and to understand why the authorities have consistently opted for coercive measures aimed at isolating such people from society at large, we first need to consider the wider legal context in which these practices take place. In this chapter, we begin by addressing the overall issue of the post-Mao legal reforms – the steps taken to rebuild the legal system after the Cultural Revolution, how these have been characterized and assessed by China law scholars elsewhere, and the implications or potential of this continuing process of legal reform for an expansion of citizens' rights of various kinds – and also the extent to which China today can be said to be operating and abiding by the rule of law. This is followed by a more specific account of the current state of administrative law in China and, in particular, of the security authorities' continuing widespread use of an elaborate system of "administrative punishments" and "administrative coercive measures" over which the judiciary is granted only a minimal and, at best, post hoc supervisory role.

As will be further argued and explained below, China's current system of compulsory forensic psychiatric confinement can best be understood, in formal legal terms, as being an officially unacknowledged, but nonetheless real and specific, type of administrative detention. This is because, although the basis for forensic psychiatric custody is contained and specified within the Criminal Law and the Criminal Procedure Law, and notwithstanding its official characterization as a "judicial" procedure, the actual adoption of the measure involves the removal of the detainee concerned from the orbit of the criminal justice system and their return to the exclusive jurisdiction of, and control by, the police or public security organs. Moreover, not only does the judiciary play no role in this process even during the stage prior to the detainee's removal from the formal criminal justice system, but also there appears to be a significant degree of confusion within the system as to whether criminal psychiatric custody measures should properly be seen as a form of pre-emptive or preventative administrative custody, or conversely as a form of administrative punishment, one aimed specifically at offenders whose mental state has rendered them ineligible for punishment under the Criminal Law. In practice, both elements are often to be found side by side, in varying proportions, in individual cases.

Also discussed in this chapter is the vexed and contentious question of "political crime" in China – officially known as "crimes of counterrevolution" for most of the past half-century – and its close and direct relevance to the main topic of this book. In addition, a short outline of China's participation in various international human rights mechanisms and conventions is provided. Finally, the chapter concludes by briefly examining the currently prevailing international system of legal and ethical norms governing compulsory forensic-psychiatric hospitalization, as defined and laid down by the United Nations, the World Psychiatric Association and the Council of Europe.

During roughly two millennia of successive imperial dynasties, nothing resembling a fair and impartial system of rule by law developed or emerged in China. From the Tang Dynasty onwards, the country had an elaborate system of codified laws and regulations, but these essentially comprised, on the one hand, a set of administrative norms for the exercise of government, and on the other, a categorized framework for the implementation of punishments against those found to have violated traditional

Confucian morality or the edicts of the government.[69] With the establishment of the Chinese Republic in 1911, fairly systematic attempts were made to implant a Western-style legal system in China, but these mostly foundered in the course of the subsequent three decades as a result of continuing domestic strife, first among the warlords and then between the KMT and the Communist revolutionary forces, and because of the presence of severe and widespread official corruption and also the persistence of a wide range of traditional cultural factors that militated against modern concepts of law and legality. As Marina Svensson has discussed, however, Chinese intellectuals paid quite extensive scholarly and political attention to the question of both civil freedoms and human rights during the Nationalist period.[70]

During the first decade after its assumption of national political power in 1949, the Chinese Communist Party made significant efforts to build a basic system of laws, notably the Marriage Law and the Agrarian Reform Law, and also to set up legal institutions, including the Procuracy and the Court system, although in practice the Public Security organs (the police) retained and exerted much greater power than either of the latter. However, the post-1949 legal regime was fundamentally hampered, at least insofar as its ability to convey a modicum of protection for individual citizens' rights was concerned, by a number of closely inter-related and highly draconian doctrines that Mao and the Party had inherited from Marx, Lenin and Stalin.

The first of these was the "class theory of law." In Marxist doctrine, law and the legal system formed one part of the social "superstructure," the underlying class nature of which was determined by the particular "economic base" or "mode of production" found in a given society. In capitalist societies, all elements of the social superstructure, including law, were viewed by Marx and his followers as serving the interests of the bourgeois ruling class; the latter was then, in Marxist parlance, said to "exercise dictatorship over the proletariat" – primarily through the legal system. According to this theory, law by definition could never be class-free or exercise a politically neutral function in society: it was always a tool used by the ruling class to suppress the various subject classes. Certain Soviet jurists of the 1920s and 30s, in particular Yevgeny Pashukanis, took this doctrine to new extremes by arguing that law was fundamentally a bourgeois institution that should be abolished entirely as socialism advanced, in train with the "withering away of the state."[71] Although it is unlikely that Mao ever read Pashukanis, many of his policies after 1949 appear to have been inspired by very similar views and sentiments. To a varying extent, the whole notion of a "socialist rule of law" would have struck both thinkers as being something of an oxymoron.

---

69 As Stanley Lubman has noted, "In both Chinese tradition and Communist practice, law was regarded as an ensemble of rules for administering a society rather than as an arrangement of norms that create rights in the person and entities in that society." (See: Stanley B. Lubman, *Bird in a Cage: Legal Reform in China After Mao*, Stanford University Press, 1999, p.297.)

70 Marina Svensson, *The Chinese Conception of Human Rights: The Debate on Human Rights in China, 1898–1949*, Department of East Asian Languages, Lund University, 1996.

71 Pashukanis was director of the Moscow Institute of Law and his ideas dominated Soviet jurisprudence until early 1937, when he was purged by Stalin and then executed. His major treatise was *Obshchaia Teoriia Prava i Marksizm,* first published in Moscow in 1924 and subsequently translated into French, German, Japanese, Serbo-Croat and into English in its third edition of 1927 as *The General Theory of Law and Marxism.* See John N. Hazard (ed.), *Soviet Legal Philosophy* (1951), Harvard University Press, Cambridge, pp. 111-225. A large selection of Pashukanis' writings in English translation can be found on the Internet at: http://home.law.uiuc.edu/~pmaggs/book.doc.

Second, law in China's new socialist society was specifically characterized by Mao and the Party as being a tool of "the dictatorship of the proletariat" – a weapon for use in suppressing the restorationist or "counterrevolutionary" efforts and conspiracies of the overthrown, but still highly dangerous, former ruling class. At various periods since 1949, including the present one, the "dictatorship of the proletariat" has been more loosely renamed – in order to convey the sense of a ruling class alliance between the workers, peasants and progressive intellectuals – as the "people's democratic dictatorship"; and during such periods, the overall scope of "class struggle" waged by the Party, and hence the politically invigilatory or punitive role of the legal system, has been substantially smaller in scale. Conversely, during the more intense or "ultra-leftist" periods of class struggle waged by the Party since 1949 – notably the Anti-Rightist Movement of 1957-58 and the Cultural Revolution decade – law was seen and used almost exclusively as a device for suppressing the Party's political enemies.

A third element of Party doctrine that served to politicize China's post-1949 legal system almost from the outset and to prevent it from developing or being seen as a neutral and class-free arbiter of justice in society was Mao's theory of the "two types of contradictions." Building on Stalin's conception of "social contradictions" as providing the motive force for national progress and development, Mao drew a sharp operational distinction between non-antagonistic "contradictions among the people" (*renmin neibu maodun*), on the one hand, and antagonistic "contradictions between the people and the enemy" or "hostile contradictions" (*di-wo maodun*), on the other. Whereas the former type of contradiction could be peacefully and harmoniously resolved through, typically, a process of mediation or consultation, Mao argued, the latter were "fundamentally irreconcilable" and hence could only be settled by methods of force and dictatorship. Of severe consequence for China's nascent post-1949 legal system, in practice Mao also insisted that use of or resort to the law should be reserved mainly for dealing with "hostile contradictions," i.e. those between the people and the enemy. For the first three decades of the People's Republic, therefore, the whole realm of law tended to be subsumed under the concept of the "dictatorship of the proletariat" and to be viewed as an adjunct political device for suppressing "counterrevolution." Above all, law was seen during this period as being a political tool or instrument to be held tightly in the hands of the Communist Party.

The legacy of that era has continued, to a greater or lesser extent, to blight the development of an objective and impartial rule of law in China right up to the present day. In particular, as Stanley Lubman, one of the leading Western academic experts on Chinese law, has noted,

> The Maoist legacy that burdens Chinese law most heavily is the treatment of dissent.... Mao distinguished between "antagonistic" and "nonantagonistic" contradictions within Chinese society, the former between the "people" and the "enemy," the latter within the "people." Methods of "dictatorship" were appropriate for the former, methods of "democracy" were to be used to solve the latter. Political dissent was, of course, consistently treated as an antagonistic contradiction for which the heaviest measures of dictatorship were appropriate.[72]

I. China's Post-1978 Legal Reforms and Progress towards the Rule of Law

During the Cultural Revolution, most legal institutions in China apart from the police were either abolished or preserved mainly in name alone. For a several-year period in the late 1960s and early 1970s, civilian security functions were exercised throughout the country by the People's Liberation

---

72   Lubman (op cit), p.136.

Army. The Procuracy was dismantled entirely, and the court system survived essentially as a mere legal-procedural arm of the Party, to be used largely for the rubber-stamping of foregone criminal verdicts against political enemies. Civil law and civil litigation of any kind simply ceased to exist after 1966.

When Deng Xiaoping returned to power at the historic Third Plenary Session of the 11th CPC Central Committee in December 1978, one of his first major policy initiatives was to announce the inauguration of a new era of "socialist democracy and the legal system" (*shehuizhuyi minzhu yu fazhi*). While progress on the former issue has remained minimal, indeed largely rhetorical, over the past two decades and more, the Party's achievements in the latter realm have been, by almost any standard of judgement, extremely impressive.

As Randall Peerenboom, another leading authority on contemporary Chinese law, has noted,

> Given the heavy reliance on Party policies rather than law during the Mao period, China [after the Cultural Revolution] lacked even the most basic laws such as a comprehensive criminal code, civil law, or contract law. The response has been a legislative onslaught the pace and breadth of which has been nothing short of stunning. Between 1976 and 1998, the National People's Congress (NPC) and its Standing Committee (NPCSC) passed more than 337 laws and local people's congresses and governments issued more than 6,000 regulations. In contrast, only 134 laws were passed between 1949 and 1978, with only one law passed during the Cultural Revolution from 1967 to 1976. Moreover, of the 134 laws passed between 1949 and 1978, 111 were subsequently declared invalid and many of the remaining ones were amended during the post-1978 reform era.[73]

Furthermore,

> The legal profession in particular has made remarkable strides over the last twenty years. While in 1981, there were just 1,465 law offices and a mere 5,500 lawyers, by 1998 there were more than 8,300 law firms and over 110,000 lawyers.... While litigation was virtually nonexistent in 1979, the total number of cases of first instance reached 3 million by 1992, and 5 million by 1996[74]

The scope of legal reform since 1978 in China has ranged across almost every major type and aspect of law, including economic law, contract law, trade law and economic dispute arbitration law; civil law, criminal law and administrative law; labour law, and legislation on occupational safety and workplace dispute mediation and arbitration; environmental protection law; law on public demonstrations and assembly, and on the registration of social bodies, non-governmental organizations, and a range of other civil society-related issues; and a series of laws on national security matters. (One of the few major legal issues that still remains to be tackled by the government is that of constitutional law.) Given the sheer scale of the topic, it is impossible to attempt here any comprehensive overview or assessment of the often bewildering profusion of laws, legal institutions and practices that now exist in China, and instead we will focus on those aspects of the legal system that most closely relate to our central theme of the protection of citizens' rights and interests.

---

73 Randall Peerenboom, *China's Long March toward Rule of Law*, Cambridge University Press, 2002, p.6.
74 Ibid, p.7.

Among the most important items of legislation that should be mentioned in passing in this regard are: the Criminal Law (1979 and 1997), Criminal Procedure Law (1979 and 1996), Procuracy Law (1979), General Principles of Civil Law (1986), Administrative Litigation Law (1989), Law on Assembly, Procession and Demonstration (1989), Judges Law (1995), Police Law (1995), Prisons Law (1994), State Compensation Law (1995), Lawyers' Law (1996), Administrative Punishments Law (1996), Administrative Reconsideration Law (1999), and Law on Legislation (2000.) In addition, numerous regulations governing a wide range of administrative punishments have been passed by various non-legislative state agencies over the past two decades, chiefly the Regulations on Labour Re-education (1979 and 1982) and the Security Administration Punishment Regulations (SAPR, 1986 and 1994), which were superseded in 2005 by the Security Administration Punishments Law. The various judicial and administrative regulations governing forensic psychiatric appraisal and custody are described at length in Chapter 5, below. Of all the above, the main laws and regulations dealing with criminal procedure and administrative punishments, and also the provisions allowing for appeals and challenges against criminal and administrative custodial rulings, are clearly of greatest concern to our present topic.

As late as the early 1980s, Chinese government officials and legal authorities continued to characterize the whole concept of human rights as being a "bourgeois fallacy" – a deceitful and illusory theory designed to "weaken the fighting spirit" of the proletariat. This stance changed dramatically from the mid-1980s onwards, after the Chinese government began to become actively involved in the human rights treaty and monitoring mechanisms of the United Nations. To date China has ratified the Convention on the Elimination of All Forms of Discrimination Against Women (1981), Convention on the Elimination of All Forms of Racial Discrimination (1982), Convention Against Torture (1988), the Convention on the Rights of the Child (1992), and the International Covenant on Social, Economic and Cultural Rights (2001); in addition, it has signed but not yet ratified the International Covenant on Civil and Political Rights (1998.)[75] China has also begun cooperating with several of the UN's thematic human rights mechanisms: in 1994, it invited the UN Special Rapporteur on the Question of Religious Intolerance to visit China; in 1996 and 1997, it invited the chairman of the UN Working Group on Arbitrary Detention; in 2003 it hosted a visit by the UN Special Rapporteur on Education; and a long-delayed visit to China by the UN Special Rapporteur on Torture took place in late 2005. In the labour rights field, China has so far ratified only three of the eight fundamental conventions of the International Labour Organization (ILO) – the Equal Remuneration Convention (No.100), the Minimum Age Convention (No.138) and the Worst Forms of Child Labour Convention (No.182.) In particular, China has not yet signed or ratified the two core ILO standards on workers' freedom of association – Conventions No. 87 on Freedom of Association and Protection of the Right to Organize, and No. 98 on the Right to Organize and Collective Bargaining; according to the ILO's 1998 Declaration on Fundamental Principles and Rights at Work, however, Conventions No. 87 and 98 are held to be so fundamental that they are regarded as binding upon all member states of the ILO, irrespective of ratification status.

---

75 In addition, prior to mainland China's return to the U.N. in 1971, the Nationalist government had ratified numerous international conventions which remained in force thereafter; among these were the UN's Protocol Relating to the Status of Refugees (1967), the Convention Relating to the Status of Refugees, the Convention on the Prevention and Punishment of the Crime of Genocide, the International Convention on the Suppression and Punishment of the Crimes of Apartheid, and the four Geneva Conventions of Aug. 12, 1949, and their two additional protocols

While in practice the Chinese government still continues all too often to treat human rights issues as being largely a "battle front" in its international relations with Western countries, especially the United States, and hence much of its activities in the human rights arena have tended to consist mainly of propaganda-type efforts aimed at refuting and dispelling international condemnation of its poor domestic human rights record in such areas as freedom of expression and association and over the still-entrenched problem of police brutality and torture, there are nonetheless increasingly clear signs of progress in China today in the direction of greater human rights protections under the law. Law centres for the study of human rights have been set up in several major Chinese universities, numerous academic books on the subject are published each year in China nowadays, extensive programmes of scholarly exchange on law and human rights are now underway between China and a range of Western countries, and Chinese legal scholars are publishing ever bolder articles on the need for greater human rights' protections of all kinds.

In addition, the Chinese government has for many years now been engaging in a programme of regular "human rights dialogue" with a number of Western governments, including the U.S., the E.U and several of its member states. Although Beijing still uses its involvement in such activities as a means of pressuring its dialogue counterparts into ceasing or soft-pedalling any public criticism of continuing human rights abuses in China (for example, the government has suspended its rights dialogue with the U.S. on several occasions in recent years in protest against Washington's attempts to have China's rights record openly debated at the UN Commission on Human Rights), there is nonetheless mounting evidence to suggest that the whole issue of human rights has now become relatively well entrenched within China's official governmental discourse, and moreover that it is being taken increasingly seriously by senior policy makers within both the executive and legislative branches of the government.[76]

On the whole, Chinese officials are nowadays "talking the talk" on human rights but not yet "walking the walk." But whereas ten or so years ago, it was fair to say that the authorities were essentially just paying lip service to human rights concerns and issues, nowadays the central question has become: what are the main continuing legal, political and institutional obstacles to the effective implementation of the range of human rights and citizens' rights that have already been laid down by the government in various laws – and how much farther can the envelope feasibly be pushed in this general direction under China's existing one-party state system? To an extent, the Chinese government's increased level of engagement both in the international human rights arena and in terms of its domestic law-making progress on rights over the past decade and more has been driven by a desire to reburnish its international image in the wake of the international public relations catastrophe created by the military crushing of the April-June 1989 Tiananmen Square democracy movement. But it would be unfair to see this as the major causal factor. Rather, the pressure for greater rights protection under the law since the early 1990s has mainly come from two broad domestic constituencies or groups of actors: first, from influential policy-making sectors, including large numbers of both government officials and prominent academics in the fields of law and other related specialties; and second, from the general public, large numbers of whom have been adversely affected by the course of economic reform and have taken

---

76 For a detailed study of China's growing involvement in the international human rights arena, and of the efforts by Western countries to promote the human rights agenda in China, see: Rosemary Foot, *Rights Beyond Borders: The Global Community and the Struggle over Human Rights in China*, Oxford University Press, 2000; and Ann Kent, *China, the United Nations, and Human Rights: The Limits of Compliance*, University of Pennsylvania Press (Philadelphia), 1999.

increasingly to pressing their demands both in public, through protest demonstrations and the like, and also through the courts.

Many writers on Chinese law have lamented the combination of "a low level of rights consciousness" on the part of most Chinese people and the general absence of a rights-based conception of law in China's historical tradition. However, there is an important sense in which the transition to modernity, of the kind that China is currently experiencing at almost break-neck speed, creates an ideological short-cut to the popular embrace and acceptance of the core tenets of rule of law – especially when the previously dominant ideology (as is also the case in China today) is undergoing rapid disintegration and collapse. Stanley Lubman writes searchingly on this point:

> As both Communist ideology and official virtue decline, the rule of law could fill the growing vacuum of belief, despite the absence of a strong rights-based tradition in Chinese society....The rule of law challenges [both Chinese] tradition and the decaying ideology that has been used to justify the Party-state. When its validity becomes generally recognized, the rule of law itself functions as an ideology that legitimates the exercise of a distinct form of power. When Chinese individuals participate in litigation they *experience* the rights-consciousness dimension of law.... Other observers have concluded that what Chinese today mean when they say that there is no law "is something very specific: the government is not restrained by its own rules, *and it should be*."[77]

Elsewhere, Lubman develops this important theme further:

> Chinese often express cynicism about the relationship between law and [Party] policy, and scepticism about the fairness of the courts, especially when cases involve persons with considerable power and influence over the judges. Most interesting of all is the fact that the standard against which they measure the performance of the Party-state in legal matters, one that is entirely understandable to the West, embodies the essence of the rule of law. Although that concept is often said to be a unique product of Western civilization and many Chinese have heard of it as an imported idea, it has roots in Chinese circumstance. The perception that they have been ruled for decades by arbitrary and frequently hypocritical cadres has led many Chinese to believe that government should be based on universally applicable rules, and that under such a government certain rights ought to be recognized and protected by the uniform application of rules. These sentiments about the rule of law suggest a heightened interest in legal institutions, and Chinese seem to be increasingly willing to litigate disputes.[78]

These observations are certainly borne out by the statistics on the numbers of lawsuits being brought by Chinese citizens in recent years. In the politically controversial field of labour rights and labour disputes, for example, the numbers of Chinese workers who have been taking either their employers or local governments to court in search of redress for their grievances has roughly doubled each year since the promulgation in 1994 of China's first Labour Law. Moreover, out of an approximate total

---

77 Lubman (op cit), pp.306-7. The passage in quotation marks is taken from Donald C. Clarke and James V. Feinerman, "Antagonistic Contradictions: Criminal Law and Human Rights in China," in Stanley B. Lubman (ed.), *China's Legal Reforms*, Oxford University Press, 1996, p.153.
78 Lubman (1999, op cit), p.126.

number of 300,000 registered labour disputes that arose in 2002, more than half failed to be resolved at the administrative "labour dispute arbitration" level to the workers' satisfaction, with the result that the workers then took their cases to court for formal legal adjudication. (Although the courts found in either total or partial favour of the workers over their employers in more than half of these cases, it should be noted that a large proportion of the judgements were subsequently ignored by the employers, and that the courts, as is true also in many other branches of the Chinese legal system, generally made little effort to enforce them.) As Mary Gallagher has tellingly noted, however, perhaps the main reason for this upsurge in labour dispute-related litigation is that Chinese workers are systematically denied the right to form independent trade unions or any other kind of shopfloor-level negotiating bodies of the kind that might have allowed their grievances to be dealt with at an early stage and in an informal, non-litigious manner.[79] The government's widespread prohibition of freedom of association in other areas of civil society, moreover, may well be driving much of the litigation that is taking place in other areas of the law as well.

In the similarly sensitive area of administrative law, which has granted Chinese citizens the previously unimaginable right to challenge the legality of actions or decisions made by the various agencies of government, an equally high level of public litigation has arisen in recent years. According to Peerenboom, the total number of administrative lawsuits in China in 1999 fell just short of 100,000, and plaintiffs prevailed "in whole or in part" in almost 40 percent of these cases. (By contrast, only 12 percent of plaintiffs prevail in similar lawsuits in the U.S. and Taiwan, and between 4-8 percent do so in Japan.)[80] Lubman, however, examining court statistics up to 1997, found that "The percentage of cases in which the courts rescinded a challenged administrative decision has remained below 20 percent since 1990 except for one year, and it fell as low as 15 percent in 1995-97." As Lubman also notes, "By subject matter, cases against the police have been the largest category in every year except 1996," and cases of this type have accounted for between 16 percent and 34 percent of all administrative lawsuits brought by citizens.

Nonetheless, it is important to note that despite the seemingly high number of administrative lawsuit cases being brought nowadays in China, the numbers are still very low when compared with the overall scale of government agency activity around the country.[81] And significantly, a high proportion of administrative cases (between 10 and 56 percent over the period 1991-97) are withdrawn by the plaintiff and so do not come to court, most likely as a result of official pressure from above on the plaintiffs. According to Veron Mei-Ying Hong, who conducted a field study in 1998-99 among citizens who had tried to sue the police, mainly in administrative lawsuits challenging sentences of "re-education through labour":

---

79 See: Mary E. Gallagher, "Use the Law as Your Weapon! The Rule of Law and Labor Conflict in China," in *Engaging Chinese Law*, Neil Diamant, Kevin O'Brien, Stanley Lubman (eds.) Forthcoming, Stanford University Press, 2005.
80 Peerenboom (op cit), p.400 and p.404.
81 As Peerenboom points out, "[T]here are still many fewer cases than one might expect, particularly given how often plaintiffs are successful. In fact there are amazingly few cases relative to the total number of specific administrative acts.... In 1996, [for example,] there were 20,000 driver license confiscations in Guangxi but not one was challenged through either administrative reconsideration or litigation. There were approximately 50,000 family planning decisions a year in Guangxi but only about 10 challenges under the ALL. And there were 1,600 cases of reeducation through labour in 1996 but only 35 requests (2.2%) for administrative reconsideration." Peerenboom, op cit, p.404.

The majority of those interviewed identified interference by administrative organs and by the Chinese Communist Party as the greatest difficulty encountered in administrative litigation. Such interference may occur during the entire course of an administrative case, but it is especially common before the case is accepted. At subsequent stages, judges may be pressured to uphold the administrative act, and aggrieved parties may be pressured to withdraw the case.[82]

Lawsuits under the Administrative Litigation Law may also be accompanied by tort actions under the State Compensation Law, indeed claims under the two statutes can be combined into a single suit. However, those claiming damages for injuries caused by the illegal exercise of authority by state functionaries must first file their complaint or claim with the agency directly concerned, before being allowed to proceed with court action under the State Compensation Law. (This is also the required procedure in most other types of administrative litigation, although the initial complaint is generally made to the next-higher level of the state agency concerned.)

There are several fundamental limitations to the administrative litigation system as it currently exists. First, any act or decision taken by the Communist Party or any of its subordinate bodies is exempted from challenge or review in the administrative courts.[83] Second, the courts are permitted neither to challenge the appropriateness and suitability of a specific administrative act (for example, a police decision to impose "labour re-education" on somebody), nor to strike down (still less declare unconstitutional) the law or regulation under which the administrative action was carried out. The courts are only empowered to rule on the technical issue of whether or not the act was lawful, in the sense of being permissible under the particular law or regulation in question.[84] In addition, since China's legal system does not follow or permit the application of case precedence, the significance of any given ruling that overturns an administrative action by a state agency goes no further than the single case in question and can therefore exert no wider legal reform function. Nonetheless, by contrast with the previous almost total absence of legal remedies available to citizens wronged or mistreated by state officials, the present system of administrative litigation represents a substantial breakthrough; and above all, it is clearly contributing to a significant escalation of popular rights consciousness at the grassroots level of society, in both urban and rural areas.

Official Chinese Conceptions of the Rule of Law

After some 25 years of intensive legal reform in China, can it now justifiably be said that China's rulers have succeeded in establishing a genuine "rule of law"? Any attempt to answer this question is inevitably beset by a host of largely intractable dilemmas and difficulties – linguistic, cultural and

---

82　Veron Mei-Ying Hong, "Improving Human Rights in China: Should Re-Education Through Labor Be Abolished?" *Columbia Journal of Transnational Law*, Vol. 42 (2003), pp.303-326, at p.322.
83　As Lubman observes, "[O]mission of the Party from the organizations whose decisions may be challenged means that the one entity that is the ultimate maker of decisions in every government organization at the present time, the Party Committee, remains unchallengeable by the courts." (Lubman, op cit, p.214.) In addition, Chinese officials have begun to develop counter-measures to avoid being sued by members of the public, such as issuing documents in the name of the CCP, since the latter is granted immunity from administrative litigation. (See Peerenboom [op cit 2002], p.403, citing Jiang Ping 1995, in Xia Yong, *Zouxiang Quanli de Shidai*.)
84　As Lubman points out, "Courts are forbidden to interpret the general validity of legislation or administrative rules and, moreover, must defer to administrative agencies' interpretation of their own rules." Lubman (op cit), p.8.

legal-conceptual. A good place to start is on the terminological level, since this will allow us to perceive more clearly how China's leaders themselves see this question. In 1978, at the outset of the reforms, the main concept officially used in China was "*fa zhi*" (法制), meaning "legal system", and the debate at that time centred on how to use legal institutions to ensure that "rule by law" (*fa zhi* 法治) would prevail over the system of unchecked "rule by man" (*ren zhi*) that had characterized the preceding 30 years of Maoist "cult of the personality."[85] The emphasis during most of the first decade of legal reform in China – as officially expressed in the phrase "*yi fa zhiguo*" (以法治国), meaning "use law to rule the country" – was on an essentially instrumentalist concept of law and legality, whereby the legal system would allow the Party and government to administer the country in a more objective, impartial and rules-based manner than had hitherto been possible.[86] In other words, China at this time had a system of rule *by* law, rather than rule of law. The idea that law should serve to create a more level playing field between the state and its citizens, with the latter being able to claim and enjoy greater rights vis-à-vis the former, was certainly discernible in official policy at this time, but it was by no means central to it.

Throughout the 1980s, however, a fast growing community of progressive-minded legal scholars in China tried in various ways to push forward the frontiers of legal reform, and calls for the protection and strengthening of individual citizens' rights were expressed with increasing force and frequency. By early 1989, as the following passage by Stanley Lubman shows, this wider campaign of legal reform had reached remarkable heights:

> A notable articulation of scholarly views appeared just before the Tiananmen events. In late April of 1989 the journal of the Legal Research Institute of the Chinese Academy of Sciences published a summary of discussions by leading legal scholars at a conference earlier in the year. Their sentiments and proposals amount to a clear call for establishment of the rule of law based on principles familiar in the West:
>
> – law is not a tool of class dictatorship, and legal institutions such as the legislature, the Procuracy and the courts must be independent;
>
> – the state and the Party must be subject to law;
>
> – the Party may not supplant the state and policy may not supplant the law;
>
> – the NPC must not be a "rubber stamp" and its members should be elected in public campaigns;
>
> – political power must be divided by a system of checks and balances, and laws should be enacted to establish a system of constitutional government that will define procedures for amending the constitution;
>
> – administrative agencies must be permitted to act only within their legal competence, and an administrative court should be established to exercise control over official arbitrariness;
>
> – legislation and implementation of law must be aimed at maximizing citizens' rights and freedoms and restricting government powers;

---

85 As Peerenboom observes, "The debate ended in a victory for the rule-of-law camp when the 1982 constitution incorporated the basic principles of a government of laws not men, the supremacy of the law, and the equality of all before the law." (Peerenboom, op cit, p.57.)
86 See Note 92, below.

– citizens' rights and freedoms may not be restricted except through the exercise of due process.[87]

Although legal reform, like most other areas of reform in China, went into relative deep freeze for a several-year period after the June 4, 1989 government suppression of the Tiananmen Square democracy movement, it was reactivated after Deng Xiaoping's spring 1992 "Tour of the South" (*nan xun)*, which inaugurated the country's definitive move towards capitalist-style economic reforms (in official parlance: the "socialist market economy".) Reforms were particularly slow in the criminal justice field, however, and even as late as 1995, the vexed and widely deplored practice of "verdict first, trial second" (*xianpan houshen*, also translatable as "decision first, trial later") was still in common use in China's criminal courts. As the Supreme People's Procuracy candidly stated that year,

> The main problem [in adjudication]…is the practice of decision first, trial later, first making the ruling, then conducting the trial; internal instructions are implemented and positions coordinated, the Court President and Division President, even the officials of higher courts, determine guilt and set the punishment, then begin adjudication in the courtroom, turning what in reality is two adjudications into one. This practice causes the division of the courts into levels to exist in name only, causes adjudication activities in court to become merely formalistic appearances, and to a certain extent deprives defendants of their right to trial.[88]

A major set of revisions to the Criminal Procedure Law, promulgated in March 1996, increased the rights of criminal defendants in a number of key areas, notably in allowing earlier access to legal counsel and in establishing a rudimentary form of the presumption of innocence (for example, criminal detainees would henceforth be known as "suspects" rather than "criminals.") But the revised law actually increased the already more than generous time limits on pre-trial detention, and most independent accounts have found that in practice, since 1996, the new array of defendants' rights has been honoured more in the breach than in the observance.[89] In particular, the continuing problem of widespread torture of criminal suspects and the extraction of forced confessions in police custody has remained a major blight on China's law enforcement scene from the early 1980s until the present.[90] Since March 1996, another source of judicial abuse has been Article 306 of the revised Criminal Law,

---

87 Cited in Lubman (op cit), pp.124-5.
88 Criminal Law Section, Legal Affairs Committee of the NPC, "Opinions of the Supreme People's Court, Supreme People's Procuracy, Public Security Ministry and Ministry of Justice on Revision of the Criminal Procedure Law," June 19, 1995. According to Stanley Lubman, who cites the above passage in *Bird in a Cage* (p.164), "This memorandum summarizes the views of participants in a conference held from Mar. 25 to Apr. 24, 1995; copy in the author's files." (Ibid, p.394.)
89 For a comprehensive assessment of the 1996 reforms of the Criminal Procedure Law, see Human Rights in China, *Empty Promises: Human Rights Protections and China's Criminal Procedure Law in Practice*, New York, February 2001. For a detailed analysis of the rights provisions of the revised Criminal Law of 1997, see: Donald C. Clarke, *Wrongs and Rights: A Human Rights Analysis of China's Revised Criminal Code*, Lawyers Committee for Human Rights (New York), December 1998.
90 It is worth noting, however, that the first major study of this problem ever produced by an international human rights group – Amnesty International's 1988 report, *Torture in China* – was in large part based on specific and detailed case reports that appeared in China's own main newspaper on the legal system, *Zhongguo Fazhi Bao* (since renamed *Fazhi Ribao*), between 1985 and 1988 exposing and detailing the use of torture by Chinese PSB officers around the country. For a more recent analysis of this problem, see: Murray Scot Tanner, "Shackling the Coercive State: China's Ambivalent Struggle against Torture", *Problems of Post-Communism*, Sept-Oct, 2000.

which specifically targets criminal defence lawyers for "fabrication of evidence"; since Article 307 of the same law provides a general prohibition on evidence fabrication, the singling out of lawyers in particular in this regard is legally redundant and serves only an intimidatory and control purpose.[91] Dozens of lawyers around the country have been arrested and jailed under this provision in recent years.

Also in 1996, President Jiang Zemin put forward the slogan of "ruling the country in accordance with law" (*yi-fa zhiguo* 依法治国), and in 1999 this concept was further expanded and then formally incorporated into the State Constitution as: "Rule the country in accordance with law and establish a socialist rule-of-law state" (*yi-fa zhiguo, jianshe shehuizhuyi fazhiguo*.) This formulation marked a substantial step forward as compared to the official thinking of the 1980s, when the dominant term in legal discourse had been the more instrumentalist one of "using law to rule the country." The subtly revised formula of "ruling the country in accordance with law"[92] implied clearly that law was henceforth to serve as the yardstick of official behaviour – and moreover, China was now officially described as being a "rule-of-law state," or at least one in which the rule of law was being actively and progressively built. In March 2004, among a series of amendments to the Constitution, the NPC included, for the first time, a specific mention of human rights. (According to Article 33 of the revised Constitution, "The State respects and preserves human rights.")[93]

In an article comprehensively reviewing the various main viewpoints and perspectives on rule of law currently held by the mainland Chinese legal community, the Hong Kong-based law scholar Albert Chen stresses that a majority is clearly in favour of a rights-based concept of law that would serve to bind the rulers as well as the people.[94] He warns, however, that leftist-conservative legal scholars have continued, in recent years, to wage a sustained and determined counterattack against this consensus viewpoint:

> The conservative scholars...attack the use of the concepts of social contract, civil society, the priority of rights and the spirit of modern law. They claim that the ideas of social contract and natural rights were ideological devices used by bourgeois writers to create the illusion of a just social order, to mask the reality of class oppression in

---

91 See: Congressional-Executive Commission on China (CECC), "Defense Lawyers Turned Defendants: Zhang Jianzhong and the Criminal Prosecution of Defense Lawyers in China," 28 May 2003; available at: www.cecc.gov/pages/news/zhang_052703.php. See also: CECC, "Zhang Jianzhong Case Update," 29 March 2004; available at: www.cecc.gov/pages/news/zhangupdate.php.
92 The terminological distinction between "using law to rule the country" and "ruling the country in accordance with law" could scarcely be finer or more subtle, since in Chinese the two phrases sound almost identical (*yi fa zhiguo*.) The separation of meaning is expressed through the first character alone, which is tonally distinct in either case: in the former phase, *yi* (以) means "to use", while in the latter, *yi* (依) means "in accordance with" or "to rely upon."
93 An interesting account of how the public security organs and the Party's "politics and law committees" are coping with this unfamiliar concept can be found in: Zhao Ling, "*Zhongguo 'Zheng-Fa Xi' Lichi 'Renquan' Huayu*" (China's "Politics and Law Network" Strives to Uphold "Human Rights" Language), *Nanfang Zhoumo* (Southern Weekend), 2 July 2004.
94 For a fascinating, blow-by-blow account of the various major issues around which progressive legal scholars have tried to campaign since 1978 in order to push forward legal frontiers in China (for example, on the presumption of innocence, the campaign for a Press Law, and a reduction in the use of the death penalty), see: Guo Daohui, Li Buyun and HaoTiechuan, *Zhongguo Dangdai Faxue Zhengming Lu* (A Record of Contention on the Science of Law in Contemporary China), *Hunan Renmin Chubanshe*, December 1998.

the capitalist state and to deceive the proletariat. There is no need for these ideas in the socialist state. "The use of these terms would only serve to beautify capitalism and destroy socialism." "Civil society" is said to be relevant only to bourgeois society in the period of *laissez faire* capitalism.[95]

Perhaps the most insightful summary of China's current progress toward rule of law is one put forward by Cai Dingjian, a law professor at the China University of Politics and Law, in which he uses the metaphors of "the knife, the baton and the bridle" to symbolize the three stages of legal evolution in China since 1978. Albert Chen presents Cai's views as follows:

> The period of "the knife" ran from 1949 to the early 1980s. Law was conceived as an instrument of class dictatorship and for the suppression of "enemies." Hence law meant primarily criminal law. The period of "the baton" began in the 1980s and continues to the present. Law is conceived as a tool for administrative management of people and the economy. This is an era of administrative law and economic law. The next period in China's legal evolution will be that of "the bridle." This will be the age of constitutionalism. Law will control the exercise of state power, prevent its abuse and protect the rights of citizens. It will attend not only to order and efficiency (the concerns of the previous eras), but also to justice, equality, freedom and democracy.[96]

"Thin" and "Thick" Rules of Law

Western academic observers of the post-Mao legal reforms have also generally taken a less than sanguine view of the current state of development of rule of law in China. According to the prominent China law scholar, William Alford, for example,

> [T]he principal state architects of China's post-Cultural Revolution law reform project have a genuine ambivalence toward their undertaking. On the one hand, they wish to reap the advantages of liberal legality in terms of its perceived capacity to support economic growth, engage the international community, and legitimate the existing regime. On the other hand, however, they aspire to do so without being unduly subject to its constraints, either in the obvious sense of explicit limits of the

---

95 Albert Chen, "Toward a Legal Enlightenment: Discussion in Contemporary China on the Rule of Law," *UCLA Pacific Basin Law Journal*, 1999/2000, Vol. 17, Nos. 2 & 3, pp.125-165. As Chen further notes, "The 'leftist' sentiment of these scholars is vividly reflected in the following passage: 'We must not exchange away Marxist principles when we borrow from, inherit or transplant Western legal and political thought and institutions.... If we allow a "contract" of exchange between Marxism and non-Marxism, if we let Marxism be auctioned in the market, then this socialist society of ours can no longer be sustained.'" (Quoted passages from Lü Shilun, "Several Theoretical Questions Relating to the Construction of the Legal System," *Gao-Xiao Lilun Zhanxian* [Colleges' Theoretical Front], 1996, No. 4; and Zheng Guosheng, "What Kind of Society is the Society under the Socialist market Economy?" *Yifa Zhiguo, Jianshe Shehuizhuyi Fazhi Guojia,* Liu Hainian *et al* [eds.], 1996, p.440.)
96 See Chen (op cit), pp.46-7. See also: Cai Dingjian, "Towards the Rule of Law: Where is the Way?" in *Yifa Zhiguo, Jianshe Shehuizhuyi Fazhi Guojia,* Liu Hainian et al (eds.), 1996, pp.395-6; and "Development of the Chinese Legal System Since 1979 and its Current Crisis and Transformation," in *Cultural Dynamics*, 1999, Vol. 11, No. 2, pp.133-166. I am grateful to Sophia Woodman, a researcher at the law department of Hong Kong University, for drawing these articles to my attention and for sharing with me her reading notes on rule of law and human rights issues in China.

type that liberal legality places on the exercise of political authority, or in the more subtle ways that adherence to a system of consistently and visibly enforced rules tends to limit even the well-intentioned exercise of discretion by those in power.[97]

Although the leadership has been drawing extensively on foreign experience in legal reform, Alford adds, it has tried to "keep within sharply circumscribed bounds" the key idea that law should "enjoy autonomy and not be subordinated to politics." According to another commentator, Geor Hintzen, even in the 1990s the mainstream of mainland legal thinking held that China should follow a combination of rule of law and rule of man, namely "the establishment of a legal system to make personal rule more routine." In his view, "In the 1990s, the phrase 'rule by law' was intended as an instrument in the hands of personal power rather than as a form of supreme legal power. In other words, law was not to limit power, but to make it even more effective."[98] Another acute observer of China's legal scene, David Cowhig, uses the example of the Chinese security authorities' decade-long crackdown on Internet freedoms to illustrate another structural problem in the rule of law equation, namely the growing lack of effective centralism in the modern Chinese state:

> When asking the question "Whose Hand is on the Switch?" about the internet in China we need to bear in mind that there are many hands and many switches. Chinese provincial and local governments and indeed various parts of the central government have far greater coordination problems than we experience among the federal, state and local governments in the United States. China might be thought of as a decentralized de facto federal state that lacks federal institutions that facilitate central control and coordination such as the federal court system and regional offices of central government ministries. China is best understood not so much as a Big Brother state but as a loose collection of thousands of provincial and local Party and government little brothers. Many of the provincial little brothers have only nominal allegiance to Big Brother in Beijing. Local officials want to control media not just for Beijing's purposes but also to prevent Beijing to know about their own shortcomings. Many orders and regulations from the central government are ignored from the outset or forgotten after only a few months.[99]

Both Lubman and Peerenboom, in their respective recent books analyzing the state of law in China today, each of which is magisterial in scope and deeply-textured in content, conclude that China is currently situated, at best, somewhere on a line of development prior to the emergence of even the most minimally defined rule of law. Of the two writers, Lubman is evidently the least optimistic in this regard, and his principal concerns or reservations are as follows:

---

97 William P. Alford, "A Second Great Wall? China's Post-Cultural Revolution Project of Legal Construction," *Cultural Dynamics*, 1999, Vol. 11, No. 2, pp.193-213; at p.198 and p.201.
98 Geor H. Hintzen, "The Place of Law in the PRC's Culture," *Cultural Dynamics*, 1999, Vol. 11, No. 2, pp.167-192; at p.179 and p.181.
99 David Cowhig, "Wired China: Many Hands on Many Switches," Statement to the Congressional-Executive Commission on China's Round-Table on Internet and Free Flow of Information in China, Washington D.C., 15 April 2002. As Cowhig further notes, "The state of the web in China reflects the uncertain state of China itself. Most Chinese, including most Communist Party members, want a more democratic and more open society. China's communist leaders fear that the development and modernization [it] brings will help…shake their hold on power and lead to social instability. A Chinese provincial vice governor said a few years ago, 'We are the guardians of a dead religion but must hold on for the sake of social stability'." For the full text of Cowhig's statement, see: http://www.cecc.gov/pages/roundtables/041502/cowhig.php.

Serious constraints on effectiveness arise out of the Party's determination to retain political control. The avowed policy of increasing legality has not been carried out firmly and consistently; law and the courts are still expected to be secondary to Party policy. The local Party-state seriously influences the day-to-day work of the courts.... One of the most striking defects of legal reform is the failure to raise the position of the judicial system from its current level; it remains at the same level as other bureaucratic hierarchies of the state and lacks authority over them....

A genuine CCP commitment to establish the rule of law would require the Party to depart from a principle it has followed since the PRC was established: policy, as defined and implemented by the CCP, must be supreme over law....[100]

However, simply promulgating new laws that create rights to challenge arbitrary officials in the courts will not remove the major obstacles that current Chinese governmental practices present to the growth of rule of law.... The rule of law will not advance as long as the courts (or some other functional equivalent within the administration) lack the power to interpret and decide on the validity of legislation and of administrative rules.[101]

For these reasons, Lubman concludes that China is still far from having achieved even a minimal-level or "thin" rule of law – which he defines as a system in which legal rules and standards objectively exist, are stable and are basically followed and supported by the populace, and where law is the supreme authority and the courts can function impartially and without direct political interference. Indeed, he would go still further:

Because of the lack of a unifying concept of law, and even more so because of the fragmentation of authority that marks China today, I have nowhere in this book referred to a Chinese legal *system*, only to Chinese legal institutions.[102]

Peerenboom, throughout his account of China's legal reforms, is consistently more ready to see the glass as being half full, and this perception extends to his assessment of the rule of law issue as well. However, he too is ultimately unwilling to accord this accolade to the Chinese legal system today:

Of course, while it may no longer be accurate to describe China's legal system as rule by law, whether the system in its current form merits the label rule of law is another matter.... In light of [its] many shortcomings...I have described China's legal system as in transition toward rule of law but still falling short of the minimal standard of achievement required to be considered rule of law. Problems such as the treatment of political dissidents and the inability of the legal system to hold senior-most officials accountable would certainly give me pause in describing Chinese system as even an imperfect rule of law. The cumulative toll of these everyday deficiencies, in my view, is sufficient to deny China's current system the title rule of law, even allowing that there is sufficient evidence of a credible normative commitment to the principle that law is to bind the state and state actors...[103]

---

100   Ibid, p.130.
101   Ibid, pp.301-2.
102   Ibid, p.3.
103   Peerenboom (op cit), p.140.

Here again, Peerenboom is applying the "thin" rule of law standard. (Both writers agree that none of the "thick" conceptions of law – whether of the State Socialist, Liberal Democratic, Neo-authoritarian or Communitarian variant forms – apply in China's case, since all four require "thin" rule of law as a minimum prerequisite.) However, where Lubman's position on the rule of law issue can best be described as one of cautious pessimism, Peerenboom appears rather to take a generally optimistic view of the system's future prospects. In particular, he downplays the significance of the Communist Party's continuing dominance over the legal system and society as a whole. As he observes,

> The most common explanation for China's troubles place the brunt of the blame on ideology and the attitudes of China's ruling elite, particularly senior Party leaders. Analyses of China's failure to realize rule of law thus typically begin, and all too often end, by noting that China remains a single party socialist state. Some critics argue that single party socialism is simply incompatible with rule of law and a limited government because the leading role of the Party cannot be reconciled with the supremacy of the law and a system in which law limits Party power....
>
> In contrast, I suggest that single party socialism in which the Party plays a leading role is in theory compatible with rule of law, albeit not a Liberal Democratic version of rule of law. Party members and government officials are required to comply with the law, and in practice their behaviour is increasingly constrained by law, especially when compared to twenty years ago. Although the CCP still often fails to abide by the circumscribed role set forth in the state and Party constitutions, on a day-to-day level, direct interference by Party organs in administrative rule-making or specific agency decisions is not common.[104]

While it is true that the Party tends to interfere less frequently in court decisions these days, the extent to which Party organs, and considerations of politics in general, continue to be granted the fundamental "leading role" over China's entire legal system can be clearly gauged from Article 3 of the PRC Law on Legislation – a law which was widely seen, at the time of its promulgation in July 2000, as marking a major step forward in the country's progress toward rule of law:

> Law making must respect and follow the basic principles of the Constitution, namely taking economic construction as the central task, upholding the socialist road, upholding the people's democratic dictatorship, upholding the leadership of the CCP, upholding Marxism-Leninism-Mao Zedong Thought and Deng Xiaoping Theory, and upholding reform and opening.[105]

For the most part, however, rather than seeking to apply either the "thin" or "thick" normative conceptions of rule of law to China's present stage of legal development, both Lubman and Peerenboom advocate the use of a less value-laden and more functionally oriented process of "thick description" – that is, a process of building up an empirically based account of what the legal system currently is, and of how it actually works in practice. As Lubman explains this approach,

> In framing research into the dynamics of Chinese legal institutions, it seems desirable to avoid high levels of abstraction and to be self-conscious about the simplest of concepts that are the basic building blocks of Western legal analysis. Suggestions

---

104 Peerenboom (op cit), pp.10-11.
105 The Law on Legislation of the People's Republic of China, passed by the NPC on 15 March 2000 and effective 1 July 2000.

for a useful approach come from Clifford Geertz, who advocates restraining the level of conceptualization that is appropriate to use in order to develop cross-cultural understanding, characterizing it as "thick description." The foreign student of Chinese law is like Geertz's ethnographer, and Geertz's suggestion is apposite here: The foreign student must begin close to the perspective of the participants themselves and keep analytical concepts grounded in thick description of the specific details of the institutions under study.[106]

As noted earlier, this approach yields rich and impressive results in both writers' cases. Where Lubman's conclusions as to the current nature and potential of China's legal reforms consistently seem to remain more firmly grounded in the bottom line or "thin" conception of rule of law, however, Peerenboom – having issued an overall "fail" mark to China in this regard – then tends to discount the salience and importance of this finding by proceeding on the implicit assumption that "thick description" is everything. A theme that runs throughout his book is that China will most likely end up with its own distinctive form of rule of law, one that differs substantially from any of the present ideal types (or "thick" variants) that are currently on offer around the world. It is hard to fault this argument: China is certainly large and powerful enough, and it has a sufficiently distinctive cultural tradition, to make such an outcome not just possible but almost inevitable. Moreover, to deny the appropriateness of such an outcome would be to risk placing an undue emphasis upon Western-derived standards and benchmarks for legal development. Where rule of law and human rights are concerned, however, there are conspicuous and persuasive grounds for fearing that the danger of falling into the opposite dilemma – that of cultural relativism – is if anything still greater. The area of Chinese law in which Peerenboom most clearly falls into error in this regard is in his treatment of the question of administrative detention in China.

Punishment without Crime

If one had to choose a single criterion or yardstick for determining whether or not a country had attained the minimum standard of observance of rule of law, then the consensus view among law and human rights scholars would probably be that freedom from arbitrary detention is the *sine qua non* standard for assessment. In the absence of this fundamental legal guarantee, attempts to safeguard and protect all other key rights – notably freedom of expression, freedom of association, and the right not to be tortured or subjected to other forms of cruel and unusual punishment – become highly problematical if not impossible. Certainly, a person being subjected to arbitrary detention is unlikely, to the extent that they have any inclination at all to ponder such abstract questions of jurisprudence, to distinguish between whether the legal system under which they are being mistreated is a "thick" one of the Statist Socialist or Liberal Democratic variant, or alternatively a less exalted legal system still struggling to make the grade as a "thin rule of law." They simply want to regain their freedom as soon as possible and to be treated as a person with basic rights and dignity. China's present legal system makes extensive provision for the police to impose a wide range of different forms of administrative detention, all of which constitute, to a greater or lesser extent, arbitrary detention, and all of which have been very widely used since the 1950s. Over the past decade or so, the Chinese government has come under increasing pressure from the human rights agencies of the U.N. – so far without success – either to abolish or to reform these time-honoured police practices by making them subject to at least a minimum level of

---

106 Lubman (op cit), p.38. See also Clifford Geertz, "Thick Description: Toward an Interpretive Theory of Culture," in Geertz, *The Interpretation of Cultures*, New York: Basic (1973), pp.1-30

judicial oversight and supervision. As Amnesty International has vividly noted, under China's present legal system, all such sentences in effect amount to "punishment without crime," since no court hearing has been held either to establish the facts or to apportion criminal responsibility.[107]

The first and most commonly used form of administrative detention in China is that provided for under the Security Administration Punishment Regulations (SAPR), issued initially in 1986 and then again in revised form in 1994.[108] Under these regulations, the police can impose sentences of up to 15 days in PSB-run detention centres (and fines of up to RMB 5,000 yuan) on people accused of harming the public order, infringing upon the personal rights of citizens or causing harm to public or private property, where such offences are deemed to be "not sufficiently serious to warrant criminal punishment." Persons subject to such sentences are technically allowed to "petition" the next-higher level of the PSB to have them reversed, and if that fails (which it almost invariably does), they can then take out an administrative lawsuit against the PSB in court. (Statistics on the number and efficacy of such lawsuits is hard to come by, but the overall success rate again seems to be very low.) However, such remedies are essentially post hoc in nature, since there is no right of habeas corpus under Chinese law and no provision is made for the detainee to gain access to legal counsel whilst in detention.

Until 1997, the most widespread form of administration detention was one known as "shelter for investigation" (*shourong shencha*), whereby criminal suspects whose identities were unclear or who were thought by the police to be engaged in cross-province criminal activity could be detained in police holding centres or camps for up to three months. In practice this measure was often unlawfully used by the police as a convenient substitute for criminal detention (which involves a degree of supervision by the procuracy), and frequently for much longer than three months. Although the revised Criminal Procedure Law of 1996 abolished this form of administrative detention, it incorporated the same general principle under a different heading and preserved several of its original defects.[109]

Another type of administrative detention that was recently abolished is "shelter for deportation" (*shourong qiansong*, also known as "custody and repatriation".) This was a measure whereby the police could detain vagrants, beggars and persons believed to be living and working in areas outside their place of "household registration" (*hukou suozaidi*) and for which they lacked the necessary residence approval documents. Once detained, such people were sent to special police holding camps for periods ranging from several days to more than a year, before being forcibly escorted back to their original place of residence. The police frequently used this measure to extort bribes from the detainees or their relatives, in order to secure the detainee's release, and conditions in the holding camps were widely reported to be considerably worse than in any other type of police detention centre in China. In March 2003, a young student named Sun Zhigang was beaten to death after being taken into "shelter for deportation" in Guangzhou,[110] and following a major public protest and outcry through the Internet over

---

107 See: Amnesty International, *China: Punishment Without Crime: Administrative Detention*, January 1993. See also: Veron Mei-Ying Hung, "Reassessing Reeducation Through Labour," *China Rights Forum* (New York), No. 2, 2003, pp.35-41.
108 The full Chinese text of these regulations can be found on the Internet at: http://www.cecc.gov/pages/selectLaws/criminalJustice/securityAdminRegs.php?PHPSESSID=c0f274d7de707b98d06377c3afe672b3.
109 For details, see Human Rights in China, *Empty Promises* (op cit.)
110 See: Amnesty International, "China: migrant worker dies in custody," July 2003, available at http://web.amnesty.org/wire/July2003/China. See also: "Court Reaches Final Decision on Sun Zhigang Case," Xinhua News Agency June 28, 2003.

this incident, in June 2003 the government finally abolished this form of administrative detention.[111] Estimates of the numbers of people subjected to "shelter for deportation" each year in China prior to its abolition range from between 10 and 20 million.[112]

In another widely reported case, in June 1999, Su Ping, a 26-year-old woman from the countryside in Hunan, was detained by police at Guangzhou railway station for being unable to produce her identity card. She explained that she had just had all her luggage stolen and that the ID card had been among the items stolen, and she instead showed the police her marriage license and local residency permit, which she had been carrying in her hand luggage. The police, however, forcibly removed her to the psychiatric wing of a hospital in the local town of Zengcheng, where she was placed overnight in a male ward. During the night, she was gang raped repeatedly by five or six men. Her husband found her there the following morning in a state of extreme physical and mental distress. According to a subsequent investigative report by the Washington Post,

> Only one man has been convicted of rape, and he has been sentenced to four years. Her biggest victory is that a court ruled in May [2000] that she is not mentally disturbed. Even that ruling was a long time in coming. After the incident, police allowed hospital officials to clean up the crime scene, destroying any evidence, according to her husband and media reports. Several of the men she identified as her assailants were released without an investigation even though she identified them in a police line-up…. A few days later, Zengcheng police called the couple and accused them of fabricating the case.[113]

Other forms of administrative detention that are still very widely used include "shelter for re-education" (*shourong jiaoyu* or *shourong jiaoyang*), under which prostitutes and their clients can receive police-imposed sentences of between six months and two years;[114] and "compulsory drug treatment" (*qiangzhi jiedu*), under which drug addicts can be detained for three to six months, with a maximum extension of up to one year in total, and made to undergo a forcible drug detoxification program (based on the "cold turkey" principle) administered by the police.[115] Significantly, China's compulsory drug treatment programme is increasingly being coordinated and implemented through the police-run Ankang custodial centres, which are also the institutions where most criminal suspects found to be not legally responsible by reason of insanity are sent for long-term treatment and custody.[116]

In June 2003, in a case with implications similar to that of Sun Zhigang, the three-year-old daughter of a female drug addict, Li Guifang, who had been sentenced to three months in a drug

---

111 Hamish McDonald, "China abolishes vagrancy law after death," Sydney Morning Herald, June 20 2003.
112 For a detailed account and critique of China's "custody and repatriation" program, see Human Rights in China, "Not Welcome at the Party: Behind the "Clean-Up" of China's Cities — A Report on Administrative Detention under 'Custody and Repatriation'," HRIC Arbitrary Detention Series, No. 2, September 1999, available at www.hrichina.org.
113 "Su Ping" was an alias used to protect the woman's identity. See: John Pomfret, "Chinese Rape Case Highlights Arbitrary Detention Policies," The Washington Post, 2 August 2000, p.A24; see also: "*Yi Nü Cuo Dang Jingshenbing, E Yun Tian Lun Jian*" (A Woman Wrongly Taken to be Mentally Ill Tragically Ends Up Being Gang Raped), *People's Daily Online*, 2 August 2000.
114 See NPC Standing Committee, "Decision on Strictly Prohibiting Prostitution," 4 September 1991; and PRC State Council, "Measures for Detention for Re-Education of Prostitutes," 4 September 1993.
115 See NPC Standing Committee, "Decision on Strictly Prohibiting Drugs," 28 December 1990; and PRC State Council, "Measures on Compulsory Drug Treatment," 12 January 1995.
116 See Note 522 below.

detoxification centre, starved to death because police officials had ignored Li's desperate pleas for them to release the young girl from her home, where Li had locked her in for safety reasons shortly before being detained and sentenced for drug taking. The child's body was not retrieved until 17 days after Li's arrest, following complaints from the neighbours about the smell emanating from her apartment. Again following a public outcry over the Internet, the two police officers responsible were a year later sentenced to two and three-year prison terms; in the meantime, however, the authorities had banned all further public discussion of the case and censors had systematically removed all postings about it from mainland Internet sites.[117]

However, the form of administrative detention in China which has rightly attracted the most severe and sustained criticism over the past two decades and more, both domestically and internationally, is "re-education through labour" (*laodong jiaoyang*.)[118] Under this measure, which has been in existence since the mid-1950s, the police are empowered to sentence suspected offenders to up to three years of administrative detention in special "camps" or "centres" for labour re-education, and the sentence can be extended to a maximum of four years in total if the person concerned fails to show contrition or to "reform" themselves properly whilst in custody. As in the case of the less serious "security administration" punishments, those sentenced to labour re-education can petition the next-higher level PSB authorities or sue the police in court in an attempt to have their sentences lifted, but the fragmentary statistics available on this topic suggest that such efforts are very rarely successful.[119] And again, the lack of habeas corpus remedies means that any such petitions or lawsuits have to be waged from the highly disadvantageous position of a police detention cell. Moreover, although detainees can in theory now seek legal counsel to help them wage an administrative lawsuit against the police to challenge sentences of labour re-education, in practice this right is largely vitiated by the fact that persons undergoing such sentences are still barred, under current regulations, from actually meeting with their lawyers. (By contrast, detainees formally held under the Criminal Procedure Law do now have the right, albeit far from sufficient, to meet with their lawyer during the investigative and pre-trial phases of custody.)[120]

---

117 Jane Cai, "Officers in Jail Over Starved Toddler," *South China Morning Post*, 23 August 2004.
118 For a very detailed recent study of this form of detention, see: Liu Jianguo (ed.), *Laodong Jiaoyang – Shiyong Duixiang, Ban'an Chengxu, Wenshuo Zhizuo* (Re-education Through Labour – Targets of Use, Procedures for Case Handling, and Completion of Documents), *Zhongguo Jiancha Chubanshe* (China Procuracy Publishing House), July 2002; volume marked: "*neibu faxing*" (internal distribution only).
119 According to Human Rights in China, "The Administrative Litigation Law of the PRC, promulgated in 1989, does entitle people to a limited right to challenge RTL decisions. However, a person held under RTL would have great difficulty in proving to a court's satisfaction that s/he was wrongly sentenced to such a term, since the regulations governing this measure give the public security departments very broad discretion. Very few cases are known to have been reversed following challenges under the Administrative Litigation Law and, to our knowledge, not a single appeal by a dissident against an RTL sentence has been successful. Of course there is the additional problem that inmates in RTL have very limited opportunities to make contact with the outside world, and thus may have enormous difficulty in getting any legal advice or representation for such an appeal." (See HRIC, *Reeducation Through Labor (RTL): A Summary of Regulatory Issues and Concerns*, New York, February 2001, p.4.
120 There are literally dozens of administrative regulations and edicts governing the use of labour re-education in China, none of which have the status of law as such, and many of which are officially designated as "confidential" (*neibu*) and therefore are not publicly available. The most important government documents on the topic are as follows: 1) NPC Standing Committee, "Resolution on Approving the Decision of the State Council on the Issue of Reeducation through Labor" (*Quanguo Renmin Daibiao Dahui Changwu Weiyuanhui Pizhun Guowuyuan Guanyu Laodong Jiaoyang Wenti De Jueding De Jueyi*), August 1, 1957. 2) NPC Standing Committee, "Resolution

Around 3.5 million people in total have been sentenced to labour re-education since the mid-1950s, and the numbers of those subjected to this measure by the police each year been rising steadily over the past twenty years. In the mid-1980s, according to China's legal authorities, around 150,000 people were serving labour re-education sentences each year, while in 2001 the figure was officially said to be approximately 260,000; other estimates placed the likely total as being nearer to 310,000.[121] According to government officials, around 60 percent of those concerned have been sentenced and detained for offences involving "disturbing public order," and around 40 percent for drug and prostitution-related offences.[122] Moreover, according to the New York-based monitoring group, Human Rights in China,

> In addition, substantial numbers of political and religious dissidents are sent into RTL camps. HRIC has documented over 30 cases of political dissidents being imprisoned in this way in the last three years. According to the Falungong group, some 5,000 members have been sentenced to RTL since the ban on the organization was issued in 1999.[123]

According to reports from political detainees and others, conditions in RTL camps are generally abusive, with overcrowded, unsanitary living conditions; inadequate food; endemic violence; and excessive working hours being among the major concerns. Nationwide, there are now close to 300 RTL centres, according to official

---

on Approving the Supplementary Decision of the State Council on the Issue of Re-education through Labor" (*Quanguo Renmin Daibiao Dahui Changwu Weiyuanhui Pizhun Guowuyuan Guanyu Laodong Jiaoyang De Buchong Guiding*), November 29, 1979. 3) "The Notice of the State Council on Circulating the Trial Practices of the Ministry of Public Security on Re-education through Labor" (*Guowuyuan Guanyu Zhuanfa Gonganbu Zhiding De Laodong Jiaoyang Shixing Banfa De Tongzhi*), January 21, 1982.

See also: Gong'an Bu Fazhi Si, *Gong'an Jiguan Banli Laodong Jiaoyang Anjian Fagui Huibian* (A Compilation of Laws and Regulations for Use by Public Security Organs in Handling Cases of Re-education Through Labour), Jing Guan Jiaoyu Chubanshe (Police Officers Educational Publishing House), October 1992; volume marked "*neibu faxing*" (internal distribution only).

121 Amnesty International, "China: Rule of Law and Human Rights—Time for Institutional Reforms" (Press Release)22 October 2002.
122 See Human Rights in China, *Reeducation Through Labor (RTL): A Summary of Regulatory Issues and Concerns*, New York, February 2001, p.1.
123 Article 10 of the Ministry of Public Security's 1982 "Trial Practices" (see Note 120) defines as follows the six categories of people punishable under RTL:

1. Those counterrevolutionaries or elements who oppose the CCP or Socialism, where their offences are minor, but do not merit criminal punishment;

2. Those who commit minor offences relating to group crimes of murder, robbery, rape and arson, but whose acts do not merit criminal punishment;

3. Those who commit minor offences such as hooliganism, prostitution, theft, or fraud but whose acts do not merit criminal punishment;

4. Those who gather to fight, disturb social order, or instigate turmoil but whose acts do not merit criminal punishment;

5. Those who have a job but repeatedly refuse to work, and disrupt labour discipline, complain endlessly, as well as disrupt production order, work order, school and research institute order and the people's normal life, but whose acts do not merit criminal punishment;

6. Those who instigate others to commit crimes, but whose acts do not merit criminal punishment.

statistics.[124] RTL detainees are mostly treated just like prisoners in the criminal justice system, although now, unlike in the past, they are generally segregated from inmates convicted of criminal offences.[125]

A striking example of the arbitrary ways in which administrative detention can be used occurred in August 2004, when a Hong Kong Democratic Party candidate for election to the Legislative Council, Alex Ho Wai-to, was detained by police in Dongguan, Guangdong Province, and sentenced without trial to six month's labour re-education for allegedly using the services of a prostitute.[126] In the great majority of such cases, first-time offenders are punished by means of either fines or, at most, up to 15 days' administrative detention under the SAPR. What gave rise to particular concern in Hong Kong, however, is that an off-duty Hong Kong policeman had been detained in Shenzhen on identical charges at almost the same time as Alex Ho but had subsequently received a sentence of only 15 days' administrative detention. The sharp discrepancy between these two administrative sentences led many Hong Kong commentators to voice fears that the mainland authorities' harsh treatment of Ho was a politically motivated act aimed at intimidating the Hong Kong Democratic Party in the run-up to the September 2004 Legislative Council elections.[127]

Technically, the authority to hand down sentences of labour re-education is vested in bodies known as Labour Re-education Administrative Committees, which are supposed to be made up of representatives from the Public Security Bureau, the Civil Affairs Bureau and the Bureau of Labour. But according to official reports, these bodies rarely if ever actually meet, and in practice such sentences are imposed solely by the PSB. The lack of any judicial involvement in or oversight of the system has led the U.N.'s Working Group on Arbitrary Detention to label China's labour re-education system as a whole as being "inherently arbitrary."[128] Attempts to encourage the Chinese government to abolish this aspect of the labour re-education system have formed the centrepiece of a continuing programme of "technical cooperation" being undertaken in China by the UN's Office of the High Commissioner for Human Rights since 2001, under the rubric of improving the legal handling of "minor crimes." Moreover, as recently as May 2000 the U.N. Committee Against Torture, in its concluding remarks after reviewing China's periodic implementation report on the Convention Against Torture, stated: "The

---

124 Shao Zongwei, "Reeducation Law Revamp Due Soon," *China Daily*, February 5, 2001.
125 For more detail, see Human Rights in China, *Detained at Official Pleasure: Arbitrary Detention in the People's Republic of China*, June 1993; and Amnesty International, *China—Punishment Without Crime: Arbitrary Detention*, September 1991.
126 According to the New York Times, "The candidate, Alex Ho, was arrested Thursday at a hotel room in Dongguan and held without access to a lawyer or to family members until he signed a confession that he had hired the prostitute, said Fred Li, a senior Democratic Party member of the Legislative Council. Mr. Li said Mr. Ho initially refused to sign, but did so when told he would be released on Monday if he signed, and when threatened with prosecution for rape if he did not sign. Instead of being released, however, Mr. Ho was then sentenced to six months in detention, Mr. Li said. The Chinese police have broad powers to detain people for 're-education through labor' without trial." (Keith Bradsher, "China Holds Candidate from Hong Kong on Prostitution Charge," *New York Times*, 18 August 2004.)
127 See, for example, Klaudia Lee and Nailene Chou Wiest, "Democrat's Punishment is Unusual, Says Scholar," *South China Morning Post*, 21 August 2004.
128 This assessment followed a visit to China by the Working Group in 1998. See: United Nations Working Group on Arbitrary Detention, "Report on the Visit to the People's Republic of China," E/CN.4/1998/44/ADD.2. See also HRIC (op cit, February 2001), p.4.

Committee recommends that the State party consider abolishing all forms of administrative detention, in accordance with the relevant international standards."[129]

The labour re-education sentencing system is at odds even with China's own recent national legislation. According to the 1996 Law on Administrative Punishments, no sentence of deprivation of liberty can be imposed on a citizen in the absence of a specific law (*falü*) providing for such a punishment. The March 2000 Law on Legislation (also translatable as the Law on Legislative Procedure) is equally specific on this point. As the China Daily noted earlier this year, in a commentary analyzing the Sun Zhigang case,

> The Law on Legislative Procedure stipulates that any provisions concerning deprivation of the human and democratic rights of citizens must be made in the form of laws by the National People's Congress (NPC) or the NPC Standing Committee. In other words, the State Council does not have the power to deprive such rights with administrative regulations.[130]

Although the Chinese government is now said to be considering the introduction of a Law on Labour Re-education, none of the existing legal norms and documents in this vast area of law enforcement possess the status of law, and as such the labour re-education system as a whole would appear to be in violation of both the Administrative Punishments Law and the Law on Legislation. Of course, it should be emphasized that the mere passage of a Law on Labour Re-education would not suffice to legitimize the system in terms of international human rights standards; only a fundamental reform of the system itself, involving the introduction of judicial determination and oversight, would be enough for this purpose.[131]

Forensic Psychiatric Committal – A Form of Administrative Detention

To the above well-known list of the different types of administrative detention in China must now be added a hitherto generally unacknowledged form of such detention: namely, forensic psychiatric custody. Indeed, this form of detention can in many ways be said to be the most severe and egregious, in basic human rights terms, of all the various forms of administrative detention found in China today.

---

129 See: "Conclusions and Recommendations of the Committee against Torture: China," (Concluding Observations/Comments, A/55/44), 9 May 2000, Paragraph 127.
130 See: "Giving Help to Those Who Need It," *China Daily*, 2 August 2004; available at: www.china.org.cn/english/China/102781.htm. According to Article 8 of the Law on Legislation: "Only national law may be enacted in respect of matters relating to: […] (v) the deprivation of the political rights of a citizen, or compulsory measures and penalties involving restriction of personal freedom." Although the NPC Standing Committee did rubber-stamp some of the existing regulations governing the use of labour re-education, they are essentially documents promulgated by and in the name of the State Council. (See Note 120 above.)
131 One possibility is that, rather than passing a separate "Law on Re-education Through Labour," the National People's Congress will instead opt for a more comprehensive "PRC Law on Security Administration Punishment" (*Zhi'an Guanli Chufa Fa*); such a law would cover both labour re-education-like measures and also the existing range of "security administration punishments," extending from fines and warnings to 15 days in police custody. (See: Li Yan, "*Zhi'an Chufa Youwang Quxiao Laojiao*" [Administrative Punishments: The Prospect for Abolition of Labour Re-education,] *Nanfang Dushi Bao* [Southern Metropolis Daily], 28 July 2004.) According to the latter article, the NPC has already begun drafting a PRC Law on Security Administration Punishment; the highlights were said to be that it contains no specific references to labour re-education, and it provides for persons sentenced to administrative detention to be granted a "hearing of evidence" (*juliu tingzheng*), presumably before a custodial judge or other competent official.

Just as in the case of labour re-education, the imposition of this measure by the police involves a lengthy deprivation of personal liberty and confinement in a police-run place of custody. And just as with labour re-education, the judiciary plays no deciding or monitoring role in the imposition of forensic-psychiatric custodial "sentences". Instead, both measures are decided upon and implemented solely by an administrative agency – the police. In addition, no Mental Health Law, or any other law, currently exists in China that would serve to legitimize the use of forensic psychiatric custody, even within the limited sense of legality as laid down by the Administrative Punishments Law. In a word, the formal attribution of the prefix "judicial" (*sifa*) to China's system of criminal psychiatric custody and treatment is functionally redundant.[132]

There are, however, two major differences between these two forms of administrative detention: first, no limitation of time attaches to the imposition of forensic psychiatric custody; and second, persons subjected to this measure are granted no right of judicial (or even administrative) review or appeal. There is not even a provision in Chinese law for a basic *habeas corpus* type of hearing to challenge the lawfulness of psychiatric committal.[133] According to officials working in the Ankang detention system, the average length of criminal-forensic psychiatric custody is around five years, and in many cases it lasts as long as 20 years or more. At no time during the period in question do those so detained, or even their families or other legal guardians, enjoy any legally specified right to challenge such detention in a court of law.

As we shall see in Chapter 8, during 2003-04 there occurred in China – for the first time ever, apparently – several cases in which people who had been forcibly committed to Ankang facilities, and had then either escaped or been released, tried to bring administrative lawsuits against the police challenging the lawfulness of their treatment and seeking to have the administrative action against them annulled by the court. Only in one such case did the plaintiff succeed – but he had died in mysterious circumstances in Ankang custody on the night prior to the court hearing.[134] In all the other cases, the police argued that they had performed "no administrative action" in carrying out the psychiatric committals in question, and the courts blandly accepted this claim and dismissed the cases. There is no known case in China (other than the instance just mentioned) of anyone having even attempted to mount a legal challenge to a police ruling of criminal-forensic psychiatric custody whilst they were still being held in an Ankang facility or other secure psychiatric hospital.

To summarize very briefly what all this means in practice: the system of forensic psychiatric custody is legally defined as being a judicial process; in reality, however, it is a judicially unacknowledged or unrecognized form of administrative detention; and in an apparently increasing number of specific

---

132 For a further discussion of this issue, see especially p.68 and Note 158 below.
133 Even if there were such a provision, a right of *habeas corpus* would not in itself be sufficient to meet the requirements for judicial review in such cases. The European Court of Human Rights, for example, has ruled that both legal remedies must be available to persons subject to this measure. According to the Council of Europe, "On 5 November 1981 the Court, in the case *X against the United Kingdom*, decided, *inter alia*, that there was a breach of Article 5, paragraph 4 of the [European] Convention [on Human Rights.] The Court found that, although X had access to a court which ruled that his detention was 'lawful' in terms of English law, a judicial review as limited as that available in the *habeas corpus* procedure, while adequate for emergency measures for the detention of persons on the grounds of unsoundness of mind, was not sufficient for a continuing confinement such as the one undergone by X until 1976." (See: Council of Europe, "Legal Protection of Persons Suffering from Mental Disorder Placed as Involuntary Patients," Recommendation No. R [83] 2, adopted by the Committee of Ministers of the Council of Europe on 22 February 1983, Strasbourg 1983, p.12.)
134 See p.268 below: "The Case of Wang Henglei."

instances nowadays, the police are trying to pass it off as a form of involuntary civil committal. We will return to these various themes and issues in subsequent chapters.

Better the Devil One Knows?

In a lengthy article published in 2004 and entitled "Out of the Pan and into the Fire: Well-Intentioned but Misguided Recommendations to Eliminate All Forms of Administrative Detention in China," Randall Peerenboom tries systematically to rebut all the arguments that human rights groups and others have been making for many years as to why China's system of administrative detention should be abolished.[135] While Peerenboom's argument is useful to the extent that it may lead human rights advocates to comprehensively revisit and fortify their thinking on this topic, on a more practical level it can only be described as tantamount to renouncing the goal of bringing China's legal system into conformity with even the "thin" standard for rule of law. Peerenboom's basic contention is that any abolition of administrative detention in China would only result in the hundreds of thousands of people currently dealt with under the system being redirected instead into the more severe, and if anything still less fair or equitable, criminal justice system. Given the government's determination to crack down on crime and the general population's insistence on harsh punishment for criminals, he argues, the sentences imposed on such people would be significantly heavier, they would mix with hardened criminals in prison, and they would emerge from the system with a formal criminal record.

Although Peerenboom develops his theme with considerable subtlety and panache, ultimately none of it is very convincing.[136] First, the principal defect of administrative detention, from a human rights

---

135 Randall Peerenboom, "Out of the Pan and into the Fire: Well-Intentioned but Misguided Recommendations to Eliminate All Forms of Administrative Detention in China," *Northwestern University Law Review*, 2004, Vol. 98, No.3, pp.991-1104.

136 Particularly unconvincing, at least for the present writer, was Peerenboom's peremptory dismissal of the problem of forensic psychiatric detention in China. (Answers to his various points and criticisms are supplied, without specific reference to the writer himself, elsewhere in this book.) He writes:

> Munro notes [in "Judicial Psychiatry in China and its Political Abuses" (2001, op cit)] that some dissidents and Falungong members accused of criminal violations have been involuntarily committed to mental institutions. In general, the total number of political cases has fallen dramatically during the 1990s. Of those persons committed to mental institutions, some unknown percentage will be genuinely mentally disturbed. The others, however, should not be committed to mental institutions, but rather should be subject to the criminal process and/or administrative detention systems. Of course, whether the activities in question should be criminalized at all is a separate issue. For present purposes, however, it is important to note that the consequence of blocking the authorities from sending those who are not mentally disturbed to mental institutions will be that they will be funneled into the administrative detention or formal criminal systems. Given the stigma that attaches to being committed to a mental institution as well as the oppressive nature of some of the treatments for mental patients, presumably most people would rather take their chances with administrative detention or even imprisonment. It bears noting that it is highly unlikely that the authorities direct many persons whom they genuinely do not believe are mentally disturbed to mental institutions. There is little reason for them to do so given that they can send the offenders to administrative detention centers or prisons. The argument suggested by Munro, that the authorities believe the threat of long-term detention in a mental institution is a better deterrent than long-term detention in prison, is not very persuasive. Even assuming detention in a mental institution would be perceived as a substantially worse fate by potential offenders, which seems likely, the tiny numbers of people committed to mental institutions would greatly reduce the deterrent effect. If the authorities were serious about using the mental institutions as a deterrent, one would expect to see many more involuntary commitments. Moreover, the post-Mao, reform-minded government has taken great steps to project the image of a more humane regime,

and due process point of view, is that it makes it far too easy for the police to put people behind bars. The introduction of judicial control over such cases would allow the facts and evidence to be tested and challenged in open court, witnesses and counter-evidence to be produced by the defence side, and the accused would benefit, more generally, from the range of greater rights protections provided for under the revised Criminal Procedure Law. Despite the relative lack of independence that China's judiciary undoubtedly still suffers from, it seems unquestionable that a substantial proportion of the kinds of people who are currently sent straight to police detention centres or labour re-education camps without any form of trial would, if administrative detention were abolished, be either exempted from criminal prosecution or have their cases dismissed by the judiciary. Moreover, the police would almost certainly press far fewer criminal charges in any case, knowing that the accused would all be allowed to have their day in court and that therefore weak prosecutions would fail in a significant or substantial proportion of cases.

Second, Peerenboom's critique of the efforts by both the international rights community and China's own reform-minded legal scholars to advocate for the abolition of the administrative detention system has a curiously ahistorical or static quality to it. In correctly claiming, for example, that the revised Criminal Procedure Law has not in practice brought many of the kinds of due process improvements and safeguards for the rights of the accused that it promised to bring, and that therefore the Chinese criminal justice and prison systems arguably represent, at present, scant improvement if any over the administrative sentencing and detention system, he neglects to point out that the criminal justice system is today, nonetheless, substantially more fair and equitable than it was prior to the introduction of the Criminal Procedure Law reforms in 1996. In other words, limited progress has been achieved – and much of the credit for that progress must go to the long-standing advocacy efforts both of China's own legal reform community and of the international rights groups that have consistently supported its efforts. The conclusion that Peerenboom should surely be drawing from his analysis of the current failings of the criminal justice system is that the authorities should put greater effort into reforming

---

establish itself as a reliable member of the international community, and implement rule of law, all of which will be undermined by allegations of Soviet-style use of mental institutions to deal with political dissidents. Munro tries to explain away this inconsistency as the government having its cake (deterrence) and eating it too (appearing humane in the eyes of the international community for treating rather than imprisoning mentally disturbed criminals). *Id.* at 122. But a more likely explanation is that the lower-level authorities who handle the cases, as well as the psychiatrists who must examine those detained, legitimately (whether rightly or wrongly) believe the persons are mentally disturbed. Of course, what may seem like mildly or even wildly eccentric beliefs in one society may be perceived as evidence of mental disorder in other societies. Believing that if one spins the dharma wheel in one's stomach, one will be able to fly or will not need medicine may be a sign of disorder and may constitute a danger to oneself and perhaps others if the person were to prevent their family members from attaining medical attention, for example. Indeed, the government claims that Falungong has been responsible for the death of more than 1400 people, including practitioners and their family members. *Id.* at 116. Similarly, given the current political environment and emphasis on stability, continually petitioning the government to establish a democratic party or passing out leaflets calling for the overthrow of the Party may seem to many observers to be evidence of someone having lost his or her senses. Nevertheless, in many cases Falungong adherents will not be a danger to themselves or others. Nor will those who are advocating political change be suffering from psychotic delusions of grandeur or paranoid fears of persecution. These individuals should not be sent to mental institutions, and the government should ensure through regulations and publicity that all within the system understand that simply expressing political ideas at odds with socialism is not sufficient grounds for involuntary commitment to mental institutions. (Peerenboom, "Out of the Pan and into the Fire…" Note 148.)

it further – and not that the current state of the criminal justice system provides an argument and justification for continuing to deprive, without any semblance of due process, hundreds of thousands of Chinese citizens of their personal liberty.

Third, if China's administrative detention system really does represent such an attractive alternative to the criminal justice system, then surely one should be arguing for a substantial expansion of the scope of administrative detention in China today. By enlarging the list of offences that could be expeditiously dealt with under the regulations on labour re-education, and removing them from the orbit of the Criminal Law, for example, one would be allowing many more Chinese citizens to enjoy the claimed comparative benefits of untried and arbitrary detention. But this would be a step too far for Peerenboom, and instead he argues simply that the system should be left more or less as it is, and that any reform efforts should be limited to gradually bringing China's administrative detention system into greater conformity with international standards of justice.

Much of what Peerenboom has to say about China's administrative detention regime is true, so far as it goes. But by taking such a determinedly contrarian or "devil's advocate" type of position on the question of what should be done about it, he ends up by overstating his case in a way that will strike many human rights specialists as both condescending and slightly absurd. The simple and direct answer to his characterization of calls for the abolition of China's administrative detention system as "well-intentioned but misguided" is that prosecutions and custodial sentences are something which, in any country, can never safely be left to the police to decide upon and implement on their own authority. This is particularly true in China, where the police and other security services have for the past five decades and more been allowed to wield grossly disproportionate power not only over the other two branches of the legal system but also, and more importantly, over society as a whole. Indeed, the power to impose administrative custodial sentences of up to four years without trial constitutes the ultimate source both of the Chinese PSB's unquestioned dominance over the legal system as a whole, and of the ubiquitous sense of fear with which the PSB is regarded by members of the general public. In a key sense, reining in the powers of the police constitutes the essential prerequisite for any future expansion of civil liberties and popular legal rights in China, and the place where this process really has to begin is in stripping the police of their power to impose lengthy administrative sentences. In particular, any serious attempt by the government to transfer real power and independence to the judiciary will require the prior abolition of this police power.

II. The Legal Handling of Political Crime in China

A contention put forward with increasing regularity by foreign observers of China's legal system since the early 1990s is that the falling numbers of political dissidents and other critics of the government who are nowadays being sent to re-education camps or prisons provide a clear sign that the Party-state is becoming more tolerant of political dissent. This claim brings to mind the example of tourists who visit the Highlands of Scotland and remark on how wonderfully "empty and natural" the countryside is, when in fact what they are viewing is an artificially created wilderness that once, prior to the Clearances of the late 18th century onwards, was filled with thriving communities of people. The relative decline in the numbers of political dissidents in Chinese prison cells today is not a sign or product of any major relaxation in the government's repressive policy towards such people. Rather, it is proof positive of how extremely effective the government has been over the past 20 years and more in signalling to the general public that any attempt to fundamentally challenge government policies, or to form politically dissident groups or networks of any kind, will be immediately and ruthlessly crushed.

Since the police allegations in most cases involving the use of politically directed psychiatry in China since 1949 have centred on the charge of "counterrevolution" (*fan'geming zui*), we should first provide a detailed historical account and description of this general category of crime, before proceeding to examine the ways in which certain specific sub-groups of counterrevolutionaries in China have been handled, in recent decades, under the criminal-psychiatric appraisals system.

The world of criminal jurisprudence was first introduced to the concept of counterrevolution during the French Revolution, in a decree issued by the Jacobins on March 10, 1793 establishing the system of "revolutionary tribunals." The works of Marx and Engels are replete with references to "counterrevolution," and Lenin eventually enshrined the concept in the Soviet criminal code after describing it as being not merely a useful legal device but also "an instrument of terror" that would awe the opponents of the Bolshevik Party into submission. The term was subsequently incorporated into the criminal codes of several Soviet satellite states, although the USSR itself later dropped the term in favour of the less political-sounding "crimes of state."[137] In China, somewhat ironically, the concept was first enshrined in law by Chiang Kai-shek, the leader of the KMT, whose government on March 9, 1928, promulgated a Temporary Law on the Punishment of Crimes of Counterrevolution, aimed primarily at the Communist Party of China.[138] Soon after establishing its first territorial base in Jiangxi Province in the late 1920s, the Communist Party took steps to establish a similar legal regime, but aimed at suppressing the "KMT bandits" and their supporters among the local rural elite. On April 8, 1934, the Communist Party enacted its first formal law in this area: the Regulations of the Chinese Soviet Republic on the Punishment of Counterrevolution.[139]

Upon the Communist Party's assumption of power in October 1949, the clear evidence of widespread wrongful executions and imprisonments perpetrated by the Party's secret police since the 1930s proved to pose no obstacle to the systematic expansion of the same kind of legal regime that had produced these earlier injustices.[140] In February 1951, the Central People's Government passed a

---

137 The Chinese term for "crimes of state" is "*guoshi zui*."
138 See *Zanxing Fan'geming Zhizui Fa* (Temporary Law on the Punishment of Crimes of Counterrevolution). According to the latter law, "All attempts to subvert the Chinese Nationalist Party and the National Government... are defined as crimes of counterrevolution." As the KMT's Judicial Yuan expressly proclaimed, moreover: "Cases involving the Communist Party are to be dealt with as counterrevolutionary offences."
139 See Han Yanlong & Chang Zhaoru (eds.), *Zhonghua Suweiai Gongheguo Chengzhi Fan'geming Tiaoli*, (Regulations of the Chinese Soviet Republic on the Punishment of Counterrevolution), in "*Zhongguo Xin Minzhuzhuyi Geming Shiqi Genjudi Fazhi*" (Legal System of the Base Areas during the Revolutionary Period of New Democracy)," in *Wenxian Xuanbian* (Selected Documents), Vol.3 (Zhongguo Shehui Kexue Chubanshe, Beijing, 1981), pp. 5-11.
140 For example, as the State Council noted in 1983: "Some work-units and individuals have recently submitted petitions on behalf of comrades who were unjustly killed during the period of the Second Revolutionary Civil War [1927-37]...requesting that these wrongly executed comrades be commemorated as martyrs" (PRC State Council, State Council Document No. 91, 1983, *Guowuyuan Pizhuan Minzhengbu Guanyu Dui Di'erci Guonei Geming Zhanzheng Shiqi Sufanzhong Bei Cuosha Renyuan de Chuli Yijian de Tongzhi* [Notification of the Ministry of Civil Affairs, As Approved and Circulated by the State Council, Concerning the (Ministry's) Opinion on How to Handle the Cases of Persons Wrongly Killed in the Course of Campaigns to Suppress Counterrevolution During the Period of the Second Revolutionary Civil War], in *Xinfang Gongzuo Shiyong Zhengce Fagui Shouce, Zhonggong Zhongyang Bangongting* [A Handbook of Policies, Laws and Regulations for Use in Petitions and Visits Work], issued by the Office of the CPC Central Committee [document marked "for internal distribution only"], Falü Chubanshe, July 1992.)

law, titled "Regulations of the PRC on the Punishment of Counterrevolution,"[141] which would serve as the main legal basis and justification for the systematic persecution of political dissidents and all other opponents of the Party for most of the next three decades. With Deng Xiaoping's return to power in late 1978, the growing trend towards an official condemnation and repudiation of both the 1957 Anti-Rightist Movement and the Cultural Revolution, together with rising public demands for the rehabilitation of the legions of counterrevolutionary political victims created during those two periods, acquired major new impetus. Over the next five years or so, virtually all of the hundreds of thousands of people who had been condemned, imprisoned, or executed for alleged counterrevolutionary offences during the Cultural Revolution decade were exonerated by the new regime and declared to have been victims of the myriad "trumped-up cases and miscarriages of justice" perpetrated by the former radical Maoist leadership, the "Gang of Four," and its followers. Similarly, the great majority of those branded as "rightists" in 1957 were finally rehabilitated, although Deng's role as Party General Secretary in overseeing the purges of that time meant that many simply had their political "hats" removed, rather than being officially pronounced innocent.

Overall, the Party's use of charges of counterrevolution against its political enemies and opponents – real or imagined – during the second half of the twentieth century undoubtedly generated more miscarriages of justice and devastated the lives of greater numbers of innocent people than any other single factor on China's judicial landscape. The only just and appropriate governmental response to such an appalling judicial track record would have been for Deng and his colleagues, in the late 1970s, to have set about dismantling the entire legal category of "crimes of counterrevolution," thereby repudiating the manifest judicial failings of the past and holding out the promise of a more politically neutral criminal justice system in the future. But instead, in July 1979, the new leadership chose to give pride of place in the country's inaugural criminal code to an entire chapter on counterrevolutionary crime, laying down penalties ranging from several years in jail to life imprisonment or even death. Since then, at least ten thousand people have been consigned to long terms in prison on charges of counterrevolution that were no less politically determined and legally unsound than in the past.

By the mid-1980s, however, the incidence of counterrevolutionary crime as a proportion of the total number of criminal offences recorded each year in China had dropped, according to official figures, to a very low level as compared with the situation during the first two decades or so of the People's Republic.[142] Until quite recently, the total number of imprisoned counter-revolutionaries was classified by the government as top secret, but the example of one province may serve to illustrate the general trend. In October 1959, Heilongjiang Province recorded a total prison inmate population of some 97,332 persons, of whom no fewer than 57,933, or just under 60 percent of the total, were counterrevolutionaries.

---

141 *Zhonghua Renmin Gongheguo Chengzhi Fan'geming Tiaoli.*
142 This reduction in the number of counterrevolutionary cases in China does not mean that the authorities have become substantially more tolerant of political criticism than before. Rather, a clear trend has been evident since 1980 towards sentencing political dissidents and other "enemies of national stability" on alternative and less obviously political legal grounds: for example, on common criminal charges such as alleged economic malfeasance, soliciting prostitutes, and even for violating restrictive regulations on the ownership of fax machines. In many cases, these charges have clearly been trumped-up and devoid of factual basis. Another recent trend has been towards imposing "administrative sentences" on dissidents and others in the form of up to three-year terms of "re-education through labour" (*laodong jiaoyang*) – an extremely widespread form of detention without trial that is applied solely at the discretion of the police authorities.

By 1981, out of a total prisoner population of 23,685, the number of counterrevolutionaries had fallen to only 577, or 2.5 percent of the total.[143]

This reduction did not occur in a gradual or phased manner, but rather took the form of a sudden drop over a brief several-year period from December 1978 onwards. By 1982, for example, the government had officially exonerated the victims of more than 27,800 counterrevolutionary cases (involving a much greater number of actual defendants)[144] that had been falsely adjudicated in courts across the country during the two-year period from September 1976, when Mao died, until late 1978, when Deng Xiaoping returned to power. Similarly, in Fujian province alone during 1977-78, altogether 750 counterrevolutionaries were sentenced by the courts, of whom ninety-three received the death penalty and were executed. Again, the great majority of those sentenced were eventually rehabilitated.[145] These various figures show the extensive use that was still being made of such charges even after the conclusion of the Cultural Revolution.

Thereafter, according to official statistics, the numbers declined sharply. From 1980 to 1984, Chinese courts tried a total of 7,123 cases of counterrevolution (again accounting for many more defendants, only a tiny handful of whom would have been acquitted).[146] The question of possible rehabilitation and release did not arise in these cases, however, since by that time the government had completed its post-Cultural Revolution "rectification of the political line," and therefore those sentenced in the 1980s and later were all considered to be "genuine" political enemies of the State. By the mid-1980s, the annual numbers of sentenced counterrevolutionaries were down to single digits in many Chinese cities. Foshan Municipality in Guangdong Province, for example, had tried and sentenced 1,861 such cases in 1951; 2,165 in 1955; 3,298 in 1959; 178 in 1972; and 275 in 1976. During the entire nine-year period from 1979 until 1987, moreover, a total of only forty-seven cases of counterrevolution were tried by the Foshan court system, representing an average of 0.5 percent of all the criminal cases tried by local municipal courts during those years.[147] As of the mid-1990s, the government's official accounting for the total number of sentenced counterrevolutionaries still held in prisons throughout China stood

---

143 Heilongjiang Provincial People's Procuracy, *Heilongjiang Jiancha Zhi* (Annals of the Heilongjiang Procuracy), (Harbin: Heilongjiang Renmin Chubanshe, 1988). Of the 577 persons imprisoned in 1981, just under half were said to be "historic counterrevolutionaries," that is, political prisoners who had probably already been held in jail for several decades.
144 Many criminal "cases" (*anjian*) in China involve multiple defendants, and this was especially true in the case of counterrevolutionary offences carried out during the early 1980s, when numerous "reactionary organizations" dedicated either to the restoration of Cultural Revolution-era policies or (at the other end of the political spectrum) to the promotion of Western-style democracy appeared in many parts of the country.
145 For documentary sources on the above statistics, see *Sichuan Shengqing* (A General Account of Sichuan Province), published "for internal use only" by Sichuan People's Press, December 1987, p.548; and "Many 'Unjust, False and Erroneous' Verdicts Also Found Among Cases Tried Between 1977 and 1978," *Renmin Sifa Xuanbian* (A Compilation of Articles from "People's Justice" Magazine), (Law Publishing House, February 1983), pp.116-8 (volume also marked "for internal use only"). Among twenty-one of the counterrevolutionaries sentenced by the Fuzhou Intermediate Court, the latter report added, "Seventeen, or 77 percent of the total, were found to have been completely innocent... The original verdict was upheld in only one case." And of nine such verdicts rendered by the Xiamen Intermediate Court, "All were found to have problems."
146 *Dangdai Zhongguo de Shenpan Gongzuo* (Judicial Work in Contemporary China), Vol.1, (Contemporary China Publishing House, 1993). According to this book, the figure of 7,123 counterrevolutionary cases accounted for 0.43 percent of all criminals sentenced during the period in question.
147 *Foshan Shi Fayuan Zhi* (Annals of the Foshan Municipal Courts), compiled and published by the Foshan Municipal Intermediate Court (year of publication not known, but probably 1988 or 1989).

at around 2,000. Current unofficial estimates suggest that at least 300 of them remain behind bars today.[148]

However, an analysis of the changing composition of cases of counterrevolution since the early 1980s, that is, the relative proportions of those convicted of the various types of counterrevolutionary offences during different periods, reveals another equally striking trend. The 1979 Criminal Law specified more than ten varieties of counterrevolutionary crime, ranging from carrying out "subversion" and "espionage" to organizing "reactionary sects" and "counterrevolutionary groups." The main judicial weapon used by the government in the punishment of non-violent acts of speech and expression, however, was the Article 102 charge of "counterrevolutionary propaganda and incitement." The specific meaning and content of this offence was explained in detail by the Supreme People's Procuracy in 1992 as follows:

> There are four main forms of expression [of Article 102 crimes]: 1) shouting counterrevolutionary slogans in public and making counterrevolutionary speeches; 2) writing, posting up or distributing in public places counterrevolutionary leaflets, banners, and big-or small-character posters; 3) extensively mailing out counterrevolutionary-propagandist letters or sending threatening and alarmist letters to [government] organs, [social] bodies, and universities or colleges; and 4) editing and issuing reactionary publications and publishing counterrevolutionary articles. The first two of these four categories...account for two-thirds of all cases of counterrevolutionary incitement.[149]

Between 1980 and 1991, the proportion of sentenced counterrevolutionaries convicted under Article 102 rose steeply. According to one authoritative account, the average incidence of Article 102 offences as a proportion of all counterrevolutionary offences during the 1980s was "approximately 20 percent."[150] By 1990, however, an official law journal noted: "During the most recent period, counterrevolutionary propaganda and incitement cases have accounted for around 80 percent of all the counterrevolutionary cases accepted and dealt with by the people's courts."[151] Far from declining after the Cultural Revolution, therefore, both the government's sensitivity to dissident-style criticism and the extent to which it was determined to punish such acts of free political expression had, by the early 1990s, significantly increased as compared to the frequency with which it prosecuted and punished other forms of alleged counterrevolution. It should be emphasized that dissident-style individuals brought for forensic psychiatric examination in China in recent decades have also, for the most part,

---

148 See Dui Hua Foundation, Note 33 above.
149 Supreme People's Procuratorate, *Xingshi Fanzui Anli Congshu — Fan'geming Zui*, (Criminal Case-Studies Series: Vol.1: Crimes of Counterrevolution), (Beijing: Zhongguo Jiancha Chubanshe, November 1992), p.238.
150 Ibid., p.238. According to the same source, the incidence of counterrevolutionary crimes as a percentage of all criminal offences committed during the period 1980-89 varied from between 0.08 percent and 0.8 percent; and "even in the highest year, it did not reach 1 percent of the total."
151 Li Li and Li Shaoping, "*Lun Fan'geming Xuanchuan Shandong Zui de Rending* (On the Determination of Crimes of Counterrevolutionary Propaganda and Incitement)," *Xiandai Faxue* (*Contemporary Jurisprudence*), 1990, No.1. One factor behind this relative surge in Article 102 offences was no doubt the government's June 1989 nationwide crackdown on the Tiananmen Square pro-democracy movement, which had been officially condemned as a "counterrevolutionary rebellion." However, the incidence of all categories of counterrevolutionary offence (notably "leading and organizing a counterrevolutionary group" [Article 97] and "counterrevolutionary sabotage" [Article 100]) rose dramatically after the June 1989 crackdown, so the high predominance of Article 102 offences at this time was still of considerable statistical significance.

been initially charged with the same offences as those singled out for attention by the Procuracy in the passage quoted above: namely, political speech making, sloganeering, leafleting and poster sticking.

In March 1997, the Chinese government finally responded to years of intense international criticism over its cavalier use of the statutes on counterrevolution as a means of suppressing peaceful political and religious dissent by ostensibly removing them from the Criminal Law. In their place, however, came a whole range of new but very similar offences known as "crimes of endangering state security."[152] In essence, the concept of peaceful and non-violent political crime in China was not abolished as a result of this move, but merely remodelled in a form ostensibly more acceptable to international legal opinion. Far from attempting to hide the fact that this was a mere change of name with little change in substance, the Chinese leadership – in what was probably an attempt to mollify domestic conservatives who feared it was another step down the road toward liberalization – went out of its way to stress this point. The first indication that it would be business as usual after the legislative changes in question came from Wang Hanbin, Vice-Chairman of the National People's Congress Standing Committee, in a speech to the national parliament introducing the revised criminal code: "The punishment meted out for crimes of counterrevolution in the past will remain valid and cannot be altered."[153] This ruled out any question of amnesty or early release for those already sentenced on such charges. The protracted legal debate that preceded the new legislation's introduction made the matter even clearer. According to one commentator,

> By altering the name of this legal weapon [the laws on counterrevolution], we will be changing neither its basic nature and tasks nor its combat effectiveness; still less will we be discarding it. All that will be involved is the adoption, in line with today's changed circumstances, of a new and more appropriate designation for the weapon.[154]

And as another pointed out, "The proposal to redesignate counterrevolutionary offences as crimes of endangering state security means nothing more than a change of name; in no way does it imply the 'deletion' or 'abolition' of those offences."[155]

Since March 1997, the Chinese security authorities have proceeded to apply the new charges to precisely the same types of people – political dissidents, ethnic rights activists, independent trades unionists, unofficial religious believers and so forth – who previously were judicially dealt with on charges of counterrevolution; if anything, the sentences passed on such people for "endangering state security" in recent years have been even harsher than those previously imposed for counterrevolutionary

---

152 A detailed analysis of the significance of these legislative changes can be found in Human Rights Watch/Asia and Human Rights in China, "Whose Security? An Analysis of "State Security" in China's New Criminal Code," *A Human Rights Watch Report*, Vol.9, No.4 (c), April 1997. Another very detailed and informative account of the topic can be found in Donald C. Clarke, *Wrongs and Rights: A Human Rights Analysis of China's Revised Criminal Code*, (New York: Lawyers Committee for Human Rights, 1999).
153 Speech by Wang Hanbin to the Fifth Session of the Eighth National People's Congress, March 6, 1997.
154 Guo Qun, "*Guanyu Fan'geming Zuizhang de Tiaozheng* (On Readjusting the Chapter on Crimes of Counterrevolution)," in Cui Qingsen (ed.), *Zhongguo Dangdai Xingfa Gaige* (*Reform in China's Contemporary Criminal Code*), (Shehui Kexue Wenxian Press, November 1991).
155 Li Wenyan, "*Fan'geming Zui Gaiwei Weihai Guojia Anquan Zui Qianyi* (My Humble Views on the Changeover from Counterrevolutionary Crimes to Crimes of Endangering State Security)," *Fazhi Ribao* (*Legal Daily*), March 14, 1991.

offences.[156] Legal reform in China since 1978 has brought many new and valuable benefits to the country as a whole. There has been no sign, however, that the authorities are prepared to slacken off or display greater tolerance in their longstanding judicial war against dissident freedom of expression and association in the key realms of politics, ideology and religion. Essentially, insofar as the country's criminal justice system is concerned, all that has changed in the post-Mao era is the specific content of what is officially held to be "counterrevolutionary" or "threatening to state security."

For this same reason, "cases of a political nature" will no doubt continue, much as before, to account for a significant proportion of offences committed by the "dangerously mentally ill" in China. For much of the past two decades, certainly, the officially reported incidence of "pseudo-counterrevolutionary" cases as a proportion of all cases of criminal-forensic psychiatric appraisal (somewhere between five and fifteen percent) has been markedly higher than the reported incidence of cases of "genuine" counterrevolution as a proportion of the total number of criminal offences committed (much less than one percent). The precise significance of these puzzling statistics is unclear, but they evidently do not point in the direction of any major systemic reforms in the legal-psychiatric authorities' handling of the former variety of cases. In summary, so long as the notion of "political crime" continues to hold sway in police stations and courtrooms around the country, forensic psychiatry in China seems set to remain mired, to a greater or lesser extent, in the unethical practices of the past, so tainting the ability of Chinese psychiatrists to perform their proper and legitimate role within the criminal justice system.

III. The Concept of Criminal Insanity

A Comparative Overview

What does the term "forensic" signify, and what are the main tasks and concerns of the forensic psychiatrist? A concise definition, and one broadly applicable to most legal systems, is provided in the standard British textbook on the subject, *Faulk's Basic Forensic Psychiatry*:

> "Forensic" means pertaining to, or connected with, or used in courts of law. A forensic psychiatrist's work may be said to start with the preparation of psychiatric reports for the court on the mental state of offenders suspected of having a mental

---

156 The following examples illustrate the draconian manner in which the new state security laws have been applied. On December 21, 1998, the veteran dissident Xu Wenli, 55, was sentenced to 13 years' imprisonment for "conspiring to subvert state power" after he attempted to legally register a peaceful opposition group, the China Democracy Party (CDP); the following day, his colleague Qin Yongmin, 49, was sentenced to 12 years' imprisonment on the same criminal charge. On December 27 the same year, Zhang Shanguang, a Hunan labour activist, was sentenced to 10 years' imprisonment after a two-hour trial held behind closed doors which found him guilty of "providing intelligence to institutions outside the borders," a charge relating to his attempts to establish an "Association to Protect the Rights and Interests of Laid-off Workers" in Xupu County. In July 1999, Yue Tianxiang, a labour rights activist, was sentenced to 10 years' imprisonment for "subversion"; Yue, who was detained on January 11 and formally charged on January 26, 1999, formed the China Labour Rights Observer in Gansu Province to protect the rights of laid-off workers. And on August 6, 1999, Liu Xianbin, a leading CDP member in Sichuan, was sentenced to 13 years' imprisonment for alleged conspiracy to subvert state power; Liu was unable to find defence counsel as a series of lawyers withdrew from the case following pressure from the authorities. In December 2002, Xu Wenli was freed and sent into exile in the United States.

abnormality. The psychiatrist will then be expected to provide or arrange treatment for the mentally abnormal offender where appropriate.[157]

Whilst the core work of forensic psychiatrists normally occurs within the context of court proceedings against criminal defendants, they also have an important secondary role to play within the civil law sphere – for example, in assessing the mental capacity of individuals to engage in litigation, inherit or dispose of property, respond to a libel suit, and so forth, or in evaluating claims of psychological damage that may be raised in connection with compensation suits. In addition, it should be noted that within the criminal law sphere – the specific area with which this book is primarily concerned – a less restrictive definition of forensic psychiatry than that provided by Faulk is in practice often applied: namely, that it encompasses the whole range of activities carried out by psychiatrists within the criminal justice system (rather than just those relating to courts of law), and in particular professional interactions between the psychiatrist and the police.

In most countries, no real conflict or incompatibility arises between the former, more narrowly drawn understanding of the role of the forensic psychiatrist (and here the alternative term "judicial psychiatry" might more appositely be used) and the latter, more inclusive definition of the profession's activities, since the validity of any findings or conclusions drawn by the forensic or police psychiatrist as to the mental state of a particular defendant will ultimately be tested and decided upon in a court of law. It is therefore important to emphasize that in China, by contrast, the great majority of criminal cases in which suspicions about the defendant's mental state have arisen are still handled solely by the police. Only a tiny proportion of such cases eventually proceed to the stage of formal prosecution and trial, and if the forensic psychiatrist certifies that a detainee or defendant is "not legally responsible" by virtue of mental defect or insanity for any alleged criminal acts, then either the police or the procuracy will dispose of the detainee as they see fit. This may take the form of involuntary committal in a mental asylum, the person's release back into society, or a range of intermediate dispositional options – all without the need for a court hearing to be conducted. This almost complete lack of judicial involvement or oversight in the forensic psychiatric process in China should be borne firmly in mind throughout the following account, since it essentially undermines or invalidates most of the due process assumptions and axioms that underpin the role played by the forensic psychiatrist in criminal justice systems elsewhere.

A second and closely-related definitional issue that should be signalled here concerns the Chinese word most commonly used to render the term "forensic psychiatry": *sifa jingshenbingxue* – i.e. "judicial" psychiatry. At first sight, given that in practice the courts usually have little or no role to play in the proceedings in question, this would seem to be a singularly inappropriate term for the Chinese authorities to adopt. The problem evaporates, however, when one recalls that, in China, the Public Security Bureau is officially viewed and defined as being one of the nation's "judicial departments" (*sifa bumen*) – alongside and ostensibly equal to (although in practice it is generally more powerful than) the courts and the prosecution authorities. In a key sense, therefore, the choice of terminology in China reflects the actual reality or praxis of the situation: the police and security services are defined as

---

[157] *Faulk's Basic Forensic Psychiatry (Third Edition)*, revised by J.H. Stone, M. Roberts, J. O'Grady & A.V. Taylor with K. O'Shea, Blackwell Science (Oxford: 2000), p.1. See also: John Gunn and Pamela J. Taylor (eds.), *Forensic Psychiatry: Clinical, Legal and Ethical Issues*, Butterworth & Heinemann, 1993.

being part of the "judicial system," and at the same time they routinely perform roles within the system that in most other countries would fall within the exclusive competence of the judiciary.[158]

Perhaps the central issue that forensic psychiatrists in most countries are called upon to elucidate (though not always to offer a direct opinion upon) is the question of a mentally disordered defendant's legal "responsibility" for the crimes they are accused of committing. Faulk presents this issue as follows:

> In all offences it must be proven that the accused physically did the act (known as the "*actus reus*"). In most offences it must also be proven that the defendant's intention or attitude of mind was as required for the crime in question (known as having the necessary "*mens rea*"). For a crime to have been committed, therefore, it is not only necessary for the accused to have done the act but there must have been intent to do it or negligence about the consequences of the behaviour. A plea of not guilty may be based on an absence of *mens rea*, e.g. the act may have been carried out in a state of distraction, at which time the person may not have formed the necessary intent....
>
> The concept of responsibility in law concerns the degree to which the accused is held accountable for the act committed. To be found guilty means to have done the act and deserve punishment. Full responsibility goes hand in hand with full rationality and consciousness (or will). Impairment of either is taken to alter responsibility.... Rationality may be so impaired by mental disorder that the offender is held not responsible for his acts resulting in the finding of not guilty by reason of insanity. Less severe mental disorder will often mitigate the sentence of the court, which will, generally, seek to give a more merciful sentence aimed at assisting the offender rather than providing punishment and deterrence.[159]

Similarly, according to the American Academy of Psychiatry and the Law,

> The insanity defence is a legal construct that, under some circumstances, excuses mentally ill defendants from legal responsibility for criminal behaviour. The ability to

---

158 For this general reason, the terms "judicial psychiatry" and "forensic psychiatry" are used interchangeably in the present study to denote all cases in China where police and psychiatrists work together, including those in which the courts and judiciary have no professional involvement, direct or otherwise. In the Chinese professional literature on psychiatry and the law, four different terms are used that are broadly equivalent to the English term "forensic psychiatry." While these tend to be used interchangeably, they nonetheless have different connotations: 1) *sifa jingshenbingxue*, meaning "judicial psychiatry"; 2) *falü jingshenbingxue*, meaning "legal psychiatry"; 3) *fayi jingshenbingxue*, meaning "legal-medical psychiatry"; and 4) *fating jingshenbingxue* or *fating kexue jingshenbingxue*, meaning respectively "court psychiatry" and "court science psychiatry." The first of these terms is somewhat misleading, since in practice the courts have had, at least until very recently, almost no role to play in the activities in question; however, it makes sense within the Chinese legal context, since the Public Security Bureau is defined as being a "judicial department." The second term is more directly descriptive and unambiguous. However, some writers use the first term in preference to the second in order to emphasize that the court *should* play a greater role in the process than it actually does. The third term tends to be used more often by full-time police psychiatrists, although they also use the first and second terms as well. The two final terms listed above are relatively new arrivals on the Chinese legal scene, first appearing only in or around the year 2000. The jurists and legal commentators who use them are usually, though not always, actively trying to promote a greater role for the judiciary in the forensic appraisals and case decision-making arena; because of the current limitations of the system, however, their proposals and analyses have so far tended to be mainly theoretical.
159 *Faulk's* (op cit), pp.23-24.

evaluate whether defendants meet a jurisdiction's test for a finding of not criminally responsible is a core competency in forensic psychiatry.[160]

The antecedents of this important legal doctrine go back at least as far as the 6th century BC, in the distinction drawn in Hebrew Scriptures between offences where fault could be found and those that occurred without fault. Examples of the latter included harmful acts committed by children, who were seen as incapable of morally evaluating their behaviour, and those committed by the retarded or insane, who were likened to children in their inherent inability to form a guilty intent. Another authoritative source explains how the same basic concept found its way into the legal thought of mediaeval England:

> In the twelfth century, issues of moral wrongfulness began to develop in pre-English law that raised the concept of "madness" as it relates to culpability. Lords of state began granting pardons to individuals who were convicted of a crime and obviously "mad".... In the thirteenth century, the moral wrongfulness requirement of English law was merged into English common law, to require both the presence of a criminal act (*actus rea*) and the presence of a guilty mind (*mens rea*).[161]

Some five hundred years later, more specific attempts were made under the common law to find appropriate and workable criteria for establishing the condition of legal insanity. For example, the "wild beast test" of Justice Tracy in the 1723 Arnold case held that a man must be "…totally deprived of his understanding and memory, and doth not know what he is doing, no more than an infant, …a brute or a wild beast." In 1800, this was refined by Thomas Erskine in the Hadfield trial to produce the "offspring of a delusion" test, the chief importance of which was that insanity, to be exculpatory, could now be partial rather than total by nature. That same year, the Criminal Lunatics Act was passed to allow for the detention in safe custody and at His Majesty's pleasure of defendants (including those accused of treason, murder or felony) who were found not guilty on the grounds of insanity. In due course, with the founding in 1816 of England's first criminal asylum – a special wing at the Bethlem Hospital (the origin of the term "Bedlam"), such custody came to mean incarceration in special psychiatric institutions for the criminally insane. The landmark text on the topic during this general period was Isaac Ray's *Treatise on the Medical Jurisprudence of Insanity*, written in 1838, which in common with the thinking of the day focused only on offenders' capacity for proper cognition or awareness of their acts.[162]

In 1840, however, the case of Edward Oxford's attempted assassination of Queen Victoria led to the introduction of a volitional or behavioural test for legal insanity, in the form of the "irresistible impulse" defence; this test allowed for a person's acquittal if, as a result of being mentally ill, he could not resist the impulse to commit the crime, and Oxford was its first beneficiary.[163] His acquittal provoked

---

160 "Practice Guideline: Forensic Psychiatric Evaluation of Defendants Raising the Insanity Defense" (hereinafter: "AAPL Practice Guideline"), Supplement to *The Journal of the American Academy of Psychiatry and the Law*, Vol. 30, No. 2, 2002, p.3. Note that under the U.S. system, "A defendant whose insanity defense is successful is adjudicated either not guilty by reason of insanity (NGRI) or guilty but not criminally responsible (NCR), depending on the [state] jurisdiction." (Ibid, p.1.)
161 *AAPL Practice Guideline*, p.4.
162 *Faulk's* and *AAPL Practice Guideline*, passim.
163 The same test was used in a number of U.S. states from 1886 onward. However, "The practical aspects of applying this defense has led to problems distinguishing between the irresistible impulse and the impulse not resisted. Thus, as of 1990 no state uses irresistible impulse as its sole insanity defense." (*AAPL Practice Guideline*, p.5.)

the stern displeasure of Queen Victoria, however, and her subsequent comments on the incident set the tone for a legal and public-opinion controversy over the criminal insanity defence that has raged ever since. In her view,

> Punishment deters not only sane men but also eccentric men, whose supposed involuntary acts are really produced by a diseased brain capable of being acted upon by external influence. A knowledge that they would be protected by an acquittal on the grounds of insanity will encourage these men to commit desperate acts, while on the other hand certainty that they will not escape punishment will terrify them into a peaceful attitude towards others.[164]

Victoria's opinion notwithstanding, only three years later, in 1843, the famous case of the attempted assassination of Sir Robert Peel, leader of the Tory Party, by a Scottish wood turner named Daniel McNaughten served to secure the position of the insanity defence within the judicial landscape not just of England, but eventually of the whole common law world. (Similar developments occurred also within the civil law systems of mainland Europe around the same time, following the judicial acceptance in early 19th-century France of defence counsel arguments to the effect that especially violent or – because seemingly quite irrational – "monstrous" acts of murder could sometimes be attributed to the presence of a recently discovered psychiatric condition known as "homicidal monomania.")[165] McNaughten had the delusional belief that Peel and the Tory Party were persecuting him, and so he tried to assassinate Peel, in the event killing the latter's personal secretary, Edward Drummond, by mistake. When the jury endorsed his plea of not guilty by reason of insanity, public opinion was outraged and the Queen again intervened, summoning fifteen Law Lords from the Upper House of Parliament to clarify five questions or issues concerning the insanity defence. Their answers to two of her questions constitute what is now known as the "McNaughten rule" or "McNaughten test":

> Every man is presumed to be sane.... To establish a defence on the ground of insanity, it must be proved that, at the time of the committing of the act, the party accused was labouring under such a defect of reason, from disease of the mind, as not to know the nature and quality of the act he was doing; or if he did know it, that he did not know he was doing what was wrong.[166]

---

164 *Crime and Insanity in England*, N. Walker, Edinburgh University Press, 1979, p.193.
165 See: "About the Concept of the 'Dangerous Individual' in 19th Century Legal Psychiatry," Michel Foucault, in *Law and Psychiatry: Proceedings of an International Symposium Held at the Clark Institute of Psychiatry*, Toronto, Canada, February 1977, Pergamon Press (1978), pp.1-28.
166 "M'Naghten's Case, 10 Cl. & F.200, 8 Eng. Rep. 718 (H.L. 1843)," cited in *AAPL Practice Guidelines*, p.5. The McNaughten Rules are generally held to have three separate "limbs," which *Faulk's Basic Forensic Psychiatry* describes (at p.57) as follows:

(1) That by reason of such defect from disease of the mind he did not know the nature or quality of his act (this means that he did not realise what he was physically doing at the time); or

(2) by reason of such defect from disease of the mind that he did not know what he was doing was wrong (i.e. that he did not know that what he was doing was forbidden by law or that the act was morally wrong according to the standards of ordinary people); or

(3) where a person is under an insane delusion that prevents the true appreciation of the nature and quality of his act, he is under the same degree of responsibility as if the facts were as he imagined them to be. If for example whilst deluded he believes his life to be in grave danger and acts in self-defence, he would be treated as though acting in self-defence. However if whilst deluded he acts to gain revenge, then he is punishable.

A finding of not guilty under this rule is customarily known as the "special verdict." The McNaughten test became the law of the land in England and was subsequently imported into the U.S. legal system also. In 1870, the New Hampshire Supreme Court introduced a considerably more expansive standard for adjudicating on the insanity defence, one known variously as the "product test" or "the Durham rule." According to this rule, "No man shall be held accountable, criminally, for an act which was the offspring and product of mental illness." This much looser standard was widely abused in practice, however, and by 1972 it had been abandoned by all U.S. jurisdictions apart from New Hampshire and the Virgin Islands. Nowadays, a majority of the State tests governing the insanity defence in the U.S. incorporate language that directly evokes the core criterion of the McNaughten rule, namely that there must exist "a defect in reason caused by disease of the mind (mental illness), which impairs a person's ability to know the wrongfulness of one's conduct."[167] Finally, in the aftermath of the public outrage aroused by John W. Hinckley's 1981 assassination attempt on President Reagan and the court's subsequent rendering of a verdict of not guilty by reason of insanity, the U.S. Congress in 1984 enacted the Insanity Defense Reform Act, which placed substantial restrictions on the future use and conduct of the insanity defence. (For example, the burden of proof shifted from the prosecution, which previously had to prove the defendant was sane beyond a reasonable doubt, to the defence, which now had to establish affirmative evidence of the defendant's insanity; in addition, the current test states that the defendant's mental illness must be "severe" in order to be exculpatory.)

Variants of the insanity defence mechanism, and concomitant arrangements for the compulsory hospitalisation of those ascertained as being criminally insane, are nowadays to be found in most other national jurisdictions around the world. The common feature of all these systems, at least in countries laying valid claim to observance of the rule of law, is that any rulings or measures adopted in either of these two areas must first be authorized by a court of law and there must be a right of judicial appeal.[168] In the separate field of civil psychiatric committal, considerable debate and controversy surrounds the relevant laws and practices commonly found in many countries, especially – though by no means exclusively – in the more underdeveloped parts of the world.[169] The criteria for civil involuntary hospitalisation, based mainly on local understandings and interpretations of the "psychiatric dangerousness" criterion, and also the extent and quality of judicial involvement found in the committal process, vary widely from country to country. (Within the Asia region, Japan's mental health system has long been the focus of particularly intense international criticism on human rights grounds; the great majority of mental hospital patients there are compulsorily admitted and detained, often being held in locked wards for 24 hours a day, and legal-institutional provisions for appeal or review of such status are minimal.)[170]

---

167 *AAPL Practice Guideline*, p.5.
168 See below, section IV.
169 A detailed comparative account of the civil psychiatric committals systems in England, Singapore, Hong Kong, Canada, Taiwan, Japan and the United States is presented in: "Conference Briefing Papers: International Conference on Mental Health Law, Taipei, Taiwan, June 1-3, 1992." (Place and date of publication unknown.)
170 See for example, "Japan's New Mental Health Law: More Light Shed on Dark Places?," Stephan M. Salzberg, *International Journal of Law and Psychiatry*, 1991, Vol. 14, pp.137-169; and "Human Rights in Mental Health," Larry Gostin, *International Journal of Law and Psychiatry*, 1987, Vol. 10, pp.353-368. (The latter article summarizes the five-point "Kyoto Principles" on mental health and human rights, which were drawn up by a group of international scholars on law and mental health in 1987 largely in response to the dire civil and human rights situation found within Japan's mental hospital system. The five principles affirmed at Kyoto were: 1) the right to humane, dignified and professional treatment; 2) voluntary admission should be encouraged whenever treatment is necessary; 3) the right to a full and impartial judicial hearing before involuntary loss of liberty; 4) the right to a

Variation on a Theme – The Insanity Prosecution

A few fundamental observations should now be made concerning the ways in which, in China, the various legal principles and practices outlined above are understood and applied in the context of "cases of a political nature," that is of cases involving political detainees who are suspected of being mentally ill. All Chinese textbook accounts of criminal forensic psychiatry follow and endorse the same general principles as those discussed above: the issue of "legal responsibility" is placed at centre-stage, and the McNaughten rule is held up as a model standard both for the judicial handling of mentally disordered offenders in general, and for the conduct and application of the insanity defence in particular. But there the similarities tend to cease.

The first unusual or paradoxical aspect that emerges, upon closer examination of the source material, is that in China's case it is almost never the counsel for the defence who raises the insanity argument;[171] it is either the police or the prosecution who do so – "on the defendant's behalf," as it were. This is the precise opposite of what occurs in other countries, where virtually all insanity pleas are made by the defence. At one important level, this simply reflects the fact that, under the PRC Criminal Procedure Law, detained suspects have only very limited access to counsel until shortly before the trial; any moves to have the detainee examined by a forensic psychiatrist will therefore normally have been carried out by the police or prosecution long before any access to counsel has been granted (in most cases, forensic appraisal occurs during the early stages of pre-trial detention.) But by the same token, this hardly inspires a high degree of confidence in the general workings of the system.

The official statistical evidence indicates that in the majority of criminal cases in China where forensic psychiatric procedures are invoked, the crimes at issue are those of murder, assault, rape, arson, and other similarly grave acts. Given that the legal authorities everywhere tend to be highly suspicious of the insanity plea, regarding it in most cases as being a mere ploy by the defendant to avoid criminal punishment, one assumes that the majority of Chinese defendants who "benefit" from police moves to have them declared criminally insane must have displayed fairly conspicuous signs of mental disorder, either at the time of their arrest or at some point in the subsequent course of their detention. On the other hand (as will be discussed further in Chapter 5),[172] Chinese forensic psychiatrists themselves have begun recently to complain, in articles written for the professional journals, that a so-called "presumption of insanity" is all too often applied in the course of these forensic appraisal procedures. So the true picture remains far from clear.

Where "political cases" falling within the legal or forensic psychiatric appraisals category are concerned, however, the fact that in all known or reported cases it is the police who raise the question of the defendant's sanity and hence of their capacity to bear legal responsibility for the alleged crimes, and not the detainees themselves or their lawyers who do so, inevitably gives rise to the suspicion that

---

free and open environment and free communication; and 5) the right not to be discriminated against on grounds of mental illness. (For a useful and informative account of legal reforms in this general area in Taiwan, see "Taiwan's Mental Health Law," Stephan M. Salzberg, *International Journal of Law and Psychiatry*, 1992, Vol. 15, pp.43-75.)

171 There are signs that this may slowly be changing: in the past few years, a series of cases have been publicized in the Chinese press where the lawyers of people accused of murder have successfully raised the insanity defence on their client's behalf, thereby saving them from execution. This in turn has provoked widespread public outrage, amid accusations that the insanity defence is tantamount to the granting of a "murderers' license" (*sharen zhizhao*.) For further detail on this issue, see p.168 below.

172 See p.179 below.

the process in question has little, if anything, to do with the insanity defence as understood and applied elsewhere. Indeed, it is hard to avoid rather quickly suspecting that it actually constitutes something which should more properly and accurately be described as the "insanity prosecution." The general pattern which emerges from the numerous case examples of alleged mentally ill dissidents, and in the many extracts from the official forensic psychiatric literature cited below, seems clearly to point to such a conclusion, despite the authorities' claim that the purpose of the system is a humanitarian one.[173]

This general pattern comes into still sharper focus when one considers that in the vast majority of cases in China, no judicial oversight or verification at all is exercised over the forensic psychiatric finding that a criminal detainee is suffering from a severe mental disorder rendering him or her incapable of bearing legal responsibility for the alleged criminal acts. What instead happens is that either the police or the procuracy (usually the former) order and initiate the psychiatric evaluation, they then make the decision as to whether or not the examining psychiatrists' conclusions as to the defendant's state of mind and level of legal responsibility should be accepted, and if in the end they endorse a finding of "not responsible on grounds of insanity," then they are free to dispose of the defendant in any of the various ways earlier listed. In short, the defendant is simply removed from the criminal justice process and denied all further rights, including that of any judicial hearing to determine a) whether the finding of criminal insanity was in fact sound and accurate; b) whether the defendant or his/her lawyer wish to present a second medical opinion on the matter; and c) whether the dispositional measures adopted by the police or procuracy were in any way appropriate or lawful in nature. Equally vital to remember is that where China's non-violent "political cases" are concerned, the so-called crimes from which society is ostensibly being protected throughout this whole process are entirely different in nature from the heinous acts of violence which the now internationally accepted mechanism of granting legal exculpation to mentally disordered offenders was originally designed to address.

The Role of Due Process Safeguards

In order to appreciate the importance of the role played by judicial oversight in the proper functioning of the legal-psychiatric appraisals process elsewhere, and to see how serious are the consequences of the lack of any such involvement by the judicial bench in China's case, it may be helpful for us to look briefly at the wider due process implications, in the context of the British criminal justice system, of the forensic psychiatric evaluation of the "legal responsibility" issue. The purpose here is not to compare a primitive system against an "ideal" one (the U.K. system is far from being that); rather, it is to illustrate how the various key elements of the relevant legal process are in principle meant to fit together, and to identify the specific legal safeguards against abuse that require to be upheld. The most important point to be borne in mind is that there is a fundamental difference, in due process terms, between the role of

---

173 A superficially similar situation arises occasionally in other countries when a judge wishes to impose a plea of insanity on a defendant who refuses to make such a plea on his own account, but who is clearly not mentally competent enough to see that it is in his or her best interests to plead insanity. In the United States, for example, at least seventeen jurisdictions permit insanity defences to be entered over the objections of defendants. (See: Robert D. Miller, MD, "*Hendricks v. People*: Forcing the Insanity Defense on an Unwilling Defendant," *Journal of the American Academy of Psychiatry and the Law*, 2002, Vol.30, No.2, pp.295-7.) But this clearly does not, in any sense, constitute an insanity "prosecution"; rather, it is done in the defendant's legal interests. The other basic difference in China's case is that a judge has no say in the process anyway: it is the police who raise the "insanity prosecution" and it is the police who then endorse the finding of insanity and proceed to dispose of the detainee as they see fit. The detainee, needless to say, also has no say in the matter.

a forensic psychiatrist who has been hired by defence counsel to support a plea of exculpatory insanity, and the role of a forensic psychiatrist who has been hired by the police or the prosecution to investigate a defendant's mental condition and capacity for legal responsibility.

In present-day Britain, the relevant legislation includes the Mental Health Act 1983, the Criminal Procedures (Insanity and Unfitness to Plead) Act 1991, the Crime (Sentences) Act 1997, and various acts dealing with probation. The range of legal interventions covered by these various laws is much wider than just the insanity defence. As Faulk observes, "Mental abnormality may be grounds for mitigation, a reason to be excused trial, a reason for diminished responsibility, or grounds to be excused guilt."[174] There is no reason in principle why the police or prosecution side should not, on occasion, take the initiative towards any of these various outcomes – and indeed, the police in countries other than China sometimes do refer criminal detainees for forensic psychiatric examination, especially in the early post-arrest or remand stages. But in practice, pleas and requests for mitigation, excusal from trial, diminished responsibility and (naturally enough) verdicts of not guilty on grounds of insanity are almost always raised by the defence. In all cases, moreover, the judiciary plays the key role in determining the actual outcome; and if the defence side has objections to any police-initiated moves, it then has prompt recourse to the courts in pursuit of remedy.

During the various stages of the criminal process, a range of rights safeguards are available under British law to detainees suspected by the authorities of having a mental disturbance or in cases where affirmative findings of this nature have already been made. The following passages from *Faulk's Basic Forensic Psychiatry* provide a rough and schematic overview of how the system works. First, as regards court orders for psychiatric evaluation,

> Section 35 of the Mental Health Act 1983 provides for a remand to hospital so that a report on the accused's mental condition may be compiled....It should be noted that the section does not allow the patient to be treated against his will....In order to effect this section there must also be a report from a doctor approved under Section 12 of the Mental Health Act 1983 to convince the court (oral or written evidence) that there is reason to suspect mental illness, severe mental impairment, mental impairment or psychopathic disorder, and a recognition by the court that a report on bail is impracticable....The defendant can arrange his own private psychiatric report or appeal against the remand....

And concerning compulsory committals,

> Section 36 of the 1983 Act provides for remand of an accused person to hospital for treatment, and is used for mental illness or severe mental impairment....In practice, Section 48 of the Mental Health Act is more usually employed. This section can be employed by the Crown Court only and is an alternative to prison remand. It may be done in the pre-trial period (in which case it may get a defendant well enough to be tried) or during the trial.... Note that the order cannot be applied to those with psychopathic disorder or mental impairment alone, presumably because these disorders would never be thought to require emergency treatment in their own right....The patient is subject to "consent to treatment regulations" and therefore may be treated against his will....The Mental Health Review Tribunal has no powers to discharge the patient....

---

174 Faulk (op cit), p.39.

If the case then proceeds to trial,

> Under the Criminal Procedure (Insanity and Unfitness to Plead) Act 1991 the courts have powers to deal with persons found not guilty by reason of insanity or unfitness to plead....[In the latter case,] the plea must be proven, on the balance of probabilities (if raised by the defence), or, beyond reasonable doubt (if raised by the prosecution.) A new jury is empanelled just to decide the question. If the matter is not proven then the original trial goes on....Following a verdict of unfit to plead, proceedings move to a "trial of the facts", where a jury hearing evidence determine if the accused "did the act or made the omission against him". The important issue to grasp is that this does not amount to a finding of guilt. If not satisfied on this issue, they return a verdict of acquittal. If they are convinced, a finding that the defendant did the act is recorded....

If the verdict is not guilty by reason of insanity, the court's options then include:

> ...in a case of murder, an admission order to a hospital specified by the Secretary of State (effectively a hospital order with a restriction order unlimited in time); or in other cases the possibilities are an absolute discharge, a guardianship order (under Section 37 Mental Health Act 1983), or a supervision and treatment order....[In the latter cases,] medical advice must be given that compulsory detention for treatment is not needed, and the court must be satisfied that release into the community will not pose an unacceptable risk....
>
> The other possibility is an admission order to a hospital specified by the Secretary of State.[175] This works like a Section 37 from the date of the order. The court has the option of adding a restriction order. If the jury is unconvinced of the disability then the accused is found fit to plead. The trial proper then begins and a new jury is empanelled.
>
> Under the old Act someone found under disability was automatically detained as though under a hospital order with a restriction order unlimited in time. This dissuaded seriously ill people from this plea when the offence was a minor one. The present Act with its wide range of disposals will encourage more people to plead that they are under disability and may, for the same reason, lead to more insanity defences.

And finally, in the most serious cases, the following option is available:

> Section 41 restriction order: The purpose of this section is to protect the public by ordering that a patient detained on a hospital order will not be allowed to leave the hospital without the Home Secretary's permission. The order can be made for a stated period of time (several years) or unlimited in point of time (i.e. potentially to last for the rest of the patient's life.) This interference with the patient's liberty is so great that only a judge in a higher court can make the order. Judges are recommended to make the order [only] where there is a risk of the patient causing serious harm to others if set at large....The patient under a Section 41 order can apply to the Mental Health

---

175 There are currently three such "special hospitals" in England: Broadmoor Hospital in Berkshire, Rampton Hospital in Nottinghamshire and Ashworth Hospital in Merseyside; in Scotland, the equivalent is Carstairs Hospital in Perthshire, and in Ireland, Dundrum Hospital in Dublin.

Review Tribunal after six months. The tribunal does have the power to discharge the patient either conditionally or absolutely but other powers are limited.[176]

As can be seen, this is in no sense a relaxed or overly liberal kind of legal regime; indeed, the U.K. Mental Health Act is often publicly attacked by its many critics as "draconian."[177] Nonetheless, the frequent reference in the above to the role of judges, juries, time limitations and recourse to review tribunals is all deeply reassuring as compared to the equivalent legal regime in China, whose parliament has still not enacted a national mental health law of any kind, and where judges, juries, time limits and review tribunals are wholly absent from the criminal-psychiatric evaluations and committals process. In China, by far the most frequently adopted measure in the case of persons determined as criminally insane is indefinite compulsory hospitalization in a police-run mental asylum. The key differences between this practice and the U.K.'s severest court option, a Section 41 restriction order, is that in China's case it is applied solely on police authority and there is no subsequent right of judicial or even administrative review.

The forensic psychiatrist's role in assessing the legal competence or "responsibility" of a criminal suspect varies widely from one country to another. In the U.K., for example, examining psychiatrists are expected to avoid pronouncing on this issue,[178] whereas in the U.S. it is one of their main duties to do so.[179] Despite this seemingly sharp divergence between the two countries, however, it should again be emphasised that in both cases it is again the court which ultimately decides whether or not the defendant is mentally ill, and hence if they should be held legally responsible or not. The psychiatrist only offers his or her professional assessment of the matter, and that assessment can be vigorously challenged and disputed in court through alternative psychiatric testimony supplied by the defence side. In China, there is no court hearing and the determination of criminal defendants' capacity or otherwise to bear legal responsibility for their alleged crimes is entirely a private or "internal" affair of the police and the

---

176 Faulk (op cit), pp.44-49 and p.56. For a useful summary of the ethical precautions and safeguards that forensic psychiatrists (especially those acting on behalf of the prosecution) should observe when examining criminal defendants, see *AAPL Practice Guideline*, pp.17-20.

177 Moreover, plans announced by the Home Office in 2002 to introduce legislation that would allow persons diagnosed as suffering from "personality disorders" to be pre-emptively hospitalised merely for posing a potential threat to society have aroused a storm of opposition from within the U.K. psychiatric and mental healthcare community. See, for example: Sameer P. Sarkar, MD, "A British Psychiatrist Objects to the Dangerous and Severe Personality Disorder Proposals," *The Journal of the American Academy of Psychiatry and the Law*, 2002, Vol. 30, No. 1, p.6-9.

178 In Britain, "[T]he psychiatrist is generally not asked to comment on 'responsibility' and to use the term may lead to confusion. The court is very much more pragmatic and requires simply an account of the patient's mental abnormality, its effect on the patient, its prognosis and the treatment arrangements which can be made. Without mentioning the word 'responsibility' the legal representatives of the offender will hope to use the psychiatric report as mitigation in any particular case." (Faulk, op cit, p.24.) The same source adds, "Psychiatrists, in providing a psychiatric report dealing with the question of responsibility (intent, disordered mental states, diminished responsibility, insanity, etc.) enter into an area in which, it may be argued, the psychiatrist is being taken beyond the boundaries of his expertise....Psychiatrists should be especially careful in compiling pretrial reports (fitness to plead, insanity, diminished responsibility) where the defendant denies the charge. The psychiatrist is best advised to avoid discussion of the offence and issues relevant to sentencing where the charge is denied." (Ibid, p.229.)

179 In the U.S., "The opinion section is the most critical part of the forensic report. It should summarize pertinent positives and negatives and answer the relevant forensic questions, based on that jurisdiction's legal definition for being found not criminally responsible....If the defendant is charged with more than one offence, the issue of criminal responsibility on each charge should be individually addressed." (*AAPL Practice Guideline*, p.S25.)

procuracy. The forensic psychiatrist's primary duty is to pass judgement on the responsibility question, and since he or she is acting on behalf of the authorities and not the detainee, the police or procuracy in most cases simply adopt the psychiatric opinion proffered and dispose of the case accordingly.

Particularly troubling in this regard is the fact that most Chinese dissidents known to have encountered this treatment have ended up, on account of their allegedly "anti-government" viewpoints or behaviour, being labelled by police psychiatrists as suffering from "paranoia." In the majority of such cases, the following fundamentally flawed sequence of legal events then ensues: first, the dissident's "paranoid condition" (or similar) is declared by the forensic psychiatrist to be sufficient grounds for a finding of lack of legal competence or responsibility; second, an associated judgement will be rendered – by the police or procuracy – that the "anti-government" viewpoints or activities in question pose a severe risk or danger to society; and finally, a decision will be made on the basis of these two points to compulsorily hospitalise the dissident on an indefinite basis.[180]

Finally, it should be remembered that on both sides of the Atlantic and elsewhere, insanity defence pleas are in point of fact extremely rare – and for very good reason. In most criminal cases, a guilty defendant who successfully pleads insanity can very easily end up spending a substantially longer period of time in a secure mental asylum than the term of regular imprisonment that he or she would have served had they not so pleaded. In the case of a relatively minor offence, this may mean the difference between indefinite compulsory hospitalisation and a few years in jail at most.[181] For this reason, the insanity defence has historically tended to be used only as a measure of last resort, for example in murder cases in countries that still retain the death penalty.[182]

As we have seen, the Chinese authorities' own statistics on the proportion and total numbers of criminal suspects found not legally responsible on grounds of mental illness reveal that an alarmingly high proportion of them have been non-violent political dissidents or dissident-type individuals, rather than genuine criminal offenders of any kind. The fact that the great majority of those concerned have probably ended up spending longer periods of time in state custody than would have been the case had they never benefited from China's equivalent of the insanity defence provides further grounds for believing that the latter should more accurately be termed the "insanity prosecution." The acknowledged prevalence within the Chinese legal system of a "presumption of insanity" in such cases serves only to confirm this suspicion.

---

180 In the U.K., by contrast, in order to qualify as unfit to plead: "It is not enough simply that the accused might act against his own interests (e.g. in paranoia) or that he conducts his defence unwisely; the disorder must involve such disability that the defendant is unable to properly make a defence to the charges against him." (Faulk, op cit, p.56.)
181 "Insanity defense pleas are exceedingly rare. Even an experienced defense attorney may have tried only a few insanity defense cases. The experienced forensic psychiatrist can educate the defense attorney about the risks and consequences to the defendant of a successful defense in a case involving a minor crime where the potential jail time is minimal, but where the potential time of criminal commitment to a mental hospital may be substantial and the stigma greater. In such cases the defense evaluator may recommend alternative dispositions, such as a guilty plea with probation conditioned on receiving mental health treatment." (*AAPL Practice Guideline*, pp.17-18.)
182 Even this, however, can seriously backfire: "Evaluating a defendant in a case where the prosecution has given notice of intent to seek the death penalty raises additional issues for defense evaluators. Mental state and detailed behavioral data that evaluators obtain from the defendant that seemingly support a finding of insanity may, if the insanity defense fails, be used by the state to argue for the death penalty." (Ibid, p.18.)

IV. International Legal and Ethical Standards on Psychiatric Custody

In evaluating China's past and current practices in the field of forensic psychiatry, it is important also to be aware of the more widely applicable standards of law and ethics that have been established by the international community in the general area of mental healthcare and psychiatry in recent decades. The bodies chiefly responsible for defining these standards are the United Nations, the World Psychiatric Association (WPA), and the various psychiatric professional organizations of different countries.[183] The pre-eminent or overarching relevant provisions – namely, that people everywhere enjoy equal rights to freedom of the person, freedom of political and religious belief, freedom of expression, the right to a fair trial and so forth – are comprehensively set forth in the Universal Declaration of Human Rights[184] and in the International Covenant on Civil and Political Rights (ICCPR).[185] The Council of Europe has also extensively addressed the issue of involuntary psychiatric committal and treatment and has issued a series of important rules and protocols in this area.

---

183 Several Western psychiatric associations have formulated national-level ethical guidelines in recent years. One example is the Canadian Medical Association's "Code of Ethics Annotated for Psychiatrists," approved by the board of directors of the Canadian Psychiatric Association in October 1978; see http://www.cma.ca/eng-index.htm. In the area of forensic psychiatry, one of the more noteworthy examples is the "Ethical Guidelines for the Practice of Forensic Psychiatry," adopted by the American Academy of Psychiatry and the Law in May 1987 (and revised in October 1989); see http://www.cc.emory.edu/AAPL/ethics.htm.

184 According to Article 2 of the Universal Declaration of Human Rights (adopted and proclaimed by General Assembly Resolution 217 A (III) of 10 December 1948), "[N]o distinction shall be made on the basis of the political, jurisdictional or international status of the country or territory to which a person belongs"; in other words, all rights listed in the document apply equally to all citizens of any country. Article 5 states, "No one shall be subjected to torture or to cruel, inhuman or degrading treatment or punishment"; Article 9 adds, "No one shall be subjected to arbitrary arrest, detention or exile"; and Article 10 continues, "Everyone is entitled in full equality to a fair and public hearing by an independent and impartial tribunal, in the determination of his rights and obligations and of any criminal charge against him."

On more specific related matters, the Declaration states, in Article 18, "Everyone has the right to freedom of thought, conscience and religion; [including the right…] to manifest his religion or belief in teaching practice, worship and observance"; in Article 19, "Everyone has the right to freedom of opinion and expression…"; and in Article 23 (4), "Everyone has the right to form and to join trades unions for the protection of his interest."

Finally, addressing the general question of states of emergency and national security-related measures, Article 29 specifies: "In the exercise of his rights and freedoms, everyone shall be subject only to such limitations as are determined by law solely for the purpose of securing due recognition and respect for the rights and freedoms of others and of meeting the just requirements of morality, public order and the general welfare in a democratic society."

185 The relevant rights as set forth in the Universal Declaration are enlarged and elaborated upon in the International Covenant on Civil and Political Rights (ICCPR) (adopted Dec. 16, 1966, G.A. Res. 2200A [XXI], entered into force March 23, 1976, signed by China in October 1998, not yet ratified) in the following provisions: Article 2 (non-discrimination on the basis of political and religious opinion, ethnicity or similar grounds), Article 4 (exclusion of the right to freedom of thought, conscience and religion from the scope of rights that States Parties may derogate from in times of national emergency), Article 7 (freedom from torture), Article 9 (ban on arbitrary arrest or detention), Article 12 (no restriction allowed on key rights except as necessary to protect national security, public order, public health or morals or the rights and freedoms of others), Article 14 (right to a fair and impartial trial), Article 18 (freedom of thought, conscience and religion), Article 19 (freedom of expression and the right to hold opinions without interference), Article 21 (right of peaceful assembly), Article 22 (freedom of association, including the right to form and join trades unions), and Article 26 (equality before the law and prohibition of discrimination on grounds such as race, colour, sex, and political or other opinion).

The United Nations

In the early 1980s, in response to growing international concern over the political misuse of psychiatry in the Soviet Union, its satellite states and a small number of other countries (notably, South Africa under *apartheid*),[186] the United Nations undertook a major investigative review of mental healthcare provision around the world. In particular, the world body focused on the rules, procedures and practices pursued by various countries in the area of involuntary psychiatric committal and treatment. In 1983, Special Rapporteur Daes presented the results of the investigative review in a report to the U.N., and the following passage figured prominently in her conclusions:

> [W]e are painfully aware that:
>
> Psychiatry in some States of the international community is often used to subvert the political and legal guarantees of the freedom of the individual and to violate seriously his human and legal rights.
>
> In some States, psychiatric hospitalisation treatment is forced on the individual who does not support the existing political regime of the State in which he lives.

On the basis of these findings, the Special Rapporteur recommended that the U.N. Commission on Human Rights should, among other things, urge all member States "[To] prohibit *expressis verbis* psychological and psychiatric abuses, in particular for political or other non-medical grounds."[187] After several years of discussion and drafting work within the UN, this initiative bore legislative fruit in December 1991, when the world body's General Assembly adopted a wide-ranging set of provisions entitled "Principles for the Protection of Persons with Mental Illness and for the Improvement of Mental Health Care." According to Principle 4 of this important U.N. document,

> A determination that a person has a mental illness shall be made in accordance with internationally accepted medical standards.
>
> A determination of mental illness shall never be made on the basis of political, economic or social status, or membership in a cultural, racial or religious group, or for any other reason not directly relevant to mental health status.

---

186 In a major report of 1986 submitted to the U.N.'s Sub-Commission on Prevention of Discrimination and Protection of Minorities, for example, the Sub-Commission's Special Rapporteur stated:

> Between 8,000 and 9,000 [black] Africans suffering from mental disorders are detained against their will in privately owned institutions in the Republic of South Africa... There is not a single black psychiatrist in South Africa and vital decisions about thousands of African mental patients are made by part-time physicians who do not even speak the language of the patients... Recent legislative measures of the Government concerning the "rehabilitation" of African pass [law] offenders equate in a dangerous way the non-observance of the *apartheid* laws with mental disorder... These conditions and policies, being a direct effect of *apartheid* in the health field, are inimical to the letter and spirit of the Constitution of the World Health Organization...

(Erica-Irene A. Daes, Special Rapporteur of the U.N. Sub-Commission on Prevention of Discrimination and Protection of Minorities, *Principles, Guidelines and Guarantees for the Protection of Persons Detained on Grounds of Mental Ill-Health or Suffering from Mental Disorder* [New York: United Nations Publications, 1986] E/CN.4/Sub.2/1983/17/Rev.1, p.8.)

187 Ibid, p.30.

> Family or professional conflict, or non-conformity with moral, social, cultural or political values or religious beliefs prevailing in a person's community, shall never be a determining factor in the diagnosis of mental illness.
>
> A background of past treatment or hospitalisation of a patient shall not of itself justify any present or future determination of mental illness.
>
> No person or authority shall classify a person as having, or otherwise indicate that a person has, a mental illness except for purposes directly relating to mental illness or the consequences of mental illness.

Among other important general provisions, the Principles state: "Every patient shall have the right to be treated in the least restrictive environment and with the least restrictive or intrusive treatment appropriate to the patient's health needs and the need to protect the physical safety of others" (Principle 9). "Medication shall meet the best health needs of the patient, shall be given to a patient only for therapeutic or diagnostic purposes and shall never be administered as a punishment or for the convenience of others" (Principle 10). "Physical restraint or involuntary seclusion of a patient shall not be employed except in accordance with the officially approved procedures of the mental health facility and only when it is the only means available to prevent immediate or imminent harm to the patient or others" (Principle 11.11). "Psychosurgery and other intrusive and irreversible treatments for mental illness shall never be carried out on a patient who is an involuntary patient in a mental health facility..." (Principle 11.14). "In the cases specified [where involuntary committal or treatment is involved] the patient or his or her personal representative, or any interested person, shall have the right to appeal to a judicial or other independent authority concerning any treatment given to him or her" (Principle 11.16). And according to Principle 13, all mental patients shall have "the right to full respect for his or her...freedom of communication...and freedom of religion or belief."

Principle 20 deals specifically with the rights of mentally-ill criminal offenders and reads as follows:

> The present Principle applies to persons serving sentences of imprisonment for criminal offences, or who are otherwise detained in the course of criminal proceedings or investigations against them, and who are determined to have a mental illness or who it is believed may have such an illness.
>
> All such persons should receive the best available mental health care as provided in Principle 1 above. The present Principles shall apply to them to the fullest extent possible, with only such limited modifications and exceptions as are necessary in the circumstances. No such modifications and exceptions shall prejudice the persons' rights under the instruments noted in paragraph 5 of Principle 1, above.[188]
>
> Domestic law may authorize a court or other competent authority, acting on the basis of competent and independent medical advice, to order that such persons be admitted to a mental health facility.

---

188 Paragraph 5 of Principle 1 reads: "Every person with a mental illness shall have the right to exercise all civil, political, economic, social and cultural rights as recognized in the Universal Declaration of Human Rights, the International Covenant on Economic, Social and Cultural Rights, the International Covenant on Civil and Political Rights and in other relevant instruments, such as the Declaration on the Rights of Disabled Persons and the Body of Principles for the Protection of All Persons under Any Form of Detention or Imprisonment."

> Treatment of persons determined to have a mental illness shall in all circumstances be consistent with Principle 11 above.[189]

Thus, the U.N. General Assembly ruled that no derogation from or restriction of fundamental civil and political liberties was to be permitted, or otherwise viewed as justifiable, in the case of detained criminal offenders who were ascertained by governmental authorities as being mentally ill.[190]

The Council of Europe

The increased attention given internationally to the political misuse of psychiatry in the Soviet Union and a number of other countries, including South Africa, together with several landmark cases in this general area heard by the European Court of Human Rights, prompted the Council of Europe in the early 1980s to begin formulating specific rules and protocols on the use of involuntary psychiatric committal and treatment and to strengthen legal safeguards for those concerned. The first of these documents was the "Rules Concerning the Legal Protection of Persons Suffering from Mental Disorder Placed as Involuntary Patients," issued by the Council of Europe in February 1983. According to Article 2 of the Rules,

> Psychiatrists and other doctors, in determining whether a person is suffering from a mental disorder and requires placement, should do so in accordance with medical science. Difficulty in adapting to moral, social, political or other values, in itself, should not be considered a mental disorder.

Article 3 then addressed the key issue of "psychiatric dangerousness":

> In the absence of any other means of giving the appropriate treatment:
>
> a. a patient may be placed in an establishment only when, by reason of his mental disorder, he represents a serious danger to himself or other persons;
>
> b. states may, however, provide that a patient may also be placed when, because of the serious nature of his mental disorder, the absence of placement would lead to a deterioration of his disorder or prevent the appropriate treatment being given to him.

The 1983 Rules also stated (in Article 4):

> 1. A decision for placement should be taken by a judicial or any other appropriate authority prescribed by law....

---

189 U.N. General Assembly, report of the Third Committee, *Principles for the Protection of Persons with Mental Illness and for the Improvement of Mental Health Care* (New York: United Nations, December 17, 1991), A/46/721. For a wider discussion of the ethical aspects of compulsory psychiatric hospitalisation, see Robert Miller, "The Ethics of Involuntary Commitment to Mental Health Treatment," in Sidney Bloch and Paul Chodoff (eds.), *Psychiatric Ethics* (Oxford University Press, 1991) pp.265-289.

190 The UN is currently engaged in drafting an international convention on the rights of disabled people, including the mentally ill. See: Aaron A. Dhir, "Human Rights Treaty Drafting through the Lens of Mental Disability: the Proposed International Convention on Protection and Promotion of the Rights and Dignity of Persons with Disabilities," Cornell Law School LL.M. Papers Series, 2004; available at: http://lsr.nellco.org/cornell/lps/clacp/2.

2. Where a decision for placement is taken by a non-judicial body or person, that body or person should be different from that which originally requested or recommended placement. The person should immediately be informed of his rights and should have the right of appeal to a court which should decide under a simple and speedy procedure.

Regarding the civil rights' entitlement of a person subjected to involuntary committal, the Rules specifically stated (in Article 9, paragraph 1): "The placement, by itself, cannot constitute, by operation of law, a reason for the restriction of the legal capacity of the patient." In an Explanatory Memorandum issued at the same time as the Rules, the Council of Europe elaborated on this point as follows:

43. The purpose of paragraph 1 is to ensure that placement is not regarded as a ground for restricting the patient's legal capacity *ipso jure*. Any such restriction must comply with the principles (and procedures) of ordinary law, which generally provides that legal capacity may be restricted only where the person concerned is unable to understand or defend his interests.[191]

In April 1994, the Council of Europe issued a second key document in this area, Recommendation 1235 on Psychiatry and Human Rights, which reiterated and further strengthened the above provisions on involuntary committal. According to Article 7 (i) of the Recommendation, for example,

b) in the event of compulsory admission, the decision regarding placement in a psychiatric institution must be taken by a judge and the placement period must be specified. Provision must be made for the placement decision to be regularly and automatically reviewed;

c) there must be legal provision for an appeal to be lodged against the decision;

d) a code of patients' rights must be brought to the attention of patients on their arrival at a psychiatric institution;

e) a code of ethics for psychiatrists should be drawn up inter alia on the basis of the Hawaii Declaration approved by the General Assembly of the World Psychiatric Association in Vienna in 1983.[192]

In January 2000, the Council of Europe published a comprehensive White Paper on the rights of persons placed as involuntary patients in psychiatric facilities and announced that it would soon be drawing up a new legal instrument in this area that would be applicable to all member states. The White Paper set forth detailed provisions concerning the role and function of the police, courts and prisons in implementing, and monitoring the lawfulness of, involuntary psychiatric custody. It also returned unequivocally to the question of the political misuse of psychiatry:

2.2 In respect of personality disorders, account was taken of the judgement of the European Court of Human Rights in the Winterwerp case, which reads as follows:

---

191 See: Council of Europe, "Legal Protection of Persons Suffering from Mental Disorder Placed as Involuntary Patients," Recommendation No. R (83) 2 adopted by the Committee of Ministers of the Council of Europe on 22 February 1983, in Strasbourg.
192 Council of Europe, "Recommendation No. 1235 (1994) on Psychiatry and Human Rights," adopted by the Assembly on 12 April 1994 (10th Sitting); see also Document 7040, report of the Committee on Legal Affairs and Human Rights, Rapporteur: Mr Stoffelen; and Document 7048, opinion of the Social, Health and Family Affairs Committee, Rapporteur: Mr Eisma. See below for details of the WPA's Hawaii Declaration.

"...Article 5.1 [of the Convention][193] obviously cannot be taken as permitting the detention of a person simply because his views or behaviour deviate from the norms prevailing in a particular society." ...

2.4   Involuntary placement should under no circumstances be used for political ends. (In this respect, reference could in particular be made to Recommendation No. R (83)2 of the Committee of Ministers to member States on legal protection of persons suffering from mental disorder placed as involuntary patients, which states that "Difficulty in adapting to moral, social, political or other values, in itself, should not be considered a mental disorder.")[194]

In addition, all of the above documents stipulate that psychosurgery and any other such "treatment which is not yet generally recognised by medical science or presents a serious risk of causing permanent brain damage" is in no circumstances to be given without the informed and written consent of the patient, especially if he or she is in detention.[195] Finally, a document issued jointly by the Office of the European Commissioner for Human Rights and the World Health Organization in February 2003 emphasized the need for regular outside monitoring of all custodial psychiatric facilities by a range of independent bodies:

In addition to effective internal complaint procedures, the frequent visiting of psychiatric institutions by independent inspection mechanisms greatly reduces the potential for human rights abuses. The access to such institutions by appropriate NGOs, user and advocacy groups is also to be encouraged.... It is particularly important, in this context, that the confidentiality of information disclosing abuses is respected and that whistle-blowers are protected.[196]

The World Psychiatric Association

Within the international psychiatric community, increasing reports in the 1970s and thereafter concerning the political abuse of psychiatry in the former Soviet Union and elsewhere provided a powerful impetus to efforts by concerned professionals to establish clear ethical codes aimed at eliminating political and other forms of unwarranted outside interference from the practice of psychiatry in all countries. The first major outcome of these efforts was the Declaration of Hawaii, passed by the General Assembly of the World Psychiatric Association in July 1977 and updated at its July 1983 world congress in Vienna. According to the preamble of the Declaration,

---

193 European Convention on Human Rights, Article 5.1: "Everyone has the right to liberty and security of person. No one shall be deprived of his liberty save in the following cases and in accordance with a procedure prescribed by law: ..."

194 Council of Europe, "White Paper on the Protection of the Human Rights and Dignity of People Suffering from Mental Disorder, Especially Those Placed as Involuntary Patients in a Psychiatric Establishment," 3 January 2000, DIR/JUR (2000) 2; the document was drawn up by a Working Party of the Steering Committee on Bioethics and was "published for public consultation purposes, with a view to drawing up guidelines to be included in a new legal instrument of the Council of Europe."

195 For details of these provisions, see Note 536 below.

196 Office of the Commissioner for Human Rights, "The Protection and Promotion of the Human Rights of Persons with Mental Disabilities," CommDH (2003)1, Seminar organized by the Commissioner for Human Rights and hosted by the WHO Regional Office for Europe, 5-7 February 2003, in Copenhagen.

It is the view of the World Psychiatric Association that due to conflicting loyalties and expectations of both physicians and patients in contemporary society and the delicate nature of the therapist-patient relationship, high ethical standards are especially important for those involved in the science and practice of psychiatry as a medical specialty. These guidelines have been delineated in order to promote close adherence to those standards and to prevent misuse of psychiatric concepts, knowledge and technology.

The WPA statement continued,

If and when a relationship is established for purposes other than therapeutic, such as in forensic psychiatry, its nature must be thoroughly explained to the person concerned... As soon as the conditions for compulsory treatment no longer apply, the psychiatrist should release the patient from the compulsory nature of the treatment and if further therapy is necessary should obtain voluntary consent... The psychiatrist must on no account utilize the tools of his profession once the absence of psychiatric illness has been established. If a patient or some third party demands actions contrary to scientific knowledge or ethical principles the psychiatrist must refuse to cooperate... The psychiatrist should stop all therapeutic, teaching or research programs that may evolve contrary to the principles of this Declaration.[197]

At its world conference in Athens in October 1989, moreover, the WPA adopted a further resolution stating, among other things: "A diagnosis that a person is mentally ill shall be determined in accordance with the internationally accepted medical standards.... Difficulty in adapting to moral, social, political, or other values, in itself should not be considered a mental illness."[198] In addition, the Athens resolution affirmed a number of key subsidiary protections for the rights of the mentally ill. For example: "The final decision to admit or detain a patient in a mental health facility as an involuntary patient shall be taken only by a court or a competent independent body prescribed by law, and only after an appropriate and proper hearing... They have the right of appeal and to be heard personally by the court or competent body." Also, "Patients who are deprived of their liberty shall have the right to a qualified guardian or counsel to protect their interests."[199] In August 1996, the WPA's General Assembly reiterated and further strengthened these various principles in its Declaration of Madrid.[200] The Chinese Society of Psychiatry, the country's sole professional body in this field, is a full member of the WPA.

---

197 Declaration of Hawaii, 1983, as included in Appendix II of Bloch and Reddaway, *Soviet Psychiatric Abuse: The Shadow Over World Psychiatry*, pp.237-239.
198 The World Federation for Mental Health (WFMH) adopted the same principle in its January 1989 "Declaration of Human Rights and Mental Health." According to the document's preamble, "Whereas a diagnosis of mental illness by a mental health practitioner shall be in accordance with accepted medical, psychological, scientific and ethical standards...and whereas persons have, nonetheless, been at times and continue to be inappropriately labelled, diagnosed and treated as mentally ill...difficulty in adapting to moral, social, political or other values in itself shall not be considered a mental illness" (from a pamphlet issued by the WFMH, on file with author).
199 "WPA Statements and Viewpoints on the Rights and Legal Safeguards of the Mentally Ill," adopted by the WPA General Assembly in Athens, October 17, 1989; in Geneva Initiative on Psychiatry, *Human Rights and Professional Responsibilities of Physicians in Documents of International Organizations* (Amsterdam and Sofia, 1998), pp.70-71.
200 "World Psychiatric Association: Madrid Declaration on Ethical Standards for Psychiatric Practice," approved by the WPA General Assembly on 25 August 1996; available at: www.wpanet.org . See also: *Mental Health Reforms* (Journal of the Geneva Initiative on Psychiatry), 1997, No.1, pp.8-9. Among new provisions included in

Taken together, the UN's 1991 Principles and the WPA's Declarations of Hawaii and Madrid provide the core set of international standards upon which the ethical and legal practices of psychiatrists around the world should properly be evaluated. By detaining large numbers of non-violent political and religious dissenters and subjecting them to forensic psychiatric assessment and compulsory hospitalisation, China's legal-psychiatric establishment is acting in violation of almost all of these international legal and ethical standards. In Chapter 9, which describes an international campaign launched in early 2001 against the political abuse of psychiatry in China, we will see how the World Psychiatric Association has responded, since then, to the challenge posed by the Chinese authorities' delinquent behaviour in this area.

Cruel and Unusual Punishment

In terms of international human rights law, the incarceration of a sane political dissident or other peaceful critic of the government in an institute for the criminally insane can best be described as an act of arbitrary detention involving "cruel, inhuman or degrading treatment or punishment" as defined in the UN's Convention Against Torture, which China ratified in 1988 and is therefore bound to uphold. This characterization is supported and implicitly endorsed by the fact that the successor state to the former Soviet Union, the Russian Federation, was requested by the U.N.'s Committee Against Torture to provide an accounting of its practices in the mental health arena in its periodic implementation reports to the Committee, following the USSR's ratification of the Convention in 1987. In 1990, in its response to the first periodic implementation report of the USSR, the Committee stated:

> With reference to Article 13 of the Convention, members requested further details on the right of appeal of those in custody, in pre-trial detention or psychiatric hospitals, whether there were systematic controls on such detention, and whether they were carried out by the institutions themselves or by an external authority.... The representative [of the USSR] stated that, as of 1988, all psychiatric institutions, formerly run by the Ministry of Internal Affairs, had been placed under the jurisdiction of the Ministry of Health. He added that earlier in the year the USSR had been readmitted to the World Psychiatric [Association], and that psychiatric institutions in the country had been visited by a group of American psychiatrists.[201]

---

the Madrid Declaration were that "psychiatrists should devise therapeutic interventions that are least restrictive to the freedom of the patient," and that "no treatment should be provided against the patient's will unless withholding the treatment would endanger the life of the patient and/or those who surround him or her."

201 U.N. Committee Against Torture, "Consideration of the Initial Report of the Union of Soviet Socialist Republics (CAT/C/5/Add.11), 15 November 1989," CAT A/45/44 (1990.) For purposes of the Convention, the CAT defined psychiatric-medical forms of "cruel, inhuman or degrading treatment or punishment" as falling under Article 16, which provides that:

> Each State Party shall undertake to prevent in any territory under its jurisdiction other acts of cruel, inhuman or degrading treatment or punishment which do not amount to torture as defined in article 1, when such acts are committed by or at the instigation of or with the consent or acquiescence of a public official or other person acting in an official capacity. In particular, the obligations contained in articles 10, 11, 12 and 13 shall apply with the substitution for references to torture of references to other forms of cruel, inhuman or degrading treatment or punishment.

Six years later, the Russian Federation, in its second periodic report to the Committee, devoted four whole pages to listing the major and systematic overhaul of the country's psychiatric system that had been carried out since the demise of the Soviet Union. The following are some of the highlights:

> 101. The Act of the Russian Federation on psychiatric care and safeguard of citizens' rights during such care, which came into force on 1 January 1993, contains a number of provisions confirming the Russian Federation's commitment to the norms of international law in this sphere. Thus the preamble to the Act states, in particular, that one of its aims is to prevent "the use of psychiatry for non-medical purposes", which might be "detrimental to the health, human dignity and rights of citizens." ...
>
> 103. Article 10 sets out in particular rules for utilizing drugs and medical techniques, stating expressly that they may be employed "only for diagnostic and treatment purposes, according to the nature of the morbid condition, and must not be used to punish persons suffering from psychiatric disorders or in the interests of other persons." ...
>
> 105. The psychiatric Care Act has provided legislative endorsement of the reorganization carried out in 1988 in connection with the transfer to the authority of the public health agencies of all enforcement measures of a medical character applied by the courts to persons with psychiatric disorders who have committed dangerous actions covered by the criminal law. Until 1988 the Special Psychiatric Hospitals for persons constituting a particular threat to society were under the authority of the Ministry of Internal Affairs, a situation that resulted in unwarranted restriction of the freedom of patients, and infringement of their rights and legitimate interests....
>
> 106. It should be added that since 1988 the Criminal Code in force in the Russian Federation has contained an Article 126 providing for criminal responsibility in case of "illegal placement in a psychiatric hospital."
>
> 107. ... In 1994 the Board of the Russian Association of Psychiatrists in plenary session adopted the Psychiatrist's Code of Professional Ethics, a number of provisions of which reflect the aims and principles of the Convention. One of the sections of Article 4 of this Code in particular states: "A psychiatrist shall not be entitled to employ medical techniques or drugs in order to punish a patient, or for the convenience of staff or other persons, or to take part in the torture, abuse or other forms of cruel or inhuman treatment of people."[202]

Only a handful of countries or territories to which the Convention Against Torture formally applies have been requested by the Committee to respond to allegations concerning the misuse of psychiatry – and interestingly, Hong Kong (to which the United Kingdom extended its own ratification of the Convention prior to the territory's return of sovereignty to China in 1997) has been one of them.[203]

---

202 U.N. Committee Against Torture, "Second Periodic Report of States Parties Due in 1992: Russian Federation, 07/02/96

203 The questions raised by the CAT in Hong Kong's case concerned the possible over-use of the involuntary committal provisions of the Mental Health Ordinance and also the possible over-use of electroconvulsive therapy (ECT.) See: U.N. Committee Against Torture, "Consideration of Reports Submitted by States Parties Under Article 19 of the Convention – Third Periodic Report of States Parties Due in 1997 (Addendum): China," Paragraphs 168-179, 4 May 1999.

As the sovereign power, China now submits Hong Kong's implementation reports to the U.N. on the Special Administrative Region's behalf. The historical precedent of the former Soviet Union and its successor state having had to provide answers to the Committee Against Torture on psychiatry-related human rights questions, coupled with the fact that the Chinese government has already done likewise in respect of Hong Kong, suggests that Beijing might also, at some future date, be invited or required by the Committee to answer charges that the psychiatric incarceration of sane political dissidents and other similar people in mainland China constitutes – as it did in the former Soviet Union – a cruel and unusual form of punishment.

PART TWO
POLITICIZED PSYCHIATRY UNDER MAO

CHAPTER 3
Law and Psychiatry from 1949 to the Early 1960s

I. Judicial Treatment of Insanity Prior to 1949

Chinese historical records from the past two millennia contain occasional references to cases of insane persons who committed violent crimes but were pardoned or treated leniently by the courts on account of their mental disorders; also recorded are the cases of several famous individuals who successfully avoided punishment by feigning insanity. Over the last few hundred years of the imperial era, however, more systematic legal norms were gradually applied in this area of the criminal justice system. According to one scholarly account,

> The Ch'ing government came to grips with the problem of criminal insanity soon after the consolidation of its rule in the late seventeenth century. It initially relied on the voluntary efforts of the families and neighbours of insane persons to keep them under control, but this soon gave way to the more interventionist measure of registration and confinement, designed to isolate the insane from the rest of society. Mandatory confinement of all insane persons was soon followed by the introduction of prison sentences for insane killers.[204]

Where family members were ordered to take charge of the care and custody of a mentally ill person, they assumed collective legal responsibility for their ward's good conduct and could be punished by up to forty blows with a bamboo stave if the person subsequently committed an offence.[205] Moreover, according to a contemporary Western observer, "Lunatics are in general required to be manacled, and the relatives must not remove the manacles without proper authority."[206] The death penalty for murder, normally mandatory in such cases, was not applied in cases where the offender was shown to be insane at the time of the crime, even when the victim was one of the offender's own parents. An exception to this rule of clemency was made, however, if the victim was one of the grandparents.[207] The death penalty was applied also in the case of multiple homicides by the insane.

After the founding of the Chinese Republic in 1911, a new criminal law was passed stipulating that punishment was to be waived or reduced in the case of crimes committed by the mentally ill. China's first specialized mental hospital was established in Guangzhou in 1898, with others following in Beijing (1906), Suzhou (1929), Shanghai (1935) and Nanjing (1947). In 1922, the country's first teaching centre for psychiatry was established at the Xiehe Hospital in Beijing; and in 1932, the Nationalist government established an Institute of Forensic Medicine, headed by Lin Ji, who is today renowned as the father of the discipline in China. Also in the early Republican era, a new and more specialized type

---

[204] Vivien W. Ng, "Ch'ing Law Concerning the Insane: An Historical Survey," *Ch'ing Shi Wen-t'i* (*Problems in Ch'ing History*), Vol.4, No.4 (December 1980), p.84.
[205] Technically, the maximum number of blows with a heavy bamboo stave prescribed by law was one hundred; in practice, however, this would often have been fatal, so the lesser number was used as a maximum instead. See Derk Bodde & Clarence Morris, *Law in Imperial China* (University of Pennsylvania Press, 1967), p.77.
[206] Ernest Alabaster, *Notes and Commentaries on Chinese Criminal Law* (Luzac & Co., 1899), p.93. See also Andrew H. Woods, M.D., "A Memorandum to Chinese Medical Students on the Medico-Legal Aspects of Insanity," *Journal of the National Medical Association of China*, Vol.9 (September 1923), pp.203-212.
[207] "And the sentence (slicing to pieces) is [in such cases] to be carried out in all its horror, even though the lunatic be already dead" (Alabaster, *Notes and Commentaries*, p. 96).

of institution known as the "psychopathic hospital" gradually began to appear in major Chinese cities. The earliest such institution was apparently located in Guangzhou (Canton), where opium addiction, syphilis, vagabondage and concubinage were among the more common social causes of crime-related mental illness. According to a contemporary Western account,

> The only separate psychopathic hospital in China up to 1933 was a mission hospital in Canton, the John G. Kerr Hospital for the Insane. In 1924 this institution had 726 patients, half of whom were men... There are special psychopathic wards in a few general hospitals, such as in Soochow, Peiping[208] and Shanghai but these are small. China urgently needs modern special hospitals for mental disease in the large centres. In 1930 the [KMT] Ministry of Justice announced its intention to erect special reformatories and "lunatic asylums" in various large cities. There is a dearth of trained psychiatrists in China.[209]

The equivalent institution in the Chinese capital, the Peiping Municipal Psychopathic Hospital, was by 1935 responsible for the custody and care of around 250 criminally insane and other mentally disordered persons of various types. Of these, around a third had been referred to the hospital by "families, institutions or relatives," while as many as two thirds had been directly placed there by the police authorities.[210] The average length of stay for inmates was between one month and eighteen months, and hospitalisation (especially for the "police cases") was essentially compulsory,[211] although there seems to have been no formal legislation in this area at the time.

The psychopathic hospitals differed in two important respects from the earlier forms of compulsory custody for the mentally ill practiced during the pre-Republican period. First, their main purpose was to provide medical care and treatment, whereas the previous legal measures had simply been a prolonged form of preventive detention. Second, however, the scope of admissions was now considerably broader, with the types of offending behaviour ranging from "killing mother with an axe," "attacking parents," "attempted suicides," "lying on the street and scolding people" and "appearing naked in public" at one end of the spectrum, all the way through to "ideas of grandeur," "burning of incense," and "restless patients with reports of jumping around, singing, laughing, [and] clapping hands" at the other.[212] Significantly, contemporary accounts give no indication that expressions of political deviance or heterodox thinking, whether as a symptomatic manifestation of mental pathology or otherwise, were seen or used by the authorities as grounds for imposing psychiatric incarceration at this time.[213]

---

208 The name used for Beijing during much of the Republican era.
209 H.D. Lamson, *Social Pathology in China*, (Shanghai: The Commercial Press, 1935), p.434.
210 Francis L.K. Hsu, "A Brief Report on the Police Co-operation in Connection with Mental Cases in Peiping," in R. Lyman et al. (ed.), *Social and Psychological Studies in Neuro-Psychiatry* (Beijing: Henri Vetch, 1939), pp.202-230.
211 "The police considers it a custodial place" (Ibid, p.225).
212 Ibid, pp.210-211.
213 However, a detailed study by the scholar Hugh L. Shapiro of numerous psychiatric medical records from the 1920s and 1930s at the Peking Union Medical College (PUMC), relating to the cases of patients referred to it from the Peking Municipal Psychopathic Hospital, did find that in a surprising proportion of the cases involved the patients' mental symptoms were broadly inspired by or related to the often traumatic political events of the day. See: *The View from a Chinese Asylum: Defining Madness in 1930s Peking*, Hugh L. Shapiro; unpublished doctoral dissertation: Harvard University, Graduate School of Arts and Sciences, January 1995; see especially Chapter 8: "The View of Politics from the Asylum."

If anything, the law tilted more towards a lackadaisical approach in its construal of the "dangerousness" criterion, sometimes even in the most violent of cases. For example,

> The police will loosen the control of any mental patient if his family is willing to bear the responsibility. One of the best examples of this kind is found in case No. 513, in which the patient chopped up more than ten people fatally with a knife during one of his attacks, but was allowed by the police to be discharged against the advice of the hospital because the patient's wife repeatedly petitioned the Bureau [of Public Security] that she would take all possible care to guard against the recurrence of a similar incident.[214]

It should be noted in passing that, in the 1980s and 1990s, it remained a common complaint within the Chinese psychiatric profession that once a determination of "absence of legal responsibility" on the grounds of mental illness had been made, even the most violent of offenders could still, in many cases, be released straight back into society.[215] While the reasons for this hazardous practice stem mainly from the country's lack of secure psychiatric facilities, it contrasts sharply, nonetheless, with the apparent frequency with which those involved in "cases of a political nature" are officially deemed to be in need of custodial care.

II. Inauspicious Beginnings: The Early Years of the People's Republic

By 1949, after several decades of virtually continuous warfare and national revolution, there were no more than fifty or sixty qualified psychiatrists to be found in the whole of China.[216] As the Communist Party began rebuilding the country, it turned primarily to the Soviet Union for scientific and technical assistance throughout the 1950s. While many of the earlier trained psychiatrists, some of whom had studied in the West, played a key role in expanding the professional infrastructure during these early years, they increasingly became a target of official suspicion for their alleged "bourgeois ideology." As one psychiatric journal succinctly put the matter: "With the arrival of advanced Soviet medical science, China's psychiatric workers were liberated from the ideological influence of the reactionary academic doctrines of Europe and America."[217] The new generation of psychiatric professionals that emerged in China after 1949 was thus overwhelmingly influenced by Soviet psychiatric theory and doctrine. And in particular, according to one of China's leading authorities on the subject, "Soviet forensic psychiatry

---

214 Francis L.K. Hsu, op cit, p.222.
215 See, e.g., Zhang Jun, *Xingshi Cuo'An Yanjiu* (*Research on Miscarriages of Criminal Justice*), (Beijing: Qunzhong Chubanshe, 1990), pp.110-111.
216 See Shen Yucun (ed.), *Jingshenbingxue (Psychiatry) 3rd Edition* (Beijing: People's Health Publishing House, May 1997), p.16. Other official sources give a figure of as low as thirty psychiatrists for the whole country. Sixty psychiatrists for the population of China at that time works out at approximately one per eight million inhabitants. The figure for general physicians was approximately 670 for every one million inhabitants (see "Fifty Years of Progress in China's Human Rights," Xinhua News Agency, February 17, 2000, p.1). There are currently said to be around 12,000 psychiatrists in China (see *Psychiatric News*, June 16, 2000, available at http://www.psych.org/pnews/00-06-16/china.html). And according to an official Chinese news source, there are currently altogether 575 hospitals and 77,000 doctors and nurses dealing with mental diseases in China (see "Nation's Mentally Ill Need More Care," *China Daily*, November 27, 2000; available at http://www.chinadaily.com.cn/cndydb/2000/11/d2-1ment.b27.html).
217 See Li Xintian, "One Decade of the Clinical Application of Artificial Hibernation Therapy in China," *Zhonghua Shenjing Jingshenke Zazhi (Chinese Journal of Nervous and Mental Diseases)*, 1959, No. 6, p.351.

exerted a very great influence after it was first introduced into China."[218] Within a few years, forensic-psychiatric assessment centres organized along Soviet lines had been set up in the cities of Nanjing, Beijing, Shanghai, Changsha and Chengdu;[219] clinical practice in the area of forensic psychiatry developed steadily thereafter. While psychiatry in general received relatively little support from the authorities, legal assessment work appears to have been given (perhaps unsurprisingly, considering the government's clear emphasis at this time on national and public security-related matters) significant priority.

The Serbski School of Forensic Psychiatry and its Adoption in China

It was during this same period that the Soviet psychiatric establishment began to apply, especially in the field of forensic assessment, the now widely deplored range of unorthodox clinical theories whereby particular forms of political and religious dissent were seen as being attributable to certain specific (though in other contexts, oddly rare) varieties of "dangerous" mental illness. The most frequently used diagnosis of this type was "sluggish schizophrenia," a diagnostic concept that was first formulated and used briefly by American psychiatrists during the 1930s, and then later adopted and radically developed by Academician Andrei Snezhnevsky, the leading figure in Soviet psychiatry from the 1940s until his death in 1987. Under the directorship of Georgi Morozov, a key student and follower of Snezhnevsky who applied the latter's doctrine of "sluggish schizophrenia" with increasing enthusiasm to cases of alleged ideological deviance, the notorious Serbski Institute of Forensic Psychiatry in Moscow served, from 1953 until the late 1980s, as the main theoretical and practical stronghold for the political abuse of psychiatry in the USSR.

Underlying the strange complicity between law and psychiatry in the Soviet Union was the official view that, since socialist society was inherently superior to capitalist countries and thus the former social sources and causes of crime had mostly been eradicated, the continued occurrence of criminal or dissenting acts must be due to flaws in the offender's mental state. As the Soviet leader Nikita Khrushchev himself explained:

> A crime is a deviation from the generally recognized standards of behaviour [and is] frequently caused by mental disorder. Can there be diseases, nervous disorders among certain people in Communist society? Evidently yes. If that is so, then there will also be offences which are characteristic of people with abnormal minds.... To those who might start calling for opposition to Communism on this basis, we can say that...clearly the mental state of such people is not normal.[220]

The key features of "sluggish schizophrenia," so called because of its slow rate of progression, which more often than not gave outsiders the impression that the reform-minded "sufferer" was mentally quite normal, were described as follows by Sidney Bloch, a Western psychiatrist and co-author of one of the major studies on Soviet psychiatric abuse:

> Characteristically, patients given this diagnosis are able to function almost normally in the social sense. The symptoms may resemble those of a neurosis or take a paranoid

---

218 See Jia Yicheng (ed.), *Shiyong Sifa Jingshenbingxue (Applied Forensic Psychiatry)*, (Anhui Renmin Chubanshe, September 1988), p.10.
219 See the Internet site of the Beijing Institute of Forensic Medicine and Science (*Beijing Shi Fating Kexue Jishu Jianding Yanjiusuo*) at http://www.fmedsci.com/sfjs/sfjs6.htm.
220 *Pravda*, May 24, 1959.

quality. The patient with paranoid symptoms retains some insight into his condition, but overvalues his own importance and may exhibit grandiose ideas of reforming society... The concept of sluggish schizophrenia [thus] facilitated the application of a label of disease of the most serious kind to people whom psychiatrists in the West would regard as either normal, mildly eccentric, or at worse neurotic. In other words, it does not require much to be labelled as mad by the Snezhnevsky-trained psychiatrist.

Professor Georgi Morozov...states: "Schizophrenia is a disease in which patients are with rare exceptions deemed not responsible." Yet he concedes that: "Forensic psychiatrists often experience difficulties when...symptoms are mild and the presence or absence of schizophrenia must be established." The diagnosis may then be made on a history of psychiatric symptoms in the past, that is long before the offence was committed, and, also possibly in the *absence of symptoms* at the time of the offence. Thus, the defendant may appear normal when under psychiatric examination, but according to the Snezhnevsky school, still harbour the disease.[221]

Another catch-all diagnosis that was commonly applied to people detained for particularly "puzzling" or "flagrant" acts of ideological dissent in the Soviet Union from the 1950s onwards was "paranoid psychosis." A wide repertoire of nonconformist behaviours was, however, shared between both sets of sufferers. These included: "reformist delusions," "litigation mania," "overvalued (or excessive) religiosity," "serious illegal acts [such as] the writing of complaints," "slander and dissemination of false information," "persistent ideas of reform that tend to be convincing to others and tend to cause recurrent illegal actions" and even "an interest in poorly-understood and bizarre foreign fashions and trends in art, literature and philosophy, and discussion of such interests."[222] As Bukovsky and Gluzman wrote, in their *samizdat* pamphlet, "A Manual on Psychiatry for Dissenters,"

> Doctors of Medical Sciences Pechernikova and Kosachev, experts at the [Serbski] Institute of Forensic Psychiatry, openly state: "Ideas of fighting for truth and justice most frequently arise in personalities with a paranoid structure"; or: "The litigious-paranoid state develops following psychotraumatizing circumstances which affect the interests of the person concerned, and is typified by accusations of encroachment upon the legal status of the individual"; or: "A characteristic feature of these (overvalued – the authors) formations is the conviction of the individual's own rightness, an obsession with asserting his 'trampled rights', the importance the sick person attaches to his own feelings as an individual,"; or: "They use the court hearing as a platform for making speeches and appeals."[223]

---

221 Sidney Bloch, "Soviet Psychiatry and Snezhnevskyism," in Robert van Voren (ed.), *Soviet Psychiatric Abuse in the Gorbachev Era*, p.56. See also G.V. Morozov and Ia.M. Kalashnik (eds.), *Forensic Psychiatry*, International Arts and Sciences Press, Inc. (White Plains: New York), 1970; the original Russian edition is titled: *Sudebnaia Psikhiatriia* (Juridical Literature Publishing House, Moscow 1967.
222 This list of symptoms is taken from a series of translations from official Soviet forensic psychiatric reports that appear in Semyon Gluzman, *On Soviet Totalitarian Psychiatry* (International Association on the Political Use of Psychiatry [IAPUP] Amsterdam, 1989), pp.39-44.
223 Bloch and Reddaway, *Russia's Political Hospitals* (op cit), p.428. The WHO's International Classification of Diseases (ICD-10) lists "litigious paranoia" as a mental abnormality. However, the WHO certainly did not intend to include, as symptoms of such a condition, the kinds of activities listed by Soviet psychiatrists as being typical of this condition. Above all, the WHO did not intend for persons who may genuinely be suffering from an overly-

The State's medico-legal punishment for such activities, moreover, was severe. According to a report on the authorities' handling of nineteen such cases:

> Their pattern of adaptation changes to such a degree that their life undergoes a fundamental change; they dedicate their activities entirely to the struggle for their idea, which they often characterize as a "struggle for justice"... [However,] environmental change, the strict regime of a psychiatric ward, the impossibility of a continuation of their pathological litigious activity, sedative and neuroleptic medication, all served to normalize their behaviour rather quickly.[224]

The standard Soviet textbooks on forensic psychiatry were required reading for Chinese legal psychiatrists from the mid-1950s onwards, and numerous Soviet psychiatric writers continued to be cited favourably in Chinese psychiatric publications long after the Sino-Soviet Split had brought an end to all direct contact or cooperation between the two countries. Even in the 1990s, favourable references to the Soviet school of forensic psychiatry were quite commonly found among the pages of the Chinese professional literature, and several Chinese textbooks published during this period contained the full or partial texts of the main Soviet-era laws and regulations on the compulsory hospitalisation of mentally ill offenders.[225]

In classifying the schizophrenic condition, the Russian term *vyalotekushchaya* can be rendered in English as either "sluggish" or (more broadly) as "latent", while in the Chinese medical lexicon, the equivalent term used is *qianyinxing jingshen fenliezheng*, which translates into English as "latent schizophrenia."[226] As late as 1994, this mental condition was still listed as being one of several officially acknowledged "borderline states" in China;[227] from the 1980s onwards, however, it rarely appears in the

---

litigious or "querulous" mindset to be arrested and sent to institutes for the criminally insane – as was done in the former Soviet Union and as is still done today in China.
224 L.N. Diamant, "Issues in Clinical Evaluations and Compulsory Treatment of Psychopathic Personalities with Paranoid Delusions and Overvalued Ideas," cited in Gluzman, *On Soviet Totalitarian Psychiatry*, p.40. Contrary to what is widely believed, the political misuse of psychiatry in the Soviet Union extended well beyond the forensic psychiatric domain. In perhaps a majority of cases, Soviet political dissidents and others were committed to regular mental hospitals rather than to institutes for the criminally insane, and this was done mostly by police authorities acting in collaboration with regular psychiatrists. However, such practices can perhaps best be seen as an "informal extension," or *ad hoc* outgrowth into society at large, of the formal forensic-psychiatric committals process. In this sense, the latter was still certainly of primary importance.
225 For example, the now discredited Soviet laws on forensic psychiatric hospitalization are extensively quoted in two Chinese textbooks published as late as 1992 (when the Soviet Union was finally collapsing). See Li Congpei (ed.), *Sifa Jingshenbingxue*, pp.404-406. See also Chen Weidong et al., "Chapter 9: Litigation Procedures for the Adoption of Coercive Medical Measures," in *Xingshi Tebie Chengxu de Shijian yu Tantao (Practice and Explorations in Special Criminal Procedure)* (People's Court Publishing House, 1992), pp.467-505. See also Shen Zheng (ed.), *Falü Jingshenbingxue (Legal Psychiatry)* (China Politics and Law University Press, 1989), pp.64-68.
226 The Chinese term "*qianyinxing jingshenfenliezheng*" was specifically used, for example, by the leading forensic psychiatrists Jia Yicheng and Ji Shumao in a brief account of criticisms made against Soviet political psychiatry at an international academic conference in 1977 (see Jia Yicheng (ed.), *Shiyong Sifa Jingshenbingxue*, p.15). Note that the Chinese term for "sluggish schizophrenia" is not to be confused with that used for "chronic schizophrenia": "*manxing jingshenfenliezheng*."
227 See Zhai Jian'an (ed.), *Shiyong Fayixue Cidian (A Dictionary of Applied Forensic Science)*, (People's Health Publishing House, September 1994), p.18.

relevant literature.[228] In the earliest known examples of political-style psychiatric diagnosis in China, which date from the early 1960s, the less specific term "schizophrenia," in either an undifferentiated or a "paranoid" form, appears to have been the most prevalent label used.

In China, as in the former Soviet Union, the diagnosis of schizophrenia was and continues to be made in a far higher proportion of mental illness cases than in most other countries. Moreover, where diagnosed schizophrenics commit crimes and are brought for forensic psychiatric assessment in China, a finding of "absence of legal responsibility" – leading to the high likelihood of compulsory forensic hospitalisation – is almost invariably made. For example, among 386 cases of schizophrenic offenders forensically assessed in the Beijing and Tianjin areas between 1978 and 1987, no fewer than 97.5 percent of the examinees were found to be "not legally responsible" for their actions.[229] Furthermore, other studies indicate that "cases of a political nature" have accounted for a very high proportion of the targets of assessment. In a study of 181 cases of schizophrenic offenders forensically examined at the Harbin No.1 Special Hospital between 1976 and 1980, political cases involving "reactionary speeches," "sticking up posters with absurd content" and "shouting reactionary slogans" amounted to 59 in number, or 33.3 percent of the total.[230] Another authoritative account from the same period, moreover, put the inverse relationship for the country as a whole at an overwhelmingly high level: "In [psychiatrically appraised criminal] cases involving political speech and expression, schizophrenia sufferers accounted for 91 percent of the total, and 70 percent of these were chronic schizophrenics who had been living at large in society."[231] The shadow of Soviet-era political psychiatry looms conspicuously in all these reports.

From the late 1970s and early 1980s onwards in China, the diagnosis of choice in political cases appears to have shifted towards "paranoid psychosis" and its various sub-categories (in particular: "litigious mania"), although schizophrenia continued also to be diagnosed. As we shall see, while the medical connotations are substantially different, the diagnosis of "paranoid psychosis" shares many of the characteristic features of vagueness, non-specificity and "apparent normality" found in the case of Soviet-style "sluggish schizophrenia."[232]

---

228 Where "sluggish schizophrenia" is mentioned in Chinese sources, it is usually accompanied by cautionary remarks about the need to avoid "over-diagnosing" the condition. The principal objection, however, seems not to stem from any concerns about the possible use of political psychiatry, but is rather that the diagnosis of this "borderline condition" in the case of criminal offenders, and a resultant finding of non-imputability, can lead to their escaping punishment for serious crimes. One author, for example, recounts the case of a rapist who was diagnosed as having "sluggish schizophrenia" and was then promptly released by the police, to the consternation of the victim's family; a fresh forensic appraisal was arranged and the man was eventually ruled to bear "partial legal responsibility" for his crime (Jia Yicheng, *Shiyong Sifa Jingshenbingxue*, pp.196-198).
229 Li Congpei, et al., "An Analysis of Forensic Psychiatric Evaluations in Cases of Schizophrenia," *Chinese Journal of Nervous and Mental Diseases*, 1987, Vol.20, No.3, pp.135-138. Incidentally, one of the scholarly sources referred to in this article is a book by Georgi Morozov.
230 Wu Xinchen, "An Exploration of the Hallmarks of Criminal Behavior Among Schizophrenics," *Chinese Journal of Nervous and Mental Diseases*, 1983, Vol.16, No.6, pp.338-339.
231 Luo Dahua (ed.), *Fanzui Xinlixue (Psychology of Crime)*, (Qunzhong Chubanshe [volume marked "for internal distribution only"], 1984), p.216. The Chinese phrase "living at large in society" (*sanju zai shehuishang*) is a somewhat pejorative term generally used in respect of "socially undesirable elements" whom the authorities feel should be placed under some form of supervision or restriction; in this case, it probably signifies that the alleged schizophrenics had not previously been institutionalised in any way.
232 As two expert observers of the Soviet psychiatric scene later remarked, a diagnostic shift in a broadly similar direction also occurred in the Soviet Union around the same period. (One of the experts, Richard Bonnie,

A brief outline of the therapeutic regime that came into being in the Chinese psychiatric field in the 1950s may also be useful. In light of the intense controversy that exists in the West over several of these therapies, it is important to bear in mind that the therapeutic resources available to psychiatrists throughout the world at that time were highly limited in both range and effectiveness, especially with respect to the major psychiatric diseases such as schizophrenia. Until the early part of the twentieth century, psychiatrists everywhere were largely helpless to relieve the catastrophic symptoms of these illnesses, and sufferers were for the most part simply warehoused in primitive insane asylums. During the inter-War period, however, several new treatments marked a major turning point in psychiatric clinical practice. One was insulin coma therapy, discovered in 1927 by Manfred Sakel, a Polish neurophysiologist and psychiatrist;[233] another was electroconvulsive shock therapy (ECT), discovered by the neurologists Ugo Cerletti and Lucio Bini in Rome in 1937; a third was the psychosurgical technique of prefrontal lobotomy, discovered in 1936 by Egas Moniz, a Portuguese neuropsychiatrist. The history of psychiatry is replete with major instances and patterns of the abuse of all these forms of treatment, especially in America and Europe in the 1940s and 1950s.[234] With the next important

---

participated in an American psychiatric delegation's 1989 visit to the USSR to assess a number of psychiatrically-detained Soviet dissidents.) As they observed,

In the mid-1980s, Soviet psychiatric officials began to acknowledge that a pattern of "hyperdiagnosis" had resulted in inappropriate psychiatric labeling and unnecessary hospitalization in the USSR. It was therefore noteworthy that Soviet psychiatrists who interviewed the twenty-seven patients concurrently with the U.S. team in 1989 found no current evidence of schizophrenia in the cases of fourteen patients who were thought to be without mental disorder by the U.S. psychiatrists. However, it is also noteworthy that the Soviet psychiatrists nonetheless still retained *some* psychiatric diagnosis for most of these patients. In this respect, the U.S. delegation found continuing evidence of "hyperdiagnosis," particularly in the tendency to characterize these patients as having "psychopathy," a term that seems to be roughly equivalent to the general concept of personality disorder. Specific examples of "psychopathic" symptoms identified in the interviews by Soviet psychiatrists included "unitary activity," which related to a high level of commitment to a single cause, such as political reform, and "failure to adapt to society," which was used to describe a dissident patient who was "unable to live in society without being subject to arrest for his behavior." One of the Soviet psychiatrists was asked whether a patient who had been sent to a special hospital for distributing anti-Soviet leaflets presented a danger to society. "Of course not," he responded, "everything the patient distributed can be read in the newspapers now." As this observation implies, what had changed was the meaning of a socially dangerous act, not the meaning of mental disorder.

(Richard J. Bonnie and Svetlana V. Polubinskaya, "Unraveling Soviet Psychiatry," *The Journal of Contemporary Legal Issues*, 1999, No.10, pp.285-286.)
233 In the course of treating diabetics, "Sakel discovered accidentally, by causing convulsions with an overdose of insulin, that the treatment was efficient with patients afflicted with psychosis, particularly schizophrenia" (Renato M.E. Sabbatini, "The History of Shock Therapy in Psychiatry," *Brain and Mind*, No.4 (Dec. 1997-March 1998) (electronic magazine on neuroscience, found at http://www.epub.org.br/cm/history_i.htm).
234 The best overview of the extensive misuse of somatic therapies in the West is Elliot S. Valenstein, *Great and Desperate Cures: The Rise and Decline of Psychosurgery and Other Radical Treatments* (Basic Books, February 1986). Tens of thousands of lobotomies were performed in the United States from 1936 until around 1952. The most egregious practitioner was the American neurologist Walter Freeman, who invented a technique known as "ice-pick lobotomy," which took no more than a few minutes to perform. According to one account, "This procedure was so ghastly, however, that even seasoned and veteran neurosurgeons and psychiatrists could not stand the sight of it, and sometimes fainted at the 'production line' of lobotomies assembled by Freeman." Moreover, "[Lobotomies were] widely abused as a method to control undesirable behavior, instead of being a last-resort therapeutic procedure for desperate cases…Families trying to get rid of difficult relatives would submit

breakthrough in the treatment of mental illness – the synthesis and widespread dissemination from the early 1950s onwards of major antipsychotic medications such as chlorpromazine – the use of these earlier therapies greatly declined in most countries.

It is clear from the Chinese psychiatric literature of the late 1950s and early 1960s that ECT and insulin coma therapy were in widespread clinical use in China (as in the U.S. and other Western countries) by that time, and that the theory and practice of these techniques had been learned directly from the Soviets.[235] Viewed in historical context, and when used for genuine therapeutic purposes, neither therapy would appear to be particularly controversial. According to reports from former victims of political psychiatric abuse in China, however, both insulin coma treatment and ECT (without concomitant use of sedatives or muscle relaxants) were often used by psychiatric staff from the 1960s onwards as methods of punishment rather than of treatment. ECT remains in widespread use in Chinese mental hospitals today.

Regarding the use of psychosurgery, an official source states that Chinese neurosurgeons carried out numerous cases of human prefrontal lobotomy between 1949 and 1955 at hospitals in Tianjin, Nanjing, Shanghai, Beijing and Xian, but that the practice was discontinued for many years thereafter.[236] This was due to the fact that psychosurgery was banned from the mid-1950s onwards in the Soviet Union, where it was seen as contravening the "conditioned reflex" orthodoxies of the Pavlov school. The same source adds, however, that in 1986 a number of Chinese hospitals began to perform such operations once again, reportedly of a kind involving less drastic surgical intervention than had been required in the earlier series of operations.[237]

---

them to lobotomy. Rebels and political opponents were treated as mentally deranged by authorities and operated [upon]" (Sabbatini, *The History of Shock Therapy*). The use of psychosurgery did not really end in the U.S. until the 1970s (partly as a result of the influence of the film "One Flew Over the Cuckoo's Nest"), and since then there have continued to be voices (so far, mainly in the wilderness) seeking to bring it back. Finally, according to a leading authority on medical ethics, "ECT stands practically alone among the medical/surgical interventions in that its misuse was not so much an overzealous effort to cure patients but to control them so as to benefit hospital staff." (David J. Rothman, Director of the Center for the Study of Society and Medicine at the Columbia College of Physicians and Surgeons, New York; personal communication to the author, July 11, 2002.)

235 For example, while acknowledging insulin coma treatment to be a "radical therapy with very severe side effects," one study reported that at the Nanjing Mental Hospital in 1958 (the peak year of Mao's "Great Leap Forward," when the entire nation was being urged to make "greater, faster, better and more economical" strides towards Communism), doctors had begun applying the therapy to some 500 patients "on a continual daily basis… omitting the [previous] weekly rest day" (Tao Guotai et al., "Clinical Observations on 2,663 Cases of Insulin Shock Treatment," *Chinese Journal of Nervous and Mental Diseases*, No.1,1960, pp.19-24; Bao Zhongcheng et al., "Clinical Observations on 400 Cases of Electro-shock Therapy," *Chinese Journal of Nervous and Mental Diseases*, No.1, 1960, pp.28-30; and Wang Jingxiang, "China's Achievements Over the Past Decade in Insulin Shock Therapy Work," *Chinese Journal of Nervous and Mental Diseases*, No.6, 1959, pp.349-351.) Another form of treatment that was apparently widely used in Chinese mental hospitals at this time was "artificial hibernation therapy" (*dongmian liaofa*), a prolonged state of deep sleep induced by means of either chlorpromazine hydrochloride or wintermin (*dongmian ling*); a less radical version of this treatment was known simply as "sleep therapy" (*shuimian liaofa*).

236 Shen Zheng, *Falü Jingshenbingxue*, pp.1016-1017; and Zhu Qihua et al. (eds.), *Tianjin Quanshu (An Encyclopaedia of Tianjin)* (Tianjin People's Publishing House, December 1991), p.630.

237 For details of China's resumption of psychosurgery in Ankang criminal-psychiatric custody centres from the mid-1980s onwards, see p.249 below.

Three Patterns of Legal-Psychiatric Abuse

Three general varieties of ethically suspect or abusive psychiatry will be singled out for attention in the following discussion. The first involves a phenomenon known within the psychiatric profession as "hypodiagnosis," or the under-diagnosing of mental illness. In China, within the legal or forensic domain, this was most often seen in the cases of people who apparently were suffering from some form of mental illness, but whose symptoms included random or disconnected "political ravings" of a kind that the police viewed as being reactionary or "anti-government." Owing to the extreme sensitivity of political discourse in post-1949 China, forensic psychiatrists came under strong implicit pressure from the authorities to interpret such utterances in a literal, or face-value, sense; the "offenders" would then be found "legally responsible" for their acts or statements, and duly sentenced as political enemies of the State. This represents one important instance (or medico-legal trope) of the "totalitarian" distortions of psychiatry found first in the Soviet Union and later, especially during the Cultural Revolution, in China.

The second relevant category is that of "hyperdiagnosis," or the excessively broad clinical determination of mental illness. Within the legal domain in China, this has been reflected in a tendency on the part of forensic psychiatrists to diagnose as severely mentally ill, and therefore legally non-imputable for their alleged offences, certain types of dissident or nonconformist detainees who were perceived by the police as displaying a puzzling "absence of instinct for self-preservation" when staging peaceful political protests, expressing officially banned views, pursuing legal complaints against corrupt or repressive officialdom, etc. This particular ethical distortion, which was perhaps the main hallmark of Soviet-era "totalitarian-style" psychiatry, is the one that has been most conspicuously in evidence, or readily apparent, in China for the past two decades and more.

A third category of politically motivated ethical abuse within the field of Chinese legal psychiatry can be summed up under the heading of severe medical neglect. In certain respects, the problem of hypodiagnosis can be seen as one major sub-form of the latter, since it resulted in numerous mentally ill individuals being sent to prison as political "counter-revolutionaries" and then denied all medical or psychiatric care for many years in an environment bound only to worsen their mental condition. But there was also a much broader aspect to the phenomenon, reflected both in the absence of medical-care provision for mentally ill prisoners in general, and, more specifically, in the deliberate withholding of such care from political offenders whom the authorities had already clearly diagnosed as being mentally ill.[238]

---

238 The nature and significance of such medical neglect appears to have been different during the two main historical periods since 1949. Prior to 1978, it seems mainly to have resulted from a policy of deliberate official discrimination against mentally ill political offenders, who were seen as being too "heinous" in their crimes to merit any humanitarian attention, let alone proper psychiatric care; at that time, somewhat ironically, the fact that China's mental healthcare resources were much scarcer and even less well-developed than they nowadays are seems to have been a factor of secondary importance in the absence or denial of psychiatric care. In the post-Cultural Revolution period, by contrast, there is little evidence to suggest that psychiatric care has continued to be withheld from mentally ill prisoners on solely political grounds, and it is instead the persistent scarcity of such resources more generally that mainly explains the continuing problem of widespread medical neglect within the country's prison system. However, for the apparently small minority of psychiatrically incarcerated offenders in the post-1978 era who may, in fact, have been mentally ill at the time of committing their "political crimes," forced psychiatric custody also represents an abusive type of treatment that might best be described as a politically-motivated form of medical neglect. In such cases, the authorities' fallacious ascription of a criminal nature and purpose to the acts of mentally disordered speech or behavior in question means that the sufferer, whilst being

The Cases of Lu Ling and Hu Feng

Specific case examples from the period of the 1950s of the first two forms of politically-inspired psychiatric abuse in China have not as yet come to light, no doubt because of the general paucity of official documentation that exists for psychiatry as a whole during the first decade of the People's Republic. However, as one authoritative writer on the topic of crime and mental illness noted in August 2000, in a major two-volume study that was officially published in Beijing, "As experts familiar with the situation regarding psychiatric appraisals in the 1950s and 1960s have pointed out, the proportion of political-style cases was also extremely high during both those periods."[239]

One of the best-documented examples of the third form of abuse arose in the late 1950s and concerned a prominent Chinese writer named Lu Ling. From 1952 to 1955, a group of leading figures on the Chinese literary scene, including Lu Ling and led by the famous writer Hu Feng, came under increasing attack from the Party's cultural commissars for their alleged repudiation of Mao's doctrine that arts and literature should follow the path of "socialist realism" and serve the interests of the workers and peasants, and for their stubborn adherence to such "bourgeois notions" as the literary genre of "subjective inner realism." In July 1954, both Hu and Lu issued long written rebuttals of the charges against them, and the following year, the Party launched its first major political crackdown against China's intellectual establishment since 1949. Hu Feng was sent to jail for more than twenty years and many of his associates received lesser prison terms.

Lu was married, with three daughters, and was thirty-three years old at the time of his initial arrest in June 1955. During his first few years in detention, his refusal to admit any serious wrongdoing led to ever-harsher treatment at the hands of the authorities, and he eventually began to show clear signs of mental disturbance. In June 1959, after four years of solitary confinement without formal charge, during which he had been forced by his inquisitors to write endless screeds of self-denunciatory material, he finally exploded and wrote a second major rebuttal of all the charges against him. For this "odious act of resistance," he was transferred to China's primary detention facility for high-ranking political criminals, the secretive and much-feared Qincheng Prison, located just north of Beijing. For further resisting "ideological reform" and for moaning or shouting incoherently, he was often left bound and handcuffed by his jailers, although still held in solitary confinement. Finally, in early 1961, his sanity deteriorated to the point where the authorities decided to transfer him for secure custody and treatment to the capital's Anding psychiatric hospital. After three years of intensive medication, he was deemed ready for release and allowed to return home on conditions of medical bail. For a year, he sat quietly at home, in an apparently catatonic state of post-traumatic stress, and then in 1965 he began writing a long series of "petition letters" to the authorities seeking redress for his treatment at their hands. According to a recently published account of Lu's case, these writings were largely incoherent:

> Oh, but what letters they were! Some were left unaddressed, others had no recipient's name written on them; most of them were incomprehensible, or filled with random abuse as if written by a small child; some were even marked for the attention of

---

denied access to proper and appropriate forms of medical care, is also placed in a coercive judicial setting that can only exacerbate his or her mental condition, especially if the underlying illness is of a paranoid nature.
239 Liu Baiju, *Jingshen Zhang'ai Yu Fanzui* (Mental Disorders and Crime), Beijing: *Shehui Kexue Wenxian Chubanshe* (Social Sciences Documentary Publishing House), August 2000, p.663. The author of this 857-page, two-volume work is a Researcher at the Chinese Academy of Social Sciences' Bureau of Scientific Research, and a graduate of the law department of Chinese People's University.

"Queen Elizabeth" and suchlike, bringing to mind the various mad characters of Chekhov's plays. They were filled with a cold and remote sense of despair...[240]

The security authorities, however, interpreted these sad scribblings differently, and in November 1965 Lu was rearrested and sent back to Qincheng Prison on charges of engaging in "active counterrevolutionary activities." He was to remain there, in continuous solitary confinement and reduced to spending most of his waking hours muttering incoherently at the cell wall, until June 1974, by which time he had lost all semblance of sanity. In 1979, after several years spent sweeping the streets of the capital "under supervision by the masses," he received an official letter of rehabilitation from the Beijing Intermediate People's Court:

> This Court has carried out a review and determined the following. On the question of Lu Ling's participation in the Hu Feng [Anti-Party] Clique, the Ministry of Public Security reached a conclusion on the matter in 1969 and thus no further action will be taken. As regards the more than thirty counterrevolutionary letters that Lu Ling wrote and mailed out between July and November1964: since these actions resulted from the fact that he was afflicted by mental illness at the time, he should not be held criminally responsible for them.[241]

Some months later, Lu received a second letter from the court, stating: "Regardless of whether [you were] sane or insane, the expression of 'politically hostile'[242] language should never be seen as grounds for bringing charges of counterrevolution." This statement probably marked the high point of official efforts to reform China's highly repressive laws on political dissent; as we shall see, however, it proved to be little more than an ephemeral blip on the country's law enforcement horizon.[243]

---

240 Zhu Hengqing, *Lu Ling: Wei Wancheng de Tiancai (Lu Ling: A Talent Unfulfilled)*, (Shandong Wenyi Chubanshe, April 1997), pp.112-113. This book provides the most detailed account to date of all aspects of Lu Ling's case.
241 Ibid, p.113.
242 The Chinese term used was *gongji*: technically, this means simply "hostile" or "attacking," but when used in Chinese legal discourse (especially in the phrase "*e'du gongji*" – "viciously attacking") in connection with proscribed acts of speech or writing, it invariably means "politically hostile."
243 The same sentiment as that expressed in the court decision on Lu Ling's case appeared in March 1979 in one of the country's main daily newspapers: "In order genuinely to protect the democratic rights of the Chinese people, the following must be clearly and unequivocally written into the Constitution and the law: 'Speech shall not be taken as a grounds for the crime of counterrevolution. Whoever determines the crime of counterrevolution on the basis of a person's acts of expression shall himself be guilty of a criminal offence'" (*Guangming Ribao*, March 10, 1979). (For the full background story on the publication of this remarkable article, see Xu Bing and Min Sheng, "Reminiscences on the Article '*Speech is No Crime* and *Making Speech a Crime*'," in Guo Daohui et al. (eds.), *Zhongguo Dangdai Faxue Zhengming Shilu* [*A Record of the Contention on the Science of Law in Contemporary China*], [Hunan Renmin Chubanshe, 1998], pp.183-189.) Ten years later, however, this bold opinion was roundly dismissed in the following terms in a textbook on criminal law: "Viewpoints such as this run contrary to the stipulations of China's Criminal Law and are therefore wrong" (Gan Yupei (ed.), *Xingfaxue Zhuanlun* [*Essays on Criminal Law*] [Beijing University Publishing House (volume marked: "for internal use only"), November 1989], p.512).

The *locus classicus* post-Cultural Revolution document on why "hostile speech or statements" (especially those directed against State and Party leaders) were still to be dealt with as a criminal offence is the CPC's Central Political-Legal Commissions' *Opinion on the Question of Whether Viciously Attacking or Slandering Central Leading Comrades Constitutes a Crime*, December 17, 1981; a full translation (by Donald C. Clarke) can be found on the Internet at http://faculty.washington.edu/dclarke/public/clpc-opinion.htm.

A decade later, in 1990, the full story of the sad fate of Lu Ling's close colleague and mentor, the writer Hu Feng himself, appeared in a biographical study written by Hu's son, Zhang Xiaoshan. As Zhang reveals in this account, his father, while lying in a Beijing hospital bed in 1979 recovering from the long-term political persecution he had endured during the Cultural Revolution, and longing for news of his rehabilitation by the Central Committee, also became severely mentally disturbed:

> The quiet hospital room in no way served to calm father's nerves. One morning, sitting on the sofa and with eyes staring fixedly ahead, he told me he had received a message through the air saying that Vice Premier Deng [Xiaoping] had delivered a speech calling for several people to be punished, and that five people had been stripped of their Party membership and taken away in handcuffs. News of this event would shortly be appearing in the newspapers: 3,890,000 copies had already been printed and had sold out immediately… That afternoon, he said he had received another message through the air, telling him to take a helicopter and leave right away; he began to put on his overcoat and tried to go out to board the helicopter, and despite all our efforts we were unable to prevent him from going outside.
>
> Some days later, his mental condition had still not improved. He slept only very rarely and so we took turns to watch over him constantly. On one occasion when I'd locked the door, he kept demanding that I open it, and father and son ended up having a pitched fight over the matter. He said that a political coup had taken place within the Central Committee, that someone had seized power from Deng Xiaoping and that the Central Committee had sent someone over to try and save him… One night, while mother was standing watch over him, father was suddenly overcome by an indefinable sense of fear and dread, and he began trying to jump out of the third-floor window. When mother struggled to prevent him doing this, he lashed out at her with his stick, breaking the glass in the door to his room. At 2.00 AM that night, father was finally admitted to the psychiatric wing of the Beijing No.3 Hospital.
>
> Father was far from being the only person to become mentally deranged as a result of the 1955 affair (i.e. the false branding of Hu Feng and others as being a "counterrevolutionary clique.") Many more such incidents also occurred during the Cultural Revolution, when the psychiatric wing of the Beijing No.3 Hospital alone was filled with untold numbers of prominent senior Party cadres.[244]

For several decades in China, therefore, two distinct but closely related forms of political abuse have coexisted within the broad domain of Chinese law and psychiatry: on the one hand, an official reluctance to extend appropriate medical care to mentally ill prisoners convicted of political offences, on the implicit grounds that the heinous nature of their offences rendered them ineligible for even the most basic humanitarian consideration; and on the other, a parallel and rather more sophisticated tendency, inherited from the Soviet psychiatric tradition, according to which the uninhibited expression of ideologically unorthodox views was seen, in certain cases, as indicative of "mental pathology" in an ostensibly legal and medical sense. Indeed, where the politically sensitive field of forensic psychiatry is concerned, there appears to have been little, since 1949, in the way of a stable middle-ground between these seemingly divergent tendencies, both of which were equally disreputable from the point of view

---

244 Zhang Xiaoshan, "A Fragmentary Reminiscence: In Commemoration of the Fifth Anniversary of the Death of My Father, Hu Feng (*Pianduan de Huiyi: Jinian Fuqin Hu Feng Shishi Wu Zhounian*)," in *Historical Materials on the New Literature (Xin Wenxue Shiliao)*, 1990, No.4.

of international standards. With the onset of the Cultural Revolution, however, the distinction in China between "political crime" and "political insanity" was lost entirely.

CHAPTER 4
The Cultural Revolution

As for China, no reliable evidence of psychiatric abuse is available to us. But the apparently widespread practice of trying to cure mental illness by inculcating Maoism into patients so that they should think "correctly" arouses the suspicion that psychiatrists may also be involved in the "thought reform" practised on dissenters in labour camps.

— Sidney Bloch and Peter Reddaway, 1977[245]

Political cases: These are very seldom mentioned in the literature of other countries. According to a survey done by this author of forensic psychiatric appraisal cases carried out at the Shanghai Municipal Mental Health Centre over the period 1970-71, however, political cases accounted for 72.9 percent of the total. This had to do with the particular historical circumstances of that time.

— Zheng Zhanpei, 1988[246]

As the above statement by one of China's foremost forensic psychiatrists[247] and numerous similar items of official testimony cited below serve to demonstrate, the numbers of detained political activists sent to institutes for the criminally insane during the Cultural Revolution apparently exceeded, by far, the combined total of genuinely psychotic murderers, rapists, arsonists and other violently mentally ill offenders dealt with under China's forensic psychiatric system at that time. This fact alone points to a scope and intensity of politically-inspired psychiatric abuse in China during this period that is probably unprecedented in the annals of world psychiatry. It certainly went well beyond the equivalent Soviet experience. Moreover, as further official testimony provided below shows, many genuinely mentally ill people were either sent to prison or shot as "counterrevolutionaries" in the course of Mao's decade-long "revolution to touch men's souls."

Clearly, any attempt to defend Chinese legal or forensic psychiatry against the current allegations of political abuse, on the basis of the acknowledged fact that many psychiatrists were themselves persecuted for upholding ethical standards during the Cultural Revolution, must at the same time confront and deal with the equally significant fact that many other psychiatrists were, for whatever reason, active participants in the wholesale ethical abuses of that infamous decade. Little mention of law or legality will be found in this chapter, for the simple reason that law and legality had very little to do with anything during the Cultural Revolution, and the field of psychiatry was certainly no exception to this rule. A clear appreciation of what happened in Chinese psychiatry during this period, however,

---

245 Bloch and Reddaway, *Russia's Political Hospitals* (op cit), p.466.
246 Shen Zheng (ed.), *Falü Jingshenbingxue*, p.314.
247 According to an official biography of Zheng Zhanpei published in 1999, "He has worked at the Shanghai Municipal Institute for the Prevention and Treatment of Mental Illnesses (now called the Shanghai Municipal Mental Health Centre) from 1960 up to the present" (Xie Bin, "*Sifa Jingshenbing Xuejia Zheng Zhanpei Jiaoshou*," in *Falü Yu Yixue Zazhi* [*Journal of Law and Medicine*], 1999, Vol.6, No.3, p.99). Among many other posts Zheng now holds, he is concurrently Chairman of the Shanghai Municipal Experts Committee for Psychiatric Judicial Appraisals and Adviser to the Shanghai Municipal Bureau of Reform Through Labour

is indispensable to understanding why political dissidents and other similar individuals have continued to be sent to mental asylums by the authorities long after Mao's "revolution to touch men's souls" passed into history.

I. Forensic Psychiatry in Crisis

The Case of Chen Lining: "A Madman for the New Era"

On the afternoon of January 7, 1967, as China sank ever deeper into the social and political turmoil of the Cultural Revolution, a bizarre conversation took place at the Anding Hospital, Beijing's foremost psychiatric institution, between a group of Red Guard activists and two of Chairman Mao's closest colleagues in the new ultra-leftist Party leadership, Qi Benyu and Wang Li. The topic of discussion was a group of mental patients who had earlier been detained for treatment at the hospital after making "reactionary statements" about President Liu Shaoqi, Mao's erstwhile senior colleague but now principal adversary in the Party leadership, and whom the Red Guards had recently "liberated" from their confinement. The conversation went, in part, as follows:

> *Qi Benyu*: You Red Guards are the pioneers of rebellion in China's mental asylums, you are rebels against Revisionism; in the future, the Soviet Union will need to carry out a Cultural Revolution and do the same kind of thing!
>
> *Red Guard*: I request permission…to conduct similar revolutionary liaison activities in mental asylums throughout the country.
>
> *Wang Li*: Our purpose in coming here today is to support you.
>
> *Qi Benyu* (to a recently discharged mental patient): Are you mad?
>
> *Wang Fuxian*: No…I just had different views and opinions from other people; I was in the minority. When I rebelled against the authority of my local Party Secretary, they said I was mentally ill.
>
> *Qi Benyu*: How does that make you mentally ill? They're the ones who are mad! … If the revisionists ever came to power, they'd have Wang Li and me declared "mentally ill" too![248]

This obscure incident from over thirty years ago provides a rare glimpse into the elusive history of political psychiatry in China. The central figure in the Anding Hospital incident was one Chen Lining, a Party member who had incurred the wrath of Mao's political opponents in the early 1960s by writing articles and wall-posters criticizing the "revisionist" policies of President Liu Shaoqi. As a result, between 1962 and 1966, Chen was incarcerated seven times in mental hospitals and placed under secret arrest by the security police. By January 1967, however, the political tables had been turned and Liu was being attacked nationwide as China's "No.1 Capitalist Roader." Upon learning that Chen Lining's criminal case records were being held at Qincheng Prison, where he had been detained

---

[248] Transcript taken from "Red Guard Publications: Part III — Special Issues," Vol.16, Center for Chinese Research Materials, Association of Research Libraries, Washington D.C. (1975), pp.5186-5187 (conversation edited here for purposes of conciseness). Grateful acknowledgement is due to Lalagy Pulvertaft for providing extensive source materials on both Chen Lining and the Anding Hospital incident and also (as discussed below) the case of Yan Weibing, wife of propaganda chief Lu Dingyi.

for several months before being transferred to the Anding Hospital, several dozen Red Guards broke into the prison one night and removed them.[249] After the records had been made public, Chen was released from the mental asylum and proclaimed by his Red Guard supporters to be the "Madman of the New Era" (*xin shidai de kuangren*).

In a speech given at the Chinese Academy of Sciences two months later, Chen described a part of his ordeal in forensic-psychiatric detention as follows:

> During my political persecution at the Hunan Provincial Mental Hospital, I was subjected to numerous bouts of drug interrogation,[250] given electro-convulsive therapy more than 40 times and insulin-coma shock therapy altogether 29 times, and was fed large quantities of chlorpromazine. They treated me like an experimental object and it was all a disguised form of physical torture. It was extremely painful, and by the end, I was left trembling and sweating all over and my memory had started to go.

The details of Chen's medical record from that time are highly revealing. According to an entry made by a psychiatrist in December 1963: "The patient's mental illness has recurred; his counterrevolutionary statements are none other than a pathological mental symptom of his longstanding reactionary views. Diagnosis: schizophrenia." The following year, a psychiatrist at Anding Hospital added a further entry: "Patient's mental condition: thinking clear and alert, interacts well with others, answers questions appropriately… But lacks self-knowledge and is unclear as to why he was placed under criminal investigation in the first place. Initial diagnosis: schizophrenia (paranoid type.)"[251]

A psychiatrist who had sympathized with Chen Lining during his incarceration gave a speech at a Red Guard rally shortly after Chen's "liberation" from the mental hospital, in which he added the following colourful details to the story:

> The black hands of the reactionary line headed by Liu [Shaoqi] and Deng [Xiaoping] subjected Chen Lining to political persecution, secretly arresting him and transferring him from the mental hospital to a detention centre in Beijing, where he was frequently interrogated and tortured over a long period. They tormented him daily by not letting

---

249 See: "*Jingshenbing? Zhengzhifan?*" (Mentally Ill Person? Or Political Prisoner?), undated, Tao Dejian, available at: www.taosl.net/fy024.htm.

250 *Mazui fenxi* is a practice whereby patients were drugged and questioned in an attempt to find out if they were feigning symptoms of mental illness. Most Chinese psychiatrists now regard this practice as inhumane and contrary to human rights, but Li Congpei – the *eminence grise* of Chinese forensic psychiatry – was still advocating its use as of 1990 (Li Congpei [ed.], *Sifa Jingshenbingxue*, pp.73-74). See also: "*Zai Sifa Jingshen Jianding Zhong Kefou Yong Jingmai Mazui Fenxi?*" (When Carrying Out a Judicial Psychiatric Appraisal, Is it Permissible to Use Intravenous Drug Interrogation?), *Linchuang Jingshen Yixue Zazhi* (Journal of Clinical Psychological Medicine), 1999, No.1. See also: Chen Zhongbao (ed.), *Yingyong Sifa Jingshenbingxue* (Applied Forensic Psychiatry – Chapter 7: The Use of Medications in Drug Interrogation), Shanghai Kexue Jishu Chubanshe, August 1988.

251 See "Red Guard Publications: Part III – Special Issues." Less than a year later, however, when Chen Lining was found to have also said "crazy" things about Chairman Mao, the Red Guards swiftly repudiated him as a political role model and once again branded him a "heinous counterrevolutionary element." A detailed account of this dramatic reversal in Chen's political fortunes (and also in those of his erstwhile patron, Qi Benyu) can be found in "*Cong Chen Lining Anjian Kan Bianse Long Qi Benyu zhi Liu de Fan'geming Zuilian (The Case of Chen Lining Shows Us the Counterrevolutionary Features of the Chameleon-like Qi Benyu and His Ilk)*," published in the Red Guard journal *Xin Bei-Da — Changcheng* (New Beijing University — Great Wall, March 20, 1968), pp.1-4.

him read any books, not even the Selected Works of Mao Zedong, and he was totally cut off from the outside world in prison. Only after he went on hunger strike did they relent and provide him with a copy of [Mao's 1949 article] "On the People's Democratic Dictatorship." After I learned of all this, I realized that as a doctor in a mental hospital of a socialist country, I shouldn't neglect politics and that my primary duty was to take responsibility for the mental patients' political welfare. As Chairman Mao has said, "Without a correct political standpoint, one has no soul."[252]

A number of key pointers to the history of psychiatric abuse in China can be discerned from the above account. First, as the quotation from People's Daily cited on the opening page of this book shows, the Chinese leadership was aware of the main facts about Soviet political psychiatry by at least the early 1960s. Second, it transpires that very similar abuses were also to be found in Chinese forensic psychiatry by around the same period. And third, it is clear that a significant campaign – albeit a highly politicised and ultimately destructive one – of public exposure of such practices took place in China well before the existence of Soviet political-psychiatric abuse was even known about in the West or, indeed, had become a focus of Soviet dissident concern.

As the Cultural Revolution unfolded, however, the distinction between political crime and mental illness – one that had apparently been tenuous even at the best of times – was effectively abandoned in Chinese public life. For a decade and more, until roughly 1978, both legal and medical specificity were discarded outright in favour of an essentially pre-modern concept whereby, much as in Europe during the Middle Ages, the political or religious dissenter was viewed as being possessed by a deeply wicked, or "counterrevolutionary," form of madness; while for their part, the genuinely mentally ill were all too often condemned and punished as dangerous political subversives.

China's Forensic Psychiatric Inquisition

As a direct consequence of Qi Benyu's "important directives" at the Anding Hospital meeting of January 1967, a sinister campaign of persecution – later dubbed the "tide of reversing psychiatric verdicts" (*jingshenbing fan'an feng*) – was launched and carried out by Red Guards around the country. A certain number of mental patients were, as in Wang Fuxian's case, released after being found to have the requisite "revolutionary thinking," while others, mostly senior cadres or their relatives, were accused by the ultra-leftists of having been diagnosed as mentally ill and admitted to the hospital solely as a means of protecting them from the political purges then underway. In many more cases, however, genuinely mentally ill people, especially those whose symptoms had included pseudo-political "ravings" against Mao, were dragged out of mental asylums and brutally coerced into "confessing" that they had been sane all along. These unfortunate individuals were then officially reclassified as counterrevolutionaries

---

252 "'Kuangren' Ri Ji – Zalan Liu-Deng Fan'geming Zhuanzheng" (Diary of a "Madman" – Smash the Counterrevolutionary Dictatorship of Liu and Deng), Qinghua Daxue Jinggangshan Bingtuan Bianyin (Issued by Qinghua University Military Corps), February 1967. With thanks to Francis Deron of Le Monde for providing a copy of this document. In a recent memoir, a former ultra-leftist official revealed that in 2001, Chen's younger sister told him that the Ministry of Public Security had concluded in the late 1970s that Chen was indeed mentally ill. She added that he was currently being treated for mental illness at his home in Xiangtan, Hunan. (See: "'Chen Lining Shijian' Shi-mo" [Full Story of the Chen Lining Incident], Wang Guangyu, 7 March 2005, available at: www.cnd.org/HXWZ/ZK05/zk422.gb.html.) The title "Madman of the New Era" was inspired by Lu Xun's short story "Diary of a Madman"(1918), which in turn echoed Gogol's work of the same name.

and either jailed or summarily executed. As Guan Xin, an official of the Zhejiang High People's Court, explained in a restricted-circulation official report of 1981.

> In the course of reviewing trumped-up cases and miscarriages of justice (*yuan jia cuo an*) from that period, numerous cases have been discovered of people who were obviously mentally ill but who were wrongfully imprisoned or even executed as "political lunatics."
>
> During the ten years of the Cultural Revolution, owing to interference and sabotage from the ultra-leftist line, the issue of the forensic-scientific evaluation of mental illness was for the most part consigned to the rubbish heap. Mentally ill people were convicted of crimes on the basis of their strange utterances and wild language, thereby creating the notion of the so-called "political lunatic" (*zhengzhi fengzi*) – a hodgepodge of the two unrelated terms "politics" (signifying class struggle) and "lunatic" (a state of biological pathology.)[253]

Similarly, Yang Desen, one of China's leading forensic psychiatrists, noted in 1985: "During the ten years of chaos, a minority of mentally ill people were wrongfully executed or imprisoned as 'counterrevolutionaries.'"[254] One example may serve to convey the extent of the medico-legal confusion that prevailed during those years and of the cruel judicial absurdities that often resulted. The case description appears in a two-volume study on crime and mental illness that was published only in late 2000. (It is worth noting, however, that even at such a recent date and in such a clearly unjust case as this one, the author of the study failed to indicate that the case had been a miscarriage of justice.)

> Mr. A, a local-level cadre. A family history of mental illness (both grandfather and father were sufferers). Joined the revolution at the start of the War of Liberation [1945-49.] In 1958, he opposed the "tide of exaggeration,"[255] and for this was dismissed

---

[253] Guan Xin, "How to Discern Mental Illness and Ascertain Legal Capacity," *"Renmin Sifa" Xuanbianben 1981 Nian* (*A Compilation of Articles from "People's Judiciary" 1981*) (volume marked "for internal use only"), (Law Publishing House, 1983), p.590. As Guan concludes from this grotesque record: "Professional experience has clearly shown us that in order to avoid the wrongful conviction and execution of the mentally ill, it is vital that we should disseminate basic knowledge about forensic psychiatry with a view to correctly identifying the mentally ill and ascertaining the question of their [legal] responsibility."

[254] Yang Desen, "On the Legal Responsibility of Mentally Ill Persons for Their Illegal Conduct," *Chinese Journal of Nervous and Mental Diseases*, 1985, Vol.11, No.5, pp.310–312. Yang Desen (also known as Young Derson) is head of the psychiatry department at Hunan Medical College. As the American psychiatrist and anthropologist Arthur Kleinman observed in his landmark 1986 study of Chinese psychiatry, *Social Origins of Distress and Disease: Depression, Neurasthenia and Pain in Modern China*, p.9, Yang was himself the target of political attacks during the Cultural Revolution: "During these years, Dr. Young, Professor Ling's [i.e., Ling Ming-yu, then head of the HMC psychiatry department] former student and successor, received equally harsh treatment from the Red Guards because of his defense of the core psychiatric position that mental illness is an illness, and not wrong political thinking as the Maoists held."

[255] "*Fukua feng*": The term officially used in China today to denote the tendency by Party officials at all levels during the Great Leap Forward (1958-60) to grossly over-report production statistics (especially grain output) in their localities, as a means of convincing the central government that they were implementing Mao's Great Leap Forward directive to do everything "more, better, faster, and more economically" (*duo-kuai-hao-sheng*). This wholesale fabrication of production figures is now generally acknowledged to have been the main reason for the disastrous famine that ensued in China in the early 1960s, in which at least 27 million people died of starvation and related causes.

from his leadership post in 1960 (he was officially rehabilitated in 1962.) Because of the stress caused by this, from 1961 onwards he developed schizophrenia and was then given medical treatment and placed under the guardianship of his family; he lacked either self-awareness or the ability to look after himself, and at times when his illness worsened he would walk around naked and without any sense of shame.

In common with several of the other individuals whose cases we have already encountered,

> Over a several-year period prior to the Cultural Revolution, he wrote numerous letters to Chairman Mao and the Party Central Committee, all filled with incomprehensible nonsense. After carrying out several investigations, the authorities ascertained that he had written these letters because he was mentally ill, and thereafter the local post office used to destroy the letters whenever they found them. Everyone around him knew that he was mentally ill.

Unusually for the era in question, however, Mr. A seems to have had a relatively lively knowledge of the post-war international order – a feature of his case that was swiftly to prove disastrous for him:

> During the early part of the Cultural Revolution, he wrote a series of letters to Premier Zhou [Enlai], saying: "The United Nations should quickly send troops to crush [the protests]," and other similar things. In December 1968, he was arrested as an "active counterrevolutionary," and a month or so later he was sentenced by the court to ten years' imprisonment. Because he kept on uttering strange and incomprehensible statements while in prison, in 1974 he was given a death sentence for engaging in [further] "active counterrevolution"; the death sentence was not approved by the provincial high court, however, and Mr. A died in prison in 1977.[256]

Even the mentally retarded, at that time, were not safe from the country's political correctness enforcement squads. Indeed, according to Shen Zheng, another leading authority on forensic psychiatry, among an unspecified number of mentally retarded people who were submitted for forensic-psychiatric evaluation for alleged criminal offences during the period 1960-76, "the main subgroup (31.2 percent) consisted of political cases."[257] And as another expert writer observed in 2000: "If an epilepsy sufferer

---

256 Liu Baiju, *Jingshen Zhang'ai Yu Fanzui* (Mental Disorders and Crime), Beijing: *Shehui Kexue Wenxian Chubanshe* (Social Sciences Documentary Publishing House), August 2000, p.674 ("Case No. 224.")

257 Shen Zheng, *Falü Jingshenbingxue*, p.217. Similarly, another writer reports: "[B]etween 1960 and 1976, a certain hospital dealt with a total of 40 mentally retarded persons who had committed crimes, and ten of these were cases of a political nature, making this the most frequent of the various offences committed." Wang Zenghui, "An Analysis of 116 Cases of Forensic Psychiatric Appraisal of the Mentally Retarded," *Linchuang Jingshen Yixue Zazhi* (Journal of Clinical Psychological Medicine),1996, No.6.

Even in the late 1990s, mentally impaired or disabled people were still being arrested on political charges and then subjected to forensic psychiatric assessment. For example, a study published in April 2000 examining the question of crimes committed by epileptics noted that the sample group included one person detained for making "anti-social speeches" (Wei Qingping et al., "*Dianxian Huanzhe Weifa de Sifa Jingshen Yixue Jianding Fenxi* [An Analysis of Expert Psychiatric Testimony on Epileptic Patients' Illegal Actions]," *Chinese Journal of Nervous and Mental Diseases*, 2000, Vol.26, No.2, pp.65-67). Similarly, on the case of a mentally retarded man who was arrested on charges of espionage, see: Shen Zheng, *Sifa Jingshenbingxue* (*Legal Psychiatry*), (Zhongguo Zheng-Fa Daxue Chubanshe), p.220.

In a comprehensive study on the subject of crime and mental illness in China, also published in 2000, one writer has sought to explain and justify the current persistence of these abusive legal-psychiatric practices as follows:

kills someone in the course of an epileptic seizure in which they have lost normal consciousness, their choice of target in the attack will generally be quite random; during the Cultural Revolution era, however, if the victim happened to be a Party member or a cadre, it would most likely be treated as a case of "counterrevolutionary murder."[258]

The profound crisis into which China's entire psychiatric profession was thrown during the Cultural Revolution led to the effective dismantling of mental healthcare institutions across the country. Also, numerous Chinese psychiatric professionals, possibly a majority, were labelled as "bourgeois academic authorities" and either purged outright from their positions or sent down to the countryside, often for many years, to perform manual labour and "learn from the peasants." Medicine in general, and psychiatry in particular, had long been a low-status profession in China, but during these years psychiatrists ranked close to the very foot of the social and political ladder. Virtually the entire intellectual domain of psychiatry and human psychology was officially repudiated, to be subsumed under a crude Maoist universalism whereby "correct political ideology" served not only as the key to social survival, but was moreover equated with mental health in general – and vice versa. Thus, in what little remained at that time of the country's mental healthcare institutions, official wall slogans proclaimed to mental patients: "Without a correct political standpoint, one has no soul."[259] Under this reductionist doctrine, psychiatry and psychiatrists became superfluous, and therapy for the mentally ill consisted largely, until the late 1970s, of group "study sessions" on the works of Mao.[260]

"People suffering from impairments of the intellect can also engage in negative political speech and action. Such impairments impact, primarily, in two separate ways on the emergence of negative political speech and action. The first is that impairments of the intellect prevent those affected from being able to properly understand or construe the various items of political information they receive, with the result that they may uncritically adopt undesirable political ideas. The second is that these impairments prevent them from making appropriate judgments, on the basis of existing knowledge, in respect of the various political questions at issue, thereby leading them into careless and wild behaviour. Whatever other people say or do, they will also say or do, although very few of them have any real insight into the nature and significance of their speech and actions. At certain times, they express "revolutionary" views, and at other times they express "counterrevolutionary" views; the listeners, however, will probably only notice the "counterrevolutionary" content of their statements and hence will regard them as being "counterrevolutionaries." While such people may have real or practical motives for engaging in negative political speech and action, nonetheless, not all of these will be directly related to politics; for the most part, they tend to be motivated by lower-level factors such as obtaining material gratification or getting attention from others. For example, one mildly mentally retarded person created and spread a horrifying political rumour, but he did so just because it amused him and he found it enjoyable." (Liu Baiju [op cit], p.677.)

258 See Liu Baiju (op cit), p.264. Under China's pre-1997 Criminal Law, "counterrevolutionary murder" was viewed as being a more heinous offence than murder committed without any political motive.

259 "*Meiyou zhengque de zhengzhi guandian, jiu dengyu meiyou linghun.*" This quotation from Chairman Mao appears in his 1957 article "On the Correct Handling of Contradictions Among the People," in *Selected Works of Mao Tse-tung, Vol. 5* (Beijing, 1977), pp.384-421; the official translation of the quoted sentence differs slightly from that given above.

260 Given the virtual collapse of the country's mental healthcare system at that time, it is surprising to learn that in the legal or forensic area of psychiatric work, things apparently continued much as they had before the Cultural Revolution. As can be seen from the passages cited above, large numbers of "dangerously mentally ill offenders" apparently continued to be arrested, brought before panels of forensic-psychiatric assessors and then dispatched to secure mental hospitals around the country during the Cultural Revolution. But Communist dictatorships sometimes behave in very strange ways. Pol Pot, for example, in planning his new, improved version of Stalinism and Maoism, made provision for a mental hospital in his Democratic Kampuchea utopia. Construction of this facility for the treatment of insanity was planned in 1976, before his Communist Party had reached the conclusion

The extreme political pressures of this era inevitably led to pervasive ethical corruption within the field of psychiatry and forensic medicine in general. As one writer put the matter, "In the past, owing to the influence of the extreme 'leftist' line, [forensic psychiatrists] overemphasized 'putting class struggle to the fore' and 'making vocational work serve politics,' to the extent that issues of an academic or technical nature were sometimes turned into a question of one's basic political standpoint."[261] According to another official account,

> During those years when class struggle was at the forefront of everything, some [forensic doctors] paid no attention to the principle of seeking truth through facts, and instead took the slogans 'Always be highly conscious of the class struggle' and 'Maintain the highest level of revolutionary vigilance" as their basic guiding ideology for performing forensic evaluations... Some forensic doctors who insisted on upholding the truth were taken in for interrogation, thrown into jail and branded as counterrevolutionaries... Others, however, submitted to political pressure and went against their own consciences, making wrongful forensic evaluations... Still others went so far as to use their scientific knowledge to turn truth and lies upside down, saying black was white, and acting entirely in the service of particular individuals or groups.[262]

In the winter of 1978, a young man named Wei Jingsheng, who was to become China's best-known dissident and who later spent seventeen years in prison for advocating human rights and democracy, wrote an article in China's *samizdat* pro-democracy press describing conditions at Qincheng Prison during the Cultural Revolution. His account was probably the first to reveal that psychiatric techniques were being misused in China for purposes of political repression:

> The most common form of torture is simple beating. The prisoner is summoned and surrounded by a group of men who slug and kick until he is bruised, bloody, and completely breathless. Even more common is for prisoners to be so heavily drugged that they become mentally unstable. The justification for administering these drugs is to cure "mental illness." Sometimes people are sent to the hospital for further "treatment." One person who had received the treatment recalls that after taking the medication he had talked to himself constantly for days on end. Naturally, such monologues were recorded for use during the next interrogation. Among the hospitals

---

that everything that was going wrong with the revolutionary society it was trying to build was the result of CIA-KGB-KMT-Vietnamese plots. This paranoid delusion on the part of Pol Pot and other Party leaders led them to decide to apply mass execution, rather than psychiatry, to solve social and political problems, and the hospital was never built. For the plans, see David A.T. Chandler (ed.), "The Party's Four-Year Plan to Build Socialism in All Fields, 1977-1980," *Pol Pot Plans the Future, Yale University Southeast Asian Studies Monograph No.33* (New Haven: 1988), p.109. With thanks to Dr. Stephen R. Heder, Lecturer in Politics at the School of Oriental and African Studies, London, for this information.
261 Jia Yicheng et al., "On Several Basic Concepts in Forensic Psychiatry," *Chinese Journal of Nervous and Mental Diseases*, 1983, Vol.9, No.2, p.119.
262 Zhao Haibo, "On the Fundamental Principles and Methods of Forensic Medical Investigation," in Cui Jian'an (ed.), *Zhongguo Fayi Shijian (China's Forensic Medical Practice)*, (Police Officers' Educational Press, August 1993), pp.47-48.

that participate in such practices are the Fuxing Hospital, Hospital 301, and Anding Hospital.[263]

Subsequent testimonies from high-ranking government officials who had been incarcerated at Qincheng Prison authoritatively confirmed Wei's general account. According to one former inmate, for example: "Especially inhuman was the practice of…force-feeding you a kind of drug that induced hallucinations."[264] The most vivid and detailed account is that of Mu Xin, a former editor of the *Guangming Daily*, who was arrested in 1968 and held for several years at Qincheng Prison on trumped-up charges of conducting an "anti-Party conspiracy." In his memoir of this period, Mu wrote,

> In the nearly four years from the moment I was thrown into Qincheng Prison to the downfall of Lin Biao, they continuously gave me stimulants. This would happen at least ten to fifteen days every month… They did this with the intention of destroying my brain, not just to impair my memory but also to make me unable to write anything anymore… Even after I returned to my home, having suffered several years of this continuing drugging and poisoning, my brain was severely damaged and traumatized.[265]

The Case of Yan Weibing

As mentioned earlier, many mental patients, especially senior cadres or their relatives, were accused during the Cultural Revolution of having feigned their illnesses as a means of avoiding punishment for their political opposition toward Mao. One such case involved a woman named Yan Weibing, wife of the then Minister of Propaganda, Lu Dingyi, who was one of the first senior victims of the Cultural Revolution purges. This little-known case bears more than a passing resemblance to the infamous

---

263 Wei Jingsheng, "A Twentieth-Century Bastille," in James D. Seymour (ed.), *The Fifth Modernization: China's Human Rights Movement*, (New York: Human Rights Publishing Group, 1980), p.217. Wei's article originally appeared in the March 1979 issue of *Tansuo (Explorations),* a dissident journal founded and edited by Wei the previous winter.
264 Wang Li, "Wang Li's Testament," *Chinese Studies in Philosophy*, Vol.26, nos. 1-2 (Fall-Winter 1994-95), p.5.
265 Mu Xin, "Inmate No. 6813 in Qincheng Prison," *Mao's Great Inquisition: The Central Case Examination Group, 1966-1979*; *Chinese Law and Government*, Vol.29, No.3 (May-June 1996), pp.74-75. The bizarre lengths that prison guards at Qincheng went to in order to manipulate and control the inmates was related by Mu as follows:

"Before they delivered the newspaper that carried the news of the death of Mr. Dong [Biwu] [one of the founders of the People's Republic, who had fallen from official grace during the Cultural Revolution], they surreptitiously gave me a drug that suppresses tears (in fact, many of the female 'prisoners' were given this drug before they met with their children who came to meet them in prison). This drug makes it impossible, somehow, for a person to shed tears, no matter how badly he or she might feel. On the other hand, before they delivered the newspaper that carried the news of [the death of] Chiang Kai-shek, they deliberately doped me with some drug that had the opposite effect of the first one. In spite of all this, however, it was most certainly unlikely that I would feel the slightest bit of 'grief' at the death of a public enemy of the people like Chiang Kai-shek, and I most certainly would not be able to bring myself to shed tears on his account. Those people were able, in fact, to sense this, and so they ordered the 'guard' to pour some liquid sulfuric acid – which attacks one's eyes severely and makes one's eyes all runny – on the ground right outside the door of my cell, and then they tried to fan the fumes into my room in an effort to force me to shed tears, thus allowing them to make a report on my 'counterrevolutionary sentiments'." (Ibid, pp.92-93.)

"Doctors' Plot" concocted in the Soviet Union shortly before Stalin's death.[266] It claimed numerous senior political casualties and delivered a traumatic blow to China's psychiatric profession in general. According to an account of the case compiled by Red Guards in June 1968,

> The active counterrevolutionary element Yan Weibing, wife of the counterrevolutionary revisionist clique leader Lu Dingyi, over the six-year period from March 1960 to January 1966 wrote dozens of anonymous counterrevolutionary letters that insanely attacked Deputy Commander Lin Biao, the close comrade-in-arms of our most dearly beloved leader Chairman Mao, and members of his family; she insanely opposed Comrade Lin Biao, and is [thus] an active counterrevolutionary element who has committed towering and heinous crimes.[267]

---

266 The *Encyclopaedia Britannica* provides the following summary of this notorious incident:

"Doctors' Plot: (1953), alleged conspiracy of prominent Soviet medical specialists to murder leading government and party officials; the prevailing opinion of many scholars outside the Soviet Union is that Joseph Stalin intended to use the resulting doctors' trial to launch a massive party purge. On Jan. 13, 1953, the newspapers Pravda and Izvestiya announced that nine doctors, who had attended major Soviet leaders, had been arrested. They were charged with poisoning Andrey A. Zhdanov, Central Committee secretary, who had died in 1948, and Alexander S. Shcherbakov (d. 1945), who had been head of the Main Political Administration of the Soviet army, and with attempting to murder several marshals of the Soviet army. The doctors, at least six of whom were Jewish, also were accused of being in the employ of U.S. and British intelligence services, as well as of serving the interests of international Jewry. The Soviet press reported that all of the doctors had confessed their guilt."

"The trial and the rumoured purge that was to follow did not occur because the death of Stalin (March 5, 1953) intervened. In April Pravda announced that a re-examination of the case showed the charges against the doctors to be false and their confessions to have been obtained by torture. The doctors (except for two who had died during the course of the investigation) were exonerated. In 1954 an official in the Ministry of State Security and some police officers were executed for their participation in fabricating the cases against the doctors. In his secret speech at the 20th Party Congress (February 1956), Nikita S. Khrushchev asserted that Stalin had personally ordered that the cases be developed and confessions elicited, the "doctors' plot" then to signal the beginning of a new purge. Khrushchev revealed that Stalin had intended to include members of the Politburo in the list of victims of the planned purge." (See http://www.britannica.com/seo/d/doctors-plot/.)

Significantly, a Soviet official who tried to denounce the "Doctors' Plot" was promptly declared criminally insane. As Bloch and Reddaway relate:

"In January 1953 Sergei Pisarev, a party member since 1920 and for many years a party official, submitted a report to Stalin criticizing the secret police for its fabrication of the non-existent 'plot' to poison leading figures. Before long he was arrested. Pisarev spent the initial seven weeks of his detention in the Serbsky Institute for Forensic Psychiatry and then, having been declared insane, he was confined for four months in the psychiatric section of the hospital in Moscow's Butyrka Prison, and for nearly a year and a half in the Leningrad Prison Psychiatric Hospital. The diagnosis reached by the Serbsky psychiatrists was schizophrenia, yet later on three occasions during his Leningrad hospitalization Pisarev learned that his psychiatrist there, Dr L.A. Kalinin, had reported that he was 'healthy and fully capable of accepting responsibility for his actions'." (See: *Russia's Political Hospitals*, pp.58-9.)

267 Documentation Group of the Revolutionary Committee of Beijing College of Politics and Law and Documentation Group of the Capital Red Guards Committee's Politics and Law Commune, "A Shocking Case of Counterrevolution: An Investigative Report into the Attempt by Peng Zhen, Lu Dingyi and their Sinister Lieutenants to Concoct a Counterrevolutionary Phoney Medical Diagnosis Aimed at Shielding the Active Counterrevolutionary Element Yan Weibing," *Xingxing-Sese de Anjian: Liu Deng Peng Luo Shixing Zichanjieji Zhuanzheng de Yangban*

In fact, Yan had been under psychiatric diagnosis and treatment, including frequent insulin coma therapy, for several years for a mental condition that senior Chinese psychiatrists had determined to be some form of paranoid behavioural disturbance.[268] She suffered frequent outbursts of uninhibited anger, much of which was apparently aimed at Lin Biao's wife, Ye Qun, and to whom she had been sending copious amounts of politically coloured "hate mail" in recent years. In the months leading up to the full-scale outbreak of the Cultural Revolution in May 1966, her husband Lu had been considering having her compulsorily admitted to the Anding Hospital for treatment. In the event, all of the psychiatrists and senior government officials responsible for Yan's earlier care and treatment (including Shen Yucun, who survived to become the principal editor of the major PRC textbook on psychiatry after 1978 and head of the WHO's mental health liaison office in Beijing) were branded by Red Guards as having been centrally involved in a "counterrevolutionary conspiracy" to falsely diagnose Yan as mentally ill so that she could be spared punishment for her "insanely hostile" letters against Lin Biao and his wife; at least one of them committed suicide as a result.[269]

The real target of the Red Guards' displeasure, of course, was Lu Dingyi himself, and the evidence of his wife's letters formed a crucial plank in their efforts, soon thereafter successful, to have him dragged from power. Yan's persecutors thus had little time for diagnostic niceties and their final verdict on her mental state was as follows: "What was Yan Weibing's real mental illness? A counterrevolutionary disease of the heart![270] Her mind was extremely alert...and her state of anxiety [reflected only] her high degree of counterrevolutionary vigilance." She had been under investigation by the Ministry of Public Security for many months on account of the letters to Lin Biao's family, and on April 28, 1966, the central authorities ordered her arrest on charges of counterrevolution. Yan and her husband were to

---

(All Types of Cases: Model Examples of the Bourgeois Dictatorship Exercised by Liu, Deng, Peng and Luo), June 1968, pp.18-33.

A whole separate study could fruitfully be done on the topic of the close convergence of political and popular-psychological language during the Cultural Revolution, and on the wholesale semantic degradation that resulted. When the Red Guards accused Mrs. Yan of "insanely attacking" Lin Biao, for example, they meant it both as a serious political allegation and also, more randomly, as a form of sheer political abuse. On a deeper discursive level, however, they seem also to have been acknowledging that she probably was mentally ill, and the phrase "insanely attacking" may thus have been intended as a kind of pseudo-medical, politically reductionist explanation for her allegedly deviant mental behavior. On a much simpler level, of course, the question inevitably arises: who was the more "crazy," she or they?

268 The precise diagnosis, made by psychiatrists two weeks after Yan was formally arrested, was: "Paranoid state on the basis of a sub-acute hysterical personality type" (Ibid, p.31).

269 The psychiatrist was Shi Shuhan, an official at the Ministry of Health; he took an overdose of barbiturates on August 25, 1966. Among the numerous senior psychiatrists and health officials denounced and punished as "counterrevolutionary conspirators" as a result of the Yan Weibing "false diagnosis" case were: Qian Xinzhong, Minister of Public Health; Huang Shuze, deputy Minister of Public Health and head of the ministry's healthcare bureau; Xue Bangqi, director of the East China Hospital in Shanghai; Shen Yucun, a psychiatrist in the brain medicine department of Beijing Hospital (and wife of Qian Xinzhong); Su Zonghua, director of the Shanghai Hospital for the Prevention of Mental Diseases; Xu Yunbei, a former Party Secretary at the Ministry of Health; Zhang Ziyi, former deputy head of the Party's Propaganda Department; Zheng Xuewen, head of the medical treatment department of the Ministry of Health; and Geng Dezhang, the personal physician of Lu Dingyi.

270 *"Fan'geming de xin bing."*

spend the next twelve and a half years in solitary confinement at Qincheng Prison, during which time they were denied even a single meeting together.[271]

The Case of Mr. C

Accounts from senior-level cadre victims of the Cultural Revolution purges go only a small way toward explaining, however, the extremely widespread incidence of forensic-psychiatric "cases of a political nature" that was later reported to have occurred during those years. A perhaps more typical story was one related many years later to a Western human rights organization by a former political prisoner, identified only as "Mr. C," who spent a total of more than sixteen years in various labour camps, detention centres and prisons for the "mentally disordered" in China. His account conveys with great clarity the grotesque ironies and injustices that characterized legal psychiatry at that time:

> Summer 1969. After I was arrested as a counterrevolutionary, I was interrogated three times. I did not want to accept any charge for a crime that I had not committed, nor did I want to name any person as having committed any crime. Therefore I was sent to Jiangwan Number 5 [in Shanghai]. This place was known as the "Institute for Diagnosing Mental Disorder" – the setting of my most terrifying experiences during my entire 16 years of imprisonment.
>
> The whole "institute" was a large cage from within which one could not see the skies. Inside this large cage there were many small cages, which were only half as high as an average person. One could only squat or lie in them, and I had to crawl in and out of mine. They were no better than chicken houses. All those detained in the "institute" were suspected of mental disorder, but being there would truly drive a mentally normal person insane. There, one could constantly hear frightening screams. The wardens tried to stop people from screaming and, when failing to do so, would administer drugs to cause people to lose consciousness and thus become silenced. Once awakened from the drug, one felt very dull, depressed and uncomfortable.
>
> People sent to this institute were mostly those who had committed serious counterrevolutionary crimes such as shouting anti-Mao slogans in public. In order to avoid sentencing of death, these people pretended to be mentally abnormal by screaming nonsense, only to be cruelly beaten and drugged. They were allowed to go out of their small cages to be "aired" once a day, and were given two meals of very thin porridge each day.
>
> Whenever the wardens appeared, I would tell them that I was not mentally disordered and that I would like to talk to them about my problems if only they would let me out of the "institute." Usually, people insisted on their lunacy in order to receive a reduced sentence. Therefore, when I very soberly proclaimed that I was normal, they truly believed me to be a madman.

---

[271] For a detailed account of Lu Dingyi's and Yan Weibing's persecution during the Cultural Revolution, see Chen Qingquan and Song Guangwei, *Lu Dingyi Zhuan* (*A Biography of Lu Dingyi*), (Zhonggong Dang Shi Chubanshe, Beijing, December 1999). Prior to the publication of this book, it was not known what became of Yan following her arrest in April 1966 (Ibid, p.541).

I did not know how long I would be treated like an animal in a place where fear alone could suffice to drive a person crazy. Many of the inmates I met had been there for more than ten years; some had been imprisoned there for over twenty years. Worse still, when an inmate was diagnosed to be a normal person, he or she would either be executed, given a more severe sentence, or shut up in the cage forever as a "politically insane" criminal.

I was there for only about 100 days. A good-hearted warden, knowing that I was a college student from reading my personal files, secretly released me. I hid for a while, then was arrested again soon after.[272]

The place where Mr. C was held – "Jiangwan No. 5" – is believed to be the same institution that in 1987 was renamed as the Shanghai Public Security Bureau's Ankang Centre for the Custody and Treatment of the Mentally Ill, located just south of the Fudan University campus on Guoquan North Road. Apart from the appalling conditions of detention that Mr. C describes, what is most striking about his story is the Orwellian complexity and intricacy of the classification of the inmates. Most were arrested "counterrevolutionaries" who had shouted banned political slogans and then been suspected of mental illness. Others, presumably "genuine" counterrevolutionaries, had adopted the survival stratagem, after their arrest, of feigning mental illness in order to avoid being executed for shouting such slogans. Meanwhile Mr. C himself, another political offender, was regarded as indisputably insane by the warders because he had actively chosen to reject this stratagem by declaring himself quite sane. The normal language and conceptual armoury of forensic psychiatric science would seem to be of little direct use as a means of understanding or construing a situation of such utter medico-legal absurdity as this one.

II. General Psychiatry in Crisis

In the field of psychiatry during the Cultural Revolution, people called mental illness a "political sickness" and "ideological illness," and the three main psychiatric treatments (chlorpromazine, ECT and insulin shock therapy) were denounced as "three magic weapons for harming the working class." [273]

The persistence and further expansion of the political misuse of legal psychiatry in China during the Cultural Revolution presents us with a baffling question. At a time when legal norms nationwide had broken down almost completely, and when the national psychiatric care system had in large part been dismantled in favour of the "revolutionary" policy of dispersing mental patients back into the community and sending their former physicians and carers into "re-educational" exile in the countryside, why did those who remained within the system go to the elaborate and quite sophisticated lengths of developing and applying a theory that equated political and ideological dissent with varying degrees of severe mental pathology? A much more obvious outcome of the official repudiation of both law and psychiatry that occurred during the Cultural Revolution would surely have been for the authorities to

---

272 "Shanghai Detention Center for the Mentally Disordered: An Interview with Mr. C," *Human Rights Tribune* (journal of the New York-based monitoring group Human Rights in China), Vol.1, No.5 (October 1990), p.16; HRIC's journal is now called *China Rights Forum*.
273 Xu Taoyuan, "*Zhongguo Jingshenbingxue Sishi Nian*" (Forty Years of Psychiatry in China), *Shanghai Jingshen Yixue*, 1989, Vol.1, No.1, pp.7-9.

consign all further thought of legal and forensic psychiatry to Lenin's often-revisited "rubbish bin of history." But this is not at all what actually happened.

We have seen, in the preceding section, how in the sub-specialist field of criminal psychiatry both the professional infrastructure and the Soviet-inspired guiding theory whereby political opposition or dissent was seen as being a primary symptom of serious mental illness not only survived the political storms of the early phase of the Cultural Revolution, but grew substantially in scope and intensity thereafter. What is considerably more surprising, however, is to learn that parallel developments within the much broader field of the general psychiatric-care system in China at this time proved to be even more radical and far-reaching in nature than those occurring within the forensic psychiatric domain – affecting the lives of far greater numbers of people, and in ways that in countless cases must have been disastrously traumatic for those concerned.

In brief overview, what transpired in Chinese psychiatry at this time is that while the Serbski-school theory of "political insanity" continued to be applied within the forensic field against many criminal detainees accused of "opposing Mao Zedong Thought" and other such heretical behaviour, within China's general psychiatric care domain a new and still more pernicious trend of thought arose. This was the belief that mental illness itself was caused by an underlying range of subjective politico-cognitive conditions that could conveniently be summed up under the catch-all heading of "incorrect or improperly-reformed political worldview." This new theory of mental illness was later, in October 1978, summed up as follows by one of its critics:

> Some years ago, a viewpoint emerged whose influence was soon to sweep across the entire nation. It held that ideological problems were the direct cause of all the functional mental illnesses, and that the fundamental roots of such illness lay in the bourgeois worldview of the patients and in their metaphysical philosophy of life.[274]

As a result of the steady ascendancy of this medically ultra-heterodox notion from the early 1970s onwards, those suffering from virtually all forms of mental illness in China began to be viewed, in essence, as not only being personally responsible for their distressing psychological conditions, but also, in many cases, as being potential or concealed "anti-Party" dissident elements. Consequently, the mentally ill in China came increasingly to be seen as falling within the fast-burgeoning categories of citizens who formed the direct targets of the Cultural Revolutionary "mass dictatorship." With this development, the personal had become wholly political – and a direct identification was drawn between medical "madness" on the one hand, and political or legal "badness" on the other.

"All Mental Illness is Political"

The approximate genesis of this dire and astonishing new school of psychiatric thought can be traced back to the opening months of 1966 (the same general period in which Yan Weibing, the wife of the Minister of Propaganda and first prominent casualty of the Cultural Revolution, Lu Dingyi, found herself being accused of feigning mental illness as a means of concealing her alleged political hostility toward Marshall Lin Biao.) It should be noted in passing that the real story of how Chinese psychiatry degenerated, during the Cultural Revolution, into a punitive set of theories and practices that targeted

---

274 "*Yiqie gongnengxing jingshenbing de bingyin dou shi sixiang wenti, zong genzi zaiyu bingren de zichanjieji shijieguan he xing'ershangxue de fangfalun.*" See: Yan Shanming, "*Guanyu Jingshenbing Benzhi Wenti de Tantao*" (An Inquiry into the Essential Nature of Mental Illness), *Xin Yixue Fukan – Shenjing Xitong Jibing (New Medicine Review – Series on Diseases of the Nervous System)*, 1978, No.4, pp.109-10.

the sufferers rather than the illness remained virtually unknown about outside of China until the time of the present research study. The principal source from which the following account of one of the darkest aspects of the entire Cultural Revolution experience has been assembled is a series of articles that appeared in "internal use only" editions of mainland Chinese psychiatric journals during the 1970s.

The overall thrust and tenor of the "revolutionary new thinking" that began to emerge within Chinese psychiatry in early 1966 can be gauged from an official Party slogan that appeared on the inside front cover of the April 1966 issue of the *Chinese Journal of Neurology and Psychiatry*. Printed in one-inch-high Chinese characters and occupying the entire page, the slogan read:

> We Must Think Constantly About the Class Struggle and the Dictatorship of the Proletariat, Give Full Prominence to Politics at All Times, and Remember Always to Raise High the Great Red Banner of Mao Zedong Thought.

A lengthy accompanying article exhorted China's entire psychiatric community to "Raise High the Great Red Banner of Mao Zedong Thought and Actively Participate in the Socialist Cultural Revolution." Offering a tantalizing glimpse of the tectonic upheaval that was about to hit the Chinese psychiatric profession, and whose dire effects were to last for the ensuing decade and more, the journal's editorial article then proceeded to spelled out the main political tasks and challenges that the profession was now being officially urged to tackle. Entitled "Give Full Prominence to Politics and Follow China's Own Path toward the Cure and Prevention of Psychiatric Illness," the editorial began by noting that:

> Many problems still exist in our work, foremost among them being that some psychiatric workers are still quite heavily influenced and affected by bourgeois medical ideology; …they are concerned only with the situation inside their hospitals and ignore the situation beyond the hospital walls; they use too many drugs and pharmaceuticals to treat patients and fail to mobilize the positive factors within the patients themselves, and so end up treating the illness rather than the person; … and their ideology is lacking in the self-consciously revolutionary spirit of self-reliance, hard work and thriftiness, and wholeheartedly serving the people.

However, continued the editorial,

> For the past year and more, medical health workers throughout China have been resolutely implementing the directives of the Party Central Committee and Chairman Mao by taking part in the Three Great Revolutionary Movements;[275] large numbers of doctors and pharmacists have been going "up to the mountains and down to the villages" in order to relieve the peasant masses of their pains and illnesses; and while healthcare work has been greatly reinforced in the countryside, a revolution has been taking place in the urban healthcare field. Most important of all, an ardent high tide in the universal study of Chairman Mao's works has been unleashed, allowing us to raise our level of ideological awareness, to give full prominence to politics, and to criticize and condemn the bourgeois ideological preference for working in isolation from politics, the masses and reality.

Intriguingly, in common with much of the reforming zeal that arose in other walks of life during the opening months of the Cultural Revolution, Chinese psychiatry appears at this time to have tried to address certain real and pressing problems in the care of the mentally ill – in particular, the over-reliance

---

275 In Maoist parlance, these are: the struggle for production, the class struggle, and scientific experimentation.

on medication and institutional confinement that was found also in most other parts of the world at that time – and moreover, to have done so in a way that could possibly, if domestic political circumstances had been more favourable, have turned out quite differently. For the first time in China, for example, the non-biological approach of "psychotherapy" (*xinli zhiliao*) began to be used as an alternative therapy within the mental healthcare system. As this and similar articles of the time showed, however, the form of psychotherapy actually used from early 1966 onwards consisted of increasingly intense political indoctrination sessions in which mental patients were exhorted to cure themselves by studying the works of Mao and adopting a "proletarian" political outlook.[276] As the editorial continued,

> In Chengdu in March of this year, at a national symposium to exchange research-work experiences in the fields of psychiatry and neurology, the question of the content and essential nature of "psychotherapy" was quite extensively discussed. In the view of the conference, China's "psychotherapy" is fundamentally different in nature from the old-style "psychotherapy" found elsewhere. The main difference is that it has a clear and distinctive class nature: it employs a variety of means to help the patients strengthen their resolve to fight their illnesses for the sake of the revolution, and to do so self-confidently; and it firmly opposes the subjective-idealist ideological standpoints adopted by the bourgeois schools of psychoanalysis and psychobiology. The second main difference is that it emphasizes the importance of mobilizing the patient's inner subjective dynamism[277] during the treatment process...
>
> "Psychotherapy" is therefore a kind of ideological re-education, the essence of which is to instil in the patients a revolutionary worldview and outlook on life... Although for the meantime we are using the term "psychotherapy" to denote this treatment method, it may well turn out to be a rather inappropriate term. We will need to reconsider what name to use for it in the light of subsequent practical experience.[278]

Elsewhere in the same issue of the *Chinese Journal of Neurology and Psychiatry*, staff members from a Gansu Province mental hospital elaborated as follows on the editorial's main themes:

> In the early period after the founding of our hospital, we lacked experience in clinical management and so tried to study and emulate the experiences of other local hospitals. But we basically continued to follow the capitalist managerial model, with patients being confined in isolation, spending long periods in a boring and depressing environment and undergoing a gradual mental decline. In the course of the 1957 Anti-Rightist Movement and the struggle to annihilate capitalism and assert

---

276 Somewhat confusingly, given its generally positive image in the West, in China psychotherapy (known variously as "*jingshen zhiliao*" or "*xinli zhiliao*") was essentially a Maoist ultra-leftist invention whereby the mentally ill were subjected to compulsory political and ideological re-education. To some extent, the term "psychotherapy" retains these negative connotations in China even today.
277 The concept of "subjective dynamism" (*zhuguan nengdongxing*) was a prominent strand in radical Maoist thought from the early 1960s onward; it reflected Mao's belief that China under socialism could develop at a much faster rate than the backward material and economic conditions of the country would otherwise allow, provided the population fully believed in and utilized the transformative powers of human subjective will. In a colloquial sense, it amounted to a kind of "mind over matter" belief system, the principal target or adversary of which was the orthodox (Soviet) Marxist doctrine of "economic determinism."
278 "*Tuchu Zhengzhi, Zou Woguo Jingshenbing Fangzhi Gongzuo Ziji de Lu,*" Chinese Journal of Neurology and Psychiatry, 1966, Vol.10, No.2, pp.95-97.

the proletarian worldview,[279] however, the level of ideological awareness among our medical personnel rose greatly and we made initial progress in critiquing the bourgeois viewpoint that "mental illness is protracted and incurable" and so nothing much can be done about it…

In line with the gradual unfolding and deepening of the Great Socialist Education Movement,[280] we have been conducting a major campaign to study the works of Chairman Mao and to learn from the People's Liberation Army… Every human activity has an ideological basis, and the mentally ill are no different in this regard. Where problems of an ideological category are concerned, it is no use just relying on giving medicine and injections. What we really have to focus on is helping mental patients to give full prominence to politics, raise their levels of class-consciousness, and embrace the ideology of becoming well for the sake of the revolution and of waging conscious battle against their illnesses.

The claim that Mao's notorious Anti-Rightist Movement, in which hundreds of thousands of intellectuals were sent to prison or otherwise severely persecuted as "anti-Party elements," had in any way served to advance the cause of public mental health in China can only be described as risible. In its subsequent account of the more specific and practical details of the mental hospital reforms then being undertaken in Gansu, moreover, the article vividly illustrated the process of galloping politicisation that had begun to invade mainland Chinese thinking on mental illness in general as the Cultural Revolution got underway:

Among the patients themselves, depending on their individual circumstances, we have set up groups for the living study and living application of Chairman Mao's works, organized newspaper-reading classes, and held education sessions on current political affairs and on the advanced example set by the heroes of the revolution. Moreover, especially among the long-term inmates, we have compiled textbooks that take account of their particular mental conditions and which we use for purposes of re-educating them. The mental patients have found these very interesting, and when used in combination with psychotherapy and appropriate clinical management they have proven to be quite effective. In addition, we have purposefully arranged for the patients to view films such as "Be Eternally Loyal to the Party" and "The Spark of Life," to visit exhibitions on political class education, to take part in "recalling past bitterness and remembering present happiness"[281] sessions, and to hold group classes where they enthusiastically sing revolutionary songs. All of this has helped to release the patients' subjective positivity and has imbued them with a spirit of revolutionary optimism.

In short, the everyday atmosphere in the sick wards is increasingly brisk, lively and dynamic. One mental patient, for example, wrote to us after being discharged from

---

279 *"fan youpai, xing-wu mie-zi de douzheng"*
280 The Socialist Education Movement began in the early 1960s, first in the countryside and then later in the cities, and was the immediate forerunner of the Cultural Revolution.
281 *"Yi ku si tian"*: political consciousness-raising sessions in which people would hear tales from the elderly about how harsh and exploitative life had been before 1949 and then dwell upon all the ways in which life had improved under Communism. These sessions were a regular feature of daily life in China from the early 1950s until the late 1970s.

hospital: "My stay in hospital this time was just like being in a school of politics – you cured both my physical illness and also my ideological sickness. I want to thank the Party for all the warmth and concern it has shown me."[282]

Lastly, elsewhere in the journal, another mental patient provided the following similarly glowing testimonial to the efficacy of China's new, politically-oriented psychiatric reforms:

In the past, when the doctor told me: "To cure your sickness you must be guided by correct ideology," I felt quite upset and offended. How could correcting one's ideology ever make one recover from mental illness? Wouldn't this mean that I actually had some kind of ideological sickness? Now that I've gained an understanding of the dialectical relationship between ideology and illness, however, I realise why all the medicine I used to take had no effect and I've become confident of being able to cure myself.[283]

China's Mental Patients in the Dock

With the full-blown onset of the Cultural Revolution in May 1966, all of China's professional psychiatric journals abruptly ceased publication, most of them for more than a decade. A several-year gap in the official documentary record of the legal-psychiatric events and theories in question thus emerges at this point. Indeed, so virtually complete was the lack of any scholarly or professional psychiatric publications of any kind within China throughout the Cultural Revolution decade – whether books, journals or even occasional papers and monographs – that the broader history of Chinese psychiatry as a whole during this period remained more or less a blank sheet for Western scholars until fairly recently. The narrative resumes, however, in the summer of 1972, in a series of articles that came to light almost thirty years later in the archives of the National Library in Beijing.[284] The articles in question all appeared in a rare and previously unknown "restricted circulation" (*neibu*) medical journal that was published in Guangzhou between 1972 and 1978 – and they chart in vivid and painful detail the practical outcome of the quickly thwarted initiatives of the opening months of the Cultural Revolution to reform Chinese psychiatry in the direction of a more humane and patient-centred approach.

The various articles took the form of a far-reaching debate and enquiry by numerous leading Chinese psychiatrists at that time into the question of what constituted the "essential nature of mental illness." By the late 1960s, Mao's longstanding insistence upon the Promethean role and virtue of human will and subjective political ideology had attained its apotheosis in a corollary belief, on his part, that *incorrect* thinking or mentality was therefore tantamount to a crime against the revolution. This punitive doctrine pervaded all walks of life in China during the Cultural Revolution, but it found especially fertile soil for development within the field of Chinese psychiatry. In the Chinese language, fortuitously or not, the words for "ideology" and "mentality" are one and the same (*sixiang*.) The outcome of all this was that individual mental problems soon came to be seen, in simplistic and

---

[282] "Give Full Prominence to Politics and Revolutionize the Clinical Management of Mental Illness," ("*Tuchu Zhengzhi, Cujin Jingshenbing Linchuang Guanli Gongzuo Geminghua,*"), by psychiatrists from Tianshui Mental Hospital, Gansu Province, *Chinese Journal of Neurology and Psychiatry*, 1966, Vol.10, No.2, pp.107-108.
[283] *Chinese Journal of Neurology and Psychiatry*, 1966, Vol.10, No.2, p.114.
[284] The articles were found at the library by the present author during a research trip to Beijing in January 2001.

reductionist fashion by the ultra-Maoists, as being not merely reflective of, but as actually *caused by*, incorrect or deviant political thinking on the part of the sufferer.

The Chenzhou Experience

First, let us see the viewpoint that prevailed in China throughout most of the 1970s, as reflected and exemplified in an article – "Analysis of a Survey of 250 Cases of Mental Illness" – published in the Guangzhou *neibu* medical journal in August 1972. The article presented the "model findings" of a wide-ranging psychiatric study carried out several months earlier by a group of ultra-Maoist civilian and military psychiatrists from Chenzhou District in Hunan Province (significantly: Mao's home province), and its central thesis ran as follows:

> When objective reality is reflected within the minds of people whose worldview has not been properly reformed and in whose thinking the word "private" is playing havoc,[285] or because their ideological methodology for the handling of contradictions is incorrect, an intensified struggle arises among the various contradictions in their mind, thereby leading to an imbalance in the biological functioning of certain parts of the brain and hence to the emergence of a whole series of psychiatric symptoms – namely, mental illness. Mental illness is therefore not, as the bourgeois scholars would have us believe, a "supra-class, solely biological phenomenon," but rather something that is inextricably linked with the class struggle and with the clash between the two major worldviews.[286]

> Human personality is mainly acquired, not innate, and is a reflection of one's overall worldview. With people who are relatively heavily imbued with bourgeois ideology, we generally find that their personalities are narrow-minded, intolerant, solitary and withdrawn, or else show a mixture of fragility and arrogance. Unless people like this diligently and earnestly study Marxism-Leninism and Mao Zedong Thought and conscientiously reform their own worldviews, they will generally become obsessed with thoughts of personal gain or loss and fail to apply the methodology of "one divides into two"[287] in dealing with problems, and instead end up making nit-picking self-justifications and putting their own personal interests in first place.

> Under the socialist system, a clash will thus inevitably develop between the word "public" and their own preoccupation with the word "private," engendering a contradiction within their minds between these two things. And unless this contradiction can be correctly resolved, the ideological struggle within their minds

---

285 "*'si'zi zuo guai*," i.e., they still retain "selfish" ideas that conflict with the Communist or socialist values of public ownership and communal living.
286 i.e., the proletarian worldview and the capitalist or bourgeois worldview.
287 The phrase "one divides into two" (*yi fen wei er*) is a key term in late Maoist or ultra-leftist Chinese political philosophy. Mao advocated the concept constantly in his various philosophical writings on the Marxist-Hegelian dialectic, using it as a byword for the primacy of the class struggle under socialism. His chief adversary in this debate, which began in the late 1950s, was the philosophy professor Yang Xianzhen, who rashly proposed the alternative formula of "two combine into one" (*he er wei yi.*) Mao denounced Yang's ideas as providing, among numerous other heinous things, a theoretical justification for the Soviet policy of "peaceful coexistence" with the United States, and Yang himself was purged and became the object of a nationwide hate campaign by the Party from the early 1960s onwards

will intensify and may produce partial imbalances in the functioning of their cerebral cortices; so people like this can very easily develop mental illnesses.

As the Hunan psychiatrists sternly concluded from these remarkable "research findings":

> The reason why most patients become mentally ill is connected to the class struggle, and the fundamental causal factor in the majority of cases is that they still retain a bourgeois worldview and methodology.

Having thus identified the basic problem, the authors of the "250 Cases" report then proceeded to prescribe what they viewed as being the necessary diagnostic and treatment regime. Eschewing the taxing diagnostic complexities of "bourgeois" psychiatric method, they declared that all types of mental illness should henceforth be subdivided into four broad categories: namely, "manic type," "depressive type," "hallucinatory or delusional type" and "chronic type." (The degree of oversimplification that this involved can be seen from the fact that nowhere in the article was schizophrenia, by far the most widespread and serious of the major mental illnesses, even mentioned.) Moreover, not only were the recommended courses of treatment for all four types of mental illness almost entirely political in nature and orientation, but also (in common with most schools of quackery elsewhere in the world) they were said to be quite miraculously fast and efficacious. The key, declared the subtitle of the report, lay in "According Mao Zedong Thought the Commanding Role at Each and Every Stage in the Process of Treating Mental Illness." By adhering unswervingly to this simple axiom, the pioneering Hunan psychiatrists reported,

> [W]e managed to cure 198 of the patients and substantially improved the condition of a further forty-nine, resulting in a complete recovery rate of 79.2 percent and an effective cure rate of 98.8 percent; the average course of treatment was forty-six days.

Such outstanding results went so far beyond the generally very modest treatment and cure rates for severe mental illness reported in all other parts of the world as to require some rather major methodological explanation. The relevant details were accordingly set forth in the "250 Cases" study from 1972 as follows:

Using Mao Zedong Thought to Re-Educate and Reform the Mentally Ill

> In firmly seizing the fundamental task of using Mao Zedong Thought to re-educate and reform the mentally ill, we persisted in organizing the patients into groups to study the works of Chairman Mao, held frequent and numerous lecture meetings and mass criticism sessions, exchanged experiences among ourselves, unfolded mutual assistance programs and conducted one-on-one discussions with the patients. Throughout this, we comprehensively educated them on the following four main topics:
>
> 1) Political class education. When applying class education, we focused on "recalling past bitterness and remembering present happiness" and on "recalling past bitterness and remembering our present empowerment,"[288] and by so doing we were able to raise the patients' level of class consciousness and make them bear firmly and constantly in mind that their personal emancipation has been entirely due to the Communist

---

288 *"yi ku si quan"*

Party and that they have Chairman Mao to thank for all of their present happiness and good fortune.

2) Education on political line. We frequently lectured the patients on the history of the two-line struggle [within the Party] and held profound sessions of revolutionary criticism and denunciation, during which we purged the patients' minds of the residual poisonous influence of the traitor Liu Shaoqi and his black "six theories," while at the same time raising their level of awareness of the political-line struggle and of the need to self-consciously defend Chairman Mao's revolutionary line and to take the initiative in doing battle with all kinds of undesirable ideological tendencies.

3) Education on the current situation. Focusing on major events within China and abroad, we gave the patients frequent and extensive lectures on the excellent nature of the overall current situation, thereby making them pay attention to national affairs and the world situation and arousing their revolutionary spirit and ardour.

4) Education on worldview. We organized the patients repeatedly to study articles by Chairman Mao such as "Serve the People," and thereby, taking the "three glorious examples" as a model,[289] encouraged them to take a correct outlook on matters of life and death, happiness and suffering, love and marriage and so forth, to struggle consciously against capitalism and revisionism, and to implant within themselves the proletarian worldview.

5) Education on the theory of dialectics. In addition, we organized the patients to study Chairman Mao's glorious philosophical thinking by repeatedly doing a good job of both studying and applying the fundamental principles of "one divides into two," "practice first," "the relationship between internal causal factors and external ones" and "the turning around and resolving of contradictions," and thereby eliminating idealism and metaphysics and upholding the theory of materialist dialectics.

6) Education on doing battle with one's illness. In accordance with the different ideological realities of the individual patients, we organized them to take part in a variety of study groups in which we explained to them the causes of their mental illnesses and helped them to properly identify the principal contradictions in their thinking; by this means, we fully mobilized their inner subjective dynamism and enabled them to dig out the real roots of their illnesses by eradicating "private" thoughts and implanting the concept "public" in its place, thereby reinforcing their sense of self-confidence in waging battle with their illnesses.

Other key elements of the treatment regime involved, first, a similarly intensive program of the "living application of Mao Zedong Thought" within the minds of the medical and nursing staff themselves; and second, the medically rather more orthodox approach of "providing a supplementary combination of Western and Chinese medical treatment in order to help restore the biological functioning

---

289 Namely, the Canadian doctor Norman Bethune, a Red Army soldier named Zhang Side and the "Foolish Old Man of North Mountain," about whom Mao wrote, respectively, in his celebrated three articles titled "In Memory of Norman Bethune" (1939), "Serve the People" (1944) and "The Foolish Old Man Who Removed the Mountains" (1945). These three articles were at the core of all Communist Party educational efforts in China after 1949.

of the patients' brains."[290] Even the latter measures, however, were prefaced with a warning that "only the use of Mao Zedong Thought to re-educate and reform the mentally ill [can] remove the causes of illness at the fundamental level."

Similarly, in the small number of cases (amounting to 20.2 percent of the total) where mental patients were reported to have later suffered relapses after being "cured" by the above method, the chief blame for illness recurrence was once again laid at the door of the sufferers themselves:

> First, after being discharged, the patients did not show a high enough level of self-awareness in studying Mao Zedong Thought and they had insufficiently emphasized the task of carrying out [ideological] self-reform...

In this way, any residual stubborn failures of the "miracle cure" identified by the Hunan researchers could be attributed to the complexity and intractability of class struggle and politics, rather than to any failings or incompleteness in the current state of Chinese medical science. For as they explained:

> In socialist society, there are still classes, class contradictions and the class struggle. The reformation of people's ideology will never be fully completed. As soon as one contradiction is resolved, a new contradiction arises in its place. Mentally ill people are no exception to this rule, and so the recurrence [of mental illness] and the struggle to avoid such relapse is absolute.

In conclusion, the authors of the "250 Cases" study from Hunan reiterated their two main findings as follows:

> 1. Mao Zedong Thought and Chairman Mao's glorious philosophical thinking is the powerful ideological weapon that guides and directs our understanding, treatment and prevention of mental illnesses. The decisive factor in treating and curing mental illness is to mobilize the "two enthusiasms"[291] and employ Mao Zedong Thought to re-educate and reform the patients.

---

290 The physical therapies and their effects were tabulated in the report as follows. (Note that "new-style acupuncture" refers to the use of electrically-charged acupuncture needles, a technology that first came into use in China in the early 1970s and is now also quite widely used elsewhere.)

Statistics on Treatment Outcome by Group:

	New-style acupuncture	New-style acupuncture + wintermin	Herbal medicine + new-style acupuncture + wintermin
Total number of cases	89	152	9
Complete recovery	51	103	4
Near recovery	19	19	2
Condition improved	18	29	2
No change	1	1	1

291 The meaning and significance of this term is not known.

2. The reason why most patients become mentally ill is connected to the class struggle, and the fundamental causal factor in the majority of cases is that the patients still retain a bourgeois worldview and methodology.[292]

The above psychiatric research study, which quickly became known as the "Chenzhou Experience," was widely propagated in mental hospitals across China and became hugely influential within the country's psychiatric profession from the time of its appearance in 1972 until the late 1970s. The theory had two closely related hallmarks: first, a type of medical-scientific reductionism that sought to simplify the clinical diagnosis of mental illness to a point where only the immediate presenting symptoms of the patient were seen as being important and relevant;[293] and second, a crude and extreme form of political universalism whereby "Mao Zedong Thought" was believed to hold the answer to all ideological issues and phenomena – up to and including those properly belonging to the realm of mental pathology or illness in the strictly psychiatric sense.

Unsurprisingly, the Chenzhou Experience did not go entirely unchallenged within Chinese psychiatric circles at that time: a small number of psychiatrists were bold enough openly to question its main diagnostic findings. For example, in an article published in the Guangzhou *neibu* medical journal in 1973, a group of psychiatrists from Jiangxi Province wrote anonymously as follows:

> From the point of view of psychiatry as a branch of science, we feel it is inappropriate to regard problems of worldview and methodology as being the fundamental causal factor in the emergence of mental illness as a whole…
>
> For if so, then the majority of ordinary people would also be likely to develop mental illness, since at the present stage of social development a very large section of the population still cleaves to the word "private" and has an improperly reformed worldview. But why, then, is the rate of mental illness among China's population still running at the level of only several people per thousand? Pursuing this logic further, if the word "private" functions as the "hotbed" of mental illness and if reactionary ideology lies at the root of all such illnesses, then people whose thinking is most heavily laden with the concept "private" – namely, those whose worldview is basically bourgeois or capitalist in nature – should all surely become mentally ill. But in actual practice, we discover no such rule or regularity as this.
>
> In our view, problems relating to worldview and methodology can only partially explain the emergence of mental illnesses and cannot be regarded as the primary causal factors behind mental illness as a whole.

---

292 "Analysis of a Survey of 250 Cases of Mental Illness," *Xin Yixue – Shenjing Xitong Jibing Fukan (New Medicine – Supplementary Series on Diseases of the Nervous System)*, 1972, No.8, pp.12-16. This journal was published on a monthly basis "for internal use only" (*neibu faxing*) by the Zhongshan Medical College in Guangzhou and was one of only a tiny handful of medical journals produced in China during the Cultural Revolution.

The Chinese public, however, was provided with a brief introduction to the "Chenzhou Experience" as early as August 1971, in the form of a feature article in the People's Daily. See: "*Kao Mao Zedong Sixiang Zhihao Jingshenbing*" (Rely on Mao Zedong Thought to Cure Mental Illness), *Renmin Ribao*, August 10, 1971.

293 After all, if all mental illness was caused by "incorrect political worldview" and thus could be cured simply by the continuous and earnest study of Mao Zedong Thought, then the task of precise illness classification became to a large extent redundant. All that was required of the psychiatrist was to make a rough-and-ready diagnosis or categorization based on the patients' immediate symptoms of illness, and then to forge ahead promptly with the all-important task of politically and ideologically re-educating them.

Under the circumstances prevailing in China in the mid-1970s – the height of the political power of the "Gang of Four" – however, the one thing that no Chinese commentator could safely do was to challenge the basic proposition that Mao Zedong Thought provided a panacea for all of society's problems, no matter how seemingly unrelated to politics the issues in question might be. Even the dissenting psychiatrists from Jiangxi, therefore, went to considerable pains to heap enthusiastic praise and endorsement upon the political-style "psychotherapy" regime for the mentally ill that constituted the core of the Chenzhou Experience. After first stressing that the latter had "achieved outstanding results and is eminently deserving of our emulation," they thus declared:

> [W]e ourselves at all times persist in using Mao Zedong Thought to re-educate, reform and manage the mentally ill, and practice has shown us that doing this task well always has a positive effect on their treatment and management and helps to prevent their illnesses from recurring. In studying and learning from the Chenzhou experience, we have gained an even deeper understanding of these matters…
>
> Studying the Chenzhou experience has further strengthened our determination to employ Mao Zedong Thought as a means of re-educating and reforming the mentally ill, and we have now begun pursuing this task in a variety of different ways. Practice has shown that when we do a good job in this area, the political atmosphere in the wards becomes rich and all-pervasive, the mental patients' thinking and ideology undergo a total transformation, and an orderly and well-structured climate for treatment and cure is thereby created.[294]

In short, by cloaking their heterodox theory of mental illness so heavily and comprehensively in the mantle of Mao Zedong Thought, the Hunan psychiatrists had in effect rendered it politically unchallengeable. For to question the theory on any fundamental level – and in particular, its political-style "treatment" aspects – would have been tantamount, in the eyes of China's ever-vigilant political censors at that time, to repudiating the wisdom and omnipotence of Mao himself. The true scale of any "silent opposition" that may have existed toward this theory among China's psychiatrists during the mid- to late-1970s remains unknown, but it seems reasonable to assume that it was probably quite extensive. In practice, however, as was the case with so many other deeply unpopular ultra-leftist doctrines that were imposed as sacrosanct wisdom from above by the country's political leadership during that period, the Hunan psychiatrists' exclusively class-based theory of mental illness appears to have continued to predominate over all competing medical points of view throughout Mao's final years. Indeed it became, if anything, even more harsh and punitive in nature – and from any normal standpoint of medical or psychiatric ethics, downright offensive – as time went on.

"Lancing the Boil": Thought Reform for the Mentally Ill

Probably the most complete and systematic expression of the various constituent elements of the theory – the medical reductionism, the crude political universalism, and the insistence that the mentally ill had only their own "unreformed bourgeois worldviews" to blame for their unfortunate state of health – can be found in an article written by Jia Rubao (a psychiatrist from Shaanxi Province and one of those who had participated in the original "250 Cases" survey) that appeared in the above-mentioned

---

[294] "Study and Discussion Notes on 'Analysis of a Survey of 250 Cases of Mental Illness'," by unnamed authors from Yichun District Mental Hospital, Jiangxi Province, *Xin Yixue (New Medicine)*, 1973, Vol.4, No.3, pp.176-178; cover date March 15, 1973.

Guangzhou medical journal in April 1977. Jia began his account by assigning overall primacy to the forces of politics and the class struggle in the genesis of mental illness:

> It is social existence that determines people's consciousness and the realities of the class struggle that determine people's ideology and emotions. "In class society everyone lives as a member of a particular class, and every kind of thinking, without exception, is stamped with the brand of a class." (Chairman Mao, "On Practice," [1937] *Selected Works of Mao Zedong*, p.272.) For this reason, the content of the psychiatric symptoms of the mentally ill (their thoughts, emotions, behaviour and also the imbalance between these things and the environment) is all closely bound up with the reality of the three great revolutionary struggles[295]; that is to say, [these symptoms] are a reflection of the different ideologies, cultures, customs and beliefs, emotions and sentiments of different societies (classes.)

Since class struggle lay at the heart of the mental healthcare enterprise, it followed that the principal task of psychiatrists now became, in effect, to "pursue politics by other means" – that is, to wage virtual class warfare within the minds of mental patients throughout the country's mental hospital wards. But were the mentally ill themselves to be viewed and treated as the "victims" or as the "culprits" in this process? Puzzlingly enough, the ultra-Maoist theory concerning the "essential nature" of mental illness appears, in practice, to have assigned them both roles simultaneously. In practice, however, the emphasis was placed firmly on the latter role. As Jia stridently explained:

> Mental illness, therefore, is not, as the bourgeoisie would have us believe, a "supra-class, solely biological phenomenon," but rather something that is inextricably linked with the class struggle and with the clash between the two major worldviews. Indeed, the pathological thoughts [harboured by the mentally ill] are simply a continuation of the normal thoughts that existed prior to the onset of illness. As we know from their own post-recovery accounts, the mentally ill are often people who previously were obsessed with considerations of personal gain and loss, were backward and had no desire to make progress in life, had failed to employ the methodology of "one divides into two" in dealing with their problems and resorted instead to mere hair-splitting and self-justification, and who were drowning fast in the sea of individualism. They paid no attention to the advice of others and so the struggle between contradictions became more and more intense in their minds, leaving them in a constant state of agitation and insomnia, with no interest in food, and increasingly withdrawn and isolated.
>
> The process goes exactly like this: under the socialist system, it is impossible for these people to satisfy their selfish desires and so the "boil" cannot be lanced; at first, the normal thoughts and the pathological thoughts coexist side by side, but as the pathological thoughts steadily gain the ascendant in their minds, they begin to sing, dance and run around aimlessly, tearing off their clothes and going around naked, and sometimes injuring or killing people – that is, they become mentally ill. We see, therefore, that bourgeois worldview and methodology are the fundamental

---

295 In Maoist political discourse, the phrase "three great revolutionary movements" (*san-da geming yundong*) denoted "the struggle for production, the class struggle and scientific experimentation."

> causal factors in the emergence of mental illness; indeed this is the essential nature of mental illness.
>
> Some people will ask the question: in capitalist society, then, is mental illness more commonly found among the bourgeois class? Yes, there are certainly more mentally ill people from this class background than elsewhere. But…the bourgeois scholars absolutely never try to study or analyse the problem in this light…

According to Jia's theory, therefore, the problems of the mentally ill could be traced directly back to their own inner-subjective state of "political backwardness" – that is, their alleged selfishness or obsession with personal gain, and their alleged rampant individualism. Moreover, all of these personal political defects were seen, in turn, as being reflections or products of the continued stubborn adherence of those concerned to the "bourgeois worldview" (specifically, their alleged nostalgia for the private ownership system) and hence – most serious of all – to their perceived underlying hostility toward the "proletarian worldview," the public ownership system and indeed socialism in general. As was noted above, the ineluctable logic of this analysis was that the mentally ill should henceforth be treated, in essence, as being among the targets of the much-feared "dictatorship of the proletariat." All of this, of course, was said to be for the patients' own good: as mentally ill people, their victim status could scarcely be denied, and the ostensible purpose of the political-style "treatment" process was therefore to restore them to a rude and archetypically proletarian state of mental well-being and vigour, as widely depicted in the posters and murals of contemporary socialist-realist art.[296]

As Mao famously observed, "a revolution is not a dinner party" – that is, to make an omelette one must break eggs. And in this particular case, it was clearly also vital (to cite another of Mao's favourite sayings) "to cure the illness in order to save the patient." Mao used this latter phrase in a metaphorical sense: in waging major political struggles, he observed, it was useless to focus only on "symptoms" and instead vital to correctly diagnose and treat the underlying "sickness." However, the dictum is doubly apt in the present context, since the stated purpose of the ultra-leftist "psychotherapy" process that Chinese psychiatrists like Jia were so zealously advocating during the mid- to late-1970s was simultaneously medical and political in nature: namely, to "cure" the mentally ill of their psychic and emotional afflictions by relentlessly and systematically breaking down their perceived political resistance to socialism and the "proletarian worldview." In practice, therefore, the country's mental patients were expected to undergo, much as in the case of sentenced criminals in China after 1949, a sustained process of "thought reform" (*sixiang gaizao*: the "brainwashing" of Cold War popular parlance) – an essentially punitive process designed to rid them of their pathologically "anti-social" thoughts and tendencies and to reconstruct them afresh in the image of Mao's "socialist new man."

The main elements of this "therapeutic" process – the actual results of which, in the case of the many thousands of people suffering from such severe mental conditions as chronic paranoid schizophrenia who were actually subjected to it, can scarcely be imagined – were exhaustively enumerated by Jia in the following check-list of tasks:

> Our own approach, by contrast [with that of bourgeois psychiatry], is: "Examine the symptoms, find the causes, and treat the illness at its source."
>
> [In practice,] this means combining Chinese and Western medicine; persisting in using Mao Zedong Thought to re-educate and reform the mentally ill and also arming

---

296 See, for example, *Picturing Power in the People's Republic of China: Posters of the Cultural Revolution*, Harriet Evans and Stephanie Donald (eds.), Rowman & Littlefield Publishers, Inc., 1999.

their minds with the weapon of Mao Zedong Thought; fully mobilizing within them the positive role of subjective dynamism;[297] ... using class education and political-line education to profoundly re-educate the mentally ill in the proletarian worldview, and thereby implant within them a correct conception of human destiny, romantic love, and personal pleasure and hardship; hooking them up with reality by educating them about both the current [political] situation and the principles of dialectical materialism, and by raising their awareness of the class struggle, the struggle over political line, and the necessity of continuing the revolution under the dictatorship of the proletariat; digging out the roots of mental illness by overthrowing the concept of private ownership and establishing the principle of public ownership, and in so doing wage a stubborn battle against disease by engendering the lofty and far-sighted ideals of Communism and convincing the patients of the inevitability of victory; ...

If we do all these things well, then the overwhelming majority (90 percent) of mentally ill people can be completely cured.... Moreover, as the socialist revolution deepens over time, and as the new-style medical science of combining Chinese and Western medicine unfolds and develops, not only will a broad new vista emerge on the mental illness preventative front in China, but also the non-organic mental illnesses[298] will become more and more rare, eventually disappearing altogether.[299]

The logical corollary of this theory, of course, was that the massed ranks of the international bourgeoisie and imperialist class would all, in the fullness of time, go completely and irrevocably mad. But here, Jia's analytical courage seems to have failed him and this most startling of political-psychiatric conclusions was left unstated.

Some Preliminary Observations

As the above account shows, the scale and severity of the politically-inspired corruption of psychiatric ethics that occurred in China during the Cultural Revolution decade went well beyond anything of a similar nature that had already taken place, or was yet to occur, within the former Soviet Union and certain of its satellite states. Indeed, China's negative experience during those years appears to have been of both a quantitatively and a qualitatively higher order altogether. Where Soviets psychiatrists for the most part had confined their application of the concept of "political insanity" to a relatively small subsection of the nation's political and religious dissident population, and moreover had restricted its clinical use to the single and rather rarely-invoked diagnostic label of "sluggish schizophrenia," during the mid- to late 1970s their Chinese counterparts succeeded in universalising the underlying concepts and practices of political psychiatry to the point where almost every kind of mental illness was seen as falling within its "therapeutic" orbit. The result of this global politicisation of the psychiatric profession

---

297 See Note 277, above.
298 Psychiatrists generally distinguish between "organic" mental illnesses, i.e. those caused by external damage to the brain or by physical pathology within it, and the "non-organic" or "psychogenic" mental illnesses that result from psychic or emotional conflicts and trauma.
299 Jia Rubao, "More on the Essential Nature of Mental Illness," (Employees' Hospital of the Huashan Metallurgy and Vehicle Repair Plant, Huayin, Shaanxi Province), *Xin Yixue – Shenjing Xitong Jibing Fukan (New Medicine – Supplementary Series on Diseases of the Nervous System)*, 1977, Vol.3, No.2, pp.142-143; article dated April 1977. It is clear from this article that the author was also one of the authors of the above-cited "Analysis of a Survey of 250 Cases of Mental Illness."

in China was that huge numbers of ordinary and entirely non-dissident mental patients around the country came to be treated, in effect, as if they were the "class enemy."

This phenomenon was vividly outlined by a psychiatrist from Beijing, writing in 1979 at a time when the Cultural Revolution had only just been formally repudiated by the Party and government:

> In recent years, owing to past sabotage by the "Gang of Four," it is not surprising that we psychiatrists often still have a sense of fear and trepidation. For example, when we discuss the role played by "negative mood" (*fuxing qingxu*) in the illness-course of neurasthenia, we are criticized by people who insist that in China, any mention of "negative mood" is the equivalent of talking about "feelings of dissatisfaction" (*buman qingxu.*) According to this logic, because China has an advanced and superior socialist system, people should not be suffering from unhappy feelings of any kind – whether anxiety, depression, sadness or just low spirits – and if people do feel any of these things, it is because they harbour "dissatisfaction toward socialism" (*dui shehuizhuyi buman.*)[300]

It is sobering to ponder just how far this disastrous trend might ultimately have gone had not the death of Mao finally intervened, in September 1976, prompting the return to power of Deng Xiaoping some two years later and the start in China of what thereafter became known as the "era of opening and reform". A major element in the growing official critique of the Cultural Revolution that unfolded after Mao's death was the charge that the ultra-leftist leadership had deliberately fostered an "artificial expansion of the scope of class struggle" in all walks of life in China during that period. Viewed in this light, China's mentally ill population may be seen as merely one social subgroup among many that contributed to the tragically high overall numbers of victims produced by the nation's ten-year encounter with extreme Maoist fanaticism.

There was, however, a certain singularity or uniqueness about the way in which the ultra-leftist authorities in China attempted to deal with the mentally ill population, as compared to their handling of other, similarly problematical target groups in society. The reason for this appears to have stemmed, in the first instance, from the fact that the phenomenon of mental illness in general, being essentially a disorder of the brain and of the normal thought processes, proved to be uncomfortably close to – indeed, for the ultra-Maoists, intimately intertwined with – the all-important realm of political thought and ideology. Mao had always placed inordinate emphasis on the importance of implanting "correct political ideology" among each and every citizen, and during the Cultural Revolution unprecedented quantities of official energy were expended in trying to uphold, reinforce and police this same principle – above all, through the rooting out of "incorrect" or "erroneous" political thoughts wherever they could be found. Consequently, the vast majority of the population made substantial and very conscious efforts to bring their individual speech and behaviour into close conformity with the officially presented paradigm of political virtue and rectitude – and not infrequently, such assiduous "toeing of the Party line" required quite spectacular feats of ideological gymnastics, since the line itself was constantly changing and in flux.

---

300 See: Zhong Youbin, "*Dui Woguo Jingshenbingxue Xianzhuang de Jidian Yijian Ji Dui Zhuanye Kanwu de Xiwang*" (Several Viewpoints on the Current State of Psychiatry in China and Some Hopes for Our Specialist Journals and Periodicals), *Shenjing Jingshen Jibing Zazhi* (Journal of Nervous and Mental Diseases), 1979, Vol.5, No.4, pp.220-1.

But mentally ill people, especially those who were quite severely disturbed, tended to behave very differently and in ways that would surely have struck the Party's ubiquitous "thought police" as being deeply suspect and unsettling. Typically, the mentally ill would display little or none of the kind of self-protective caution, or constant political circumspection and self-censorship, in which ordinary members of the Chinese public since 1949 have become, of necessity, the virtual world experts. Depending on the specific nature of their illness, they would either behave quite uninhibitedly – speaking their minds frankly and openly on any and all topics of conversation that might arise, however politically controversial; or they would be unusually withdrawn and taciturn – hence failing to provide the requisite enthusiastic public endorsement (*biao tai*) of whatever new policy the Party might be espousing at that particular moment. Either way, they would have laid themselves wide open to the diligent and enthusiastic attentions of the Cultural Revolution's "political correctness" squads.

What greatly compounded the ultra-leftist authorities' dilemma in dealing with such people was the fact that – as scholarly fieldwork by Chinese psychiatrists has subsequently shown quite clearly[301] – a surprisingly high proportion of the inmates of China's mental hospitals at that time had become seriously mentally ill as a direct consequence of the incessant political campaigns that the Party had been waging throughout the country since 1949. In numerous other cases, moreover, people who had become mentally ill for reasons not directly connected with politics had nonetheless been so heavily influenced by those same campaigns that they, too, tended to express their illnesses symptomatically in the form of politically coloured thought, speech or behaviour. Most dangerously of all for those concerned, this very often took the form of uninhibited outbursts of anger directed specifically against Mao and the Communist Party.

There is as yet no specific documentary evidence to support this idea, but a preliminary working hypothesis as to why Chinese psychiatry became so rapidly and highly over-politicised during the Cultural Revolution would be that when the Red Guards first entered China's mental hospitals in the summer of 1966 to begin pursuing their campaign of "reversing the psychiatric verdicts," they were aghast to discover that substantial numbers of the inmate population appeared to be openly and flagrantly hostile towards both Mao and the Party. Given the broader social and political atmosphere of the time, whereby for example the inadvertent wearing of a Mao badge in an upside-down position by an ordinary citizen could be taken as proof positive of a "counterrevolutionary conspiracy," what could the mostly teenaged political zealots who made up the ranks of the Red Guards at that time reasonably be expected to make of a mentally ill person who shouted "Down with Chairman Mao!" straight in their faces – other than that the hospital in question was in all likelihood a veritable hotbed of dangerously anti-government thought and activity?

The Post-Mao Counterattack: Humane Psychiatry Responds

Significantly, the first major challenge mounted by a Chinese psychiatrist against the Cultural Revolutionary diagnostic and treatment model, an article published in the same Guangzhou *neibu* medical journal in the summer of 1976, sought directly to grapple with several of the themes and issues just mentioned. It was written by Professor Yang Desen, a veteran psychiatrist from the Hunan Medical College who had himself endured much persecution during the Cultural Revolution, and who is now one of the most influential and respected psychiatrists in China. What is most remarkable about Yang's article is that it was written one month before the death of Mao, at a time when even the slightest

---

301 See articles cited at Notes 415–417 below.

form of criticism of the Cultural Revolution – public or private, direct or veiled – and its associated policies could easily bring disgrace, arrest or worse to the person making it. (The Cultural Revolution was formally and openly repudiated by the new Deng Xiaoping government only in October 1979.) It would thus be hard to overstate the degree of personal bravery that Yang showed at this time, in frontally challenging the Cultural Revolution orthodoxy whereby all mental illness was said to be caused by politically deviant thinking on the part of the sufferer.

Refuting the "Ideological Defect" Theory

Professor Yang's August 1976 article, entitled "Mental Disease Cannot be Regarded as an Ideological Defect: An Opinion on the Essential Nature of Mental Illness,"[302] evoked over the subsequent two years a tide of written responses from other psychiatrists around China expressing almost unanimous support for his position. At the outset of his article, Yang boldly broached the central issue of whether or not mentally ill people ought to be held politically responsible for their "erroneous" thoughts and statements:

> Distorted reflections of objective reality can be found in normal people's thinking as well as in the minds of the mentally ill. In the latter case, this is caused by the presence of disease in the brain, and one of the ways it expresses itself is through mentally pathological thoughts. In the former case, the brain itself is not defective, and the various manifestations – such as erroneous thoughts and ideology, the presence of [philosophically] idealist theory, religious superstitions, and prejudiced and one-sided notions of various kinds – are all rooted in the question of [political] class and epistemology. When erroneous ideas emerge in the minds of normal people, they can usually be resolved in the course of social practice and through persuasion and re-education. But mentally pathological thoughts and ideas are produced by illness, arising in train with the development of the disease and then disappearing once the illness has been cured; so they do not amount to a simple question of epistemological error, and the two situations are essentially different. While in general terms one can say that mentally pathological thoughts also fall under the heading of incorrect cognition and understanding, it is nonetheless quite wrong to lump these two things together.
>
> What points of commonality and difference exist, then, between the pathological thoughts of the mentally ill (for example, hallucinatory and delusional content) and the erroneous ideology of normal people? This question has not yet been openly discussed in China. Comrade Stalin gave an explication of this issue in his writings on the relationship between Marxism and linguistics;[303] and in China in the 1960s, when our philosophers discussed the question of the unity between thought and existence, the majority viewpoint held that erroneous thoughts and [social] existence also occur in unity. All this provides a source of enlightenment for us in the present discussion.

---

302 Yang Desen, "Mental Disease Cannot be Regarded as an Ideological Defect: An Opinion on the Essential Nature of Mental Illness," *Xin Yixue–Jingshen Xitong Jibing Fukan* (New Medicine–Supplementary Series on Diseases of the Nervous System), 1976, Vol. 2, No. 3, pp.187-189.
303 See: J.V. Stalin, *Marxism and Problems of Linguistics*, first published in the June 20, July 4, and August 2, 1950 issues of *Pravda*.

The seminal philosophical debate of the late 1950s and early 1960s in China on the relationship between "thought and existence" (*siwei yu cunzai* or *yishi yu cunzai*: also translatable as "being and consciousness") centred primarily on the question of whether thought, consciousness and ideology were the product of external social conditions and circumstances, or if on the contrary (as Mao seemed often to believe) it was the former that mainly "determined" the latter.[304] The debate was extremely complex and wide-ranging and had numerous sensitive political ramifications.[305] Significantly, as Vladimir Bukovsky explained, the same set of ideological concerns had also loomed large in the context of Soviet forensic psychiatry:

> The ruling doctrine asserts that being determines consciousness. As Socialism has been built in the USSR, and Communism is being built, the consciousness of people must be exclusively Communist. Where then, can belief in God appear from, if for 60 years atheism has been propagated and the preaching of religion outlawed? And from where does an opponent of Communism come – in a Communist society?
>
> Within the confines of Communist doctrine there are only two possible explanations: the cause must lie either in subversive activity directed from abroad – i.e. every dissenter has been bought or recruited by the imperialists; or in mental illness: dissent is just a manifestation of pathological processes in the psyche.
>
> As life in the USSR does not develop freely, but is "interpreted by the Party", these two principles mean that every dissenter whom it is difficult or inconvenient to pursue under the first heading is automatically assigned to the second.[306]

This again was essentially the "hyperdiagnosis" model of legal or forensic psychiatry. The more specific, and subtly different, issue that Yang Desen wanted to consider in this context, however, was that of whether the pathological thoughts, fantasies and delusions expressed by the mentally ill could – as his ultra-leftist colleagues had insisted – be traced back to and explained by the patients' pre-illness political and ideological worldviews. As was suggested earlier in our discussion, this latter doctrine was more the hallmark of a particularly pernicious form of psychiatric "hypodiagnosis": the view that the mentally ill were really the victims of their own political backwardness, and that the diagnosis and treatment of mental illness could therefore be reduced to – or rather replaced by – a process of political analysis and indoctrination. Doubtless lest he be accused of fundamentally opposing Maoist epistemological verities, Professor Yang began by making the following tactical concession to his adversaries' argument:

---

304 The philosopher Yang Xianzhen was one of the chief protagonists in this debate; see Note 287 above.
305 The "correct" epistemological standpoint on such matters, as laid down by Stalin among others, was the orthodox Marxist view that individual thought and consciousness were the direct product, or "reflection" within the human brain, of external and material social realities. (Thus, for example, a citizen living under the socialist system could be expected "naturally" to cleave to the proletarian worldview; while on a more abstract political level, the "economically determinist" implications were that it would be pointlessly premature for the Communist Party to pursue a program of radical socialist change on the basis of a still backward and underdeveloped agrarian economy.) This general understanding of the issues, however, came into sharp and awkward conflict with Mao's parallel insistence on the transformative power of the human will – a key feature of his political philosophy and one that he invoked often during the early 1960s and beyond by stressing the unique value of "subjective dynamism" (*zhuguan nengdongxing*.)
306 From Bukovsky's Foreword to Bloch and Reddaway, *Russia's Political Hospitals* (op cit), p.14.

> What must be clarified here is that the pathological thoughts of mentally ill people do constitute a distorted reflection of objective reality. This is a fundamental question relating to our continued staunch adherence, in the field of psychiatry, to the materialist theory of reflection.[307] The content of the delusions in the minds of the mentally ill has a clear social nature and a clear class nature.
>
> With delusions of grandeur, for example, a person's belief that he or she is an emperor, prime minister or general would be a reflection of the feudal social consciousness; while in the case of those believing themselves to be model workers, it would serve to reflect the social consciousness of the socialist system. Similarly, a [mentally ill] person's belief that he or she was a landlord or a capitalist would, under the psychiatric symptomatology of the old [pre-1949] society, have manifested itself as a delusion of grandeur accompanied by a sense of elation; whereas the same belief in the new society would serve to express something quite different: namely a delusion of guilt or culpability, accompanied by feelings of depression...
>
> All this shows us that the content of mental delusions changes over time and in accordance with the trends of social change and development, and that such content is entirely a transplanted and distorted reflection of objective reality.

Having adroitly covered his political back in this way, Yang then proceeded to the real nub of his argument:

> We should now consider the further question: what is the nature of the interrelationship between the pathological thoughts and ideology of the mentally ill and the normal thoughts and ideology they had prior to falling ill?
>
> Some people maintain that pathological thoughts are simply a continuation of the normal thoughts found prior to the onset of illness, and that if any changes occur, these can only be quantitative and not qualitative in nature. Putting the matter bluntly, they maintain that the pathological thoughts provide a naked, wholesale revelation of the true thoughts and ideology that the mental patients had prior to falling ill. And moreover, they attribute the fact that the patients concerned did not express such thoughts before they fell ill, and that they hastily try to repudiate such thoughts after recovering their mental health, to mere phoney and disingenuous attempts by the patients to conceal their true thoughts. They then conclude that the patients' expression of pathological thoughts provides the clearest possible indication of the essential nature of their underlying ideology...
>
> According to this general perspective, all the symptoms of mental illness are fundamentally rooted in the patient's pre-illness ideological and political-class background, and moreover a positive identification of the patient's ideological awareness and character can be made on the basis of these symptoms.

As Yang swiftly pointed out, however, a wealth of practical clinical experience flatly contradicted any such simplistic and mechanistic theory of causation as this:

---

307 "*weiwuzhuyi fanyinglun*": the Marxist epistemological doctrine whereby all human mental activity is seen as being rooted in, and ultimately reflective of, events and circumstances occurring in the "material" realm.

> [A] great many of the pathological thoughts found among those suffering from the most common form of severe mental illness, schizophrenia, cannot be explained at all on the basis of this theory: for example, a schizophrenic from a stable and harmonious family background who starts suspecting that his mother or spouse is trying to poison him or that his infant son is keeping him under surveillance; or the case of a revolutionary cadre who, because of his mentally disordered condition, starts claiming that he has committed major crimes of counterrevolution. In these cases, no causal interconnection whatsoever can be found between the patient's pre-illness thoughts and ideas and those that arise after the onset of illness; the latter are diametrically opposed to the former, and the patients themselves, after recovery, see them as absurd and ridiculous.

In a still more telling example, Yang then took direct aim at the ultra-leftist school of psychiatry's cynical readiness to interpret the "politically hostile" utterances of many mentally ill people at that time wholly at face value:

> Another example is that of a schizophrenic who suffered from auditory hallucinations in which he heard his neighbour swearing and cursing at him. In reality, the neighbour was a bad person, but the patient's psychiatric symptoms then assumed the form of a determination on his part to do battle against all bad people and things. Eventually he moved house, but the auditory hallucinations then began to contain the voice of his new neighbour – who happened to be a leading official in his work unit. The patient's mental symptoms took the form of making frequent complaints and bizarre statements [about the leading cadre], and in the end they escalated to the level of an outright and open confrontation between him and the entire organizational leadership. As an indicator of his [political] ideological awareness, therefore, the psychiatric symptoms of the very same patient were transformed, in essence, into their own diametrical opposite… It is hard to connect or reconcile any of these kinds of phenomena with the pre-illness ideological realities of those concerned.

Professor Yang's forthright and eloquent conclusion on all of this was as follows:

> By indiscriminately and matter-of-factly applying the methodology of analysing normal people's thinking to the task of analysing the pathological thoughts of the mentally ill, and in the process equating the latter with the erroneous ideological tendencies of normal people and hence overestimating the role played by mental factors in the genesis of different types of mental illness, it becomes all too easy to start seeing mental illness itself as constituting an "ideological defect" (*sixiang maobing*.)

> But the absurd content of the pathological thoughts generally eludes any such kind of strict ideological source analysis, and attempts to extrapolate from these pathological thoughts to the nature of the patient's pre-illness ideological consciousness can therefore easily lead one to an extremely superficial conclusion: namely, that all mental illness is caused by the extreme and unchecked development of individualism.[308] Public opinion in general, and also people who have done no serious investigation or systematic observation of the essential nature of mental illness, are all too ready

---

308 *"jingshenbing dou shi gerenzhuyi jiduan fazhan de jieguo"*

to accept and give credence to this kind of conclusion. This in turn easily creates a public mindset whereby mentally ill people are universally looked down upon and discriminated against, to the point even where certain individuals try to prosecute and hold mentally ill people legally responsible in all kinds of ways for their pathological speech and behaviour, although those concerned have no actual capacity to bear such responsibility.

Mental disease, therefore, cannot be equated with defective ideology. Severe mental illness can result in death or long-term disablement, and what the patients urgently need is medication and treatment. There is a world of difference between their situation and that of normal people who display ideological defects, and the two must not be put on a par.

Finally, it is indicative of the all-powerful hegemony that the Party's perception of nonconformist or dissident speech and behaviour as posing a fundamental political threat to society had come to exert in Chinese public discourse since 1949 that even Yang, in his closing remarks, felt the need not only to partially endorse the positive role of Maoist-style ideological indoctrination in the treatment of the mentally ill, but also to stress the need for those whose symptoms assumed the unfortunate form of banned political expression to be forcibly hospitalised. As he explained,

Precisely because mentally ill people still retain a certain amount of normal brain activity, they are able, just like normal people, to benefit from re-education based on Marxism and Mao Zedong Thought; their inner subjective dynamism can be mobilized and they can engage in battle against their illnesses. Psychotherapy is very important, [but] it neither precludes nor can totally substitute for pharmaceutical medications. The speech and behaviour of mentally ill people may well have adverse influence and effects upon society, and all erroneous things should of course be subjected to appropriate criticism and must not be permitted to spread unchecked or to threaten public order and stability. [Such people] should be subjected to compulsory treatment and we should reinforce management over them; this is essential for purposes of safeguarding both the interests of society and also the personal interests of the mentally ill.

In a sense, the closing line of Yang's last paragraph said it all. For his implicit meaning was that so personally dangerous had Chinese society become, at that time, for anyone expressing political views departing from the official line, that if mentally ill people who did so even for purely psychopathological reasons were not locked safely away in mental hospitals they would instead, in all likelihood, be arrested by the police and imprisoned as "counterrevolutionary criminals."

Chinese Psychiatry Awakens from the Nightmare

In the short space of the two months following the publication of Yang's August 1976 article, two historic events occurred that were eventually to change China's social and political landscape almost beyond recognition: Mao's death on September 9, and the summary arrest by an elite unit of the PLA several weeks later of his most senior political followers and henchmen in the Communist Party leadership, the so-called Gang of Four. A several-year period of intensive intra-Party purges then ensued across the country, in which many thousands of ultra-leftist officials who had risen to power during the Cultural Revolution decade were public denounced either as "vicious anti-Party conspirators" or as "residual poisonous dregs of the Gang of Four" and then likewise placed under arrest. Many of them later received sentences of life imprisonment and a substantial minority were eventually executed.[309]

During the same period, an unprecedented renaissance occurred within most branches of the social and natural sciences in China, as the nation's intelligentsia proceeded joyfully and exuberantly to rid itself of the ideological straitjacket of rigidly ultra-leftist orthodoxy in which it had been so stiflingly wrapped for over a decade. The sense of unalloyed relief that accompanied this dramatic "movement for the liberation of thought," as the post-Mao government soon dubbed it, was no less widespread and intense within the country's psychiatric profession than in all other walks of life in China at that time.

As mentioned above, Yang Desen's preliminary critique of Cultural Revolutionary policies and practices in the field of mental healthcare drew forth an enthusiastically supportive response from many of his colleagues around the country, and two years later, in August 1978, he was invited by the editors of the Guangzhou medical journal that had carried his original piece to wrap up the debate by presenting a condensed version of the main points and highlights of the best of these various contributions. (It should be noted in passing that this medical journal still only appeared on a *neibu* or "restricted circulation" basis, and that it was one of only a tiny handful of such journals published throughout China at that time; none of the country's specialist psychiatric journals had as yet resumed publication.)

The general tone of this concluding contribution to the crucial two year-long debate was laid down in an accompanying editorial note:

> Since issue No.3, 1976, this journal has given space to an academic debate on the question of the essential character and nature of mental illness. This debate has attracted the widespread support and attention of our readership and many people have sent us manuscripts expressing their viewpoints. All this became possible only after the smashing of the "Gang of Four" by our brilliant leader Chairman Hua Guofeng and the Party Central Committee and as a result of their promotion of the policy of "letting a hundred flowers bloom and a hundred schools of thought contend."

Yang's August 1978 article was so well argued and comprehensive in scope, and so quietly devastating in its impact, that little would be gained and much of value lost by any attempt merely to summarize it. The complete article reads as follows:

Subjective Conjecture is no Substitute for Scientific Research[310]

(A Summary of Readers' Views)

Yang Desen, August 1978

> The article by Comrade Yang Desen in Issue No.3, 1976 of this journal and the article by Comrade Jia Rubao in Issue No.2, 1977 presented fundamentally opposite views on the question of the essential nature of mental illness.[311] Both these viewpoints are quite influential both within domestic social opinion as a whole and among medical personnel in the psychiatric field. The debate has attracted strong interest and support

---

309 Robin Munro, "China's Ultra-left on Trial: The Purge of the Gang of Four," 1988, unpublished research paper for Amnesty International.
310 *Xin Yixue– Shenjing Xitong Jibing Fukan* (New Medicine – Supplementary Series on Diseases of the Nervous System), 1978, Vol.4, No.5-6 (cover date August 20, 1978), pp.329-332. The translation of Yang's article, and of all the other primary source documents cited in this book, was done by the present author.
311 See the articles cited at Notes 299 and 302 above.

from everyone and has been closely followed, understandably enough, by many mentally ill people and their families. We have received eleven separate articles supporting Yang's position,[312] and since for reasons of space we cannot publish these articles in their entirety, we have instead put together a summary digest of the main points and arguments.

1. First of all, we must define more narrowly the real scope of this debate; otherwise the controversy will remain diffuse and unfocused. (Manuscripts 1 & 2.)

Apart from the neuroses and mental retardation, mental illnesses generally fall into one of three main categories, and opinions were basically unanimous on the first two of these categories, with controversy being focused mainly on the last category. First, there are the organic and symptomatic mental illnesses, caused by infection, poisoning, external injury or somatic disease; opinions were unanimous and no conflict of views arose with regard to this category of illness. Second, there are the psychogenic and reactive psychoses, which appear in susceptible individuals as a result of intense psychological pressures and stimuli; cases of this type are few in number, with such reactions being much more commonly found among neurosis sufferers, and again opinions were pretty much united in regard to this category. And third, there is the major category known as the endogenous mental illnesses, foremost among which is schizophrenia, whose causal factors still remain to be discovered; the controversy was centred primarily on this category of mental illness.

On the one hand, while some outstanding research discoveries have been made in the fields of psycho-biochemistry, genetics, neuropathology, psychopharmacology and experimental psychiatry, these have still not produced any affirmative conclusions on the question in hand. On the other hand, only in certain specific cases [of schizophrenia] can we observe, prior to the onset of illness, the presence of any clear and conspicuous elements of psychological pressure or stimulus. Thus far, [schizophrenia] has always been known as a "functional" psychosis; some scholars, however, both at home and abroad, now regard it as being similar in nature to idiopathic epilepsy, that is to say, they see it as being an organic brain disorder caused by certain as yet unknown genetic defects or metabolic disorders. The controversy over the nature of the factors causing schizophrenia has therefore centred upon two main issues: first, the question of how to assess the role played by psychological pressure or stimuli in the genesis of the disease; and second, the question of the connection between the formation of mental illness and the nature of the sufferer's worldview and methodology.

---

312 The various readers' contributions to the debate were listed and identified in the article as follows: 1) Zhu Xixi, "My Views on the Question of the Essential Nature of Mental Illness"; 2) Yu Zhanfei, "Some Rough Opinions on the Causes and Treatment of Mental Illness"; 3) Liu Hengwen, "A Discussion of the Causal Factors Leading to Mental Illness"; 4) Long Yaxian, "Reflections Upon Reading [Jia Rubao's] 'More on the Essential Nature of Mental Illness'"; 5) Sun Ru, "Taking Issue with Comrade Jia Rubao on the Question of the Essential Nature of Mental Illness"; 6) He Xingqing, "Subjective Conjecture is No Substitute for Scientific Research"; 7) Zhang Jiejie, "Mental Illness is Not an 'Ideological defect'"; 8) Ding Qinzhang, "Do 'Ideological Problems' Play the Leading Role in the Causation of Mental Illness?"; 9) Cao Songyao, "Marxist Philosophy Provides a Compass for Understanding the Essential Nature of Mental Illness"; 10) Yan Shengmei, "The Study of Dialectics is the Guide to Medical Practice"; and 11) Lu Lizhao, "Taking Issue with Comrade Jia Rubao."

2. Mental illness is a common disease that afflicts the ordinary working populace; it has always existed and can be found both in China and all other countries. Just as in the case of high blood pressure-induced ulcers or other disorders, mental illness knows no class boundaries or divisions. (Manuscripts 3 & 4.)

Comrade Jia maintains that in capitalist societies "there are certainly more" mentally ill people from within the bourgeois classes than from elsewhere in society. Some people questioned whether any actual survey data exists to support this view, while others maintained that the exact opposite is true: that since there is usually a direct link between poverty and illness, it is by no means clear that the working people of capitalist societies – given the oppression and exploitation they are under, the psychological distress and practical difficulties they experience in daily life, and also their lack of access to medical treatment – are at all less likely than others to be afflicted by mental illness. According to surveys by certain foreign scholars, the incidence of mental illness (including mental retardation) among the population has been found to be inversely proportional to family income and standard of living, that is, it occurs more frequently among the impoverished social classes, and it would be wrong for us to discount these findings as having no basis in fact. Seen in this light, mental illness is rather like tuberculosis, in that, whether in the old society or the new, it strikes disproportionately against the working population.

We cannot, therefore, in disregard of the plight of large numbers of working people who suffer from mental illness and in the absence of any compelling scientific evidence, simply claim that mental illness is a disease of the bourgeoisie, a disease of capitalist society. In our own view, within the field of health and hygiene, the superiority of the socialist system lies mainly in the fact that socialism seeks, by universally expanding disease prevention work and the social welfare system, to reduce the incidence of diseases of all kinds among the working population and to wipe out the serious infectious illnesses. In the case, however, of certain illnesses whose causes are still unknown – for example cancer, cardiovascular disease and schizophrenia – thus far, and irrespective of national boundaries, the disease incidence rates have shown no sign of declining; to the contrary, as mortality rates fall, they have been steadily rising. The objective existence of schizophrenia, therefore, cannot be explained away as being the product of any particular social system; indeed, there is a much more conspicuous causal connection to be seen between certain organic mental illnesses, such as those induced by syphilis, alcoholism and narcotic addiction, and the particular nature of the social system. Under the superior kind of social system that we live in today, what we ought to be doing is widely to publicize a correct understanding of the essential nature of mental illness and diligently to pursue the tasks of disease prevention and cure. What we should not do is either to commit the error of thinking that by acknowledging the objective existence of mental illness in our society we will somehow be harming China's reputation, or to prematurely set ourselves the goal and task of eliminating all mental illness, in the belief that it is somehow incompatible with our [superior] social system.[313] Neither of these approaches is at all conducive to a facts-based resolution of the problem.

3. We cannot accept that bourgeois worldview and methodology is the main and fundamental factor causing mental illness. (Manuscripts 1-11.)

The contributors were unanimous in rejecting Comrade Jia's contention that "A bourgeois worldview and methodology are the fundamental causal factors in the emergence of mental illness; indeed this is the essential nature of mental illness." They opposed this viewpoint from a range of angles and on various different grounds, which may be summarized broadly as follows:

a) The character of a mentally ill person, prior to the onset of illness, may display certain weaknesses or defects, such as having a shy and solitary disposition or being narrow-minded and intolerant, but these are not necessarily all attributable to the "vanity and arrogance" and "putting self first-ism" (*geren diyizhuyi*) found in the bourgeois worldview. A person's character or disposition cannot be equated with his or her worldview, for within a given social class, one comes across many people who share the same worldview but whose characters are quite different. There are only two basic worldviews, the proletarian and the bourgeois, but individual character comes in endless shapes and sizes: for example, the brave or timid types, the frugal or spendthrift types, the profound or superficial types, and the well-adjusted or over-solitary types. Furthermore, given that all of us need to reform our worldviews and that no one is in a position to say they have finally succeeded in this task, the claim that mental illness is the consequence of a failure to properly reform one's worldview could plausibly be applied to everyone who has ever been afflicted by any kind of mental illness, and is therefore devoid of any specific meaning or significance. Trying to understand and explain the particularity of a given contradiction by considering only its universal aspect, as, for example, in the attempts of some people to explain the mental activity of the brain by reference to the contradictory motion of atoms, is at once the most economical of approaches and also the one least likely to produce a solution to specific problems.

We often say that one important reason why people make mistakes is that they have not done a good enough job of reforming their worldview, so if we now also identify this problem as being the reason why people become mentally ill, it becomes all too easy to start equating becoming mentally ill with making mistakes, and to start seeing mental illness itself as constituting an "ideological defect" (*sixiang maobing*); at the very least, the distinction between these things becomes blurred and vague. None of this tallies with what we actually observe in the course of clinical psychiatric practice. To stick the accusatory labels of

---

313 This notion that the mentally ill were a national embarrassment, or even an "affront to socialism," continued in China for several years after Mao's death. As a psychiatrist from the Capital Steel Mill Mental Hospital noted in October 1979, "During the period when the 'Gang of Four' were running amok, psychiatric professionals didn't even dare to raise the subject of China's rate of mental illness; the belief was that under the socialist system in our country, any and all types of mental illness ought to be steadily declining." (See Zhong Youbin: article cited at Note 300 above.).

"putting self first-ism" and "improperly reformed worldview" onto large numbers of mentally ill workers, peasants and soldiers is neither fair nor just. People with widely divergent worldviews and all different levels of political consciousness fall victim to schizophrenia. In our clinics and sick wards, we come across numerous workers, peasants and soldiers, and also many cadres and intellectuals, who suffer from this disease, among them Party officials, model workers and other advanced individuals of various kinds, and both during their illnesses and afterwards, they all show warm love and affection for the Party, an enthusiasm for labouring on behalf of socialism, the qualities of loyalty and reliability, and a willingness to help others; while at the same time, we come across some patients whose minds are filled with selfish ideas of all kinds and in whom individualism is running relatively unchecked. Both situations exist side by side, and we must not take a one-sided view of things or seek to characterize the whole on the basis of a part, far less try to draw any blithe theoretical generalizations.

b) During the initial onset of illness and also prior to any relapses, many schizophrenia sufferers show no conspicuous signs of being under adverse psychological pressure or stimuli, or of having been caught up in any obvious clash or conflict of personal interest; the attribution by others, after the onset of illness, of so-called psychogenic factors in their cases is often quite forced and arbitrary. Even going by Comrade Jia's own statistics, we see that not all of his cases showed psychogenic causal factors; and even if those that didn't amounted to only a few percent of the total, how then can he explain either the reasons for these people becoming mentally ill or the essential nature of their mental illnesses? In children, schizophrenia can emerge before the age of ten, and at this early age, strictly speaking, they cannot yet be said to have formed any particular worldview. Simple schizophrenia can also strike suddenly and without warning in childhood or early youth and then progress slowly thereafter. Countless numbers of chronic schizophrenics are left disabled for many years by the disease, unable to take care of themselves and more or less completely isolated from the outside world, but no pre-existent adverse psychological pressures or stimuli can be found in their cases. And in those cases where psychogenic factors were identified at the onset of illness, such factors have mostly long since disappeared from the scene. In all such cases, the chronic course of the illness is remarkably similar to that of the organic diseases, and it is very hard to explain such an outcome by reference either to psychogenic factors or to the nature of the sufferer's worldview.

c) In many cases of schizophrenia, prior to the sufferers being hospitalised and with a view to resolving any ideological contradictions or unfulfilled desires that may be present in their minds, the work units, colleagues, families and friends of those afflicted have often made extensive efforts to educate, persuade, comfort and reassure them, and also to improve their living environments, but the effect and outcome of all this work is generally quite minimal; the illness continues to develop as before, and eventually those afflicted have to be sent to mental hospitals for treatment. Once in hospital, they can get relief from their symptoms only if given drug therapy; or if that too fails, they will be discharged as incurable. In all countries around the world, large numbers of schizophrenia sufferers improve as a result of drug therapy alone, and after recovery their individual worldviews remain, as one would only expect, entirely the same as before. Truth knows no boundaries and is equally valid everywhere, so a correct theory of medical treatment must be equally applicable to patients overseas and those living in China. While not denying the importance and significance of ideological re-education and psychotherapy, we do not believe that bourgeois worldview and methodology is the universal and fundamental causal factor leading to onset of the endogenous mental illnesses.

4. The case findings from numerous other medical surveys conducted in China [Manuscripts 1, 2, 3 & 9] do not support the "overwhelming majority" conclusions derived by Comrade Jia from his survey.

In his article, Comrade Jia says that his survey of several hundred cases of mental illness established that there were "three overwhelming majorities," namely, that in an overwhelming majority (94 percent) of the cases he studied, the cause of illness was adverse psychological pressure or stimuli; that in an overwhelming majority of cases (92 percent), the sufferers had "failed to reform their worldviews properly and used incorrect ideology in dealing with contradictions"; and that the overwhelming majority of mentally ill people (90 percent) can be completely cured. And Comrade Jia also states: "The pathological thoughts are simply a continuation of the normal thoughts that existed prior to the onset of illness." Our various contributors put forward the following set of dissenting opinions on these points:

a) Comrade Jia overestimates the role played by psychological pressures and stimuli prior to the onset of illness, and also the extent to which these factors actually exist. Without contradictions there would be no world, and inasmuch as mental contradictions are a reaction to the contradictory existence of objective matter, we can all be said to have mental contradictions. These naturally exist also before people fall mentally ill, but a large proportion of them do not directly cause the illness, and indeed may have no causal connection with the illness whatsoever. But Comrade Jia's survey stresses the key role played by psychogenic causal factors, so whenever such factors appear, he adamantly and confidently ascribes to them the decisive role in the illness's overall genesis.

b) Under the special circumstances [of China's recent past], "When evildoers are in power, the good people suffer." But even when these evildoers' worldviews have been of the most extremely reactionary kind, they themselves did not become mentally ill. Many good people, on the other hand, were attacked, persecuted, killed or driven insane by them. By what kind of bizarre logic are we now supposed to ask those who became mentally ill as a result of all this to start "re-examining their worldviews" in an effort to find the "causes" of their illnesses, not to mention the absurdity of attributing their mental problems to "putting self first-ism"? The pathological factors leading to mental illness include, among other things, being so grief-struck at the death of a family member through accident or natural disaster that one falls seriously ill. Are we supposed also to lump this kind of mental illness under the heading of "improperly reformed worldview"? Just what kind of a theory is this?

c) The results obtained to date in the treatment of schizophrenia, both at home and abroad, are very far from satisfactory. In the case of those with acute or short-term illnesses, the rate of recovery or near-recovery is no more than around 70 percent; and in the case of chronic sufferers whose illnesses have been going on for a long time it is less than 20 percent. Claims that the overwhelming majority of sufferers can be cured of the illness are generally based on loose and inaccurate diagnostic criteria (for example, including hysteria sufferers in the sample group) or on excessively broad criteria for identifying recovery (for example, the inclusion of sufferers who have improved to the extent merely of having their excitement states brought under control), and they simply ignore any residual negative symptoms or impairments of self-awareness that may exist; and usually, no follow-up examinations of the patients have been carried out either.

d) Among mental patients we find those who, because of delusions of jealousy, kill their own wives and children; those whose delusions of self-guilt drive them either to refuse all food or to eat their own excrement; people who, because of their shallowness of emotion, stand muttering and laughing in front of their dead mother's body; others whose conflictual auditory hallucinations drive them to curse and swear into the empty air; and still others who – in Comrade Jia's own words – "sing, dance and run around aimlessly, tearing off their clothes and going around naked, and sometimes injuring or killing people." In none of these cases, however, would it be plausible to assert, "The pathological thoughts are simply a continuation of the normal thoughts that existed prior to the onset of illness." It is unimaginable that all such abnormal and pathological thoughts, statements and actions as those just mentioned were prefigured by, or existed in, the normal thinking of those concerned prior to the onset of their illnesses, or that there was any kind of systematic connection between their eventual pathological behaviour and their initially normal mentality.

5. Marxism-Leninism and Mao Zedong Thought can only be a guide to psychiatric research; it cannot be a substitute for it.

a) To regard mental illness as being an ideological defect, and hence to substitute ideological re-education work based on Marxism-Leninism and Mao Zedong Thought in place of pharmaceutical drug therapy; to substitute the philosophical concepts of internal and external causality in place of the medical theory whereby specific internal and external causal factors are sought within the various mechanisms leading to each different disease; to regard psychiatry itself as being a social science rather than a branch of medical science; and to repudiate the biological basis of mental illness, and hence deny the validity of natural-scientific research in this field – none of these approaches accords, in any way whatsoever, with the principles of Marxism-Leninism and Mao Zedong Thought.

b) Comrade Jia writes,

"In addition, there is the school of experimental research that studies mental phenomena in isolation from their social context, repudiates the class nature of mental activity, denies the counteractive force of mind upon matter (the brain)...and carries out certain anatomical, physiological and biochemical work that is independent of human society. This is all a reflection, within the field of psychiatric research, of the one-sided and mechanistic doctrine of mechanical materialism, and it bears no relation at all to objective reality."[314]

Comrade Jia correctly emphasizes here the social nature and class nature of mental phenomena; the latter cannot be "reduced" simply to physiological or biochemical phenomena. But two further points need to be made in this connection. First, the "counteractive force of mind upon matter" means, in philosophical terms, that mental or spiritual factors can become transformed, in the course of practice, into physical or material factors; in other words, it signifies the real counteraction of the spiritual world upon the material world. It does not, however, mean "the counteractive force of mind upon matter (the brain)"; mental activity is a function of the brain itself, and therefore can exist neither in isolation from the brain nor in opposition to it. Second, mental illness is the consequence of pathological changes occurring in the physical matter that makes up the brain, so it is vital that dissections, physiological and biochemical studies and other forms of scientific research be carried out on the brain; there is simply no substitute for this. Provided the research findings are properly construed and understood, there are no grounds for dismissing such work as "mechanical materialism."

c) In Comrade Jia's view: "The process of reforming and raising one's ideological level is a never-ending one; as soon as old contradictions are resolved, new ones will keep on emerging. Therefore the recurrence [of mental illness] and the attempt to avoid such relapses is absolute." But he then goes on to say that "the non-organic mental illnesses will become more and more rare [as socialism advances] and will eventually disappear altogether." As several contributors to the discussion pointed out, these two statements are self-contradictory: according to the former, the task of reforming and raising one's ideological level (i.e. the struggle between contradictions) is eternal; while in the latter, it is predicted that the non-organic psychoses will eventually become extinct (i.e. the struggle between contradictions will cease, or at least will never again flare up or intensify.)

d) According to Comrade Jia's understanding, every recurrence (relapse) of a mental illness is due to the emergence of a new contradiction, and each time a recurrence of illness is cured, it is because the contradiction has been resolved. The question of the recurrence and remission of mental illness becomes, therefore, one of a struggle between contradictions in the realm of ideology, or rather a reflection of the ongoing struggle between the two major worldviews. This kind of attempt to use philosophical concepts to explain the natural course of illnesses, such as the remission and recurrence of schizophrenia and mania, is hardly very plausible or convincing. Even in the case of episodic hysteria, there will not necessarily be

---

314 "Mechanical materialism" was the pejorative term used by Marx to describe the system of thought of the German philosopher Ludwig Feuerbach (see, for example, Marx's famous 1845 essay, "Ten Theses on Feuerbach," and also his 1886 article "Ludwig Feuerbach and the End of Classical German Philosophy"). Marx claimed to have "redeemed" Feuerbach's materialism by removing the "mechanistic" aspects and replacing them with a (similarly cleansed) version of Hegel's theory of dialectics; Marx called the resultant theory "dialectical materialism."

any psychogenic factors in evidence; somatic illness, pain in the internal organs, or just excessive work can also spark off the condition.

Having thus systematically demolished all the key tenets and arguments of his Cultural Revolutionary adversaries in the field of psychiatry, Professor Yang then concluded by adding the following more personal set of observations concerning the appalling damage that they had inflicted on the profession during what had by now come to be known in China as the "Ten Years of Disaster":

Compiler's Postscript

The question of the correct understanding of the essential nature of mental illness is something that has direct relevance both for the treatment of millions of mentally ill people and also for the future development of our profession, and the present debate has been an important struggle between truth and fallacy in this arena. Moreover, this is a debate that has been going on since ancient times, and it continues to this day all over the world. In the past, when mental illness was believed to be the result of possession by ghosts or spirits, people used to scorch the flesh of the mentally ill with burning sulphur in an attempt to purge them of evil, or would lash them with peach branches until their bodies were a mass of bleeding wounds. Subsequently, when mental illness was believed to result from unfulfilled erotic urges, the mentally ill would be tricked or forced into sudden arranged marriages, thereby making their lives even more unmanageable, with children left destitute and uncared for, and creating an even greater burden for society. Our ignorance about the essential nature of mental illness has resulted in endless forms of random and harmful treatment being applied, including starvation, bloodletting, anacarthsis [forced vomiting] and the use of drastic abdominal purgatives, with the sufferers often being left on the verge of death. At other times, techniques of fear and intimidation were employed, for example, firing guns in the air, submerging the sufferers in water, or spinning them around in mid-air until they were almost unconscious from shock. And then along came other treatments, such as artificially raising the patient's body temperature, applying electric shocks to their brains and surgically removing parts of the frontal lobe. In short, the impotence of science has exacerbated the sufferings of the mentally ill in manifold ways.

After the founding of New China, the Party and the People's Government made great efforts to improve the health of the population and actively pursued all kinds of disease prevention work, especially in regard to tuberculosis, leprosy and mental illness. Large numbers of hospitals, convalescent homes and reception centres were set up, many new medical staff and specialists were educated and trained, and numerous medical journals and publications were established. In universities and colleges, courses in psychiatric medicine were set up and, guided by Chairman Mao's revolutionary line in healthcare, enormous progress was made in this field, as in other branches of medical science in China.

After Lin Biao and, especially, the Gang of Four started to peddle their reactionary political line – a line that was "left" in form but right in essence – the country was plunged into deep disaster. Every aspect of official life in China suffered the noxious consequences of their doctrines, and the damage wrought in the field of psychiatry was certainly no less serious and profound than elsewhere. They threw people's thinking into complete chaos, and metaphysics and idealism became rampant. As part of their nakedly careerist plan to seize political power within the Party and the government, they even, at one point, instigated mental patients to "rise up in rebellion," and those who did so were then lauded as being "madmen of the new era." They claimed that mental patients were being "persecuted" in our socialist hospitals, and they vilified the broad mass of revolutionary medical workers by accusing them of exercising "bourgeois dictatorship" over mental patients. They characterized all the currently effective, though far from ideal, forms of treatment and therapy used for mental illness in China and the rest of the world as being "instruments of torture designed to destroy patients' health." They even laid down a "class line of demarcation" in respect of the dosages of medication that could be prescribed. Old therapies would be suddenly banned, and new ones imposed, solely by administrative fiat. As a result of all this, in the worst hit mental hospitals, recovery rates and sickbed rotation rates began to decline and medical staff became so demoralized that they left psychiatry altogether.

Eventually, [the ultra-leftists] claimed that the real reason people became mentally ill was that their heads were filled with an "excess of selfish ideas and personal concerns" and that mental illness was the product of "an extreme development of individualism." Simplistic techniques of ideological re-education then became the principal form of treatment and cure for mental illness in China. Mentally ill people were made to undergo re-education at the hands of the medical staff and ordered to dig out, from within their own minds, the "ideological roots" of their illnesses. In some mental hospitals, patients who uttered banned thoughts or engaged in banned forms of behaviour because of their illnesses were held criminally responsible, and even their families were wrongfully implicated. This conception of mental illness as being an ideological sickness and a disease of the bourgeoisie, the belief that it is a product of the capitalist social system, holds in lofty disdain the sufferings of countless numbers of working-class mentally ill people and has served to consign psychiatry to the distant margins of public health work in our country. Is it not now incumbent upon us, therefore, to expose and criticize to the fullest extent possible all these absurd theories and pernicious policies of the Gang of Four, these perversions of medicine that have inflicted such harm and damage upon the mentally ill and upon the great majority of those working in our profession?

As Chairman Mao taught us,

> Idealism and metaphysics are the easiest things in the world, because people can talk as much nonsense as they like without basing it on objective reality or having it tested against reality. Materialism and dialectics, on the other hand, need effort. They must be based on and tested by objective reality. Unless one makes the effort, one is liable to slip into idealism and metaphysics.[315]

---

315 Ironically, this passage by Mao comes from his Introductory note to "Material on the Hu Feng Counterrevolutionary Clique" (May 1955); translation taken from *Quotations from Chairman Mao Tse-tung*, (Peking: Peking Foreign Languages Press, 1966). Hu, a writer, was one of the first intellectuals to be severely persecuted by the Party after 1949. (see Chapter 3 above.) In Marxist and Maoist philosophy, idealism and metaphysics are viewed as being "reactionary" in nature and diametrically opposed to materialism and dialectics.

No matter what the circumstances, we must always have the courage to uphold the truth, rectify our mistakes, seek truth from facts and study with humility. Only thus will we be able to contribute to the cause of socialist reconstruction by realizing the Four Modernizations, including the modernization of science and of psychiatric medicine.

Yang's eloquent and moving testimonial requires little further analysis or commentary here. After reading it through, one is left in no doubt as to the sheer havoc and mayhem that occurred within Chinese psychiatry during the Cultural Revolution as a result of the ultra-leftists' perverse eradication of the vital conceptual distinction between the issue of political heterodoxy on the one hand, and the question of mental illness on the other. This historical experience left behind a profound legacy of damage, one from which Chinese psychiatry was not to recover for many years afterwards, and one which was to continue – though in subtly different ways – to underpin the authorities' use of legal or forensic psychiatry as an adjunct tool against political and religious dissent well into the post-Mao period also.

All that remains to be observed at this point, as regards the main theme of this book – the nature of the relationship between psychiatric medicine and criminal justice in post-1949 China – is to note that in the latter field, nothing remotely approaching the degree of critical self-reflection and systemic reform that was prompted in the psychiatric field as a result of the devastating experiences of the Cultural Revolution subsequently transpired. Despite all the countless politically-inspired miscarriages of justice that were officially acknowledged to have taken place throughout China during that decade, the Chinese legal system after 1976 continued, just as before, to send large numbers of political dissidents and nonconformists to prison on charges of "counterrevolution," merely for peacefully expressing banned or unorthodox political ideas.

The sharp imbalance or asymmetry between the considerable progress that has been made in the field of general psychiatry in China since 1978, on the one hand, and the minimal progress made in the area of the criminal justice system dealing with political dissent, on the other, has meant in practice that in the specific field of police-related or forensic psychiatry, the system has continued to be plagued by the same kinds of politically-motivated legal defects and abuses that were so characteristic of forensic psychiatry in the Soviet Union. As we shall see in the next chapter, the failure of the criminal justice system in China after 1978 to abandon the longstanding legal prohibitions on political free speech and activity has continued to impose a clear and inescapable limit upon the ability of reform-minded psychiatrists, throughout the post-Mao era, to divest their profession as a whole of its disturbing historical legacy of political psychiatric abuse.

III. Medical Neglect and Prison Psychosis

One further issue that should be briefly addressed here, by way of concluding this account of law and psychiatry in China during the Mao era, concerns the extent and quality of psychiatric care extended by the authorities to criminal offenders in general since 1949. The focus of the following observations is on the theme, as briefly touched upon earlier, of medical neglect, rather than of either hypodiagnosis or hyperdiagnosis, although in practice these various divergent themes were often complexly intermingled.

The U.N.'s basic document in this area, the Standard Minimum Rules for the Treatment of Prisoners, stipulates that seriously mentally ill persons are not to be held in prisons and that less severely disturbed inmates should be given appropriate medical care.[316] Since prison systems in most countries are notoriously under-resourced in terms of their ability to provide psychiatric treatment for mentally ill offenders, in practice these provisions are often widely ignored. China's shortcomings in this respect should thus, in principle, occasion little surprise or blame. For decades after 1949, however, the PRC prison authorities applied a policy of actively withholding appropriate medical care in the case of major political prisoners suffering from mental illness. According to Article 37 of the 1954 *PRC Regulations on Reform through Labour*, prison authorities were not permitted to take custody of offenders suffering from mental illness or other serious diseases, "except in the case of major counterrevolutionary criminals."[317] Since the great majority of all convicted prisoners in China during the 1950s and 1960s were "counterrevolutionaries," this discriminatory policy inevitably meant that large numbers of mentally-ill political prisoners were denied access to proper care throughout their imprisonment. Another abusive practice that seriously compounded this general problem was that, until fairly recently, both sentenced counterrevolutionaries, irrespective of their mental state, and common criminals suffering from mental illness were frequently held in solitary confinement cells throughout their term of imprisonment.[318] An extreme example of the conditions of squalor and misery that could result from this practice was related in a 1983 directive from the Ministry of Public Security:

> In December 1980, the authorities at Yingshan Prison, Guangxi Province, placed a mentally disturbed prisoner in solitary confinement and kept him there for more than two years. They afforded him neither medical treatment nor ideological education. No one cleared away the prisoner's excrement and urine, with the result that a mound of faecal matter thirty-five centimetres high accumulated inside the cell. During the winter of 1982, the prisoner was not supplied with any additional clothing or bed quilt, and as a result of the extreme cold and the noxious gases created by the

---

316 See especially Article 82 of the Standard Minimum Rules and Procedures for the Effective Implementation of the Rules, (United Nations [New York: Department of Public Information, 1984]), adopted by the United Nations on August 30, 1955: "(1) Persons who are found to be insane shall not be detained in prisons and arrangements shall be made to remove them to mental institutions as soon as possible. (2) Prisoners who suffer from other mental diseases or abnormalities shall be observed and treated in specialized institutions under medical management. (3) During their stay in a prison, such prisoners shall be placed under the special supervision of a medical officer. (4) The medical or psychiatric service of the penal institutions shall provide for the psychiatric treatment of all other prisoners who are in need of such treatment."

317 See also Xu Shoubin, "The Legal Protection and Restriction of Rights of the Mentally Ill," *Fazhi Shijie (World of Legality)*, 1994, No.6, p.26. The prohibition on penal institutions taking in mentally ill prisoners was reiterated by the Ministry of Public Security (whose No.11 Bureau ran all such facilities until July 1983 when jurisdiction was transferred to the Ministry of Justice) in Article 9 of the Ministry's 1982 "Detailed Rules on the Disciplinary Administration of Prisons and Labor-Reform Detachments (Trial Draft)," in *A Compilation of Standard Interpretations of the Laws of the People's Republic of China: Supplementary Volume* (Jilin People's Publishing House, 1991), p.798. However, the provisions of Article 37 of the 1954 Regulations remained in force.

318 Even common criminals with mental illnesses were rarely dealt with according to the provisions of the 1954 Regulations, since virtually no mental healthcare facilities were to be found anywhere in the country's prison system; as late as 1988, the penal network reportedly still contained only two specialized mental hospitals ("Penal-System Medical and Health Work Has Been Greatly Strengthened and Developed in Recent Years," *Fanzui Yu Gaizao Yanjiu [Research in Crime and Reform]*, 1994, No.4, pp.53-55).

fermentation of the decaying excrement, the prisoner died in January [1983] from the combined effects of cold exposure and gas poisoning.[319]

The same directive ordered that mentally ill prisoners were henceforth not to be placed in solitary confinement and must be given proper medical care and attention. In March 1998, however, a leading southern Chinese newspaper reported the case of a violent prisoner suffering from chronic schizophrenia who had been kept locked by police in an outdoor cage for at least the previous five years. As a result of the publicity, the man was subsequently freed from the cage and placed in a secure mental asylum. According to the newspaper account,[320]

> Reporters found Deng Qilu, the "man in the cage," at Beitan Village, Nanxiang Township, Xuwen County last weekend. The cage had been made [by the police] by welding together reinforced steel pipes and had an area of approximately two square meters inside but had no exit. It was situated in an open yard at the side of the village. The caged man looked to be a little over 40 years old, had grown long whiskers, and was stark naked. When we strangers walked close to the cage, his eyes showed fear and panic.[321]

A related issue concerns the question of prisoners who went insane or were driven mad during their time in prison. This type of phenomenon, known as "prison psychosis," is common to prison systems

---

[319] "Notification of Bureau No. 11 of the Ministry of Public Security On Strengthening and Reorganizing the Management of Solitary Confinement Cells (July 12, 1983)," *Zhonghua Renmin Gongheguo Falü Guifanxing Jieshi Jicheng (A Compilation of Standard Interpretations of the Laws of the People's Republic of China)*, (Jilin People's Publishing House, October 1990), pp.1591-1593. (A heavily censored version of the same directive appears in: *Zhonghua Renmin Gongeheguo Jiancha Yewu Quanshu (A Compendium of PRC Procuratorial Work)*, (Jilin People's Publishing House, July 1991), pp.1496-1497.) The directive ordered an immediate tightening up of the administration of solitary confinement units throughout China. For a full translation of China's regulations at that time on the administration of solitary confinement cells (Articles 60–64 of the Ministry of Public Security's February 1982 "Detailed Rules for the Disciplinary Work of Prisons and Labour Reform Detachments"), see Asia Watch (now Human Rights Watch), "Democracy Wall Prisoners: Xu Wenli, Wei Jingsheng and Other Jailed Pioneers of the Chinese Pro-Democracy Movement," Vol.5, No. 6, March 1993, pp.21-23.
[320] "Man Detained in Iron Cage for Ten Years in Guangdong," *Yangcheng Wanbao*, March 28, 1998; translation from BBC Summary of World Broadcasts, April 13, 1998. (Chinese press reports on the case varied on whether the man had spent five or ten years in the cage.) The background to the case was described in another news report as follows:

On 29th May, 1999, Deng was detained for investigation after he suddenly stabbed and inflicted serious injury upon a police officer with a sharp weapon measuring 80 cm in length. On 30th July of the same year, the Zhanjiang City Hospital for the Prevention and Treatment of Mental Disease and a forensic psychiatry appraisal team of Zhanjiang City determined: "Deng Qilu has been suffering from dementia praecox for a period of 16 years… In this connection, it is suggested that he be placed under long-term, intensified custody to prevent him from committing violence and injuring others." ("'Caged Man' Set Free," *Yangcheng Wanbao*, March 29, 1998; also in BBC Summary of World Broadcasts, April 13, 1998.)
[321] In a recently reported case of this type, in October 2002, a mentally ill man named Wu Xiaoyong, who had murdered his neighbour during a psychotic episode and then been released from jail after a forensic psychiatric finding of incapacity to bear legal responsibility, froze to death in a small hut where he had been left permanently shackled by his family. (See: *"Jingshenbingren Side Qi 'Suo'"* (A Mentally Ill Man Dies from his "Shackles"), *Nanfang Zhou Mo* (Southern Weekend), 13 March 2003.

around the world, but it was especially frequent and severe in China during the Cultural Revolution.[322] In particular, the police pressure on those arrested for alleged political offences was often so great that many people began to believe that they actually had committed "towering crimes against the people" – notably conspiracy, espionage and political subversion – and in the course of their daily forced-confessional writing sessions in prison, they began to reinterpret large sections of their own pasts in lurid and entirely confabulatory terms. In some cases, this unusual and highly specific form of "politically induced" prison psychosis was driven, at some vestigial level of the person's sanity, by a realization that it was only by constantly amplifying the scale and seriousness of the imagined crimes that one might hope to prolong the police investigation and thereby postpone the day of eventual punishment, which not infrequently meant death.[323] Clinically speaking, the people concerned were already acutely mentally disturbed, but their flights of confessional fantasy, of whose veracity they themselves were quite convinced, would frequently be given blanket credence by the authorities and taken as grounds for criminal conviction.

In 1979, soon after Deng Xiaoping's return to power, the judicial authorities issued a directive instructing that – "in the interests of revolutionary humanism and so that these offenders do not die in prison" – a nationwide review be carried out of the cases of all "aged, weak, sick and disabled or mentally ill prisoners," and that the majority of such persons be set free.[324] As late as the 1990s, however, reports from the legal-medical literature indicated that many severely mentally ill prisoners in China continued to be held in solitary confinement cells in regular prisons, watched day and night by a roster of prison guards and assigned prisoner "trusties," due to the continued widespread lack of secure psychiatric treatment facilities.[325]

---

322 Recent data, however, show that the condition was rarely if ever diagnosed in China until fairly recently. According to one local study published in 1998, no cases were recorded during the 1980s, but during the 1990s the condition was said to have accounted for 9.2 percent of all cases of forensic psychiatric examination (Zheng Chengshou et al., "*80 Niandai yu 90 Niandai Sifa Jingshenbingxue Jianding Anli de Duizhao Yanjiu* [A Comparative Study on the Case Expertise of Forensic Psychiatrics Between the 1980s and 1990s]," *Zhonghua Jingshenke Zazhi* [Chinese Journal of Psychiatry], 1998, No.4, pp.228-230). See also: Lü Chengrong et al, "*Jujinxing Jingshen Zhang'ai 30 Li*" (Thirty Cases of Prison Psychosis), Shanghai Jingshen Yixue (Shanghai Archives of Psychiatry), 1996, Vol. 8, No. 2, p.101.
323 One especially vivid and complex such case from the Cultural Revolution is described at length in Shen Yucun (ed.), *Jingshenbingxue*, pp.1106-1107. See also Jia Yicheng, *Shiyong Sifa Jingshenbingxue*, p.513. This particular condition is referred to in Chinese psychiatry as either "delusion-like fantasy syndrome" (*lei wangxiangxing huanxiang zheng*) or "reactive confabulatory syndrome" (*fanyingxing xugou zheng*); the latter diagnosis may be clinically related to a condition known elsewhere as "Korsakoff's syndrome."
324 "Joint Directive of the Supreme People's Court, Supreme People's Procuratorate and Ministry of Public Security Concerning the Clearing Out of Aged, Weak, Sick and Disabled or Mentally Ill Prisoners," April 16, 1979. All mentally ill (or otherwise infirm) prisoners serving sentences of death with a two-year suspension of execution (*si-huan*) were, however, specifically excluded from the scope of this official amnesty order. A sanitized version of the April 16, 1979, directive, omitting the statistical and other details cited above, appears in many PRC legal anthologies; the unexpurgated version referred to here can be found in *Jiancha Gongzuo Shouce* (*A Handbook of Procuratorial Work*), Vol.1 (Kunming: Yunnan Sheng Renmin Jianchayuan, December 1980), pp.281-283. Grateful acknowledgement is due to Lalagy Pulvertaft for kindly providing the uncensored version of this document.
325 See, e.g., Lin Huai (ed.), *Jingshen Jibing Huanzhe Xingshi Zeren Nengli He Yiliao Jianhu Cuoshi* (Capacity of Mental Illness Sufferers for Criminal Responsibility and Measures for Their Medical Guardianship), (Renmin Fayuan Chubanshe, 1996), p.67.

The total number of mentally ill prisoners falling within the scope of the government's 1979 amnesty order was officially said to be 4,600, many of whom were over eighty years old and one third of whom had already been in prison for ten years or more. Among this large group of prisoners were no doubt many of those former mental patients from the early 1960s whose psychiatric symptoms had included "strange political utterances" and who had been harassed and beaten into "confessing their sanity" during the Cultural Revolution. The main lesson of experience drawn by the authorities in the late 1970s, however, was not that "political lunatics" of this sort should never have been criminally detained in the first place. Instead, the new and reform-minded viewpoint was simply that they should henceforth be relieved of their "criminal liability" and be placed in police-run psychiatric custody, rather than in regular prisons or labour camps as before.

In December 1994, a new Prisons Law of the PRC (passed on December 29, 1994, at the 11th Session of the Standing Committee of the 8th National People's Congress) finally superseded the 1954 PRC Regulations on Reform Through Labour (see *Laodong Gaizao Tiaoli*, in *Gong'an Fagui Huibian* (1950-1979), Qunzhong Chubanshe, 1980, pp. 397-409). Surprisingly, the current law entirely omits the previous "strict" prohibition on prisons accepting mentally ill offenders into penal custody; this move may perhaps be attributable to the authorities' decision several years earlier to set up the Ankang network of facilities specifically for this purpose, but it still merits further examination. According to Article 17 of the new law, "Prisons shall perform physical examinations on all prisoners turned over to them for punishment. If through physical examination either of the following conditions is found in a prisoner sentenced to life imprisonment or to fixed-term imprisonment, they may temporarily not admit the prisoner into prison custody: 1) A serious illness that requires release on bail for medical treatment; 2) pregnancy, or nursing of an infant." Besides omitting any mention of the previous prohibition on prisons accepting mentally ill offenders, Article 17 uses a much less emphatic phrase than before to describe the action to be taken in respect of the types of offenders who are still mentioned. Whereas now, prison authorities "may temporarily not admit the prisoner into prison custody", previously they had "to refuse to take into custody" not only the two categories of offender cited above but also any prisoner suffering from mental illness.

PART THREE
POLITICIZED PSYCHIATRY AFTER MAO

CHAPTER 5

The Legal Context for the Handling of Mentally Ill Offenders

In some countries in the West, the relationship between law and human rights often ends up in a self-contradictory predicament. The so-called human rights of the mentally ill, such as the right to refuse treatment and the right to refuse hospitalisation, are clear examples of the kind of phoney human rights advocated by Western jurisprudence.

— Chinese textbook on forensic psychiatry, 1989[326]

I. A Nuanced Reversal of Policy

If the political misuse of psychiatry had ended with the inauguration of the Deng Xiaoping era in 1978, the above account of the first thirty years of forensic psychiatry in China would be of primarily historical interest. The official repudiation of the Cultural Revolution in the late 1970s and the commencement of the policy of "opening and reform," however, did not bring an end to such practices. Over the next two decades, China's forensic psychiatrists continued to diagnose certain categories of dissident-type individuals as being "dangerously mentally ill" and to send them to long-term custody in special mental asylums. According to official accounts, there was a substantial decrease in the overall scale and incidence of these practices after the Cultural Revolution. For example, a retrospective study of forensic psychiatric assessments carried out at the Hangzhou No. 7 People's Hospital, published in June 1987, reported:

> According to this hospital's statistics, cases of antisocial political speech and action accounted for 54 percent of all cases [examined] during the year 1977; currently, the proportion of such cases has fallen to a level of 6.7 percent. This shows that the present situation of stability and unity in China has resulted in a marked fall in the number of cases arising from such factors.[327]

While highly welcome, this reduction in the overall scale of political psychiatric abuse in China needs to be viewed and evaluated in an appropriate conceptual context. The statistics generally cited for the incidence of "cases of a political nature" in Chinese forensic psychiatry during the Cultural Revolution decade (in this case, 54 percent, and in Shanghai's case, as much as 73 percent)[328] are, by any objective standard of assessment, quite staggeringly high. They point to a situation whereby miscarriages of legal and medical justice were so widespread and pervasive as to be almost mind-boggling in their ethical implications. By contrast, the 1987 figure of 6.7 percent for such cases appears low. However, even the latter statistic would suggest a rate of political psychiatric abuse in China

---

326 Chen Shouyi, in preface to Shen Zheng, *Falü Jingshenbingxue*, p.9.
327 Zhong Xingsheng and Shi Yaqin, "A Preliminary Analysis of 210 Cases of Forensic Psychiatric Medical Assessment," *Chinese Journal of Nervous and Mental Diseases*, 1987, Vol.20, No.3, pp.139-141. As Veronica Pearson has commented, regarding this report from 1987, "There is no discussion of whether this is an absolute drop in numbers due to a decrease in that kind of crime, or whether the officials of the Public Security Bureau now only take notice of such behaviour if it is very extreme" (Pearson, "Law, Rights and Psychiatry in the People's Republic of China," p.413).
328 See quotation from Zheng Zhanpei at p.105 above.

during the past two decades that is substantially higher than that reported in the case of the former Soviet Union.[329] Furthermore, as we saw in Chapter 1, official sources give alternative statistics on this count for China during the period since 1978 that go well beyond 6.7 percent. What accounted for all this?

Over the past two decades, mainly as a result of the courageous stance taken by Yang Desen and other veteran Chinese psychiatrists around the time of Mao's death, the Chinese psychiatric profession has gradually evolved to the point where, nowadays, its theory and practice is in general based on internationally accepted diagnostic and ethical standards. (The decision of the Chinese Psychiatric Association in 2001 to remove homosexuality from the country's list of officially recognized mental disorders provides a clear illustration of this trend.[330]) Where Chinese criminal or forensic psychiatry was concerned, however, the deeper conceptual and institutional roots of the late-Maoist psychiatric orthodoxy that equated mental illness with political deviancy survived substantially intact. In practice, it underwent what can best be termed a "nuanced reversal": As we have seen, during the Cultural Revolution decade, more or less all mentally ill people were seen as being that way because of their "bourgeois ideological defects"; from the late 1970s onwards, however, the view became that *some* people who displayed these same ideological defects (namely a specific subgroup of political and religious dissidents or "counterrevolutionaries") held the offending views in question *because they were mentally ill*.[331]

This subtly revised theory entailed a return to the classic "hyperdiagnosis" model of psychiatry (the politically inspired over-diagnosis of mental illness) that prevailed in the Soviet Union at that time. The model persisted in China throughout the 1980s and then steadily declined in influence during most of the 1990s, in line with the sharp fall in the numbers of "counterrevolutionary offenders" arrested in China during the latter period. But the basic doctrine remained intact within the legal or forensic branch of Chinese psychiatry, and since the start of the campaign against Falun Gong in mid-1999 it has been pressed back into widespread service by the Chinese police and their forensic psychiatrist colleagues.

An article that appeared in a Shanghai psychiatric journal in autumn 1987 revealed the findings of the most detailed retrospective survey thus far carried out in China on the question of the nature and main targets of forensic-psychiatric appraisals work throughout the country during the period from the 1950s to the late 1980s. The survey was based on a dozen separate local survey reports on this topic that had been presented at a major academic conference in June of that year. According to the article's author, Jia Yicheng, who at the time was China's senior authority on forensic psychiatry, the average incidence of "political cases" dealt with under the system throughout this four-decade period in the various localities examined had amounted to more than 20 percent of the total criminal psychiatric

---

329 For a detailed discussion of the statistical size and extent of the political psychiatry problem in China since 1980, see p.22 above. For the equivalent data in the Soviet case, see p.33 and Note 68.
330 As in earlier versions of the American psychiatric profession's *Diagnostic and Statistical Manual* (DSM), the residual category of disorders caused by lack of self-acceptance on the part of homosexuals has still been retained in China. See: Wan Yanhai, "*Zhonghua Jingshen Kexue Hui Renwei Tongxinglian Xingwei Shi Zhengchangde*" (The Chinese Society of Psychiatry Views Homosexual Behaviour as Normal), *Aizhi*, 3 March 2001, available at: http://www.aizhi.org/xljk/ccmd-3.htm.
331 To rephrase this slightly more clearly: according to the Cultural Revolutionary analysis, all mental illness arose as the result of hostile or reactionary political viewpoints and ideology; while in the post-Mao era, the view became that some reactionary or hostile political viewpoints and ideology were caused by mental illness. The latter were still, however, "objectively" regarded as being crimes.

caseload. The total number of "political cases" in these unidentified regions of China, moreover, had been alarmingly high:

> As can be seen from the statistical data provided in the twelve articles [under study], altogether 1,621 (or 21.05 percent) of the 7,699 criminal cases under examination involved reactionary or counterrevolutionary speech or action (*fandong huo fan'geming yan-xing*), placing this category in a high second position [after murder: 23.03 percent] on the overall statistical list of dangerous behaviours.[332]

The report thus provided, for the first time, a specific indication of the absolute numbers of victims (or at least, their general order of magnitude) generated by several decades of the practice of political psychiatry in China. At the same time, the total figure of 1,621 by no means accounted for the true scale of the problem; rather, it was merely an initial and partial accounting based on a relatively small number of locally-based research studies carried out during the mid-1980s.

Professor Jia's commentary on these statistics also provided a useful summary and confirmation of the broader historical trend mentioned above:

> When viewed from a periodic perspective, however, a very clear distinction emerges. Six of the articles contained statistical data on appraisals carried out during the post-Cultural Revolution period of 1981-86, and among the 2,019 criminal defendants who were appraised during this period, only 59 (or 3.12 percent) had engaged in counterrevolutionary speech or action. The other six articles contained statistical data from the period beginning in the 1950s and ending in 1976, and among the 5,680 criminal defendants appraised during this period, the relevant figure was 1,562 persons, or as much as 27.5 percent. This was clearly a result of the Cultural Revolution period and of the ultra-leftist ideological trend that preceded it.[333]

As the quotation presented on the opening page of this book vividly shows, by 1998 the same writer was acknowledging publicly that these cases had been of a "similar" politically abusive nature as those that had elicited worldwide concern and condemnation in the case of the former Soviet Union. It is important to note, however, that Jia's figure of 3.12 percent for criminal-psychiatric "political cases" during the early to mid-1980s was substantially lower than the average incidence of such cases (some 7–15 percent) found in numerous local forensic psychiatric studies carried out during the 1980s as a whole by other researchers. And crucially, it was only with the sharp percentage reduction in such cases that occurred in the early 1990s, to a level of between 1 and a few percent, that China's level of political psychiatric abuse began, finally, to fall to approximately the same level as that found at the height of similar phenomena in the Soviet Union during the 1960s and 1970s. Hitherto, China's incidence rates for "political cases" appear to have been much higher than those found under Soviet psychiatry. Equally important, moreover, with the widespread psychiatric detentions of Falun Gong protestors that have occurred since mid-1999, the incidence curve in China has again started to rise. (The Falun Gong caseload will be discussed in more detail in Chapter 7.)

---

332 In addition, Jia noted that out of 489 of these cases in which specific diagnoses of schizophrenia were made, no fewer than forty-one, or 8.38 percent of the total, were "cases of reactionary or counterrevolutionary speech and action."
333 "Summary and Analysis of Papers Submitted to the First National Academic Conference on Forensic Psychiatry," by Jia Yicheng (Psychiatric Teaching and Research Group of the Shanghai Railways Medical College), September 1987, *Shanghai Archives of Psychiatry* (*Shanghai Jingshen Yixue*), 1987, No.3, pp.118-24.

The official psychiatric literature since the early 1980s has also been quite specific in noting that persons arrested for dissident activities who are then found non-prosecutable or not guilty by reason of insanity are, in most cases, sent for involuntary and indefinite psychiatric committal – either in an Ankang hospital or (in the many areas of China which do not yet have this kind of specialized police-run facility) the closed wards of general mental hospitals. For example, according to an article entitled (candidly enough) "An Analysis of Forty-One Mentally Ill People Involved in Cases of a Political Nature," written by three psychiatrists from the Hangzhou Ankang facility and published in one of China's national-level psychiatric journals in late 1996:

> Instances whereby mental illness sufferers, owing to the severe weakening or outright loss of their powers of recognition and control, become involved in cases of a political nature are by no means rare. After committing these crimes, once ascertained in the course of forensic psychiatric evaluation as being not legally responsible for their actions, the majority of such people are sent to Ankang hospitals.

Concerning the numbers of those involved,

> During the period 1978-89, the Hangzhou Ankang hospital admitted 41 patients of this kind, accounting for 7.8 percent of all admissions. The largest numbers were admitted in 1978 and 1989, when they accounted for 17.1 percent and 14.6 percent of total admissions respectively – markedly higher than in other years...

As the authors themselves obliquely indicated, the reason why such a high proportion of "political case" admissions took place in 1978 and 1989 was that the former was the year of the Democracy Wall movement (the first phase of China's modern dissident/human rights movement) and the latter was the year of the nationwide pro-democracy movement based in Tiananmen Square. Moreover, the article continued,

> According to reports in the Chinese literature, the proportion of mentally ill persons subjected to expert judicial appraisal who have committed political offences is between 15.7 percent and 20.5 percent; this is second only to cases of murder and injury, although there has been a marked decrease in such cases since the 1980s.

> The majority of those in the case group had schizophrenia, but unlike the situation in other kinds of criminal cases, they were all suffering from the paranoid variety. This shows that paranoid schizophrenics tend to commit "anti-government" activities much more readily than those suffering from other variants of the disease, probably as a result of their delusions of persecution, delusions of influence, and delusions of grandeur, as well as their impaired thought processes.

As if to erase all doubt as to the actual nature of the "anti-government activities" in question, the article then went on to identify the five main criminal offences for which these 41 "patients" had been arrested in the first place. They were: "sending reactionary letters," "writing reactionary slogans," "petitioning and litigating," "shouting reactionary slogans" and "spreading rumours to delude the masses." In other words, none of the 41 individuals forcibly held and treated at the Hangzhou Ankang hospital during 1978-89 on grounds of criminal insanity were involved in any acts of violence or other authentic crime. Rather, they had been carrying out peaceful acts of free political expression.

In addition, the article even provided a table showing the precise psychiatric diagnoses that had been made for those falling within the various criminal subgroups:

Table 3: Clinical Diagnoses and Types of Crime in 41 Political Cases

Type of Crime / Diagnosis	Sending reactionary letters	Writing reactionary slogans	Petitioning and litigation	Shouting reactionary slogans	Spreading rumours to delude the masses	Total
Schizophrenia (paranoid type)	15	8	4	3		30
Paranoid psychosis			3			3
Depressive illness	1		1			2
Mania				1	1	2
Psychogenic mental disorder	2			1		3
Mental retardation					1	1
Total	18	8	8	5	2	41

As can be seen, the most frequently listed offences were "sending reactionary letters," "writing reactionary slogans" and "petitioning and litigation," and in the great majority of cases the forensic psychiatrist's official diagnosis was "paranoid schizophrenia." The same general pattern emerges in numerous other such survey reports in the Chinese legal and psychiatric literature.

The article also provided cursory but revealing summaries of several of the cases. For example, "Three of the paranoid schizophrenics were dominated by systematic delusions that led them to make ceaseless complaints and accusations against their so-called 'persecutors'." Moreover,

> Among the eight cases of petitioning and litigation, the majority involved people who kept barging into [government] offices and ceaselessly quibbling and arguing, in an indiscriminate and directionless manner that took no account of whether or not they were having the desired effect; this again was markedly different from petitioning and litigation by normal people.

As the various case studies of "persistent complainants and petitioners" presented in subsequent chapters of this book illustrate, local Chinese officials have increasingly been exploiting the country's lack of procedural safeguards in this area in order to have citizens who raise allegations of corruption or malfeasance against them wrongfully declared mentally ill and arbitrarily detained for long periods in mental hospitals. Indeed, cases of this type probably account for the majority of all cases of politically motivated misuse of the legal-psychiatric custody system in China today.

Turning to the question of "reactionary" document writers, the article by the Hangzhou Ankang psychiatrists notes that one of the detainees had "shouted reactionary slogans while undergoing an acute episode accompanied by disturbance of consciousness." As they further explained,

> As regards the modus operandi of the various offences, in the overwhelming majority of cases – whether it was sending letters or writing reactionary slogans – the methods employed were all relatively simple, stupid, or self-contradictory and inconsistent.... A minority of the sufferers wrote long screeds that went on for thousands of words, but these documents were vague, general and repetitive in content, and lacking in any clear or purposeful sense of logic. As for the "reactionary slogan" writers, most used

> cigarette packets or other pieces of scrap paper to write down their thoughts on, so the pathological nature of their activities was obvious to others, and clearly different from most other cases of counterrevolutionary crime.

The injustice and irony of the situation emerges clearly from this passage: had the writings of these political pamphleteers or slogan writers struck the police investigators as being logical and well-ordered in content, the detainees concerned would have received fixed-term jail sentences as counterrevolutionaries. As it was, however, the perceived vagueness, repetitiveness and illogicality of the political views in question meant that their hapless authors instead ended up being sentenced without trial – and on the basis of essentially literary evaluations performed by police officers whose educational level, by the government's own admission, is nowadays almost uniformly low – to an indefinite period of confinement in an institute for the criminally insane.

As the authors concluded from their study,

> Cases of political crime created by the mentally ill usually exert a highly negative influence in society and have extensive ramifications. They take up large amounts of human and material [investigative] resources, and they pose a definite disruptive threat both to the normal functioning of state offices and to the political stability of the country.[334]

Given the particular nature of the various cases under consideration, their official characterization here as "posing a definite disruptive threat...to the political stability of the country" will probably strike many readers as absurd. The fact remains, however, that the Chinese security authorities actually do see such cases as being highly serious – indeed that is the unsettling conundrum that lies at the core of our present enquiry. In a sense, suspension of normal disbelief is almost a prerequisite for being able to follow and understand the Chinese authorities' legal handling and treatment of political-style criminal insanity cases.

As was further discussed in Chapter 1, literally dozens of similarly specific references as those cited above to "political case" percentages among forensic-psychiatric sample groups appear throughout China's professional psychiatric literature. In fact, virtually all of the country's leading specialists in the field have written about this issue at length over the past twenty-five years. In Chapter 6, we will examine a representative cross-section of the actual individuals whose life stories have contributed to these alarmingly high statistics on "political lunacy" cases in the post-Mao era. But first, we need to take a more detailed look at the wider legislative and procedural context within which the forensic-psychiatric appraisal and disposition of alleged mentally-ill dissident detainees has been conducted in China since the late 1970s. At the start of this period, a basic distinction was drawn by the legal authorities between "genuine" political offenders, that is counterrevolutionaries, on the one hand, and mentally disordered political offenders, or what the authorities colloquially call "political lunatics" and we have termed the "pseudo-counterrevolutionaries," on the other. This was certainly progress as compared to the situation of forensic psychiatry during the Cultural Revolution, when the dividing line in this area became grotesquely blurred. But what did not change after 1978 was the authorities' firm insistence that, in both types of situation, a serious political crime had been committed.

---

334 "An Analysis of Forty-One Mentally Ill People Involved in Cases of a Political Nature," Luo Jiming, Li Shenlu and Tang Xiaofeng (Hangzhou Ankang Municipal Hospital), December 1996, *Journal of Clinical Psychological Medicine* (*Linchuang Jingshen Yixue Zazhi*), 1996, Vol.6, No.6, pp.356-357.

II. Legal Norms and Procedures for the Handling of Psychotic Offenders

In an article published in 1974 in the British Medical Journal summarizing his findings from a recent study visit to Soviet psychiatric hospitals, the British psychiatrist J.K. Wing expressed with neat precision the unusual ethical dilemma he encountered in evaluating his Soviet colleagues' handling of cases of political offenders alleged to be mentally ill. After discussing two other problematic issues that arose,[335] Wing wrote,

> The third conceptual problem concerns [legal] "responsibility." This is the most difficult one for the British psychiatrist to comment on since it means trying to answer a ludicrous non-question: should a person who is not severely mentally ill by our standards be regarded as responsible for an action which we would not regard as a crime?[336]

The same central issue hovers disquietingly over any discussion of the formal legislative and procedural aspects of the ways in which "political lunacy" cases are handled in the Chinese forensic psychiatric context. The range of cases falling within the system's scope and purview is much wider, of course, than this one specific category, and it seems reasonable to assume that the great majority of cases dealt with under the system involve the commission of genuine and serious offences (such as murder, rape and arson) by mentally ill people. The following descriptive account thus has a general applicability, and critical observations are directed toward the significant minority of cases where the system claims and applies jurisdiction over people, such as peaceful dissidents, sane or otherwise, who have not committed any internationally recognized criminal offence.

Until 1979, the main judicial yardstick in this field was a brief directive issued by the Supreme People's Court in 1956, according to which persons found to have been mentally ill at the time of committing criminal offences were not to be held legally responsible for their actions.[337] The mental state of the defendant was to be ascertained by "the relevant medical departments" and through interviews with the person's neighbours.[338] In 1979, the first Criminal Law of the PRC codified this longstanding

---

335 These were, the fact that "there is nothing in our criminal law equivalent to the Soviet category of crimes against the State," and secondly, that "the concept of mental illness, particularly of schizophrenia, is a good deal wider [in the USSR then, as in China today] than in the U.K."
336 J.K. Wing, "Psychiatry in the Soviet Union," *British Medical Journal*, No.1 (March 9, 1974), pp.433-436. After Wing's visit to the Serbski Institute of Forensic Medicine in July 1972, Moscow Radio quite shamelessly put the following words into his mouth: "I admire the Soviet system because in the USSR everything is done to restore the patient to normal life.... I cannot find anything to criticize. I find everything is beautiful." See Bloch and Reddaway, *Russia's Political Hospitals* (op cit), p.285.
337 See "Reply of the Supreme People's Court on the Question of the Handling of Crimes Committed by Mentally Ill Persons," June 2, 1956. Soon after the Cultural Revolution, during which legal norms had collapsed almost entirely, the Supreme People's Court reiterated the validity of the June 1956 directive (Supreme People's Court, Document No. 17 [78], August 4, 1978).
338 The directive also stipulated: "Counterrevolutionary elements and their families, or landlords and rich-peasant elements, should not be dealt with differently." This seems to run counter to Article 37 of the 1954 Regulations on Reform through Labour, which excluded "major counterrevolutionary offenders" from the rule that prisons were not allowed to admit criminals suffering from mental illness. In practice, however, any contest at that time between the court system and the prison system (which was run by the all-powerful Ministry of Public Security) would generally have ended in the latter's favour.

policy, although in somewhat simpler terms than before.[339] Then in March 1997, an extensively revised version of the Criminal Law was promulgated which significantly amended the previous provisions in this area:

> Article 18. If a mental patient causes harmful consequences at a time when he is unable to recognize or control his own conduct, upon verification and confirmation through legal procedure, he shall not bear criminal responsibility, but his family members or guardian shall be ordered to keep him under strict watch and control and arrange for his medical treatment. When necessary, the government may compel him to receive medical treatment.
>
> Any person whose mental illness is of an intermittent nature shall bear criminal responsibility if he commits a crime when he is in a normal mental state.
>
> If a mental patient who has not completely lost the ability of recognizing or controlling his own conduct commits a crime, he shall bear criminal responsibility; however, he may be given a lighter or mitigated punishment.
>
> Any intoxicated person who commits a crime shall bear criminal responsibility.[340]

The main changes were as follows. First, "expert forensic evaluation" must now be performed in order to ascertain whether or not a defendant was mentally ill at the time of committing an offence. Except during the Cultural Revolution, in practice this was hitherto also generally the case, but the statutory inclusion of a forensic-psychiatric appraisal procedure is still important. Second, the new law stipulated for the first time that mentally ill defendants may be ordered by the government to undergo "compulsory medical treatment." While not specifically mentioned, involuntary committal was certainly among the intended range of available legal options. Again, this merely codified a longstanding police prerogative, but the new law's mention of compulsory medical treatment has particular significance in light of the Chinese government's post-1987 program for creating a nationwide network of Ankang institutions. Finally, whereas previously a judgment of either full legal responsibility or total absence of such responsibility had to be officially rendered when evaluating a defendant's mental state, the intermediate option of "limited legal responsibility" (*xianding zeren nengli*) can now be adopted; while

---

339 According to Article 15 of the 1979 Criminal Law (Adopted July 1, 1979 and effective as of January 1, 1980; available in *U.S. Journal of Criminal Law and Criminology*, Spring 1982): "A mentally ill person who causes dangerous consequences at a time when he is unable to recognize or unable to control his own conduct is not to bear criminal responsibility; but his family or guardian shall be ordered to subject him to strict surveillance and arrange for his medical treatment. A person whose mental illness is of an intermittent nature shall bear criminal responsibility if he commits a crime during a period of mental normality. An intoxicated person who commits a crime shall bear criminal responsibility."

340 Similar provisions appear in the 1996 PRC Law on Administrative Punishments (passed by the National People's Congress on March 17, 1996 and effective as of October 1, 1996, see BBC Summary of World Broadcasts, FE/2585, April 13, 1996), which governs all of the wide-ranging forms of non- or extra-judicial punishment currently available to law enforcement agencies in China. According to Article 26 of this law, "If a mental patient commits an illegal act at a time when he is unable to recognize or cannot control his own conduct, no administrative penalty shall be imposed on him, but his guardian shall be ordered to keep him under close surveillance and arrange for his medical treatment. Administrative penalty shall be imposed on a person whose mental illness is of an intermittent nature and who commits an illegal act when he is in a normal mental state." The same general provisions appear also in Article 10 of the 1994 revised version of the PRC Regulations for the Punishment of Public Order Offences (see *Guowuyuan Gongbao* [Bulletin of the PRC State Council], 1994, pp.440-448), which allow police to impose (without trial) custodial sentences of up to fifteen days for minor offences.

this too was frequently done in the past, it is now fully lawful. (This category is equivalent to the English legal term "diminished responsibility," which may be invoked in the specific context of a defence against the charge of murder.) Significantly, the lack of such an intermediate option in the legal code of the former Soviet Union was a frequent target of criticism from the dissident community there.

The legislative basis for conducting "expert evaluations" had been formally laid down in March 1996 in a revised version of the Criminal Procedure Law of the PRC. According to Article 119 of that law, "When certain special problems relating to a case need to be solved in order to clarify the circumstances of the case, experts shall be assigned or invited to give their evaluations." Article 120 of the same law added, "If an expert intentionally makes a false verification, he shall assume legal responsibility." And Article 121 continued: "The investigation organ shall notify the criminal suspect and the victim of the conclusion of the expert verification which will be used as evidence in his case. A supplementary expert verification or another expert verification may be conducted upon application submitted by the criminal suspect or the victim." An especially problematic area where criminal defendants suspected of mental illness are concerned relates to the lawful time limits on pre-trial detention. According to Article 9 of the government's 1984 "Supplementary Provisions" on this question, all time limits on detention specified in the 1979 Criminal Law could be dispensed with during the period that a criminal defendant was being held in custody for forensic-psychiatric appraisal,[341] and Article 122 of the revised Criminal Procedure Law proceeded to formalize this dubious legal practice: "The period during which a criminal suspect is undergoing appraisal for mental disorder shall not be included in the calculation of time limits for handling the case."[342]

Separately, the police are accorded wide legal powers to detain and hospitalise alleged offenders who are suspected of being mentally ill. According to Article 14 of the 1995 Law of the People's Police of the PRC,

> The people's policemen of public security organs may take protective measures to restrain a mentally ill person who seriously endangers public security or other people's personal safety. If it is necessary to send the patient to a designated institution or place for guardianship, the matter shall be reported for approval to the public security organ of a people's government at or above the county level, and his or her guardian shall be notified without delay.

This law does not require the police to arrange either prior or subsequent forensic psychiatric assessment of persons whom they decide to send to a "designated institution," which in practice may be either an Ankang custodial facility or, in the case of lesser offences, the secure ward of a regular

---

341 See Supplementary Provisions of the Standing Committee of the National People's Congress Regarding the Time Limits for Handling Criminal Cases (*Guanyu Xingshi Anjian Ban'an Qixian de Buchong Guiding*, passed by the NPC Standing Committee on July 7, 1984; in Wang Huai'an et al (eds.), *Zhonghua Renmin Gongheguo Falü Quanshu*, Jilin Renmin Chubanshe, 1989, p.223).

342 Another relevant provision of the new Criminal Procedure Law (adopted on March 17, 1996 and effective as of January 1, 1997, see "PRC: Amended PRC Criminal Procedure Law," FBIS, April 10, 1996), Article 48, reads as follows: "All those who have information about a case shall have the duty to testify. Physically or mentally handicapped persons or minors who cannot distinguish right from wrong or cannot properly express themselves shall not be qualified as witnesses."

mental hospital; they merely have to report the matter to a superior police authority.[343] The police may choose, at their discretion, to send the detainee for forensic psychiatric examination; and in cases where the alleged offence was a serious one, the procuracy, the prosecuting authority, would no doubt require that such an examination be carried out and a subsequent finding made of non-imputability by reason of mental illness as a precondition for agreeing to suspend criminal proceedings against the person. However, Chinese law remains highly vague in this general area, and in practice offenders suspected of being mentally ill may end up being first committed by the police, and then left in prolonged custodial limbo while other authorities decide if and when an expert evaluation of their mental state is needed. In most criminal cases, the authority of the courts is circumvented at an early stage, since either the police or the procuracy normally suspend criminal justice proceedings once a forensic finding of non-imputability has been made. The latter authorities then decide, on the basis of their assessment of the "degree of dangerousness" of the offence in question, whether or not custodial care is required.

Moreover, since China broadly follows the "commensurability principle" of forensic psychiatric practice, whereby an offender deemed to be legally non-imputable by reason of insanity for a given crime is generally held in secure psychiatric custody for at least as long as the period of penal incarceration to which they would have been sentenced if ascertained to have been sane at the time of committing the offence, the authorities' inclusion of certain types of peaceful political prisoners (alongside psychotic murderers and the like) among the "most serious and dangerous" category of alleged mentally ill offenders means that such people can end up being psychiatrically detained on an indefinite or even permanent basis.[344]

In 1985, a prominent authority in the field of legal psychiatry, Wu Jiasheng, acknowledged the urgent need for China to take legislative action in this area:

> Legislation to protect and safeguard society in the area of mental illness should be promptly formulated. The most pressing problems are those concerning compulsory custodial treatment; at present, there are no clear guidelines on the applicable scope of such treatment, on the means by which it should be carried out, the types and methods of treatment, the time limits on detention, or the rights of the mental patient. From the viewpoint of building a healthy and complete socialist legal system, it is essential that we formulate relevant laws and regulations soon.[345]

The same year, the Chinese government began preparing to enact comprehensive national legislation on the treatment of the mentally ill, and since then, no fewer than 15 different draft versions

---

343 The police in many countries are empowered, in emergency situations, to take suspected mentally ill people into custody and to transfer them to psychiatric hospitals if they fear that dangerous consequences might otherwise ensue. In the case of China, however, it is the lack of any clear legal requirement for prompt forensic psychiatric evaluation then to be conducted that renders this police power liable to misuse and therefore problematic from a human rights point of view.

344 The same principle was also applied in the USSR. As Bloch and Reddaway observed, "No matter how severe the conditions of an incarceration, the knowledge of release after a definite period gives the prisoner a sense of hope and anticipation, and the passage of each day reinforces it. Not so in the case of the patient committed involuntarily to a psychiatric hospital…. The court often seems to apply a formula whereby the duration of internment should match the sentence which the dissenter would have received for his (alleged) offence, had he been ruled legally responsible." (Bloch and Reddaway, *Russia' Political Hospitals* [op cit], pp.212-3.)

345 Wu Jiasheng, "*Qiantan Jingshenbingren Weifa Zhaohuo Xingwei de Zeren Nengli* (A Brief Discussion of the Legal Capacity of Mentally Ill Persons Who Behave Unlawfully and Create Disastrous Incidents)," *Faxue (Jurisprudence)*, 1985, No.40, pp.43-45.

of a "Mental Health Law of the PRC" have been produced and widely circulated among psychiatric professionals around the country;[346] the World Health Organization has also provided input on the draft law.[347] The question of involuntary psychiatric committal and treatment has been addressed in considerable detail by the law's drafters, with provisions on such matters as the criteria for compulsory admission, the civil legal capacity of those committed, and the permissible use of restraints on inmates. In addition, the draft law contains several stipulations on the basic rights and interests of the mentally ill (for example, that "inhumane treatment of patients is not allowed" and that those compulsorily hospitalised should have their mental state "systematically assessed at least once every half year"); and it even briefly addresses the rights of mentally-disordered criminal defendants and provides a basic legal framework for the operation of forensic psychiatric custodial centres.[348] The passage of a well-crafted mental health law is clearly vital to any attempt to reform the system and safeguard the rights of those psychiatrically detained.[349] However, there is no indication that the government intends to enact formal legislation regulating official behaviour in this sensitive area anytime soon.

Judging from numerous articles that have appeared in the Chinese legal press in recent years, it seems likely that a primary reason for the government's reluctance to pass a national mental health law is that the authorities fear it would confer rights on criminal defendants which could be "misused" by

---

346 See: Zhang Lizi, "*Baohu Jingshenbingren Quanyi – Lifa Zhengzai Jinxing Shi*" (Protect the Rights and Interests of the Mentally Ill – Legislation Currently Underway), Jiankang Bao (Health News), 31 March 2004.

347 The law-drafting group is headed by Professor Liu Xiehe of the Institute of Forensic Medicine at the West China Medical University in Chengdu. The most recent joint initiative between China and the WHO on drafting a mental health law was a high-level symposium held in Beijing on November 11, 1999, attended by Dr Gro. Harlem Brundtland, the WHO's Director-General, and thirteen vice-ministerial-level Chinese officials. The full text of Brundtland's speech at the conference can be found at http://www.who.int/director-general/speeches/1999/english/19991111_beijing.html.

348 In the 1988 draft, these were referred to as "Guardianship Hospitals for the Mentally Ill" (*Jingshenbingren Jianhu Yiyuan*), which were to be organized and led by the Public Security departments; such hospitals were therefore clearly the same as the ones now more commonly referred to as "Ankang."

349 For useful and authoritative practical guidelines on this field of legislation, see World Health Organization, *Mental Health Care Law: Ten Basic Principles*, 1996 (WHO/MNH/MND/96.9). The legislative experience of the former Soviet states in this area also provides an important comparative frame of reference. According to two well-qualified observers,

> Establishing a proper legal foundation for mental health care has been the top priority for reformers in transforming psychiatry in practically all post-Soviet and post-socialist countries… The [July 1992] Russian law merits particular attention because it has provided a sound model for the other countries of the former Soviet Union. The law has many positive features that will help to facilitate the transformation of Russian psychiatry. (1) It codifies the fundamental norms and principles that should guide psychiatric care, including confidentiality, informed consent, and medical necessity. (2) It declares and reinforces the fundamental idea that psychiatrists are expected to be independent in making their decisions, which – as the law states – should be based only on "medical indications, medical duty and the law." (3) It establishes formal procedures for judicial review of involuntary hospitalisations, and of alleged violations of the rights of hospitalised patients. (4) Finally, the law opens psychiatric institutions to outside scrutiny and thereby promotes accountability to patients' families and to the society at large. The State is directed to "set up a service independent of health agencies for the protection of rights of psychiatric patients," and the law also specifically authorizes associations of psychiatrists, families or other citizens to monitor the observance of patients' rights and to file complaints on behalf of aggrieved patients. Enactment of this law was itself a remarkable achievement…

(Bonnie and Polubinskaya, "Unraveling Soviet Psychiatry," pp.292-294.)

them in ways that would reduce the awe and majesty of the law. In particular, much public attention has been given to a series of controversial cases in which accused murderers succeeded in pleading insanity and were then exempted from trial and punishment. In some cases, the offenders concerned were even released back into society, where they are said to have continued to threaten and injure innocent members of the public, safe in the knowledge that they had in effect been granted a "murderer's licence" (*sharen zhizhao*) by the court.[350] In a number of these reported cases, the general public's anger and dismay was greatly heightened by the fact that powerful local officials – sometimes relatives or friends of the murder – had actually bribed the forensic psychiatric assessors to issue false certificates of mental illness on the accused's behalf.

In a major case that took place in Wuhan in May 2000, for example, a prominent local gang leader named Yang Yiyong chopped a factory manager to death in broad daylight in a public hospital. A few weeks later, police psychiatrists from the Wuhan Ankang Hospital forensically examined Yang and declared that he was suffering from "acute general brain disease syndrome" (*jixing naobing zonghezheng*) and that he was therefore "not legally responsible" for his actions. Yang was thereupon released and promptly resumed his duties as a criminal gang leader. More than a year later, a diligent police investigator reopened Yang's case and eventually discovered what had happened: another member of Yang's gang had spent a total of 100,000 yuan to bribe the local PSB Bureau Chief and one of his subordinates (surnamed Ji and Gao respectively) into conspiring with a forensic psychiatrist (surnamed Zhu) from the Wuhan Ankang hospital to provide Yang with a false medical certification of exculpatory mental illness. Yang was subsequently rearrested, tried and executed for multiple murders, but official press reports stated only that Officers Ji and Gao had been "suspended from duty while investigations continued", and that the procuracy had sent Psychiatrist Zhu's case back for "further investigation" because it disagreed with the PSB's characterization of the case as an "occupational crime" (*zhiye fanzui*.)[351]

In September 2002, senior Chinese forensic psychiatrist Li Congpei commented: "It is precisely because China is currently so backward in its mental health legislation work that people like this are able to exploit the psychiatric appraisals system for corrupt ends and purposes."[352] Around the same time, an article in People's Daily stated:

> At present, the institutional management of psychiatric evaluations work is quite chaotic. Some forensic assessors act irresponsibly and even engage in corrupt activities. However, any certifications bearing their official seals are treated as valid and authoritative.... Furthermore, forensic assessors who issue false or

---

350 See for example, "*Jingshenbing Jianding Zenme Chengle 'Sharen Zhizhao'*" (How Psychiatric Evaluation Has Become a "Murderer's License"), *Beijing Qingnian Bao*, 16 July 2002; and "*Henan Tongbai: Jia Fuyuan 'Jingshenbing' Sharen An*" (A Case of Murder by "Mentally Ill" Jia Fuyuan in Tongbai, Henan Province), in Liu Bin (ed.) *Ershi Shiji Mo Pingfan Yuan-Jia-Cuo An Anli Jishi* (A True Record of Rectifying Wrong and Unjust Criminal Cases in the Late 20th Century), available at: www.shuku.net.

351 See "*Gong'an Juzhang Weifu Sifang 'Jingshenbing Shashou' Yuan Shi Hei Laoda*" (PSB Bureau Chief Privately Intercedes on Behalf of a "Mentally Ill Murderer" Who Turns Out to be a Major Gang Leader), *Wuhan Wanbao*, 11 November 2001; see also Si Wen, "*Cong Suowei 'Sharen Zhizhao' Kan Falü Zhidu de Zhubu Wanshan Guocheng*" (A Case of the So-called "Murderer's License" Shows How the Legal System is Being Gradually Perfected), *Renmin Wang*, 9 July 2002, available at: www.qglt.com/wsrmlt/wyzs/2002/07/09/070914.html.

352 See Yang Yonggang, "*Cong 'Youbing Wuzui Lun' Dao Jingshen Weisheng Lifa*" (From the "Innocent-Because-Ill Theory" to Mental Health Legislation), *Zhong Fa Wang* website, 23 September 2002; at: www.china1laws.com/china/popular/lawnews/default.asp?Programid=26&lawnews=225.

phoney psychiatric evaluation certificates are very rarely held legally responsible and criminally prosecuted. In this way, murderers only have to buy themselves a "murderer's license" and they can get away with literally anything.[353]

The contrast between, on the one hand, the situation of murderers in China who, correctly or falsely, are exempted from punishment on grounds of insanity and then released back into society and, on the other hand, that of political dissidents and other non-violent critics of the government who are subjected to what we earlier called the "insanity prosecution" and are then sent to the Ankang for many years, because the authorities deem them to be too "dangerous" to release, could hardly be starker. However, it appears that the Chinese government would prefer to continue with a system that grants virtually no procedural or substantive rights to mentally-ill criminal defendants, and to reserve for the police and procuracy the legal initiative on any plea-making in this area, rather than to enact national mental health legislation that might lead to an increase in the number of "opportunist" insanity pleas by serious criminal offenders.[354] The proven potential for official corruption in this area of the law has no doubt only confirmed the government in its resolve to make haste as slowly as possible on introducing the PRC Mental Health Law.

In August 1989, the government issued a long-awaited set of formal rules – the Temporary Regulations for Judicial Appraisal of the Mentally Ill – specifying legal procedures for the conduct of expert psychiatric appraisals in criminal, civil, administrative and other types of cases.[355] According to Article 1 of the Temporary Regulations, they were intended, among other things, "to safeguard the lawful rights of mental illness sufferers," but in fact they contained almost no specific provisions on this topic. On more institutional matters, the Temporary Regulations instructed that Psychiatric Judicial Appraisal Committees were to be established at all provincial, regional and major municipal levels of government, and that these should comprise "responsible officials and experts" from the courts, procuracy, and public security, judicial administration and health departments. These committees were also to appoint, for specific cases that arose, Technical Appraisal Groups consisting of not less than two expert assessors, and the latter's expertise was to be sought in all cases where questions of mental competence had arisen in respect of criminal defendants, parties to civil or administrative litigation, persons undergoing administrative punishment (primarily, those sentenced without trial to up to three years in "re-education through labour" camps), criminal offenders serving custodial sentences, and also "other persons involved in the case who require [such] appraisal." The only "right" specifically accorded

---

353 "...*ji ke wan shi da ji*." See Si Wen (op cit), p.2.
354 There are also, however, certain institutional pressures in the other direction. According to one senior official source, the Ministry of Public Security in late 1987 drafted a national-level document entitled "Regulations on the Custody and Treatment of Mentally Ill People Who Seriously Endanger Public Order" (*Shourong Zhiliao Yanzhong Weihai Shehui Zhi'an de Jingshenbingren Tiaoli*), but because of the government's continuing delay in promulgating the PRC Mental Health Law, it had not been possible for the Ministry to actually finalize and enact these Regulations. (See: "*Gong'an Bu Fubuzhang Tian Qiyu zai Quanguo Jingshenbing Fangzhi Kangfu Gongzuo Huiyi Kaimushi-shang de Jianghua*" [Deputy Minister of Public Security Tian Qiyu's Speech at the National Work Conference on Mental Illness Prevention, Cure and Recovery], 13 May 1993, available at: www.cdpf.org.cn/nj/ala071/.)
355 See *Guanyu Jingshen Jibing Sifa Jianding Zanxing Guiding* (Temporary Regulations for Judicial Appraisal of the Mentally Ill), issued jointly by the Supreme People's Court, Supreme People's Procuracy, Ministry of Public Security, Ministry of Justice and Ministry of Civil Affairs, July 11, 1989. The regulations came into force on August 1, 1989. This followed an earlier set of rules on the same topic issued in October 1985 by the Anding psychiatric hospital in Beijing, which were "to be adopted by all provinces" in China (see Pearson, "Law, Rights and Psychiatry in the People's Republic of China," p.411).

to the subject of the appraisal appears in Article 8: "The Appraisal Committee may, depending upon the circumstances, accept a request from the person being examined for a supplementary appraisal, a fresh appraisal or a review of the [original] appraisal to be performed."

The principal task of the appraisers was to ascertain whether or not, at the time of "carrying out dangerous behaviour," the person concerned was mentally ill, and, if so, to identify the specific nature and severity of the illness. Depending on the type of case involved, the appraisers would also be charged with ascertaining the level of mental capacity and responsibility of those being examined in one or more of the following areas: overall legal responsibility for criminal acts committed; capacity to distinguish between right and wrong actions; ability to control one's behaviour and actions; capacity to stand trial (capacity for litigation); to serve a sentence or undergo other punishment; to testify or provide evidence; and (in the case of mentally ill victims of alleged sexual assault) to exercise either self-defence or sexual consent.[356] Two other important points should be made. First, only the "judicial organs" (i.e., courts, procuracy, police) were accorded the right to present a person for forensic psychiatric appraisal. Second, although the Temporary Regulations do not state as much, it was clearly understood that the findings of the expert appraisers were not binding on the judicial organs and that any final decision on whether to institute charges or to proceed to trial would be made solely by the latter.

The 1989 Temporary Regulations are still China's authoritative governing document in this area. In early 2000, however, the Ministry of Health issued a "recommendatory draft" version of a new document entitled "Administration Methods for Psychiatric Judicial Appraisal,"[357] the final clause of which states that the 1989 Temporary Regulations are to be superseded by the new document once it comes into force. The Administration Methods themselves were based to a very large extent on a similar document issued by the Beijing municipal government in January 1998,[358] and it is likely that they are already being implemented on a trial basis in several parts of China. It should be noted at the outset that none of these regulations list or refer to the enjoyment of any statutory rights or protections by the person being evaluated, and no provision is made for the lodging of appeals against eventual committal on grounds of criminal insanity.

The main additional measures and stipulations found in the new draft regulations are as follows. First, a new national-level governing body is to be instituted. According to Article 5, "The Supreme People's Court, Supreme People's Procuracy, Ministry of Health, Ministry of Justice and Ministry of Public Security shall jointly form a State Committee for the Coordination of Psychiatric Judicial Assessments, which shall be responsible for coordinating all such work throughout the country." This State Committee will stand at the apex of the system of provincial-level Psychiatric Judicial Appraisal Committees created in virtue of the 1989 Temporary Regulations, and will establish offices in the various health departments under the jurisdiction of the State Council, China's highest administrative body. Second, the new draft regulations stipulate a wide range of new measures aimed at imposing

---

356 The Chinese terms for these various criteria are (in order of listing above): "*xingshi zeren nengli,*" "*bianren nengli,*" "*kongzhi nengli,*" "*susong nengli,*" "*fuxing (shou chufa) nengli,*" "*zuozheng nengli,*" and "*ziwo fangwei nengli.*"
357 See Ministry of Health, *Jingshen Jibing Sifa Jianding Guanli Banfa* (Administration Methods for Psychiatric Judicial Appraisal), issued informally sometime in early 2000. The full Chinese text of this document can be found on the Internet at http://www.fmedsci.com/sfjs/sfjs11.htm.
358 See Beijing Municipal Bureau of Health, *Beijing Shi Jingshenbing Sifa Jianding Guanli Banfa* (Beijing Municipal Psychiatric Judicial Appraisal Management Rules [1998]). The full Chinese text is available on the Internet at http://www.fmedsci.com/sjfs/sfjs3.htm. The document came into force on January 1, 1998.

tighter regulation over the existing forensic-psychiatric appraisals system, especially in respect of the legal and academic accreditation of Technical Appraisal Groups and of individual expert assessors, the various time limits within which appraisals must be applied for, organized and completed (for example, assessors are to complete their appraisal within 30 days of first examining the person), and the requirement that complete case documentation, including all relevant police files, must be provided to the assessors before they can proceed. And third, the draft regulations introduced a number of significant legal-procedural safeguards. For example, officials or assessors having a close family connection with the examinee or any other personal interest in a case must withdraw themselves (the rule of recusal), and the examinee or other concerned persons have the right to request this. Technical Appraisal Groups must comprise no fewer than three assessors, and any expert opinions dissenting from the group's final recommendations should be separately noted on the official record. Also, private individuals and bodies may now also apply for expert appraisal to be carried out.

In December 2001, the Shanghai municipal legislature approved a new set of local rules – the Shanghai Municipal Mental Health Regulations – which went somewhat further than the various national-level regulations in laying down protections for basic patient rights. For example, Article 6 of the Shanghai regulations states: "The civil rights and personal dignity of the mentally ill are protected by law. It is forbidden to discriminate against, humiliate, abuse or abandon a mentally ill person." Under Article 28, a patient who disagrees with a hospital's diagnosis of his or her mental state has the right to apply to the municipal judicial psychiatric-appraisal committee for a second evaluation and diagnosis. And for the first time, under Article 46, the regulations specifically state that if any concerned party disagrees with a particular administrative act or decision taken by a hospital authority, then they have the right either to apply for a review of the decision under the Administrative Reconsideration Law, or to sue the hospital authority under the Administrative Litigation Law. (Although the regulations do not specifically mention patients as being among the "concerned parties" [*dangshiren*], one assumes that they are so included.) Also welcome is the prohibition (in Article 43) on carrying out experimental treatments or neurosurgery upon patients without their written consent. However, the stipulations governing involuntary civil committal (Articles 30-32) contained little new, other than stating that a hospital must make a full diagnosis of a forcibly hospitalized person's mental state within 72 hours of his or her admission. And the question of involuntary criminal committal is nowhere addressed in the Shanghai regulations.[359]

All of these current or pending reforms are no doubt worthy and laudable, and they may well have an important impact on ensuring the overall accuracy, quality and consistency of mental health care and forensic psychiatric appraisals in China. The bottom line, however, as far as our main topic – the treatment of alleged mentally ill political offenders – is concerned, is that none of the experts or officials working in the various committees and groups listed above have any say or discretion in the selection of the people whom they are required to examine. The identity of these individuals is determined solely

---

359 *Shanghai Jingshen Weisheng Tiaoli* (Shanghai Municipal Mental Health Regulations), passed by the Standing Committee of the Shanghai Municipal People's Congress on 28 December 2001 and effective as of 7 April 2002; available at: www.lawhighway.com.cn/falvshuju/content.asp?num=60964. The Shanghai Regulations are being billed in China as the country's "first local mental health act," and it is possible that they will give a much-needed boost to the continuing efforts to pass a national mental health law. (See: Zhang Xinkai, "*Zhuanti Taolun – Jingshen Weisheng Yu Fa*" (Special Discussion – Mental Health and the Law), 9 January 2003, *Zhongguo Jingshen Weisheng Wang* (China Mental Health Net), available at: www.21jk.com.cn/p. See also: Xie Bin and Zhang Mingyuan, "*Shanghai Shi 'Jingshen Weisheng Tiaoli' Jianjie*" (An Introduction the "Shanghai Municipal Mental Health Regulations"), *Zhonghua Jingshenke Zazhi*, November 2002, Vol.35, No.4.

by the nature of the country's criminal justice system; if the law says that a certain action is a crime, and if the offender is then arrested and brought for forensic psychiatric assessment, the expert assessors are required, unless they are ill or have some other acceptable reason for declining the job, to carry out an appraisal of the person's mental condition. It is not their task to determine whether or not a crime was actually committed, but rather to evaluate the detainee's sanity and then reach a conclusion as to whether or not he or she should bear "legal responsibility" for whatever offence the police claim was committed.

When the charge in question is a political one, however, this task immediately becomes, for the expert assessor, not only highly politicised in the general sense, but also, given China's overall history and track record in this particular area, potentially fraught with considerable personal risk. The safest course of action in such cases, undoubtedly, is for psychiatric assessors to "go by the book" – and as we have seen, Chinese forensic psychiatric textbooks still, even today, define certain types and instances of the uninhibited public expression of officially banned views and ideas as being clearly indicative of mental pathology. We do not have any first-hand accounts from Chinese forensic psychiatrists as to how they feel in such situations, but the following account of the situation of their former Soviet counterparts may provide some useful comparative insights into the matter:

> When the psychiatrist is finally confronted with the dissident, he knows he is dealing with someone who stands accused of committing what is considered by the authorities to be a serious crime. He is on his toes. He probably does not know, in most cases, whether a high-level decision has been made by the KGB to hospitalise the dissident, or whether the KGB investigator had genuine doubts about the dissident's mental health. The safer course is to assume that the KGB would like the dissident to be hospitalised. The psychiatrist himself is often in a special group to begin with: he is a forensic psychiatrist, usually a consultant to the KGB, and is particularly sensitive to the expectations of authorities. If he is sure that the expectation of hospitalisation exists, then much less evidence of illness is needed to establish a diagnosis. If he does not know, then his need to play it safe may influence him to see more symptoms than he ordinarily would – sufficiently more to justify a diagnosis of illness.[360]

At another level, moreover, ethically conscientious assessors face the following invidious choice: to find the defendant to be sane and hence "legally responsible" for the alleged political offence, in which case he or she will almost certainly be found guilty and sentenced to a long term of imprisonment; or to make a finding of insanity and legal non-imputability, in which case the person will most likely be committed for an indeterminate period to an Ankang or similar-style centre for psychiatric custody and treatment?[361]

---

360 Walter Reich M.D., "Diagnosing Soviet Dissidents," *Harper's*, August 1978, pp.31-37. At the time of writing this article, Dr. Reich was Lecturer in Psychiatry at Yale University and chairman of the program in the medical and biological sciences at the Washington School of Psychiatry. Over the previous six years he had interviewed a number of Soviet dissidents and psychiatrists.

361 In his report to the *British Medical Journal*, J.K. Wing posed a tantalizing ethical question that might also be asked of Chinese legal psychiatry: "Assuming for the moment that the Soviet psychiatrists have made their diagnosis in good faith, the question looks quite different to them: is a person who is suffering from a slowly developing form of schizophrenia responsible for an action that is likely to land him, at the very least, in a labour camp for three years? The Soviet doctor claims that he is acting humanely and that, in essence, the part he plays is no different from that of the American psychiatrists who saved Ezra Pound from execution" (J.K. Wing, "Psychiatry in the Soviet Union").

III. The Psychiatrist and the Dissident: Some Thorny Legal-Medical Issues

The Dangerousness Criterion

Under currently prevailing international legal and medical standards, a number of key principles are held to be paramount in the field of legal psychiatry. First, compulsory hospitalisation is, in most cases, only justified where the patient's mental state poses a direct danger, usually physical, either to his or her own health and safety, or to that of others; alternative considerations, such as concern by the authorities that a person's mental state or behaviour may prove injurious to "social stability," do not meet the requirements of this key "dangerousness" criterion.[362] As a U.N. Special Rapporteur noted in 1983,

> It is not satisfactory to generalize about "dangerousness" in the abstract. One must distinguish between "danger to self", "danger to others", and "danger to the public"… The argument of "overprediction of dangerousness" poses a grave threat to the human rights and fundamental freedoms of the patient.[363]

Second, it is a commonplace of international law, starting with the Universal Declaration of Human Rights, that no person may be subjected to detention, arrest, trial or any other form of persecution on account of their peacefully held political or religious views and activities.[364] And third, as a logical extension of these two principles, it is flatly impermissible for government authorities to subject any person, whether mentally ill or otherwise, to involuntary psychiatric treatment or hospitalisation on criminal charges relating to the person's political or religious views and beliefs – or indeed, to do so for any other reasons of governmental convenience.

---

362 The U.N. Principles for the Protection of Persons with Mental Illness and for the Improvement of Mental Health Care (discussed above at p.80) contain broader criteria for involuntary hospitalisation than just that of dangerousness; for example, they also permit involuntary commitment in the case of a person suffering from mental illness whose judgment is impaired and who is likely to suffer further psychiatric deterioration if not hospitalised. This aspect of the Principles clearly goes well beyond the question of dangerousness to self or others, and as such is viewed as controversial by many experts in the field. For a detailed critique of this and other aspects of the December 1991, U.N. document, see Eric Rosenthal and Leonard S. Rubenstein, "International Human Rights Advocacy under the 'Principles for the Protection of Persons with Mental Illness.'" *International Journal of Law and Psychiatry*, 1993, Vol.16, p.257. However, while the Principles may create a certain potential for abusive practices by allowing involuntary commitment on the grounds of possible further deterioration in the patient's subjective mental condition, they nonetheless still define the objective "dangerousness" criterion quite narrowly. Since the Chinese authorities invariably cite this particular criterion (and in the much wider form, moreover, of a putatively "social" or "political" type of dangerousness) when explaining why certain types of political nonconformists require to be psychiatrically detained, it is important to emphasize that China is in violation of international standards in this specific and key respect. Certainly, official concern that the mental state of those involved might "further deteriorate" unless they are forcibly committed never appears, in the Chinese legal-medical literature, as being either the whole or partial grounds for such action having been taken by the authorities. Finally, it is again vital to stress here that one is talking, in the Chinese case, about people being *criminally* detained and then subjected to *forensic* psychiatric appraisal – a very different matter from the kinds of involuntary civil commitment cases to which the psychiatric "deterioration" provisions in the U.N. Principles might well give rise.
363 Erica-Irene A. Daes, *Principles, Guidelines and Guarantees*, p.20.
364 See for example, Articles 9, 18 and 19 of the Universal Declaration of Human Rights.

The following questions should be borne in mind, therefore, in seeking to evaluate the cases of those described as "mentally ill political offenders" in China. Were the individuals concerned in fact mentally ill? If so, did they pose a genuine and direct danger to themselves or to others? And did their activities, as officially described, in any way justify their being placed under arrest and subjected to the authority of the state's criminal-psychiatric assessors? The first question is, in most cases, difficult if not impossible to answer on the basis of the fragmentary case material available, although certain useful insights can often be gleaned. The remaining two issues boil down, in essence, to the dangerousness criterion and how it is defined and interpreted by the authorities. The understanding of dangerousness as a medico-legal category varies considerably in legal systems around the world,[365] but the question of a mentally ill person's potential for doing physical harm to himself or others is of central and primary concern in most jurisdictions; secondary considerations may include psychological harm, danger to property, or damage to the environment.[366] China, however, is today the only country known specifically to include "political harm to society" within the scope of what the medico-legal authorities officially regard as being dangerous mentally ill behaviour.[367]

How high or prominently, then, do so-called political cases figure in the Chinese psychiatric establishment's general hierarchy or ranking of "serious crimes committed by the mentally ill"? This important issue has a close bearing upon the further question of whether the offenders concerned, once evaluated as being "not legally responsible" for their actions, will end up, variously: a) being set free and placed under a "family surveillance and control" order, or instructed to undergo either outpatient or

---

365 For an informative account of this topic, see Timothy Harding and Cleopatre Montandon, "Does Dangerousness Travel Well? A Cross-National Perspective on Medico-Legal Applications," in John R. Hamilton and Hugh Freeman (eds.), *Dangerousness: Psychiatric Assessment and Management* (Gaskell, 1982), pp.46-52. A fuller and more in-depth discussion of the various issues involved can be found in John Gunn, "Dangerousness," in John Gunn and Pamela J. Taylor (eds.), *Forensic Psychiatry: Clinical, Legal and Ethical Issues* (Butterworth & Heinemann, 1993), pp.624-645.

366 The dangerousness criterion is a contentious issue among psychiatrists at the best of times, even when it is narrowly restricted to the potential for committing physical violence. According to one source,

> Furthermore, the evidence is pretty overwhelming that psychiatrists are not very good at predicting dangerousness; their success rate in correctly identifying future violence varies from a high of 40 percent...to a low of something like 0.3 percent... The role of psychiatrists in sentencing and detaining procedures is also challenged, on the grounds that they cannot even agree amongst themselves on a definition of dangerousness. I myself like the simple one of it being the potential to cause serious physical harm to others, although there is a case for psychological harm to be included also.

(Hamilton and Freeman, *Dangerousness*, pp.1-3.)

367 This is not to say that no other countries still practice political psychiatry; a handful do, notably Cuba. For the background history, see Charles J. Brown and Armando M. Lago, *The Politics of Psychiatry in Revolutionary Cuba* (Freedom House, 1992). For a more recent case report, see "Dissidents Stage Fast to Protest Reincarceration," Agence France Presse, February 27, 1998; in FBIS same day. But so far as is known in these other cases, the notion of political harm is not actually written into the formal definition of psychiatric dangerousness. It is also worth noting that even where the dangerousness criterion is validly and legitimately applied, "The level of security applied to a patient should always be the minimum level which is compatible with safety and good management" (John Gunn and Pamela J. Taylor, *Forensic Psychiatry*, p.635). In practice this means that unless a crime has already been committed, a violent mentally ill person may be detained in, for example, the secure ward of a normal mental hospital; those who commit serious crimes of violence may, by contrast, end up in a secure prison mental hospital. In China, as the Ankang admissions criteria listed on p.256 below clearly indicate, non-violent and alleged mentally ill "political offenders" are among those most likely to receive the latter kind of treatment.

inpatient psychiatric treatment at a normal hospital; b) being placed under involuntary committal in the secure ward of a regular mental hospital or, for those with no means of financial support, in a similar closed section of one of the numerous Ministry of Civil Affairs-run "social welfare institutes"[368] found throughout the country; or c), being forcibly confined without limitation of time in an Ankang institute for the criminally insane.

In a fundamental sense, this question can be readily answered simply by looking at China's Criminal Law, which has always defined political offences of various kinds – peaceful or otherwise – as constituting the most serious possible form of crime. This was made clear both in the 1979 Criminal Law, which dealt with all the various "crimes of counterrevolution" under Chapter 1 of the "Special Provisions" section of the Law, and also in the 1997 revised version of the same law, which dealt in the same way with the newly defined range of "crimes of endangering state security." It comes as no surprise, therefore, to learn that "cases of a political nature" are generally deemed by China's forensic psychiatric community to rank among the most serious and dangerous of all possible offences committed by the mentally ill.

This point emerges clearly in the following passage from a major retrospective survey of criminal psychiatric cases that was published in China in 1988:

> Of the 222 cases in the present group where diagnoses of schizophrenia were made, sixty-six cases (or 29.7 percent) involved murder or serious injury (a figure closely approximating the findings of Li Congpei *et al* in their study); there were fifty-five cases of a political nature; and forty-eight cases involved disturbances of social order. The combined total for these three categories came to 169 cases, accounting for 76.1 percent of all cases committed by schizophrenics. From this, we can ascertain the major gravity of the threat posed to social order and personal safety by schizophrenia sufferers who commit crimes, and also the severity of the consequences thereof.[369]

In other words, so-called political cases and also ones involving "disturbance of public order"[370] are evidently viewed by China's legal-medical authorities as representing no less serious and dangerous a threat to society than cases of murder and injury committed by genuinely psychotic criminal offenders. According to this logic, it is only natural that the authorities should treat psychiatric detainees from

---

368 These institutes serve, simultaneously, as warehouses or dumping grounds for indigent elderly people, abandoned or orphaned infants and small children and also the destitute mentally ill. For further information, see Human Rights Watch/Asia, *Death By Default: A Policy of Fatal Neglect in China's State Orphanages* (New York: Human Rights Watch, 1996), Chapter 2 and *passim*.

369 Shen Muci et al (op cit), p.166-168. As can be seen, "cases of a political nature" accounted for as much as 25 percent of all the schizophrenia cases forensically examined in this study.

370 Many cases of "disturbing public order" in China also merit inclusion under the general heading of "cases of a political nature," since state-appointed forensic examiners frequently diagnose such persons as suffering from "litigious mania" (*susong kuang*) also known as "processomania." The latter diagnostic category was reportedly first posited by a French psychiatrist in the 19th century, and was widely applied by Soviet forensic psychiatrists (who generally regarded it – as do their Chinese counterparts today – as being a subspecies of "paranoid psychosis") in the cases of politically dissident detainees up until the late 1980s. Western systems of law acknowledge a category of persons known as "vexatious litigators"; but this term is applied only in civil cases (most commonly, in judicial denial of the right to bring suit on the grounds that the plaintiff's allegations are frivolous or unwarranted), and certainly not as a psychiatric label leading to incarceration on the grounds of criminal insanity. The various different types of "disturbing social order" in China that also properly qualify as "political cases" are further discussed below.

both the above categories as prime candidates for long-term admission into the Ankang system. Significantly, the very same logic was applied by forensic psychiatrists in the former Soviet Union. According to the findings of a case survey carried out at the Serbski Institute and other major Soviet mental hospitals in the early 1970s,

> Compulsory treatment in Special Psychiatric Hospitals should be recommended in cases involving brutal murders motivated by delusional ideas, in cases of persistent litigious behaviour, and in the case of persistent "ideas of reform" which tend to be convincing to others and tend to cause recurrent illegal actions.[371]

But the official view in China goes still further than this, for it sometimes seeks actually to equate violence and dissidence, by depicting the latter as being a form of "violence" in itself. A prime example of this mode of thinking can be seen in the following passage written by Li Congpei, one of the foremost forensic psychiatrists working in China today, and several of his colleagues on the question of crimes committed by schizophrenics:

> Among the cases under discussion, outbursts of violent behaviour[372] were characterized by several unusual features: for example, the person's "criminal" motive would frequently be vague and unclear or the reverse of what it originally seemed to be, and was thus difficult to fathom; or the person would often display absolutely no sense or instinct of self-preservation, for example by openly mailing out reactionary letters or pasting up reactionary slogan-banners in public places – and even, in some cases, signing his or her real name to the documents; and in cases where the "criminal" behaviour had been relatively savage,[373] the person would later maintain an air of cool indifference.[374]

At the outset of this analysis of 386 cases of criminal behaviour by schizophrenics, Li and his colleagues stated that the diagnostic criteria applied in the study were based, among other things, upon the psychiatric classification models laid down in the World Health Organization's International Classification of Diseases (ICD-9) and the American medical profession's Diagnostic and Statistical Manual of Mental Disorders (DSM-III). The authors' explicit characterization, however, of the relatively mild acts of public political protest referred to above as representing typical examples of violent psychotic behaviour will no doubt dismay psychiatric professionals around the world who actually do base their work on these standard medical reference texts. The only real threat or danger that peaceful dissidents, sane or otherwise, might conceivably be said to pose in China today is to the indefinite continuance of the Communist Party's arbitrary and un-elected tenure of national political power. But from the authorities' point of view, neutralizing even the remotest possibility of any such threat is the whole point of the exercise.

---

371 A.L. Kosachev, "Clinical and Forensic Evaluation of Psychopathy of a Paranoid Type," Moscow 1973 (publisher unknown); cited in Gluzman (op cit), p.40.
372 "*shixing baoli xingwei*"
373 "*jiaowei xiongcan*"
374 Li Congpei, Li Yongzhi, Liu Jinsheng and Fang Mingzhao, "*Jingshen Fenliezheng Sifa Jingshenbing Jianding An Li Fenxi* (An Analysis of Cases Involving the Forensic-Psychiatric Evaluation of Schizophrenia)," *Chinese Journal of Nervous and Mental Diseases*, 1987, Vol.20, No.3, pp.135-138. It is worth noting also that the works of Georgi Morozov were cited as an authority in the footnotes to this article.

"Presumption of Insanity" and "Lack of Instinct for Self-preservation"

A useful and pithy working summary of the abnormal mental condition allegedly responsible for driving dissidents to question or challenge the government's political line and policies, and of the two main forms that such activity generally takes, was provided in 1994 in a textbook on forensic psychiatry written by a leading police psychiatrist at the Beijing Ankang institute:

> Paranoid psychosis manifests itself, in clinical practice, in two different ways: one form is "litigious mania," in which delusions of persecution tend to predominate; the other form is "political mania," where the dominant role is played by "political delusions." The content of the delusions in "political mania" concern the line and policies of the State; those afflicted do avid research into politics and put forward a whole set of original theories of their own, which they then try to peddle by every means possible, thereby leading to court action.[375] For this reason, such people are sometimes viewed as being political dissidents.
>
> For example, one middle-aged person who was suffering from "political mania" wanted to do research into "modern humanism" and spontaneously resigned from his job. He spent all his time shut up at home, writing manuscripts tens of thousands of characters in length, which he then sent to the Academy of Social Sciences and the editorial departments of various newspapers and journals, hoping they would accept them. When all his efforts failed, he got in touch with some foreigners and asked them to publish his articles abroad, thereby causing a great deal of trouble.[376]

The close similarity between this twofold capsule definition of politically-related mental illness and the diagnostic theories developed and applied by forensic psychiatrists in the Soviet Union over several decades is readily apparent; indeed, the two definitions are virtually identical. As Bukovsky and Gluzman explained in their 1974 *samizdat* document "A Manual on Psychiatry for Dissenters," forensic psychiatrists trained in the Serbski school of thought typically identified two forms of "paranoid development of the personality" as being chiefly responsible for the commission of acts of political dissent by Soviet citizens. The mental conditions in question were:

a) Reformist delusions: [the belief that] an improvement in social conditions can be achieved only through the revision of people's attitudes, in accordance with the individual's own ideas for the transformation of reality.

---

375 "...*cong'er yinqi susong*" literally means "thereby leading to litigation." The text is ambiguous as to whether it is the dissident or the government who initiates the "litigation" in question. Since there is no known case of any Chinese political dissident having ever launched court action against the government for pursuing "erroneous politics" (i.e., an "incorrect" form of Marxist socialism), the above reference to "litigation" or "court action" can only be understood as a somewhat euphemistic indication by the author that the dissident in question was criminally prosecuted for his contrarian political views and writings. This would also explain why he was being subjected to forensic psychiatric examination: he had already been detained or arrested for alleged political crimes.

376 Long Qingchun (ed.), *Sifa Jingshen Yixue Jianding Zixun Jieda*, pp.83-84. Interestingly, the author adds: "The incidence of unlawful and calamitous behaviour, however, is markedly less common in the case of paranoid psychotics than in the case of schizophrenics. The vast majority of such behaviour is caused by the sufferers' paranoid delusions... And in cases where, under the dominant influence of delusions of grandeur or persecution, 'reactionary speech or action' ensues, then it will usually do so in public places, for example with the person concerned handing out leaflets or sticking up big-character posters, signed with his or her real name, in crowded public places."

b) Litigation mania: a conviction, which does not have any basis in fact, that the individual's own rights as a human being are being violated and flouted; the reasons become "clear" to him, and he begins to send in complaints and demands to have "justice" restored.[377]

We shall return to these two important categories in the next chapter, in an examination of how specific individuals and cases of both types have been dealt with by the Chinese legal and psychiatric authorities. Before doing so, however, we should first consider a number of other important legal-medical diagnostic issues that commonly arise in the context of the forensic psychiatric evaluation of "political cases" in China.

The first such issue concerns the high rate at which findings of lack of legal competence or legal non-imputability on grounds of mental illness are made. In an extensive and wide-ranging review of a total of 931 cases of forensic psychiatric evaluation that had been performed at Beijing's Anding hospital during the period 1983-87, Tian Zu'en and other senior physicians at the hospital established, among other things, that altogether 301, or 32.3 percent, of the criminal detainees concerned were found to have "impaired ability to recognize" their actions; a further 307 persons, or 33 percent, were found to have "impaired ability to control" their actions; and 323 others, or 34.7 percent, were found to have "no impairment of legal capacity."[378] These findings are significant because, like numerous other officially published statistics on the same point, they indicate that a far higher proportion of criminal defendants brought before psychiatric evaluation panels in China, altogether 65.3 percent in Tian's case study, are found to be legally incapable by reason of insanity than is the case in most other countries.[379] An even more striking finding of the same study was that out of nineteen "political cases" among the survey

---

[377] *Russia's Political Hospitals* (op cit), p.427.

[378] The Chinese terms for these categories, in order of above listing, are: "*bianren zhang'ai*," "*kongzhi zhang'ai*" and "*falü nengli wu zhang'ai*." See Tian Zu'en, Yu Qingbo, Qi Wei, Wang Ping, Chen Lifeng and Yu Tian, "*Jingshenbingren de Xingshi Falü Nengli* (Criminal Legal Capacity of the Mentally Ill)," *Chinese Journal of Nervous and Mental Diseases*, 1988, Vol.21, No.3, pp.169-171. Under Chinese law the presence of either "impaired recognition" or "impaired control" constitutes, by itself, sufficient grounds for a finding of "lack of legal responsibility."

[379] According to Richard J. Bonnie, Professor of Law at the University of Virginia School of Law and Director of the University's Institute of Law, Psychiatry and Public Policy:

In the United States, where most psychiatric evaluations of criminal responsibility are initiated by defence attorneys, forensic examiners find a clinical basis for an insanity defence in approximately 10-20 percent of cases, depending on the state. See, e.g., Warren, J.W., Rosenfeld, B., Fitch, W.L., and Hawk, G., "Forensic Mental Health Clinical Evaluation: An Analysis of Interstate and Intersystemic Differences," *Law and Human Behavior*, Vol. 21, 1997, pp.377-390. (In 1987-88, opinions favoring insanity were rendered by forensic examiners in 7 percent of evaluations in Michigan, 9 percent of evaluations in Virginia, and 13 percent of evaluations in Ohio.) Interestingly, forensic examiners in the former USSR tended to render opinions of non-imputability in a substantial majority of cases in which the defendant was found to have a mental disorder. (See Bonnie, R.J., "Coercive Psychiatry and Human Rights: An Assessment of Recent Changes in the Soviet Union," *Criminal Law Forum*, 1990, No.1, pp.319-346, at page 334: '[N]onimputability determinations ... occur in a much larger proportion of criminal cases than appears to be the norm in the united States and other Western countries.') That practice appears to have continued in Russia.

(Richard J. Bonnie, personal communication to author, December 7, 2000).

See also "Statistics of Mentally Disordered Offenders 1999 — England and Wales," U.K Government, available at http://www.homeoffice.gov.uk/rds/pdfs/hosb2100.pdf; see in particular Table 6, p.12.

group that were specifically defined as being "counterrevolutionary" in nature, fourteen detainees, or 73.7 percent of the total, were determined to have "impaired recognition" of their allegedly criminal acts, while the remaining five detainees, or 26.3 percent of the total, were found to have "impaired control" over their actions.[380] None of the nineteen "pseudo-counterrevolutionaries" was diagnosed as being mentally normal.[381]

These various figures suggest either that the standard of proof and evidence for determining criminal insanity is considerably less rigorous in China than elsewhere, or else that far fewer cases of a frivolous, implausible or opportunist nature are presented for expert medical evaluation. The latter possibility can effectively be ruled out since virtually all such cases in China are put forward by the police or the state prosecutor, rather than, as generally occurs in the West, the counsel for the defence. Either way, it is clear that criminal defendants' chances of being "acquitted" of the suspicion of mental illness is in practice extremely low – a situation broadly similar to that found in the criminal trials system, where less than one percent of defendants are eventually found to be innocent.

A volume published in 1999 by three experts from the Institute of Forensic Medicine at the West China Medical University in Chengdu, including Liu Xiehe, one of China's top forensic psychiatrists, sheds important light on this issue. Liu and his colleagues began by calling for his Chinese colleagues to adopt, along the lines of certain stipulations found in the Criminal Code of Canada, a "presumption of sanity" when conducting forensic psychiatric appraisals. As they explained,

---

380 Curiously enough, however, where the question of "criminal motive" (*fanzui dongji*) was concerned, Tian and his co-authors found that while the illegal political behaviour of eleven of the nineteen "counterrevolutionary" forensic examinees had been inspired by "pathological motives" (*bingli dongji*), and that of three others by "unclear motives" (*buming dongji*), the remaining five examinees were said to have been prompted by "real" or "authentic" motives (*xianshi dongji*) – meaning (in the authors' own words): "motives arising from the conflicts and requirements of reality and having no direct or evident relationship to the mental illness from which the person is suffering." In other words, the five "mentally ill" individuals in question appear, by the authorities' own admission, to have been entirely sane and rational at the time of staging their banned political manifestations (Tian Zu'en et al., "Criminal Legal Capacity of the Mentally Ill," pp.175-177). The same article also discussed the correlation between motive and legal responsibility: out of the total group of 931 forensic-psychiatric examinees, all the 323 persons who were determined to bear "full legal responsibility" for their criminal acts were also said to have been inspired by "authentic" motivating factors, suggesting an officially perceived one-to-one correlation between these elements under normal circumstances; a roughly similar number of persons (352) were found to bear "limited responsibility" for their actions despite also having been prompted by real or authentic motives; and only twenty-three persons found to be similarly motivated were determined to bear "no legal responsibility" for their acts. Of 163 persons whose crimes were officially attributed to "pathological motives," all were declared to be not legally responsible, as were eighteen others who were said to have acted from "mixed motives." The remaining 52 persons from the group were said to have had "unclear" motives, and all were similarly held not legally responsible (Ibid., p.176).
381 But again, they were caught on the horns of what might be called "psychiatric justice with Chinese characteristics." For had they been found to be sane, they would have proceeded to trial and almost certain conviction on charges of counterrevolution, the most serious offence in the Criminal Law. Since, however, the ostensibly political activities that brought them into the orbit of the criminal justice system in the first place are viewed by the government as being so "socially dangerous" that such persons must on no account be allowed to continue manifesting their "pathological symptoms" within society at large, the fact that they were determined to be mentally ill meant that they would instead, in all probability, be placed in closed psychiatric prison wards where they would be forced to undergo indefinite medical treatment for their exotic psycho-political disorders. For China's hapless "political lunatics," in short, freedom is seldom a viable outcome.

At present in China there are two main modes of thought. First, the "clinical mode of thought," which is mainly found among appraisals experts who have worked for many years as clinical psychiatrists and also, part time, as judicial psychiatric appraisers. When psychiatric experts of this kind have to perform judicial appraisals, they make a presumption that the person being examined is either mentally abnormal or afflicted by some form of mental illness. The reason for this is that they assume that the examinee would not have been sent for appraisal in the first place unless he or she was in fact mentally abnormal or suffering from mental illness; or else, they feel that the person must indeed have been behaving in some unusual kind of way, otherwise the judicial officers, lawyer or family members concerned would not have raised the request for an appraisal to be carried out. As a result of this general presumption, or feeling of probability, the appraiser will then go to great pains to avoid "being negligent," either by searching through the case files for any possible evidence of mental abnormality or mental disease, or by urging the judicial officers, lawyer or family members to provide as much evidence of this nature as they can.[382]

The second main mindset, which the three writers call "the judicial appraisal mode of thought," was one generally found among full-time police forensic psychiatrists, who tended to take the opposite approach and presume that all criminal suspects sent for psychiatric appraisal were mentally normal. The reason they did so was in order to ensure that as many offenders as possible would receive due punishment for their actions. In the view of the book's authors, both of these tendencies were biased and unscientific, and they concluded by calling for China to adopt a similar "presumption of sanity" rule as that found in the Canadian legislation.

The situation described here clearly gives much cause for general concern. Where "cases of a political nature" are involved, however, the implications become more complex and troubling still. Basically, these have to do with the same general problem identified elsewhere in this discussion, namely the essentially specious nature of the Chinese judicial authorities' distinction between "genuine" and "mentally ill" counterrevolutionary offenders. At least where internationally recognized criminal offences are concerned, the two "modes of thought" identified above might result, at worst, in either a mentally ill offender being sent to a regular prison and not receiving any medical treatment, or in a sane offender being wrongly diagnosed as mentally ill and sent to a forensic psychiatric asylum.[383] In China's "political cases," however, no internationally recognized offence has been committed, but simply an

---

382 Zhang Wei, Huo Kediao and Liu Xiehe, "*Fayi Jingshenbingxue Jianding de Siwei Fangshi* (Modes of Thought in Forensic Psychiatric Appraisals)," in *Fayixue Jinzhan yu Shijian* (*Advances and Practices in Forensic Medicine*) (Chengdu Science and Technology University Press, 1999). The passage quoted above can be found at http://www.legalmed.org/ref/99z1.html.

A case of this type was reported in the official media in January 2002. A man named Qiu Changgui had got into a fight with a leader of his work unit and been arrested and then sent to a mental hospital for 14 days. According to the news report, the police argued that it was not up to them to prove that Qiu was insane; rather, it was Qiu's responsibility to prove that he was sane. As the journalist observed, "Saying 'He is presently unable to find evidence to prove that he is not suffering from mental illness' amounts to a psychiatric 'presumption of guilt'." (See: Ma Shaohua, "Bu Shi Jingshenbing, Xuyao Shenme Zhengju" (Why Should Evidence be Required to Show that Someone is Not Mentally Ill?), *Zhongguo Qingnian Bao* (China Youth Daily Online), 18 January 2002.

383 There is, of course, a third possibility, namely that the person sent either to prison or a mental asylum will eventually turn out to have been innocent; such miscarriages of justice occur, from time to time, in all legal systems around the world.

act of free expression protected by international law, so the general picture assumes a significantly different quality and character than this. Presumably, the former type of Chinese psychiatrist will tend to rush to assume that a person detained for political offences is indeed mentally ill and needs to be forcibly committed, whereas those of the second mindset will insist that "due punishment" be meted out and that the person be sent immediately to jail. In short, political detainees are presumed to be either guilty, or insane. Given this essentially punitive medico-legal climate, whichever variety of expert appraiser the hapless Chinese dissident, or "pseudo-dissident," happens to encounter, it is evident that his or her chances of being allowed to walk free at the end of the day are effectively nil.

As if this were not unjust enough, there is sometimes a further subtle twist to the situation. One of the tasks of forensic psychiatrists everywhere is to ascertain whether or not the examinee is feigning symptoms of mental illness as a way of avoiding trial or punishment. This phenomenon, generally referred to as "malingering," was discussed in the context of the psychiatric examination of political offenders by one Chinese source as follows:

> Counterrevolutionary behaviour by the mentally ill: In most cases, the mental illness takes the form of either delusions of grandeur or delusions of persecution. When the mentally ill person exhibits behaviour that endangers the People's Republic of China, it is usually in the form of speech or writing, such as writing reactionary posters or banners, shouting reactionary slogans, or drafting reactionary manifestos. The hallmark of such counterrevolutionary behaviour by the mentally ill is that one can generally find no immediate or proximate cause for it. The thoughts and actions appear illogical. The counterrevolutionary behaviour is carried out in public, with no apparent fear of the consequences, in broad daylight and in a brazen and flagrant manner. However, one must be on the alert in such situations: the person concerned may simply be feigning mental illness as a cover for their actions, while all the time engaging in genuinely counterrevolutionary plots.[384]

The implied scenario – of a dissident being caught in the street red-handed by the police while pasting up banned political material, and then being forensically examined to see if he or she was only "pretending to be mad" – surely takes some beating, even by official Chinese standards of political diligence and correctness.

The above passage also raises another diagnostic emphasis, or clinical predisposition, that appears to be central to the official forensic psychiatric mindset in cases of this type. In essence, this can be colloquially summed up as the belief: "You'd have to be crazy to do things like that in China." Underlying this assumption, which itself is a reflection or facet of the "presumption of insanity" issue, is the common understanding that any Chinese citizen in his or her right mind would surely be aware that to publicly challenge the government on questions of political ideology is an extremely high risk activity that most likely will lead to one's arrest by the police. One writer succinctly conveyed the official psychiatric viewpoint on this question in a book published in 1989:

> Political offences of this kind are usually perpetrated in public places. The person concerned will write out reactionary documents, sign them in full, and then sometimes – as if afraid that people won't know his or her real identity – even add their full

---

384 "...*jiu keneng shi yi weizhuang jingshenbing shouduan wei yanhu, jinxing zhenzhengde fan'geming goudang.*" See *China Encyclopaedia of Public Security*, p.1967. The most suitable diagnostic label for such crafty and devious political offenders would perhaps be "pseudo-pseudo-counterrevolutionaries."

addresses and give details of their work unit. In other cases, the person involved will write out slogan-banners and then go walking down the street, in broad daylight and into crowded areas, with a whole pile of the things draped over his or her arm and begin pasting them up all over the place. When other people start noticing this performance and come over to see what's happening, the person often tries to "act casual" and pretend that he or she is some kind of a "big hero."[385]

With unintended irony, other Chinese forensic psychiatrists frequently note that the mental instability of people of this type is further apparent because, in "openly signing their real names" to such documents and then "failing to run away" afterwards, they have clearly demonstrated a "lack of any instinct for self-preservation."[386] The above passage, however, could easily have been referring to the kinds of peaceful protest actions that took place on a daily and hourly basis in Tiananmen Square, and most other parts of China, during the May 1989 pro-democracy movement. While such activities are understandably irksome to authoritarian governments who insist upon a high degree of public conformity to official standards of thought and behaviour, and while it is possible that some, or perhaps even many, of the "political offenders" concerned may have been mentally or emotionally disturbed in some way, the fact remains that none of these people, according to the official account, committed murders, raped or molested anyone, set fire to public buildings, attacked important government leaders, or even exposed themselves naked in the street. Any of them who were indeed mentally ill should have been provided with prompt and appropriate medical care, while the rest should have been allowed, in conformity with internationally recognized standards, to go about their public business in a free and unrestricted fashion.

Civil-style Psychiatric Appraisals in Political Cases: The Case of Li Mou

So far, we have dealt almost exclusively with the criminal law aspects of forensic psychiatric assessment and custody. It is important, however, also to address the civil law dimension of involuntary psychiatric committal in China, since as we shall see in the various case studies presented in Chapters 6 and 8 below, the Chinese police appear to be resorting with increasing frequency to various bogus forms of "involuntary civil committal" nowadays as a means of silencing whistleblowers and other similar kinds of social critics.

The question of the civil rights entitlements and "capacity for civil action" of mentally ill people in China is dealt with in various provisions of the 1987 General Principles of the Civil Law of the PRC and also in Articles 170-173 of the 1991 Civil Procedure Law.[387] For example, Article 13 of the General Principles states: "A mentally ill person who is unable to recognize his own conduct shall be a person having no capacity for civil conduct and shall be represented in civil activities by his agent *ad litem*."

---

385 See Shen Zheng (ed.), *Falü Jingshenbingxue*, p.305; the quoted passage was written by Zheng Zhanpei.
386 See, for example: Mao Shulin et al., "Chapter Seven: Psychopathology and Crime," *Fanzui Xinlixue (Psychology of Crime)*, (Beijing: Qunzhong Chubanshe, 1985), p.222; see also Jia Yicheng, *Shiyong Sifa Jingshenbingxue*, p.38. Similar references to the "lack of instinct for self-preservation" shown in cases of this type can be found throughout the Chinese legal-medical literature.
387 Civil Procedure Law of the PRC, Section Four: "Cases of Ascertaining Citizens' Incapacity or Restricted Capacity for Civil Action":

> Article 170. An application for ascertainment of a citizen's incapacity or restricted capacity for civil action shall be raised by a close relative or other interested party at the basic people's court in the place of the residence of the citizen in question.

It continues by saying that those "unable to fully recognize" their own conduct shall be regarded as having "limited capacity" for civil conduct and may engage in "civil activities appropriate" to their state of mental health. In other articles of the same law, issues relating to the legal guardianship of mentally ill people are addressed. The General Principles do not, however, contain any provisions on such important matters as the legal procedures and criteria for the compulsory hospitalisation and treatment of the mentally ill. Indeed, simply by virtue of being ill, mentally ill people in China who have committed no offences often encounter significant reduction of their civil rights at the authorities' hands, for example through deprivation of the right to vote. In addition, confidential regulations even state that the police "should delay issuing [citizens'] identity cards to...persons who are mentally ill" – thereby placing them in a broadly similar official category to that of persons placed under formal arrest or serving terms of imprisonment, who are to be denied identity cards altogether.[388]

This assumption of general civil incompetence on the part of the mentally ill, especially those subject to compulsory hospitalisation, is at sharp variance with accepted international legal and ethical standards. As one Western authority on law and psychiatry has noted,

> The applicable human rights principle is stated in the Daes Report [to the U.N.] (1982):[389] Every patient has the right "to exercise all his civil, political, social or cultural rights," including the right to manage his own economic affairs, control the disposition of his assets, and vote. The only limitation is where a court makes a

---

The written application shall clearly state the facts about and the grounds for the incapacity or restricted capacity of the citizen in question.

Article 171. Where necessary, the people's court, having accepted the application for ascertainment of a citizen's incapacity or restricted capacity for civil action, shall conduct a corroboration on the citizen in question. Where the applicant has provided a conclusion of expert corroboration, the people's court shall examine the conclusion.

Article 172. Where necessary, in handling a case of ascertainment of a citizen's incapacity and restricted capacity for civil action, shall appoint a close relative of the citizen in question other than the applicant as his representative. Where the close relatives shirk the responsibility, the people's court shall appoint one of them as representative. The people's court shall ask the opinion of the citizen in question if his health permits.

If the people's court, in handling the case, concludes that the application is based on facts, it shall make a judgment ascertaining the citizen's incapacity and restricted capacity for civil action; if it finds that the application it not based on facts, it shall reject the application.

Article 173. Where the people's court, in accordance with an application by the person who has been ascertained to be incapable for civil action or to have only restricted capacity, or by his guardian, confirms that the cause of the said citizen's incapacity or restricted capacity has been removed, it shall make a new judgment and reverse the original judgment.

388 See Liu Guangren (ed.), *Hukou Guanlixue* (*The Administration of Household Residence*), (Beijing: Zhongguo Jiancha Chubanshe [volume marked "for distribution within the public security organs only"], 1992), p.324.
389 Erica-Irene A. Daes, Special Rapporteur of the U.N. Sub-Commission on Prevention of Discrimination and Protection of Minorities, *Principles, Guidelines and Guarantees for the Protection of Persons Detained on Grounds of Mental Ill-Health or Suffering from Mental Disorder* [New York: United Nations Publications, 1986] E/CN.4/Sub.2/1983/17/Rev.1.

specific finding that the person is incompetent to exercise the right; detention in hospital in itself does not justify a finding of incompetence.[390]

In particular, there appears to be little if any in the way of legislative interconnect or cross-over in China between, on the one hand, the handling of mentally ill offenders under the Criminal Law and, on the other, the broader issue of their civil rights entitlement as laid down in the General Principles. Whatever may be the situation of those subjected to civil psychiatric committal in China,[391] it is clear from the relevant official literature that criminal detainees found not legally responsible by reason of insanity automatically lose, by virtue of this finding, most if not all of their civil rights.[392] In practice, moreover, it is often hard to tell from the individual case accounts – especially in certain dissident-style petitioner or whistleblower cases – whether the detainees in question have been handled under civil forensic evaluation and committal procedures or, alternatively, under the criminal-law forensic process.

The following case account, involving a factory worker turned whistleblower, illustrates the complex and sometimes baffling interrelationship between civil and criminal-style legal norms and practices that is often to be found in cases of this type. It appeared in a textbook on forensic psychiatric assessments work published in Beijing in 1994:

> After a man named Li Mou[393] had accused his factory director on numerous occasions of financial impropriety, he was diagnosed by Hospital A as suffering from mild mania, and hence as bearing no legal responsibility [for his alleged crime]. On the basis of this finding, the court then ruled that Li Mou had no capacity for civil action. Hospital B, however, evaluated Li Mou and found that he was capable of civil action. How should this case be assessed and what decision should be made?

---

390 Larry Gostin, "Human Rights in Mental Health: A Proposal for Five International Standards Based upon the Japanese Experience," *International Journal of Law and Psychiatry*, Vol. 10, 1987, pp.353-368. As Gostin points out, similar problems are, if anything, even more widespread in the case of Japan: "The mentally ill person in Japan is still the subject of discrimination under outmoded assumptions of general incompetency. There are dozens of laws, regulations and customs which deny basic rights and privileges to mentally ill people as a class. The mentally ill technically are prohibited from entering public places such as swimming pools, baths, public libraries, local legislative assemblies, and public monuments such as castles. The mentally ill are also excluded from professions such as barbers, beauticians, guides, interpreters, drivers and doctors. Finally, mentally ill people are not entitled to welfare benefits, services, and employment protection available to the physically disabled and mentally retarded." (Ibid, pp.365-366.)

391 For a detailed discussion of the civil law aspects of the treatment of mentally ill people in China, see: Pearson, "Law, Rights and Psychiatry in the People's Republic of China," pp.417-420.

392 Specific procedures for the courts to make findings of civil competence and incompetence are set forth in Articles 170-173 of the Civil Procedure Law of the PRC (adopted by the 4th session of the 7th National People's Congress on April 9, 1991 and effective as of same date); see Note 387, above, for the full text of the relevant Articles. Courts may declare a mentally ill person to have "lost the capacity for civil action" and they may also reverse such rulings (Article 19 of the General Principles of Civil Law, adopted at the 4th Session of the 6th National People's Congress on April 12, 1986 and effective as of January 1, 1987), although the former (as in other countries) is not an essential prerequisite for compulsory civil psychiatric committal. In the case of criminal psychiatric committal, however, the courts in China appear to have an almost negligible role to play, either in terms of authorizing and approving such treatment, or as regards providing those psychiatrically detained with legal channels for appeal and possible redress.

393 The "Mou" portion of Li's name is a generic substitute for his actual given name – equivalent to calling him "Li So-and-so" – and was added by the book's author to protect the man's identity.

Summary of appraisal by Hospital A: Li Mou, male, 37 years old, educated to lower-middle school level, a worker. From 1985 onwards, Li made numerous accusations to the higher authorities, saying that his factory director was guilty of financial impropriety (*you jingji wenti*.) It was suspected that Li was mentally ill, and in July 1988 he was referred for a forensic evaluation to determine whether or not this was the case and to ascertain if he was capable of bearing legal responsibility for his actions.

As the account then made clear, Li Mou had been arrested and charged with a criminal offence – most likely "false accusation" (*wugao*) – after denouncing his factory manager for economically corrupt activities of some kind. The case account continued,

Psychiatric examination findings: Despite being held in prison at the time, he displayed a high-spirited mood during the investigation, was loquacious, and spoke in a humorous and jocular fashion. He had an overly high opinion of himself, claiming that he was "an enthusiastic worker, and those around me are always full of praise for me;" and that "if I were the factory manager, I'd certainly be much better at it than Mr. Wang is." He said that he had denounced the factory director in order to protect the [national economic] reforms and therefore it had been a public-spirited act. He insisted that the details of the accusations he had made were all true, and that "the investigation team failed to check the evidence properly." His memory of the several-year-long course of events surrounding his accusations – the dates and times, figures and statistics and so forth – was all quite clear.

Appraisal conclusions: Affective psychosis (minor mania), no capacity to bear legal responsibility (*wu zeren nengli*.)

Reading between the lines, it appears that Li was then released from prison following a forensic finding that – on account of "minor mania," no less – he had no capacity to bear legal responsibility and so could not be criminally prosecuted for denouncing his factory manager. However,

In August 1988, Li Mou's work unit applied through the law court to have Li Mou declared as being a person with no capacity for civil action (*wu minshi xingwei nengli*), and in December the same year the court made a formal ruling to that effect. Subsequently, Li Mou began petitioning the higher authorities in an effort to have his case overturned and to be granted compensation.

By this point in the account, a fairly clear picture is emerging of a concerted official campaign to discredit and silence Mr. Li. First, there was the abortive criminal prosecution, and now his own work unit – presumably in the person of the factory manager himself – had succeeded in having him declared as being without capacity for civil action as well. Such a declaration by the court, if not physically silencing Li, would nonetheless have effectively served to invalidate any testimony he might subsequently make to any other government or judicial body regarding the factory manager's alleged corrupt behaviour. In continuing to challenge the findings of first the forensic examiners and then the court, however, Li was facing a dangerous double-edged sword. For if his petitions to the higher authorities arguing for both his sanity and his capacity for civil action were successful, he would then become liable to face trial on the original criminal charge of "false accusation."

In August 1992, Hospital B conducted a second forensic appraisal of Li Mou, and its analysis and findings were as follows: As a child, Li Mou had developed and matured quite normally and had been an average achiever at school; and as a worker, he had performed his duties diligently and responsibly. In terms of personality, he was introverted and stubborn, but his personal relations with others were quite satisfactory. From 1985 onwards, he frequently denounced and reported his factory director, Mr. Wang, for acts of financial impropriety, and since 1988 he had been constantly petitioning the higher authorities for his own rehabilitation. Prior to 1985, his performance at work had been exceptional and he was socially very well-adjusted; so there was no paranoid-type personality disorder, and neither did he show any signs of having an affective psychosis. Li Mou's accusations against the director and his subsequent petitioning activities together formed a connected and integrated whole, and moreover there was a factual basis to them (in August 1986, a joint municipal investigation team concluded that the various facts Li had reported to them were basically correct, although there were some discrepancies in the precise figures); in other words, there was a logical relationship of cause and effect [between the accusations and the later petitioning activities.] Under psychiatric examination, Li showed good cognitive and discriminatory abilities whilst recounting the story of his denunciations against the director, setting forth all the details clearly and fully.

It is striking that only now do we learn, almost in passing, that an official investigation team had concluded in August 1986 – that is, almost two full years before Li was criminally detained and examined by forensic psychiatrists to ascertain whether or not his mental state was such as to allow him to undergo prosecution and trial for "false accusation" – that his allegations of financial impropriety against the factory manager were "basically correct" all along! Yet still, the compiler of the case account found it necessary to dwell at considerable length on the seemingly obvious non-issue of Li's basic sanity:

From the psychiatric medical viewpoint, it would be incorrect to maintain that Li's denunciatory activities during 1985-88 were caused by "mild mania" and hence constituted pathological behaviour, whilst maintaining at the same time that the petitioning activities he carried out after 1988 were normal and rational in nature, since such a pattern would be at variance with the normal course of illness in cases of this type. As regards the symptoms, the "indomitable and unyielding" type of accuser or complainant is more likely to be a person suffering from a paranoid state,[394] rather than someone who is just being meddlesome or over-officious. And from the illness pattern point of view, Li's behaviour was not that of someone suffering from either intermittent or chronic "minor mania." The clinical diagnosis of "minor mania" [made by Hospital A] was thus inappropriate. Li Mou was well aware, beforehand, of both the nature and the likely consequences of the accusations he intended to make [against the director], and he was capable both of recognising his actions and of exerting self-control over them. He therefore had [legal] capacity for action.

The writer of this case account – a leading forensic psychiatrist from the Beijing Ankang hospital – then gave a trenchant verdict on the behaviour of both Hospital A and the court that had declared Li Mou to have no capacity for civil action:

---

394 As noted elsewhere above, complainants and petitioners of this type are frequently diagnosed in China as suffering from "litigious mania" (*susong kuang*), sometimes also known as "processomania."

At first sight, the above case appears to be very complicated and hard to unravel. Moreover, trying to establish a person's capacity for action with respect to events that occurred seven years earlier is certainly fraught with many difficulties. In fact, the case is really not that difficult. First, the court's verdict [of lack of civil capacity] was handed down on the basis of Hospital A's forensic finding that Li Mou should not be held legally responsible for his acts. Since no forensic conclusion had been given as regards Li's capacity for [civil] action, however, the verdict itself was incorrect. Capacity for action and legal responsibility [for crimes committed] are two entirely separate and distinct legal concepts, and a finding of absence of legal responsibility is by no means equivalent to a finding of lack of capacity for action. In general, patients suffering from minor mania do possess the capacity for action. Furthermore, the diagnosis of minor mania made in Li's case was a questionable one: Hospital A's evidence for making this diagnosis was insufficient and unconvincing, whereas Hospitals B's refutation of the diagnosis was logically and comprehensively argued, presenting a thorough analysis that took account of all the relevant diagnostic, course-of-illness and rules-of-disease aspects of the case.

Hence, the forensic finding of Hospital B should be accepted, and in handling the case of Li Mou's denunciations of the factory director for his involvement in financial impropriety, Li should be treated as having full capacity for action. That is to say, if his accusations were true, then the issues in question should be appropriately resolved; and if they were intentionally fabricated then he should be held legally responsible.[395]

So ultimately, the requirements of legal truth and justice appear to have been reasonably well served in this case. In fact, however, since the book in which this case account appeared is dated 1994 and its author was unable to do more than speculate about what the case's final outcome might be, it seems clear that six years after Li Mou's initial arrest and his forensic appraisal as being unable, by virtue of insanity, to bear legal responsibility for the charge of "false accusation" against a factory manager whom the authorities themselves had found to be "basically" guilty of the alleged crime, Li still had not succeeded either in clearing his own name or in ridding himself of the wholly undeserved taint of insanity. And the factory manager, for his part, was apparently still no closer to being relieved of his duties – let alone of standing trial for his criminal misdeeds. In all probability, Li Mou is even today still travelling down the endless, and generally quite fruitless, road of "petitioning the higher authorities" (*shangfang*) in search of vindication and justice.

---

395 From Long Qingchun (op cit), pp.200-202.

CHAPTER 6
Close Encounters of the Legal Psychiatric Kind

In the previous chapter, we saw how China's system of legal psychiatric appraisal and committal is theoretically supposed to work. In this chapter, we will approach the issue from a more practical and empirically based level: on the one hand, by presenting a series of actual cases of political dissidents, whistleblowers, and complainants and petitioners of various kinds who have been sent by the police for forensic psychiatric assessment and then confined in mental asylums for political rather than valid medical reasons; and on the other, by examining a series of official documents in which the legal and psychiatric authorities provide detailed professional explanations of how they perceive and deal with cases of these various types.

I. Counterrevolutionary Behaviour by the Mentally Ill

Before going any further, it may be helpful to have before us a capsule definition of what, precisely, the Chinese judicial and psychiatric authorities have in mind when they speak of "political cases" involving the commission of crimes by the allegedly mentally ill. The following passage, taken from a textbook on forensic psychiatry produced in 1983 by the official publishing house of the Ministry of Public Security, provides a clear and concise overview of how the problem was officially viewed during the early years of the Deng Xiaoping era. Published less than five years after the official denunciation of the Cultural Revolution, it affirms and incorporates key elements of the still deeply-entrenched abusive concepts and practices of that period, while at the same time seeking – in accordance with the more modern and "scientific" official ethos of China in the 1980s – to cloak them in the terminology of modern medical science. Moreover, the passage provides a virtual roadmap of the political abuse aspects of the system of forensic psychiatric evaluation and custody which, some four years later, was to be formally adopted and developed by the Chinese government as the Ankang regime.

Manifestations of Counterrevolutionary Behaviour by the Mentally Ill[396]

As Article 90 of the [1979] Criminal Law points out: "All acts carried out with the aim of overthrowing the political power of the dictatorship of the proletariat and the socialist system, and which endanger the People's Republic of China, are crimes of counterrevolution." Under the dominant influence of pathological thinking and other symptoms of psychological disease, mentally ill people may engage in behaviour that sabotages the proletarian dictatorship and the socialist state. In terms of form and consequence, these acts constitute crimes of counterrevolution. The most commonly encountered pathological states involving counterrevolutionary behaviour by the mentally ill are delusions of grandeur and delusions of persecution.

A mentally ill person suffering from delusions of grandeur, for example, may think that he is the "head of the Central Committee" or a "leading political figure" (*lingxiu renwu*), and may formulate "guidelines" and "policies" as a replacement for existing policies, laws or decrees that he thinks are unreasonable. In one case, a mentally ill

---

396 See Liu Anqiu (ed.), *Sifa Jingshenbingxue Jichu Zhishi* (*Basic Knowledge in Forensic Psychiatry*), (Beijing: Qunzhong Chubanshe, 1983), pp.18-19.

person proclaimed himself as a "peasant revolutionary leader" and called for a new political party to be set up in order to carry out a second revolution, and he openly drew up a manifesto and handed out leaflets.

People suffering from delusions of persecution with a certain specific content, for example those who deludedly harbour feelings of suspicion towards the Party organization, government departments and certain leading officials, may adopt all kinds of retaliatory measures against them, thereby occasioning counterrevolutionary behaviour. Still other kinds of mentally ill people, those suffering from disorders of thought and logic, try to interpret and understand the present political situation [in China] from the standpoint of pure theory. A mentally ill person, for example, owing to his divorcement from reality, applied the former political orthodoxy to China's present-day context: the patient insisted that the Cultural Revolution had been entirely necessary and extremely timely, and he even went around publicly arguing his case with others. In addition, people with pathological personality disorders may also engage in various kinds of counterrevolutionary behaviour.

Identifying Counterrevolutionary Behaviour by the Mentally Ill

Counterrevolutionary behaviour carried out by mentally ill people is to be distinguished from the commission of such behaviour by genuine counterrevolutionary elements. The following basic hallmarks will assist us in ascertaining those in the former category:

In analysing the personal history of an individual engaging in counterrevolutionary behaviour, no historical origins or social background showing any logical relationship [with the behaviour in question] can be identified. That is to say, no conformity can be found between the nature of the counterrevolutionary behaviour and the person in question's previous political demeanour, ideological make-up and moral or ethical quality.

The content of the behaviour displays a certain degree of absurdity and lack of commensurability with the actual status and capacity of the person concerned. For example, an ordinary student expressing the wish to become a major and important figure: most people would regard this as being something quite unimaginable. Or a person who groundlessly suspects the leadership of persecuting and harming him and then proceeds to focus his resentment upon the entire Party organization: this represents a marked deviation from normal logical reasoning and inference.

The person concerned carries out the counterrevolutionary behaviour in a brazen and flagrant manner and with no sign of scruples or misgivings. In a publicly confrontational manner, he or she will hand out leaflets in broad daylight and deliver speeches on the main road or at street corners. Naturally, some mentally ill people may act in a more covert manner than this; yet as soon as they are caught, they admit to everything quite frankly and unreservedly. In addition, mentally ill people may write anonymous letters, but often these are not genuinely anonymous but rather a manifestation of some mental impairment. For example, a person suffering from mental illness wrote a letter to all Military Regions in the country and to the Central Committee, signing his name as "Chen Zhenli" ["Chen the Truth"]; this was not his real name, but he still wrote his actual address on the envelope. After the case was cracked and he had been caught, the person was asked why he had written this anonymous letter. He replied that it was actually an open letter: he'd used the name "Chen Zhenli" because he had the truth on his side and the viewpoints he expressed were all "true."

The various elements of the counterrevolutionary-behaviour process are generally only loosely interconnected and may be logically self-contradictory. These can also show a lack of consistency over time – sometimes active and positive, but at other times passive and negative – and may even be self-repudiatory in nature.

The most important grounds for ascertaining the commission of counterrevolutionary behaviour by the mentally ill is where, necessarily, a correspondence exists between the particular manifestation of mental abnormality and the mental illness in question. A detailed investigation of the person's background and medical history may reveal additional psychiatric symptoms, and the counterrevolutionary behaviour will then be seen as simply one manifestation or symptom of the mental illness.

The official literature on forensic psychiatry in China in recent decades is replete with formulations expressing, more or less overtly, all of the theoretical themes and contours mentioned above. With the above general definition in mind, we shall now proceed to examine a series of specific cases in some depth and detail. One of the most frequent grounds on which Chinese citizens have been placed under criminal arrest and labelled as "counterrevolutionaries" by the country's security forces since the end of the Cultural Revolution is that of attempting to form unauthorized political groupings or parties. Doomed attempts of this nature were particularly numerous on both sides of the political spectrum in China during the several-year period immediately following the death of Mao. On the one hand, residual ultra-leftists who were resentful of the more meritocratic and market-based policies introduced by Deng Xiaoping often formed underground political groups dedicated to the reinstatement of Cultural Revolutionary policies; while on the other, a certain number of reform-minded or "rightward-leaning" citizens sought to test the limits of the official reform programme by setting up groups and associations dedicated to China's political democratisation and the protection of human rights.[397] The security and legal authorities drew no practical distinction between the two tendencies, however, dismissing and suppressing both with equal vigour as being "counterrevolutionary" in nature.

The Case of Mr Liu

The following officially-published case account – concerning an intellectual who had been politically discriminated against for many years because of his overseas family origins, was sent to prison during the Cultural Revolution for stubbornly criticizing the Communist Party, and who eventually, after Mao's death, tried to form an independent political party – is broadly illustrative of the forensic psychiatric handling of the second of the two varieties of post-Mao dissident organisational activity mentioned above.[398] The account first appeared in a book published in China in 1992:

---

397 For information on China's "Democracy Wall" movement, see: James D. Seymour, *The Fifth Modernization: China's Human Rights Movement, 1978-1979*, Earl M. Coleman Enterprises, 1980; and Robin Munro, "China's Democracy Movement: A Midwinter Spring," *Survey: Journal of East-West Studies*, No.121 (Summer 1984), pp.70-98.

398 No cases of underground "leftist" activists and organisers being declared criminally insane have as yet come to light, although there have been several notable cases of non-clandestine "left-Marxist" theorists who have been

Mr. Liu, 47 years old, a university graduate and returned overseas Chinese. After immigrating to China in 1962, he went to one of Beijing's most famous universities, graduating in 1968. That year was the harshest phase of the Cultural Revolution, and because of his class status and family background he was sent down to a state farm to perform manual labour. In 1972, he was sent to work in a research institute. He was generally enthusiastic in his work and achieved outstanding results, but he kept himself to himself most of the time and was stubborn and self-willed.

Throughout his time at college, the state farm and the research institute, Liu applied several dozen times to join the Communist Party of China, but he was always turned down because of his overseas connections. Because of this, he wrote numerous letters to the leading officials concerned, stating that he himself was free from any [political] taint, that there must be dissidents within the Communist Party of China, and asking the Party Central Committee to clean up the membership. The relevant departments criticized and educated Liu many times on this account. He was even subjected to criticism and struggle sessions and sentenced to a period of reform through labour. But Liu continued to uphold his own viewpoints.

After the end of the Cultural Revolution, he again wrote numerous letters to the competent departments expressing these viewpoints. Later, he wrote another letter, saying that in the mid-1980s he had organized and set up a political party called the "China Party for Democratic National Reconstruction" (*Zhongguo Minzhu Jianguo Dang*.) In addition, he wrote a detailed and tightly argued "Party Charter" that was tens of thousands of words in length, in which he declared his intention "to unite with all advanced intellectuals at home and abroad," in order to assist the Communist Party "to clean up the membership." Liu made many copies of this document and distributed them within society, and he also sent a copy to a leading official of the Communist Party Central Committee.

He was subsequently taken into custody for criminal investigation. Suspecting that he was mentally ill, the authorities sent him for forensic psychiatric examination. Appraisal findings: paranoia; no capacity for criminal responsibility.[399]

Significantly, there was nothing in this forensic psychiatric case account to suggest that Liu actually was suffering from any form of internationally recognised mental disorder or illness; to the contrary, he appears merely to have been a person with a quite understandable political chip on his shoulder – someone who, after enduring many years of unwarranted political persecution at the hands of the authorities, decided to take the dangerous and irrevocable step of becoming a classic-style political dissident by defiantly setting up his own, apparently wholly peaceful and non-violent, political party. Although the case account gives no specific indication of what finally happened to Mr. Liu, the most likely outcome of his perceived "paranoid" insanity in conducting these "counterrevolutionary" activities is that he would have been spared trial and imprisonment, and instead sent to an institute for the criminally insane.

---

dealt with in this way. One of these – "The Case of Mr. Zhu" – is discussed below at p.196.
399 Sun Dongdong, *Jingshenbingren de Falü Nengli* (Legal Capacity of the Mentally Ill), Xiandai Chubanshe, 1992, p.127; cited as "Case No. 225" in Liu Baiju (op cit), pp.674-5.

Another very common context or situation in which the label of "counterrevolution" has been affixed to political activists in China since 1949 is where the individuals concerned have publicly expressed political viewpoints and policies that are at variance with, or which flatly contradict, those espoused by senior-level Party officials or prominent local-level power-holders. The following case, which dates from more or less the same period in China as that in which the above-quoted lengthy definition of "counterrevolutionary behaviour by the mentally ill" was written, affords a vivid and disturbing illustration of how the general theory of "political insanity" was applied in practice against dissenting individuals by Chinese forensic psychiatrists during the 1980s.

The Case of Wang Fumian

Although one of the earliest known cases of politically-motivated psychiatric abuse from the post-Cultural Revolution era, the case of Wang Fumian is also one of the best and most reliably documented, since the details were published in separate eye-witness accounts written by two former PRC journalists, Liu Binyan and Cao Changqing (both of whom later went into overseas exile.) Liu, internationally renowned and respected, was for many years China's foremost investigative journalist, and he had campaigned for the rehabilitation of numerous victims of political persecution over the years. But as he was later to write of this particular case: "The image of Wang Fumian haunted me. We had met only a few times, but of all the victims of persecution, he was the one for whom I felt the most."

In March 1984, while working as a senior columnist on the People's Daily, Liu was visited at his home in Beijing by Wang Fumian, a worker from Yichun city in Heilongjiang Province, with a request for help in publicizing the story of his recent political persecution by the Heilongjiang Party leadership. Wang's principal adversary was a powerful official named Wang Fei, a former ultra-leftist who had risen to prominence during the Cultural Revolution and who – having skilfully avoided falling victim to the anti-"Gang of Four" purges of the late 1970s – had recently become head of the Party's provincial Organisation Department. During the Cultural Revolution, Wang Fumian had headed an opposing political faction in Yichun city, and after Mao's death in 1976 he publicly denounced Wang Fei as being a die-hard Gang of Four supporter who had persecuted countless innocent people during the Cultural Revolution and who was now conspiring to place his former political cronies in senior positions throughout the city's Party and governmental apparatus.[400] Wang Fei responded by having him arrested on trumped-up criminal charges and thrown into prison for four years. Released after completing his sentence, he had come to Beijing to petition the authorities for official redress of this injustice and for a full investigation to be launched into Wang Fei's politically and economically corrupt activities in Heilongjiang.

As Wang left Liu Binyan's home that night, he was seized on the street by a group of six police officers who had driven all the way down from Yichun, and was forcibly taken back to Yichun by car. (Liu was distraught: "That night, I wrote in my diary: 'Today is the darkest day in my whole life!'") On Wang Fei's orders, Wang Fumian was then forensically examined by three psychiatrists, who duly

---

400 As Liu Binyan explained, "During the Cultural Revolution, when he was ruling it over the city, [Wang Fei] had outdone himself in calling meetings to repudiate the capitalist-roaders, to study the theory of the dictatorship of the proletariat, and to condemn Deng Xiaoping. In fact, Wang Fei had done such a thorough job that he had been cited for good performance by Vice-Premier Sun Jian, who was serving under the Gang of Four. Wang Fei then printed Sun Jian's words in praise of himself and distributed them far and wide. Now if Wang Fei were to expose people who had been involved with the Gang of Four, as Wang Fumian called for, where would it lead to but his own door?" (*A Higher Kind of Loyalty*, p.228.) Liu Binyan died in exile in the U.S. in December 2005.

declared him to be suffering from "paranoia" (*pianzhikuang*.) Wang was thereupon incarcerated in the Heilongjiang Provincial Public Security Bureau's Hospital for the Custody and Treatment of the Mentally Ill – the forerunner of the Heilongjiang Ankang facility – situated some 50 kilometres from Harbin, the provincial capital.

For the next two years, Liu Binyan tried to find out what had happened to Wang Fumian, but he encountered a wall of official silence from Heilongjiang until the summer of 1986, when a substantial easing in the national political climate made it possible for him to get permission from the People's Daily to travel to Yichun with several other of the paper's journalists to investigate the case in detail. Once there, however (as Liu later wrote): "In all the years I had been a reporter for the People's Daily, rarely had I come across such a reign of terror as I encountered in Yichun." For weeks, his group sought fruitlessly either to find Wang Fumian or even to gain access to any of the legal or medical records relating to his case. As a result of relentless political pressure and threats emanating directly from Wang Fei's office, everyone with any knowledge of Wang's case had been frightened into complete silence and non-cooperation.

Eventually, through the assistance of Cao Changqing, a fellow journalist and personal friend of Liu's who had worked for several years in the Heilongjiang provincial mental hospital during the 1970s, Liu was put in direct contact with the director of the police-run asylum (a former colleague of Cao's) where Wang Fumian was being held. In due course, the two journalists gained the director's permission to interview Wang in person at the hospital. As Cao later wrote of this "special hospital",

> It was set in a remote and barren part of the countryside, with no sign of people anywhere around, and was surrounded by high walls and barbed wire, with a steel gate at the front. The place was just like a prison. The doctors and nurses all wore police uniforms under their white [medical] tunics.

Of their meeting with Wang, Liu Binyan observed as follows:

> Neither the head of the ward nor the two doctors in charge could detect any sign of mental illness in him. We talked to him and taped the conversation. He sounded sane, even logical. We saw no signs of mental illness…. But now, he had been pronounced a "maniac"[401] and was locked up in a psychiatric ward. This kind of disease had no cure; it was life imprisonment,[402] worse than if he had been sentenced to twenty years on criminal charges. What did Wang Fei have against the man to do this to him?

Before the meeting, Liu had met with the three doctors who, under Wang Fei's orders, had originally diagnosed Wang as mad. Two of them, both qualified psychiatrists, had found him to have merely a "personality disorder," but the third, who was actually a horse veterinarian who had been reassigned to a psychiatric department two years earlier, insisted that it was a case of "paranoia"; more impressed

---

401 As Cao Changqing's account, which was published in Chinese, makes clear, the actual diagnostic term used was "paranoia" (*pianzhikuang*); Liu's use of the term "mania," in the English version of his autobiography, was probably the result of a medically imprecise translation.

402 Criminal detainees determined to be "non-imputable" for their alleged offences by reason of insanity are usually placed in involuntary psychiatric custody on an indefinite basis; they can only be released after an eventual finding by forensic psychiatrists that they have sufficiently recovered as to no longer pose a "danger" to themselves or society. According to an official Chinese source, the average length of stay for mentally ill offenders in the Ankang system is five and a half years, with some inmates being held for as long as twenty years. (See source cited at Note 520 below.)

by the sound of the latter diagnosis, Wang Fei had ruled in favour of its use in the forensic assessment report. Later, Liu looked up the PRC medical textbook definition of this psychiatric diagnosis:

> It read: "A rare kind of mental disease. Symptoms are overconfidence, extreme wilfulness, found mostly in people of advanced cultural background. They are biased and tend to distort facts, although their delusions are not wholly divorced from reality. Taken for normal at an early age, the patient gradually asserts his (her) willpower more and more forcibly; he (she) rushes about offering petitions, writing endless letters of accusation. A few are deluded into thinking they are making exceptional contributions to humanity…"
>
> My hair stood on end and my blood curdled as I read these words. The definition seemed specifically phrased to match Wang Fumian's case! "Overconfidence," "biased," "delusions of grandeur"…these were exactly the words Party leaders used to denote intellectuals with any independent thinking.[403]

Liu's conclusion on the case was that Wang Fei and his political cronies, knowing that they had insufficient evidence against Wang Fumian to secure a second criminal conviction against him – and moreover that even if sentenced he would eventually be released and would then certainly resume his petitioning activities in Beijing – had decided to silence him indefinitely by having him declared criminally insane. "Apparently necessity was the mother of invention," wrote Liu. "They looked up three psychiatric doctors and had him pronounced mentally ill. It met the legal requirements, and satisfied the dictatorship of the proletariat." Upon returning to Beijing, Liu wrote up his damning findings on the Wang Fumian case and submitted them to the Party General Secretary, Hu Yaobang, and other top officials, calling both for Wang's release and for a high-level investigation into Wang Fei's tyrannical rule in Heilongjiang. Two months later, however, in January 1987, the nationwide campaign against "bourgeois liberalization" got underway in China: Hu Yaobang was toppled from power, and Liu Binyan was dismissed from his job at the People's Daily and expelled from the Party. His petition on Wang's case to the top Party leadership was thereupon shelved.

Several years later, Cao Changqing received a letter from Wang Fumian, saying he had eventually been freed and was now living in Shenzhen. As Cao recorded in his account of the case, which was published in Hong Kong in late 2002,

> [Wang] had finally submitted. Aware that there was no longer anyone who could save him, and not wanting to be kept locked up as a paranoiac in the lunatic asylum for the rest of his life, he had "confessed his crimes" and endorsed everything that the Public Security Bureau had ever said about him. Moreover, he had signed a document they had prepared containing four pledges or guarantees: 1) after his release he would make no more petitions or complaints to the higher authorities; 2) he would strictly control all his speech and actions; 3) he would have no further contact or communication with "bad elements" like Liu Binyan; and 4) he would submit to discipline and the law, and would never seek to have the case against him overturned (*yong bu fan'an*).

Cao Changqing's conclusion on the case was as follows:

---

403   *A Higher Kind of Loyalty*, Liu Binyan, Pantheon Books (New York), 1990, pp.221-232.

It was evident from the manner in which the Heilongjiang Department of Public Security finally released Wang Fumian that the police had not in fact regarded him as suffering from paranoia, since asking a mentally ill person to sign such "guarantees" as these would have been illogical and at variance with all common sense. What it proved, quite to the contrary, was that they regarded him as being a mentally normal person, and that they had merely been using the label of mental illness as a way of punishing him for his dissenting views.[404]

II. How to Distinguish a Paranoiac from a Political Dissident

Far from declining in influence as the economic "opening and reform" policies of Deng Xiaoping deepened and progressed, the concept of "political paranoia" continued to hold significant sway within Chinese forensic psychiatric circles through the late 1980s and well beyond. To demonstrate that the general theory is alive and well in contemporary China, it will suffice to cite at length one further authority, Long Qingchun, a leading forensic psychiatrist at the Beijing Ankang institute. In a textbook which he edited in 1994, Long included the following intriguing item of comparative forensic-psychiatric analysis (titled as in the original Chinese):

What Is the Difference Between a Paranoiac and a Political Dissident?[405]

There is a certain type of person with the mental illness of paranoid psychosis (*pianzhixing jingshenbing*.) The content of the fantasies and delusions of such persons does not come from their having been persecuted, but is mainly about state policies and principles. Such persons continually submit petitions, and are often taken by non-specialists to be political dissidents (*chi butong zhengjianzhe*.) But there is a difference in nature between the two.

Paranoiacs, commonly known as "document maniacs" (*wen fengzi*), manifest [their illness] through their loss of reason in political theory. With respect to all sensitive [political] issues, they listen only to themselves and think, "Only I am right." Although they might focus on one or two specific issues, generally they have both historical problems and current problems.[406] Their political theory and their political stance are mutually contradictory; although they oppose the [government's] general line and policies, they also support Marxism-Leninism and materialism. Political dissidents are relatively specific. They have dissenting opinions about certain specific issues, and don't simply oppose everything.

---

404 "*Zhongguo Jingshenbingyuan li de Zhengzhifan*" ("Political Prisoners in China's Mental Asylums"), Cao Changqing; reprinted in *Da Ji Yuan* (Epoch Times), New York, September 2, 2002; article originally published in *Zheng Ming* (Contention) magazine, Hong Kong, September 2002.
405 See Long Qingchun (ed.), *Sifa Jingshen Yixue Jianding Zixun Jieda* (Consultative Questions and Answers for Forensic-Psychiatric Medical Evaluations), (Beijing: Chinese University of Politics and Law Publishing House, 1994), pp. 58-59. Don Clarke kindly provided the translation of this article.
406 "...*wangwang shi ji you lishi wenti, you you xianshi wenti*." In China, the phrase "having historical problems" generally indicates that the person in question was accused of (and usually punished for) "bourgeois" or "counterrevolutionary" views or activities in the past; similarly, the phrase "having current problems" often indicates that the person is a current target of such political suppression (c.f. the terms "*lishi fan'geming*" and "*xianxing fan'geming*," meaning "historical counterrevolutionary" and "active counterrevolutionary"). A better translation of "*wenti*" in this context might thus be "political record" or "political taint."

> Paranoia is a kind of morbidity; therefore, the delusions and fantasies are self-contradictory. They are not plausible and consistent, and have no capacity to spread to others. That which is expressed by political dissidents is logical and has a certain capacity to spread to [literally: "infect"] others.
>
> A paranoiac will take any opportunity to peddle his views, without regard to time, place, or audience. A political dissident will choose the time, place, and audience for expressing his views; he will not start talking to just anyone he runs into.
>
> The acts and views of paranoiacs do not match their education, reading, and status. There was, for example, an old retired worker with only three years of elementary school education who worked untiringly to write a "Manifesto of Scientific Communism." He bought a typewriter and printer with his own money and sent his "work" out everywhere. Neither his wife nor his children could convince him to stop. The acts and views of political dissidents are consistent with their learning and their status; moreover they generally have better sense than to pursue something in complete disregard of the [legal] consequences.

Disarmingly enough, the basic distinction that Long appears to be drawing here between political lunatics and dissidents is that while the former engage in nonsensical rambling, what the latter say makes a lot of sense and is broadly convincing to others. Two more central points should be noted in this context however. First, the political dissidents in question, while escaping psychiatric incarceration for their oppositional viewpoints, would for the most part have been severely dealt with under criminal law provisions against "counterrevolution," since 1997 renamed as "crimes of endangering state security." Second, those diagnosed as being "paranoid psychotics" following their arrest on similar charges of political subversion will, in most cases, neither be freed from police custody nor given appropriate treatment, whether out-patient or in-patient, for their alleged politico-psychiatric disorders. Rather, they will be declared "not legally responsible" and then placed indefinitely in Ankang custody or similar. A third vital issue also arises in all such cases: whether the person concerned was genuinely suffering, in fact, from an internationally recognized mental disorder.

The Case of Mr Zhu

Elsewhere in the same volume, Long Qingchun provided a lengthy summary of the case of the elderly retired worker alluded to above. The deeply ironical aspects of this case should be readily apparent: a worker in a socialist state being declared criminally insane for upholding his belief in egalitarian Marxism (in this instance, a once ubiquitous but now officially repudiated variant of late Maoist-era radicalism.) The case account reads in full as follows:

> *A retired worker threw himself wholeheartedly into the study of political economy, tirelessly and laboriously writing "A Manifesto of a Scientific Communist." Why did this constitute mental illness?*[407]
>
> Subject of [forensic-psychiatric] evaluation: Zhu, male, 57 years old, married. Ethnically Han, lower middle school educational level, worker in a coalmine. No unusual aspects in his development since childhood. Upper-primary school

---

[407] See Long Qingchun, *Sifa Jingshen Yixue Jianding Zixun Jieda*, pp.174-175 (italics indicate subtitle of passage, in original).

[sic] educational level, entered the army in 1956, joined the Party in 1961, and enthusiastically studied the works of Chairman Mao. Was demobilized in 1963 and began work at the coalmine. During the "Cultural Revolution," served as vice-chairman of the mine's Revolutionary Committee and was quite an activist. His achievements in "grasping revolution and promoting production" were, moreover, publicized in the People's Daily, and because of this Zhu regarded the Cultural Revolution as the sole path to the realization of Communism.

In 1979 he began to get ideas about writing books on political theory, and after he retired in 1986 he often used to seek out members of the leadership and expound his thoughts and ideas to them. In his view, [the policy of] taking economic construction as the focus [of national work] was entirely mistaken, and he completely negated the principles and policies laid down [by Deng Xiaoping in December 1978] at the Third Plenum of the Party's 11th Central Committee. He maintained that the international communist movement had already entered a third high tide, that China had produced its leader, and that this leader was none other than himself.[408] Furthermore, he wrote a 100,000-character-long document entitled "A Manifesto of a Scientific Communist" and mailed it out to all the leading organs at central, provincial and municipal levels. Zhu had discussed all these views with the leadership of his work unit. He was normally a fairly quiet man, and he never used to discuss politics with ordinary members of the masses.

Most leaders of Zhu's work unit felt that while his political viewpoints were wrong, they were not reactionary in content; moreover, he had relayed them all to the leadership and the organization, he had not disseminated them among the masses, and when mailing them out he had signed his real name to them. Also, Zhu had spent several thousand yuan of his own money to buy a printing machine, which his wife used to print out his various writings, and so his behaviour had seemed orderly and logical and he didn't appear to be mentally ill.

---

408 Many Western-trained psychiatrists might also identify this particular aspect of Zhu's behaviour as a possible sign of mental instability – as being, say, indicative of "delusions of grandeur" or other forms of "overvalued ideation." Both these diagnostic concepts appear with particular frequency, however, in Chinese forensic psychiatric discussions of "political cases" (the Chinese terms used are, respectively, "*kuada wangxiang*" and "*chaojia guannian*"), where those being psychiatrically assessed at the same time face serious criminal charges for activities that a Western-trained examiner would be viewing, at worst, as a potential medical problem. Moreover, it should be noted that much of China's political culture during the first three decades after 1949, especially the "individual heroic" mode of leadership embodied in the exemplary person and history of Chairman Mao, served to instil in many Chinese people a strong and no doubt exaggerated sense of personal responsibility for the entire "fate of China." A good example is that of Chen Erjin, a young dissident who in 1974 wrote a book entitled *Lun Wuchanjieji Minzhu Geming* (On the Proletarian Democratic Revolution), in which he called for national democratic change in the direction of a socialist two-party system. In 1982, he was arrested and sentenced to ten years of imprisonment as a counterrevolutionary for attempting to set up a "second Communist Party" in China. According to several reliable informants who knew Chen well, however, he was in no way mentally impaired or unstable (Chen Erjin, *Crossroads Socialism: A Manifesto for Proletarian Democracy*, translated and with an introduction by Robin Munro [London: NLB/Verso Editions, 1984]; Chen's book was first published in the June 1979 issue of the Beijing dissident journal *Si-Wu Luntan [April Fifth Forum]*). In 2000, Chen escaped into Burma and eventually made his way to Bangkok, where he was granted political refugee status by the UNHCR. He now lives in exile in Denmark and maintains, under the name Chen Yangchao, a website at: www.cnfr.org.

According to the masses, Zhu's everyday speech was quite logical; he behaved in a respectable manner, was always polite in his dealings with people, and had an orderly and regular lifestyle. In their view he wasn't mentally ill, just highly eccentric, and so they regarded him as being a political dissident.

In March 1987, Zhu was expertly evaluated and found to be suffering from paranoid psychosis, on the following main grounds:

The content of Zhu's "theories" was conceptually chaotic: for example, he maintained that "during the period of scientific socialism, it is the State that engenders [social] classes, the superstructure that determines the economic base, and the mode of rule that determines the mode of production," etc. He maintained that all the principles and policies laid down since the Third Plenum of the 11th Central Committee were wrong. He was the leader who would guide the international communist movement during its third high tide. All this was a form of "political delusion," a pathological mental disorder, and Zhu's behaviour was thus obstinate, impervious to reason, and insoluble through criticism or discussion.

Under the influence of his "political delusions," Zhu's pathological willpower grew ever stronger. Upon his retirement, he declared that he would "keep on writing until his very last breath." He saved more than 4,000 yuan to buy a printing machine. Even after these materials had been sent back,[409] he continued writing and mailing out his articles just as before, thereby manifesting utter political lunacy.[410]

Zhu's views and utterances were incompatible with his status, position, qualifications and learning; the great disparities here clearly demonstrated his divorcement from reality.

Paranoid psychosis differs from schizophrenia in that, in the former, mental activity remains well balanced, the delusions are relatively systematic and not entirely absurd in content, and the integrity of the personality remains relatively intact. Aside from his "political delusions," therefore, Zhu's overall mental activity remained normal, he was able to lead a quite normal life, and even his own family had difficulty believing that he was mentally ill.

Crucially, this account contains no indication that Zhu had engaged, by international standards, in anything of a remotely criminal nature. From the case details provided, it seems clear that he was simply a committed leftwing thinker, of the kind to be found everywhere in China during the Cultural Revolution decade, but one who – inexplicably and inexcusably from the government's point of view – had failed to perform the requisite ideological *volte face* after the 1978 return to power of Deng Xiaoping and the Party's repudiation of Cultural Revolution-era political theory. It should also be noted that over the several years following Mao's death and the ascendancy of the new political line, thousands of Zhu's fellow "die-hard ultra-leftists" across China were arrested and sentenced to long terms of imprisonment on various counts of counterrevolution.[411] So why was Zhu, following his initial detention or arrest on such charges, not dealt with in similar fashion, but rather referred by the police for

---

409 Presumably after their confiscation by the authorities.
410 "*biaoxianchu zhengzhi-shang de fengkuangxing*"
411 The official sobriquet generally applied to such people at the time was "residual poisonous dregs of the Gang of Four."

forensic-psychiatric assessment and then found to be mad? Zhu's case affords several vital clues that help elucidate the curious dividing line drawn by China's legal-medical authorities between "political crime" and "political insanity."

The first aspect of Zhu's case that seems to have raised forensic psychiatric eyebrows was the fact that Zhu had in no sense acted covertly or "conspiratorially" in the way he developed and publicized his contrarian political theories: as was noted earlier, this is widely taken in China to be a prima facie indication of mental instability, on the implicit assumption that "proper" political dissidents have "sufficient sense of self-preservation" to assiduously conceal their activities from the authorities, through fear of the stern judicial punishment they would otherwise encounter.

Second, the authorities evidently saw Zhu's endeavours in the realm of political theory as somehow "incompatible" with his status as a mere worker. This condescending attitude may seem surprising in view of the strong emphasis placed by Mao on the importance of China's fostering of a new generation of "worker intellectuals" after 1949. But Zhu was a long-time Party member who had at one time risen to the relatively important position of vice-chair of his local Revolutionary Committee, so he was surely entitled to have more than a passing interest in political theory. What the authorities appear to have taken primary exception to, however, is Zhu's original authorial efforts in this field, and in particular their detailed and extensive nature. In the official medico-legal view, only academic scholars or Party theorists are supposed to engage in this type of activity; for ordinary members of the public to do so is apparently seen as being not just eccentric, but also – and especially where dissident-type theories are being advanced – indicative of an underlying mental abnormality.

Third, there was the alleged "conceptual chaos" of Zhu's theoretical writings: this represents perhaps the most sinister aspect of the authorities' forensic psychiatric "case" against his sanity. What is significant, however, is that no substantive evidence was raised to suggest that Zhu was in any way cognitively impaired, or that his thoughts were indeed "chaotic" or disconnected. To the contrary, he was officially said to be "logical…respectable…polite" and to have "an orderly and regular lifestyle." The evidence that was officially given pertained solely to his ideas and theories themselves: these were "wrong," "obstinate" and "politically deluded," and the fact that Zhu persisted in holding them, even after receiving an official warning, was identified as a sign of "utter political lunacy."[412] The authorities' stated belief that Zhu's "overall mental activity remained normal" and their observation that even his own family viewed him as sane, was seen, not as undermining the final diagnosis of "paranoid psychosis," but rather as in effect confirming it. As noted earlier, this particular diagnostic contradiction was the very hallmark of the Soviet-era political diagnosis of "sluggish schizophrenia."

The real clincher of Zhu's "insanity," from the authorities' point of view, was that he stubbornly continued to espouse the now-discredited political ideas of late-era Maoism, despite the potentially dire legal penalties for so doing. In other words, it was essentially his "failure to keep up with the times" (*gan bu shang qingkuang*) in the highly fluid world of official Chinese political dogma, pure and simple, that had sealed his forensic-diagnostic fate.

---

412 In point of fact, all the various theoretical viewpoints attributed to Zhu by the authorities (for example, that "the superstructure determines the economic base") are typical of mainstream Maoist thought from the late 1950s until Mao's death in 1976, and moreover are held in common by numerous 20th century Western schools of Marxism, in a tradition extending from Trotsky through to the various "New Left" European schools of thought of the 1960s and 70s. Zhu may well have been slightly "megalomaniac" by disposition, but then so, by some accounts, were many European New Left theorists.

The above case is not one drawn from the obscure archives of China's revolutionary past. It was published in Beijing in 1994 in an official training manual for Chinese forensic psychiatrists. It was thus presumably seen as a typical illustrative case, the concluding diagnosis being one fully appropriate for study and emulation by others working in the legal-psychiatric profession.

III. Authentic and Borderline Cases: "Folie Politique"

We will now consider a number of official forensic-psychiatric case reports involving persons drawn from the important subgroup of detainees whom we earlier called the "pseudo-counterrevolutionaries" – namely, those detained on politically-related criminal charges who may well have been suffering from internationally recognised mental disorders of various kinds, and whose symptoms assumed the unfortunate and highly dangerous form of "politically hostile" thought, speech and action. Since the late 1950s, according to the official psychiatric literature, these symptoms have consisted primarily of political "ravings" against Mao, the Cultural Revolution and the current Chinese leadership.

The dissident Soviet psychiatrist Semyon Gluzman provides the following insightful discussion of this unusual medical problem:

> Should we automatically suspect a psychiatrist of abuse if he notes delusional ideas of a political nature? Are all those who "deliriously expound on social and political life" actually mentally healthy?
>
> Of course not. Every psychiatrist can recall cases of colourful, systematized delusions of a political nature in people who were quite obviously mentally ill. For example, I had a patient, a young woman with an economics degree, who said: "The Jews killed Lenin, now they want to kill me." This idea formed the basis of the behaviour which had brought her to a psychiatric ward. The KGB was not interested in her; hers was a classic case of schizophrenia, of which the above statement was but one manifestation.
>
> In the final analysis, if our patients talk of their "enemies" blasting them with cosmic rays, or their meetings with beings from other planets, what is so different about saying that "the CIA watches me day and night, they even read my thoughts" (I had such a patient myself once)? Delusions involve an erroneous, unreal judgement which completely dominates the consciousness of the patient and cannot be corrected by rousing him and explaining his mistake. Cosmic rays, books about beings from other planets, newspaper articles about the CIA (they do follow people sometimes) – all these exist in our present-day world.[413]

As Gluzman further interestingly notes:

> In the middle of the 19th century, psychiatrist Belhomme defined as a specific nosological form, "political psychosis," *folie politique*.... [And] Grizinger, a famous psychiatric authority, insisted: "Political discourse during the time of the revolution gives content and colour to the delusions of many patients. These effects, however, in a majority of cases, represent a superficial and accidental phenomenon and can only impress the ignorant."[414]

---

413 Gluzman, *On Soviet Totalitarian Psychiatry* (op cit), p.25.
414 Ibid, p.37.

Owing to the relentless intrusion of politics into all aspects of social life in China since 1949, however, this specific pattern or syndrome appears to have been unusually common there, especially during the Mao era and its immediate aftermath. In many such cases, there is an intrinsically slender borderline to be drawn between sanity and mental illness. (As Golda Meir is said to have told Henry Kissinger: "Even paranoids have enemies.") Chinese researchers studying the wide range of unusual or "culture-bound" symptomatology found among mental illness sufferers in China in the 1970s, for example, found that one such common symptom was:

> Delusions of impending arrest: Contrary to any objective evidence, a patient assumes that the authorities intend to send security cadres of policemen to arrest him. This delusion is generally primary.

But of course such ideas often turned out, at that time, to be all too true. Other culturally specific symptoms identified by the same researchers during the late Mao period included: "delusion of imminent catastrophe," "delusion of being slandered," "delusion of being examined" and "delusion of being despised." Again, in countless cases of the period such anxieties were anything but delusory, and a psychiatrist of the time would often have had great difficulty in distinguishing between paranoia and normalcy.

As the researchers observed of their 1981 survey findings,

> During the past 15 years or so, we have discovered many new manifestations of schizophrenia in this hospital, where patients come from almost every part of the country. These clinical features were rarely seen before Liberation and in the early years thereafter. Since then, however, they have appeared with increasing frequency and now have become common clinical phenomena in our schizophrenic patients. No suitable terms for these new manifestations are to be found in our current authoritative textbooks or journals.[415]

Almost a decade later, in 1990, the first of the authors of this article teamed up with seven other psychiatrists from the Shanghai Mental Health Centre to produce a much more comprehensive study of the same topic – covering the entire period from 1949 to 1982, and based on an analysis of altogether 1,604 cases of delusional schizophrenia from that period. The researchers' main finding was that because of the virtually unending series of harsh political campaigns carried out in China since 1949, the overwhelmingly predominant subtype of delusional schizophrenia found in the country since the founding of the PRC had been that of "persecution delusion" schizophrenia (*beihai wangxiang jingshen fenliezheng*) – a category that accounted for as much as between 63 percent and *98 percent* of the entire sample group under examination, depending on the particular sub-period in question.[416]

More generally, as one Chinese expert on crime and mental illness has recently written,

---

415 Hsia Yu-fen, M.D., and Tsai Neng, "Transcultural Investigation of Recent Symptomatology of Schizophrenia in China," *American Journal of Psychiatry*, November 1981, Vol. 138, No.11, pp.1484-6. Other typical symptoms cited in the study were: "delusion of being cultivated by superiors," "delusion of being experimented on," and "delusion of leadership lineage." (The latter referred, in most cases, to people who believed they were related to or descended from an important Communist Party official.)

416 See: Xia Yufen, Zheng Zhanpei et al, "*Woguo Wangxiangxing Jingshen Fenliezheng de Zhengzhuang Bianqian*" (The Changing Symptomatology of Delusional Schizophrenia in China), *Shanghai Jingshen Yixue* (Shanghai Archives of Psychiatry), 1990, Vol.2, No.3, pp.133-6.

Politics is something that intimately involves each and every person; everyone is affected by politics, even if they seek to stay as far away from it as possible. Indeed, politics can even become a direct causal factor or circumstance in the development of certain mental illnesses, for example schizophrenia, reactive psychosis, and neurosis. In China, politically stressful events have always been recognized as a major causal factor in mental disturbances.

Using their "Inventory Table for the Assessment of Factors Leading to Mental Disturbance," Zheng Yanping and Yang Desen have produced a hierarchy of forty-three such factors, and the third most common causal element they identified in their study – after death of a spouse, and death of the main family member – was "being attacked in the course of political movements."[417] Similarly, in the "Inventory for the Assessment of Life Events" formulated by Zhang Mingyuan et al, "coming under political attack" ranked high on the list of relevant life events, closely preceded only by such events as the loss of a spouse, death of children or parents, and divorce.[418]

Especially during the periods when politics was all encompassing and the political atmosphere had descended to an especially vicious level, the role played by political factors [in generating mental illness] was even more pronounced. At those times, some people were unable to withstand the politically-induced mental stresses they experienced after coming under political persecution and attack; others could not adapt to the psychological pressures they had to endure as a result of the cruel and harsh political environment; still others were unable to deal with the psychological blow of being discovered to have "political problems"; and others again were incapable of adapting to or dealing with the sudden dramatic changes that so often occurred in the political climate. As a result, they either suffered from short-term mental-abnormality reaction states or else developed full-blown mental disorders.

Elsewhere, the same writer notes:

[D]uring the decades of "politics always to the fore" (*zhengzhi diyi*), politics formed the single most important topic of daily life and everyday language was filled with political terminology of all kinds; everyone talked non-stop about politics and even small children became infected with the habit, so how could mentally ill people living in the same social environment manage to completely avoid such influences? In those times, politics even penetrated into the symptomatology of mental illness. For example, some sufferers would walk only on the left-hand side of the road, believing that this would prove they were "leftists"; others developed delusions of guilt that they were agents or spies; and others would have auditory hallucinations in which they heard messages sent to them by the central Party leadership.[419]

---

417 See Zheng Yanping and Yang Desen, "Life Events, Mental Anxiety and Neurosis," *Chinese Journal of Nervous and Mental Diseases*, 1983, No.2.
418 See Liu Baiju (op cit), p.664. For the article cited in this passage, see: Zhang Mingyuan et al., "An Inventory for the Assessment of Life Events: Some Common-Pattern Outcomes," *Chinese Journal of Nervous and Mental Diseases*, 1987, No.2. Until recently (c. 2003), Zhang Mingyuan was President of the Chinese Society of Psychiatrists.
419 Liu Baiju (op cit), p.666.

In another intriguing example, the author discusses the case of people suffering from "compulsive antithetical thought disorder," a condition whereby those affected feel impelled to respond to any statement, concept or proposition put to them with a diametrically opposite one. In China, he notes,

> With some sufferers, the compulsive antithetical thoughts extend to politics.... Provided the content of these compulsive thoughts is not actually expressed or put into action, no real harm can arise. In the course of China's past political campaigns, however, some afflicted people actually gave voice to their compulsive thoughts and intentions, and as a result they were subjected to mass criticism and struggle sessions for displaying "reactionary ideology."[420]

Finally, the author poignantly cites yet another subcategory of this type: "In the case of those suffering from depressive illness who engage in negative political speech and action, sometimes their aim in doing so is to commit an indirect form of suicide (self-punishment.)"[421] This formulation speaks volumes as to the wider state of freedom of political thought and expression in China today. Indeed, the most important fact to bear in mind when considering these "pseudo-counterrevolutionary" cases in China is that – in sharp contrast to the situation in other countries where genuine cases of politically coloured mental illness also arise – the individuals concerned have almost invariably been placed under criminal arrest. The principal purpose of their subsequent examination by police psychiatrists has been, not to establish how best to make them mentally well again, but rather to ascertain if they were capable of standing trial for their alleged "counterrevolutionary" offences. If not, they would mostly be placed in forensic psychiatric custody instead of in a prison. In the authorities' view, to set free someone expressing such patently "dangerous" political thoughts and ideas would be far too socially risky an option.

Although primarily of relevance to the Mao era, this curious mental phenomenon – the "pseudo-counterrevolutionary syndrome" – continued to afflict many of those in the early post-Mao period who in fact had been made seriously mentally ill by the genuine political insanity of the Cultural Revolution years. Both of the case examples presented below date from the 1980s, when the severe psychological after-effects of the trauma of the Cultural Revolution were still being felt by many ordinary Chinese citizens. The first one qualifies more as a "borderline case" of this kind – that is to say, it appears from the details given that the person concerned might indeed have been afflicted by some kind of mental disorder, but at the same time the case presents a number of conspicuous similarities with those of the evidently quite healthy Mr Liu and Mr Zhu, as discussed above.

The Case of Mr L.

> Mr. L, 32 years old, a worker, educated to lower-middle school level. He became ill immediately after the Cultural Revolution, believing that he was "the son-in-law of a fourteenth-generation descendant of Zheng Chenggong"[422] and that he could lead

---

420 Ibid, p.679. The mental condition referred to here, "*qiangpoxing duili siwei*," is also translatable as "compulsive antagonistic mentality." See also Li Congpei, *Forensic Psychiatry* (op cit), p.270.
421 The passage in question continues: "Some mentally ill people of this kind write letters to the relevant departments informing them that they're planning to carry out such-and-such an act which endangers state security, adding their real names and work-unit details to the letter, and they then sit back and await their punishment."
422 Zheng Chenggong (1624-62), also known as Koxinga, was a Chinese military leader of the late Ming and early Qing dynasties. He launched a military campaign against the new Manchu government from his base in Fujian Province, and captured Taiwan from the Dutch in 1662. His name is a byword in China for loyalty and devotion to the nation.

the whole of China in carrying out reforms. He proposed to replace the Chinese Communist Party with a "Labour Party of China" (*Zhongguo Laodong Dang*), with himself as "Chairman," and he proceeded to formulate a "Party Charter" and "Party Constitution" and also to recruit members into the party. Three ignorant youths joined this organization. He also drafted a "Law of the People," a "Cadres Law," a "Military Law" and a "Law on Science," the contents of which were a total mishmash and full of nonsense, so that no one could make head or tail of them. Later on, he and his collaborators distributed several thousand leaflets throughout all areas of the city, thereby creating an extremely bad influence. He was then arrested on charges of committing "counterrevolutionary crimes."

During his investigation and questioning, it was discovered that although he confessed unreservedly both about the events in question and about his criminal motives, there were certain absurd and unusual elements in his account. He was then sent for forensic psychiatric appraisal. In the course of the appraisal, it was ascertained that he had a family history of mental illness, with several of his relatives afflicted. Upon psychiatric examination, it was found that while his consciousness was normal and his memory and intellect were both sound, he nonetheless had marked delusions of grandeur and his ideological outlook was fallacious and unrealistic. He requested and urged the government not to destroy the various "laws" he had formulated, saying that although he would have to go to prison and so would be unable to complete his "enterprise," these "laws" should still be preserved for the benefit of future generations, to serve as the basis for carrying out a scientific reformation of the country.

Appraisal findings: paranoid schizophrenia; crime caused by delusions of grandeur during an active phase of the illness; no capacity for criminal responsibility.[423]

Like many cases of this variety, it is impossible to draw any firm conclusions from the officially supplied evidence as to whether or not Mr L. was mentally normal at the time of attempting to form his unauthorized political party. On the face of it, the forensic examiners offer little in the way of hard evidence that he was not. First, there is the reference to Mr L.'s belief that he was the descendant of an important historical figure, which may or may not have been true (such beliefs are not uncommon among the mentally normal, in China as elsewhere); and second, there is the official claim that his "ideological outlook was fallacious and unrealistic" and contained "certain absurd and unusual elements."

But as we have seen in the case of Mr Zhu, China's forensic psychiatric examiners jump readily to such conclusions when faced with any outspoken dissidents who happen to pursue their "ridiculous" political ideas with a high degree of authorial vigour and enthusiasm. In describing L.'s efforts to draft detailed legislation for the future society, for example, the authorities' claimed that "they were full of nonsense" and that "no one could make head or tail of them." However, since the forensic psychiatric report on L. clearly stated that "his consciousness was normal and his memory and intellect were both sound," an alternative explanation for the alleged confusion in his legal thinking might simply be that his formal education had gone no further than lower-middle school level – or even that he was just not very bright. Finally, the police psychiatrists' claim that L.'s desire to replace the Communist Party

---

[423] Jia Yicheng (ed.), *Shiyong Sifa Jingshenbingxue* (*Applied Forensic Psychiatry*), (Anhui Renmin Chubanshe, 1988), pp.192-193; cited as "Case No. 226" in Liu Baiju (op cit), pp.675-6.

with a new political party, created and led by himself, amounted unequivocally to the "delusions of grandeur" characteristic of such a severe illness as "paranoid schizophrenia" must surely be seen as failing the "Gluzman litmus test" on such matters. In L.'s case, there were apparently no cosmic rays, creatures from outer space, or delusions of being persecuted by China's equivalent of the CIA to be found. (Although in the circumstances, the latter fear would have been well-enough founded.)

At most, the available official evidence in this case indicates that L. might possibly have been mentally disordered in some way. If he was truly a paranoid schizophrenic, however, then the underlying injustice of the way he was treated becomes even more apparent: instead of being treated in a medically humane and appropriate manner, he was branded by the legal and psychiatric authorities as being "criminally insane" and thus destined to spend long years incarcerated alongside psychotic and mostly violent offenders.

The Case of Ms. Li

This second case of "pseudo-counterrevolution," involving a female worker who developed florid and systematic delusions about an impending apocalyptic plot by the Chinese government, appears to be much more clear-cut and conclusive, in medical terms, than the case of Mr. L. However, the legal and human rights implications of the case are basically the same, and therefore no less troubling.

> Ms. Li, 37 years old, a worker, educated to upper-middle school level. Normally quite introverted by character. In 1981, she and her husband were divorced on grounds of emotional incompatibility. In 1982, after she violated labour regulations and undertook private work projects,[424] she was punished by being dismissed from her job but retained on payroll for a one-year probationary period. Thereafter she began to show signs of mental abnormality, suspecting that her former husband, neighbours and work-unit leadership were saying insulting things about her, and she filed a court lawsuit making accusations against the leaders of her work unit; she also frequently got into arguments at her work unit, demanding that they revoke the punishment imposed upon her.
>
> Subsequently, she formed the belief that the government was putting poison into food and vegetables, as part of a plan to cause people's deaths from chronic poisoning and thereby to fulfil its goal of restricting China's population and allowing the ants to rule the world. On March 10, 1991, on a certain university campus, Li was caught red-handed while in the act of pasting up a small-character poster that had negative political content and was titled "Nuclear War in Peacetime"; a search of her person then produced a large quantity of other small-character posters. During the pre-trial criminal investigation, Li made a series of strange and incomprehensible statements and it was decided to send her for forensic psychiatric examination.
>
> Appraisal findings: schizophrenia; the small-character leaflets were posted up while she was in the grip of her delusions; no capacity for criminal responsibility.[425]

---

424 "*si bao gongcheng*." In 1982, before China's market economy began, citizens were normally not allowed to undertake paid work outside their state-appointed jobs.
425 Lü Xianrong (ed.), *Sifa Jingshen Yixue Anli Ji* (*A Compilation of Forensic Psychiatric Medical Cases*) (Ankang Hospital of the Wuhan Municipal Public Security Bureau, 1992), p.137; cited as "Case No. 227" in Liu Baiju (op cit), p.676.

The evidently severe nature of Ms. Li's mental illness serves only to highlight the tragedy and injustice of the fact that, rather than being placed by the authorities in a mental hospital where she could receive appropriate medical attention, she instead wound up in police custody facing serious criminal charges on account of her systematic and politically florid delusions. At the risk of repeating the obvious, it should be pointed out that in this case too, Ms. Li's schizophrenic delusions had not led her to present any real or genuine threat to public safety – there had been no attempt on her part to take any physical or violent action to forestall the imagined social calamity; instead she had tried merely to "warn" the public about the impending disaster by writing and distributing a number of leaflets about it on a college campus.

Also clear from this case is the absurd degree of literalism with which the authorities often pursue their investigations into "political cases" of this type. In particular, the mention of a government plot "to allow the ants to rule the world" should surely have rung early warning bells in the minds of the police – but no, po-faced throughout, they still proceeded to arrest and charge her with hatching a serious political crime. The final outcome of this sad process – the declaration that Ms. Li was not criminally responsible by reason of insanity – would in the U.K. legal context be the improbable equivalent of the police arresting a wild-eyed billboard carrier at Speaker's Corner for proclaiming "The End of the World is Nigh!" and then having the unfortunate free thinker committed to Rampton or Broadmoor indefinitely on grounds of criminal insanity.

IV. A Theory of "Political Insanity" for the New Millennium

A chapter from a major two-volume study on mental illness and crime which was written by a law researcher at the Chinese Academy of Social Sciences, Liu Baiju, and was published as recently as August 2000, represents the current "state of the art" thinking within Chinese forensic psychiatry on the question of "political crimes" committed by alleged mentally ill dissidents. It is therefore well worth examining in some detail. Titled "On Negative Political Speech and Action," the chapter begins by stating,

> Acts that endanger the nation and threaten the social system can, when severe in nature, constitute crimes. Offences of this type are customarily referred to as political crimes… Mentally ill people, owing to the pathological factors that beset them, may also engage in behaviour that endangers the state and the social system, and the most commonly seen forms of such behaviour are the writing of banners, distributing leaflets and flyers, sending letters, making speeches, and shouting out slogans… [However,] to describe this as "counterrevolutionary behaviour" or as "behaviour that endangers state security" would obviously [since those concerned are mentally ill] be "inappropriate." To call it "reactionary behaviour" would also not be good, since the term "reactionary" has excessively vague connotations. In the end, this writer has decided to use the term "negative political speech and action" to denote such behaviour.[426]

So far so good: the author appears to be making an effort to "downgrade" the seriousness of the political offences committed by dissidents in cases where they are perceived by the authorities

---

426 Liu Baiju (op cit), p.662. For a full English translation of the section on "negative political speech and action" from this book, see Munro, *Dangerous Minds: Political Psychiatry in China Today and its Origins in the Mao Era*, Human Rights Watch and Geneva Initiative on Psychiatry (New York and Hilversum), August 2002, pp.257-274.

to be suffering from mental illness. However, while he brings to his topic a degree of analytical sophistication going well beyond that found in most other Chinese forensic-psychiatric discussions of this question, he remains severely hampered in this endeavour by the awkward and insoluble fact that all the dissident activities in question are still held under China's criminal law to constitute the most serious possible forms of crime. Hence, his adoption of the ostensibly more liberal and user-friendly rubric of "negative political speech and action" in place of the formerly prevalent terms "reactionary" and "counterrevolutionary" to denote such activities turns out to have no practical legal consequences for the detainees concerned: they must still be sent either to institutes for the criminally insane or to locked wards in general psychiatric hospitals.

Concerning the frequency with which such cases have occurred in China over the past 30 years or so, Liu had this to say:

> A review of the literature on forensic-psychiatric medical appraisals shows us that while the expression of negative political speech and action by the mentally ill is hardly a common occurrence, it is also by no means rare.
>
> - In a report by Zhong Xingsheng *et al* on 210 cases of forensic appraisal that were carried out during 1981-84, fourteen out of the 181 crimes at issue (or 7.73 percent) were ones of anti-social speech and action.
> - In a report by Shen Muci *et al* on 654 cases of forensic appraisal conducted during 1973-86, out of a total of 566 crimes, 103 were cases of a political nature, or 18.2 percent. (Eighty of these cases dated from 1980 or earlier.)
> - Xu Shenghan, in a report on 708 cases of forensic appraisal carried out during 1982-86, found that 32 of the 638 offences committed (or 5.02 percent) were crimes of counterrevolutionary behaviour.
> - In a report by Liu Guangyu *et al* on 931 forensic appraisal cases dating from 1979-90, among a total of 667 offences committed, 27 (or 4.05 percent) were identified as being political cases. [427]
>
> Among these various studies, the one by Shen Muci *et al* [which included data from the 1970s] showed the highest proportion of such cases, at 18.2 percent, while in the other reports [which all dealt with the post-Mao period] the proportion of cases that were political in nature averaged out at 5.6 percent.... Naturally, however, an incidence rate of 5.6 percent is by no means something that we can afford to ignore, and it fully justifies treating acts of negative speech and action by the mentally ill as being a problem requiring special study and attention.

It should be noted that the author wrote this not twenty or more years ago, but in the year 2000. One of the more interesting and subtle aspects of Liu Baiju's analysis is his discussion of the seemingly large subgroup of criminal psychiatric detainees for whom we have coined the term "pseudo-counterrevolutionaries." His account of this issue, however, serves mainly to throw into even sharper relief than before the two main questions that have arisen throughout this book: first, were the detainees in question in fact suffering from any genuine mental illness; and second, if so, why were they subsequently consigned to institutes for the criminally insane, rather than sent for treatment in

---

427 For source details of the first two of these reports, see Notes 46 and 327 above.

regular mental hospitals? As will be seen, there is a strongly oxymoronic quality to Liu's treatment of the first of these topics:

> If the mentally ill person was actively concerned about politics and had independent views on the subject before becoming mentally ill, or if he or she was the innocent victim of psychological trauma arising from political attacks, then he or she might engage in negative political speech and action after falling ill. For example, if those who become mentally abnormal as a result of suffering political persecution then develop delusions of persecution, the content of these delusions may have a negative political coloration, and such people may therefore develop hostile feelings toward the political environment. However, the fact that such a history existed before the mental illness arose by no means implies that the negative political speech and action expressed by the mentally ill person concerned is necessarily rational in nature. For sufferers of this kind, the influence of the pre-illness history occurs at the unconscious level.

In other words, even though "sufferers" of this type were in fact the targets of severe political persecution in the past, their resultant long-term feelings of persecution are still, in the author's view, to be attributed to mental illness ("unconscious delusions" against the Party) rather than to any rational and accurate subjective understanding or construal of their past traumatic experiences. Thus, any hapless *bona fide* dissident who had actually encountered previous episodes of official persecution on ideological grounds would be hard-pressed indeed to argue that he or she was not, contrary to the official perception, "pathologically deluded" in the present. Considerable caution is therefore called for when evaluating even this, seemingly more self-evident, subgroup of what the authorities colloquially term "political lunacy" (*zhengzhi fengzi*) cases in China today. The least that can be said here is that it would surely require a physician trained to a very high level of sophistication in the theories of Chinese-style political psychiatric diagnosis to be able to differentiate correctly between, on the one hand, a victim of past political persecution whose current activities in pursuit of official redress, rehabilitation or compensation from the authorities should properly be perceived as being rational, or psychiatrically normal, in nature; and on the other, a victim of past political persecution whose broadly identical current activities deserved, by contrast, to be interpreted as being the acts of someone who had been rendered clinically paranoid by the past political injustices they had suffered.

Secondly, on the question of why many mentally ill detainees of this kind end up falling within the orbit of the criminal justice system, Liu makes the following very pertinent observation:

> While the speech and actions of some mentally ill people may, in themselves, be devoid of any real political meaning or significance, they may nonetheless, under certain specific kinds of circumstances, be elevated in the minds of others to the high realm of politics. For example, schizophrenics suffering from delusions of grandeur sometimes believe and declare themselves to be the Emperor or the President; in normal times, people would pay little or no attention to statements like that, but during periods when the political atmosphere is tense, such statements may well be seen as constituting "counterrevolutionary speech."

Forensic psychiatrists in most developed countries are familiar with a specific subcategory of violent criminal offenders who commit their crimes because they suffer from systematic paranoid delusions broadly related to politics: they may believe, for example, that the Queen of England or the President of the United States is trying to persecute and punish them, or (most commonly in the case of schizophrenics) that they have had electronic bugging devices implanted in their brains by the security services; they then feel compelled to fight back, sometimes in a violent and indiscriminate manner. The crucial distinction in China's case, however, is that in the great majority of officially reported cases of this type no internationally recognized criminal offence has taken place, and the alleged mentally ill detainees in question are found criminally insane solely on account of their peacefully expressed "anti-government" thoughts and viewpoints. Again, if genuinely mentally ill, such people should in all cases be afforded humane and appropriate medical care in a non-coercive psychiatric setting. They should not be incarcerated in high-security mental institutions simply because their political or religious views happened to upset the Chinese Communist Party.

However, as Liu's subsequent elaboration on this general theme strikingly but inadvertently reveals, the more precise "legal-medical profile" of many of these politically demented detainees turns out, upon closer inspection, to be remarkably similar to the familiar Western profile of the mentally normal, classic-style political dissident living in a repressive communist state. As he explained,

> Foremost among the pathological factors leading mentally ill people to engage in negative political speech and action are delusions, and impairments of thought and logic. The content of the delusions that can lead to negative political speech and action is always related, directly or indirectly, to questions of politics. Among the various categories of delusion, the ones that most readily give rise to negative political speech and action are delusions of persecution and delusions of grandeur.
>
> If the identity of the persecutor that is fabricated [in the mind of the detainee] by virtue of the delusions of persecution happens to be either the ruling political party, the state institutions, or individual members of the leadership, then inevitably the sufferer will develop feelings of hostility and over-vigilance toward the ruling political party, the state institutions or individual leaders, and they may then start "exposing," "denouncing" and "condemning" the latter's various "conspiracies" and "crimes." In general, the targets of these delusions of persecution are limited to certain specific individuals, but in some cases the scope of hostility may become constantly amplified in the sufferer's mind, progressing from one individual to a number of different people, and then onward to include the whole [Party] organization, the government, or even the whole of society.
>
> [Moreover,] those suffering from delusions of grandeur, may develop political mania (*zhengzhi kuangre*) and become excessively interested in political matters – believing, for example, that they themselves have some political mission to fulfil and that they are destined to become (or already are) political leaders. If they proceed to propagate such views publicly, they will inevitably come into sharp conflict with the external environment. In some cases, the sufferers not only exaggerate their own importance, but also seek to deny or negate that of others, and they may even try to usurp the latter's role, so leading to even greater complications.

Finally, according to Liu,

> They also enjoy propagating their viewpoints in public and in front of many onlookers, and they strive hard to convince people that they are correct, thereby giving rise

to the impression that they are engaging in "counterrevolutionary propaganda and incitement."[428]

While not excluding or discounting the possibility that, in a certain number or proportion of the cases involved, some of those falling within the various "political-style" forensic psychiatric groups and categories outlined above may in fact have been suffering from some form of genuine mental disturbance, the key question must again be posed: for what possible legitimate reason could any of these people, irrespective of which of the various diagnostic labels they were eventually given, have ended up being subjected to the invasive scrutiny of China's forensic psychiatric examiners? The answer, by all currently prevailing international standards of criminal justice and legal psychiatry, is a resounding "None." The sole reason for the arrest and subsequent psychiatric assessment of such people to determine their "capacity for legal responsibility" appears to have been that their original presenting activities or statements were viewed by the police, at the time of their commission, as being politically hostile or overly provocative in nature and hence as constituting grave political offences under the Criminal Law.

We shall now examine a number of specific cases dating from the 1990s, by way of affording a practical illustration of how the revised and updated theory of "political lunacy" presented by Liu Baiju and other recent writers on forensic psychiatry in China has actually been interpreted and applied by the country's security authorities during the recent past. A significant feature of the more recent caseload that has come to light is that, whereas in previous decades the great majority of officially reported cases concerned political activists who had been arrested on charges of "counterrevolution," over the past few years there has been an increasing number of cases reported involving detainees drawn from other social groups.[429] These include, notably: persistent complainants and petitioners; independent trades unionists and workers rights activists; whistleblowers who expose corruption or malfeasance in the workplace; unrepentant Falun Gong practitioners; and homeless migrant workers or other indigent and rootless members of society who get into trouble with the local police authorities for various reasons.

Workers Rights Activists

The Case of Xue Jifeng

As we have seen from several of the cases cited above, the committed espousal of banned or "outdated" radical left-wing views by ordinary citizens in China since the Cultural Revolution, or attempts to form unauthorized workers' political parties, can easily lead both to the arrest of those concerned and also, in due course, to civil or criminal-style forensic diagnoses of "paranoid" insanity and legal incapacity. During the past few years, moreover, several cases have come to light of factory workers and others who have received similar treatment for trying to carry out independent trades union-style activities – for example, leading their fellow workers in protest against unjustified or arbitrary factory closures, misappropriation of pension funds by management, or non-payment of redundancy

---

428 Liu Baiju, (op cit), p.265-6 and p.270-1; the passages shown above are taken from Chapter 7: "*Xiaoji Zhengzhi Yan-Xing*"..
429 Whether or not this signals a relative decrease in the proportion and number of political dissidents now being dealt with in this manner by the forensic psychiatric authorities is unclear; it may simply be that cases of the various other types mentioned here have only recently started to come to public attention in China and overseas. (In the case of Falun Gong, of course, the movement itself dates only from the early 1990s.)

or unemployment compensation and the like. The following two cases, both of which involved actual attempts to set up independent labour unions, illustrate well this apparently fast-growing category of psychiatric abuse in China. Moreover – by contrast with virtually all of the other cases we have considered thus far – both were widely reported in the international news media. Also, there was a strong "whistleblowing" aspect to each of these cases, since both the workers concerned were seeking to expose economic misdoings and financial irregularities at their workplaces.

The plight of Xue Jifeng, a retired railway conductor from Henan Province who in 1998 became active in leading a workers' protest movement against local corruption, was first highlighted in a news report by *Agence France Presse* in November that year. As the article explained,

> More than 2000 people staged a demonstration in a central Chinese city after they lost their savings in a failed investment firm, a Hong Kong-based human rights group said Monday. The protestors marched [on] Sunday in front of the Communist Party offices in the Henan provincial capital Zhengzhou demanding their money back and that three of their representatives be freed from detention, the Information Centre of Human Rights and Democratic Movement in China said. Two of the three jailed representatives, Ma Ling and Gao Zhifeng, were taken in for questioning after leading 400 protestors on October 10 in blocking a main Guangzhou-Beijing railway…
>
> The third, Xue Jifeng, was taken from his home last Monday and placed in a psychiatric asylum after accusing the Henan authorities of being responsible for the failure of the Three Stars investment group. The provincial government in May announced the closure of the three-year-old group, which collapsed owing about 10,000 investors more than three billion yuan (360 million dollars), the Information Centre said. Local Communist Party authorities told AFP they had no knowledge of the protest or the closure of the Three Stars group.[430]

Most of the investors in the failed scheme were workers and employees of Three Stars and many of them lost their entire life savings when the company was later declared bankrupt by the local government. The investment scheme itself was officially found to have been nothing more than an illegal fund-raising scam, and the company's executives had even leaked news of the impeding wind-up so that their families and friends could withdraw their own investments before the company folded. In response, Xue and other affected employees formed a local action group – the Preparatory Office of the Workers Association, which later evolved into the Zhengzhou Workers Association – and began publicly issuing leaflets and flyers calling upon the government to help them recover the workforce's lost investment funds and for the company officials responsible for the scam to be criminally prosecuted. On November 9, Xue was detained by police and forcibly admitted to the Henan Xinxiang City Mental Hospital; one week later, after Zhengzhou citizens staged a large protest demonstration against his arrest, Xue was released from the hospital.

A year later, however, the workers' grievances had still not been resolved, and Xue and his colleagues decided to stage a large public protest in central Zhengzhou. On December 19, the day of the protest and about a week after he had tried unsuccessfully to legally register the recently-formed Zhengzhou Workers Association with the city authorities, Xue was again detained by police and forcibly returned to the Xinxiang Mental Hospital. Intent on silencing him, the authorities this time kept him in psychiatric incarceration for a period of six months, during which he was held in a ward with seriously

---

430 "AFP Reports 2,000 protest Against Failed Investment Firm," *FBIS Daily Report*, November 16, 1998.

disturbed patients who harassed him day and night and was force-fed powerful psychotropic drugs that he said had severe side effects.[431] Subsequently, the police tried to pressure his wife into signing a declaration saying that he had been "cured," but she refused to do so on the grounds that he had never been mentally ill in the first place. In a telephone interview with AFP from the hospital, Xue himself stated: "People who know me and the staff in the hospital do not think that I have a mental illness.... I was put here by the Zhengzhou Public Security Bureau on orders from the government." Eventually, on June 20, 2000, he was released from the mental hospital after agreeing to sign a muzzling order that contained (according to the New York-based Human Rights in China) "conditions restricting his rights without any legal process at all."[432] Unsurprisingly, there have been no reports of Xue's having engaged in any further workers' rights-related activity since that time.

The Case of Cao Maobing

A second fairly recent case of a psychiatrically detained worker activist, that of Cao Maobing, attracted still greater international press attention. In November 2000, Cao, 42 years old, was an electrician at the Funing Silk Factory in Jiangsu Province, some 185 miles north of Shanghai, and for the previous year he had been active in organizing workers at the factory to protest against corrupt managers who had solicited money from them to buy stock but then failed to issue them with the stock certificates. In addition, since a management reorganization move earlier in the year, hundreds of workers at the factory had not been paid their basic wages and benefits. The workers therefore decided to set up their own union, and during the second half of 2000 Cao applied on their behalf several times to the authorities for legal recognition of the group and for permission for it to be affiliated with the official All-China Federation of Trade Unions (ACFTU.) The authorities refused even to consider the application, and Cao himself was detained and briefly held by the police on no fewer than ten occasions between June and November. During this period, Cao led a small delegation of workers to Beijing to seek the intervention of the central authorities, but their requests were ignored.[433] On November 11, around 1,800 members of the factory's workforce went out on strike, and similar protest actions soon began to be staged by workers in other factories around the city. One month later, having still made no progress in the dispute, the silk workers decided to take their case to the international news media; Cao was chosen as their spokesman.

Reports of the Funing Silk Factory workers' attempt to set up an independent trade union made world headlines; articles on the incident ran in all the main wire services, and the New York Times and Washington Post both published extensive interviews with Cao.[434] On December 16, the day after he had spoken with reporters from these two papers, however, Cao was ordered by the chief of security at the silk factory to undergo a psychiatric examination, and later the same day he was taken by police to

---

431 "Rights Group Says China Sent Labour Activist to Mental Hospital," *Agence France Presse*, April 11, 2000.
432 For a full account of Xue's case, see: "Xue Jifeng: Detained in a psychiatric hospital for championing worker rights," *China Rights Forum*, Summer 2000, pp.28-29. Several photos of Xue, taken during his second confinement at the Xinxiang Mental Hospital, together with a series of court documents relating to his case are held on file by the present writer.
433 See: "Assistance for Jailed Labour Activist Still Needed," *China Labor Watch* press release, January 7, 2001.
434 "Leaders of Independent Chinese Labor Union Fear Crackdown," John Pomfret, *Washington Post*, December 15, 2000; and "Silk Workers in Standoff with Beijing Over Union," Erik Eckholm, *New York Times*, December 15, 2000.

the Yancheng No. 4 Mental Hospital and involuntarily hospitalised there. His fellow workers responded almost immediately by issuing the following protest statement to the international press:

> Mr. Cao Maobing is a worker at Funing Silk Factory, Jiangsu, China. He led the workers to organize a union, advocate labour rights, hold the management and government to national laws and human rights standards, pressure the management to come up with long-owed wage payments, demand that the government maintain the minimum living standard of laid-off and retired workers, and pay minimum wages to those still working [at the factory.] Mr. Cao is an upright, kind and law-abiding citizen, and a brave and intelligent worker. He has made a lot of personal sacrifices to help other workers to uphold their right to a basic living.
>
> However, the Yancheng municipal government and the Funing County government have maliciously labelled Mr. Cao as being mentally ill and have had him illegally and forcibly admitted to the Yancheng No. 4 Mental Hospital, where he is being subjected to inhumane mental and physical abuse. The workers at Funing Silk Factory hereby call upon the government to stop this unlawful act of persecution forthwith, to allow us to exercise our union rights, and to accept the other rightful demands that we have made. The vile and mean treatment [shown to Cao] is unbecoming of a government, and if it continues, the people will lose their trust and confidence in the government...[435]

At the mental hospital, according to his wife, Yao Guifang, doctors "demanded Cao Maobing take medicine that they would not identify and forced him to swallow the pills when he refused... He's absolutely not insane and refuses to take the medicine. But eventually they forced him to take it." Yao also confirmed that her husband had been compulsorily admitted to the hospital by the Public Security Bureau, adding that the latter had "refused to say why he has been committed or when he might be allowed to return home."[436] The same day, another international news agency discovered that the former manager of the Funing Silk Factory had been arrested on charges of corruption three months earlier, a fact which clearly suggested that the workers original allegations and grievances had been justified.[437] Medical staff at the mental hospital swiftly denied the charges of forced medication;[438] but two months later, in February 2001, the New York Times reported on its front page that "[Cao] has protested his incarceration with a hunger-strike, been forcibly drugged and been subjected to electroshock therapy..." Moreover, according to the same article,

> The director of the hospital where Mr. Cao was being held said that an intensive examination by experts had determined that he was suffering from paranoid psychosis...Reached by telephone Thursday, the hospital director, Li Hu, said that Mr. Cao was [first] sent by the police for a forensic psychiatric evaluation in 1998 and that doctors concluded then that he was paranoid, but released him... "We handled Mr. Cao's case with great care," Mr. Li said. "In the second half of January, before

---

435 Document provided by Li Qiang, director of China Labor Watch (*Zhongguo Laogong Guancha*), a New York-based NGO; the group's website address is: www.chinalaborwatch.org.
436 "Wife: China Union Leader Drugged," Christopher Bodeen, *Associated Press*, December 17, 2000.
437 "Worker Demand Release of Chinese Unionist from Mental Asylum," *Agence France Presse*, December 17, 2000.
438 "Detained unionist no longer drugged," Vivien Pik-kwan Chan, *South China Morning Post*, December 19, 2000.

the Chinese New Year, seventeen experts, including specialists from the Nanjing Brain Hospital took part in the exam. They were able to identify a group of symptoms that led to the same conclusion we reached in 1998 – Mr. Cao suffers from paranoid psychosis."[439]

Following official statements of concern to the Chinese government about Cao's situation by the U.N's Working Group on Arbitrary Detention, and after a series of high-level protests that the International Confederation of Free Trades Unions (ICFTU) had lodged with the ILO's Committee on Freedom of Association during the first half of 2001,[440] Cao was finally, after almost seven months of incarceration, released from the Yancheng No. 4 Mental Hospital and allowed to return home. A few days afterwards, the director of the hospital, Mr. Li, reiterated to the foreign press that Cao was suffering from "paranoid psychosis." However, "He's a little better," the hospital chief said in a telephone interview. "He's not fully recovered yet. It's very hard to cure."[441] There has been no further news about either Cao Maobing or the Funing silk workers' struggle for an independent trade union since that time.

A communication addressed to the Chinese government by the Working Group on Arbitrary Detention in June 2001 provides a telling postscript to Cao's case:

> The allegations of the source and of the Government referred to above are basically contradictory. Against the detailed allegations of the source that the detention of Cao Maobing was politically motivated (he was detained immediately after giving an interview on international radio, the hospital is run by the Public Security Bureau, his relatives have been under pressure from the authorities), the Government limited its comments to stating that Mr. Cao's detention is exclusively attributable to his mental illness and that the allegation that he has been taken into custody because of his trade union activities is utter nonsense.
>
> The Government did not provide information in support of its allegation concerning the mental illness of Mr. Cao, nor did it provide specific information to convince the Working Group of the existence of sufficient safeguards against arbitrary detention of political opponents or trade union activists for alleged mental illness, namely information concerning the legal provisions governing the admission to and the holding of people with mental disorders in psychiatric hospitals, the system of monitoring the admission and stay in such institutions by an independent body in order to prevent abuse, and the remedies available to psychiatric patients and their families to obtain review of continued detention.
>
> The Working Group cannot but conclude that the detention of Cao Maobing in a psychiatric hospital…is motivated by his trade union or political activities. Therefore, on the basis of the information available to it the Working Group is convinced that Cao Maobing is being detained for having peacefully exercised his right to freedom

---

439 "China is Said to Abuse Promoter of Factory Union," Erik Eckholm, *New York Times*, February 9, 2001.
440 See, for example, "China: ICFTU Complaint to ILO: Additional information - Cases n° 1930 and 2031 (Appeals and Protests, 2/6/2002)," and "People's Republic of China: Annual Survey of Violations of Trade Union Rights (2002) (Country Reports: Annual Survey of Trade Union Rights, 6/1/2002)," both available at the ICFTU's website: www.icftu.org.
441 "Chinese activist released after 6-month detention," Frank Langfitt, The Baltimore Sun, July 19, 2001. For a good overall summary of Cao's case, see "The Case of Cao Maobing," *China Rights Forum*, Spring 2001, p.7.

of opinion and expression, as guaranteed by article 19 of the Universal Declaration of Human Rights.[442]

Petitioners and Complainants Persecuted by Corrupt Officials

This type of political psychiatric abuse was commonly found also in the former Soviet Union. In 1973, for example, the main *samizdat* journal of the Soviet dissident movement, *Chronicle of Current Events*,[443] reported as follows:

> A number of facts indicate that the [public] reception rooms of the highest official bodies in Moscow either have an ambulance from the psychiatric first-aid service on permanent duty, or are in direct contact with this service. In many cases people who have come with complaints, usually of a non-political nature, to the reception rooms of the Party Central Committee, the Council of Ministers, the Presidium of the Supreme Soviet, the All-Union Central Council of Trade Unions, the KGB and other organizations have not been allowed to put their case, but instead have been forcibly driven off to a Moscow psychiatric hospital, and then, after assessment, to a hospital near their home.[444]

One such example was that of Mrs. Gusyakova, a 61-year-old housewife who had herself sought to defend a local official who had been psychiatrically incarcerated on false medical grounds. In November 1973, she went to the Presidium of the Supreme Soviet of the Russian Republic to complain about the illegal acts of the district authorities, only to encounter the following treatment:

> As the lower officials give no help to us petitioners I asked to be received by one of [chairman] Yasnov's deputies. Mrs Duritsnaya agreed to receive me in room 10, but told me to wait in the corridor. An hour later I was called into the room, and three tough men grabbed me and shoved me through a door into the yard (in room 10 there is such a door.) They pushed me into a car and drove me off to Psychiatric Hospital No.13.... For the hospital doctors it was a very awkward situation: I did not need treatment, at home I had a seriously ill husband, yet the authorities demanded I be kept in a mad-house, as I was complaining about illegal acts by the authorities.[445]

She was held there for one week. As Sidney Bloch and Peter Reddaway, the chief historians of Soviet political psychiatry, observed of this case:

> Gusyakova was fortunate of course: she escaped the last stage. But her summing-up of the situation, in an open letter to *Pravda*, is damning. It indicates...how psychiatry is probably abused just as much in suppressing ordinary citizens as well-educated dissenters: "Simple people [she wrote,] cannot obtain elementary justice: the most persistent protestors, those who doggedly press for fairness, are dispatched to lunatic

---

442 See: "Civil and Political Rights, Including the Question of Torture and Detention. Opinion No. 20/2001 (China): Communication addressed to the [Chinese] Government on 26 June 2001 Concerning Cao Maobing," 59th Session of the Commission on Human Rights, Item 11 (b) of the provisional agenda, E/CN.4/2003/8/Add.1, pp. 47-49.
443 *Ekspress Khronika*, No.20, 1973.
444 *Russia's Political Hospitals* (op cit), p.271
445 Ibid.

asylums from the reception rooms of the Supreme Soviet Presidium and the Central Committee. No, not dissenters, just the persistent – to stop them complaining."[446]

As this case illustrates, the political misuse of psychiatry in the Soviet Union extended well beyond the formal forensic psychiatric domain. Contrary to what is often believed, Soviet dissidents, petitioners and complainants and others were committed, in perhaps a majority of cases, to regular mental hospitals rather than to forensic custody institutions, and this was done mostly by local government or police officials acting in collaboration with regular psychiatrists. The same holds true in China today.

The Case of Zhang Gonglai

Zhang Gonglai, a 46 year old former nursery school teacher from Harbin and a cadre in the Communist Youth League, encountered very similar treatment to that just described; moreover, her case is typical of a growing number of such cases that have begun to be publicly reported in the official Chinese press since the late 1990s. A graduate from a local teachers' training college, in 1988 Zhang was hired to teach at a nursery school attached to the same college. Apparently, she had agreed not to have a child for at least two years after starting work there, but the following year she became pregnant. Angered by what they viewed as a breach of contract, the nursery school leadership refused to allow her to return to work after she had completed her maternity leave. Over the next two years, Zhang repeatedly petitioned both the municipal and provincial governments, demanding reinstatement of her job, restoration of her good name and compensation for lost income. Eventually, in 1991, the city authorities ordered the nursery school managers to admit wrongdoing and allow her to return to work after a further six-month leave-of-absence or "cooling off" period. Half a year later, however, when Zhang attempted to return to work, nursery school officials again refused to let her do so.

Over the next seven years, Zhang doggedly continued to petition the local authorities about the matter, but all to no avail. Finally, on July 29, 1998, she decided to stage a mini-demonstration at the Harbin provincial government office, by displaying inside the office a small placard listing her various complaints and demands. Thereupon, according to a detailed account of her case, written by a personal friend of hers and published in a Hong Kong monthly magazine in November 2000,[447]

> A cadre came out and said to her: "Come on in, we're definitely going to solve your problem today." When she entered the visits and complaints office, she saw that the headmasters of both the teachers' training college and the nursery school [Teng Xiuzhi and Zhang Ruifang] were there waiting. Four men wearing white coats then appeared, grabbed hold of her and, without offering a word of explanation, tied her hands behind her back and dragged and kicked her outside toward a waiting car. She was driven straight from the municipal government offices over to the local mental hospital, and on arrival, the two headmasters signed the committal papers

---

446 Ibid, p.272.
447 "An Account of the Evil Misdeeds of the Heilongjiang Provincial Mental Hospital: Petitioners persecuted by being psychiatrically incarcerated," Chen Qi, *Kaifang* (Open) magazine, November 2002; reprinted in *Da Ji Yuan* (Epoch Times), November 7, 2002. All of the details in Chen's account were later confirmed in a personal statement issued by Zhang Gonglai herself on May 25, 2002; see "Detained in Psychiatric Institution for Petitioning Authorities About Abuse," Zhang Gonglai, *Ren Yu Renquan* (Chinese-language website affiliated with Human Rights in China), January 2003, available at www.hrichina.org.

– ostensibly as her "legal guardians" – and handed over the money to cover her hospitalisation fees.

According to her own subsequently published account, Zhang, whom the headmasters had told staff was suffering from "paranoia," was kept in a filthy and crowded mixed-sex ward at the hospital alongside severely disturbed patients, who regularly hit her and tried to pull out her hair. She was given regular forced injections of unknown medications from the outset of her incarceration at the hospital, and was punished by such methods as being tied to her bed for long periods and given electric shock treatment if she so much as dared to question or complain about any aspect of her treatment and experiences there. During her first two months at the hospital, she was not even allowed to go outside for the daily fresh air and exercise period enjoyed by most of the other patients. Her family members, who had not been informed of her whereabouts for over a week after her forced admission to the mental hospital, were appalled to find, when they finally saw her there, that she was covered in bruises and had fleas all over her body.

Thereafter the family appealed frequently for help to the local Women's Federation office on her behalf, but an official there told them: "If she's willing to sign a statement guaranteeing that she'll never again try to petition the authorities about her case, then she can be released!" Moreover, the Women's Federation repeatedly pressured the family to sign a statement acknowledging that Zhang was mentally ill, and granting it the role of serving as her "legal guardian." The family refused these demands, and Zhang continued to be held at the hospital for the next four years. In late 2000, moreover, in an apparent attempt to intimidate her into accepting the diagnosis of mental illness and agreeing to refrain from any more petitioning activities in future, the hospital authorities moved all the other woman patients out of her ward, leaving her there alone with the male mental patients for several days.

She was finally discharged from the hospital by its director, Zhang Congpei, in extremely poor health after her protracted ordeal, in either June or July of 2002. Soon thereafter, she travelled to Beijing in order to seek redress and compensation from the central government for the abuse and ill-treatment she had suffered over the preceding four years. However, on August 20, she was arrested for allegedly assaulting a woman who shared her room at the Yun Lai Hostel in Beijing's West District. A report on the incident later issued by Human Rights in China (HRIC) described what had occurred as follows:

> According to a source familiar with the situation, Zhang did have a dispute with the woman in question, but merely kicked her in self-defence while the other woman was assaulting her, and the woman suffered no lasting harm. This source claims that Zhang was arrested after Beijing and Heilongjiang officials conferred over how to put an end to Zhang's endless petitioning.

Moreover, continued the statement,

> According to HRIC's sources, Zhang Gonglai's situation is by no means unique. Reliable information indicates that over the past few months more than 30 petitioners have been committed to the Harbin Psychiatric Hospital against their will. Information regarding these incarcerations is found in court records, Public Security Bureau records, Sanitation Bureau records, and other official documents. In addition, if petitioners want to escape the deplorable conditions of the Harbin Psychiatric Hospital they have to agree to desist in their petitioning, refrain from all contact with the news media, and never speak to others about conditions at the

psychiatric hospital. Anyone who breaks any of these conditions after release risks being arrested and readmitted for "psychiatric relapse."[448]

Zhang Gonglai's court hearing was scheduled for January 9, 2003, but there were no subsequent reports as to the final outcome of her case.

The Case of Huang Shurong

Our final case in this chapter concerns a second female petitioner who was arbitrarily detained in the same mental hospital in northeast China, and again on the instructions of the same officials whom she was complaining about, on five separate occasions between 1998 and 2002. The case of Huang Shurong, a 42-year-old woman from Suileng County, Heilongjiang Province, who encountered this treatment after becoming embroiled in a land dispute with her local government in 1998, led Elisabeth Rosenthal (the Western journalist who first brought Huang's case to public attention) to speculate that the detention of persistent petitioners and complainants in mental hospitals in China is nowadays "far more common" than that of political dissidents.[449] Rosenthal's long investigative report on the case appeared on the front page of the New York Times in February 2002, and it finally prompted, several months later, the first major public debate within China itself on the problem of the political misuse of psychiatry by local officials as a means of silencing their critics.

Ms. Huang's problems began in 1998, when local officials in her home village of Baoshan carried out a redistribution of local land that allocated some of the best plots to themselves and which, in the process, stripped Huang's family of a portion of her best piece of cornfield. Five villagers, including Huang, lodged formal complaints with the Suileng County petitions and appeals office, accusing the local officials of engaging in corrupt activities, but to no avail. Eventually, Huang took her case to the relevant authorities in both Harbin, the provincial capital, and also to Beijing, lodging complaints with the State Council and the Agriculture Ministry; the former instructed the Heilongjiang government to "appropriately deal with" her complaints. According to Rosenthal,

> That was when the real trouble began. In early June 1998, while she was walking home from yet another visit to the county appeals office, an unmarked car carrying police officers and officials pulled up beside her, she said. Without explanation, they bundled her into the car, bound her hands and sped off, leaving her two young children alone at the roadside.
>
> Amid tears, screams and protests, she was driven four hours to a psychiatric hospital – the Harbin Specialist No. 1 Hospital – where she said she was admitted, without examination, to a locked ward. Her children were not informed where their mother had been taken.

On this first occasion, she was released after 47 days. Since then, however,

> Ms. Huang, who is 42 and divorced, has spent a total of 210 days under lock and key, at times subjected to powerful drugs and electroshock therapy, although friends and

---

448 "Harbin Woman Allegedly Persecuted for Exercising Her Right to Petition," Human Rights in China (press release), January 7, 2003. For additional information on Zhang's case, see "Large Numbers of Healthy People Are Incarcerated at the Heilongjiang Mental Hospital," Chen Qi, *Da Ji Yuan*, November 26, 2003.
449 "In Rural China, Mental Hospitals Await Some Who Rock the Boat," Elisabeth Rosenthal, *New York Times*, February 15, 2002.

family, experts in Beijing and even some of the psychiatrists who have hospitalised her say she is perfectly sane…

To bolster her land case and clear her name, she travelled to Beijing for an extensive psychiatric evaluation at the prestigious Beijing Medical Sciences University. In their December 1998 report, psychiatrists described her as "clear-minded" and "talking to the point," with "good self-awareness and no signs of mental illness." But that paper has not helped her plight. The last three years of Ms. Huang's life have been a vicious cycle of continued protests, forced hospitalisations at the behest of county officials and subsequent release by doctors…

The last time she was hospitalised, at a large psychiatric hospital in Harbin, the local officials who dropped her off told the psychiatrists on duty that she was a madwoman who screamed and cursed at officials. The officials paid up front for six months of treatment – about 10,000 yuan, or about [US] $1,200 – and said she had been categorized as paranoid before…

Fearing that she would be recommitted if she remained in her hometown, she recently fled with her two teenage children to Beijing, where she survives by selling discarded trash…

"The police wouldn't take me in, since I'd done nothing illegal, so they sent me to a psychiatric ward where they had some connections to shut me up and humiliate me," she said over tea at a restaurant in Beijing.…[450]

Around the same time as the above report was published in the New York Times, Huang Shurong's story was taken up by several investigative journalists from China's most bold and outspoken newspaper, the Guangzhou-based *Nanfang Zhoumo* (Southern Weekend.) Four months later, in June 2002, the magazine published a several thousand-word exposé of the case, presenting a whole series of new and still more disturbing details about Huang's lengthy experience of psychiatric persecution at the hands of the Suileng County officials. The *Nanfang Zhoumo* piece was swiftly reported on and discussed in numerous other mainland Chinese newspapers, journals and radio and television stations, and within days the case had become a national *cause celebre*.

At the outset, the magazine's reporters established unequivocally, through interviews with higher-level officials who had subsequently investigated them, that Huang's original allegations of corruption against the Suileng officials were true and accurate; as a result of those investigations into the misallocation of land and related matters, the Baoshan Party Secretary, the village chief, the village accountant and the village cashier had all been sacked from their posts. Nonetheless, the confiscated land was still not returned to Huang and the other complainants, and a core group of hostile county officials – notably a woman named Wu Yufang, head of the Suileng Visits and Complaints Office, and others from the same department – had continued to harass her. As described above, after she had taken her complaints against them all the way to Beijing, these same officials arranged for her to be abducted and taken to the Harbin Specialist No. 1 Hospital for forensic psychiatric examination. (Among the more unsavoury details of the case that emerged in the *Nanfang Zhoumo* report were that when Ms. Huang had begged to be released so that she could look after her children, "It was useless: each time I asked, they tied me to the bed for up to 18 hours, and I even had to urinate on the bed.") Huang's family had not been informed as to where she was being held, and the hospital staff refused to let her telephone

---

450   Ibid.

or write to them; eventually a kindly nurse agreed to secretly post off a letter from her telling them of her whereabouts. Only after the family agreed to pay a sum of 800 yuan to the hospital for "medical expenses," and also a further 600 yuan to the Suileng officials and the hospital doctors, was Huang finally permitted to leave the hospital on this first occasion.

The ostensible purpose of the psychiatric examination carried out at the Harbin mental hospital was to establish Huang's mental capacity or otherwise for civil action and responsibility, and it should therefore have been conducted in accordance with Articles 170-173 of the Civil Procedure Law of the PRC, promulgated in April 1991 and which stipulates that any findings of lack or reduction of civil capacity by reason of insanity must be made by a court of law.[451] According to *Nanfang Zhoumo*'s investigations, due process had been flouted and ignored, and instead, after a mere two-hour-long "forensic examination," Huang had been declared by three psychiatrists from the hospital to have lost all capacity for civil action – including (as the psychiatrists were at pains to specify in their report) the right and ability to continue pursuing her complaint against the county officials – because she was said to be suffering from an unspecified though allegedly severe "paranoid condition."[452]

In an attempt to unearth the facts and obtain additional medical opinions, the Chinese journalists then proceeded to interview two of the three psychiatrists concerned – Zhang Congpei, Party secretary and deputy director of the hospital, and the same person, it turned out, who had been responsible for Zhang Gonglai's "medical care" also (see previous case study) and Teng Xiuying, head of the medical department – together with most of the Suileng County officials involved in the case. The journalists also interviewed several top forensic psychiatric specialists from other hospitals in Heilongjiang.

What they discovered from these various interviews was both alarming and shocking. First, they asked Drs. Zhang and Teng why Ms. Huang's forensic appraisals record contained no witness statements from members of her family or her neighbours concerning her mental condition and general state of health prior to her initial detention, when the record nonetheless stated that such testimony had not only been provided at the forensic examination session, but also that it had included such statements as that Huang was "mentally unwell" and that she was known locally by the nickname "Huang the Madwoman" (*Huang Fengzi*.) Zhang and Teng replied that in fact no villagers had either been present at, or supplied testimony to, the forensic appraisal examination session, and that all the information about Huang's alleged history of mental illness had been provided by the Suileng County officials who had brought her to the hospital.

In addition, the two doctors' evaluation report stated that they had read through a case file (*juan zong*) consisting of several volumes of documents on Huang before conducting their appraisal, that this case file had been supplied by the same county officials, and that the information contained in it this had allowed them to form a complete clinical picture of her mental health condition prior to the examination. Zhang and Teng were unable to produce the case file, however, and asserted that it was

---

451 For details of the relevant CPL provisions, see Note 387 above.
452 When interviewed by the *Nanfang Zhoumo* journalists later, Dr. Zhang Congpei stated: "In the course of her petitioning and complaining, [Huang Shurong's] thought processes became afflicted by relational delusions, and a series of fixed ideas formed in her mind, such as that certain people were trying to get at her and persecute her; her willpower became pathologically reinforced, to an ever increasing degree, and she then began petitioning and complaining incessantly. This caused harm to her capacity for recognition and self-control (*bianren ji zi-kong nengli*), so that in the course of her petitioning and complaint activities she lacked any real or effective capacity in these two respects. She was neurotic and psychologically disturbed to the point of being mentally ill, in the broad sense. The type of illness she had is usually both lifelong and incurable."

stored at the Suileng Visits and Complaints Office. But when the journalists later asked Wu Yufang, the head of that office, about the case file, she flatly denied that it had ever existed. Furthermore, it transpired that the local government office which Drs. Zhang's and Teng's forensic appraisal record explicitly stated had "referred" Ms. Huang for psychiatric examination at the Harbin hospital – namely, the "Sihai Dian Township Visits and Complaints Office of Suileng County, Heilongjiang Province" – also did not exist. (The two officials who had claimed to represent this non-existent office and who had actually signed the referral papers on its behalf were Wu Yufang herself, and one He Qingxiang, the Party Secretary of Ms. Huang's home village.) The conclusion reached independently by three nationally renowned forensic psychiatrists whom the journalists consulted on the whole affair was that, from both the medical and the legal points of view, the forensic appraisal of Ms Huang conducted at the Harbin mental hospital had been invalid and unlawful from start to finish.

What most outraged press and public opinion throughout China, however, was the unusually frank response that Dr. Teng Xiuying gave to *Nanfang Zhoumo* on the question of why he and his colleagues had rendered "this forensic psychiatric appraisal that had no legal or medical-procedural basis." Said Teng, "To be honest, we were simply taking care of an awkward problem for the government – solving a headache for them. That's really what it was all about. The county authorities went to the provincial visits and complaints department, and they in turn came to us for help." Equally revealing of the Suileng County officials' real motive in sending Huang Shurong to the Harbin mental asylum was the comment one of them made to her immediately after her initial release from the hospital: "So now they say you're not mentally ill, right? Fine, we'll send you off for re-education through labour (*laodong jiaoyang*) or have you criminally sentenced (*pan xing*) instead. We've already prepared all the documents!"[453] Finally, the intrepid reporters interviewed Wu Yufang herself, the principal villain of the piece, and asked her: would it not have been quite unlawful for them to send Huang to jail in this way? With no apparent sense of irony or embarrassment, Wu proceeded to shed the following crocodile tears over the whole incident:

> Aiya! You talk about law. Some laws in China are capable of being implemented, but others are not, in fact most of them are like this. To tell the truth, the laws really exist only on paper, and that's why we can't carry them out. For now, we're still living under "rule by man" (*ren zhi*), and in most parts of China [the rule of] law still doesn't amount to very much. I've learned this from bitter experience.[454]

As the reporters left Wu's office, they noticed that two award plaques were hanging on the wall. The certificates read: "Advanced Collective Unit – Heilongjiang Provincial Visits and Complaints Department" and "Superior Collective Unit – All-China Visits and Complaints Department." Eventually, after her fifth forced hospitalisation, at the Heilongjiang Provincial No. 3 Hospital, Huang Shurong was examined by a group of no fewer than twenty psychiatrists, and after fifty days of intensive clinical observation, was pronounced to be entirely sane. In fact, the psychiatrists concluded, "She showed no signs whatever of having even the most minor form of mental illness."

---

453 Wu Yufang later confirmed this point to the *Nanfang Zhoumo* reporters. According to Wu, "We planned to have her psychiatrically evaluated after her return from Beijing. If she turned out to be mentally ill, we would have her medically treated, and if she wasn't mentally ill then we would put her into administrative detention."
454 "*Zhong-Gong guo mei chu shuo-li: Shangfang funü jing bei xin-fang xitong youxiu jiti guanjin jingshenbing*" ("Nowhere in the Chinese Communist Party's nation to seek redress: A female petitioner is locked up in a mental hospital by a "superior collective unit" of the Visits and Complaints network"), *Nanfang Zhoumo* (Southern Weekend), June 6, 2002.

As mentioned, the press response from around China to the *Nanfang Zhoumo* report was intense. *China Youth Daily*, for example, suggested that Huang Shurong's case represented the tip of an iceberg:

> In recent years, there have been frequent reports in the press exposing cases of the false or unlawful diagnosis of mental illness. Moreover, many of those diagnosed in this way have been petitioners or complainants (*shangfangzhe*) who have taken their cases to higher levels of authority, thereby angering government officials from their own localities; the government officials then brand these people as being "elements harmful to stability" and eventually contrive, by fair means or foul, to have them labelled as "mentally ill."[455]

The same point was made two days later by no less an authority than *China Procuracy Daily*, the organ of the country's chief prosecution agency. According to the newspaper,

> In recent years, the numbers of petitioners and complainants who have been sent either to detention centres or to mental hospitals is such that they can no longer be regarded as merely isolated cases. What we see, in fact, is that it has now become "common knowledge" within the departments concerned that they can "deal with" petitioners and complainants in this way, and that certain relief agencies [i.e. detention centres and mental hospitals] are willing to "closely collaborate" with them in so doing.... In the case of Huang Shurong, the local visits and complaints office even paid the mental hospital to take her in, and furthermore insisted repeatedly that it should "not let her escape."[456]

Other journalists in China, however, pressed the critique substantially further, by openly calling for punishment to be meted out not only to the corrupt officials who perpetrated these injustices, but also to the psychiatrists and other medical staff who collaborated in them. For example, *SinoLaw*, a website linked to the *Procuracy Daily*, carried a scathing article on June 11 entitled "What a Way to 'Solve Headaches for the Government'." According to the article,

> One form of retaliation against petitioners and complainants that has become common (*liuxing*) in certain parts of the country these days is to forcibly incarcerate them in mental asylums, in order to completely break their spirit.... People usually direct their feelings of anger about this phoney use of medical treatment as a means of psychological persecution towards the government officials who resort to this form of retaliation against petitioners and complainants, while overlooking the sinister and evil collaborative role that the mental health professionals themselves perform in this process. When [mentally] normal citizens end up being put in mental asylums thanks to the "great contribution" performed by the medical staff, however, it is precisely the latter's various "appraisals" and "rulings" which have allowed these punitive and persecutory acts against citizens to be passed off in the name of "science" and "legality." The medical staff are an essential link in the chain of evil that produces

---

455 "J*ingshenbing jianding youguan wenti*" ("Problems in the appraisal of mental illness"), Chen Jieren, *Zhongguo Qingnian Bao*, June 17, 2002.
456 "*Jiuzhu jigou, jiu zheyang chengquan le renzhi*" ("Here's how the relief agencies prop up rule by man"), Jian Lushi, *Jiancha Ribao*, June 19, 2002.

these abuses, and this should not be forgotten about when apportioning blame and punishment.

The article then took direct aim at the lame excuse for Huang Shurong's persecution which had been offered up by Dr. Teng:

> What [the psychiatrists] were actually doing was "solving a headache" not for the government, but for corrupt and specific individual officials...and what was knowingly sacrificed in the process was a citizen's lawful rights and interests, along with her personal dignity. Their ultimate motive in doing all this was to ingratiate themselves with the officials concerned and thereby reap personal profit and advantage from the situation.[457]

Perhaps the most serious outcome of Teng's "perverted notion" of "solving headaches for the government," concluded the article, was that it had served to "demolish the image and prestige of science and medical ethics" in the eyes of the entire local populace.

The extensive domestic and international news reporting on Huang Shurong's case in 2002 and the intense public concern which the case evoked around the country served finally to bring the whole issue of arbitrary and politically motivated psychiatric detention out of the shadows and into the public arena in China. One more bastion of secrecy still remained: the country's police-run network of institutes for the criminally insane. In Chapter 8, we will examine the Ankang system in detail and see how it, too, from the second half of 2003 onwards, began finally to be opened up to outside scrutiny and criticism. But first, we must pause to consider what has undoubtedly been the darkest page in the Chinese government's human rights record since the June 4, 1989 massacre by the PLA of hundreds of unarmed pro-democracy demonstrators in Beijing: the nationwide crackdown against the Falun Gong spiritual movement.

---

457 "*Ruci zheban 'wei zhengfu paiyou jienan'*," SinoLaw (*Zhongguo Fazhi Wang*: available at www.sinolaw.net.cn), June 11, 2002.

CHAPTER 7

The Falun Gong: Chinese Dissent Goes Cosmic

In April 1999, a hitherto obscure though numerically large spiritual community in China calling itself the *Falun Dafa* (Great Wheel of Buddha's Law) or *Falun Gong* (Cultivation of the Wheel of the Law)[458] staged an unannounced peaceful protest demonstration outside Zhongnanhai, the main Communist Party leadership compound in central Beijing. According to reports, more than 10,000 practitioners from the group, whose devotional activities centre on the practice of a traditional form of Chinese physical and mental exercises known as *qigong*, took part in the silent, day-long vigil.[459] The source of their dissatisfaction was an escalating campaign of official criticism of the Falun Gong movement, and of its leader, a middle-aged former government official named Li Hongzhi. The public demonstration was the largest held in China since the Tiananmen protests of May 1989, and it apparently caught the government's security services completely by surprise. A flurry of official condemnations quickly followed, but no overt action was taken against the Falun Gong until July 19-20, when dozens of the group's leading organizers and practitioners were suddenly arrested by police in the middle of the night. Two days later, and thus retroactively, as far as those already detained were concerned, the government announced that the Falun Gong was a proscribed organization and that it was to immediately cease all activities throughout the country.[460]

Over the subsequent few years, tens of thousands of practitioners nationwide were detained, arrested and sent to detention centres or labour re-education camps for periods of several months or years; in a minority of cases, they were criminally charged and sentenced to terms of up to 18 years' imprisonment.[461] During the first two years or so of the anti-Falun Gong campaign, practitioners

---

458 "*Falun*" is the Chinese rendering of the Sanskrit word "*dharma*" (Buddhist law).
459 The practice of qigong has undergone a massive popular revival in China since the early 1980s. A detailed account of this phenomenon can be found in Zhu Xiaoyang and Benjamin Penny (eds.), "The Qigong Boom," *Chinese Sociology and Anthropology*, Vol.27, No.1 (Fall 1994). On September 15, 2000, as part of the government's continuing crackdown on Falun Gong practitioners, the State Sports General Bureau issued new rules tightening up controls over the practice of qigong throughout China. See *Jianshen Qigong Guanli Zanxing Banfa* (*Temporary Methods for Administering Bodybuilding and Qigong*), available at http://www.sport.gov.cn/qigong.htm.
460 Proclamation of the Ministry of Public Security of the People's Republic of China, July 22, 1999. Using unusually strong language, the Ministry called for the Falun Gong to be "outlawed and extirpated" (*yuyi qudi*) throughout China. In a comprehensive denial of the civil rights of all Falun Gong practitioners, moreover, the proclamation stated: "It is forbidden to undertake assemblies, marches or demonstrations in defence or propagation of the Falun Dafa (Falun Gong), whether by means of sit-ins, petitioning the authorities, or any other such activities."
461 As the trials of Falun Gong leaders unfolded, the sect's main overseas support network issued the following translation of a directive that it claimed had recently been issued by the Beijing Bureau of Justice, imposing restrictions on detained sectarians' right of independent access to legal defence:

> To All Law Firms and District and County Judicial Departments: All consultations and retainers in respect of Falun Gong issues must be reported immediately. Particular requirements are: 1) In no circumstances may a lawyer accept a retainer involving any client involved in Falun Gong issues. Such cases should be reported to the Regulation Section (telephone: 6340-8078) and will be decided upon only after being reported. 2) In any event where consultations are requested by a client involved in Falun Gong issues, any advice or explanations proffered by attorneys offices must conform to the law and be strictly in conformity with the tone of the Central Government. 3) All recent consultations and retainers on Falun Gong issues must be documented and faxed

continued, on an almost daily basis, to travel to Beijing and other major cities to stage peaceful protests and sit-ins in public areas; they were invariably arrested within minutes and carted off to police holding centres to await their punishment.[462] As of August 2004, according to detailed reports issued by overseas-based Falun Gong rights monitoring groups, no fewer than 1,024 detained practitioners had died as a result of torture or other severe ill treatment at the hands of the authorities.[463] Although the continuing repression against the Falun Gong movement in China still, five years after it had begun, made it impossible for international human rights groups to independently verify most of these shocking reports, investigative reports by foreign journalists based in China confirmed the truth of the allegations in numerous individual cases and established a clear pattern of police resort to violence and brutality against Falun Gong practitioners in detention facilities around the country.[464]

I. The Reappearance of the "Ideological Defect" Theory

The most distinctive aspect of the government's protracted campaign to crush the Falun Gong, aside from its sheer scope and intensity, was the flood of reports that began to appear in the second half of 1999 indicating that large numbers of detained practitioners were being forcibly sent to mental hospitals by the security authorities.[465] Given the officially-reported steep decline in the incidence of "political cases" in Chinese forensic psychiatry since the late 1980s, this sudden development was both unexpected and highly disturbing. By October 2003, overseas Falun Gong support groups had documented approximately 1,000 such cases in which the victims' names, places of psychiatric detention and other such key details were known, and some fifteen detained practitioners were reported to have died as a direct result of their physical ill treatment in mental hospitals.[466] Again, these various

---

immediately to the Regulation Section on or before August 2, 1999. (fax: 6340-8034) ("An Announcement in Regards to Falun Gong Issues from the Regulation Section, Judicial Bureau of Beijing City," available at http://www.clearwisdom.net/eng/china/judicial_announcement.html.).

462 For detailed accounts of the human rights violations involved in the government's anti-Falun Gong campaign, see Amnesty International, *People's Republic of China: The Crackdown on Falun Gong and Other So-called "Heretical Organizations,"* March 23, 2000 (ASA 17/011/2000); and *Dangerous Meditation: China's Campaign Against Falungong*, Human Rights Watch, January 2002. See also: Danny Schechter, "Is Falun Gong Going Crazy?" Index on Censorship, 2001, No.4.

463 See, for example, European Falun Gong Information Centre, "48 Falun Gong Deaths Reported in June and July" (press statement), 20 August 2004; available at: www.clearharmony.net.

464 See in particular Ian Johnson's Pulitzer Prize-winning trilogy of articles: "Death Trap: How One Chinese City Resorted to Atrocities to Control Falun Dafa," *Wall Street Journal*, 25 December 2000, p.1; "Falun Dafa Fight Stifles Others, Too: Beijing's Blitz Squelches Unorthodox Views," *Wall Street Journal*, 6 February 2001; and "Burden of Belief: As Crackdown Grows, Falun Gong's Faithful Face a New Pressure," *Wall Street Journal*, 28 March 2001. See also: Philip P. Pan, "Torture is Breaking Falun Gong: China Systematically Eradicating Group," The Washington Post, 5 August 2001, p.A01.

465 See, e.g., Elisabeth Rosenthal, "China is Said to Hold Devotees of Sect in a Psychiatric Hospital," *New York Times*, January 21, 2000. The Soviet authorities also used to send religious dissenters and nonconformists to psychiatric hospitals. See Bloch and Reddaway, *Russia's Political Hospitals* (op cit), pp.269-70. In recent years, religious sectarian movements in Russia have once again come under direct legal and medical attack from government authorities. See, e.g., "Duma Appeal on Dangerous Religious Sects," *Moscow Rossiyskaya Gazeta*, December 28, 1996; translated in FBIS, same date; and Lev Levenson, "Psychiatrists and Officers in Defense of Traditional Values," *Ekspress Khronika*, January 31, 1997.

466 See documents cited at Note 23 above. See also: Dr. Shiyu Zhou et al. (eds.), *A Report on Extensive and Severe Human Rights Violations in the Suppression of Falun Gong in the People's Republic of China — August*

reports have not yet been independently confirmed by international human rights groups or similar organizations, and instances of factual error or misreporting may eventually come to light; however, there has as yet been no reason or evidence for doubting their overall veracity.[467] Numerous Western journalists who witnessed police raids on Falun Gong demonstrators, in Beijing and elsewhere, reported seeing detainees being severely beaten up in broad daylight, so there are scant grounds if any for believing that such people have been accorded any more polite or humane treatment after their removal from the public arena. In one particularly graphic and clear-cut account, published in the Washington Post in August 2002, a Chinese-American journalist recorded how a PSB officer whom he had personally interviewed had been sent to a mental hospital for continuing to practise Falun Gong, had later escaped from the asylum, been rearrested and sent back inside again, and had then died in custody shortly thereafter. The journalist interviewed the police officer during his brief period of escape from the mental hospital, and he obtained direct confirmation of the man's death from the hospital authorities concerned.[468]

The accounts of the abusive treatment meted out to psychiatrically detained Falun Gong practitioners in several dozen mental hospitals around the country after July 1999 make frequent and consistent reference to the following kinds of practices: the detainees were drugged with various unknown kinds of medication, tied with ropes to hospital beds or put under other forms of physical restraint, kept in dark

---

2000 Update (Chapter 3: Detention and Abuse in Mental Hospitals), Golden Lotus Press, August 2000, pp.65-82. The information in this report was compiled by activists and researchers associated with the Falun Gong overseas support network. (The full text of the report can be found at http://hrreport.fldf.net.) According to the same source, the circumstances of three of the earliest Falun Gong practitioners' deaths after the crackdown began were as follows:

1) In December 1999, Yang Weidong, 54, a medical inspector in Weifang city, Shandong, was forcibly committed to the city's Kangfu mental hospital. Already in poor health after several weeks spent in police custody as punishment for having gone to Beijing to petition against the anti-Falun Gong crackdown, Yang developed oedema of the liver while at the mental hospital. According to the account, "Even the doctor in Kangfu Hospital was frightened upon seeing his condition. He told the guard who watched Yang Weidong: 'He is in a state of physical collapse, how come you do not send him home? His illness is already incurable.'" Yang reportedly died on December 25, several days after being released from the hospital.

2) In May 2000, a woman named Shi Bei reportedly died after being forcibly held and given psychotropic medication at the Hangzhou No. 7 Hospital, Zhejiang (see p.229 below for further details of Shi's case).

3) In June 2000, a 32-year-old man named Su Gang, a graduate in computer science and employee at a chemicals plant in Zibo city, Shandong, died after nine days of forcible hospitalization and medication at the Changle Mental Hospital. He had earlier been held in police detention for around 130 days for his Falun Gong activities. According to the account, "At 6 p.m. on May 31, the security staff of Su Gang's workplace sent him back to his father, Su De'an. After nine days of brutal 'treatment,' which included daily over-dose injections with damaging effects on the central nervous system, Su Gang looked miserable…he was very slow in reacting and his limbs appeared stiff…He was not able to recover from the severe mental and physical damage he had suffered in the mental hospital. After a period of painful struggle, he left this world on the morning of June 10, 2000." Su's death in psychiatric custody was also reported in "Bad Medicine in China" (editorial), *The Washington Post*, June 23, 2000.

467   The ethical teachings of Falun Gong reportedly make its practitioners so frank and honest that, when stopped by police while travelling on trains during the first year or so after the crackdown began and asked if they were going to Beijing to petition or demonstrate on behalf of the banned sect, they invariably felt obliged to give a truthful reply, thereby leading to their immediate forcible eviction from the trains, and often much worse outcomes.

468   Philip P. Pan, "The Silent Treatment from Beijing: Mental Hospitals Allegedly Used to Quiet Dissidents, Falun Gong," *The Washington Post*, 26 August 2002, p.A01.

hospital rooms for long periods, subjected to electro-convulsive therapy or painful forms of electrical acupuncture treatment, and denied adequate food and water and allowed only restricted access to toilet facilities. After several weeks or months of such treatment, they would typically be pressured by the medical staff into writing and signing confessional statements renouncing their belief in Falun Gong, as a precondition for their eventual release; in many cases, they were reportedly then required to pay fines or unreceipted charges of several thousand *yuan* for their board and treatment at the hospitals. Among the numerous confirmed victims of these various practices have been university professors, medical workers, government functionaries, members of the police and armed forces (including several senior officers), farmers, students, housewives, and a judge.[469]

Hundreds of individual case accounts of this type have been published by the Falun Gong support network since July 1999 and many of them are highly graphic in nature and make distressing reading. The following account will suffice to convey a clear and vivid picture of the conditions and practices obtaining at mental hospitals across China where Falun Gong practitioners have been "treated" against their will over the past five years.[470]

> My name is Ms. Zhou Caixia and I was the former Party Branch Secretary and Director of Jiaozhou City's Rubber Factory. My work performance and popularity were well known among my co-workers. I learned Falun Dafa in the spring of 1996.
>
> The Chinese constitution gives every citizen the basic right of appeal. Since the beginning of the persecution of Falun Dafa, I had gone to Beijing to appeal. I was escorted back by personnel from the Jiaozhou City Police Department and detained for seven days and nights. The authorities deprived me of sleep during the entire time so they could force me to say words to renounce Falun Dafa on TV. They mentally tortured me in an agonizing way. In October of the same year (1999) as I was reading Dafa books with a group, Zhongyun Police abducted me and handcuffed me for four days and nights. Then, I was transferred to a place they called the "House of Refuge," a place Jiaozhou City authorities were using to detain Dafa practitioners from the beginning of the persecution. They used a few old and deteriorated rooms in a wing of the Nantan Village Committee. In a room smaller than 120 sq ft., 17 Dafa practitioners were being detained. We all ate and slept under extremely crowded

---

[469] According to an Associated Press report on February 11, 2000, "A judge in southern China has been put in a psychiatric hospital and forced to take narcotics for refusing to renounce his belief in the banned Falun Gong spiritual movement, a rights group said today. The case of Huang Jinchun is the latest troubling sign that the communist government is using mental institutions to punish political or religious dissenters. Huang displayed no symptoms of mental illness either at work or after being sent to the hospital nearly three months ago, the Hong Kong-based Information Centre of Human Rights and Democratic Movement in China reported, citing former colleagues and nurses. But at the Longqianshan Psychiatric Hospital in the southern Guangxi region, medical personnel gave Huang daily injections of a narcotic that left him sleepy and muddled, after he refused to stop practicing Falun Gong, the nurses said. 'The doctors and nurses made fun of me: "Aren't you practicing Falun Gong? Let us see which is stronger, Falun Gong or our medicines?" Huang related in an appeal posted earlier this week on an overseas Falun Gong website.'"

[470] "Letter from the Former City Rubber Factory Director in Jiaozhou City, After Being Involuntarily Admitted to a Mental Hospital and Tortured for Practicing Falun Gong," 29 June 2004; this first-hand account, which is presented above in unedited form, was included in a recent statement issued by China Mental Health Watch. (See: "'Misdiagnosis and Lack of Training' are Deliberate Cover-Up for Severe Violations of WPA Madrid Declaration," August 2004, China Mental Health Watch; available at: www.chinapsychiatricwatch.org.)

conditions. Each one had to pay a daily "fee" of 50 Yuan for living expenses. The food consisted of one small steamed bun and one small pickle. Drinking water was not always provided. By December 27, 1999, no one was released, until the authorities collected a so called "fine" from each one of 5,000 Yuan.

Newspapers and television fabricated even more wild and terrible lies and viciously defamed and attacked Dafa. The unreasonable persecution against Dafa had escalated, but even so, they inspired our determination to appeal and clarify the truth about the persecution to the public. In May 2000, I went to Beijing again to ask for justice for Dafa, resulting in even more savage persecution. Zhongyun Police officers detained me four days and nights and deprived me of sleep. Because I would not renounce my belief in Falun Dafa or give up my cultivation practice, Wang Zhongxiao from the office directed Luo Qingchun to take me against my will to the Jiaozhou City Mental Hospital to be subjected to further torture.

Normally, a hospital is a place of healing, and the doctors are supposed to be humanitarians that redeem and rescue others. This hospital, however, was a living hell used by Zhang Yuanfu (former Jiaozhou City Committee Secretary), Liu Zuojing (former political and judiciary committee secretary) and others to persecute Falun Dafa practitioners. The people at this hospital indiscriminately commit crimes and torture good people. A nurse, without moral constraint screamed, "Give me money! I will even kill people if you tell me to." How could this kind of person deserve to be on the hospital staff! Using medication on a healthy person in an arbitrary manner will poison that person's body or will lead to paralysis or even loss of life, particularly if strong medications for treating mental illnesses are given in abnormally high doses to practitioners who are not mentally ill.

The injections designed for use on mental patients are usually administered only once a month, but the Dafa practitioners were injected with them daily, and some were even continuously injected seven times a day which had the effect of severely destroying the practitioner's central nervous system and gave them a strange and frightening appearance from the side effects which caused them to lose control of their basic functions such as speaking, and motor coordination.

Jiang Dengfa, head of the facility, and Dr. Yang Chengchao in particular were responsible for many incidents of abusing Dafa practitioners. Several people held Dafa practitioners down and forcedly injected them with drugs. I refused to cooperate with this kind of medical mistreatment and pulled their needles out. Since they used very large-diameter needles for Dafa practitioners, blood spurted from the hole where the needle had been pulled out, spraying onto the ceiling. Administrator Jiang Dengfa used this to terrify and intimidate other Dafa practitioners saying, "Did you see this? The blood on the ceiling came from Zhou Caixia; no one can escape!"

Yang Chengchao beat Dafa practitioner Wang Weihe to the ground then kicked him with his leather boots, dragged him out of the room by his leg into the hallway and dragged him back into the room. He then tied Wang Weihe to a metal bed with his arms and legs stretched out tightly for eleven hours. The medical staff administered drug injections to him throughout the day and night for a total of seven times. This kind of drug makes the person lose consciousness very quickly. Their internal organs are in extreme and unbearable pain. The medical staff has tortured Dafa practitioners with these drug injections causing practitioners eyes to stare, unblinking. Practitioners' bodies became completely rigid after receiving these injections and they could not move their necks because it became stiff. Their bodies remained frozen tight in hunched over positions with bent legs. The drugs caused them to be paralyzed in these positions and at night their eyes stayed wide open during sleep and their fingers were stiff and could not be bent.

Wang Weihe was tortured so severely that he didn't dare to open his mouth for a long period of time; once he opened his mouth, the saliva would run uncontrollably down to the floor. He could not lift his arms, and could not even pick up a rice bowl. Later, Wang was transferred to the Zhang Jiatun Brainwashing Class. The political and judiciary committee deputy secretary Liu Xuedong threatened him, saying, "If you don't obey, we will send you to the mental hospital again." These vicious authorities use the mental hospital as a place for torturing and terrorizing Dafa practitioners until they agree to renounce their belief.

Jiang Dengfa, head of the mental hospital, often beat Dafa practitioners. When Chief Judge Xiao Zhirui from Jiaozhou City's Court practiced the exercises with practitioners, Jiang Dengfa suddenly kicked his back and slapped him violently. When I started to protest this kind of barbaric abuse with a hunger strike, the vicious staff maliciously force-fed me. Chief nurse Guo Xiumei and five other people started to insert tubes down my throat. When they pried my mouth open, they smashed down four front teeth (I can't eat easily, even now), both my mouth and nose bled very badly, soaking a big roll of toilet paper. Nearly 40 Dafa practitioners were tortured there by those people.

Zhang Yuanfu, Liu Zuojin and a gang of other people changed the hospital – they made it from a place of healing into a place to fiendishly torture Dafa practitioners. Using this mental hospital to torture Dafa practitioners by following Jiang's persecution policies against Falun Dafa was the first such example in the nation, and the staff was awarded distinction by the Jiang's regime. This became one of the big "political credits" which gave Zhang Yuanfu his start in Jiaozhou City.

I was tortured in the mental hospital for almost five months. I strongly felt that we were innocent, and we should not be persecuted! This was not where Dafa practitioners should remain. I ran away from that evil place. The hospital staff searched for me everywhere and attempted to arrest me. The methods they used were vicious.

Among the Falun Gong practitioners reported to have died as a result of their ordeals in Chinese mental hospitals was a woman named Shi Bei. Under pressure from the police, hospital staff reportedly gave her forced injections of high dosage sedatives and denied her food for one week in order to prevent her from propagating her spiritual beliefs inside the hospital; her precise cause of death remains unknown.[471] The hospital in question, however, was said to be the Hangzhou No. 7 People's Hospital

---

471 The overseas Falun Gong support network stated in its report: "Shi Bei was simply starved to death." This was unlikely to have been the sole cause of death, however, since she was reportedly denied food for only a week.

– the same institution about which (as was noted in Chapter 5 above)[472] three of its staff psychiatrists had optimistically stated in 1987:

> According to this hospital's statistics, cases of antisocial political speech and action accounted for 54 percent of all cases [examined] during the year 1977; currently, the proportion of such cases has fallen to a level of 6.7 percent. This shows that the present situation of stability and unity in China has resulted in a marked fall in the number of cases arising from such factors.[473]

Remarkably, the Chinese authorities have admitted quite openly during the crackdown that Falun Gong practitioners were being admitted to mental hospitals in large numbers. In a volume officially published in late 1999, for example, they stated:

> According to doctors at the Beijing University of Medical Science, since 1992 the number of patients with psychiatric disorders caused by practicing "Falun Gong" has increased markedly, accounting for 10.2 percent of all patients suffering from mental disorders caused by practicing various *qigong* exercises. In the first half of this year, the number rose further, accounting for 42.1 percent.[474]

Another official spokesperson went still further, however, making the patently absurd claim in September 1999 that "Falun Gong practitioners now account for 30 percent of all mental patients in China."[475] In neither of these reports was the coincidence between the very sizeable increase in Falun Gong admissions to mental hospitals during 1999, and the fact that it was during this same period that the government prepared and implemented its nationwide crackdown upon the sect, deemed to be worthy of mention.

The authorities' current attempt to partially "psychiatrize" the Falun Gong question by claiming that the group's spiritual doctrines and practices drive its members insane represents, as we have seen, only the most recent phase in a well documented history of political psychiatric abuse in China that stretches back almost half a century.[476] What is particularly noteworthy about this latest phase, however, is the unsettling similarity between the government's claim that belief in Falun Gong produces severe nervous

---

472 See p.157 above
473 Zhong Xingsheng et al., "A Preliminary Analysis of 210 Cases of Forensic Psychiatric Medical Assessment," pp.139-141.
474 Ji Shi, *Li Hongzhi and His "Falun Gong" — Deceiving the Public and Ruining Lives* (New Star Publishers, Beijing 1999), p.12. Similarly, in a July 1999 report from Xinhua, the official Chinese government news agency, Dr. Zhang Tongling, a psychiatrist at the No. 6 Attached Hospital of the Beijing Medical University, was quoted as saying: "I myself have witnessed a rocketing rate of mental illness among Falun Gong practitioners since 1996." She quoted statistics from the psychiatric departments of two Beijing hospitals as showing that mentally diseased Falun Gong followers now accounted for 42 percent of all mental patients, compared with only 10.01 percent in 1996. "It is an indisputable fact that practicing Falun Gong can lead to many kinds of mental disorders, which however has never been admitted by Falun Gong advocates," said Cai Zhuoji, also a psychiatrist at the Beijing Anding Hospital" ("Medical Scientists Reveal Falun Gong Fallacies," *Xinhua News Reports*, July 24, 1999; reproduced in FBIS, same date).
475 The claim is made in a video CD-ROM entitled *Falun Gong—Cult of Evil*, issued by the Chinese government in September 1999 as a companion item to Ji Shi, *Li Hongzhi*.
476 The USSR authorities also used to send religious dissenters and nonconformists to psychiatric hospitals. See Bloch and Reddaway, *Russia's Political Hospitals* (op cit), pp.269-70. In recent years, religious sectarian movements in Russia have once again come under direct legal and medical attack from government authorities. See, e.g., "Duma Appeal on Dangerous Religious Sects," *Moscow Rossiyskaya Gazeta*, December 28, 1996;

breakdowns and mental illnesses, and the ultra-leftist medical doctrine propagated during the Cultural Revolution whereby all or most mental illness was said to be the product of a "bourgeois reactionary worldview" on the part of those afflicted. After 1978, the authorities had wisely abandoned this clearly untenable doctrine in favour of a more nuanced approach which partially reversed the claimed line of causality: some dissidents, it was now stated, held their bourgeois-reactionary viewpoints because they were mentally ill. In the case of the crackdown on Falun Gong, however, the basic argument in China has once again become that it is politically incorrect thought and belief – or what in the early 1970s were termed "ideological defects" (*sixiang maobing*) – that causes people to become mentally ill.[477]

II. Legal and Medical Justifications for the Crackdown

In October 1999, the Standing Committee of the National People's Congress issued a proclamation stating the following:

> Heretical cult organizations shall be resolutely banned according to law, and all of their criminal activities shall be dealt with severely. Heretical cults, operating under the guise of religion, qigong or other forms, employ various means to disturb social order and jeopardize people's lives and property and economic development, and they must be banned according to law and punished resolutely. People's courts, procuratorates, public security, national security, and judicial and administrative organs shall fulfil their respective duties and join efforts in carrying out these tasks.[478]

Although widely reported overseas as being "a new anti-cult law," this decision in fact merely reinforced an existing set of provisions contained in Article 300 of the 1997 Criminal Law legitimising the suppression of what the authorities termed "heretical cult organization" (*xie jiao*); the maximum

---

translated in FBIS, same date; and Lev Levenson, "Psychiatrists and Officers in Defense of Traditional Values," *Ekspress Khronika*, January 31, 1997.

477 Certain echoes of this ideologically determinist notion can be found in various Western neo-Marxist writers, from Gyorgy Lukacs to Louis Althusser and others, on the phenomenon of "false consciousness."

478 Decision of the Standing Committee of the National People's Congress on Banning Heretical Cult Organizations and Preventing and Punishing Cult Activities, adopted at the 12th Session of the Standing Committee of the Ninth NPC on October 20, 1999; English translation in *Beijing Review*, 1999, No.45. This Decision, in turn, was essentially a brief public notification of a more complex and detailed set of rules that had been formulated by the Supreme People's Court and Supreme People's Procuracy on October 8, 1999, explaining how Article 300 and other relevant provisions of the Criminal Law were to be applied in the course of the "anti-cult" crackdown. See *Explanations of the Supreme People's Court and Supreme People's Procuracy Concerning Laws Applicable to Handling Cases of Organizing and Employing Heretical Cult Organizations to Commit Crimes*, adopted at the 1079th Meeting of the SPC on October 9, 1999 and at the 47th Meeting of the Ninth Procuratorial Committee of the SPC on October 9, 1999; English translation in *Beijing Review*, 1999, No.45. The latter document is highly reminiscent of a similar set of guidelines issued by the same two bodies in August 1989 explaining how the various Criminal Law statutes on "counterrevolution" were to be applied in practice in the course of the ongoing legal campaign to suppress the nationwide pro-democracy movement of April-June 1989. See "*Zuigao Renmin Fayuan, Zuigao Renmin Jianchayuan Guanyu Banli Fan'geming Baoluan he Zhengzhi Dongluan Zhong Fanzui Anjian Juti Yingyong Falü de Ruogan Wenti de Yijian* (Opinion of the Supreme People's Court and Supreme People's Procuracy on Several Questions Concerning the Specific Application of Law in the Handling of Criminal Cases Committed During the Counterrevolutionary Rebellion and Political Turmoil)," August 1, 1989, in *Sifa Shouce* (*Judicial Handbook*), Vol.6 (People's Court Publishing House, Dec. 1990), pp.100-105.

penalty under Article 300 for such crimes is life imprisonment.[479] Since the start of the crackdown, the Chinese authorities have frequently asserted that Falun Gong is an "evil cult" displaying the same abusive and life-threatening organizational characteristics as the Aum Shinrikyo cult in Japan, which released sarin poison gas on the Tokyo subway in 1995, the Branch Davidians cult, dozens of whose members were killed when the U.S. law-enforcement authorities stormed its headquarters in Waco, Texas in 1993, and the Solar Temple cult, many of whose members committed collective suicide in Switzerland in 1994.[480] On this and other implicitly political grounds, the government has further branded the Falun Gong movement as posing a serious "threat to state security."

An additional major justification given for the sect's suppression has been the authorities' claim that the sect tries to prevent its members from seeking proper medical attention when they fall ill. According to officially released data, more than 1,400 Falun Gong practitioners or their family members have died as a result of this malign sectarian doctrine.[481] Sect leaders and members, however, have consistently

---

[479] Harsh as this seems, it actually represented an improvement over the 1979 Criminal Law, Article 99 of which (in conjunction with a September 1983 "anti-crime campaign" decision by the National People's Congress) defined the offence of "organizing and leading a superstitious or reactionary sect or society" (*fandong hui-daomen*) as being a counterrevolutionary crime punishable, at maximum, by the death penalty. Under this law, literally hundreds of leaders of banned religious and other sects were executed or sentenced to up to life imprisonment in China during the 1980s. Interestingly, the term officially used since March 1997 for banned sectarian activities – *xie jiao* – is a reversion by the authorities to the term traditionally used by the Confucian authorities over the past millennium and more to suppress ideological heterodoxy in Chinese society. For further details of contemporary China's religious sectarian movements and their suppression by the Chinese government, see Robin Munro (ed.), "Syncretic Sects and Secret Societies: Revival in the 1980s," *Chinese Sociology and Anthropology*, Vol.21, No.4 (Summer 1989). For numerous case examples of religious sectarians and members of similar-style groups sentenced in the 1980s under Article 99 of the pre-1997 Criminal Law, see Human Rights Watch, *Detained in China and Tibet: A Directory of Political and Religious Prisoners* (New York: Human Rights Watch, 1994), pp.251-271 and pp.343-350.

[480] See, e.g., "Cults Endanger National Security," *Xinhua News Reports*, September 27, 2000; English translation in FBIS, same date. If comparisons between the Falun Gong and other major sects or cults are to be drawn, then groups such as the Jehovah's Witnesses or (at a stretch) the Church of Scientology would seem to be more apposite and reasonable models of comparison than the very extreme examples of sectarianism raised by the Chinese authorities. One of the best English-language sources of objective information and analysis on the Falun Gong phenomenon is an Internet website assembled by the scholar Barend ter Haar: "Falungong: Evaluation and Further References," available at http://www.let.leidenuniv.nl/bth/falun.htm.

[481] Hundreds of these fatal cases and other alleged tragedies are documented by the authorities in Ji Shi, *Li Hongzhi and His "Falun Gong" — Deceiving the Public and Ruining Lives*. It would be wrong to dismiss these official claims of widespread fatalities as false, but it would be equally inappropriate to accept them as necessarily true – or for that matter, as having the abusive significance ascribed to them by the government – until they have been independently verified and studied, something which has not yet been done. In particular, such an assessment would need to examine whether the number of reported fatalities departed significantly, in either direction, from the normal mortality rate statistics for such a large subgroup of the Chinese population as that accounted for by the Falun Gong (many millions); it is not immediately apparent that it does. And second, the officially claimed causal connection between those deaths and the practice of Falun Gong by those who died would need to be further explored and evaluated by independent medical assessors. Finally, there is no obvious reason to suppose that Falun Gong practitioners are any less susceptible to major mental illnesses, including those of the most florid and potentially dangerous kinds, than is the Chinese population in general; indeed, many if not all of the tragic cases of "Falun Gong-induced" psychopathology recounted by the Chinese authorities may eventually turn out to have been attributable to this general epidemiological factor, rather than (as is officially claimed) to the practice of Falun Gong.

denied this key government allegation. It is worth noting, however, that for the majority of China's population, the economic market reforms that have been pursued since the late 1970s have made affordable access to Western-style and even to traditional Chinese-style medical treatment become largely a thing of the past. Much of the current popularity among Chinese today of various kinds of "alternative medicine" or "self-treatment" approaches to curing illness can be directly attributed to the severe practical and financial difficulty that many people experience in trying to gain access to more mainstream or professional forms of medical care. Falun Gong practitioners themselves claim that the mental and physical discipline they follow is highly efficacious in helping to maintain good health; the results of two wide-ranging epidemiological surveys and analyses conducted in Beijing in 1998, that is, prior to the government crackdown on the sect, would certainly seem to substantiate this claim.[482] Above all, the question must be asked: why, if Falun Gong has such deleterious effects upon its practitioners as the Chinese government alleges, have there been no reports of similar outbreaks of mental and physical illness occurring among the numerous and very sizable overseas-based Falun Gong communities in recent years?

Whatever the underlying truth of the matter may be, and while there are no doubt certain aspects of the Falun Gong belief system that many liberal-minded or non-religious people may find to be unacceptable,[483] the fact remains that the Chinese government has thus far presented no plausible evidence to support its central allegation that the sect poses such a threat to national security, or so fundamentally endangers public safety, as to justify, under internationally accepted standards, the imposition of an effective state of emergency requiring the nationwide suspension both of the Falun Gong's constitutional right to exist and also of the fundamental civil liberties of millions of the sect's adherents.[484]

---

482 The first survey examined the cases of 1,449 Beijing residents who practiced Falun Gong, and was conducted by a group of senior physicians in the capital, including Wang Qi, chief physician at the General Hospital for Armed Police; Li Naiyuan, chief physician at the Stomatological Hospital of Beijing Medical University; Zheng Lihua, deputy chief physician at the People's University of China Hospital; Qu Zengqiu, a pharmacist at the same hospital; Tian Xiulan, managing physician at the Beijing Hospital of Nuclear Industry; and Jing Lianhong, a physician at the Dongshi Hospital for Women and Children. The survey addressed a wide range of medical conditions found among the target patients (including diseases or complaints of the cardiovascular, digestive, musculoskeletal, respiratory, urinary, endocrine and nervous systems, as well as gynaecological, skin, haematological and ear, nose and throat disorders), and the tabulated results of the study indicated that the practice of Falun Gong led to marked improvements in all these categories of health; only one patient (suffering from a digestive ailment) was reported as showing a deterioration in health (*The Effect of Falun Gong on Healing Illnesses and Keeping Fit: A Survey Among Practitioners in Beijing Zizhuyuan Assistance Center, October 18, 1998* [February 2000], available at: www.falundafa-pa.net/survey/survey98-2_e.html.) The second survey in 1998 examined the health effects of Falun Gong practice on a much larger sample group of practitioners in five districts of Beijing; it was also conducted by numerous highly qualified medical personnel (trained in both Western and traditional Chinese medicine), and its findings were broadly similar to those of the first survey (*Falun Gong Health Effect Survey of Ten Thousand Cases in Beijing*, available at: www.falundafa-pa.net/survey/survey98-1_e.html.)
483 Possible examples of the latter include the sect's underlying hostility towards homosexuality and its belief, as taught by Master Li Hongzhi, that human intelligence and civilization were originally brought to planet Earth by aliens from outer space.
484 The true size and extent of the Falun Gong movement remains open to question, but it is clearly extremely large. The sect itself claims to have around 100 million practitioners worldwide, most of them in China; the Chinese government acknowledges a figure of only several million practitioners inside the country.

Certainly, the United Nations' body with primary responsibility for monitoring and enforcing human rights standards around the world has failed to be convinced that any such situation presently exists in China. In a declaration issued in August 1999, the U.N. body stated:

> We are convinced that the banning by the People's Republic of China on 22 July 1999 of the spiritual movement Falun Gong/Falun Dafa and the subsequent arrest of leaders, massive destruction of publications and audio-visual material, and the prohibition of assembly of its practitioners are direct violations of the spirit and provisions of the Declaration on the Elimination of All Forms of Intolerance and of Discrimination Based on Religion or Belief, and of Article 18 of the International Covenant on Civil and Political Rights.[485]

Besides the clear and unambiguous legal proscription of sectarian activities of all kinds in China today, however, the authorities also have at their disposal a medical justification, of sorts, for waging such an intense campaign of persecution against the Falun Gong. Since the late 1980s, the Chinese psychiatric establishment has identified a unique set of mental disorders that it says can arise from the practice of traditional *qigong* forms of exercise and self-cultivation,[486] and also from a more heterogeneous range of thought and behaviour broadly termed as "feudal superstitious belief" (*fengjian*

The following provides a useful summary of the limits specified under international legal standards on governments' freedom to restrict civil liberties and human rights in the name of national security:

> The International Covenant on Civil and Political Rights provides for the rights of free expression, assembly and association, but qualifies them by allowing restrictions in the interest of protecting national security. Such restrictions, however, are only valid if they are prescribed by law and 'necessary.' The latter requirement means that the restriction must be proportional to its purpose in severity and intensity and the least restrictive means of achieving that purpose. Thus interference with a right must be interpreted narrowly in cases of doubt and not presumed to be the rule. In the case of freedom of association and assembly, a restriction must be 'necessary in a democratic society,' that is it must not only meet the above requirements but must also be respectful of the democratic values of pluralism, tolerance, broad-mindedness and popular participation in the political decision-making process... A threat to national security is not the same as a threat to any given government of the nation, and mere criticism of a governing party or its policies should not be restricted in the name of national security. (Human Rights Watch/Asia and Human Rights in China "Whose Security," pp.4-5.)

See also "Johannesburg Principles on National Security, Freedom of Expression and Access to Information," drafted by an international team of human rights experts, including legal scholars, U.N. rights specialists and diplomats, at a conference in Johannesburg, South Africa, in 1995 convened by the London-based NGO Article 19. The full text of the Johannesburg Principles is available in *The New World Order and Human Rights in the Post-Cold War Era: National Security vs. Human Security*, papers from the International Conference on National Security Law in the Asia Pacific, November 1995 (Korea Human Rights Network, 1996). According to the Principles, "The peaceful exercise of the right to freedom of expression shall not be considered a threat to national security or subjected to any restrictions or penalties."

485 *The Banning of the Falun Gong and Subsequent Arrests of Practitioners*, Report of the United Nations Sub-Commission on Prevention of Discrimination and Protection of Minorities, August 4, 1999. Article 18 of the International Covenant on Civil and Political Rights (ICCPR) guarantees the right to freedom of thought, conscience and religion.

486 Qigong is a traditional Chinese form of mind-body exercises that shares certain features of yoga, meditation and other non-Western self-cultivation practices; according to Chinese psychiatry, if practiced improperly or too intensively, it can produce, alongside its many acknowledged benefits, a series of mental imbalances ranging from minor cognitive disorders to occasionally more serious, psychosis-like conditions. (For a very informative account of this topic, see: Nancy N. Chen, *Breathing Spaces: Qigong, Psychiatry, and Healing in China*, Columbia University Press, July 2003.)

mixin.) In 1989, the country's medical authorities formally recorded this category of psychiatric ailments in the Chinese Classification of Mental Disorders (2nd Version, also known as the CCMD-II), under the heading "mental disorders closely related to culture."[487] The international psychiatric community recognizes a range of mental conditions known as "culture bound syndromes,"[488] and there seems to be no reason to suppose that the improper or excessive use of *qigong* may not, in certain circumstances and cases, lead to various forms of mental imbalance or disorder. It is surely remarkable, however, that there so suddenly occurred, according to the official version of events, such a massive epidemiological outbreak of *qigong*-related mental illness across China during the precise period immediately before and after the start of the government's crackdown on Falun Gong in July 1999. Still more puzzling is the fact that, in the Chinese government's main English-language compilation of evidence concerning the severe psychological damage that the practice of Falun Gong is alleged to induce in its practitioners,[489] the sufferers are, in all recorded cases, said to have contracted an exotic mental disorder known as "dysphrenia" – a condition that is apparently either so rare or so mild that, not only does it not appear in the World Health Organization's ICD-10, it is also entirely absent from the CCMD-II, the Chinese medical establishment's own official listing of mental disorders.[490]

---

487   The Chinese terms used are "*qigong ban-fa jingshen zhang'ai*" and "*qigong suo zhi jingshen zhang'ai*" (mental disorders associated with or induced by qigong). Detailed clinical and diagnostic discussions of this culture-bound psychiatric condition can be found in the following articles: Shan Huaihai et al., "Clinical Phenomenology of Mental Disorders Caused by Qigong Exercise," *Chinese Medical Journal* (in English), 1989, Vol.102, No.6, pp.445-448; Shan Huaihai et al., "A Study of the Comparison Between Hysteric-like Episodes Caused by Chinese Qigong (Deep Meditation) and Hysteria with Psychosocial Stress," *Chinese Journal of Nervous and Mental Diseases*, 1992, Vol.18, No.3, pp.156-158; Xu Shenghan, "Psychophysiological Reactions Associated with Qigong Therapy," *Chinese Medical Journal*, 1994, Vol.107, No.3, pp.230-233; Shan Huaihai, "*Qigong Suo Zhi Jingshen Zhang'ai de Linchuang Ziliao yu Zhenduan* (Clinical Material and Diagnosis on Mental Disorders Induced by Qigong)," *Chinese Journal of Nervous and Mental Diseases*, 1999, No.3; Yang Desen, "*Qigong Neng Zhiliao Shenjingzheng yu Jingshen Jibing ma?* (Can Qigong Cure Neurosis and Mental Illness?)," *Chinese Journal of Nervous and Mental Diseases*, Vol.26, No.1 (2000), pp.52-53; He Jiali et al., "*Butong Shiduan Qigong Suo Zhi Jingshen Zhang'ai Linchuang Duizhao Yanjiu Ji Zhenduan Biaozhun Tantao* (A Clinical Comparative Study of, and Diagnostic Criteria for, Qigong-induced Mental Disorders Over Various Periods)," *Chinese Journal of Nervous and Mental Diseases*, Vol.26, No.2 (2000), pp.116-117; and Zheng Hongbo et al., "*Lian 'Falun Gong' Yinzhi Jingshen Zhang'ai 4 Li Baogao* (A Report on Four Cases of Mental Disorders Induced by 'Falun Gong')," *Chinese Journal of Nervous and Mental Diseases*, Vol.26, No.3 (2000), pp.142. Finally, a number of individual studies of this type involving cases where criminal charges were brought can be found in Zheng Zhanpei, *Sifa Jingshen Jianding de Yinan Wenti Ji Anli* (*Thorny Problems and Case Examples in Judicial Psychiatric Appraisal*), (Shanghai Medical University Press, 1996), pp.275-309.
488   These include, for example, "*koro*," a type of panic reaction among males, especially in Asia, characterized by intense fear that the penis is shrinking inside the body; "*amok*," a form of violent mass hysteria that is typically found in Malay society; and "*latah*," a condition found in many parts of Africa and characterized by fear that the soul is being taken away from the body. For a detailed discussion of these issues, see Ari Kiev, *Transcultural Psychiatry* (Free Press, 1982).
489   See Ji Shi, *Li Hongzhi and His "Falun Gong"* (op cit.)
490   Only a handful of references to "dysphrenia" can be found on the Internet. First, the website of Rick's College, Idaho (an institution run by the Church of Jesus Christ of Latter-Day Saints, or Mormons), contains the following cryptic definition: "Dysphrenic: bad brain" (a literal translation of the original Greek term). Second, an Italian neurological website mentions the term in passing in a brief note on "migraine madness." And third, Amnesty International provided the following information in a recent report on the anti-Falun Gong crackdown in China: "The word 'dysphrenia' is not widely recognized by Western psychiatric professionals and does not appear to be defined in Western medical books. The only references found by AI's expert medical advisor is

Another very striking feature of the widespread psychiatric incarceration of Falun Gong practitioners since 1999 is that, in the great majority of reported cases, it has been carried out by the police without even the pretence of due legal process. The victims have simply been detained without charge and then subjected to arbitrary committal in normal mental hospitals. (In this respect also, the activities in question indicate a worrying reversion to the widespread pattern of arbitrary political-psychiatric abuse that prevailed during the Cultural Revolution.) All such cases are said by the legal and medical authorities to have been involuntary civil committals, and all – implausibly enough – are claimed have been "legal guardianship" cases where the police acted only on the direct instructions of the patients' families.[491] In the previous chapter, we identified some of the most likely reasons why this approach is being taken with increasing frequency in China in politically motivated cases of psychiatric detention, and the same reasons seem clearly to be in evidence in the case of the Falun Gong psychiatric detentions. The use of compulsory civil committal allows the police to avoid entirely the various steps and formalities legally required for placing a suspect in criminal psychiatric custody, and it is no doubt particularly convenient for the authorities to take this approach when large numbers of such committals are being carried out within a relatively short space of time. In addition, as we shall see from the case studies presented in Chapter 8, in practice it has proved to be extraordinarily difficult for the victims of these PSB-directed "involuntary civil committals" to subsequently bring administrative lawsuits challenging the legality of their treatment; in effect, the courts have granted the police a blanket exemption from such lawsuits. In the highly repressive atmosphere of the continuing crackdown on the Falun Gong movement, all these difficulties are undoubtedly magnified several times over. Significantly, there are no known cases, out of the roughly 1,000 that have so far come to light, of psychiatrically detained Falun Gong practitioners having later even tried to challenge the legality of their ordeals by filing administrative lawsuits against the police agencies and hospitals concerned.

As indicated earlier, there have been relatively few reports of Falun Gong practitioners having been sent to Ankang facilities in the course of the crackdown since mid-1999. Partly this is because at present only a couple of dozen cities and provinces in China have built such facilities, and partly it is a reflection of the security authorities' apparent preference for using compulsory civil committal in cases of this type. It has recently emerged, however, that from the early 1990s onwards, a number of city governments in China began setting up "Ankang Wards" (*Ankang Bingfang*) on the premises of regular psychiatric hospitals at local level. According to the Dalian municipal regulations of November 1992, for example: "County-level (Municipal) and District-level Governments can establish Ankang Wards in mental hospitals under their administrative jurisdiction in order to carry out, upon authorization from the Dalian City PSB, the custody and treatment of mentally ill people who have provoked incidents or disasters."[492] Clearly, this move blurs further the already hazy and tenuous institutional distinction

---

related to neurological movement disorders which occur as side effects of drug treatment for schizophrenia or a psychopathic disorder of communication – 'psychopathic' meaning a psychiatric illness" (Amnesty International, *People's Republic of China: The Crackdown on Falun Gong and Other So-called "Heretical Organizations,"* March 2000 [ASA 17/011/2000]).
491 This claim was made repeatedly by one of China's top forensic psychiatrists in Yokohama in August 2002, on the occasion of the World Psychiatric Association's World Congress, during a meeting with the present author and Dr. Jim Birley, a former president of the Royal College of Psychiatrists.
492 "*Dalian Shi Jianhu Zhiliao Guanli Zhaoshi Zhaohuo Jingshenbingren Tiaoli*" (Dalian Municipal Regulations on the Guardianship, Treatment and Management of Mentally Ill People Who Create Disasters or Incidents), passed by the Standing Committee of the Dalian Municipal People's Congress on 4 November 1992 and effective as of 17 December 1992.

in China between places of civil psychiatric committal and institutions for the criminally insane. Or to put the matter another way: the Ankang system is now spreading its tentacles into the country's regular mental healthcare facilities. We will now look at several individual cases that were almost certainly dealt with in the Ankang Wards of ordinary mental hospitals.

III. The Forensic Assessment of Falun Gong Detainees: Four Cases

Since all Falun Gong followers practice a variant form of qigong, it was originally believed that the diagnosis of "*qigong*-induced mental disorder" served as the Chinese authorities' main medical justification for psychiatrically detaining large numbers of Falun Gong activists. A number of Western commentators have even argued that no unethical misuse of psychiatry or other human rights abuse has been involved in these cases because those concerned probably were suffering from qigong-related mental disorders.[493]

However, a number of psychiatric studies published in China over the past few years have contradicted this assumption by stating that the diagnosis of qigong-related mental illness is not to be used in the case of Falun Gong detainees, since they are in fact suffering from something much more serious. According to one such article, "Falun Gong is entirely different from ordinary body cultivation techniques, and no clear definition of the type of mental disorder that it produces can be found within China's currently used body of diagnostic criteria for mental illness." Instead, the entirely new diagnostic label of "evil cult-induced mental disorder" (*xiejiao suo zhi jingshen zhang'ai*) has now been coined by Chinese psychiatry, for exclusive use against the Falun Gong and any other unorthodox spiritual movements in China that happen to have been banned by the Communist Party and government. In effect, the legal authorities' post-Mao formulation that "some dissidents commit political crimes because they are mentally ill" has now been supplemented by the issuance of a Chinese government "health warning" to the public: "Spiritual or religious beliefs banned on political grounds can drive people mad." Again, the close similarity between this notion and the Cultural Revolution doctrine that mental illness is caused by politically deviant thinking should be readily apparent.

In the article mentioned above – "A First Look at the Forensic Psychiatric Evaluation of Falun Gong Cases" – four different cases studies are presented, and each case illuminates in different ways the persecutory essence of this new forensic psychiatric diagnosis.[494] Since the Falun Gong caseload represents the most recent and conspicuous phase in China's longstanding misuse of psychiatry as a means of political repression, and since so much controversy currently surrounds this particular group of detainees, it is worth examining these four cases in some detail.

The first case discussed concerns a 45-year-old woman who (according to the two psychiatrists who wrote the article) "went to Beijing to petition the authorities and was then placed under criminal detention, but still she persisted in practicing Falun Gong." In other words, the reason for her arrest was

---

493 See, for example, Arthur Kleinman and Sing Lee, "Psychiatry in its Political and Professional Contexts: A Response to Robin Munro," *Journal of the American Academy of Psychiatry and the Law*, Vol.30, No.1 (2002), pp.120-125. See also Robin Munro, "On the Psychiatric Abuse of Falun Gong and Other Dissenters in China: A Reply to Stone, Hickling, Kleinman and Lee," *Journal of the American Academy of Psychiatry and the Law*, Vol.30, No.2 (2002), pp.266-274.
494 Shen Jun and Gong Yantao, "*Falun Gong Anjian Sifa Jingshenbing Jianding Chutan*" (A First Look at the Forensic Psychiatric Evaluation of Falun Gong Cases), *Linchuang Jingshen Yixue Zazhi* (Journal of Clinical Psychological Medicine), 2000, Vol. 10, No. 5, pp.313-314.

not that her mental condition had posed any immediate physical or psychological danger to herself or to anyone else, but rather that she had been brave or foolhardy enough to openly express her peaceful opposition to the government's relentless campaign of suppression. The forensic examiners' conclusion was: "Mental disorder caused by practicing an evil cult; no capacity to bear legal responsibility [for her crimes]; recommend medical treatment." The mental symptoms cited by the examiners to justify this conclusion consisted almost entirely of a list of the patient's Falun Gong-inspired spiritual beliefs. (While some of these admittedly would strike a Western observer as being highly unusual, it is surely not the job of psychiatrists to pass judgment on their patients' spiritual or religious convictions.) The remaining "symptoms" cited by the forensic examiners included: "flagrantly telling everyone how much she was benefiting from her practice of Falun Gong" and "refusing to be dissuaded from her beliefs and continuing to gather people to practice Falun Gong...even after the government declared it to be an evil cult."

The second case concerns a 62-year-old man who, after suffering from insomnia for a long time, took up Falun Gong in 1995. According to the forensic case report,

> He soon became solitary and un-talkative, and he began giving people valuable presents for no reason. He always ate less than other people and would buy the cheapest of foods, to the point even of buying and taking home items that others had turned down. He said that [this was because] he wanted to be a genuinely "truthful, compassionate and forbearing" person.[495]

There was nothing in the case account that would plausibly indicate that the detainee posed any psychiatrically related danger to himself, others or society. Again, the sole reason for this person's arrest was that, according to the forensic report, "After the government declared Falun Gong to be an evil cult, he not only ignored all efforts to dissuade him from continuing to practice Falun Gong, but also joined with other practitioners in travelling to Beijing to 'uphold the dharma' on behalf of Falun Gong." It is clear from the final diagnosis – "mental disorder caused by practicing an evil cult; should bear partial legal responsibility for his crimes" – that the examining psychiatrists partially acknowledged that the "danger" he posed was basically unrelated to his alleged mental condition; however, the immediate consequence of the detainee's being found only "half mad" was that, in their view, he must face criminal trial for his non-violent beliefs.

Here we see the ethical dilemma faced by Chinese psychiatrists in all such cases: had they found, as international standards require, that the patient was basically quite sane, he would certainly have been sent to prison for his "crime" of peacefully demonstrating in Beijing. A finding of complete insanity would have been ethically absurd in this case, so they instead opted for the middle course. While we are not told about the final disposition of this case, being set free was certainly not an option: the detainee would either have received a reduced prison sentence or, perhaps more likely, have been sent for some form of custodial psychiatric care.[496]

The third case concerns a young male worker and Falun Gong practitioner who appears to have been genuinely mentally ill: said by the forensic examiners to have already been suffering from

---

495 "*Zhen Shan Ren*": the three cardinal teachings of Falun Gong.
496 Purists might argue that the examining psychiatrists' only ethically correct course of action in this case would have been to inform the police: this man is both sane and also innocent of any crime; in reality, though, the psychiatrists would probably have suffered harsh retribution from the political authorities had they dared to suggest any such thing.

symptoms of schizophrenia prior to taking up Falun Gong, he claimed that he "could tell what was going on in people's minds without the use of any instruments of detection; and that his soul had been fully realized and he was able to maintain frequent contact with aliens from outer space." The examining psychiatrists' verdict was: "[S]chizophrenia; behaviour and actions completely dominated by pathological factors, and hence no capacity to bear legal responsibility." From the case details supplied, this forensic conclusion seems to be an accurate and ethically appropriate one. But we still need to look further. Why was the person arrested? It was because, once again, he had gone to Beijing to petition peacefully against the crackdown on Falun Gong – "thereby exerting an extremely bad influence in society" – and not because his schizophrenic symptoms or behaviour had posed any perceptible threat to public safety. Having been accused of this grave "national security" offence, the inevitable outcome of the forensic diagnosis was that he would be sent to a custodial facility for criminal offenders (either the locked ward of a regular mental hospital or an Ankang institution.)

Perhaps the greatest irony here is that, as most expert outside observers acknowledge, China's national psychiatric care system is so severely under-funded that the great majority of mentally ill people, even schizophrenia sufferers, currently receive no medical care, institutional or otherwise. The schizophrenic worker discussed above, in common with countless other Falun Gong practitioners suffering from other medical ailments for which they simply cannot afford to be treated under China's increasingly expensive government-run healthcare system, was recommended to join the Falun Gong because it claims dramatically to improve practitioners' health.[497] Is it ethically appropriate that extremely scarce psychiatric resources should be allocated in such a way that a schizophrenic posing no evident threat to society, and who would otherwise probably have gone totally untreated, is sent by the police for custodial medical care of a kind which, according to all accounts so far provided by Falun Gong psychiatric detainees, amounts to an extrajudicial form of physical and psychological punishment?[498]

The final case illustrates yet another permutation of the whole sorry business. It concerns a 41-year-old female government official who began practicing Falun Gong in 1996 and then went on to become a leader and organizer of the movement in her area of residence. According to the forensic report issued after her arrest, "Consciousness clear and alert; thinking logical and well-ordered... apart from being emotionally over-excited, she showed no signs of hallucination, delusions or other conspicuous mental abnormalities. Forensic finding: not mentally ill; should be held legally responsible for her crimes." On the face of it, no ethical abuse was involved in this case because the examinee was found to be mentally normal and hence no psychiatric treatment was ordered. However, the key issue highlighted here concerns Chinese forensic examiners' attitude toward the question of a detainee's "legal responsibility" for peaceful dissident offences. Had the psychiatrists involved in the examination

---

497 Incidentally, several wide-ranging medical surveys conducted by numerous top Chinese physicians prior to the July 1999 crackdown on Falun Gong concluded that, in the case of most common illnesses, it actually does so; schizophrenia, of course, is quite another matter, but it should also be noted that this particular detainee apparently had the condition well before taking up Falun Gong. For details of two of the pre-crackdown medical surveys, see Note 482.

498 On a related point, several Western commentators offer an alternative "scarce resources" argument against the political abuse allegations. They consider it to be highly improbable that the Chinese authorities would send mentally normal dissident offenders for custodial psychiatric care, when prison is a much cheaper and more obvious option. In fact, it costs the government a substantial amount nowadays to house a convicted prisoner, whereas Falun Gong and other dissenting involuntary inmates of psychiatric institutions are usually billed, directly or through their families, for all hospitalisation and treatment charges.

of this and other similar cases simply confined their conclusions to the medical side of things, then the issue of psychiatric abuse would not have arisen and it would have been just another case of political persecution under the Chinese criminal justice system. But no, the examining psychiatrists first confirm that the only reason for the female Falun Gong practitioner being placed under police arrest was that, "rejecting all efforts to persuade and educate her away from the cult, she continued to organize groups of practitioners to carry out petitioning activities on its behalf." They then, in the medical diagnostic portion of their report, saw fit to make the wholly political comment and judgment: "she defended with extreme vigour the various advantages of practicing Falun Gong, and in so doing slandered and vilified [China's] present social realities." In other words, the psychiatrists appear to have felt under intense political pressure to endorse – enthusiastically and without reservation – the spurious criminal charge that had been laid against the detainee. Either that, or they did so freely and willingly.

As if to underscore this same point, the authors of this report on the four Falun Gong cases conclude by saying: "If we exercise comprehensive judgment, it is usually not difficult to make a diagnosis of evil cult-induced mental disorder. At the same time, [recently established criteria] will help us to identify and maintain our guard against any die-hard Falun Gong elements who might try to feign mental illness as a way of escaping legal punishment for their crimes." So there we have it: the examining psychiatrists evidently saw it as being one of their most pressing concerns to help weed out, on the government's behalf, any Falun Gong detainee who might deviously wish to pretend to be mad as a means of avoiding stern punishment for what, by international standards, was the entirely non-criminal act of belonging to an unorthodox spiritual group.[499] It is in cases like this that one sees perhaps the clearest and most striking evidence of complicity and collaboration by psychiatrists in the Chinese security authorities' continuing suppression of peaceful political and religious belief.

---

499 For a marginally more subtle, in medical terms, analysis of this issue, in which the term "Falun Gong-related mental disorder" (*Falun Gong xiangguan de jingshen zhang'ai*) is deployed in preference to "evil cult-induced mental disorder," see: Shan Huaihai, "Falun Gong Wei Shenme Hui Youfa Jingshen Zhang'ai" (Why Does Falun Gong Induce Mental Disorder?), *Xinli Jiankang Tongxun* (Bulletin of Psychological Health), 2002, No.1; available at: www.21jk.com.cn/p/law/.

CHAPTER 8

The Ankang: China's Special Psychiatric Hospitals

I. Background

In 1977, the psychiatrist Sidney Bloch and his academic co-author Peter Reddaway described as follows the Soviet Union's countrywide network of institutes for the criminally insane – the so-called Special Psychiatric Hospitals (SPH):

> Conditions prevailing in the SPHs have, by comparison with those in the Ordinary Psychiatric Hospitals, proved consistently stark and punitive. The SPHs are essentially prison-like institutions and were in fact until recently termed prison-psychiatric hospitals. Their function is to house, compulsorily, persons who have committed serious crimes – murder, rape, arson and an array of other violent offences – and who have been diagnosed as suffering from a mental illness and declared not responsible. Following the procedure of criminal commitment, such mentally ill offenders are ordered by the court to enter an SPH for an indeterminate period, until their mental condition improves sufficiently to warrant their release. In addition to a supposed therapeutic function, the SPH also serves to protect society from dangerous offenders...
>
> The SPH is under the control of the Ministry of the Interior (MVD) rather than the Ministry of Health. This is an important point as the MVD is also responsible for the administration of the ordinary police (as opposed to the secret police or KGB) and all penal institutions. The MVD's prime interest is law and order. As in its prisons, so in the SPHs, the maintenance of security is its principal concern; the health and welfare of inmates are secondary issues..... All personnel are employees of the MVD; the hospital director, senior administrative staff and psychiatrists are MVD officers holding a military-style rank.[500]

---

500 Bloch and Reddaway, *Russia's Political Hospitals* (op cit), p.191. Concerning the origins of the SPH network and its overall extent by the late 1970s: "The first SPH proper was in existence in the 1930s, situated in Kazan....After 1945 SPHs were set up in Sychyovka in the Smolensk region, and in Leningrad. The latter is usually referred to as the 'Arsenalnaya' because of its location on Arsenalnaya Street. (It has been the place of internment of dissenters such as Alexander Volpin, Pyotr Grigorenko in 1964, Vladimir Bukovsky, Victor Fainberg and Vladimir Borisov.) The Leningrad SPH was established in a building which served as a women's jail up to 1948. The Chistopol SPH may have been opened at about the same time....More than a decade elapsed before the development of other SPHs. The period between 1965 and 1972 saw the establishment of several new hospitals scattered throughout the Soviet Union. An SPH in Chernyakhovsk in the Kaliningrad region opened in 1965 in the building of a former German convict prison (Grigorenko's second hospitalization was here). Another SPH was established in Dnepropetrovsk in the Ukraine in 1968, also occupying a former prison. In the early 1970s SPHs opened in Oryol, south-west of Moscow; in Blagoveshchensk, near the Pacific coast; in Kzyl-Orda in Kazakhstan; and in Smolensk, west of Moscow. Other SPHs exist in Tashkent and Alma-Ata; but we do not know when they began to function. And an ex-inmate of the Arkhangelsk OPH has reported that when he was interned there in 1967-69 he was often threatened with dispatch to a nearby SPH at Zharovikha, which could be seen in the distance. This SPH, and others in Rostov, Ukhta and Perm, are as yet the subject only of individual, unconfirmed reports. Other SPHs have apparently been established in recent years, but as yet we know little about them." (*Russia's*

As the two writers further observed,

> No matter how severe the conditions of an incarceration, the knowledge of release after a definite period gives the prisoner a sense of hope and anticipation, and the passage of each day reinforces it. Not so in the case of the patient committed involuntarily to a psychiatric hospital.... A person once admitted to a SPH loses all basic rights – he is powerless. No matter how unjust his view of the treatment, no matter that he be beaten or over-medicated or punished unfairly, he has no legal redress whatever. The lot of an inmate is in this respect far worse than a person held in a prison or labour camp.[501]

China's present-day network of Ankang institutes for the criminally insane is functionally identical to the SPH system of the former Soviet Union and is likewise administered by China's equivalent of the MVD, the Ministry of Public Security. The only discernible discrepancy between the above account and China's case today is that no court order is sought or required for the committal of a criminal suspect into Ankang custody; instead, all such decisions are directly made and implemented by the police. Although the term "Ankang" only began to be used for these institutes from 1987 onwards, China's system of forensic psychiatric custody in fact had been in place since the early to mid-1950s – the era of close cooperation with the country's Communist "elder brother," the USSR. Owing to their highly secretive nature, almost nothing is known about the conditions of detention and treatment within these police-run psychiatric custody centres during the first few decades of the People's Republic.

One first-hand account of conditions at the Shanghai facility on the eve of its transformation into an Ankang centre, however, painted a disturbing picture of widespread fear among the inmates arising from the frequent resort by warders and nursing staff to various abusive methods of punishment. The account was written by a female dissident and former political prisoner who had been placed in the Shanghai facility in early 1987.[502] According to the dissident, the ward in which she was placed held twenty women, three of whom were also political dissenters of various kinds. One of the latter had been incarcerated in the asylum simply because: "She had gone onto the streets to make a speech protesting about the high increase in the cost of living. She had said that skyrocketing prices were making people's lives worse, and that political corruption nowadays meant officials could make a fortune out of their posts, something that would not have happened in Mao Zedong's day."

The writer of the account described as follows the regime of fear maintained by the Shanghai asylum's staff in the late 1980s:

> The only difference between [the hospital and prison] was that the two used different methods of punishment. The instruments of punishment in prison were common handcuffs, whereas the hospital used medical equipment....
>
> If patients were disobedient in the hospital, the doctors would increase their medication. Apart from eating, they only felt like sleeping and often suffered from cramps. This was not a civilian hospital that you could leave after three to five months. There, three to five years was considered to be a short time. Moreover, you

---

Political Hospitals, pp.192-3.) The total number of known or suspected SPH facilities in the Soviet Union at that time was therefore somewhere around twenty, or roughly the same number as China's Ankang facilities today.
501 Bloch and Reddaway (op cit), p.210 and p.212.
502 The woman, whose handwritten account was circulated among various human rights groups in 1995, cannot be identified for reasons of personal safety.

had to work for seven hours a day. Those who were on higher doses of medication dribbled saliva constantly. Their eyes would roll upwards helplessly in their sockets. They walked slowly and stumbled frequently.

If an inmate was marked down for punishment, her bed would be taken to the area between the dining hall and the workshop, and she would be tied by her four limbs to the bed by straps looped through the metal bed frame. In this way the nurses could supervise her from morning till night. In the daytime during working hours the dormitory was locked. Sometimes two people would be punished at once. During the daytime when everyone was working, we would look at the women's hands and feet tied to the bed. We would all keep silent, lower our heads and carry on working. In the evening when we returned to the dormitory, we would watch the bed be carried away, and see the empty space where it had stood. A cold shiver would go through your heart. You never knew when it would be your turn. Maybe you would be punished because the doctors discovered you had smuggled a letter out to some visitors, or perhaps because you'd had an argument with the doctors or nurses. When they wanted to punish someone, the alarm outside the dormitory (in the dining room) would sound and several police would arrive all at once and tie you to the bed.

Another kind [of punishment] was injections. One kind was muscular injection and the other intravenous, which was much more painful. I saw some patients who'd had intravenous injections whose tongues were so swollen that they bulged out of their mouths. After a few days of injections, their facial muscles went all stiff, and their eyes became fixed and staring. Their faces were like waxwork masks – they couldn't turn their heads, and would have to slowly turn their whole body around if they wanted to look at something.

Yet another kind of punishment was acupuncture with an electric current. The patients called it the "electric ant."[503] It uses electrically controlled acupuncture needles. There are three levels of current. The higher the current, the more painful, and the amount of pain also depends on the acupuncture points used. There is the *taiyang* point (on the temple), the *hegu* (also known as *hukou*, on the palm of the hand between the thumb and the index finger) and the heart point on the sole of the foot. People who have experienced this say the heart point is the most painful. In civilian hospitals, when a patient is subjected to electric shock treatment it is forbidden to let the other patients watch, but in this place, treatment was no longer about curing illness and saving peoples' lives. It had become the penal code that the doctors used to maintain control. When they wanted to punish someone, they would make all the other patients stand around her bed while the patient twitched in agony, crying pitifully: "I won't do it next time… I won't do it again, please let me go..." After it was all over, the nurses would admonish the other patients, saying that whoever violated the rules next would

---

503 The treatment method of electric acupuncture, which is in widespread use in China (and is found also as an "alternative" therapy in many other countries nowadays) is to be differentiated from the use of ECT. When properly administered, electric acupuncture has no ethically abusive connotations. Like many other legitimate medical treatments, however, electric acupuncture can, as the above account indicates, be misused for purposes of inflicting pain and punishment.

suffer the same treatment as her. We would lower our heads for fear that our faces had gone pale.

According to the woman's account, "Inmates convicted of murder were allowed to talk freely together, but the political prisoners were not permitted to do so." An article published in the Shanghai Archives of Psychiatry in 1987 (the same year as the above events) revealed that no fewer than 11.6 percent of the inmates held at the same Shanghai asylum at that time had been placed there either for engaging in "anti-social speech or action" (*fanshehui yan-xing*) or for "disrupting government offices" (*chongji zhengfu jiguan*) – a clear reference to persistent complainants and petitioners.[504]

There are also confirmed reports of four other political dissidents having been sent to the Shanghai Ankang during the 1990s. In September 1993, a 28-year-old man name Xing Jiandong was confined there after holding a peaceful one-man demonstration outside the Australian Consulate in Shanghai. According to an report issued by Amnesty International the following month,

> The Public Security Bureau have reportedly informed Xing Jiandong's family that he is mentally ill, but the relatives have not been shown any documentation by doctors at the hospital to support this claim. It is further reported that the family were pressured by the Public Security Bureau to give their consent to Xing Jiandong's confinement in the psychiatric hospital and were told that Xing Jiandong would be sent to a labour camp for between one and three years if they did not give written permission, After his transfer to the hospital Xing Jiandong was allegedly tied to a bed for three days and nights, then locked up with mentally disturbed patients.[505]

In late April 1993, a worker named Wang Miaogen, said to be an orphan, was sent to the Shanghai Ankang after staging a desperate protest action outside his local police station in Shanghai one night in which he hacked off four fingers from his left hand with a cleaver. Wang had spent two or three years in prison after June 1989 for having helped to organize the Shanghai Workers Autonomous Federation during the nationwide pro-democracy movement of April-May that year. Among the charges against him at that time were that he had "spread rumours, distributed leaflets and incited strikes." After his release, he alleged that the local PSB had instructed his neighbours to harass him constantly, and on the night in question he had gone to the police station to lodge a formal protest against the latest such round of harassment. According to friends of Wang's to whom he later gave a detailed account of the incident, two police officers then took him outside into the street and gave him a severe beating, kicking him repeatedly as he lay helplessly on the ground. He then went home, got a large knife and returned to the police station and performed his act of self-mutilation in front of the police station entrance. While it is possible that Wang was temporarily suffering from an acute mental disturbance at the time, Amnesty International later reported:

> According to unofficial sources, Wang Miaogen is not suffering from mental illness and there is no justification for him having been committed to hospital.... [Moreover,] while held in police custody before his committal to the hospital, Wang Miaogen was

---

504 See: Yang Xingmei and Ge Meifang, "*Yanzhong Yingxiang Shehui Zhi'an de Jingshen Jibing Huanzhe 81 Li Chubu Diaocha Fenxi*" (Analysis of a Preliminary Investigation into 81 Cases of Mentally Ill Persons Who Seriously Affected Public Order), *Shanghai Jingshen Yixue* (Shanghai Archives of Psychiatry), 1987, Vol.1, No.1, pp.32-4.
505 See: Amnesty International, "China: Prisoner of Conscience Imprisoned in Psychiatric Hospital" (ASA 17/WU 16/93), 19 October 1993.

[reportedly again] beaten up by police, kicked in the head, tied up and gagged with a sock on several occasions.⁵⁰⁶

As of August 2004, Wang Miaogen was still, eleven years after the incident, being held incommunicado at the Shanghai Ankang facility; nothing else was known about his current situation.⁵⁰⁷ In 1995, another Shanghai dissident, Zhu Fuming, an activist in his early 30s associated with the Shanghai-based Association for Human Rights, which had been campaigning for over a year for Wang Miaogen's release, was himself forcibly committed in the Shanghai Ankang for several months. The most recent confirmed case of a political dissident being sent to the Shanghai Ankang facility is that of Li Da, a young worker at an electrical appliances firm in the city who had apparently also been involved in the May 1989 pro-democracy movement. On three separate occasions, prior to his arrest in July 1998, he had stood outside the Shanghai No. 1 Department Store handing out leaflets calling for the rehabilitation of victims of the June 4, 1989 government crackdown, for greater political democracy in China, and for the right to commemorate Taiwan's National Day. Li Da's case was briefly reported on by Voice of America in February of the following year, on the basis of a letter he had smuggled out of the Shanghai Ankang facility. There has been no further news of Li since then.⁵⁰⁸

II. The Ankang Custody and Treatment System

In the mid-1980s, China's leaders, perceiving the emergence of an "ideological vacuum" among the populace, caused mainly by the official downplaying of politics in national life since the Cultural Revolution, launched a campaign to build "socialist spiritual civilization"⁵⁰⁹ across the country. The purpose was to create a spiritual counterpart to China's already fairly well developed "material civilization" – the national infrastructure and the economy. Since in Chinese the words for "spiritual" and "mental" are the same, the new movement was also an attempt to expand "mental civilization," and thus had important implications for the field of mental health work. In October 1986 in Shanghai, the ministries of health, civil affairs and public security convened the country's Second National Conference on Mental Hygiene Work, the first national-level meeting of this kind in almost thirty years.⁵¹⁰ The main issue on the agenda was the sharp increase in the rate of mental illness among China's population in recent years: since the 1970s, the rate was said to have risen from 7 per thousand

---

506 See: Amnesty International, "Medical Letter Writing Action: Wang Wanxing, Wang Miaogen, Xing Jiandong" (ASA 17/44/93), 22 December 1993.
507 It should not be assumed that extreme acts of self-injury or suicide are necessarily indicative of severe mental illness, or even of any mental illness. They can sometimes, as seems to have been true in Wang's case, constitute an extreme act of political protest in circumstances where all other avenues to justice have been denied. In this sense, Wang's sad case may be broadly compared to that of Jan Palach, the 21-year-old student who died after setting himself on fire in Wenceslas Square in Prague on 16 January 1969 to protest the Soviet-led invasion of Czechoslovakia in August the previous year. Palach's action made him a national hero, and he is commemorated in Prague today by a bronze cross embedded at the spot where he fell outside the National Museum; there is also a square in the city named in his honour.
508 In 2003, the U.S. State Department reported that both Wang Miaogen and Li Da, together with two previously unknown dissidents about whom nothing further is known – Wang Chanhao and Pan Zhiming – were still being incarcerated at the Shanghai Ankang. (See: "China: Country Reports on Human Rights Practices – 2003," Bureau of Democracy, Human Rights, and Labor, February 25, 2004; available at: www.state.gov/g/drl/rls/hrrpt/2003/.
509 *Shehuizhuyi jingshen wenming.*
510 The first one had been held in 1958.

members of the population to as many as 10.54 per thousand.[511] The level of violent crime in society was also rising rapidly, and China's severe lack of healthcare facilities for the mentally ill was identified as being a major causal factor.

In April 1987, the three concerned ministries drew up a list of proposals designed to address these problems. According to the resulting policy document,

> An especially urgent need is for the public security organs immediately to set up institutions for the custody and treatment of mentally ill persons who break the law and create disastrous incidents... Owing to the lack of management over the mentally ill, many of them are spread over society at large and they create endless disastrous incidents that pose a very serious threat.[512]

The ministries' main policy recommendations were threefold: first, to speed up the passage of a national mental health law; second, to further develop forensic appraisals work; and third, to establish a national network of police-run centres for the custody and treatment of severely mentally ill offenders. Further important meetings swiftly followed. In June the same year, the First National Academic Symposium on Forensic Psychiatry was held in the southern city of Hangzhou, and in December, the First National Public Security Conference on Custody and Treatment of the Mentally Ill took place in Tianjin.[513]

At some point in the course of these meetings, it was officially decided that the name "Ankang," meaning "Peace and Health," would be used as a uniform designation for the proposed new network of custodial facilities for severely mentally ill offenders. In December 1987, the Ministry of Public Security formed a National Ankang Work Coordinating Group, one of whose deputy chairmen was Wang Guiyue, director of the Tianjin Ankang facility and the recent founder of a "stereotactic brain

---

511 According to a website run by the Beijing Institute of Forensic Medicine and Science (*Beijing Shi Fating Kexue Jishu Jianding Yanjiusuo*), in 2000 the rate of mental illness among China's population stood at 13.47 per thousand. See http://fmedsci.com/sfjs/sfjs09.htm. This figure was reiterated in an article published in China Youth Daily on October 10, 2002: "China's Mentally Ill Number 16 Million." According to another official source, however, the total number of mentally ill people in China that year stood at 17.4 million, of whom 1.2 million were said to pose a severe and immediate threat to public safety; see "*Tebie de Guanhuai – Anhui Sheng Hefei Shi Gong'an Ju Ankang Yiyuan Jianwen*" (A Special Kind of Care – Record of a Visit to the Ankang Hospital of Hefei City PSB, Anhui Province) *Fazhi Ribao*, 10 November 2000.
512 "*Weisheng Bu, Minzheng Bu, Gong'an Bu Guanyu Jiaqiang Jingshen Weisheng Gongzuo de Yijian* (Opinion of the Ministries of Health, Civil Affairs and Public Security on the Strengthening of Mental Health Work)," April 20, 1987, in *Zhonghua Renmin Gongheguo Weisheng Fagui Huibian 1986-1988* (*PRC Compilation of Laws and Regulations on Health, 1986-1988*), (Law Publishing House, June 1990), pp.366-369.
513 This latter meeting was held at the Tianjin Public Security Bureau's Custody and Treatment Centre for the Mentally Ill, which was shortly thereafter renamed as the Tianjin Ankang institute. Since that time, "National Academic Symposiums on Forensic Psychiatry" have been convened in various Chinese cities approximately every two years. The first was in Wuhan in May 1988 (see *Renmin Gong'an Bao* [People's Public Security News], May 20, 1988), the third was in Hangzhou in October 1990 (see *Hangzhou Ribao* [Hangzhou Daily], October 24, 1990), and the eighth was in Changsha on 16-19 August 2003 (see Zhonghua Jingshen Weisheng Wang [China Mental Health Net], 31 January 2003, available at: www.21jk.com.cn/p/.) At the December 1987 conference in Tianjin, a "16-character slogan" was decided upon to guide China's criminal psychiatric custody work: "*Yifa Guanli, Kexue Zhiliao, Guan-Zhi Jiehe, Weihu Zhi'an*" (administer in accordance with the law, use scientific treatment methods, combine custody with treatment, uphold public order)

surgery" unit there.[514] After the April 1987 conference decision, moves to establish institutions of this type proceeded apace, and by May of the following year, it was announced that a total of sixteen Ankang centres had been established and brought into service around the country. According to psychiatrists from the Hangzhou Ankang, writing in 1996, "Fifteen of the [Ankang] hospitals were built since the start of the 1980s…" In fact, however, as many as 18 institutions for the criminally insane had been in existence in China for many years prior to 1987 (known locations include Beijing, Shanghai, Tianjin, Harbin, Dalian, and Gongzhuling in Jilin Province.) The first of these appears to have been the Hangzhou facility, which was established in 1954,[515] the Tianjin Ankang was founded in 1963[516], and the Beijing Ankang, currently located in Fangshan County, was founded in 1965.[517] It thus seems likely that many of the "new" Ankang facilities were simply either renamed or enlarged versions of the criminal-psychiatric custody centres that already existed.

A series of guiding documents was then drawn up by Ministry of Public Security, including the "Administration Methods for Ankang Hospitals," "Detailed Implementation Rules for Nursing Work in Ankang Hospitals" and "Rules for the Admission and Treatment of Mentally Ill People Who Seriously Endanger Public Security."[518] By 1992, the total number of Ankang facilities in China had risen to twenty, with several others reported to be under construction; and by 2001, altogether twenty-two such asylums had been brought into service in seventeen provinces, autonomous regions and directly-administered municipalities around the country, leaving fourteen major regional administrative units that had not yet set one up.[519] According to a report in the *Chinese Journal of Nervous and Mental*

---

514 *Renmin Gong'an Bao*, May 24, 1988, p.1. For the source of information on the brain surgery unit, see Note 531 below.
515 See Kang Ming, "*Ankang Yiyuan de Xingzhi, Renwu, Zuoyong*" (The Nature, Tasks and Function of the Ankang Hospitals), available at the website of the Hangzhou PSB Ankang Hospital: www.ak-hospital.com/lwsx.htm. The article is undated; however, it is listed elsewhere as having been presented by the author at an academic conference in Zhejiang Province in 2001. (For details see: http://mis.511511.com/lwwx/wxdctail.asp?id=256746.)
516 See: Tianjin Ankang website: http://www.abc-tj-abc.com/ankang/. For a fascinating book-length account of daily life and work at the Tianjin Ankang, written by a deputy bureau chief of the Tianjin PSB, see: Liao Jiangsen, *Jingshenbing Beiwanglu* (A Memorandum of Mental Illness), *Jingguan Jiaoyu Chubanshe* (Police Officers Publishing House), Beijing, December 1994; volume marked: *neibu faxing* (restricted circulation.)
517 See: Ren Lijun and Liu Yongsheng, "*40 Nian Shouwang Feichang Shijie*" (Forty Years of Standing Guard Over an Extraordinary World), *Fazhi Wanbao*, 21 July 2004.
518 These regulations are mentioned in *Renmin Gong'an Bao*, May 18, 1990; however, no copies of the documents have as yet come to light.
519 Long Qingchun (ed.), *Sifa Jingshen Yixue Jianding Zixun Jieda*, p.152. The twenty places having Ankang facilities as of 1992 were the cities of Tianjin, Beijing, Shanghai, Shenyang, Haerbin, Dalian, Tangshan, Wuhan, Xi'an, Suzhou, Chengdu, Hangzhou, Hefei, Fuzhou, Gongzhuling (Jilin), Ningbo, Jinhua and Shaoxing; and also, Ningxia Autonomous Region, and Inner Mongolia Autonomous Region (city locations for the latter two are unknown). As of late 1999, the total number of Ankang facilities was reportedly still twenty (Zheng Zhanpei et al., "*Woguo Sifa Jingshenbingxue Jianding Gongzuo de Xianzhuang ji Zhanwang* [Present Situation and Future Prospects of China's Judicial Psychiatric Appraisals Work]," *Chinese Journal of Psychiatry*, 1999, Vol.32, No.4, p.201). The source for the 2001 figure of 22 Ankang facilities is Kang Ming, op cit.

Finally, an Internet search by the present author in August 2004 found a further nine confirmed or suspected Ankang facilities, on top of the twenty that were known as of 1992. They are located in Guangzhou, Changsha, Handan, Jining, Qingdao, Zhengzhou, Shihezi (Xinjiang Uighyur Autonomous Region), Hainan Province, and Jiangxi Province (city locations for the latter two are unknown).

Diseases, the average length of stay for mentally ill offenders in the Ankang system is five and a half years, with some inmates being held for as long as twenty years.[520]

Large Ankang centres can accommodate around 1,000 inmates;[521] and the largest one, the Tianjin facility, is believed to have a considerably higher capacity. Moreover, the total number of people admitted to the Ankang system over the past fifteen years or so is remarkably high. According to the Ministry of Public Security, there were 35,000 admissions during the period 1988-93; and a further 75,000 admissions – 30 percent of whom had committed homicide – took place over the subsequent decade. The same source noted that as of 1993, the total capacity of mental hospitals of all kinds in China (including hospitals run by the ministries of health, civil affairs and public security) was only 90,000 beds, of which 6,072 were located in Ankang hospitals. So it seems clear that despite the substantial number of inmates who are held for five or more years, there is also a high turnover of shorter-term patients within the system. Many of these are likely to be drug addicts compulsorily admitted for detoxification programs – an area of work in which, along with HIV-AIDS testing and treatment, the Ankang system has become increasingly active in recent years[522] – and also voluntary, non-criminal patients (both the Tianjin and Hangzhou Ankangs, for example advertise their services to the general public), together with involuntary civil commitment cases. In addition, Ankang psychiatrists were said to have performed a total of 24,000 forensic psychiatric appraisals between 1993 and 2003, while the Ministry increased the total number of police officers assigned to work in the Ankang network by a figure of 3,500 over the same period.[523] The government's stated goal is eventually to establish one

---

520 Gu Xiangdong et al., "*Shehui Jineng Xunlian Dui 32 Li Zhuyuan Manxing Jingshenfenliezheng Huanzhe de Liaoxiao Guancha* (An Examination of the Efficacy of Social Skills Training for 32 Chronic Schizophrenic Patients)," Chinese Journal of Nervous and Mental Diseases, Vol.20, No.2, pp.85-87.
521 Lin Huai, *Jingshen Jibing Huanzhe Xingshi Zeren Nengli He Yiliao Jianhu Cuoshi*, pp. 54-55.
522 As of February 2004, altogether 13 Ankang hospitals had set up compulsory drug detoxification centres. (See: Liu Zhenqing and Chen Jingyi, "*Zhongguo Gong'an Xitong de Jingshen Weisheng Fuwu*" (China's Public Security System of Mental Health Services), *Shanghai Jingshen Yixue* (Shanghai Archives of Psychiatry), 16 February 2004; available at: http://www.21jk.com.cn/p/.) According to the website of the Tianjin Ankang, more than 8000 people have undergone drug rehabilitation there since 1992 (see: http://www.abc-tj-abc.com/ankang/index.htm.) For a detailed account of the drug detoxification programme at the Beijing Ankang, see Ren Lijun and Liu Yongsheng, op cit. For an account of the same programme at the Tianjin Ankang, see "*Jiedu Suoli Duguo 100 Xiaoshi Nü Jizhe Tiyan 'Jiedu'*" (A Female Reporter Experiences "Drug Detox" during a 100-hour Visit to a Drug Rehabilitation Centre), *Mei Ri Xin Bao*, 6 April 2002, available at: http://news.sina.com.cn/s/2002-04-06/1615537425.html. For a detailed description of various unlawful punishment methods commonly used by police in the Ankang drug addiction treatment centres, see: Lao Yan, "*Qiangzhi Jiedu Suo Shi Zenmoyang Jinxing Wenming Guanlide?*" (What are the "Civilized Management Methods" Used in Drug Rehabilitation Centres?), 7 June 2003; available at: members.lycos.co.uk/sixiang002/Shame/ShouRong/ShouRong015.txt.

Significantly, China's Ankang network is now also playing a key coordinating and implementation role in the country's HIV-AIDS testing and treatment programme. See, for example: "*Beijing Jiang Dui Ben Shi Aicibing Ren Shixing Mianfei Kangbingdu Yaowu Zhiliao*" (Beijing Set to Supply Free Antiviral Medical Treatment to the City's HIV-AIDS Sufferers), *Beijing Wanbao*, 14 July 2003.
523 See: "*Gong'an Bu Fubuzhang Tian Qiyu zai Quanguo Jingshenbing Fangzhi Kangfu Gongzuo Huiyi Kaimushi-shang de Jianghua*" (Deputy Minister of Public Security Tian Qiyu's Speech at the National Work Conference on Mental Illness Prevention, Cure and Recovery), 13 May 1993; *Gong'an Bu Fubuzhang Luo Feng*, "*Zai Quanguo Di Sanci Jingshen Weisheng Gongzuo Huiyi-shang de Jianghua*" (Speech by Deputy Minister of Public Security Luo Feng at the Third National Conference on Mental Health Work), 2003 (exact date not given), available at: http://www.cdpf.org.cn/; and Kang Ming, op cit. According to the latter source, as of approximately 2001, the total capacity of the Ankang network had risen to 7,352 beds.

Ankang centre for every city in China with a population of one million or above.[524] The entire Ankang network is directly administered by Bureau No. 13 of the Ministry of Public Security (*Gong'an Bu Shisan Ju*)[525] – the same police department that runs all the country's pre-trial criminal detention centres (*kanshousuo*) and also Qincheng Prison, the ultra-secure facility that since 1954 has housed many of China's top political prisoners.[526]

Involuntary Psychosurgery

One of the most worrying features of the Ankang custody system today is the considerable and growing interest that has been shown by police psychiatric specialists over the past two decades in the use of brain surgery as a means of treating severe mental illness. As we briefly noted in Chapter 3, Chinese psychiatrists experimented with psychosurgery in the early 1950s but abandoned it thereafter under doctrinal pressure from their Soviet colleagues. Starting in the early to mid-1980s, however, major mental hospitals in China once again began to develop surgical capacity and experience in carrying out this most controversial of psychiatric treatments. These operations have reportedly involved less drastic forms of surgical intervention than those performed in the 1950s, but they are nonetheless

---

524 *Renmin Gong'an Bao*, May 24, 1988, p.1.
525 See: Liu Zhenqing and Chen Jingyi, "*Zhongguo Gong'an Xitong de Jingshen Weisheng Fuwu*" (China's Public Security System of Mental Health Services), *Shanghai Jingshen Yixue* (Shanghai Archives of Psychiatry), 16 February 2004. According to this article, "some Ankang facilities are run by the Public Security purely as prisons" (*youde shi chun gong'an de jiansuo guanli*). The article is the most detailed currently available on the logistical aspects of the Ankang network.
526 The MPS's Bureau No.13 used to run all of the country's prison facilities for sentenced criminals as well, but in July 1983 – in an important move to separate the criminal investigative and the judicial custodial functions of the legal system – these were transferred to the jurisdiction of the Ministry of Justice (MoJ). However, the MPS retained control over Qincheng Prison and certain other "specialized" detention units in China thereafter. According to a 1990 confidential police publication,

> Qincheng Prison, for example, and also the labour reform units in Tibet, fall under the administration of the public security authorities; and in Xinjiang, several dozen labour reform units are run by the Production and Construction Corps." (See: Thoughts on Reforming the Labour Reform System's Administrative Structure," *Laogai Laojiao Lilun Yanjiu* [Theoretical Studies in Labour Reform and Labour Re-education], 1990, No.2, p.43.)

The MPS also operates an unknown number of other secret facilities similar to Qincheng Prison, as the following passage from a joint MPS and MoJ directive of June 1983 makes clear:

> In view of the ongoing requirements of our struggle against the enemy, , the public security departments will need to continue to maintain a number of prisons across the country for the incarceration of spies, espionage agents and other major criminals, and also for criminals with knowledge of state secrets. Detailed plans for this are to be drawn up by the Ministry of Public Security and submitted to the CPC Central Committee for approval and authorization. (See: "Various Regulations by the Ministry of Public Security and the Ministry of Justice Concerning the Detailed Implementation of the Central Committee's Transferral of the Work of Labour Reform and Labour Re-education Over to the Judicial Administrative Departments," 6 June 1983, in Zhonghua Renmin Gongheguo Falü Guifanxing Jieshi Jicheng (A Collection of Standard Interpretations of the Laws of the PRC – Supplementary Volume, Jilin People's Press, December 1991, p.813.)

hazardous and irreversible.[527] According to a Western scholar who performed extensive field research in Chinese mental hospitals during the 1980s,

> Psychosurgery is also re-emerging. During a visit to Guangzhou in 1988 I was told that one hospital had provided 20 patients to undergo this kind of surgery in the previous two years. In a visit to a hospital in Beijing in 1989, I discovered that doctors in Beijing and Tientsin [Tianjin] were collaborating on a psychosurgery project. It was clear from reading some of the files of the patients, who had had psychosurgery in Guangzhou, that selection and monitoring before or after the operation, as well as the procedure itself, gave great cause for concern.[528]

Other studies published by Chinese psychiatrists themselves have indicated a further rise in the use of psychosurgery in China since then.[529] Furthermore, much of the country's medical effort in this area appears to be going on behind Ankang hospital walls. According to a reliable eyewitness report, the Ankang forensic-psychiatric facility in the city of Tianjin had by 1987 established a large and technically advanced unit for carrying out psychosurgical operations; the director of the institute at the time was a neurosurgeon, and dozens of lobotomies and similar brain operations were reportedly being performed on inmates there each year.[530] The existence of this PSB-administered brain surgery unit was officially confirmed three years later by an article in the *People's Public Security News*.[531]

Articles in the Chinese medical literature over the past decade reviewing and assessing the results of the country's psychosurgery programme have emphasized how effective it has proved to be in reducing not only violent behaviour (*baoli xingwei*) by the mentally ill, but also what is termed merely "impulsive behaviour" (*chongdong xingwei*) on their part. The reports also indicate that the main

---

527 Technical advances in recent decades have led to the widespread use internationally of less invasive forms of psychosurgery than those generally used before. Known as "stereotactic" techniques (in Chinese: *liti dingxiang shoushu*), these allow more precise and less damaging surgical interventions – for example, leucotomy, cingulotomy and capsulotomy – to be carried out in place of the previously used "broad spectrum" lobotomy procedure.

528 Veronica Pearson, "Law, Rights and Psychiatry in the People's Republic of Psychiatry," p. 420. Pearson continues by saying, "Other matters for concern are the lack of consent to treatment, (particularly hazardous and irreversible practices), the custodial nature of most settings, the lack of any effective protection against compulsory detention, the summary removal of civil status, and the lack of an appeal mechanism." It should be noted, however, that she then states: "Reading through hundreds of case files, I have found no evidence that sane people are being detained for political offences. When the direct question has been put as to why this does not happen in China, the consensus is that there is no need. There are other ways of dealing with dissidents that do not require the inappropriate utilization of a scarce and expensive hospital bed." Pearson continues, "There are undoubtedly people in psychiatric hospitals whose breakdowns have been precipitated by political events, or persecution for political reasons, but that is a different matter." Although a correct and reasonable observation in itself, the latter point by no means exhausts the wide repertoire and typology of "cases of a political nature" found in China since 1949. In particular, it misses the core question of why, in China, such people are commonly dealt with on the forensic (criminal) psychiatric track, rather than under normal mental healthcare procedures.

529 See, for example: "Observations on the Effectiveness of Stereotactic Brain Surgery in Cases of Schizophrenia with Aggressive Behaviour," *Chinese Journal of Nervous and Mental Diseases*, 1992, Vol.18, No.3, pp.153-155; and "A Follow-up Review of Stereotactic Brain Surgery in Cases of Chronic Schizophrenia," *Zhonghua Shenjing Waike Zazhi (Chinese Journal of Neurosurgery)*, 1992, Vol.8, No.4, pp.263-265.

530 The source of this information is a Western doctor who wishes to remain anonymous.

531 See: "*Gong'an Xitong Jingshenbing Guan-Zhi Gongzuo Chengxiao Xianzhu* (Public Security System's Work of Custody and Treatment of the Mentally Ill Achieves Conspicuous Results)," *Renmin Gong'an Bao (People's Public Security News)*, May 18, 1990, p.1.

targets of these surgical practices have been persons subjected to involuntary psychiatric committal. According to one such study published in 1993, and written by psychiatrists from the Shanghai Mental Health Centre:

> All the subjects were chronic mental patients who displayed extremely severe forms of impulsive behaviour, and who for many years, for lack of any effective cure, had been kept in isolation and placed in leather handcuff restraints all day long. Starting in April 1985, we performed multi-target stereotactic brain surgery on numerous patients.[532] According to subsequent short-term clinical observations, either a conspicuous reduction or a complete cessation of impulsive behaviour was achieved in more than 75 percent of the cases, along with an overall reduction in other mental symptoms.[533]

After long-term clinical observations carried out seven years later, the success and effectiveness rate had reportedly risen to 89 percent. The psychiatrists concluded from this study that such psychosurgery was "uniquely effective" in treating both aggressive mental patients and also those suffering from "intractable mental conditions characterized by impulsive behaviour." Psychosurgery has even been used in China to "treat" schizophrenia – a form of mental illness that in other countries is regarded as a specific contraindication for any form of brain surgery. [534]

While psychosurgery has undergone a cautious revival in the West in recent years, the medical consensus is that it should be used only in very rare and carefully selected cases. According to a recent study by two physicians in the U.S., for example,

> [T]here remains a small percentage of patients with treatment refractory psychiatric diseases that might be considered for surgical treatment. However, because of the ethical, legal and social implications of psychosurgery, only a limited number of surgical procedures are carried out at a handful of medical centres in the world today.[535]

---

532 See Note 527 above. In this case, however, the "multi-target stereotactic surgery" (*duo ba liti dingxiang shoushu*) was far from being a minor operation, since according to the article it involved the surgical lesioning or ablation of three separate parts of the brain: the cingulum, amygdala, and nucleus caudatus. It should be noted that most forms of brain surgery are not controversial either from a medical or a human rights standpoint – its use for the removal of brain tumours being only the most obvious example. China, like many other countries, has extensive experience and capacity in these latter, quite legitimate forms of neurosurgery. (The country's leading authority in this field is Wang Zhongcheng, author of the textbook *Shenjing Waikexue* (Neurosurgery), Hebei Kexue Chubanshe, May 1998.) It is psychosurgery – the use of brain surgery to change human behaviour – that has attracted general international criticism and condemnation over the past several decades.
533 Wu Lieming, "*Nao Liti Dingxiang Shoushu Zhiliao Manxing Jingshenbing Suoban Chongdong Xingwei de Qinian Suifang*" (A Clinical Review of the Use of Stereotactic Brain Surgery to Treat Chronic Mental Illness Accompanied by Impulsive Behaviour), *Shanghai Jingshen Yixue* (Shanghai Archives of Psychiatry), 1993, Vol. 5, No. 2, pp.134-5.
534 See: Xu Peijiang et al, "*Nao Liti Dingxiang Shu Zhiliao 6 Li Manxing Jingshen Fenliezheng 7 Nian Suifang*" (Seven-year Clinical Follow-up on the Use of Stereotactic Brain Surgery in Six Cases of Chronic Schizophrenia), *Zhongguo Minzheng Yixue Zazhi* (China Civil Affairs Medical Journal), 1996, Vol.8, No.3, pp.145-6.
535 See: G. Rees Cosgrove MD and Scott L. Rauch MD, "Psychosurgery" (undated), p.2; available on the Internet at: http://neurosurgery.mgh.harvard.edu/Functional/psysurg.htm. The authors work at the Departments of Neurosurgery and Psychiatry, Massachusetts General Hospital, and at Harvard Medical School, Boston

It can be stated with certainty that in the vast majority of countries these do not include institutions for the criminally insane, where patients' "informed consent" to such hazardous and irreversible procedures is, by definition, impossible to obtain.[536] Any medical operations of this nature are expressly banned under the U.N.'s 1991 "Principles for the Protection of Persons with Mental Illness and for the Improvement of Mental Health Care," Article 11.14 of which states: "Psychosurgery and other intrusive and irreversible treatments for mental illness shall never be carried out on a patient who is an involuntary patient in a mental health facility."

The precise extent of the use of psychosurgery in China's Ankang facilities today is of course not known. More than an inkling, however, can be gleaned from the official website of just one of these facilities – the Shandong Province Ankang Hospital, which is located in the city of Jining. According to an article by Chen Chengyu, a chief surgeon at the Shandong Ankang, this police-run custodial institution established a "stereotactic brain surgery unit" in 1988. The unit, Chen states, "was one of the earliest to be set up in Shandong province"; it currently provides "procedures that are to be found nowhere else in the province"; its surgical ward "occupancy rate is greater than 90 percent" and its "surgical treatment success rate is over 96 percent."[537] While there have been no reports of political dissidents or other such detainees being subjected to brain operations in China, the infliction

---

Massachusetts. See also: "Hazardous and Irreversible Treatments in Psychiatry: Who Decides?" SK&F Publications (London), 1980, Vol. 3, No. 6.

536 The rules on psychosurgery issued by the Council of Europe may be taken as indicative of the mainstream of international legal and medical opinion on this topic. In its February 1983 *Rules Concerning the Legal Protection of Persons Suffering from Mental Disorder Placed as Involuntary Patients*, the Council stated (in Article 5.2):

"A treatment which is not yet generally recognised by medical science or presents a serious risk of causing permanent brain damage or adversely altering the personality of the patient may be given only if the doctor considers it indispensable and if the patient, after being informed, has given his express consent."

Similarly, the Council of Europe's *Recommendation 1235 on Psychiatry and Human Rights*, issued in April 1994, states in Article 7(ii) b:

"Lobotomies and electroconvulsive therapy may not be performed unless informed written consent has been given by the patient or a person, counsellor or guardian, chosen by the patient as his or her representative and unless the decision has been confirmed by a select committee not composed exclusively of psychiatric experts."

Finally, the Council of Europe in its January 2000 "White Paper" on the rights of involuntary mental patients stated:

"[T]he effectiveness of psychosurgery has not been established by appropriate controlled research. Thus, where States continue to sanction the use of it, the consent of the patient should be an absolute prerequisite for its use. Furthermore, the decision to use psychosurgery should in every case be confirmed by a committee which is not exclusively composed of psychiatric experts. The Working Party [on Bioethics] considered that in each member State the legislators should establish special protocols for the administration of psychosurgery. In so far as there is no clear proof of the effectiveness of psychosurgery, countries which still permit its use should introduce a system for recording full information about any operations carries out." (Council of Europe, *White Paper on the Protection of the Human Rights and Dignity of People Suffering Mental Disorder, Especially Those Placed as Involuntary Patients in a Psychiatric Establishment*, 3 January 2000, Strasbourg.

537 See: Chen Chengyu, "*Liti Dingxiang Ji Gongnengxing Shenjing Waike Zhiliao Zhongxin*" (The Stereotactic and Functional-Neurosurgery Treatment Centre), 30 March 2004; available on the website of the Shandong Province Ankang Hospital at: www.jsby.cn/Article_Show.asp?ArticleID=539. The article includes several photos of the brain surgery unit and also of a person undergoing brain surgery there.

of psychosurgery on detainees of any kind can only be described as ethically repugnant and legally deplorable.

In addition, Ankang neurosurgeons are currently directly involved in experimental psychosurgery in China to treat drug addiction. This is particularly troubling because most or all of the country's Ankang facilities now also operate large, compulsory drug rehabilitation centres. According to a series of reports in the official news media in 2004, these surgical operations involve the partial destruction of the brain's "reward mechanism" centre, a procedure claimed to remove the addict's craving for drugs. In a widely-publicized first such operation in the northeast of China, in July 2004 the director of the Shenyang Ankang facility, a Dr. Xie, together with a neurosurgeon from the Guangzhou Airforce Hospital, performed this operation on a young female drug addict named Li Hong.[538] Numerous similar operations are reported to have been carried out at the San Jiu Brain Hospital in Guangzhou since 2001,[539] and in May 2004 *The Australian* newspaper carried the following commentary on one particular instance that had recently been performed there:

> "I am not aware of it being done anywhere else in the world at the moment. It is highly experimental and I would be very sceptical about its efficacy," said Jefferey Rosenfeld, director of neurosurgery at The Alfred Hospital and Monash University in Melbourne. It sounded like a revamped version of the "psychosurgery" used to treat homosexuals and violent prison inmates in the 1950s, he said. It also carried risks such as brain haemorrhage, infection, abscesses, meningitis and epilepsy – "and that's just for starters", said Professor Rosenfeld.[540]

As we shall see in Chapter 9, the Chinese government has thus far refused all requests by the World Psychiatric Association to send a delegation of independent medical inspectors to China to visit, among other things, the country's Ankang facilities. The existence of a steadily expanding programme of involuntary psychosurgery in these institutions is probably high on the government's list of reasons for refusing to permit any such outside scrutiny of their work and activities.

Criteria and Procedures for Admission to Ankang Custody

The institutional model for the new Ankang forensic-psychiatric regime set up in China after 1987 was the Shanghai Municipal Hospital for Custody and Treatment of the Mentally Ill, which had been

---

538 See: "*Zhiji Dongbei Shouli Jiedu Kai'eshu 2 Xiaoshi 45 Fen Shoushu Chenggong Wancheng*" (An Eyewitness Account of Northeast China's First Successful Frontal-Lobe Brain Operation, Lasting 2 Hours and 45 Minutes, to Cure Drug Addiction), *Dongbei Xinwen Wang* (Northeast News Net), 5 July 2004; available at: www.fx120.net/news/news-map/2004070509502388801.htm.
539 See: "Will Operations Root Out Desire for Drugs?" People's Daily Online, 4 July 2004; available at: www.xinhuanet.com.
540 See "Brain Surgery 'Cure' for Heroin Addicts," *The Australian*, 29 May 2004; available at: www.sunnetwork.org/news/science/science.asp?ID=5266. Apparently, similar brain surgery on drug addicts has been carried out in Russia in recent years. According to a recent article, the Institute of the Human Brain in St. Petersburg has performed 335 such operations since 1999; however, following adverse side effects in a number of cases, the city's Prosecutor's Office ordered a ban on any more such operations in August 2002. See Nick Paton Walsh, "Russia Bans Brain Surgery on Drug Addicts," *The Guardian*, 9 August 2002; available at: http://www.guardian.co.uk/Archive/Article/0,4273,4478290,00.html.

first established in May 1985.[541] This institute, now known as the Shanghai Ankang, is located in the same part of the city that previously housed "Jiangwan No. 5," the scene of Mr. C's ordeal during the Cultural Revolution;[542] indeed, it is highly probable that they are one and the same place.[543] It is also where the female dissident whose account was cited at the start of this chapter was detained in the late 1980s.

In April 1986, the Shanghai government took the national lead by promulgating a detailed set of regulations for the compulsory hospitalisation of mentally ill people who "create incidents or disasters" (*zhaoshi zhaohuo*).[544] These regulations are still the most specific thus far issued in China on the crucial procedural matter of how mentally ill offenders actually get admitted to Ankang care: expert forensic psychiatric appraisal of the detainee was to be performed, but once a finding of legal non-imputability had been made, the public security authorities were then accorded complete authority to issue the necessary paperwork for compulsory psychiatric admission; the courts had no visible role in the process.[545]

The same complete absence of any role by the judiciary can clearly be seen from supplementary regulations issued by the Shanghai legal authorities as late as 2003:

> If the public security organs discover that a criminal suspect or defendant during a stage of the criminal procedure has a mental illness and lacks the capacity to undergo trial, they should annul the case and deliver the person to the Ankang Hospital of the Municipal PSB to undergo compulsory custody and treatment in accordance with law.[546]

---

541 The Chinese name for this institute was "*Shanghai Shi Jingshenbing Guan-Zhi Yiyuan.*" In 1987, it was renamed "*Shanghai Shi Gong'an Ju Ankang Jingshenbing Guan-Zhi Yuan*" (Shanghai Municipal Public Security Bureau Ankang Institute for the Custody and Treatment of the Mentally Ill). The same wording is now used (after substitution of the specific city or province name in question) as a uniform designation for all the various Ankang centres in China.
542 See p.116 above.
543 The Shanghai Ankang was for many years located on Guoquan Bei Lu, just north of Fudan University; as of August 2004, however, its address was listed as being No. 2 Yin Gao Lu, which is just around the corner from Guoquan Bei Lu. While this may simply be the institute's main administrative office, it is also possible that a new Ankang facility has recently been built at the Yin Gao Lu site.
544 "*Shanghai Shi Jianhu Zhiliao Guanli Zhaoshi Zhaohuo Jingshenbingren Tiaoli* (Shanghai Municipal Regulations on the Guardianship, Treatment and Management of Mentally Ill People Who Create Incidents or Disasters)," promulgated on August 29, 1986, in *Shanghai Gong'an Nianjian, 1988* (*Shanghai Public Security Yearbook, 1988*), (Shanghai Social Sciences Publishing House [volume marked: "for internal distribution only"], December 1988), pp.343-346. The regulations came into force on October 1 the same year. See also Shanghai's "*Zhaoshi Zhaohuo Jingshenbingren de Shouzhi Guiding*" (Regulations on the Admission and Treatment of Mentally Ill People Who Create Incidents or Disasters), undated copy available at: http://police.shqp.gov.cn/gb/content/2003-07/09/content_324.htm. Elsewhere, "incidents" (zhaoshi) are defined as misdemeanours punishable under the Security Administrative Punishment Regulations, while "disasters" (zhaohuo) correspond to offences punishable under the Criminal Law.
545 An argument that the courts should be given a leading role in this process is made in Lin Huai, *Jingshen Jibing Huanzhe Xingshi Zeren Nengli He Yiliao Jianhu Cuoshi,* pp.53-54.
546 "*Shanghai Shi Gaoji Renmin Fayuan, Shanghai Shi Renmin Jianchayuan, Shanghai Shi Gong'an Ju Guanyu Banli Fanzui Xianyiren, Beigaorenzai Xingshi Susong Qijian Huan Jingshenbing de Anjian de Guiding*" (Provisions of the Shanghai Higher People's Court, Shanghai Municipal People's Procuracy and Shanghai Municipal Public Security Bureau on the Handling of Cases Where Criminal Suspects or Defendants Become Mentally Ill During

The fact that the Shanghai Higher People's Court was itself one of the three law enforcement bodies that issued these regulations only serves to show that the complete exclusion of the judiciary from the criminal-psychiatric committals process is not the consequence of any accidental oversight or lack of adequate forethought about due process concerns. Rather, Shanghai's senior judicial authorities themselves appear to be quite uninterested in deciding or monitoring the fate of criminal suspects and defendants whom the police identify as being mentally ill and incapable of undergoing trial. In recent years, municipal and provincial governments elsewhere in China, including Tianjin, Guangdong, Shenyang, Heilongjiang, Dalian and other cities and provinces, have all issued similar sets of regulations.[547]

According to an article written by several Ankang psychiatrists in 1996,

> Ankang hospitals...are meant to be specialized hospitals that serve the goals of public order by taking in and treating mentally ill people who create disastrous incidents of various kinds. As the Ministry of Public Security calculated in 1993, there are approximately 12 million severely mentally ill people in China, more than 1.3 million of whom pose a serious danger to public order; it is therefore essential that every province in China should establish its own Ankang hospital.[548]

As we saw earlier, alleged mentally-ill political dissidents figure prominently on the authorities' target list of those who "create disastrous incidents" and who must therefore, for the protection of society, be incarcerated in Ankang facilities. The article as a whole painted a depressing picture of conditions within the Ankang hospital system as of early 1996: a very high patient-to-doctor and nurse ratio, severe underfunding by the government, and serious lack of capacity leading to a dense overcrowding of inmates. This scenario will be broadly familiar to those working in high-security institutes for the criminally insane in most countries, but in China's case it serves to dramatize the

---

the Criminal Process), Document *Hu-Jian-Fa* [2003] No.272 (month and day of issue not available); available on the Internet at *Dongfang Lüshi Wang* (Eastern Lawyers Network): www.lawyers.org.cn.

547 See "*Tianjin Shi Shouzhi Guanli Weihai Shehui Zhi'an Jingshenbingren Banfa* (Tianjin Municipal Methods for the Shelter and Management of Mentally Ill People Who Endanger Public Order)," undated and unpublished document on file with the author; "*Guangdong Sheng Shourong Anzhi Zhaohuo Zhaoshi Jingshenbingren Zanxing Banfa* (Guangdong Provincial Temporary Methods for the Shelter and Settlement of Mentally Ill People Who Create Disasters or Incidents)," issued by the Guangdong Provincial People's Government on January 17, 1990, in *Guangdong Sheng Fagui Guizhang Huibian* (*A Compilation of Guangdong Provincial Laws, Regulations and Rules [January 1989-December 1990]*), edited and published by the Office of the Guangdong Provincial People's Government, pp.275-276; "*Dalian Shi Jianhu Zhiliao Guanli Zhaoshi Zhaohuo Jingshenbingren Tiaoli*" (Dalian Municipal Regulations on the Guardianship, Treatment and Management of Mentally Ill People Who Create Disasters or Incidents), passed by the Standing Committee of the Dalian Municipal People's Congress on 4 November 1992 and effective as of 17 December 1992, available at: www.dl.gov.cn/togov/law/local/688_15942.htm; "*Heilongjiang Sheng Jianhu Zhiliao Guanli Weihai Shehui Zhi'an Jingshenbingren Tiaoli*" (Heilongjiang Provincial Regulations on the Guardianship, Treatment and Management of Mentally Ill People Who Endanger Public Order), passed on 9 February 1996 and effective as of 1 March 1996; and "Shenyang Shi Shouzhi Weihai Shehui Zhi'an Jingshenbingren Banfa" (Shenyang Municipality's Methods for the Custody and Treatment of Mentally Ill People Who Endanger Public Order), promulgated by the Shenyang Municipal People's Government (date unknown), available at: www.obv.cn/flyz/dffg/004/8841298.htm.

548 Tang Xiaofeng et al, "A Survey of the Current State of China's Ankang Hospitals," *Shanghai Archives of Psychiatry*, 1996, Vol. 8, No.1, pp.24-5; a full translation of this article appears in: Robin Munro, *Dangerous Minds: Political Psychiatry in China Today and its Origins in the Mao Era* (op cit), pp.248-52.

plight of the peaceful dissidents and religious nonconformists who end up being confined in such conditions alongside genuinely psychotic and dangerous offenders.

Specific criteria outlining the various types and categories of mentally ill offenders who are to be compulsorily admitted to Ankang custody can be found in several published sources in China. These criteria vary slightly from source to source, but the most complete and exhaustive version appears in an official encyclopaedia of police work published in 1990. The encyclopaedia begins by explaining the three main types of people who are to be taken into police psychiatric custody:

> The first are those commonly known as "romantic maniacs" (*hua fengzi*),[549] who roam around the streets, grab food and drink from others, expose themselves naked, or look unkempt and dishevelled, and so have an adverse effect on social decorum.
>
> The second are those commonly known as "political maniacs" (*zhengzhi fengzi*), who shout reactionary slogans, write reactionary banners and reactionary letters, make anti-government speeches in public, and express opinions on important domestic and international affairs.
>
> The third are those commonly known as "aggressive maniacs" (*wu fengzi*), who beat and curse people, pursue women, elderly people and children, smash up public property, commit murder or arson, or who otherwise endanger people's lives and the safety of property.

The police encyclopaedia then lists the following more specific and operational criteria for dealing with mentally ill people falling within the three categories:[550]

> The public security organs have primary responsibility for the management and treatment of the following five kinds of severely mentally ill persons, all of whom pose a relatively grave threat to social order:
>
> 1. Persons carrying knives who commit violent or injurious acts; those who are suicidal; and those who commit arson or other acts that seriously disturb social order, with definite consequences.
>
> 2. Persons who disrupt the normal work of Party and government offices or who disrupt normal work and production in enterprises, scientific and educational institutions, thereby posing a danger.
>
> 3. Persons who frequently expose themselves naked, or otherwise harm social morals, in busy crowded areas or in public places.

---

549 The term "*hua fengzi*" (literally: "flower crazies") is a euphemistic one whose broad meaning encompasses aspects of the English terms "hippy," "nutcase," and "sex maniac"; however, it does not have the often violent or non-consensual overtones of the latter term.

550 Another important category of persons liable to be sent to Ankang facilities is those who develop "prison psychoses" of various kinds (as discussed above) during their confinement in regular prisons. The incidence of this type of mental illness has apparently risen sharply in China in recent years. One significant subgroup of such sufferers is reportedly those sentenced to death and awaiting execution; if the stress and anxiety of impending execution leads them to become mentally ill, they are regarded as "incompetent to undergo punishment" and are then placed in Ankang custody for treatment until they become sane enough to be executed. Moreover, prisoners who stage hunger strikes in jail are often regarded as suffering from a subtype of this particular illness and are therefore also sent to Ankang centres for secure psychiatric treatment. For more information on prison psychosis, see p.151 and Note 322 above.

4. Persons who shout reactionary slogans, or who stick up or distribute reactionary banners and leaflets, thereby exerting an undesirable political influence.[551]

5. Mentally ill people who drift in from other areas and disrupt the public order of society.

Upon encountering any of these five types of people, the public security organs are to take them into custody for treatment.[552]

As was noted earlier, most countries find it necessary to maintain institutions for the criminally insane in order to protect members of the public from psychotic offenders who pose a genuine danger to society. At least in the modern era, however, few countries have ever regarded the kinds of mentally ill people listed under points 2 and 4 above as being legitimate targets for any form of forced psychiatric custody, far less confinement in an institute for the criminally insane. The former Soviet Union was the most prominent such country, and to the extent that it now follows a similar set of practices, China's revamped and enlarged Ankang system is performing much the same role as that of the Soviet Special Psychiatric Hospitals, where hundreds and possibly thousands of peaceful political dissidents, petitioners, religious dissenters and whistleblowers of various kinds were incarcerated without valid medical or legal justification.

Finally, the police encyclopaedia noted: "The taking of mentally ill people into custody is especially important during major public festivals and when foreign guests arrive for visits, and it should be appropriately reinforced at such times." In a speech given as recently as 2003, moreover, China's Deputy Minister of Public Security specifically reaffirmed the "necessity and importance" of these preventive custody-style operations. According to the Deputy Minister,

During major festivals or holidays and at other sensitive periods, the basic-level public security organs must, as a matter of urgent priority, increase surveillance and control over mentally ill complainants and petitioners…in order to prevent them from making any trouble or creating sudden disturbances….The police must be ready to pounce at a moment's notice.[553]

---

551 "*Huhan fandong kouhao, zhangtie sanfa fandong biaoyu, chuandan, zaocheng buliang zhengzhi yingxiangde.*"
552 *Zhongguo Gong'an Baike Quanshu* (China Encyclopaedia of Public Security), (Jilin People's Publishing House, February 1990), p.1964. A similar set of criteria for enforcing police custody of the mentally ill is listed in Zeng Wenyou et al. (ed.), *Jing Guan Bi Du* (*Essential Reading for Police Officials*), (Police Officials Publishing House, Beijing, October 1992), (volume marked "for internal circulation only"), p.163. A more readily accessible source, giving roughly the same kinds of guidelines and discussing the role and purposes of the Ankang system more generally, is Liu Dechao, "*Dui Weihai Shehui Zhi'an de Jingshenbingren de Chuli* (On the Handling of Mentally Ill People Who Endanger the Public Order of Society)," *Xiandai Faxue* (*Modern Jurisprudence*), 1990, No.2, pp.69-71. In addition, a 1996 study states that the various criteria for compulsory Ankang admissions were first formulated at the First National Public Security Conference on Custody and Treatment of the Mentally Ill, held in Tianjin in December 1987. See Lin Huai, *Jingshen Jibing Huanzhe Xingshi Zeren Nengli He Yiliao Jianhu Cuoshi*, p.111.
553 See: *Gong'an Bu Fubuzhang Luo Feng*, "*Zai Quanguo Di Sanci Jingshen Weisheng Gongzuo Huiyi-shang de Jianghua*" (Speech by Deputy Minister of Public Security Luo Feng at the Third National Conference on Mental Health Work), 2003 (exact date not known), available at: http://www.cdpf.org.cn/. The rounding-up by police of mentally ill citizens in advance of important public events and visits by foreign dignitaries was also a highly characteristic feature of political psychiatry in the former Soviet Union.

The Case of Wang Chaoru

As the following case serves to illustrate, urban "clean-up operations" of the kind mentioned above are implemented with brutal thoroughness by China's police and can sometimes prove fatal for those concerned. In March 1993, as part of China's bid to host the 2000 Olympic Games, a delegation from the International Olympic Committee arrived in Beijing to inspect the city's sporting and other facilities. Over the preceding few weeks, among other preparations designed to enhance China's chances of winning its bid for the games, the Beijing authorities had removed large numbers of homeless, indigent or mentally ill people from the streets of the city and shipped them out of town either to their original place of residence or to temporary holding centres, and in the case of mentally ill targets of this "cleanup" operation, the Beijing Ankang facility was also used for this purpose. One such person was a 41-year old mentally retarded man named Wang Chaoru, who lived with his parents in the southern part of the city. According to a detailed account of Wang's case that was subsequently written by Nicholas Kristof and Sheryl WuDunn, the Beijing correspondents of the New York Times during that period, a policeman arrived at the family's door, accompanied by a woman named Zhang from the local Street Committee, two days before the IOC delegation's arrival in Beijing:

> The policeman wanted to take Wang away, but the retarded man began shrieking his protests. So the policeman and Zhang left. The next morning, Zhang returned, this time with two policemen. They had no arrest warrant, no detention warrant, and they didn't suggest that Wang had broken any law or endangered anybody. They didn't give any reason for wanting to take him away, but they insisted that he had to leave with them. "I don't want to go," Wang cried out in fear. "Mama, Papa!" He raced to the corner of the big bed, shielding his head with his arms. His parents knew that it would be futile to resist, so they watched helplessly as the two policemen dragged away their terrified son. Wang had reason to be frightened. A year earlier, as part of their efforts to beautify Beijing in preparation for the annual session of the National People's Congress, the police had taken him to a sanatorium on the outskirts of Beijing and beaten him to a pulp. A few days later, they drove him to the Temple of Heaven, where they deposited him in a wounded clump at the front gate. It took Wang two hours of walking to find his way home.

As the Olympic delegation toured Beijing's sports facilities on March 7, Wang's parents waited anxiously for news about their son. Two days later, shortly after dawn,

> A police car came to pick them up, but the police officer said that only one of the parents could go. The parents, now desperate with worry, imagining their son beaten bloody, perhaps even in a coma, insisted that they both go. The police backed down and drove them out to Fangshan, a hospital closely associated with the Public Security Bureau... When they arrived, the police took the parents into an office that was bare except for several chairs and a table. "The person has died," an officer informed them matter-of-factly. "We have inspected the body." Wang Shanqin and An Yulian were devastated. They felt responsible for their son, who had depended on them. He had pleaded with them to let him stay, yet they had allowed the police to take him away.

Wang's father demanded to see the body, and he and his wife were then led down a long corridor to the hospital's morgue. Later, the couple described to the foreign journalists what they found on arrival:

"There was blood all over his face," the father recalled slowly and hesitantly, like a man fighting with himself, negotiating between his desire to tell the world and the pain of remembering. "His hair was all red with blood. His lips were cut up, and his eyes – they were pierced, as if they had burst open and then swollen shut." ... In his back, there was a big hole. Someone must have stuck a police baton into his back, boring it into the flesh. And his behind was all bruised" ... "The back of my son's legs," he continued, as he rubbed his hands under his kneecaps, "had these huge bumps, these swellings. I told them I wanted to sue, and you know what they said? 'You'll never win.' On the day we cremated him, they gave me a bag with 5,000 *yuan* in it. They didn't say what the money was for."[554]

The Beijing Public Security Bureau has a close organizational affiliation with only two hospitals in the capital: one is the Binhe Penal Hospital, located until recently within the grounds of the Beijing No. 1 Municipal Prison (this facility was torn down and relocated in the mid-1990s); the other is the Beijing PSB Ankang Institute for the Custody and Treatment of the Mentally Ill, which is located in Fangshan District, a suburban area to the southwest of the city.[555] Even today, very few foreigners living in China have heard of the name "Ankang," so it is unsurprising that the authors of the above account failed to identify the place of Wang Chaoru's death as being the Beijing Ankang facility. But that is undoubtedly where he died.

III. The Victims Go to Court: Case Notes from the Ankang, 2000-2005

One of the chief methodological difficulties in trying to interpret the copious statistical data on "political-style" criminal psychiatric cases that have been officially published in China over the past twenty-five years is that the statistics, while high by any standard of judgment, nonetheless remain almost completely anonymous and impersonal. We know that somewhere between seven and 15 percent of forensic psychiatric cases dealt with by police psychiatrists in the 1980s were political ones,

---

554 Nicholas D. Kristof and Sheryl WuDunn, *China Wakes: The Struggle for the Soul of a Rising Power* (Random House, 1994), p.98. The authorities' version of Wang's death was as follows: "'The police said that my son had died on the night of the sixth,' [said the father.] That was just hours before the Olympic delegation arrived. 'They said he went mad and died on the streets. That's impossible! When they said that, I yelled at the policemen. They were just too inhumane. How could they hate my son so much?'"

555 A detailed official description of the organization and functions of the Beijing Ankang facility can be found in Lin Huai, *Jingshen Jibing Huanzhe Xingshi Zeren Nengli He Yiliao Jianhu Cuoshi*, pp.111-116; the account was written by Zhang Hu, a leading forensic psychiatrist who formerly worked at the Harbin No. 1 Special Hospital (*Ha'erbin Shi Diyi Zhuanke Yiyuan*) and for the past ten years or so has been based at the Beijing Ankang institute. In his article, Zhang said that the Beijing Ankang is divided into three parts: a closed and highly secure zone (*fengbi qu*), where all new admissions are placed; a semi-open zone, holding around half of the inmates; and an open zone, mainly devoted to work-therapy activities, where inmates scheduled for release are held. (For a more recent account suggesting that this "triple zone" policy is also being applied in other Ankang facilities nowadays, see Kang Ming [op cit], at Note 515 above.) According to Zhang, the facility is run "fully in accordance with humanitarian principles," although he also acknowledges that "many problems remain to be solved." In his view, Ankang centres should primarily be places of treatment, rather than detention or punishment: "If the reverse were true, so that the medical objectives became secondary, and the principal purpose was simply to lock up the patients and keep them in custody, then it would be wrong, and the nature and aims of Ankang hospitals would no longer be the same" (Ibid., p.113). Another description of the Ankang regime can be found in Li Congpei, *Sifa Jingshenbingxue*, pp.385-386.

and that this percentage had dropped to between 1 and a few percent by the early 1990s. We also know, from China's official literature on psychiatry and the law, that most of these "political cases" ended up being sent to Ankang facilities or similar places of psychiatric custody. But for the most part, we have no information on the actual names and identity of the large numbers of individuals concerned. Nor do we know the details of the specific political-style incidents that led to their being arrested in the first place, or of what happened to these people once they were admitted to the Ankang or how long they were held there. Needless to say, the main reason for this has been the high degree of official secrecy which, until very recently, surrounded all aspects of the internal functioning and operations of the Ankang system. A major lapse of security clearly occurred over the years through the publication, in China's medical literature on psychiatry and the law, of the numerous and wide-ranging statistical data on political-style criminal psychiatric cases that appear in this book. But in the vast majority of cases, the actual subjects and victims of the Ankang political-psychiatric custody system have remained little more than faceless numbers on a page.

In early 2004, this situation finally began to change. Over the past two years or so, Chinese citizens have begun to use the Internet to publicize full and detailed accounts of their wrongful incarceration in the Ankang, and moreover – in a remarkable outburst of Chinese-style *glasnost* – journalists working in the official news media have begun investigating these cases, publishing their findings and conclusions, and calling for public accountability on this issue and for the punishment of officials who have misused the Ankang system as a means of persecuting and silencing their critics. As a result of this dramatic breakthrough, the previously impermeable informational walls of the Ankang have begun to crumble, and a vital degree of transparency is at last beginning to emerge. What is equally significant about these cases is that the victims have begun trying to use the legal system to defend their rights by pursuing administrative lawsuits and tort compensation claims against the Ankang authorities and the local police for wrongful incarceration. So novel are these attempts, and so fragmentary and inadequate are the rules and regulations governing the whole system of Ankang custody, however, that the courts have been finding great difficulty in deciding not only how they should be handled under the law, but also whether they should be adjudicated at all. Finally, over the past year or so, there have even been official reports of attempts to put Ankang officials on trial for criminal wrongdoing of various kinds.

As we saw in the passage from the police encyclopaedia quoted above, two of the security authorities' prime target groups for admission into Ankang-style custody and treatment are, firstly, "political maniacs," or those displaying "dangerously" political dissident-like behaviour (including "expressing opinions on important domestic and international affairs"); and secondly, people accused of "disrupting the normal work of Party and government offices" – a category which typically means the kinds of persistent petitioners and complainants whom the police regard as suffering from "litigious mania." In Chapter 6, we encountered several examples of both these categories of cases. We will now consider several cases of the latter type where the detainees are specifically known to have been sent to Ankang facilities rather than to normal psychiatric hospitals.

The Case of Qiu Jinyou

In July 1997, an elderly man named Qiu Jinyou and over 400 of his fellow farmers from the Hongshan State Farm in Xiaoshan District, Hangzhou Municipality in Zhejiang Province began a public campaign to expose extensive and systematic financial corruption on the part of the state farm's Party Secretary and legal representative, Ding Yougen, and numerous other local officials. The farmers had been attempting without success since the early 1990s to petition the local government authorities about these activities. According to detailed allegations by the farmers that later appeared on the internet, Ding and his cohorts had since 1986 embezzled several hundred million *yuan* of the farm's funds and covertly assigned ownership of numerous major farm assets, including factories and land, to their wives and other relatives. According to Qiu and his fellow farmers, the leaders of the Hongshan State Farm had never once, from 1986 up to the present time, made public any of the farm's financial accounts, despite repeated demands by the farmers that they do so as required by law.[556]

On 15 September 1997, while Qiu Jinyou was making his seventh visit to the office of the CCP Central Discipline Inspection Committee (CDIC) to call for action on the farmers' joint complaint, the head of the Xiaoshan Municipal DIC and several officers from the Hangzhou Municipal Public Security Bureau arrived on the scene and falsely claimed that Qiu was wanted by the police in connection with a case of weapons concealment and misuse of public funds. The CDIC allowed them to take Qiu away without asking to see any evidence for this claim, and he was immediately taken to the Hangzhou Sanbao Detention Centre for questioning. Over the next month and a half, the PSB focused on their real objective, which was to coerce Qiu into revealing the names of all the sources for his and the other 400 farmers' detailed information concerning the corrupt activities of Ding Yougen and his colleagues in the local government. Qiu held out for several weeks, but in the end he broke down under the pressure and signed a PSB-prepared "blood statement" (*xue shu*) pledging henceforth to cease all his complaint and petitioning activities against Party Secretary Ding and the others.

On 29 October, as soon as Qiu had signed the document, however, the police transferred him from the detention centre and placed him in the custody of the Hangzhou City Ankang Hospital. Several Ankang psychiatrists – including the Director of the Hangzhou facility, Kang Ming, and two others named Ma Yunfeng and Yu Hua – then performed a forensic psychiatric evaluation on Qiu and declared him to be suffering from both "paranoid psychosis" and "litigious mania." Five weeks later, the Xiaoshan City PSB issued the following post hoc certification for Qiu's committal:

> To the Hangzhou Municipal Ankang Hospital:

---

[556] See: Li Xinde, "*Ta Huanyou 'Pianzhixing Jingshenbing' ma?*" (Was He Really Suffering from "Paranoid Psychosis"?), *Gong-Shang Daobao* (Business Director), 25 March 2003; Li Xinde, "*Ta Shi Zenmeyang Chengle 'Jingshenbing' de?*" (How Did He End Up as "Mentally Ill"?), *Gong-Shang Daobao*, 26 March 2004, available at: www.yuluncn.com/Article_Show.asp?ArticleID=139; Qiu Jinyou, "*Shei Boduole Nongchang Zhigong de Minzhu Quanli? (Fu Tu) – Wode Shensu Zhuang*" (Who is Stripping the State Farm Employees of their Democratic Rights (illustrated with photos) – My Petition), 11 April 2004, available at: www.yuluncn.com/Article_Show.asp?ArticleID=211; Employees from the Hongshan State Farm, "*Shei Boduole Nongchang Zhigong de Minzhu Quanli? Hangzhou Shi Xiaoshan Qu Hongshan Nongchang de Zhigong Qianming*" (Who is Stripping the State Farm Employees of their Democratic Rights? List of Signatories to Petition from Employees of the Hongshan State Farm, Xiaoshan District, Hangzhou Municipality), 11 April 2004, available at: www.yuluncn.com/Article_Show.asp?ArticleID=210; Li Xinde, "*Shei Boduole Nongchang Zhigong de Minzhu Quanli? – Laizi Hangzhou Shi Xiaoshan Qu Hongshan Nongchang de Diaocha*" (Who is Stripping the State Farm Employees of their Democratic Rights? – An Investigation Report from Hongshan State Farm, Xiaoshan District, Hangzhou City), Zhongguo Yulun Jiandu Wang (China Public Opinion Monitoring Network), 17 April 2004; available at: www.yuluncn.com/Article_Show.asp?ArticleID=212; Qiu Jinyou, "*Shei Yao Jubao, Jiu Ba Shei Guanjin Kanshousuo – Du 'Guanya Li Yuchun Shi Weile Baohu Haishi Weile Fengkou' Yiwen Yougan*" (Whoever Tries to Expose Us, We'll Lock Up in the Detention Centre – Some Thoughts After Reading "Was Taking Li Yuchun into Custody a Way of Protecting Her or Silencing Her?"), *Zhongguo Weiquan Fuwu Wang* (China Rights Protection Services Network), 4 July 2004; available at: www.weiquancn.com;

> On 31 October this year, the Hangzhou Municipal Public Order Department (*Zhi'an Chu*) authorized the sending of one of this city's mentally ill people, Qiu Jinyou, to your hospital to undergo compulsory medical treatment. In view of the fact that his illness is in an active phase at present, we recommend that Qiu Jinyou be given forcible drug treatment (*qiangzhi yaowu zhiliao*), and we hereby undertake that all costs and expenses will be paid by this PSB office.
>
> Xiaoshan City Public Security Bureau   [official seal]
>
> 4 December 1997

Qiu was held at the Hangzhou Ankang for a total of 208 days, during which time none of his family members were informed of his whereabouts. He later wrote as follows about the treatment he had endured at the hospital:

> I was forcibly drugged with large quantities of medicines that badly damaged my nervous system,[557] and I truly feared that they were trying, under the pretext of "treating my illness" to kill me...During my time in the Ankang, I was forcibly administered 63 pills of one type and 144 pills of another type, which caused me to experience great pain in my brain, liver and kidneys. My hair began falling out, and I suffered from spasms and tremors, insomnia, nervous despair, memory loss and forgetfulness, food intolerance, and other such symptoms....It was just like the experiments carried out on live human beings by the Japanese fascists' 731 Army Unit.[558]

After Qiu's discharge from the Ankang, he embarked on a five-year-long effort to bring an administrative lawsuit against the hospital and the local PSB for wrongful psychiatric incarceration. He was greatly hampered in this effort, however, by the Hangzhou Ankang's consistent refusal to provide either him or his lawyer, Zhang Jinping from the Shanghai City No.1 Law Centre, with any of his hospital medical records. As an alternative, his lawyer then obtained numerous affidavits – from the head of the township committee where Qiu lived, from his employer, and also from his relatives, neighbours and friends – all stating that Qiu had never displayed even the slightest sign of being mentally ill.

On 10 November 2001, the Yuhang District Court[559] rejected Qiu's application for an administrative lawsuit against the Hangzhou Ankang and PSB, on the grounds: "The case does not fall within the scope of administrative litigation, and nor do the various particulars of the case permit us to accept it for an administrative hearing." On 22 November, the Xiaoshan District Court rejected his application for a court hearing on the same grounds. Then on 5 December, Qiu submitted an administrative appeal lawsuit to the Hangzhou Intermediate Court charging that the Hangzhou Ankang and PSB authorities had wrongfully deprived him of his liberty and subjected him to forcible medical treatment, along

---

557 Qiu named two particular medications in his statement, but the English names for them have not been found.
558 This was a secret medical experimentation and germ warfare unit operated by the Japanese Army in the vicinity of Harbin during the Second World War; thousands of Chinese prisoners were killed in these "experiments," which often involved vivisection.
559 The Hangzhou Ankang is located in the Anxi Township of Yuhang District, so this was the court of jurisdiction in Qiu's case.

with a supplementary suit claiming compensatory damages. On 22 February 2002, that court ruled as follows:

> The evidence provided by the Appellant is impossible to verify, and the applicable time limit for bringing suit in this case has now expired....The appeal is dismissed and the original ruling is upheld.

As of early 2004, the Hongshan State Farm authorities led by Party Secretary Ding Yougen were still pursuing a systematic campaign of intimidation against the farmers in an attempt to maintain their 18-year-long cover-up of financial corruption and wrongdoing at the farm. Even then, however, Ding and the others apparently still regarded Qiu Jinyou as being the "weakest link" in their wall of defence against the corruption allegations. On 16 April, upon learning that a journalist from the China Procuracy Daily would shortly be arriving to investigate the Hongshan State Farm corruption story, the local Discipline Inspection Committee chief summoned another of the protesting farmers' leaders, Qi Mingxian, and told him: "You have to guarantee that you'll tell [the journalist] that Qiu Jinyou was mentally ill. Everything else, we can compromise on."[560]

In September 2005, the Beijing correspondent of the German magazine Die Zeit travelled to Hangzhou to interview Qiu Jinyou. As well as the various punitive "treatments" already mentioned, it emerged that Qiu had been frequently subjected to electric shock treatment by officials at the Hangzhou Ankang. "The Communists are cruel. Inside the Ankang, there is nothing but terror and fear," said Qiu. "Not even the murderers there were treated as harshly as inmates of my category – people who had filed complaints or petitions with the authorities. During my time in the Ankang, I was tortured three to four times a week. I thought I was going to die there."[561]

The Case of Han Zhenxi

In 1991 in the northeastern city of Dalian, a policeman named Han Zhenxi, who along with his sister had recently started operating a private restaurant, became involved in a dispute with one of his neighbours, a local pig farmer named Ma Jingkui who had close business connections with the local government. On 18 July that year, according to the court ruling in an administrative lawsuit that Han was later to bring against his employer, the local county PSB, claiming wrongful incarceration in the Dalian Ankang:

> The Judicial Appraisal Group, acting on a referral by the Defendant (under the latter's former name of Xinjin County PSB), but without the Plaintiff's knowledge of what was being done to him, performed a psychiatric evaluation of the Plaintiff and completed a "Certificate of Judicial Medical Appraisal for Psychiatric Illness" (*Jing-Jian-Zi* No. 91060.) The diagnostic conclusion was: "Paranoid state; recommend the adoption of medical measures to prevent any unforeseen problems or events from arising."[562]

---

560 That evening, Qi Mingxian wrote a desperate letter to the *China Public Opinion Monitoring Network*, one of China's foremost citizens' rights websites, appealing for help. "I'm afraid they're going to arrest me, ransack my house, and kill me to shut me up," wrote Qi. "Please come and save me!" (See: Li Xinde, "*Shei Boduole Nongchang Zhigong de Minzhu Quanli? ...*" [op cit.]).
561 See: Georg Blume, op cit. See also above, p.13.
562 See: Qin Xudong, "*Cong Yi Fen Qiqiao de Xingzheng Panjueshu Shuoqi*" (Reflections on a Suspiciously Strange Administrative Case Judgment), *Xingzheng Yu Fazhi* (Administration and the Legal System), 2003, No.6.

Although the official press reports on Han's case do not explain the precise nature of his dispute with Ma Jingkui and the local government,[563] it is clear that his conflict with them worsened considerably after this psychiatric assessment was surreptitiously performed on him. Ma Jingkui began "petitioning" the government, and Han responded by visiting and complaining to the local PSB and government offices, where he is said to have got into various arguments with the staff. Finally, according to the court ruling mentioned above, sometime in the first half of 1997, Han "kicked open the door of the PSB Bureau Chief" and (curiously enough) "hung a bundle of grass on the PSB building's exterior wall" – thereby "seriously disrupting normal office work." Shortly thereafter, the municipal government and PSB met to discuss Han's case, and they decided that his behaviour met the criteria laid down in the Dalian City regulations governing the compulsory custody and treatment of the dangerously mentally ill. On 28 December the same year, a second judicial psychiatric evaluation was performed on Han, the findings of which were as follows:

> Paranoid psychosis. The subject of appraisal, Han Zhenxi, over the past few years has carried out numerous petitioning and complaint activities, indulged in intemperate language and behaviour (*yan-xing pianji*) and obstructed the exercise of public duties. There is a direct causal relationship between these activities and the illness from which he is suffering. He has lost the capacity to recognize and control his actions and should therefore be deemed not legally responsible for them. Since his illness is presently in an active phase, we recommend that he be taken into [legal] guardianship (*caiqu jianhuxing cuoshi*.)

The reference here to Han's being "not legally responsible" meant that he would otherwise have faced criminal charges for his disruptive petitioning activities, and on 2 March 1998, he was compulsorily admitted to the Dalian City Ankang Hospital. The court document gave no indication of what Han's treatment or experiences in the Ankang had been, but it did note that he was an "Injured and Disabled Revolutionary Armyman" – a status generally attracting great public respect in China. When he was eventually discharged from the Ankang, on 1 December,[564] and soon thereafter proceeded to bring his administrative lawsuit against the PSB and Ankang authorities, it was doubtless Han Zhenxi's membership of this elite social group that explained why the court – despite obvious pressure upon it

---

See also: "Zhewei Jingcha You Mei You Jingshenbing?" (Was This Policeman Mentally Ill?), *Beijing Qingnian Bao* (Beijing Youth News), 22 January 2002, p.23; and He Haibo, "*Quru de Sifa – Ping Han Zhenxi An Yishen Panjue*" (An Insult to the Judiciary – Assessing the Judgment of First Instance in the Case of Han Zhenxi), *Bei-Da Falü Xinxi Wang* (Beijing University Law Information Network), undated, available at: 211.100.18.62/research/lgyd/details.asp?lid=1955.

563 One possibility is that the government (or an official thereof) wanted to evict Han from his restaurant premises, either for city redevelopment purposes or because they simply wanted to take over his restaurant. The destruction of homes (*chaiqian fangwu*) of urban residents and their forced relocation by local governments around China is becoming an increasingly serious civil rights problem nowadays.

564 The court stated that Han had been "released on bail for medical treatment" (*baowai jiuyi*) and that this was still his legal status as of July 2000 when his administrative lawsuit was being heard. There is a certain irony in the use of this term in the context of the Ankang: it is a term from the Criminal Law normally used when sentenced criminals fall sick in prison and need to receive medical care in an outside hospital; in Han's case, he was imprisoned in what purported to be a psychiatric hospital because he was deemed to be criminally insane, but then when his alleged mental state improved he was "released on bail for medical treatment." This inappropriate use of concepts from the Criminal Law to describe the situation of Ankang inmates is indicative, more generally, of the legal system's ambiguity and uncertainty as to whether they are in fact being punished or medically treated.

from the local government – seemed to go out of its way to try to meet his demands for vindication and justice.

Han's administrative lawsuit requesting the annulment of the PSB's action in forcibly hospitalizing him was heard by the Pulandian Municipal People's Court of Liaoning Province on 20 July 2000. The court's ruling on the case was in many respects astonishing – both for what it said, and for what it ended up by not saying. Also interesting is the fact that the question of whether Han had genuinely been in need of custodial psychiatric treatment hardly figured at all in the court's final arguments. Instead, the court hearing focused overwhelmingly on the procedural aspects of his case. As we have seen, the court pointed out that the 18 July 1991 police psychiatrists' appraisal of Han's mental state had been carried out without his knowledge. But according to the judges' summing-up statement, there was a great deal more:

- Only five days prior to the police psychiatrists' surreptitious evaluation of Han's mental state, psychiatrists at a regular mental hospital had examined him openly (also at the PSB's behest) and "concluded that Comrade Han Zhenxi's mental state is quite normal."
- Neither Han nor any member of his family had been informed of the results of the 28 December 1998 judicial appraisal, in which the police psychiatrists had diagnosed him as a "paranoid psychotic" requiring compulsory hospitalization in the Ankang.
- Neither of the two psychiatric appraisal certificates from 1991 and 1998 had been stamped with the official seal of the Judicial Appraisal Group (or of any other body), contrary to the requirements of law. The two documents were therefore, according to the court, "for this and other reasons… both legally invalid."
- The Dalian Ankang authorities had failed to complete any of the required formal documentation either for Han Zhenxi's admission to the hospital or for his eventual discharge. As a consequence, his repeated requests to be given copies of these legally required documents had gone unanswered by the Ankang authorities – and this despite the fact that no less powerful a body than the Liaoning Provincial Department of Public Security's Discipline Inspection Committee had "specifically instructed them to provide Han with the documents."
- In October 1997, moreover, "A Joint Investigation Team, consisting of the Municipal Politics and Law Committee, the Party Discipline Inspection Committee, the Public Security Bureau, the Municipal Procuracy and the Taiping Township People's Government, studied and examined the various petitions submitted by Ma Jingkui; it then repudiated the Defendant's [i.e. the PSB's] finding that the Plaintiff [Han] had been in violation of the law in this matter. The Plaintiff is a Grade A-2 Revolutionary Injured–Disabled Armyman; in the course of his work he has frequently received the accolade of 'Exemplary Communist Party Member,' 'Civilized People's Policeman', and other such awards and distinctions."

In their closing remarks before announcing judgment, the judges made the following devastating pronouncement:

> This Court finds that the Defendant, a public security organ, is empowered to order the punishment of persons whose behaviour violates the security administration regulations. [However,] the medical appraisal performed on the Plaintiff was carried out by a Judicial Medical Appraisal Group which had not been entrusted and authorized to perform such a task by any Appraisals Committee; it was performed on a party implicated in a case in which no case file existed, no criminal grounds had been identified, and no case number had been assigned; and the certificate of its findings bears no official seal. The medical appraisal was therefore legally invalid, and the Defendant's subsequent action in dispatching the Plaintiff to the Dalian Municipal Ankang Hospital to undergo guardianship-based psychiatric treatment was a violation of the law.

Astoundingly, the judges then proceeded to declare that the Dalian municipal regulations[565] under which the local PSB was empowered to detain "mentally ill persons who create incidents or disasters" and then send them to the Ankang were themselves "legally invalid." As mere local-level regulations (*difangxing fagui*), he argued, they were at variance with China's 1996 Administrative Punishment Law, according to which any punishment involving the restriction of personal liberty has validity only when specified in law (*falü*.) Since China's judges have no authority at all to comment or adjudicate upon the validity of existing laws and regulations, one can only assume that these particular judges had reached some kind of a breaking point in their forbearance with the system as a whole, that the case before them was somehow the "straw that broke the camel's back" and that they were determined to express their views about it and put them on the record in the strongest possible terms.

However, having effectively wiped the floor with the Dalian PSB and its Ankang Hospital colleagues on all the relevant legal procedural points, and having seemingly put their own jobs on the line in the process, the judges then performed an extraordinary, abject 180-degree turn when it came to the actual judgment. First, they delivered a Parthian shot:

> According to Article 17 of the PRC General Principles of Civil Law, "If mentally ill people suffer full or partial loss of civil capacity because of their illness, the following persons shall assume guardianship over them: 1) their spouses, 2) their parents, and 3) their adult sons or daughters..." It is indisputable that the Plaintiff already had such guardians available to him. The action of the Defendant, who is the employer of the Plaintiff, in failing to seek the permission of the Plaintiff's guardians for a change of guardianship to be effected, and in then privately assuming that role itself, was in itself a violation of the law. For it then to have dispatched the Plaintiff to the Dalian Municipal Ankang Hospital to undergo guardianship-based medical treatment was a still greater violation of the law

But then, immediately afterwards, came the jaw breaker:

> However, the Defendant asserts that its action in dispatching the Plaintiff to the Dalian Municipal Ankang Hospital to undergo guardianship-based psychiatric treatment

---

565 "*Dalian Shi Jianhu Zhiliao Guanli Zhaoshi Zhaohuo Jingshenbingren Tiaoli*" (Dalian Municipal Regulations on the Guardianship, Treatment and Management of Mentally Ill People Who Create Disasters or Incidents), passed by the Standing Committee of the Dalian Municipal People's Congress on 4 November 1992 and effective as of 17 December 1992, available at: www.dl.gov.cn/togov/law/local/688_15942.htm. For details of other similar municipal and provincial-level regulations, see Notes 544 and 547 above.

was an action involving its own internal affairs (*shuyu qi neibu xingwei*), and the Court hereby upholds this assertion.

In order to uphold and supervise the administrative organs' lawful exercise of government, and to defend the lawful rights and interests of the parties concerned, this Court now rules, in accordance with Article 54 (Para 1) of the PRC Administrative Litigation Law,[566] as follows: The administrative action taken by the Defendant, Pulandian Municipal Public Security Bureau, in dispatching the Plaintiff, Han Zhenxi, to the Dalian Municipal Ankang Hospital to undergo guardianship-based psychiatric treatment is upheld.

This judgment clearly had absolutely no legal sense or logic to it. Everything the judges had said prior to pronouncing judgment showed that they believed the municipal PSB and the Ankang authorities had broken virtually every rule in the book in having Han committed to the asylum. They then, however, did the one thing that the law did not permit them to do – namely to challenge the legality of an existing administrative regulation – and they failed to do the one thing which, in view of the facts and evidence, the letter of the law virtually required them to do – which was to quash all or part of the PSB's handling of Han's case. The judges' final unqualified acceptance of the defendant's chilling assertion that the entire matter had simply been "an internal affair" of the PSB was tantamount to a judicial ruling that China's police force is, quite literally, a law unto itself.

Significantly, the press reports on this case specifically noted that "the judgment had been discussed and agreed upon by the adjudication committee beforehand" – thus explaining why the judges had been powerless to render the judgment that they so evidently favoured.[567] However, it would be wrong to assume that the buck had stopped, in this case, with the court's adjudication committee. For as one Chinese legal commentator subsequently observed,

> We are justified in suspecting here that the judges were undoubtedly toiling under some inexpressible burden of difficulty. Under pressure from the powers that be, both they as individuals and the Court as an institution were left powerless to accord the law its proper role and place. From the more subtle aspects of this case, we can clearly discern the state of awkwardness and embarrassment to which judicial dignity

---

566 According to Article 54 (Para 1): After the People's Court has heard a case, it shall make one of the following rulings, depending upon the circumstances of the case:

1) if the evidence for a specific administrative action is clear and solid, and if the law or regulation has been applied correctly and in accordance with legally prescribed procedure, then the [administrative action] should be upheld;

2) if one of the following circumstances applies to the specific administrative action, then it should be either wholly or partially quashed, or alternatively the defendant can be ordered to carry out a new specific administrative action:

a) the primary evidence was insufficient; b) the law or regulation in question was improperly applied; c) there was a violation of legal procedure; d) [the administrative body] exceeded its powers; or e) an abuse of power occurred.

567 The "adjudication committee" (*shenpan weiyuanhui*) in Chinese courts is a group of judges, usually led by the Court President, responsible for discussing and deciding the verdict (and the sentence, if any) in advance of the actual trial in all "difficult or thorny cases" (*yi-nan anjian*.) Its role is closely linked to the phenomenon of "verdict first, trial second" (*xian pan, hou shen*), as briefly discussed on p.45 above.

and legal rationality are consigned under the harsh realities of China's present legal system. As long as the judiciary continues to lack independence, the courts will be unable to play the role of a fair and impartial adjudicator and supervisor, and social justice will remain but a distant hope.[568]

The Case of Wang Henglei

On 7 January 2000, Wang Henglei, a man in his fifties and a teacher at the Changrenli Primary School in the Xincheng District of Xi'an City, suddenly went missing. For several days his wife searched frantically for him, until eventually the local police told her that Wang had been forcibly admitted to the Xi'an Ankang mental asylum. He had been in a long-running dispute with the headmaster of the Changrenli Primary School over the housing that he and his wife had been allocated by the school, and lately he had been petitioning the local government about his case. On the morning in question, Wang had made a protest speech to the other teachers in the school yard, and the headmaster had called in the police to stop him. On arrival at the school, an officer from the Xincheng District police station classified the incident as a "public order disturbance" and Wang was then detained.[569] After a brief discussion with the headmaster, the policeman then telephoned the deputy director of the Xi'an Ankang facility, Ning Laixiang, who promptly sent two of the hospital's psychiatrists over to the school. After learning that it was a public order disturbance and asking Wang Henglei a few simple questions, the psychiatrists diagnosed him as suffering from "schizoid personality disorder and paranoid psychosis." Wang was immediately bundled into a police van and dispatched to the Xi'an Ankang. No proper forensic-psychiatric evaluation of any kind was conducted on Wang, and no formal committal papers were completed or signed by the asylum authorities.[570]

Upon learning what had happened to her husband, Wang's wife hired a lawyer, who swiftly filed an administrative lawsuit in the Xincheng District Court against the Xi'an Ankang Hospital, the Xincheng District PSB Sub-Bureau, and the District Bureau of Education, requesting the court to annul the PSB's administrative action in having Wang committed to the asylum and to award compensatory damages. Meanwhile, Wang remained in the asylum, and only on May 15 – more than four months after his initial incarceration there, and only three days before the court hearing – did the Xi'an Ankang deputy director arrange for him to undergo the formal forensic psychiatric evaluation which, under Ankang

---

568 Qin Xudong, op cit.
569 A number of reports emerged around the same time saying that the Xincheng District PSB Sub-Bureau leadership was completely corrupt, and that they were the subject of fear and loathing by the local population. According to the reports, the Police Chief and his cronies had no interest in solving serious local crimes, and were constantly "on the take": any prisoner, no matter how serious his offence, could buy his freedom for the price of a hefty bribe to the Police Chief. (See, for example: Lan Tongren, "*Xi'an Shi Xincheng Gong'an Fen Ju Ba Yi Wugu Funü Meng Xiaoxia Baibai Guanzai Jingshenbing Yuan Changda Shi Nian!*" (Xi'an City's Xincheng PSB Sub-Bureau Incarcerates Innocent Woman Meng Xiaoxia in Mental Hospital for as Long as Ten Years!), *Boxun Xinwen Wang*, 27 July 2004, available at: peacehall.com/news/gb/yuanqing/2004/07/200407272240.shtml.
570 For a report on another teacher sent to a mental hospital to stop him raising complaints about his superiors around the same time, see: "*Shei You Quan Ba Zhengchang Ren Songjin Jingshenbingyuan?*" (Who Has the Right to Have a Normal Person Confined in a Mental Hospital?), Zhongguo Qingnian Bao (China Youth Daily), 4 June 2001. The victim in this case was a university professor in Guangzhou, named Zhong Huayan, who had been forcibly confined in a mental hospital six times by the university authorities after he put up wall posters on campus complaining about his work performance evaluation. For a brief summary of several other similar cases, see: Yang Qu, "You Bing" (Sick), *Zhongguo Qingnian Bao*, 2 December 2001.

regulations, was a necessary prerequisite for carrying out an involuntary committal in all but the most urgent and dangerous of cases. (Making an impromptu speech in a school yard hardly qualifies as such, even in China.)

On May 18, the court convened to hear Wang Henglei's administrative lawsuit. His lawyer argued that the question of Wang's mental state was immaterial to the case, and that the only pertinent issue for adjudication was whether or not the Ankang and local police authorities had followed due procedure in having Wang involuntarily committed. Since no formal procedures at all – legal or medical – had been followed in his committal, the case was strong and clear. The court ruled as follows:

> The primary function of Ankang Hospitals is to compulsorily take in and treat mentally ill people who threaten public order.[In Wang Henglei's case,] however, without first requiring the police to produce a written "Decision to Apply Compulsory Medical Treatment" and without informing his relatives, and relying only upon materials shown to them by the school authorities and on their own brief interview with Wang, the Ankang Hospital made a purely subjective decision that he was mentally abnormal.... The Ankang Hospital's behaviour in subjecting him to forcible medical treatment and in restricting his personal freedom thus constitutes a violation of due process (*qi xingwei weifan le fading chengxu*.) The court upholds Wang Henglei's litigation request for revocation of the compulsory treatment measures, and orders the defendants to compensate him and apologize to him for the damage caused.[571]

The amount of compensation awarded to Wang was 32.85 yuan for each day of his confinement in the Ankang. The institute's deputy director, Ning Laixiang, lodged an appeal against the ruling of first instance, however, and Wang therefore had to remain in the Xi'an Ankang until the trial of second instance had been heard – and that was not due until November 16, a full six months later. When the court duly convened on that day, Deputy Director Ning announced to the court that Wang Henglei had experienced "sudden death" (*cu si*) at the Xi'an Ankang on the previous evening and would therefore not be able to appear. (A post-mortem report by the procuracy later found that Wang had died of a ruptured blood vessel in the brain.) The judge nonetheless insisted on going ahead with the trial that day, and – while it was too late for Wang himself to benefit – the court upheld the original ruling on all points.

Unsurprisingly, Wang's untimely death provoked widespread suspicion among the local community, and even the local procuracy was convinced that the Xi'an Ankang's Deputy Director Ning had had a direct hand in it. But the police investigation against Ning proceeded with excruciating slowness. According to a report published by the Xinhua News Agency in March 2003, more than three years later:

> On 16 April 2002, a case was filed against Ning for the crime of abuse of official power, and he was taken into police detention the following day. On 30 April he was formally placed under arrest; and on 28 May he was released on bail to await trial.
>
> The procuracy has stated that the defendant, Ning Laixiang, an official in a state organ, failed to exercise his duties diligently and responsibly and wantonly abused

---

571 See: "*Meng Xiaoxia Beiju Xia-Pian (Tu): Zhuitao Gongdao de Lu Hai Yao Zou Duo Jiu*" (Meng Xiaoxia's Tragedy, Part Two (With Photos): How Much Farther Must She Journey in Search of Justice?), *Hua Shang Bao* (China Business View), 8 March 2004; available at: http://hsb.huash.com/gb/newsdzb/2004-03/08/content_882580.htm. The above-quoted passage on Wang Henglei's case appears at the end of this article.

his official powers, thereby harming the normal operation of the state organs and violating citizens' personal rights and interests. The facts of his crimes are clear, the evidence is solid and sufficient, and he should be held legally responsible for committing the crime of abuse of official power.[572]

According to a newspaper report of one year later, however,

> When our reporter enquired into this case, we learned that the procuracy had withdrawn its case against Ning Laixiang. The procuracy was unwilling to reveal to us the specific reason for this. Nonetheless, the fact that Ning Laixiang was earlier indicted on charges of abusing his power affords an indirect insight into the kinds of wrongdoings that have been going on at the Ankang Hospital.[573]

One other important point should also be mentioned. As his lawyer pointed out at the administrative trial challenging his psychiatric detention, if Wang had indeed created a "public order disturbance" at the primary school by making his speech on the day in question, then the police had a perfectly viable range of alternative options available to them – from issuing Wang with a written warning or imposing a fine on him, to sentencing him to up to 15 days in administrative detention under the Security Administration Punishment Regulations. However, in the case of persistent complainants and petitioners like Wang Henglei (and all the more so where "litigious maniacs" are concerned), such punishments probably fail – from the PSB's point of view – to exert the desired degree of deterrence. In a word, the trouble-makers just keep coming back for more: each additional short-term punishment simply gets added to the original litany of grievances and injustices that the complaint and petitioning activities were intended to resolve, which in turn leads to still more activities of this type. Sterner police measures are thus required in order to silence such people. Re-education through labour would seem to be an obvious option or tool for this purpose; but on the other hand, it entails and requires at least a modicum of due process on the PSB's part, and moreover the person sentenced has a statutory right of review and appeal. From the police point of view (or that of other officials such as Wang's headmaster), Ankang-style psychiatric custody has none of these procedural drawbacks and complexities – and what is more, it can be extended indefinitely.

The Case of Meng Xiaoxia

The next case, which also took place in the Xincheng District of Xi'an, was reported on in extensive detail in China by numerous national and provincial-level newspapers from March 2004 onwards, and in June that year it even became the subject of a major "CBS 60 Minutes"-style investigative feature programme on Chinese Central Television (CCTV.) The case provoked an outpouring of public anger,

---

572 See: Wu Wei and Qin Juan, "*Xi'an Shi Ankang Yiyuan Fu-Yuanzhang Shexian Lanyong Zhiquan Bei Tiqi Susong*" (Deputy Director of Xi'an Ankang Hospital to be Prosecuted on Suspicion of Abuse of Official Power), *Xinhua Wang* (Xinhua News Net), 18 March 2003; available at: www.xinhuanet.com. The article was originally published in *Hua Shang Bao* (China Business View), same day, at: http://hsb.huash.com/gb/newsdzb/2004-03/08/content_882580.htm.
573 See "*Meng Xiaoxia Beiju Xia-Pian...*" (op cit.).

on websites and bulletin boards around China, and led to widespread calls for the officials responsible to be swiftly brought to justice.[574]

On 21 September 1986, Meng Xiaoxia, a 34-year-old woman who worked as a supervisor at the Xi'an Shunda Plastic Shoe Factory, upbraided a young male worker named Tang Lanzhong, for breaking regulations by failing to let her inspect a batch of coal that he was bringing into the factory. Tang, who was the son of the factory's former director and was on good terms with the current manager, refused to follow Meng's instructions and moreover threatened to "do her in." When the same situation arose two days later and Meng again upbraided him for disobeying the factory's regulations, Tang knocked her to the ground with a chair and then struck her unconscious with a metal hoe. She was found several hours later by another worker and spent the next two to three months in hospital in a critical condition, and she was left permanently lame as a result of her injuries.

Upon returning to work at the factory, she found that the manager had not disciplined or punished Tang in any way, and she insisted that action be taken against him. Eventually, one year and a half later, the manager announced that one month's bonus would be deducted from Tang's salary as a punishment for assaulting Meng. Understandably dissatisfied with this outcome, Meng then submitted a complaint to the local court accusing Tang of criminal wrongdoing. The factory hired a lawyer, and many months later the court reached a "mediated" judgment characterizing the incident as an "industrial injury" case. Incensed by this, Meng began petitioning (*shangfang*) the higher authorities.

On 24 October 1989, someone slipped a note under Meng Xiaoxia's dormitory door warning her to back off, and saying that the factory leadership was planning to have her committed to a mental asylum. Two days later, in the afternoon, around a dozen unknown men burst into her room, thrust her into a van and drove her straight to the Xi'an Ankang Hospital, where the staff bound and tied her to a bed in one of the locked wards. She was placed on a daily drip-feed injection of psychotropic drugs and made to take additional medicine orally, but she devised ways to remove the needle and to spit out the pills when the staff were not looking. After a month, Meng went on a hunger strike to protest against her confinement at the hospital, and was promptly subjected to a forensic psychiatric examination and declared to be suffering from "hysteria" (*yi zheng*.) This was the first and only medical diagnosis of any kind that she was to be given by Xi'an Ankang psychiatrists during a series of six forced incarcerations at the hospital that amounted, in all, to no less than ten years out of the subsequent 18-year period.

On the first occasion, Meng Xiaoxia was released after six months, but on 5 June 1990, after she lodged a complaint with the Xi'an city government about her treatment, Meng was abducted in broad daylight by Shunda Shoe Factory officials and locked in a room at the factory for 21 days, bound to a chair with her hands tied behind her back. On the final evening, an unknown man came into the room

---

574 For a representative selection of articles on Meng Xiaoxia's case, see: CCTV.com, "<*Jishi*>: *Jingshenbing Huanzhe*" ("True Record": A Victim of Mental Illness), Parts One and Two, 25 June 2004 and 13 July 2004, both available at: www.cctv.com; "*Meng Xiaoxia Beiju Xia-Pian (Tu): Zhuitao Gongdao de Lu Hai Yao Zou Duo Jiu*" (Meng Xiaoxia's Tragedy, Part Two [With Photos]: How Much Farther Must She Journey in Search of Justice?), *Hua Shang Bao* (China Business View), 8 March 2004; Lin Tongren, "*Wei Gong Zao Da Zhi Can, Tao Gongdao Bei Qiangsong Jingshenbing Yuan Shi Nian*" (Beaten and Crippled for Upholding Truth, and Forcibly Sent to A Mental Hospital for Ten Years for Seeking Justice), *Da Ji Yuan* (Epoch Times), 27 July 2004; Yao Peng and Zhu Qian, "*Yige Nüren de Shiba Nian Shanghen*" (A Woman's 18-Year-Long Wounds), *Nüxing Wang* (Women's Network), 2 August 2004, available at: www.china-women.com/gb/2004/08/02/zgfnb/zhxw/2.htm; and Yao Peng and Zhu Qian, "*Guanyu Jingshenbing Jianding de 'Jianding'*" (An 'Evaluation' of Judicial Evaluation), *Nüxing Wang*, 4 August 2004, available at: www.china-women.com/gb/2004/08/04/zgfnb/zhxw/6.htm.

and knocked her out by banging her head against the wall. When she awoke, she found her trousers undone and discovered that she had been raped. She then escaped from the factory, bought a bottle of DDT, went to the Xi'an Mayor's office to report the incident to officials there, and then swallowed the bottle of poison down in front of them. She awoke in a hospital bed several days later, and was then discharged and sent home on 25 August.

Only a few days later, however, several more unknown men came to her home, handcuffed her, and forcibly put her back inside the Xi'an Ankang facility. Shortly thereafter, she discovered that she had become pregnant as a result of the rape, and she informed her father of this. After he complained to the factory manager, a police officer arrived at the Ankang hospital to interview Meng – but no police action was subsequently taken and she received no further news from the legal authorities thereafter. On 30 December that year, she was released from the mental asylum for the second time. She caught a train to Beijing and began frequenting the "visits and complaints" offices in the capital, in a further attempt to get the government to take action on her behalf. The Beijing authorities' response was to notify the Shunda Shoe Factory, which promptly dispatched a group of men to bring her back to Xi'an. Soon afterwards, on 14 March 1991, Meng had a bad fall and, in her ninth month of pregnancy, suffered a miscarriage.

On 30 May that year, for continuing to petition the government about her case, Meng Xiaoxia was once again, without any semblance of due process – legal or medical – forcibly incarcerated in the Xi'an Ankang institute for the criminally insane. Although locked in a secure ward with seriously disturbed patients, she managed to have a friend smuggle in a small, several-inch long metal saw blade, and whenever the wind blew strongly or it rained loudly enough to cover the noise, she would slowly cut away at one of the bars on the window of her room. On the night of July 25, she finally succeeded in cutting through the bar and was able to make her escape from the asylum. Once again, she went to the city government offices to lodge her complaint, and once again – only two days after her escape – the factory manager, having been duly notified by the government, again sent men to forcibly return her to the Xi'an Ankang.

This time, she was locked in a special high-security ward and held at the asylum for a full five years.[575] Showing daunting courage and resolve, in July 1996, she managed to escape for a second time, again by using a saw blade to cut through the bars of a window. Again she travelled to Beijing, where she survived for the next year and a half by begging and living rough in the streets. Upon returning to Xi'an, she continued to live and sleep on the city streets, afraid to return home in case the Shunda Shoe Factory authorities should learn of her whereabouts and come after her again. Eventually they did so, however, and on 24 February 1998 they seized and took her back to the Xi'an Ankang for the fifth time. Ironically, but quite revealingly, in June that year she was discharged and allowed to go home for almost two months because the factory manager had stopped paying her "medical and accommodation" bills at the Ankang; but when he rectified this oversight Meng was promptly, on 3 August, taken back to the asylum for the sixth and last time.

Her final escape from the Xian Ankang took place on the afternoon of 15 September 2000, when she took advantage of a rare outside exercise period to slip out of the hospital gates and hide until nightfall in a nearby field of high-growing millet.

---

575 The published CCTV account of Meng's case states that she was held at the Ankang for "three years" on this occasion; but from the relevant dates given in the article (30 May 1991 until July 1996) it is clear that she was actually held for more than five years

Over the next two years, Meng Xiaoxia brought a series of administrative lawsuits in the Xi'an courts against the three main parties who had conspired – all because she had dared to challenge the son of a former factory manager over his violation of the factory's own rules – to persecute her in this grotesque way over the previous decade and a half. The parties in question were the Xi'an Shunda Plastic Shoe Factory, the Xincheng District Sub-Bureau of the Xi'an Municipal Public Security Bureau, and the Xi'an Public Security Bureau's Ankang Hospital. Meng's first attempt to bring legal suit was at the Xincheng District Court on 14 December 2000, but the court rejected the suit on the grounds that what had been done to her by these various bodies had not constituted a "specific administrative action" (*juti xingzheng xingwei*), in the sense defined by the Administrative Litigation Law. After several more failed applications to bring suit, Meng finally succeeded in having her case accepted by Xi'an's Lianhu District Court; however, the latter ruled that it fell under the local jurisdiction of the Xincheng District Court, and so returned it to that court for adjudication.

Four months later, the Xincheng District Court gave its ruling on the case: Meng Xiaoxia's hospitalization at the Xi'an Ankang, it asserted, had been a "civil referral action" (*xingzheng weituo xingwei*) carried out by the Xi'an Shunda Plastic Shoe Factory; it had not been "an act of compulsory medical treatment" (*qiangzhi zhiliao xingwei*) carried out by the public security organs. For that reason, the court ruled, "it did not constitute a specific administrative action" and so: "The case does not fall within the scope of acceptance of administrative cases." So the court again rejected her suit. Meng then appealed to the Xi'an Intermediary Court, which in due course upheld the judgment of first instance. By this time, however, Meng's case had begun to attract widespread sympathy and support from the residents of Xi'an, and an elderly lawyer named Zhang Jinji, from the Shaanxi Ji Si De Law Firm, came forward to offer her legal assistance in lodging petitions for a retrial to be carried out. In early 2003, the Xi'an Intermediary Court held a formal hearing to consider this request, but eventually ruled to dismiss it.

In essence, the courts had ruled that Meng Xiaoxia's 10-year incarceration in the Xi'an Ankang – an institution owned and operated by the Public Security Bureau – had had nothing to do with the police, and that it had instead been a case of civil psychiatric committal carried out by the police on the "authorization" of the Shunda Shoe Factory manager. In principle, therefore, Meng should have been able to sue the shoe factory through the civil courts; however, by the time the various administrative courts had finally ruled that the case was none of their business, the applicable time limits for filing a civil tort lawsuit against the shoe factory had long since passed. The end result of all this was that none of the three parties directly responsible for Meng's cruel mistreatment since 1989 have ever received any form of legal censure or punishment for their actions. Nor has Meng received any apology or compensation from the PSB or Ankang authorities for her long years of persecution, suffering and lost life opportunities. Even having her story splashed all over CCTV prime-time appears to have brought her no closer to a just and final outcome.

In September 2005, interviewed in Xi'an by the Beijing correspondent of *Die Zeit*, Meng Xiaoxia said that she had been given electric shock treatment by Ankang staff on several occasions and subjected to insulin coma therapy, a frightening treatment that is nowadays condemned by psychiatrists elsewhere. "The Ankang is like hell," Meng said. "I would rather die than go there again."[576]

---

576 See: Georg Blume, op cit. See also above, p.13.

Legal Debate on Meng's case

In the aftermath of the dramatic nationwide coverage of Meng Xiaoxia's case on CCTV in June 2004, four lawyers and legal scholars in Xi'an were invited by a national newspaper to discuss and analyze the case from the legal perspective. All four agreed, to a greater or lesser extent, that the Xi'an courts' handling of the various lawsuits brought by Meng had been a dismal travesty of justice. In the course of the debate, a range of fundamental legal issues relating to the Ankang system of forensic psychiatric custody came to light and were openly debated in China, apparently for the first time ever. The highlights of the discussion by the four law experts were as follows:[577]

- Although officially claimed to be a form of "coercive shelter and treatment" (*qiangzhi shouzhi*) for the mentally ill, in practice the Ankang system "contains an essentially punitive element... involving the deprivation of personal liberty." To this extent, "It resembles the now-abolished system of custody for investigation (*shourong zhidu*)."

- If Meng's committal to the Xi'an Ankang had indeed, as the court ruled, been a "civil referral action," then under the terms of the Civil Procedure Law it should have been carried out by her parents, acting in their capacity as her immediate guardians. The Shunda Shoe Factory had no legal authority to usurp the parents' role in this regard; and in the absence of any such move by the parents, the Ankang authorities themselves "had no legal grounds for implementing an involuntary civil committal."

- Since it was actually, however, a police action and not a civil committal, then a forensic psychiatric evaluation should have been performed – but was not – prior to the committal. And second, for Meng's compulsory admission to the Ankang to be lawful, her case should have fallen under one of the five main headings of "dangerously mentally ill" persons as laid down by the Ministry of Public Security;[578] but it manifestly did not.

- Meng's confinement in the Ankang was unquestionably an "act of compulsory medical treatment" (*qiangzhi zhiliao xingwei*) carried out by the police, for the following reasons:
    - The Xi'an Ankang authorities claimed they had merely "accepted a civil referral to perform medical treatment." However, the fact that the hospital had a policy (an unofficial one) of accepting voluntary civil referrals from

---

577 See: She Jianguo et al, "*Meng Xiaoxia Anjian: Kaowen Jingshenbingren Shouzhi Zhi*" (The Meng Xiaoxia Case: An Interrogation into the System of Custody for the Mentally Ill), *Hua Shang Bao* (China Business View), 6 July 2004. The participants in the discussion on Meng's case were: Zheng Shengxun, a professor at the Xi'an College of Industry; Li Jie, a lawyer at the Shaanxi Xu Xiaoping Law Firm; Zhang Xi'an, a lecturer at the Northwest College of Politics and Law; and Zhang Maichang, a lawyer at the Shaanxi Qin Li Law Firm. The summary provided above should be taken as a rough guide only to what was a highly complex legal discussion among the four participants.

For a summary of the legal views and arguments of Meng's own lawyer, Zhang Jinji, see: Yao Peng and Zhu Lian, "*Guanyu Jingshenbing Jianding de 'Jianding'*" (An 'Evaluation' of Judicial Evaluation), *Nüxing Wang*, 4 August 2004, available at: www.china-women.com/gb/2004/08/04/zgfnb/zhxw/6.htm.

578 For the MPS list of these five categories, see p.256 above.

society was irrelevant to this case, because it had clearly acted against Meng's own wishes in the matter.

- o The Xincheng District Court's various rulings should have been legally consistent with each other, but they were not, because in a recent similar case relating to the Xi'an Ankang – that of Wang Henglei[579] – the court had ruled that "the primary function of Ankang Hospitals is to compulsorily take in mentally ill people who threaten public order"; for the same court now, in Meng's case, to argue that the Ankang "serves a dual role" (namely the provision of both voluntary and involuntary treatment) was "clearly most unconscientious" of it (*xianran shi ji bu yansude*.)

- o In December 1987, when the Ankang system was founded, the Ministry of Public Security issued a "Conference Key-Point Summary"[580] stating that all Ankang facilities belonged to and were part of the public security system; that its doctors and nurses were police officers and paid on the PSB salary scale; that Ankangs are institutions for compulsory custody and treatment; and that only persons falling under one of the five stipulated categories should be admitted for such treatment. Nowhere had the Ministry ever specified that Ankang facilities were permitted to "admit and treat patients from society at large" (*mianxiang shehui shouzhi bingren*). The court was thus doubly wrong in accepting the Xi'an Ankang's claim that this had been the basis of Meng's treatment. Since Meng's case did not fall within the five stipulated categories, moreover, her committal "was obviously unlawful."

On the key legal question of whether Meng's incarceration had constituted a "specific administrative action" by the PSB, the lawyers and legal scholars were unanimous in stating that that, despite the court's finding to the contrary, it undoubtedly did so:

- Although the sum total of the medical certification in Meng's case was one Ankang document stating that she suffered from "hysteria," both the PSB and the Ankang authorities had nonetheless issued a series of other official documents specifically "agreeing to," "authorizing" and "endorsing" each of the six involuntary committals to the Xi'an Ankang to which Meng had been subjected over the years. Moreover, each of these various documents had been stamped with the Ankang's official seal and signed by the institute's director. The court had examined these documents, the Ankang was a purely PSB entity, and the court's ruling that the police had "taken no administrative action" against Meng was thus without legal foundation.

- Moreover, local police had acted as "the evil accomplices" (*bang xiong*) of the Shunda Shoe Factory in having Meng forcibly sent to the Ankang on numerous

---

579 For details of Wang's case, see p.268 above.
580 The document referred to here is the MPS's "*Quanguo Gong'an Jiguan Di'yi Ci Jingshenbing Guan-Zhi Gongzuo Huiyi Jiyao*" (Key-Point Summary of the First National Public Security Conference on Custody and Treatment of the Mentally Ill), issued on 13 December 1987; available at: http://www.fm120.com/zt/law/laws/1/JBFZGL/BMGZ/BMGZ1005.htm. For further details of this key event, see p.246, and Notes 512 and 513, above. The "Key-Point Summary" document was issued on a classified or secret basis, probably because it includes among those to be taken into Ankang custody: "people who shout reactionary slogans and put up reactionary posters, thereby attracting crowds of onlookers and exerting a bad influence."

occasions. Indeed, so severe were the circumstances of this case that Meng would be fully justified in taking out a private criminal prosecution against the Ankang, the PSB and the shoe factory leadership.

- The court's most fundamental area of legal confusion had been in construing the "dual role" principle and axiom of the Ankang system's work – namely, the "combination of custody and treatment" (*guan-zhi jiehe*) – as meaning "custody for involuntary patients" and "treatment for voluntary patients." It was this which had led the court wrongly to accept the Ankang authorities' claim that Meng's case was one of "voluntary civil referral." What the "dual role" principle in fact meant was that only involuntary patients were to be admitted to the Ankang, and all such people were to be subjected to custody and treatment simultaneously. Thus, the Ankang authorities' claim that they only had Meng "in treatment" and not "in custody" was false.

The legal experts concluded their public discussion of Meng Xiaoxia's case by saying that since the Ankang system's formal legal foundation went no further than the Ministry of Public Security's "Conference Key-Point Summary" of December 1987 – a purely administrative document which appeared to be "in conflict with certain other laws" (an apparent reference to the Administrative Punishments Law and the Law on Legislation) – consideration should now be given to abolishing the Ankang system and to "replacing it with something more humane."

The Case of Wang Fenglai

In 1985, a young woman named Liang Caixia, from a well-off family, fell into the Zhujiang River in Guangzhou, Guangdong Province, and almost drowned. She was saved by a young man, a lower middle-school graduate named Wang Fenglai.[581] Out of gratitude, she agreed to marry him, but after a few years of marriage the educational gap between them grew wider and Liang began to treat her husband with contempt. He was quiet and introspective, while she was outgoing and lively. He worked as an orderly in a funeral parlour, while she went into business and eventually became the general manager of a successful company. She made Wang do all the cleaning and other housework, but he tolerated it patiently and out of a sense of debt since she had "married below her status." Liang eventually began openly to bring lovers home in the evenings.

In May 2003, a sudden and dramatic change arose in his wife's general behaviour towards him. She began to treat Wang warmly and kindly again for the first time in many years. One evening, she broached the topic of their retirement plans and said that he should consider quitting his job so that he could spend more time at home. Her monthly salary of 8,000 *yuan* would be more than enough for both of them. She then unfolded her plan of action to Wang Fenglai: if he could succeed in convincing his manager at the funeral parlour that he was mentally ill, he would be able to apply for early retirement on a full pension. All he needed to do was to act in a conspicuously strange manner at work for a few weeks, and eventually his manager would have to call in a psychiatrist to have him examined. Wang

---

581 See: Zheng Rong, "*'Feng' Zhangfu Zhuanggao 'Pan Jinlian' – Quan Zhangfu Bingtui, 'Chu Xin Ji Lü'*" (A "Mad" Husband Sues "Pan Jinlian" – Wife Concocts Weird Scheme to Make Husband Take Disability Retirement), *Fazhi Kuaibao* (Legal System Express), 7 June 2004, available at: www.fzkb.cn.; also available at: skb.hebeidaily. com.cn/200429/ca391213.htm.

was highly taken with the plan, and he began to think up various kinds of odd behaviour to practise at home.

When the big day arrived, on 20 June, the normally quiet and inhibited Wang arrived at work in inordinately high spirits. During the solemn funeral proceedings on that day and during the rest of the week, he giggled and made odd gestures in front of the assembled mourners. The funeral parlour office began receiving numerous complaints from angry and indignant customers, and when the manager called Wang into his office to upbraid him, Wang laughed loudly throughout the meeting. The manager then called Wang's wife, Liang Caixia – who promptly suggested that it might be a wise idea to send her husband over to the Ankang Hospital for a psychiatric examination. An appointment was duly made, and on 30 June Wang Fenglai was examined at the Guangzhou Ankang Hospital by a chief psychiatrist (*zhuzhi yisheng*) named Jia Ruowang.[582] Wang began to suspect that things were not quite going "according to plan" when Jia summoned two burly orderlies who proceeded to forcibly administer him with heavy medication. He woke up several hours later alone in a room, but was able to take advantage of a change of shifts at the entrance gate to slip out of the hospital and return home. His freedom was short-lived, however, because later that evening his wife arrived at the front door with the same two Ankang orderlies who had earlier doped him. The men bundled him into a waiting van and took him back to the hospital, where he was locked up in a room with only a metal bed in it for the next month.

On 18 July, his wife Liang made her first visit to the hospital to see him. To his dismay, instead of pleading for his release as he had still been hoping she would, she calmly informed the medical staff that Wang was "frequently violent" towards her at home, that he often "came to her office and caused disturbances," and she added for good measure that he had "sexually abused" her. Wang's outraged and angry response to these allegations was duly noted down by chief psychiatrist Jia as supporting a diagnosis of serious mental illness. Five weeks later, Wang was allowed home on medical parole, but his wife made a point of bringing a lover home that evening and of spending the night with him in the marriage bed, causing Wang to start throwing objects around the apartment in a fit of anger. Again the burly orderlies were sent to forcibly return him to the Ankang. He continued to be heavily medicated at the hospital, but after several more weeks he succeeded in persuading a nurse to smuggle out a letter to his colleagues at the funeral parlour, begging them to inform his relatives of his plight.

Soon both the relatives and the colleagues turned up at the Guangzhou Ankang, demanding that a fresh psychiatric examination be carried out on Wang Fenglai. The hospital director gave his assent, and Wang's medical records were carefully re-examined and a series of new medical tests were performed on him. When the results showed that Wang was in fact completely mentally normal, chief psychiatrist Jia Ruowang had no option but to confess that he had accepted a 3,000 *yuan* bribe from Liang Caixia in exchange for agreeing to "take good care" of her husband. Wang was then discharged from the Ankang, and Jia was promptly sacked from his job. However, neither the psychiatrist nor the wife received any legal sanction or punishment, from either the police or the courts, for conspiring together to have a mentally normal person incarcerated in an institute for the criminally insane. The only adverse consequence for Liang Caixia was that she failed to achieve the ultimate goal of her conspiracy, which was to have her husband declared as having lost his capacity for civil action because of mental illness, so that she could seize his entire savings, together with their apartment, and then divorce him.[583]

---

582 The newspaper report indicated that this name was a pseudonym.
583 In the event, it Wang Fenglai himself who sued for divorce, and on 30 November 2003 the Haizhu District Court in Guangzhou annulled the marriage and ordered that the couple's property be split between them on an

It was thus left to Wang to seek justice on his own initiative for what had been done to him. On 6 February 2004, with the help of a lawyer, he brought a civil tort suit against Liang Caixia, the Guangzhou Ankang, and Jia Ruowang and other hospital employees, claiming a total of 80,000 yuan in compensatory damages. There have been no further reports on the case, however, so the outcome of the lawsuit remains unknown.

Significantly, in late April 2004, several months prior to the first press reports on Wang Fenglai's case, several articles appeared in the Chinese news media stating that a delegation of legislators from the Guangzhou Municipal People's Congress had recently made an inspection visit of the Guangzhou Ankang – a relatively new such facility which came into commission in October 2002 but "formally commenced operations only in 2003" (the year that Wang Fenglai was sent there.) After touring and inspecting the asylum, the Guangzhou legislators voiced surprisingly outspoken criticisms of the way it was being run – "questioning both its present status and the form of management being used," according to the Southern Daily. As the newspaper then noted, "Currently, the Public Security Bureau is managing the hospital patients in accordance with the PRC Regulations on Detention Centres (*Kanshousuo Tiaoli*)."

According to the reports, out of the current Guangzhou Ankang inmate population of 105, no fewer than 95 were prisoners who until recently had been held in a temporary psychiatric ward at the Guangzhou City No. 2 Detention Centre. The Guangzhou Ankang was said to occupy 30,000 square metres of land and to consist of 13 buildings, only four of which contained patient wards and other medical facilities, the other nine being used to accommodate security personnel and administrators. As Zheng Guoqiang, Vice-Chairman of the Guangzhou People's Congress Standing Committee, remarked after inspecting the new facility, "Such a large logistical base and such a small front line!" He continued:

> The Ankang Hospital…should be run as a psychiatric institute rather than a jail… Although these mental patients committed crimes, they should not be held legally responsible. It is inappropriate to treat them as prisoners and to run the hospital like a detention centre….Instead of using the regulations on detention centres, a new mechanism should be introduced so that the place can be run like a hospital.[584]

---

approximately equal basis.

584   See: Chen Jiena, "*Shi Jingshenbingyuan Haishi Kanshousuo? Shi Ren-Da Daibiao Shicha Ankang Yiyuan Tichu Piping... Yong Kanshousuo Tiaoli Guanli Jingshenbingren Qiantuo*" (Is it a Mental Hospital or a Prison? After Inspection Visit to Ankang Hospital, People's Congress Delegates Raise Criticisms….Calling it Inappropriate to Manage Mental Patients in Accordance with Detention Centre Regulations), *Nanfang Ribao* (Southern Daily), 28 April 2004, available at: www.nanfangdaily.com.cn/southnews/jwxy/200404280630.asp. See also: "*Guangzhou Shi Shouzhi Shubai Zhong An Jingshenbingren – Bingren Ruyuan Yi, Chuyuan Nan*" (Guangzhou City Takes into Custody for Treatment Hundreds of Mentally Ill People Who Commit Serious Crimes – Going in is Easy, But Getting Out is Hard), *Xinxi Shibao* (Information Times), 28 April 2004; Chan Siu-sin, "Mental Hospital Should Not Be Run as Jail, Says Official," South China Morning Post, 29 April 2004; and "'*Ankang Yiyuan' Xia Yue Choujian*" ('Ankang Hospital' to be Built Next Month), Nanfang Ribao, 20 October 2000.

In addition, during the visit to the Guangzhou Ankang, the Secretary-General of the People's Congress Standing Committee, Yang Yongbi, rejected the view of the Deputy Director of the Guangzhou Public Security Bureau on the question of how many doctors would be required to run the new Ankang facility. According to Yang, "The size of the medical staff should be based on the number of patients in the hospital and not its capacity." (See Chen Jiena, op cit.)

A Legal Legerdemain

Perhaps the most significant and intriguing aspect of the various case accounts from 2000-04 discussed above was the argument put forward by the Ankang and PSB authorities, when challenged in the administrative courts by their victims, that they had no case to answer because the "patients" concerned had all been "civil psychiatric referrals" by third parties (though almost never, significantly, by the persons' relatives) and that consequently "no administrative action" had been taken by the PSB itself. What permits Ankang officials to make this claim with a relatively straight face in court is the adoption by the Ankang system in recent years of an ad hoc policy of providing "society-oriented reception and treatment services" (*mianxiang shehui shouzhi fuwu*) to the general public. Essentially, this is a money earning operation whereby the Ankang asylums admit fee-paying patients from the local community, as a means of boosting the no doubt quite inadequate operating funds that they receive from the government. Little is known about the nature and composition of such cases. Many of them are doubtless voluntary admissions, but many – perhaps a majority – are likely to be involuntary civil committals carried out on the instructions of the patient's families, as provided for in the relevant sections of the General Principles of Civil Law and the Civil Procedure Law. However as one of the lawyers who commented on Meng Xiaoxia's case pointed out, the Ankang system is not actually authorized, under the terms of its 1987 mandate from the Ministry of Public Security, to accept either of these two types of patients. Its role and activities are supposed to go no further than providing custody and treatment for the "five types" of dangerously mentally-ill criminal offenders.[585]

The fact that the Ankang system provides these "society-oriented services" without having the slightest legal mandate for doing so, however, means that if challenged in court over cases where – as in the examples presented above – the individual concerned was a de facto criminal detainee, but one whose admission for Ankang psychiatric treatment had been procedurally unlawful because none of the requisite legal formalities were carried out, then the police can always claim that the patient was "only" an involuntary civil committal case. What seems to be the primary advantage of this approach, from the point of view of the Ankang authorities and other officials who are the principal authors of such people's misfortune, is that the various facts and elements of the conspiracy can later be presented to the court in such a way as to support the police's case that the committals were lawful, when in fact the points in question constitute the principal evidence of official wrongdoing.

Take, for example, the lack of any formal legal- psychiatric evaluation documents: this was simply because the case at issue was "not a criminal one" and so there was no need to ascertain the detainee's capacity for legal responsibility. Likewise with the absence of documentation from the police officers who delivered the patient into Ankang custody: they failed to complete, sign and put the PSB's seal on the requisite forms – stating that a criminal suspect had been detained, that signs of mental illness were observed, that an examination was performed by properly accredited forensic psychiatrists and that the person was then compulsorily admitted to the Ankang – not through any procedural omission on their part, but simply because the nature of the case did not require them to do any of these things. The police were merely "assisting the guardians" of the patient in question (for which read: the work unit, manager, or local official with whom the person was currently having a major dispute of some kind) to carry out an urgently needed civil psychiatric committal. In a deft but not very amusing version of the "look, no hands" routine, the PSB's defence in court then became that "no specific administrative action" was undertaken by it throughout the entire process. In short, everything fits neatly together in the shadowy world of the Ankang system and everything is officially deniable.

---

585   For details of the five categories, see p.256 above.

The various cases discussed above also, however, provide a certain amount of grounds for optimism. What were the reasons for the unexpected degree of openness and candour that suddenly became evident in the Chinese news media, from early 2004 onward, on the previously off-limits subject of the country's institutes for the criminally insane? Several disparate factors can be singled out, here as in a growing range of other areas of life in China today, that appear to be interacting with one another to produce an important new kind of social synergy for China. Firstly, a more combative and independent-minded press, staffed by growing numbers of reporters willing to go out and find controversial news stories about bullying officials who violate citizens' basic rights and freedoms; second, a hesitant but still emboldening sense of confidence on the part of the victims themselves that someone out there – whether it is the local government, the courts, the news media or simply "public opinion" – might nowadays actually be ready and able to take action on their behalf; third, an increasingly influential and self-assertive community of lawyers and law firms willing to represent clients of this kind and to wage politically sensitive lawsuits on their behalf; and fourth, a steadily emerging trend towards greater public accountability within hitherto closed and autonomous sectors of the government, in particular the police force, along with initial moves by local legislatures toward monitoring and investigating matters previously seen as being the latter's purely internal and confidential affairs.

While these encouraging new developments are surely not going to lead to the demise of one-party rule and the arrival of democracy in China any time soon, they are nonetheless contributing to the creation of a vital new political space in Chinese society, one with potentially wide implications for the country's future development. In particular, the breaching of the long-standing taboo on public reporting and discussion of the Ankang system can be seen as cautiously indicative of a new kind of "social détente" between government and citizens in China today. If, as the experience of the former Soviet Union and other such countries would suggest, the willingness of a dictatorial government to open up its prison system to public scrutiny serves as a harbinger or touchstone of moves toward more general forms of public accountability, then the Chinese government's apparent readiness to start letting some sunlight into what has hitherto been probably the darkest corner of its criminal custody system may prove to have been a turning point of wider significance.

CHAPTER 9
The International Campaign

As evidence mounted in the late 1990s that large numbers of Falun Gong practitioners were being forcibly committed to mental asylums by the Chinese police, and following the publication, from early 2001 onwards, of a series of articles by the present writer showing that similar practices had been extensively used by the Chinese authorities since the late 1950s against certain types of political dissidents and other critics of the government,[586] many psychiatrists in countries around the world began publicly to express their concern over the growing evidence of human rights abuses in the field of psychiatry and the law in China. The international advocacy campaign on this issue was organized and led, in highly effective fashion, by the Geneva Initiative on Psychiatry, a non-governmental organization that had been formed in 1980 for the express purpose of campaigning against the widespread misuse of psychiatry against dissidents in the Soviet Union and Eastern Europe at that time.[587]

The Chinese government responded swiftly and in characteristic fashion to the groundswell of charges that it was misusing psychiatric detention for purposes of political control and repression. For example, in February 2001, Zhu Bangzao, spokesman of the PRC Ministry of Foreign Affairs, stated at a press conference for foreign journalists in Beijing: "Such allegations are totally groundless and unacceptable….There is no evidence to support it."[588]

At an academic conference in China later that year, Kang Ming, Director of the Hangzhou Ankang facility – and the same psychiatrist who, in October 1997, had personally diagnosed farmers' rights

---

586 See: Robin Munro, "Judicial Psychiatry in China and its Political Abuses" (op cit), and *Dangerous Minds* (op cit.). See also: Jonathan Mirsky, "China's Psychiatric Terror," *The New York Review of Books*, Vol. L, No.3, 27 February 2003, pp.38-42.

587 In 2005, the group renamed itself as the Global Initiative on Psychiatry. According to GIP's website (www.gip-global.org),

> The international foundation, Geneva Initiative on Psychiatry, sprang to life in 1980 to combat the political abuse of psychiatry which, at that moment, was widely used as a tool of repression in the Soviet Union and in a number of Eastern European countries.
>
> It was, until 1991, called the International Association on Political Use of Psychiatry (IAPUP). IAPUP spearheaded efforts of many other national and international psychiatric organizations to work together to eliminate this systematic abuse of psychiatry. IAPUP communicated with individuals in the former USSR and provided details and consultation enabling the world of psychiatry to take appropriate ethical positions to protect the human rights of victims of abuse. These efforts helped to force the then-Soviet All Union Society of Psychiatrists and Neuropathologists (AUSPN) to withdraw from the World Psychiatric Association (WPA) in early 1983.

Following the collapse of the Soviet Union, the primary focus of GIP's work shifted towards promoting a more humane and patient-centred approach to psychiatric care in Russia, the former communist states of Eastern Europe, and elsewhere; it is currently active in some thirty countries around the world. However, opposing the political misuse of psychiatry wherever it occurs remains one of the group's primary aims. The founder and current general secretary of GIP is Robert van Voren, and the group's board includes numerous internationally renowned psychiatrists, as well as several users of psychiatric services.

588 "China Slams Study Alleging Psychiatric Abuse," *Reuters*, 20 February 2001.

activist Qiu Jinyou as being a "paranoid psychotic" and "litigious maniac"[589] – delivered a paper in which he hotly defended the Ankang system against all charges of abuse. According to Kang:

> Some overseas people with ulterior motives have been making publicity saying that the Ankang Hospitals pay no attention to the human rights of mental patients, and claiming that we have been "misusing" the diagnosis of "paranoid psychosis" against "political dissidents" by curtailing their incessant "petitioning" activities and admitting them for compulsory treatment.... Such claims go against all objective facts and legal logic and serve once again to expose the odious anti-China mentality of certain ulterior-minded foreigners.... I hereby invite psychiatrists from mental hospitals in countries around the world to come and visit the Ankang Hospitals and engage in academic exchanges with us.[590]

It is debatable as to whether Kang Ming was speaking here in his capacity as a psychiatrist and physician, as someone concerned about the welfare of his patients and the good reputation of his hospital, or alternatively, as a senior officer in the Hangzhou Public Security Bureau, and whose chief concern was to combat "odious political scheming from abroad," as his article put it.[591] Certainly, the only known photograph of Kang shows him wearing not a white medical tunic, but rather a full PSB officer's uniform (badge number: 012636.)[592]

Despite the government's protestations of innocence, a series of front-page articles and editorials in newspapers around the world had by this time begun to lodge the issue firmly on the international public agenda.[593] Among the most active in pressing for action on the China question were members of the U.K.'s Royal College of Psychiatrists and the American Psychiatric Association. At its annual general meeting in July 2001, the Royal College, at the eloquent urging of two of its former presidents – Jim Birley and Robert Kendall – voted overwhelmingly in favour of the following resolution on China:

> Bearing in mind the available evidence that political dissidents in the People's Republic of China (PRC) are being systematically detained in psychiatric hospitals, we propose that the Royal College of Psychiatrists takes the following action:
>
> 1) to join with the World Psychiatric Association (WPA) to arrange a fact-finding visit to the PRC;
>
> 2) if this visit and other evidence confirm political abuse of psychiatry, to ask the WPA to reconsider the constituent membership of the Chinese Society of Psychiatrists;

---

589 For details of Qiu's case, see p.260 above.
590 Kang Ming, "*Ankang Yiyuan de Xingzhi, Renwu, Zuoyong*" (The Nature, Tasks and Function of the Ankang Hospitals); found on the official website of the Hangzhou Ankang Hospital: www.ak-hospital.com/lwsx.htm. Although undated, the article is listed elsewhere as having been presented by the author at an academic conference in Zhejiang Province in 2001. (See: http://mis.511511.com/lwwx/wxdctail.asp?id=256746.)
591 Ibid. In his article, Kang singled out the present writer by name for criticism in this regard.
592 The photograph of Kang Ming is available on the Internet at: www.zjmh.net/bri/brief_rwshow.php?id=uGain3ff9195283000. His official biography can be found at: www.worldexperts.org/9/K/K4-1.htm.
593 See, for example: Erik Eckholm, "China's Crackdown on Sect Stirs Alarm over Psychiatric Abuse: Rights Groups Cite Rise in Medical Detentions," *New York Times*, 19 February 2001, p.1; and Isabel Hilton, "The China Scandal," *The Guardian*, 22 February 2001. See also: "Contortions of Psychiatry in China," Editorial, *New York Times*, 25 March 2001.

3) to work with the WPA to provide support for those Chinese psychiatrists who are committed to ethical and evidence-based practice.[594]

It is important to note that, under the terms of the WPA's Madrid Declaration of 1996, the need to reconsider China's constituent membership of the WPA would have followed automatically from any finding of systematic political abuse of psychiatry in China; so the inclusion of point 2) above in no way served to prejudge the issue. Rather, the Royal College's carefully worded resolution was in practice aimed mainly at promoting the other two proposals: namely, that a WPA-led fact-finding mission should be undertaken to establish the veracity or otherwise of the allegations, and that meanwhile the hand of professional friendship should be extended to all Chinese psychiatrists not directly involved in the abuses concerned. This important resolution by the Royal College – which, significantly, had also taken the lead internationally in publicly opposing and condemning the psychiatric incarceration of dissidents and others in the former Soviet Union – was subsequently endorsed and supported by several WPA member societies from other parts of the world. Of particular significance, on 26 September 2001 the Russian Society of Psychiatrists voted to support the Royal College's China resolution, and this was followed in November that year by a similar expression of support from the Psychiatric Association of Lithuania – another part of the former Soviet empire where legal psychiatry had been widely used as a tool of state repression.

Soon afterwards, in October 2001, the American Psychoanalytic Association (APsaA) passed the following resolution on China:

> Mounting evidence of serious abuse of psychiatry to silence peaceful dissident voices in the People's Republic of China, including those of the Falun Gong faith, has come to the attention of the World Psychiatric Association. This abuse takes the form of incarceration without professional diagnosis, disabling doses of psychopharmacological agents, use of physical restraints and involuntary electro-convulsive shock therapy. Based upon this evidence, the American Psychoanalytic Association takes the following position:
>
> 1) That a full investigation by human rights groups and the World Psychiatric Association be conducted immediately regarding evidence of political abuse of psychiatry in the People's Republic of China.
>
> 2) Independent representatives of the international psychiatric and psychoanalytic communities do this investigation.
>
> 3) That the APsaA show solidarity with our ethical colleagues in China who are against these human rights violations, allowing them greater voice.
>
> 4) That an international conference be held to address and discuss these matters further.
>
> 5) That the APsaA's position is that any psychological disorder will not be diagnosed or considered based upon an individual's political, ethnic, religious, racial, sexual orientation or belief.[595]

---

594 Annual General Meeting of the Royal College of Psychiatrists, London, 11 July 2001; in the final vote on the China resolution, there were two abstentions and no votes against.
595 "A Position Paper on Psychiatric Abuses in the People's Republic of China, Submitted by the [APsaA's] Committee on Social Issues," 20 October 2001. (Copy on file with the author.)

In addition, in May 2001, the Medical Ethics Committee of the World Medical Association (WMA) debated a lengthy internal discussion document on the political misuse of psychiatry against dissidents in China. According to the WMA document,

> International standards allow for the detention of mentally ill people who are deemed to be a danger to themselves or others. China, however, uses the concept of "social dangerousness" whereby dissidents and non-conformists can be forcibly detained because they are seen as threatening the social order. This is in contradiction with international human rights standards which provide for freedom of expression, freedom of political and religious belief and rights to a fair trial. ...
>
> Some Chinese psychiatrists are among those who have called for reform and enactment of a mental health law.... [However,] officially defined criteria describe types of people who should be taken into psychiatric custody. Included are "political maniacs" who write reactionary letters or express opinions on domestic and international affairs, thereby exerting a political influence. Doctors are at risk themselves if they attempt to speak out or act ethically. They are faced with a dilemma in that if they declare the political activist or non-conformist sane, that person will be sent to prison for anti-social activity and threatening state security; if they declare the individual mentally ill, he or she will be committed to indefinite psychiatric custody.[596]

Following reports that similar practices had also lately been re-emerging in Uzbekistan and Cuba,[597] in June 2002 the WMA General Assembly formally adopted the following inclusive resolution:

> 1) The World Medical Association (WMA) notes with concern evidence from a number of countries that political dissidents and social activists have been detained in psychiatric institutions, and subjected to unnecessary psychiatric treatment as a punishment.
>
> 2) The WMA:
>
> 1. declares that such detention and treatment is abusive and unacceptable;
> 2. calls on physicians and psychiatrists to resist involvement in these abusive practices;

---

596 The World Medical Association, Inc., "Discussion Document on the Political Abuse of Psychiatry," DD 1/Psych/2001, submitted to the WMA Medical Ethics Committee at the 159th WMA Council Session at Divonne-les-Bains, France, 3-6 May 2001; the quoted passages appear on p.2. (Copy of document on file with the author.) According to the official record of this meeting, "The use of psychiatry as a means of political repression and torture was strongly condemned following reports of human rights abuses in Uzbekistan. Dr Delon Human, secretary general of the WMA, stated: 'The WMA strongly condemns this practice of using psychiatric treatment for political ends wherever it occurs. We note with concern evidence from a number of countries that political dissidents and social activists have been detained in psychiatric institutions and subjected to unnecessary psychiatric treatment as a punishment. The WMA urges all psychiatrists and physicians to resist involvement in these abusive practices and we call on national medical associations around the world to support physicians who resist involvement in these abuses'." (See: http://www.wma.net/e/press/2001_14.htm.)

597 See, for example, Human Rights Watch, "Uzbekistan: Dissident in Psychiatric Detention," 12 April 2001; on Cuba, see above, Note 367.

3. calls on member NMAs [national medical associations] to support their physician members who resist involvement in these abuses, and

4. calls on governments to stop abusing medicine and psychiatry in this manner, and on non-governmental organizations and the World Health Organization to support this initiative.[598]

Similar resolutions were passed by several constituent bodies of the American Psychiatric Association from early 2001 onwards,[599] and in May 2002 the APA Lifers' Committee "unanimously adopted a resolution calling on the APA to persuade the WPA to conduct its planned investigation of abuse of psychiatry in the People's Republic of China without delay."[600] In October 2001, Paul Appelbaum, the APA's president, published an article expressing firm support for an independent investigation to be carried out.[601] As Appelbaum observed, the significance of the allegations went well beyond just China:

---

598 "The World Medical Association Resolution on the Abuse of Psychiatry," initiated in the WMA Medical Ethics Committee on 20 May 2001 and adopted by the WMA General Assembly on 10 June 2002 in Washington DC. (Available at: http://www.wma.net/e/policy/a3.htm.)

599 In May 2000, for example, the American Psychiatric Association's Committee on the Abuse of Psychiatry and Psychiatrists passed a resolution at the APA's annual conference in Chicago "recommending that the World Psychiatric Association investigate the alleged wrongful detention of Falun Gong practitioners in psychiatric hospitals" ("APA Committee Calls for Investigation of Chinese Psychiatric Abuses," *Psychiatric News*, June 16, 2000, available at http://www.psych.org/pnews/00-06-16/chinese.html). According to a subsequent report, "The Board [of APA Trustees] also referred this matter to the APA Commission on International Psychiatry and the Committee on Misuse and Abuse of Psychiatry for monitoring the progress of the WPA's investigation" (*Psychiatric News*, June 16, 2000, available at http://www.psych.org/pnews/00-08-04/board.html). Additionally, when an APA delegation of sixty-five American psychiatrists attended the Second Sino-American Conference on Psychiatry in Beijing in April 2000, "[The U.S. psychiatrists] Herbert Peyser, [Allan] Tasman, [Jeffrey] Geller and other psychiatrists met with Chinese Society of Psychiatry leaders informally to convey their concerns about Falun Gong practitioners being allegedly detained involuntarily in psychiatric hospitals and injected with harmful medications for political reasons" (*Psychiatric News*, June 16, 2000, available at http://www.psych.org/pnews/00-06-16/china.html). See also the APA Area 5 Council's resolution: "Condemning the Chinese Government's Misuse of Psychiatry," passed in May 2001; the resolution referred to the Chinese authorities' "flagrant misuse of psychiatry as a means of silencing dissidents" and called upon the APA's Board of Trustees to issue a statement condemning these practices and urging it to "request the World Psychiatric Association through its review committee to pursue investigation of these allegations by all appropriate means."

That such a statement on China has still (as of this writing) not been issued by the APA as a whole is due mainly to strong opposition toward any such move by a few influential members of the APA leadership, notably Alan Stone, a Harvard University professor of law and psychiatry who espouses the revisionist viewpoint that no political misuse of psychiatry ever occurred in the former Soviet Union, and Arthur Kleinman, professor of psychiatry and anthropology at Harvard University and a leading scholar of contemporary Chinese psychiatry. For details of articles by Stone and Kleinman on this topic, see below, Note 605. See also: Alan A. Stone, "Investigating Psychiatric Abuses," *Psychiatric Times*, November 2002, Vol. XIX, Issue 11.

600 See: Abraham L. Halpern, M.D., "Lifers Take a Stand," Letter to the Editor, *Psychiatric News*, 16 August 2002, Vol. 37, No. 16, p.26. In his letter, Halpern noted that the WPA had been moving "with glacial speed" on its planned China investigation.

601 In August 2002, the American Psychiatric Association further signalled its support for the campaign against political-psychiatric abuse in China by honouring the present writer with its 2003 Award for Patient Advocacy, together with an invitation to address the APA membership at their annual meeting in San Francisco in May 2003.

> Western psychiatrists are understandably concerned when their discipline is used for political purposes. To condone such abuses anywhere is to give credence to the claim that all psychiatric diagnoses are suspect and that involuntary commitment is nothing more than a transparent effort to confine those who give voice to ideas that the dominant members of society would prefer not to hear. Thus, with the encouragement of the American Psychiatric Association and comparable organizations in other countries, the World Psychiatric Association is seeking China's permission for a delegation of foreign psychiatrists to visit the country and examine persons who claim they have been subjected to unjustified detention and treatment.

As he also noted, however,

> At this writing, the World Psychiatric Association's efforts have not met with success. The Soviet Union's acquiescence in a visit by Western psychiatrists in 1989 came only when the leaders perceived it as being in their interests to rein in the hard-liners who were then in control of the psychiatric system.[602] China's leaders today, at the helm of an economically vigorous nation, are in a very different political position from that of the heads of the tottering Soviet state.[603]

The WPA leadership at first made a reasonably sustained and conscientious effort to enter into negotiations with the Chinese government over its proposed investigative mission. In January 2002, the WPA president, Juan López-Ibor, reported the results to date of these negotiations to the various heads of the WPA's national member societies, as follows:

> As soon as the WPA received these complaints [about Chinese psychiatry], the foreseen procedure was initiated. The procedure is that the WPA Review Committee, in cooperation with the local Member Society, in this case the Chinese Society of Psychiatry, starts a process of revision of the individual cases of alleged abuse. The Review Committee and the Chinese Society of Psychiatry are working on this and have already had several meetings. Meanwhile, the [WPA] Executive Committee met with representatives of the Chinese Society of Psychiatry and received on different occasions the guarantee that this Society is fully cooperating in this task.... They are

---

602 The 1989 visit by Western psychiatrists to the Soviet Union was organized by the U.S. State Department. The delegation of experts was allowed by their Soviet hosts to interview and medically evaluate some 27 patients and former patients about whom allegations of wrongful psychiatric incarceration on political grounds had been raised. As two members of the delegation later observed, "The investigation by the U.S. delegation provided unequivocal proof that the tools of coercive psychiatry had been used, even in the late 1980s, to hospitalize persons who were not mentally ill and whose only transgression had been the expression of political or religious dissent. See: Richard J. Bonnie and Svetlana V. Polubinskaya, "Unraveling Soviet Psychiatry," *The Journal of Contemporary Legal Issues*, Vol. 10, 1999, p.280-1. For a full account of the 1989 U.S. delegation's visit to the Soviet Union, see: Richard J. Bonnie, "Soviet Psychiatry and Human Rights: Reflections on the Report of the U.S. Delegation," 19 *Law, Med. & Health Care* 123 (1990.) In early 1991, a second mission of investigation was undertaken to the Soviet Union by the UK's Royal College of Psychiatrists, led by a former President of the College, Jim Birley. The UK delegation also found overwhelming evidence to support the allegations that psychiatry had been used as a means of incarcerating sane political dissidents and other critics of the Soviet regime.
603 Paul S. Appelbaum, M.D., "Abuses of Law and Psychiatry in China," *Psychiatric Services*, October 2001, Vol. 52, No. 10, pp.1297-8.

expecting the authorisation of the Ministry of Health to include them. Unfortunately this request has not yet received an answer.[604]

López-Ibor added that he had recently written to the Chinese Minister of Health and the Minister of Public Security "to express our concerns, to offer our expertise in this area and to express the willingness of the WPA to select an international group of experts for the review process."

Nonetheless, two points soon became clear as regards the WPA leadership's stance on the China issue: first, that it was determined to limit the scope of its proposed investigation exclusively to the Falun Gong cases that had been brought to its attention, and to rule out any attempt to investigate the situation of political dissidents wrongly sent to mental asylums in China, notwithstanding the increasingly clear and abundant official evidence and statistics that had by now come to light on this latter issue (it should be emphasized, however, that none of the detailed case material presented in Chapters 6 and 8 of this book had become available at that time); and second, that the WPA leadership was determined at all costs to avoid any repetition, in China's case, of the kind of major schism and conflict that had occurred within the WPA over the issue of Soviet psychiatric abuses during the 1970s and 80s.

This difference of opinion within the world psychiatric community over how best to deal with the China question was reflected also in an important symposium of scholarly articles on the subject that appeared in the Journal of the American Academy of Psychiatry and the Law in March and June 2002. Among the eleven contributors to the debate, seven strongly supported taking action against China through the WPA and four strongly opposed the idea.[605] The view of the Journal's editor, Kenneth Appelbaum, was as follows:

> Although repression can take many forms, there is something chilling about the image of psychiatrists, who are supposed arbiters of sanity and experts in the healing of distressed minds, functioning instead as agents to discredit and punish political dissidents. We have a professional obligation to resist such misuse and perversion of our expertise and credibility. Even if misuse of psychiatry represents only a small portion of the abuses within a repressive society, it remains our unique responsibility to address such transgressions by our profession.... The issue of psychiatric abuse

---

604 Prof. Juan J. López-Ibor, "Circular Letter to All Presidents of WPA Member Societies," 24 January 2002; copy on file with the author.

605 See: "Special Section on Political Abuse of Psychiatry," *The Journal of the American Academy of Psychiatry and the Law*, 2002, Vol. 30, No. 1, pp.95-147. The various articles and contributors included: Kenneth L. Appelbaum (Editor), "Political Abuse of Psychiatry: An Introduction to the Munro Commentaries"; Robin Munro, "Political Psychiatry in Post-Mao China and its Origins in the Cultural Revolution"; Alan A. Stone, "Psychiatrists on the Side of the Angels"; Frederick W. Hickling, "The Political Misuse of Psychiatry: An African-Caribbean Perspective"; Sing Lee and Arthur Kleinman, "Psychiatry in its Political and Professional Contexts: A Response to Robin Munro"; Sunny Y. Lu and Viviana B. Galli, "Psychiatric Abuse of Falun Gong Practitioners in China"; Robert van Voren, "Comparing Soviet and Chinese Political Psychiatry"; Richard J. Bonnie, "Political Abuse of Psychiatry in the Soviet Union and China: Complexities and Controversies"; and Jim Birley, "Political Abuse of Psychiatry in the Soviet Union and China: A Rough Guide for Bystanders." See also: Robin Munro, "On the Psychiatric Abuse of Falun Gong and Other Dissenters in China: A Reply to Stone, Hickling, Kleinman and Lee," *The Journal of the American Academy of Psychiatry and the Law*, 2002, Vol. 30, No. 2, pp.266-274; and Alan Stone, "Response to Munro" (Letter to the Editor), *The Journal of the American Academy of Psychiatry and the Law*, 2002, Vol. 30, No. 4, pp.589-90.

requires caution but not silence, perspective but not indifference, and self-reflection but not incapacitating cultural relativism. Debate nurtures liberty and justice.[606]

The first major showdown within the WPA over the China issue occurred at the organization's triennial World Congress in Yokohama, Japan, in August 2002. A highly professional lobbying effort, led by the Geneva Initiative on Psychiatry, succeeded in raising widespread awareness and concern about the situation in China among the 15,000 or so psychiatrists from around the world who attended the Yokohama conference. On 26 August, the WPA's most senior decision-making body, the General Assembly, convened to discuss and decide how to proceed on the China question.[607] One of the first speakers was Mike Shooter, president of the Royal College of Psychiatrists, who argued strongly that nothing short of a full and independent investigative mission to China by the WPA would suffice, and that it was vital to ensure that the WPA delegation would get direct access to actual individuals alleged to have been wrongly incarcerated in Chinese mental asylums for political reasons. According to Shooter,

> The Royal College of Psychiatrists believes strongly that the way forward is for an investigative mission to China to be undertaken which must be independent of local organizations and government interference. In other words we believe that it has to be an inspectorate visit, not a collegiate one.

Furthermore, he warned,

> We all appreciate that the WPA Review Committee has already been looking into these matters but the College strongly believes that the WPA must take immediate further action on this matter. If they do not there will be three serious consequences:
>
> - The reputation of the WPA will be seriously damaged as it was with its years of inaction over the abuse of psychiatry in the former USSR;
> - The credibility of the WPA's various declarations of human rights and the abuse of psychiatry, most notably the recent Madrid Declaration, will be severely, if not irrevocably damaged;
> - And perhaps most important of all – the reputation and credibility of psychiatry worldwide will be seriously damaged.[608]

---

606 See preceding Note for source reference to Appelbaum's article.
607 As the head of GIP, Robert van Voren, later colourfully observed about this event: "The General Assembly was due to start at 9.30 AM and Geneva Initiative representatives were present well in advance near the registration desk for the delegates of member societies, handing out the report published [by GIP] together with Human Rights Watch. This very much symbolized the change in relations between the two organizations. Whereas in 1983 the then WPA General Secretary Peter Berner had become physical towards our representatives and had torn down some of our posters, and in 1989 the then WPA general Secretary Fini Schulsinger branded us openly as CIA-funded and Scientology-inspired, we could now easily hand out our materials, talk to delegates and were repeatedly approached by WPA Executive Committee members, albeit somewhat hesitantly and some of them clearly feeling uncomfortable." (See document cited at Note 610 below.)
608 Speech by Mike Shooter, President of the Royal College of Psychiatrists, to the WPA General Assembly, Yokohama, 26 August 2002. (Copy on file with the author.)

Although the chair of the meeting, Juan López-Ibor, succeeded in dismissing Shooter's motion calling for a full investigative mission to China by the WPA, the General Assembly was nonetheless permitted to vote on a less clear-cut set of proposals put forward by López-Ibor himself.[609] Robert van Voren, director of the GIP, later summarized the course and outcome of the General Assembly meeting as follows:

> After an introduction to the [China] issue by WPA President López-Ibor and a detailed report on the interaction with the Chinese by Review Committee chair Marianne Kastrup, Royal College President and delegate Mike Shooter spoke, calling on the WPA to send an investigative mission to China, stressing the need for it to be independent, with full access to all persons and institutions it wanted to visit. He was supported in this by the delegate from the American Psychiatric Association. López-Ibor called upon the delegates to be cautious and to go step by step, to develop a protocol for the mission first and then to nominate a working group that would carry out the mission. A request from Dr. Shooter that the Royal College be involved in the selection of working group members was turned down, and it was decided that the WPA Executive Committee would decide on who would be on the task force to prepare the mission, who would eventually go on the mission and with what protocol the mission would take place. The mission was said to have to take place before the spring of 2003, so that a report would be ready in time for the Annual meeting of the American Psychiatric Association in May 2003 and the Annual Meeting of the Royal College of Psychiatrists in July 2003. The General Assembly eventually agreed unanimously with the WPA Executive Committee's proposal, with the Royal College abstaining from voting.

---

609 The WPA Executive Committee distributed three papers on the China question to all members of the General Assembly at the start of the Yokohama conference: 1) "The World Psychiatric Association and the Abuse of Psychiatry" (undated); 2) "WPA Executive Committee Plan of Action on Falun Gong, August 25, 2002"; and "Update on the World Psychiatric Investigation on the Case of Falun Gong Practitioners Admitted to Chinese Psychiatric Hospitals," dated August 2002. (Copies on file with the author.) According to the latter document,

"The CSP [Chinese Society of Psychiatry] has offered its full cooperation in the elucidation of the alleged abuse of psychiatry, both in correspondence and in meetings on several occasions. The WPA Executive Committee and the Review Committee have received the up to now requested information from the CSP, and will probably request more in the future. The CSP has also expressed its commitment to collaborate in the development of psychiatric care in China.

"The WPA Review Committee has provided the Chinese Society of Psychiatry with lists of Falun Gong practitioners who – according to information received but not verified by WPA – are said to have been hospitalized to a psychiatric institution.

"The CSP has conducted a national meeting and a training program and the research carried out has included not only those cases submitted by WPA but all the identified Falun Gong practitioners admitted to Chinese Mental Health Hospitals. The CSP has subsequently submitted two reports to the Review Committee on the Falun Gong cases investigated."

The WPA leadership has subsequently made great play of the fact that the Chinese Society of Psychiatrists has provided it with "detailed responses" on all the known cases of Falun Gong practitioners admitted to mental hospitals – citing this as clear evidence of the Chinese side's willingness to cooperate in the WPA investigation. However, the WPA has to date failed to make public any of the actual information and details contained in these official case responses from the Chinese side.

As van Voren also noted,

> After the General Assembly, Prof. López-Ibor gave a press conference, during which he stressed that in his view the mission to China would only take place if a good protocol could be agreed upon and the delegation could meet with any person they wanted and visit any institution it wanted to see. However, he continued to refer [only] to "the Falun Gong issue." This was also the case the next day, when a press conference was held by Prof. López-Ibor. An attempt to exclude Geneva Initiative on Psychiatry representatives from attending the press conference was aborted when it became clear that it would not be possible without a scandal.[610]

Two days later, at a seminar sponsored by GIP, the incoming WPA President, Professor Ahmed Okasha – one of the principal authors of the WPA's Madrid Declaration of 1996 – made a strong public statement on the need for an independent investigative mission to China be conducted. However, he added: "I do not have an army to invade China and investigate, unfortunately. If the authorities refuse to cooperate we cannot carry out the mission."

Several weeks later, the Chinese authorities responded to the events in Yokohama with a blistering series of articles issued by *Xinhua*, the official government news agency. The following are some of the highlights:

> Xinhua reports (4 October) that the State Council Information Office held a press conference at which it rejected claims that China has used psychiatric treatment to persecute "dissidents" and "Falun Gong followers" as a "vicious slander." … Some ill-intentioned people have also been exploiting the stage of international conferences to make gratuitous accusations against China, claiming that China "is using it as a means of political and social control against its people." An official from the State Council Information Office…added that claims by "some organizations abroad" that China was exploiting psychiatric hospitals for political ends and detaining dissidents as psychiatric patients were "without the slightest basis in fact and utterly irresponsible." …
>
> The official also rejected Western media reports about Wang Wanxing and Cao Maobing,[611] both of whom were subjected to compulsory psychiatric confinement and found to be psychiatrically ill. He said: "It was proper and necessary for the local governments and public security organs to send them to hospitals for treatment, it was totally acting according to the law. During their period of medical treatment, Wang Wanxing and Cao Maobing were never subjected to any "inhumane treatment."…
>
> Concerning cults, the official said that it is universally understood that "cults are a public scourge of the world today." He also said that followers of cults are subjected to mental control which "severely traumatizes the physical and mental health of the

---

610 "The WPA World Congress in Yokohama and the Issue of Political Abuse of Psychiatry in China – A Report by Robert van Voren, September 1, 2002." (Copy on file with the author.) Among the members of the GIP delegation to Yokohama were Jim Birley, a former president of the Royal College of Psychiatrists and also former chairman of GIP, and Robin Jacoby, Professor of Psychiatry at Oxford University and current chairman of GIP. See also: Human Rights Watch, "China: WPA Action on Psychiatric Abuse Falls Short," 27 August 2002.

611 For details of these two cases, see p.6 and p.212 above.

blind worshippers." He explained that Falun Gong is a cult banned by the government. He then said:

> "In China there are indeed some Falun Gong followers whose long-term obsession with Falun Gong has led to mental and behavioural abnormality, and they have been sent to hospitals by family members so they can be diagnosed and treated." He said that hospitals used "strict procedures" to determine whether they have psychiatric disorders, and "only then are the ill received and treated." He ended by saying that accusations by "hostile Western forces" that psychiatric hospitals have been used to persecute followers are "absolutely groundless."[612]

In short, the Chinese government had decided that it was not about to play ball with any outside body, even one as large and influential as the WPA, that intended to probe into China's "internal affairs." Concerning the watered-down version of the WPA investigative mission to China that López-Ibor had hoped would take place by spring 2003 at the latest, not only did it fail to materialize on schedule, but as late as September that year the WPA's negotiations with Beijing had seemingly made no progress at all. According to a statement issued by the WPA Executive Committee that month,

> The World Psychiatric Association (WPA) informs the international psychiatric community that the plans for the site visit to China aimed to explore the alleged political abuse of psychiatry have been delayed during the past eight months by the limited collaboration on the part of the Chinese health authorities, in spite of the efforts of the Chinese Society of Psychiatry, which are gratefully recognized. The WPA Review Committee, after a prolonged period of investigation, has produced a statement that "the evidence provided is insufficient to prove conclusively whether or not there is political abuse of psychiatry in the People's Republic of China,[613] but that further clarification are needed." A meeting of the WPA President with the former Minister of Health of the People's Republic of China planned for January 28-29, 2003 has been cancelled, and no feedback has been provided to the letters subsequently sent by the WPA President to the Chinese health authorities....
>
> *The WPA addresses a public appeal to Mrs. Wu Yi,[614] asking her to authorize a visit of a WPA task force to China, with free access to mental health institutions, including those in a forensic setting. ...*

---

612 See *Xinhua* reports of 4 and 5 October 2002, "Accusation about Psychotherapy for 'Dissidents', Falun Gong Practitioners Refuted."
613 In fact, this was a serious misrepresentation of the WPA statement in question, since it clearly implied that the "insufficient" evidence in question was that supplied to the WPA by the critics of Chinese psychiatry. What the original statement by the WPA in fact said was: "*The material provided by CSP [Chinese Society of Psychiatry] reports does not prove conclusively whether or not there is abuse of Psychiatry for political purposes in the People's Republic of China, but there exist some areas that need clarification that was sent to you by the RC [WPA Review Committee] and the EC [WPA Executive Committee].*" (Emphasis added. See: "Message from WPA President on the Visit to China," February 2004; available at: http://www.wpanet.org/generalinfo/letter0204.html.) The WPA itself, having not yet met with even a single detained dissident or Falun Gong practitioner in a Chinese psychiatric hospital, was in no position to make a judgment one way or the other on the evidence placed before it.
614 Wu Yi is a Vice Premier of the PRC and was also, at that time, Acting Minister of Health.

> The WPA urges the Chinese Society of Psychiatry to persevere in its collaborative efforts to facilitate the above-mentioned visit within the current year 2003 and to provide without further delay the clarifications and documents requested by the WPA Review Committee.[615]

If Vice Premier Wu Yi was listening, she gave no obvious sign of so doing, and the WPA's negotiations with Beijing continued to lead nowhere for the next six months. Eventually, in March 2004, the WPA leadership announced that China had agreed to allow a "site visit" to the country to take place the following month. But by now, it was clear that far from being the independent, "inspectorate" kind of visit that the Royal College's Mike Shooter had earlier insisted was needed, it was in fact going to be an essentially "collegiate" type of visit. To its credit, the WPA Executive Committee appears to have insisted to Beijing that the visit would have little or no credibility unless the delegation was permitted actually to meet with at least some of the named Chinese individuals whose cases had been presented to the WPA Review Committee. But the battle of wills between the WPA leadership and the Chinese government was not long in being decided. For the Chinese leadership, this minimum precondition by the WPA represented a bridge too far, and they flatly turned it down. The WPA's President, Ahmed Okasha, duly announced that the WPA had regretfully judged it to be "prudent to suspend the WPA delegation visit to China scheduled on the 4th April 2004." The Chinese side, Okasha obliquely indicated, had decided that the WPA visit would be little more than a polite talking shop:

> Educational seminars were agreed to and the WPA looks forward to doing these with our Chinese colleagues, but they were clearly to follow, not replace, the delegation's visit to China to independently determine whether or not there had been psychiatric abuses in a selected sample of the cases of the complaints. We had clearly agreed that it was in the best interests of the CSP and the WPA to independently verify the status of some of the cases of complaint. This, it was agreed, required free access to records that had already been reviewed by Prof. Chen, face to face interviews with some patients, face to face meetings with some relatives where possible, and meetings with hospital staff named in the complaints.[616]

---

615 "Memo on the Issue of Alleged Political Abuse of Psychiatry in China," September 2003; available at: http://www.wpanet.org/generalinfo/china619.html. The entire second paragraph above was capitalized, as shown, in the WPA's original statement.

616 The following is the complete text of Ahmed Okasha's April 2004 statement (available at: http://www.wpanet.org/generalinfo/letter0404.html):

"MESSAGE FROM THE WPA PRESIDENT on the China Visit:

This is a brief message to announce the postponement of the delegation to China, that was scheduled on the 4th April for further deliberations.

Prof. Dongfeng Zhou the President of the Chinese Society of Psychiatry wrote a letter to the Chair of the delegation Dr. Otto Steenfeldt where the terms of reference of the visit did not follow the "Okasha mission agreement" to Beijing in January 2004 , with the vice minister of Health Dr. Zhu Qingsheng and members of CSP.

I sent a letter to Prof. Zhou stating that under these circumstances we feel [it is] prudent to suspend the WPA delegation visit to China scheduled on the 4th April 2004.

The terms of reference mentioned in her letter for the delegation are difficult to be accepted by the WPA, considering the General Assembly resolution, and what we have agreed about during our visit to China.

It subsequently emerged, however, that in fact it had been the Chinese side who had insisted on cancelling the April visit to China by the WPA. According to the APA's journal *Psychiatric News*,

> The CSP agreed to cooperate with an investigation of alleged psychiatric abuses involving Falun Gong that was to begin in April. Several days before it was to start, the CSP sent Okasha a letter in which it indicated that it was, at the Chinese government's insistence, postponing indefinitely acting on its earlier agreement to participate in a visit from WPA members, since the visit was to be more investigative than educational.[617]

With the Chinese authorities having clearly slammed the door in the WPA's face, and with the next triennial world congress of the organization looming ahead in Cairo in August 2005, the WPA leadership now had nothing at all to show for its post-Yokohama efforts to engage the Chinese leadership over the allegations of political misuse of psychiatry in China. Rather than facing this fact fairly and squarely, and initiating the steps mandated under its own Madrid Declaration for the censure and possible future expulsion of the Chinese Society of Psychiatry, however, the WPA leadership instead opted in essence to throw in the towel and look for a face-saving way out. Indeed, in a statement he issued in February 2004, Ahmed Okasha had already begun to prepare the ground for such an eventuality: "The purpose of our visit [to China] is a collaborative endeavour to facilitate some issues related to Falun Gong for the advantage of SCP and WPA," he wrote – thereby signalling clearly that the WPA would make no attempt to investigate any cases of political dissidents forcibly sent to mental hospitals. Okasha continued:

Educational seminars were agreed to and the WPA looks forward to doing these with our Chinese colleagues, but they were clearly to follow, not replace, the delegation's visit to China to independently determine whether or not there had been psychiatric abuses in a selected sample of the cases of the complaints. We had clearly agreed that it was in the best interests of the CSP and the WPA to independently verify the status of some of the cases of complaint. This, it was agreed, required free access to records that had already been reviewed by Prof. Chen, face to face interviews with some patients, face to face meetings with some relatives where possible, and meetings with hospital staff named in the complaints.

We do realize the sensitivities of many issues and the conciliatory role of CSP with the Chinese authorities and WPA.

The EC hopes that the WPA and the CSP can work out a plan that would allow us to respond well to the mandate of the WPA General Assembly. If the CSP is able to propose some alternative process to achieve the independent verification of these issues, the WPA will of course consider that proposal.

This is most unfortunate considering our mutual desire to bring this matter to an end. If we can not reach an agreement following the general assembly mandate , the WPA EC have no choice but to bring this matter to the attention of the General assembly of the XIII World Congress in Cairo 2005.

We continue to believe that it is in the interest of the Chinese Psychiatrists and of the WPA that we resolve this problem as soon as possible. To this effect, the WPA Executive Committee and I look forward to the CSP response and to the opportunity of continuing to work with them towards finding a satisfactory resolution to this matter.

Prof. Ahmed Okasha,
President WPA"

617 Ken Hausman, "WPA, Chinese Psychiatrists Agree on Psychiatry Abuse Charges," P*sychiatric News*, August 6, 2004, Vol. 39, No. 15, p.2.

> We need a dialogue and timetable for another visit to reach a conclusion, to abide [by] the General Assembly resolution in Yokohama.... We are aware that there is no system that is 100 percent correct or a system which adheres to all declarations of human rights, you will always find a few cases that [are] mishandled either due to lack of experience, faulty diagnosis but with good intentions and not on a systematic basis.

In a meeting with senior officials of the CSP in New York on 4 May 2004, some weeks after the Chinese side's cancellation of the planned site visit, the WPA leadership then set about reworking and further expanding upon this naively optimistic formulation. A few days later, the WPA President and the President and Vice-President of the CSP issued a joint public statement announcing that a "positive conclusion" had been reached to the two-year-long bilateral negotiations. As reported in *Psychiatric News*,

> [T]he WPA acknowledges that the CSP has cooperated in a three-year investigation of alleged psychiatric abuses of Falun Gong members who were sent to Chinese psychiatric hospitals and clinics.
>
> The CSP's investigation identified "instances in which some Chinese psychiatrists failed to distinguish between spiritual-cultural beliefs and delusions, as a result of which persons were misdiagnosed and mistreated."

The statement attributed these acts to "lack of training and professional skills of some psychiatrists rather than [to] systematic abuse of psychiatry."

In addition, the CSP agreed to take steps to "educate [its] members" about the issues that led to misdiagnosis and mistreatment and said it welcomes the WPA's "assistance in correcting this situation" and improving psychiatric diagnosis and treatment throughout the People's Republic of China.[618]

Although left unstated by the two sides, the clear implication was that as a result of this admission by the CSP that "some misdiagnosis and mistreatment" of Falun Gong detainees had occurred in China, a WPA investigative mission to China of any kind would now no longer be necessary. In the absence of any field visit to China, or of any actual meetings by WPA psychiatrists with any persons alleged to have been wrongfully committed to mental institutions on account of their political or religious beliefs, and without a single WPA official having even set foot in any Chinese police-run forensic psychiatric custody centre, the WPA leadership had agreed, for the sake of political expediency, to conclude that the few cases of misdiagnosis to which the Chinese side was prepared to admit had been caused not by any systematic or intentional misuse of psychiatry for repressive purposes, but simply by "lack of training and professional skills" on the part of the evidently tiny handful of psychiatrists concerned.[619]

---

618 Ken Hausman, "WPA, Chinese Psychiatrists Agree on Psychiatry Abuse Charges," *Psychiatric News*, August 6, 2004, Vol. 39, No. 15, p.2.
619 The full text of the joint WPA-CSP statement of May 2004 reads as follows:

"World Psychiatric Association and Chinese Society of Psychiatrists on the China Issue:

I am pleased to announce the agreement made by WPA Executive Committee, Review Committee, Task Force of the China visit and the president, vice-president of Chinese Society of Psychiatrists made in New York during the annual meeting of the American Psychiatric Association – May 2004. After much deliberation, we agreed on this summary and positive conclusion. I have received positive feedback from all WPA components commending the effort made by all parties to reach this solution.

The agreement was swiftly condemned by the main campaigning groups working on this issue. According to Abraham Halpern, a member of the APA's Lifers Committee,

> "The WPA's decision to cancel its demand for an investigative mission undercuts and renders meaningless its past high-sounding declarations concerning misuse of psychiatry," he told Psychiatric News. "The allegations of psychiatric abuse in China involve mistreatment, torture, and fraudulent diagnoses in the case of large numbers of political dissidents and Falun Gong practitioners and should not be dismissed as mere 'failures in diagnosis'."

China Mental Health Watch, a U.S.-based Falun Gong support group, was even more scathing in its criticism of the WPA's decision to abandon the China investigation:

> In place of cooperating with the independent investigation called for by the resolution of the WPA General Assembly in August 2002 in Yokohama, the Chinese Society

---

Summary and Conclusions of the Conjoint Meeting of the Executive Committee, Standing Review Committee, the Task Force on China, and the Chinese Society of Psychiatrists [and] World Psychiatric Association, at the Marriott Marquise Hotel in New York City, 4 May, 2004:

At a conjoint meeting of the Executive Committee, the Review Committee and the Task Force on China of WPA on the 4th of May 2004, to which Prof. Dongfeng Zhou, President of the Chinese Society of Psychiatry, and Prof. Yanfang Chen, Vice President participated, and the following statements and conclusions were agreed upon:

1. Following the requests of WPA and its RC, the CSP over the past 3 years has cooperated with the WPA and the WPA RC and reviewed a substantial number of cases of alleged abuse of Falun Gong practitioners within mental hospitals and mental health clinics in the PRC.

2. The CSP found instances in which some Chinese psychiatrists failed to distinguish between spiritual-cultural beliefs and delusions as a result of which persons were misdiagnosed and mistreated. This pattern of misdiagnosis and mistreatment took place because of lack of training and professional skills of some psychiatrists rather than as result of systematic abuse of psychiatry.

3. The WPA's RC and the Task Force on China reviewed the CSP's reports and independently confirmed the failure of some Chinese psychiatric colleagues to distinguish between cultural beliefs and delusions.

4. At the above meeting on May 4, 2004, the CSP acknowledged that it had identified these problems and concurred with the WPA's opinion that this failure of professional capacity to distinguish between cultural beliefs and delusions had led to misdiagnosis and mistreatment.

5. The CSP also recognized the existence of these mistakes and have undertaken steps to educate their members and are looking forward to WPA's assistance in correcting this situation, as they are themselves committed to improve the quality of psychiatric diagnosis and treatment in the People's Republic of China.

6. The CSP's representatives acknowledged that the areas in which they would specially welcome assistance are Forensic Psychiatry, Medical Ethics, Patients' Rights, Mental Health Legislation, Diagnosis and Classification.

7. Furthermore, CSP has agreed to examine case records at various hospitals where those instances of misdiagnosis and mistreatment may have occurred and to present and discuss the findings at a workshop with WPA in a collegial manner, so that we can better understand why these failures have occurred, and with the intention that these findings can be used in further educational and professional meetings at national and international levels.

Prof. Ahmed Okasha, President, World Psychiatric Association Prof. Don[g]feng Zhou, President, Chinese Society of Psychiatrists, Prof. Yanfang Chen, Vice President, Chinese Society of Psychiatrists"

(Available on the Internet at: http://www.wpanet.org/generalinfo/letter0604.html.)

of Psychiatry would admit "misdiagnosis and mistreatment" but not systematic abuse, and would welcome the assistance of the WPA in future collegial, educational meetings. This proposed "compromise" betrays the victims of psychiatric abuse in China, and damages the credibility and the integrity of the WPA.....

> The torture suffered by mentally sane Falun Gong practitioners who are involuntarily admitted to psychiatric hospitals has nothing to do with a lack of psychiatric training or professional skills of Chinese psychiatrists. The use of high doses of neuroleptic drugs to the extent of causing symptoms resembling Neuroleptic Malignant Syndrome, the force feedings, sleep deprivation and the application of high electrical voltage (not the common practice of acupuncture) are common methods to force practitioners to renounce Falun Gong. The use of these methods is not directly related to the degree of professional training. The documented deaths of previously healthy Falun Gong practitioners after being admitted or within days of being discharged from psychiatric hospitals is clear evidence of the ongoing abuse of psychiatry that has no relation to the lack of training on the part of CSP members.[620]

Once again, as has occurred so often during the past twenty years or so, the Chinese government had succeeded – simply by stonewalling and denying the allegations – in relieving itself of international pressure arising from serious human rights abuse charges. It remained to be seen whether the member societies of the WPA would be prepared to accept this face-saving compromise when they met in Cairo in August 2005 to assess the WPA leadership's progress or otherwise in implementing the Yokohama resolution. In the event, the China issue was conspicuously absent from both the conference agenda and the subsequent record of proceedings. However, it should be remembered that in the case of Soviet psychiatric abuse, it took more than ten years, from the time when the initial complaints were first received in the West, before the WPA finally galvanised itself into taking disciplinary or punitive action of any kind on the issue.

In all fairness, it should be acknowledged that the WPA – a relatively disorganized and politically inexperienced organization representing doctors – has proved itself to be simply no match for the Chinese government in the present controversy. The International Committee of the Red Cross (ICRC), a seasoned investigative and monitoring organization that regularly takes on powerful governments around the world and usually wins, has been trying without success for well over ten years now to gain access to China's prison system in order to monitor the condition of the country's political prisoner (or in ICRC parlance, "security detainee") population. If the Chinese government refuses to allow the ICRC to meet with even a single detained counterrevolutionary inside one of the country's regular prisons, it is certainly not going to accede – at least not without considerable and sustained pressure from other, more influential quarters – to polite requests from the WPA to be permitted to visit counterrevolutionaries held in high-security, police-run institutes for the criminally insane. Ultimately, the only place where the requisite pressure for change and reform of this nature can possibly come is from inside China itself.

---

620 China Mental Health Watch, "'Misdiagnosis and Lack of Training' are Deliberate Cover-Up for Severe Violations of WPA Madrid Declaration," August 2004, available at: www.chinapsychiatricwatch.org. For a recent report of a Falun Gong death in police psychiatric custody, see: "Shenyang Ankang Yiyuan Jiang Yi Falun Gong Xueyuan Guanshi Zhi Si" (Falun Gong Practitioner Killed by Being Force-Fed in Shenyang Ankang Hospital), 14 October 2002, available at: yuanming.net/articles/200210/13152.html.

CHAPTER 10
Conclusions

As this book has sought to explain, China's forensic psychiatrists unavoidably find themselves, wherever political dissident cases or ones involving Falun Gong detainees and the like are concerned, at the ethically invidious intersection of modern medical principles and an unreconstructed criminal justice system whose overriding concern remains the arbitrary suppression of dissent. We do not yet know how many, or what general proportion of, Chinese psychiatrists are directly involved in these ethically abusive practices, but it seems clear that they form a relatively small minority within the profession as a whole. It should be remembered, however, that this was also the case in the former Soviet Union; in both countries, as elsewhere, authentic cases of the major mental illnesses – in particular schizophrenia – far outnumber the phoney ones, and political and religious dissidents have therefore accounted for only a small part of the overall psychiatric caseloads. It is also possible that many of the Chinese psychiatrists who have written extensively on the topic of "political cases" dealt with in the legal-forensic domain since the early 1980s have been motivated to do so by a desire to bring the existence of this still sizeable ethical problem to a wider domestic, and possibly also international, audience. If so, the absence of overt value judgments in most of their reports would mirror their need to protect themselves against charges of disloyalty to the Party.

Excuses and rationales can always be found to explain why doctors become involved in human rights abuses of various kinds, such as in physician-assisted executions,[621] "medical supervision" over torture sessions, the procurement of transplantable organs from executed criminals' bodies,[622] and also politically repressive psychiatry. These range from the claim that expert medical involvement is required, in the case of torture and executions, in order to limit or alleviate the sufferings of the subjects of these procedures; through the more instrumental argument that, in the case of organ transplants and certain types of execution, the procedures themselves are of an inherently medical nature; to the construction of elaborate, pseudo-scientific theories that posit, as in the case of political psychiatry, false medical justifications for the state's enlistment of doctors in the criminal justice and law enforcement process. All of these practices entail, however, a fundamental corruption of the basic tenets of medical ethics – notably the principle that medical skills should be deployed only for the improvement of life and health, as summed up in the Hippocratic injunction "Do no harm."

In this study, we have outlined two of the more obvious reasons why Chinese psychiatrists allow themselves to be pressed into the unethical deployment of their skills for state-directed purposes of political and religious repression: first, the professional acculturation process, in which psychiatrists learn from the official medical literature at the outset of their training that certain types of ideologically nonconformist behaviour are attributable to severe and dangerous forms of "mental pathology;" and second, the more insidious element of personal and professional fear, inspired by a wider culture involving decades of individual and institutional experience, of the severe negative consequences of departing from the official "political line" laid down by the authorities in such matters. There are surely,

---

[621] For a detailed study of this topic, see *Breach of Trust: Physician Participation in Executions in the United States*, a joint report by the American College of Physicians, Human Rights Watch, the National Coalition to Abolish the Death Penalty, and Physicians for Human Rights (New York, March 1994).

[622] See, for example, Human Rights Watch, *Organ Procurement and Judicial Execution in China* (New York: Human Rights Watch, 1994).

in addition to those enumerated above, other more subtle reasons why Chinese psychiatrists become active partners in the political corruption of their profession.

The question remains, however: why do the authorities themselves bother? Indeed, why would any repressive regime go through such elaborate and often costly steps as adopting coercive psychiatric measures against a certain number of its political and religious opponents, when other much simpler methods of neutralizing such troublesome people – for example, execution or lengthy imprisonment – have always been readily available, and, in the case of both the Soviet Union and China, were frequently used? One possible reason has to do with the changed political landscapes that emerged, both in the USSR after the death of Stalin, and in China after the death of Mao: in these countries, the former totalitarian solution of the physical liquidation of political enemies was ended by the emergence of reformist leaderships dedicated to the curtailment of past policy "excesses." For dissidents of various kinds, this meant that being arrested by the security police no longer entailed their permanent physical removal from society, but rather long terms of imprisonment from which they had a reasonable chance of emerging alive. A sustained dissident network or movement therefore could, and did, come into being in both these countries after the deaths of their respective "great dictators." For the successor authorities, Khrushchev and Deng, however, this represented an unwanted complication of their new "liberalizing" dispensations, and more elaborate mechanisms of inducing long-term fear in the ideological enemies of the state thus had to be found.

The Soviet psychiatrist and dissident, Semyon Gluzman, has put the matter as follows:

> The totalitarian regime has grown tired and decrepit. For whatever reasons, inside the system or outside, it is no longer capable of carrying out its former reprisals. So, from somewhere deep within, comes the idea of using psychiatry to intensify fear. The victim loses his identity as well as his freedom.[623]

There are surely few more potent deterrents to dissident activity of any kind than the threat of permanent or semi-permanent forced removal to an institution for the criminally insane. A potential Chinese dissident or religious nonconformist may be prepared to face imprisonment for his or her beliefs, but indefinite psychiatric custody is probably quite another matter. Additionally, psychiatric labelling of this kind serves to stigmatise and socially marginalize the dissident in a way that regular criminal imprisonment, in the present era at least, often fails to do.

Another reason why "liberalizing" Communist governments tend to engage in such practices may derive from the *amour propre*, or self-justificatory vanity, found in historically repressive regimes of this type when they attempt to dispense with nakedly terrorist methods of dealing with ideological dissent or nonconformity. Such phenomena must still, in the official view, be crushed, but it better serves the government's self-image at such times to adopt more sophisticated and, where possible, scientific means and approaches to the fulfilment of this task. Thus, the perceived ideological enemies of the regime are officially said, in some cases, to be merely ill, rather than always or necessarily ill intentioned. While this general rationale for the use of political psychiatry may seem to contradict

---

623 Gluzman, *On Soviet Totalitarian Psychiatry* (op cit), p.12. As the same writer has elsewhere stated, "Complete totalitarianism does not resort to psychiatric camouflage. Such was the nature of totalitarianism during the time of Stalin. However, Brezhnev's totalitarianism (which I would define as 'exhausted or tired' totalitarianism) did not enjoy that absolute power, and for this reason, psychiatric repression was used as a frightening 'super weapon' which was far more horrible than the usual prisons and camps." (Semyon Gluzman, "Law and Psychiatry: The Totalitarian Experience," *Journal of the American Academy of Psychiatry and the Law*, 2001, Vol. 29, p.332.

the "deterrent" argument outlined above, in practice they are not mutually incompatible. Rather, the dissident's fear of being branded mentally ill and condemned to a lunatic asylum serves as a more subtly powerful deterrent to any further oppositional belief or activity, while the reforming government, for its part, can rest satisfied in the belief that it is acting more humanely and scientifically than its unreconstructed predecessor ever did.

A closely related reason has to do, no doubt, with the country's international image and prestige. Naked repression as conducted in the old days becomes, in the more forward-looking era of "opening and reform to the outside world," a source of increasing international embarrassment for the government. Hence, the former overtly political crimes of "engaging in counter-revolution" are reborn under the more internationally acceptable rubric of "crimes of endangering state security," while particularly flagrant or uninhibited political protestors, and more recently selected groups of Falun Gong religious detainees, are sent to mental hospitals to be "treated," rather than simply jailed as before. Again, this may appear to be paradoxical or even self-defeating governmental behaviour, given the widespread international public awareness that now exists about the malign political uses of psychiatry in the former Soviet Union and certain other countries. But the surprising fact remains that in China there has been, thus far, virtually no public discussion or dissemination of information of any kind concerning the history of psychiatric abuse elsewhere in the world, let alone of the strong reaction to such abuse that has been generated internationally over recent decades. In all the Chinese books and journals on psychiatry that have been consulted for this study, only two explicit and very brief references to the history of political psychiatric abuse in the former Soviet Union, and none to that of other countries, has been found.[624] In this regard, the Chinese legal-medical authorities may unknowingly have been a victim of the government's longstanding policy of censoring and controlling the flow of sensitive news information from around the world.

All of the above reasons may partly explain the existence of political psychiatric abuse in China today, but they cannot directly account for the fact that such practices existed there long before the inauguration of the Deng Xiaoping "new era" in the late 1970s. Here, both systemic and also more contingent factors appear to have played the determinant role. First, there was the fact that Chinese forensic psychiatry largely owed its existence, as a discipline, to the fraternal efforts and advice of Serbski Institute-trained experts from the Soviet Union in the 1950s; Chinese psychiatry thus "benefited" from psychiatric doctrines characteristic of the Khrushchev era, but at a time when China itself was still firmly in the grip of its own unreconstructed Marxist leader. This would clearly explain why the

---

624 For the first such reference, see Jia Yicheng, *Shiyong Sifa Jingshenbingxue* (op cit), p.15. The passage referred to the Soviet psychiatric practice of labelling political dissidents as suffering from "sluggish schizophrenia" and incarcerating them in mental hospitals for long periods. It added that this practice had been "severely criticized by representatives from other countries at an international academic conference on psychiatry in 1976." (It is unclear to which conference the author was referring; it was likely a mistaken reference to the WPA's Sixth World Congress at Honolulu in August 1977, the first major international event at which Soviet political psychiatry was exposed to international criticism, and where the historic Declaration of Hawaii [see above, Chapter 2] was passed by the WPA General Assembly.) Significantly, however, the passage in the Jia Yicheng volume itself contained no criticisms of the Soviet practices in question.

For the second, see: Xie Bin, Wang Shiqing and Zheng Zhanpei, "*Jingshenke Linchuang Gongzuo Zhong de Yixie Falü Wenti*" (Several Legal Questions in Psychiatric Clinical Work), *Xinli Jiankang Tongxun* (Bulletin of Psychological Health), 2001, No.3. As the article observed, "The work of psychiatric medicine has followed a dark and tortuous historical path, from the killing of large numbers of mentally ill people during the Nazi era, to the confinement of political prisoners in mental asylums during the Soviet era."

basic doctrines of political psychiatry arose at a seemingly "inappropriate" time in China's political development, and why they continued to hold significant sway in Chinese forensic psychiatry both up to and beyond the death of Mao.

Second, however, there appears to be a deeper and more systemic explanation for the phenomenon, one that has applied almost throughout the history of the People's Republic. In brief, the main underlying reason, observable throughout the official psychiatric literature from the late 1950s onwards, for why some political dissidents and other kinds of ideological nonconformists are singled out – from among the much broader ranks of their prison-bound "counterrevolutionary" or "state security endangering" colleagues – for special treatment in the form of legal-psychiatric diagnosis and forced committal, appears to be that they lack, in the experienced and discerning eyes of the police, the prerequisite hallmark of dissident "street credibility." That is to say, such people express their oppositional or contrarian viewpoints openly and with no attempt to disguise their true identities, and when detained by the police on political charges they make no effort to deny their activities or pretend that they weren't really making fundamental criticisms of the regime. As the official literature makes clear, this represents, to China's seasoned enforcers of the dictatorship of the proletariat, a rarely encountered and inexplicable form of behaviour characterized by a perplexing absence of any normal instinct for self-preservation, and thus one that can be perceived only as mentally abnormal. In the authorities' view, "proper" political dissidents and other ideological enemies behave covertly and conspiratorially, because they know the dire penalties for being caught. To act otherwise strikes the authorities, no doubt quite genuinely, as being sheer political lunacy.

This same official mindset applied also in the case of Soviet political psychiatry, which viewed the gauntlet-throwing, "here I stand, I can do no other" kind of attitude taken by particularly stubborn dissident individuals as being frankly incomprehensible in a country where one could disappear overnight into the *gulag* for doing much less. One Soviet dissident, Alexander Volpin, who was interned in psychiatric hospitals altogether five times over a nineteen-year period starting in 1957, however, succeeded in making what might be called a "necessity of a virtue" in this regard – and in so doing he probably spoke for countless similar people elsewhere in the Soviet Union, and in China too. In July 1970 he wrote,

> In my work I openly and consistently act on the principle "away with the instinct for self-preservation and moderation". Let them do what they want with me because of it, I do not mind if that is considered madness or not…for me the concept of non-adaptation must be sacred! Just for the record, let me explain that I am not against the capacity for self-preservation or an understanding of balance, but I prefer these things to be the result of free reason, not of instinct or the emotions, which can always be influenced.[625]

This more consistent and longstanding element in the Chinese official conception of criminal-psychiatric deviance or pathology is, in turn, reflective of a fundamental hallmark of Chinese-style Marxism, namely the strong emphasis always placed by Mao upon "correct thinking."[626] In China, even

---

625 A.S. Volpin, "Let Pyotr Grigorenki Have a Fountain Pen," *samizdat* manuscript dated 20 July 1970; cited in Bloch and Reddaway, *Russia's Political Hospitals* (op cit), p.72.
626 This same emphasis had, of course, much older antecedents, namely the traditional Confucian concern for correct speech and behaviour, as expressed for example in the value-concepts of "propriety" (*li*) and "rectification of names" (*zheng ming*).

more so than in Russia, the objective or material Marxian prerequisites for advanced socialism were conspicuously absent in the first half of the twentieth century, and Mao's solution to this revolutionary resource deficit was to transfer the pivotal role away from the economy and towards ideology and other such "superstructural" factors: that is, from being to consciousness, from the objective to the subjective, from the material to the spiritual, and from process to will.[627] The Soviet guardians of the faith, people like chief Party ideologist Mikhail Suslov, decried all this as being anti-materialist "voluntarism" on the part of their former colleagues in China, and even Serbski School-trained forensic psychiatrists would have demurred at the excessively diligent use made by their Chinese counterparts of the basic Soviet medico-legal theory of ideological deviance – in particular, the Cultural Revolution theory that all mental illness was caused by "ideological defects", and also the latter-day variant of that notion that is now being deployed against the Falun Gong.

Another important difference between the two systems, rather ironically, was that whereas the Soviets never admitted that psychiatric abuse had been practiced, the Chinese profession eventually acknowledged that it had occurred frequently during the Cultural Revolution. But here again, the Maoist stress on ideological factors meant that the post-1978 re-examination of "past excesses" within the profession was mainly limited to a critique of the categories and specific content of the "politically deluded" ideas that had been identified – wrongly, it was now said – as being symptomatic of criminal mental pathology. No significant challenge was raised to the core notion that thought and speech could constitute crimes, or that in certain cases these could amount also to "political lunacy" in a legal or forensic medical sense. At an important level of official Chinese discourse for the past half century, therefore, there has existed a clear and persistent epistemological identification or elision between, on the one hand, the social concept of correct political thought and action, and on the other, the ascription, in individual cases, of basic mental health and stability. All of this represents the deeper and more intractable defining layer or facet of "political psychiatry with Chinese characteristics."

The reality today, however, is that most Chinese, and certainly those of the younger generation, would no sooner think of taking to the streets and staging political protest manifestations – especially in the form of sticking up "big character posters," the most commonly cited symptom of Chinese-style "political lunacy" – than they would think of studying Das Kapital or memorizing the poems of Mao Zedong. The right to engage in street-level politics of this kind, so characteristic of the Maoist era, was excised from the Chinese Constitution in 1982, and there now exists a panoply of legislation that severely criminalizes all such unauthorized forms of political expression by China's citizens; the same is true of all types of unauthorized religious activity. What was formerly a central part of Chinese

---

627 As Stuart Schram, the leading Western expert on Mao's thought and philosophy, has written:

"Mao's contribution to the theory and practice of revolution is also characterized by an extreme voluntarism. To be sure, "voluntarism," in the sense of an accent on conscious action, is by no means absent from Marx himself. But there is no doubt that it is carried much further in Lenin, and further still in Mao Tse-tung, and in the ideology of the Chinese Communist Party. This voluntarism attained a kind of apotheosis in the theory of the permanent revolution. Consider, for example, a passage such as this (by Mao, 1958):

"Men are not the slaves of objective reality. Provided only that men's consciousness be in conformity with the objective laws of the development of things, the subjective activity of the popular masses can manifest itself in full measure, overcome all difficulties, create the necessary conditions, and carry forward the revolution. In this sense, *the subjective creates the objective.*"

(Stuart R. Schram, *The Political Thought of Mao Tse-tung* [Harmondsworth: Pelican Books, 1971], pp.135-136 [emphasis added by Schram].)

political culture is now, in the post-Tiananmen era, little more than a folk memory for most people. This fact alone would probably suffice to account for the officially recorded decline, since the1980s, in "cases of a political nature" in Chinese forensic psychiatry. It could also, however, account for the fact that for the very small number of Chinese citizens who are nowadays still prepared to risk everything by persisting in these kinds of activities, the risk of being labelled as "criminally insane" appears, if anything, to be higher now than it was during the 1980s.[628]

One other important issue should be raised in this connection. The official statistics on this question never included, and still today omit, a range of other activities that are elsewhere generally seen as being quite civic-minded or at least socially permissible in nature: persistent petitioners and complainants of various kinds (the so-called litigious maniacs), people who seek to expose corruption or malfeasance in the workplace and in government administration (the whistleblowers, or those with so-called paranoid delusions), and also nonconformist religious or spiritual practitioners of various kinds, such as the *Falun Gong* (the so-called dysphrenics). As China continues to develop and expand both its legal system and the overall principle of rule by law, and as a greater degree of rights consciousness correspondingly takes hold among the populace as a whole, examples of the former kinds of behaviour are bound to increase dramatically; thus far, however, there has been no reported decrease in the numbers of such cases dealt with as constituting crimes by the mentally ill. Indeed, the most recent cases presented above suggest that unlawful psychiatric custody is being increasingly resorted to by the police and other local officials as a means of silencing petitioners and whistleblowers in particular, at the same time as the proportion of more classic-style political dissident cases dealt with in this way has continued to fall. The most likely reason for this development is that as Chinese society has become increasingly less dominated by political ideology and dogma, the opportunities for straightforward corruption and abuse of power on the part of local officials have become ever more numerous. Similarly, although for somewhat different reasons, religious sectarianism or spiritual nonconformism is now rapidly on the rise in most parts of the country, and the authorities' extension of the "mental pathology" model to significant numbers of *Falun Gong* adherents has thus lengthened the shadow over any hopes or optimism that political psychiatry may be destined soon to disappear from the Chinese law-enforcement scene.

At the time of writing, however, cracks were beginning to appear in various key locations in the edifice of political psychiatric repression in China. As we have seen, first-hand accounts by the victims of the Ankang had begun appearing in newspapers around the country; the courts were taking tentative steps toward hearing administrative and tort compensation lawsuits brought by such people, and the Public Security Bureau found itself in the highly unaccustomed position of having publicly to explain and account for its psychiatric persecution of sane dissenters and other civic-minded members of the community. Also, local legislators had begun carrying out site inspections of Ankang facilities and raising fundamental questions about their prison-like mode of operation. Although as yet not voiced, the implicit message emanating from more enlightened legal commentators in China was that it was clearly wrong for the Public Security Bureau to be running mental asylums and that jurisdiction and control over the Ankang network should therefore be handed over to some other, more appropriate government agency.

---

628 A further important point concerns the current rapid increase in China of all types of forensic psychiatric appraisal cases; with the passage (as described in Chapter 5 above) of a series of relevant countrywide rules and regulations in recent years and the concomitant institutional build up of the legal-psychiatric appraisals system, the absolute number of such cases is now multiplying annually in China. A decline in the percentage incidence of "political" and other such cases does not necessarily mean, therefore, that fewer actual cases of these types are being dealt with under the system. The overall trend may even be in the other direction.

Behind the scenes, within the legal and psychiatric reform movement in China, things were looking similarly hopeful. Articles began appearing in the professional literature during 2004-05 raising issues never previously discussed or considered in China, including calls for systemic safeguards for the basic civil rights of mental patients; for the judiciary to be given the deciding role in all cases of involuntary psychiatric committal; for the passage of a strong mental health law incorporating the key protections set forth in international human rights law; and for an end to what one writer called the "steady and increasingly widespread expansion of the scope of coercive medical-psychiatric custody" in China.[629] In Shanghai, moreover, an important breakthrough came in late 2003 when the local authorities issued a "Code of Professional Ethics for Forensic Evaluators." Among other key provisions, the code stated that forensic experts must "defend the dignity of the nation's laws and uphold social justice" and must "perform their duties independently and free of all interference from any office or individual."[630] One lark does not a summer make, but there seemed to be more than a hint of spring-like activity in the air within China's legal psychiatric domain as the final full stop was being put to this book.

In conclusion, we return to the question of whether or not those dealt with in China as being dangerously mentally-disordered political or religious offenders really are, as the authorities claim, suffering in significant numbers from any recognizable form of mental illness. Ultimately, this is an irrelevant question to be asking in the ostensible context of the practice of forensic psychiatry, since the acts in question are not only absent from the internationally accepted definition of crime, but also specifically protected under international law as clear examples of the exercise of the right to freedom of expression. Indeed, it is this that defines the Chinese authorities' practices in this general area as constituting a fundamental abuse of human rights.

If for the sake of argument, however, one suspends all disbelief, takes the official case reports and statistics at face value and accepts that all of those dealt with in this way were in fact seriously mentally ill, then another conclusion arises: that Chinese-style "political lunacy" represents a genuinely new, post-1949 "culture-bound syndrome" of considerable size and extent, and is therefore one that deserves formal recognition in the country's official classification of acknowledged mental disorders. It is certainly true that the incessant mass political campaigns waged by the Chinese Communist Party

---

629 See for example: Long Qingchun et al, "Qiangzhi Yiliao Qianjian" (Some Undeveloped Thoughts on Coercive Medical Treatment), a paper presented at the Fifth National Academic Conference on Psychiatry, October 2003; *Shanghai Shi Sifa Jiandingren Zhiye Daode Guifan* (Shanghai Municipal Code of Professional Ethics for Forensic Evaluators) 15 October 2003; Liu Yan et al, "*Yi-Huan Shuangfang Dui Zhuyuan Jingshen Jibing Huanzhe Quanyi de Taidu Bijiao*" (A Two-Way Comparison of the Hospital's and the Patient's Attitudes Concerning the Rights and Interests of Hospitalized Mentally Ill Persons), Shanghai Jingshen Yixue (*Shanghai Archives of Psychiatry*), 12 January 2004; and Jin Juanjuan et al, "*Dui Xingshi Anjian Zhong Sifa Jingshen Yixue Jianding de Jidian Sikao*" (Various Thoughts on Judicial Psychiatric-Medical Appraisal in Criminal Cases), *21 Jiankang Wang* (21st Century Health Net), 8 February 2004. (Several of these articles are available at: www.21jk.com.cn/p/.)

630 Also, in a landmark civil court case in February and March 2004 in Shanghai, a woman named Wu Xiuli was awarded 50,000 *yuan* in compensatory damages against her husband and the Shanghai Mental Health Centre, after they had in effect conspired to have her forcibly hospitalized for a period of three days without due medical diagnosis or evidence. Although there was no political persecution involved in this case, the court ruling (which was upheld at the appeal stage) was nonetheless an important victory for patients' rights in China. (See: Wang Qian, "*Jingshenbingyuan Qiangzhi Shouzhi Zhengchangren Beipan Peichang*" (Court Orders Mental Hospital to Pay Compensation for Forcibly Hospitalizing a Normal Person), *Xinhua Wang* (Xinhua Net), 10 March 2004, available at: www.fmedsci.com/ArticleShow.asp?ArticleID=1812.) The article stated that the judges had partly based their ruling on the provisions of the 2001 Shanghai Municipal Mental Health Regulations (for details, see p.171 above.)

over the past fifty years has claimed countless lives and driven large numbers of people insane. It may well also be true that the deeper cultural effects of this longstanding history of political witch-hunts and persecution have caused many of those suffering from genuine mental illness to exhibit their disorders in the form of politically coloured language, thought, and behaviour.[631] For China's legal and medical authorities to charge psychiatrically disturbed individuals of this kind with committing serious offences and then send them to institutes for the criminally insane, however, is to add gross insult to injury.

Although there is no easy or obvious solution to the problem of politically abusive psychiatry in China, we can nonetheless discern the outlines of an appropriate and effective response by the international psychiatric and human rights communities to this issue: on the one hand, to stand in firm solidarity with the ethically sound mainstream of the Chinese psychiatric profession, while recognizing that current political conditions in China make it largely impossible for psychiatrists there, individually or collectively, to speak out openly themselves against these abuses; and on the other hand, to work in a targeted manner, through the World Psychiatric Association and its national member associations, to put sustained pressure upon the Chinese authorities to take steps to end the political misuse of psychiatry within the criminal-forensic evaluations domain, the Ankang police custodial network, and the relatively few corners of the general psychiatric system where it still persists. A minimum demand and requirement should be for the government to remove the entire Ankang network from the jurisdiction and control of the Ministry of Public Security's notorious 13th Bureau and to hand it over to another, more suitable and appropriate government agency (either the Ministry of Health or the Ministry of Justice.)[632]

Advocacy efforts by local and international psychiatric and human rights bodies will be vital in encouraging individual Western governments and the European Union to address seriously the issue of political psychiatric abuse in China, notably by placing it on the formal agenda of the various bilateral human-rights dialogue sessions that have become, in recent years, a central and regular feature of Sino-Western relations. Continuing to shine the spotlight of international publicity on the problem will also be indispensable to bringing the Chinese security authorities around, sooner or later, to the realization that it is not in the government's broader interests to continue using the mental hospital network as a long-term dumping ground for political and religious dissenters who, for one reason or another, they find it awkward or inconvenient to bring to criminal trial.

Above all, the Chinese security authorities must be prevailed upon to realize that it is contrary to the interests of society as a whole for them to continue using psychiatric custody, or any other form of arbitrary detention, as a means of silencing either the many courageous citizens around the country who are nowadays trying to blow the whistle on rampant corruption within the Party and government, or the still larger numbers of complainants and petitioners at the grassroots level who are seeking nothing more than an end to the despotic abuse of power in their communities. If civil society in China

---

631 In the case of the Soviet Union, when Western psychiatric delegations were finally, in 1989 and 1990, allowed access to alleged mentally ill dissidents held in psychiatric custody, a minority of those examined were found to be suffering from some form of mental disorder or other. In most such cases, however, these were deemed by the Western experts to be little more than harmless borderline conditions, and of a kind that should not have occasioned even civil psychiatric committal, let alone compulsory forensic-style custody. For details of the findings of one of these expert delegations, see Bonnie and Polubinskaya, "Unraveling Soviet Psychiatry," pp.279-298; see also Richard J. Bonnie, "Soviet Psychiatry and Human Rights: Reflections on the Report of the U.S. Delegation," *Law, Medicine and Health Care*, 1990, Vol.18, pp.123-131.
632 See above, p. 249 and Notes 525 and 526.

is to advance significantly beyond its present delayed and stunted level of development – in which, for example, well-connected private entrepreneurs are granted all the freedom of association they can use, while ordinary working people enjoy virtually none; if the rule of law is to be given greater authority and substance through the progressive abolition of arbitrary or "administrative" forms of detention and punishment; and if social justice is to become more than simply a slogan voiced at high-level Party conferences, then it is outspoken and public-spirited citizens like Wang Wanxing, Wang Fumian, Mr. Zhu, Xue Jifeng, Huang Shurong, Qiu Jinyou and Meng Xiaoxia – people who have challenged the system, paid the price and still come out fighting – who will deserve much of the credit for having brought these goals a step closer to reality.

GLOSSARY OF CHINESE TERMS

Pinyin Romanisation	English Equivalent	Chinese Characters
aizibing	AIDS/HIV	艾滋病
Ankang	Ankang ("Peace and Health")	安康
Ankang Bingfang	Ankang Wards	安康病房
bangxiong	evil accomplices	帮凶
baoli xingwei	violent behaviour	暴力行为
baowai jiuyi	released on bail for medical treatment	保外就医
beihai wangxiang	delusions of persecution	被害妄想
beihai wangxiang jingshenfenliezheng	persecution-delusional schizophrenia	被害妄想精神分裂症
bei jianshi gan	delusion of being under surveillance	被监视感
bei peiyang gan	delusion of being cultivated by superiors	被培养感
bei shencha gan, jiang bei jubu gan	delusion of being investigated and facing arrest	被审查感、将被拘捕感
bei wu-xian wangxiang	delusion of being slandered and persecuted	被诬陷妄想
bianren nengli	capacity to distinguish between right and wrong	辨认能力
bianzheng weiwuzhuyi	dialectical materialism	辩证唯物主义
biao tai	public stance or endorsement	表态
bingli dongji	pathological motive	病理动机
binglixing yizhi	pathological will	病理性意志
bingtai ren'ge	psychopathic personality	病态人格
buman qingxu	feelings of (political) dissatisfaction	不满情绪
caiqu jianhuxing cuoshi	take into legal guardianship	采取监护性措施
Cao Maobing		曹茂冰
chaojia guannian	overvalued ideation	超价观念
Chen Lining		陈里宁
Chenzhou Jingyan	Chenzhou Experience	郴州经验
chi butong zhengjianzhe	political dissident	持不同政见者
chongdong xingwei	impulsive behaviour	冲动行为
chongji zhengfu jiguan	disrupt government offices	冲击政府机关
cu si	sudden death	猝死
dan kuang	monomania	单狂
dangshiren	concerned party/ parties	当事人
Deng Xiaoping		邓小平
dian xiuke zhiliao	electroconvulsive therapy (ECT)	电休克治疗
dianxianzheng	epilepsy	癫痫症

di-wo maodun	contradictions between the people and the enemy	敌我矛盾
dongmian liaofa	artificial hibernation therapy	冬眠疗法
dongmian ling	wintermin	冬眠灵
falü jingshenbingxue	legal psychiatry	法律精神病学
falüxing jingshen cuoluan	legal insanity	法律性精神错乱
Falun Dafa	Great Wheel of Buddha's Law (a.k.a. Falun Gong)	法轮大法
Falun Gong	Falun Gong	法轮功
fandong hui-dao-men	superstitious or reactionary sects and societies	反动会道门
fan'geming xuanchuan shandong zui	counterrevolutionary propaganda and incitement	反革命宣传煽动罪
fan'geming zui	crimes of counterrevolution	反革命罪
fanshehuixing ren'ge zhang'ai	antisocial personality disorder	反社会性人格障碍
fanshehui yan-xing	antisocial speech or action	反社会言行
fanyingxing jingshenbing	reactive psychosis	反应性精神病
fanyingxing xugou zheng	reactive confabulatory syndrome	反应性虚构症
fanzui xinlixue	psychology of crime	犯罪心理学
fating kexue jingshenbingxue	court-science psychiatry	法庭科学精神病学
fayi jingshenbingxue	legal-medical psychiatry	法医精神病学
fayixue	forensic medicine	法医学
fazhi	legal system/ rule by law	法制
fazhi	rule of law	法治
fengbi qu	hospital secure zone	封闭区
fengjian mixin	feudal superstitious belief	封建迷信
fukua feng	"tide of exaggeration"	浮夸风
fuxing qingxu	negative mood	负性情绪
fuxing (shou chufa) nengli	capacity to serve a sentence/ undergo punishment	服刑（受处罚）能力
gan bu shang qingkuang	failure to keep up with the times	赶不上情况
geren diyizhuyi	"putting self first-ism"	个人第一主义
Gong'an Bu Shisan Ju	Bureau No 13 of the Ministry of Public Security	公安部十三局
Gong'an Ju Ankang Jingshenbing Guan-zhi Yuan	PSB Ankang Institute for the Custody and Treatment of the Mentally Ill	公安局安康精神病管治院
Gongren Zizhi Lianhehui	Workers Autonomous Federation	工人自治联合会
guan-zhi jiehe	combination of custody and treatment	管治结合
Guojia Jingshen Jibing Sifa Jianding Xietiao Weiyuanhui	State Committee for the Coordination of Psychiatric Judicial Assessments	国家精神疾病司法鉴定协调委员会

Han Zhenxi		韩振玺
he er er yi	"two combine into one"	合二而一
Hu Feng		胡风
hua fengzi	"romantic maniacs"	花疯子
Huang Shurong		黄淑荣
hukou suozaidi	place of household registration	户口所在地
huoxue huoyong Mao Zedong Sixiang	living study and application of Mao Thought	活学活用毛泽东思想
jiading jingshen yichang	presumption of mental abnormality	假定精神异常
jiading jingshen zhengchang	presumption of mental normalcy	假定精神正常
Jia Rubao		贾如宝
Jia Yicheng		贾谊诚
jiefang sixiang yundong	movement for the liberation of thought	解放思想运动
jingshenbing benzhi wenti	question of the essential nature of mental illness	精神病本质问题
jingshenbing fan'an feng	"tide of reversing psychiatric verdicts"	精神病翻案风
jingshen cuoluan bianhu	insanity defence	精神错乱辩护
jingshen fenliezheng	schizophrenia	精神分裂症
Jingshen Jibing Sifa Jianding Weiyuanhui	Psychiatric Judicial Appraisal Committee	精神疾病司法鉴定委员会
Jingshen Weisheng Fa	Mental Health Law	精神卫生法
jixing naobing zonghezheng	acute general brain disease syndrome	急性脑病综合症
juan zong	case file	卷宗
jujinxing jingshenbing	prison psychosis	拘禁性精神病
juti xingzheng xingwei	specific administrative action	具体行政行为
Kang Ming		亢明
kanshousuo	detention centre	看守所
Kanshousuo Tiaoli	Regulations on Detention Centres	看守所条例
kongzhi nengli	ability to control one's behaviour and actions	控制能力
kuada wangxiang	delusions of grandeur	夸大妄想
laogai (laodong gaizao)	reform through labour	劳改（劳动改造）
laojiao (laodong jiaoyang)	re-education through labour	劳教（劳动教养）
lei wangxiangxing huanxiang zheng	delusion-like fantasy syndrome	类妄想性幻想症
Li Congpei		李从培
Li Da		李达
Li Hongzhi		李洪志
Liang Caixia		梁彩霞
lingdaoren xuetong wangxiang	delusion of having leadership lineage	领导人血统妄想

lishi fan'geming	historical counterrevolutionaries	历史反革命
liti dingxiang shoushu	stereotactic brain surgery	立体定向手术
Liu Baiju		刘白驹
Liu Binyan		刘宾雁
Liu Xiehe		刘协和
Long Qingchun		龙青春
lübingqin	chlorpromazine	氯病嗪
Lu Dingyi		陆定一
Lu Ling		路翎
manxing jingshenfenliezheng	chronic schizophrenia	慢性精神分裂症
Mao Zedong		毛泽东
mazui fenxi	drug interrogation	麻醉分析
Meng Xiaoxia		孟晓霞
mianxiang shehui shouzhi bingren	admit and treat patients from society at large	面向社会收治病人
mianxiang shehui shouzhi fuwu	society-oriented reception and treatment services	面向社会收治服务
minshi xingwei nengli	capacity for civil action	民事行为能力
minshi weituo xingwei	civil referral (psychiatric)	民事委托行为
nao qian'e qiechushu	prefrontal lobotomy	脑前额切除术
nao waike shoushu	psychosurgery	脑外科手术
neibu faxing	for internal distribution only	内部发行
Ning Laixiang		宁米祥
pianzhi zhuangtai	paranoid state	偏执状态
pianzhikuang	paranoia	偏执狂
pianzhixing jingshenbing	paranoid psychosis	偏执性精神病
pianzhixing ren'ge zhang'ai	paranoid personality disorder	偏执性人格障碍
qigong	qigong	气功
qigong ban-fa jingshen zhang'ai	qigong-associated mental disorder	气功伴发精神障碍
qigong suozhi jingshen zhang'ai	qigong-induced mental disorder	气功所致精神障碍
qiangpoxing duili siwei	compulsive antagonistic mentality	强迫性对立思维
qiangzhi jiedu	compulsory drug treatment	强制戒毒
qiangzhi shouzhi	coercive admission and treatment	强制收治
qiangzhi yaowu zhiliao	forcible drug treatment	强制药物治疗
qiangzhi zhiliao xingwei	act of compulsory medical treatment	强制治疗行为
qianyinxing jingshen fenliezheng	latent ("sluggish") schizophrenia	潜隐性精神分裂症
Qincheng Jianyu	Qincheng Prison	秦城监狱
Qiu Jinyou		裘金友
quefa ziwo baohu nengli	lack of instinct for self-preservation	缺乏自我保护能力

raoluan shehui zhixu zui	crimes of disturbing public order	扰乱社会秩序罪
ren'ge zhang'ai	personality disorder/ psychopathy	人格障碍
renmin neibu maodun	contradictions among the people	人民内部矛盾
ren zhi	rule by man	人治
sanju zai shehuishang	living at large in society	散居在社会上
shangfangzhe	petitioners and complainants	上访者
Shanghai Jingshen Yixue	Shanghai Archives of Psychiatry	上海精神医学
sharen zhizhao	"murderer's licence"	杀人执照
shehuizhuyi jingshen wenming	socialist spiritual civilization	社会主义精神文明
shehuizhuyi minzhu yu fazhi	socialist democracy and legal system	社会主义民主与法制
shenjing shuairuo	neurasthenia	神经衰弱
shenjingzheng	neurosis	神经症
shenjing waikexue	neurosurgery	神经外科学
shenpan weiyuanhui	court adjudication committee	审判委员会
shixing fan zuo zui	reverse criminal culpability	实行反坐罪
shiyong sifa jingshenbingxue	applied forensic psychiatry	实用司法精神病学
shourong jiaoyu/ shourong jiaoyang	shelter[633] for re-education	收容教育/ 收容教养
shourong shencha	shelter for investigation	收容审查
shourong qiansong	shelter for deportation/ repatriation	收容遣送
shourong zhiliao	shelter for treatment	收容治疗
shuyu qi neibu xingwei	an action involving (the PSB's) internal affairs	属于其内部行为
sifa bumen	judicial departments	司法部门
sifa jingshenbing jianding	forensic psychiatric evaluation	司法精神病鉴定
sifa jingshenbingxue	forensic psychiatry	司法精神病学
Si Ren Bang	Gang of Four	四人帮
siwei lianxing ji siwei luoji zhang'ai	impairments of thought association and mental logic	思维联想及思维逻辑障碍
siwei yu cunzai	thought and existence ("being and consciousness")	思维与存在
sixiang	thought/ mentality/ ideology	思想
sixiang gaizao	thought reform/ "brainwashing"	思想改造
sixiang maobing	ideological defect/ defective ideology	思想毛病

---

[633] The term "shourong" literally means "shelter", but since the practice involves a form of police detention, a more accurate translation might be "informal custody". The same applies to the various other forms of "shourong" listed

Sun Zhigang		孙志刚
susongkuang	litigation mania	诉讼狂
susong nengli	capacity for litigation (or to stand trial)	诉讼能力
susong wangxiang	delusions of litigation	诉讼妄想
Wang Chaoru		王超如
Wang Fenglai		王凤来
Wang Guiyue		王桂月
Wang Fumian		王福绵
Wang Henglei		王恒雷
Wang Miaogen		王妙根
Wang Wanxing		王万星
wangxiangxing jingshen fenliezheng	delusional schizophrenia	妄想性精神分裂症
weifan fading chengxu	constitute a violation of due process	违反法定程序
weihai chengdu	degree of dangerousness	危害程度
weihai guojia anquan zui	crimes of endangering state security	危害国家安全罪
Wei Jingsheng		魏京生
weiwuzhuyi fanyinglun	Materialist "theory of reflection"	唯物主义反映论
weixianxing yuce	prediction of dangerousness	危险性预测
wen fengzi	"document maniacs"	文疯子
wu fengzi	aggressive maniacs	武疯子
wu gao	false accusation	诬告
wuli qunao	unreasonably making trouble	无理取闹
wu minshi xingwei nengli	no capacity for civil action	无民事行为能力
wu xingshi zeren nengli	no capacity to bear criminal responsibility ("non-imputable")	无刑事责任能力
xianding zeren nengli	limited capacity to bear legal responsibility	限定责任能力
xianpan houshen	"verdict first, trial second"	先判后审
xianran shi ji bu yansude	clearly most unconscientious	显然是极不严肃的
xianshi dongji	real or authentic motives	现实动机
xianxing fan'geming	active counterrevolutionaries	现行反革命
xiaoji zhengzhi yan-xing	negative political speech and action	消极政治言行
xiejiao	evil cult	邪教
xiejiao suozhi jingshen zhang'ai	evil cult-induced mental disorder	邪教所致精神障碍
xinyinxing jingshenbing	psychogenic mental illness	心因性精神病
Xing Jiandong		邢建东
xingshi zeren nengli	capacity to bear criminal responsibility	刑事责任能力
xingzheng weituo xingwei	administrative referral (psychiatric)	行政委托行为
xinlifenxixue	psychoanalysis	心理分析学

xinli zhiliao/ jingshen zhiliao	psychotherapy	心理治疗
xin shidai de kuangren	"madman of the new era"	新时代的狂人
Xue Jifeng		薛纪峰
Yan Weibing		严慰冰
Yang Desen	Young Derson	杨德森
yanxing pian ji	intemperate language and behaviour	言行偏激
yi fa zhiguo	rule the country in accordance with law	依法治国
yi fa zhiguo	use law to rule the country	以法治国
yi fen wei er	"one divides into two"	一分为二
yi ku si tian	"recalling past bitterness and remembering present happiness"	忆苦思甜
yi-nan anjian	difficult or thorny cases	疑难案件
yidaosu xiuke zhiliao	insulin coma therapy	胰岛素休克治疗
yi yan zhi zui	to make speech a crime	以言治罪
yizheng	hysteria	癔症
yuan-jia-cuo an	trumped-up cases and miscarriages of justice	冤假错案
yu wenhua miqie xiangguan de jingshen zhang'ai	culture-bound mental disorders	与文化密切相关的精神障碍
zainan lintou gan	fear of imminent catastrophe	灾难临头感
zha bing/ weizhuang bing	malingering (feigning illness)	诈病/ 伪装病
Zhang Gonglai		张共来
zhaoshi zhaohuo	create incidents or disasters	肇事肇祸
zhengquede zhengzhi sixiang	correct political ideology	正确的政治思想
Zheng Zhanpei		郑瞻培
zhengzhi fengzi	political maniacs	政治疯子
zhengzhi kuangre	political mania	政治狂热
zhengzhi pianzhikuang	political paranoia	政治偏执狂
zhengzhishang de fengkuangxing	political lunacy	政治上的疯狂性
zhengzhixing anjian	political cases	政治性案件
Zhi'an Chu	Public Order Department	治安处
Zhongguo Laodong Dang	Labour Party of China	中国劳动党
Zhongguo Minzhu Jianguo Dang	China Party for Democratic National Reconstruction	中国民主建国党
Zhongguo Shenjing Jingshen Jibing Zazhi	Chinese Journal of Nervous and Mental Diseases	中国神经精神疾病杂志
Zhonghua Jingshenke Zazhi	Chinese Journal of Psychiatry	中华精神科杂志
zhuguan nengdongxing	subjective dynamism	主观能动性
zhuzhi yisheng	chief physician (psychiatrist)	主治医生

zichanjieji ziyouhua	bourgeois liberalization	资产阶级自由化
ziwo fangwei nengli	capacity to exercise self-defence/ sexual consent	自我防卫能力
zuo'an dongji	criminal motive	作案动机
zuozheng nengli	capacity to testify or provide evidence	作证能力

TABLE OF LEGISLATION AND NORMATIVE DOCUMENTS

This appendix provides the Chinese characters for the titles of the main PRC laws, regulations and policy documents referred to in this book. To simplify the listing, the term "People's Republic of China" has been omitted from laws and regulations whose titles commence with that term. The English titles are the present author's translation from the Chinese original.

Administration Methods for Ankang Hospitals (1987)
　　安康医院管理方法
Administration Methods for Psychiatric Judicial Appraisal (2000)
　　精神疾病司法鉴定管理办法
Administrative Litigation Law (1990)
　　行政诉讼法
Administrative Punishments Law (1996)
　　行政处罚法
Administrative Reconsideration Law (1999)
　　行政复议法
Civil Procedure Law (1991)
　　民事诉讼法
Criminal Law (1997)
　　刑法
Criminal Procedure Law (1996)
　　刑事诉讼法
Dalian Municipal Regulations on the Guardianship, Treatment and Management of Mentally Ill Persons Who Create Disasters or Incidents (1992)
　　大连市监护治疗管理肇事肇祸精神病人条例
Decision of the Standing Committee of the National People's Congress on Banning Heretical Cult Organizations and Preventing and Punishing Cult Activities (1999)
　　全国人民代表大会常务委员会关于取缔邪教组织、防范和惩治邪教活动的决定
Detailed Implementation Rules for Nursing Work in Ankang Hospitals (1987)
　　安康医院护理工作实施细则
Detailed Rules on the Disciplinary Administration of Prisons and Labour-Reform Detachments (Trial Draft) (Ministry of Public Security, 1982)
　　监狱、劳改队管教工作细则（试行）

Explanation of the Supreme People's Court and Supreme People's Procuracy Concerning Laws Applicable to Handling Cases of Organizing and Employing Heretical Cult Organizations to Commit Crimes (1999, 2001)
最高人民法院最高人民检察院关于办理组织和利用邪教组织犯罪案件具体应用法律若干问题的解释

General Principles of Civil Law (1986)
民法通则

Guangdong Provincial Temporary Methods for the Shelter and Settlement of Mentally Ill Persons Who Create Disasters or Incidents (1990)
广东省收容安置肇祸肇事精神病人暂行办法

Heilongjiang Provincial Regulations on the Guardianship, Treatment and Management of Mentally Ill Persons Who Endanger Public Order (1996)
黑龙江省监护治疗管理危害社会治安精神病人条例

Joint Directive of the Supreme People's Court, Supreme People's Procuratorate and Ministry of Public Security Concerning the Clearing Out of Aged, Weak, Sick and Disabled or Mentally Ill Prisoners (1979)
最高人民法院、最高人民检察院、公安部关于清理老弱病残犯和精神病犯的联合通知

Key-Point Summary of the First National Public Security Conference on Custody and Treatment of the Mentally Ill (Ministry of Public Security, 1987)
全国公安机关第一次精神病管治工作会议纪要

Labour Law (1994)
劳动法

Law on Assembly, Procession and Demonstration (1989)
集会游行示威法

Law on Legislation (2000)
立法法

National Register of Judicial Psychiatric Appraisal Units (2003)
全国司法精神病鉴定单位名册

Notice of the State Council on Circulating the Trial Practices of the Ministry of Public Security on Re-education through Labour (1982)
国务院关于转发公安部制定的劳动教养试行办法的通知

Notification of Bureau No. 11 of the Ministry of Public Security on Strengthening and Reorganizing the Management of Solitary Confinement Cells (1983)
公安部十一局关于加强整顿禁闭室管理的通知

Notification of the Ministry of Civil Affairs, As Approved and Circulated by the State Council, Concerning the [Ministry's] Opinion on How to Handle the Cases of Persons Wrongly Killed in the Course of Campaigns to Suppress Counterrevolution During the Period of the Second Revolutionary

Civil War (State Council, 1983)
> 国务院批转民政部关于对第二次国内革命战争时期肃反中被错杀人员的处理意见的通知

Opinion of the Ministries of Health, Civil Affairs and Public Security on the Strengthening of Mental Health Work (1987)
> 卫生部、民政部、公安部关于加强精神卫生工作的意见

Opinion of the Supreme People's Court and Supreme People's Procuracy on Several Questions Concerning the Specific Application of Law in the Handling of Criminal Cases Committed During the Counterrevolutionary Rebellion and Political Turmoil (1989)
> 最高人民法院、最高人民检察院关于办理反革命暴乱和政治动乱中犯罪案件具体应用法律的若干问题的意见

Opinion on the Question of Whether Viciously Attacking or Slandering Central Leading Comrades Constitutes a Crime (CPC Central Political-Legal Commission, 1981)
> 关于对恶毒攻击、诽谤中央领导同志是否构成犯罪问题的意见

Police Law (1995)
> 警察法

Prisons Law (1994)
> 监狱法

Provisions of the Shanghai High People's Court, Shanghai Municipal People's Procuracy and Shanghai Municipal Public Security Bureau on the Handling of Cases Where Criminal Suspects or Defendants Become Mentally Ill during the Criminal Process (2003)
> 上海市高级人民法院、上海市人民检察院、上海市公安局关于办理犯罪嫌疑人、被告人在刑事诉讼期间患精神病的案件的规定

Psychiatric Judicial Appraisal Management Rules of Beijing Municipality (1998)
> 北京市精神病司法鉴定管理办法

Qingdao Municipal Regulations on the Management and Treatment of Mentally Ill Persons Who Create Incidents or Disasters (1992)
> 青岛市肇事肇祸精神病人管理治疗规定

Regulations of the Chinese Soviet Republic on the Punishment of Counterrevolution (1934)
> 中华苏维埃共和国惩治反革命条例

Regulations on the Admission and Treatment of Mentally Ill Persons Who Create Incidents or Disasters (Shanghai; date unknown)
> 肇事肇祸精神病人的收治规定

Regulations on Detention Centres (1990)
> 看守所条例

Regulations on Reform through Labour (1954)
> 劳动改造条例

Reply of the Supreme People's Court on the Question of the Handling of Crimes Committed by Mentally Ill Persons (1956)
最高人民法院关于处理精神病患者犯罪问题的复函

Resolution on Approving the Decision of the State Council on the Issue of Re-education through Labour (1957)
全国人民代表大会常务委员会批准国务院关于劳动教养问题的决定的决议

Resolution on Approving the Supplementary Decision of the State Council on the Issue of Re-education through Labour (NPC Standing Committee (1979)
全国人民代表大会常务委员会批准国务院关于劳动教养的补充规定

Security Administration Punishments Law (2006)
治安管理处罚法

Shanghai Municipal Code of Professional Ethics for Forensic Evaluators (2003)
上海市司法鉴定人职业道德规范

Shanghai Municipal Mental Health Regulations (2002)
上海市精神卫生条例

Shanghai Municipal Regulations on the Guardianship, Treatment and Management of Mentally Ill Persons Who Create Incidents or Disasters (1986)
上海市监护治疗管理肇事肇祸精神病人条例

Shenyang Municipality's Methods for the Custody and Treatment of Mentally Ill Persons Who Endanger Public Order (1996)
沈阳市收治危害社会治安精神病人办法

Shijiazhuang Municipal Methods for the Guardianship of Minors and Mentally Ill Persons (1996)
石家庄市未成年人和精神病人监护办法

State Compensation Law (1995)
国家赔偿法

Supplementary Provisions of the Standing Committee of the National People's Congress Regarding the Time Limits for Handling Criminal Cases (1984)
关于刑事案件办案期限的补充规定

Temporary Law on the Punishment of Crimes of Counterrevolution (Nanjing, 1928)
暂行反革命治罪法

Temporary Methods for Administering Bodybuilding and Qigong (2000)
健身气功管理暂行办法

Temporary Methods for Labour Re-education (1982)
劳动教养试行办法

Temporary Regulations for Judicial Appraisal of the Mentally Ill (1989)
关于精神疾病司法鉴定暂行规定

Tianjin Municipal Methods for the Shelter and Management of Mentally Ill Persons Who Endanger Public Order (1991)

  天津市收治管理危害社会治安精神病人办法

Various Regulations of Jilin Province on the Compulsory Medical Treatment of Mentally Ill Persons Who Endanger Society (2000)

  吉林省危害社会精神病人强制医疗若干规定

Various Regulations by the Ministry of Public Security and the Ministry of Justice Concerning the Detailed Implementation of the Central Committee's Transferral of the Work of Labour Reform and Labour Re-education Over to the Judicial Administrative Departments (1983)

  公安部、司法部关于贯彻执行中央将劳改、劳教工作移交给司法行政部门管理的若干规定

Xi'an Municipal Public Security Bureau: Various Regulations on Implementing the "Xi'an Municipal Methods for the Compulsory Shelter of Mentally Ill Persons Who Seriously Endanger Social Safety" (2006)

  西安市公安局:《关于贯彻<西安市强制收治严重危害社会安全精神病人办法>的若干规定》

BIBLIOGRAPHY

I. By Author:

Alabaster, Ernest — *Notes and Commentaries on Chinese Criminal Law*, Luzac & Co., 1899.

Alford, William P. — "A Second Great Wall? China's Post-Cultural Revolution Project of Legal Construction," *Cultural Dynamics*, 1999, Vol. 11, No. 2, pp.193-213.

Amnesty International — *China: Punishment without Crime: Administrative Detention*, 1991 (ASA 17/27/91.)

— "China: Prisoner of Conscience Imprisoned in Psychiatric Hospital" (ASA 17/WU 16/93), 19 October 1993.

— "Medical Letter Writing Action: Wang Wanxing, Wang Miaogen, Xing Jiandong" (ASA 17/44/93), 22 December 1993.

— *People's Republic of China: The Crackdown on Falun Gong and Other So-called "Heretical Organizations,"* March 23, 2000 (ASA 17/011/2000.)

— "China: Rule of Law and Human Rights—Time for Institutional Reforms" (Press Release), 22 October 2002.

— "China: Migrant Worker Dies in Custody," July 2003.

Appelbaum, Anne — *Gulag: A History*, Doubleday 2003.

Appelbaum, Kenneth L. — "Political Abuse of Psychiatry: An Introduction to the Munro Commentaries," *Journal of the American Academy of Psychiatry and the Law*, 2002, Vol. 30, No. 1, pp.95-6.

Appelbaum, Paul S., M.D. — "Abuses of Law and Psychiatry in China," *Psychiatric Services*, October 2001, Vol. 52, No. 10, pp.1297-8.

August, Oliver — "China Holds Rebels in Soviet-style Asylums," *The Times*, 13 August 2002.

Bao Zhongcheng et al — "Clinical Observations on 400 Cases of Electro-shock Therapy," *Chinese Journal of Nervous and Mental Diseases*, No.1, 1960, pp.28-30.

Becker, Jasper — "Dissidents 'Tortured in Asylums'," *South China Morning Post*, 19 February 2001.

Beijing Municipal Bureau of Health — *Beijing Shi Jingshenbing Sifa Jianding Guanli Banfa*, Beijing Municipal Psychiatric Judicial Appraisal Management Rules, 1998.

Birley, Jim — "Political Abuse of Psychiatry in the Soviet Union and China: A Rough Guide for Bystanders," *Journal of the American Academy of Psychiatry and the Law*, 2002, Vol. 30, No. 1, pp.145-7.

Bloch, Sidney — "Soviet Psychiatry and Snezhnevskyism," in Robert van Voren, (ed.), *Soviet Psychiatric Abuse in the Gorbachev Era*, IAPUP, Amsterdam 1989.

Blum, Georg — "China: Elektroschocks gegen das Virus Freiheit," *Die Zeit*, No.45, November 3, 2005.

Bloch, Sidney & Reddaway, Peter — *Russia's Political Hospitals: The Abuse of Psychiatry in the Soviet Union*, Victor Gollancz, 1977.

— *Soviet Psychiatric Abuse: The Shadow Over World Psychiatry*, Victor Gollancz, 1984.

Bodde, Derk & Morris, Clarence — *Law in Imperial China*, University of Pennsylvania Press, 1967.

Bodeen, Christopher — "Wife: China Union Leader Drugged," *Associated Press*, December 17, 2000.

Bonnie, Richard J. — "Political Abuse of Psychiatry in the Soviet Union and China: Complexities and Controversies," *Journal of the American Academy of Psychiatry and the Law*, 2002, Vol. 30, No. 1, pp.136-44.

— "Soviet Psychiatry and Human Rights: Reflections on the Report of the U.S. Delegation," 19 *Law, Med. & Health Care* 123 (1990.)

Bonnie, Richard J. & Polubinskaya, Svetlana V. — "Unraveling Soviet Psychiatry," *The Journal of Contemporary Legal Issues*, 1999, No.10.

Borenstein, Daniel B. — "Jailed in China: Confront the Abuse," *New York Times* (Letter to the Editor), 25 March 2001.

Bradsher, Keith — "China Holds Candidate from Hong Kong on Prostitution Charge, *New York Times*, 18 August 2004.

Brown Charles J. & Lago, Armando M. — *The Politics of Psychiatry in Revolutionary Cuba*, Freedom House, 1992.

Bukovsky, Vladimir & Gluzman, Semyon — "A Manual on Psychiatry for Dissenters," 1974; cited in Bloch & Reddaway, *Russia's Political Hospitals*.

Buruma, Ian — "Dictators of the World, it's Time to Stop Blaming Us for All of Your Problems," *The Guardian*, 2 September 2002.

Cai Dingjian — "Development of the Chinese Legal System Since 1979 and its Current Crisis and Transformation," in *Cultural Dynamics*, 1999, Vol. 11, No. 2, pp.133-166.

— "Towards the Rule of Law: Where is the Way?" in *Yifa Zhiguo, Jianshe Shehuizhuyi Fazhi Guojia*, Liu Hainian et al (eds.), 1996, pp.395-6.

Cai, Jane — "Officers in Jail Over Starved Toddler," *South China Morning Post*, 23 August 2004.

Canadian Medical Association — "Code of Ethics Annotated for Psychiatrists," approved by the board of directors of the Canadian Psychiatric Association in October 1978.

Cao Changqing — "*Zhongguo Jingshenbingyuan li de Zhengzhifan*" ("Political Prisoners in China's Mental Asylums"), reprinted in *Da Ji Yuan* (Epoch Times), New York, September 2, 2002.

CCTV.com — "*Jishi: Jingshenbing Huanzhe*" ("True Record: A Victim of Mental Illness"), Parts One & Two, 25 June 2004 and 13 July 2004, both available at: www.cctv.com.

Chan Siu-sin — "Mental Hospital Should Not be Run as Jail, Says Official," South China Morning Post, 29 April 2004.

Chan, Vivien Pik-kwan — "Detained unionist no longer drugged," *South China Morning Post*, December 19, 2000.

Chandler, David A.T. (ed.) — "The Party's Four-Year Plan to Build Socialism in All Fields, 1977-1980," *Pol Pot Plans the Future*, Yale University Southeast Asian Studies Monograph No.33 (New Haven: 1988.)

Chen Chengyu — "*Liti Dingxiang Ji Gongnengxing Shenjing Waike Zhiliao Zhongxin*" (The Stereotactic and Functional-Neurosurgery Treatment Centre), 30 March 2004; available at: www.jsby.cn/Article_Show.asp?ArticleID=539.

Chen Erjin — *Crossroads Socialism: A Manifesto for Proletarian Democracy*, translated and with an introduction by Robin Munro, London: NLB/Verso Editions, 1984.

Chen Jiena — "*Shi Jingshenbingyuan Haishi Kanshousuo? Shi Ren-Da Daibiao Shicha Ankang Yiyuan Tichu Piping... Yong Kanshousuo Tiaoli Guanli Jingshenbingren Qiantuo*" (Is it a Mental Hospital or a Prison? After Inspection Visit to Ankang Hospital, People's Congress Delegates Raise Criticisms.... Calling it Inappropriate to Manage Mental Patients in Accordance with Detention Centre Regulations), *Nanfang Ribao* (Southern Daily), 28 April 2004.

Chen Jieren — "J*ingshenbing Jianding Youguan Wenti*" ("Problems in the Appraisal of Mental Illness"), *Zhongguo Qingnian Bao*, June 17, 2002.

Chen Qi — "An Account of the Evil Misdeeds of the Heilongjiang Provincial Mental Hospital: Petitioners persecuted by being psychiatrically incarcerated," *Kaifang* (Open) magazine, November 2002; reprinted in *Da Ji Yuan* (Epoch Times), November 7, 2002.

Chen Qingquan & Song Guangwei — *Lu Dingyi Zhuan* (*A Biography of Lu Dingyi*), *Zhonggong Dang Shi Chubanshe*, Beijing, December 1999.

Chen Weidong et al — "Chapter 9: Litigation Procedures for the Adoption of Coercive Medical Measures," in *Xingshi Tebie Chengxu de Shijian yu Tantao* (*Practice and Explorations in Special Criminal Procedure*), People's Court Publishing House, 1992, pp.467-505.

Chen Zhongbao (ed.) — *Yingyong Sifa Jingshenbingxue* (Applied Forensic Psychiatry – Chapter 7: The Use of Medications in Drug Interrogation), Shanghai Kexue Jishu Chubanshe, August 1988.

Chen, Nancy N. — Breathing *Spaces: Qigong, Psychiatry, and Healing in China*, Columbia University Press, July 2003.

China Mental Health Watch — "'Misdiagnosis and Lack of Training' are Deliberate Cover-Up for Severe Violations of WPA Madrid Declaration," August 2004, available at: www.chinapsychiatricwatch.org.

Clarke, Donald C. — *Wrongs and Rights: A Human Rights Analysis of China's Revised Criminal Code*, Lawyers Committee for Human Rights (New York), December 1998.

Clarke, Donald C. & Feinerman, James V. — "Antagonistic Contradictions: Criminal Law and Human Rights in China," in Stanley B. Lubman (ed.), *China's Legal Reforms*, Oxford University Press, 1996, p.153.

Congressional-Executive Commission on China (CECC) — "Defense Lawyers Turned Defendants: Zhang Jianzhong and the Criminal Prosecution of Defense Lawyers in China," 28 May 2003.

Coonan, Clifford — "China Accused of Locking Sane Dissidents in Asylums," *The Independent*, 18 March 2006.

Cosgrove, G. Rees MD & Rauch, Scott L. MD — "Psychosurgery" (undated), available on the Internet at: neurosurgery.mgh.harvard.edu/Functional/psysurg.htm.

Council of Europe — "Legal Protection of Persons Suffering from Mental Disorder Placed as Involuntary Patients," Recommendation No. R (83) 2 adopted by the Committee of Ministers of the Council of Europe on 22 February 1983, in Strasbourg.

— "Recommendation No. 1235 (1994) on Psychiatry and Human Rights," adopted by the Assembly on 12 April 1994 (10th Sitting.)

— "White Paper on the Protection of the Human Rights and Dignity of People Suffering from Mental Disorder, Especially Those Placed as Involuntary Patients in a Psychiatric Establishment," 3 January 2000, DIR/JUR (2000) 2.

Council of the European Union — "Declaration by the Presidency on Behalf of the European Union on the Case of Wang Wanxing," Brussels, 10 November 2005; 14190/05 [Presse 292], p.126.

Cowhig, David — "Wired China: Many Hands on Many Switches," Statement to the Congressional-Executive Commission on China's Round-Table on Internet and Free Flow of Information in China, Washington D.C., 15 April 2002.

CPC Central Political-Legal Commission — "Opinion on the Question of Whether Viciously Attacking or Slandering Central Leading Comrades Constitutes a Crime," December 17, 1981; a full translation (by Donald C. Clarke) is available at: http://faculty.washington.edu/dclarke/public/clpc-opinion.htm.

Daes, Erica-Irene A. — Special Rapporteur of the U.N. Sub-Commission on Prevention of Discrimination and Protection of Minorities, *Principles, Guidelines and Guarantees for the Protection of Persons Detained on Grounds of Mental Ill-Health or Suffering from Mental Disorder*, New York: United Nations Publications, 1986, E/CN.4/Sub.2/1983/17/Rev.1.

Deron, Francis — "La Chine s'Inspire de l'URSS en Psychiatrie à Caractère Politique," *Le Monde*, 23 August 2002.

— "Prisons Psychiatriques en Chine," Le Monde, 23 August 2002.

Dhir, Aaron A. — "Human Rights Treaty Drafting through the Lens of Mental Disability: the Proposed International Convention on Protection and Promotion of the Rights and Dignity of Persons with Disabilities," Cornell Law School LL.M. Papers Series, 2004.

Diamant, L.N. — "Issues in Clinical Evaluations and Compulsory Treatment of Psychopathic Personalities with Paranoid Delusions and Overvalued Ideas," cited in Gluzman, *On Soviet Totalitarian Psychiatry*, p.40.

Documentation Group of the Revolutionary Committee of Beijing College of Politics and Law and Documentation Group of the Capital Red Guards Committee's Politics and Law Commune, "A Shocking Case of Counterrevolution: An Investigative Report into the Attempt by Peng Zhen, Lu Dingyi and their Sinister Lieutenants to Concoct a Counterrevolutionary Phoney Medical Diagnosis Aimed at Shielding the Active Counterrevolutionary Element Yan Weibing," *Xingxing-Sese de Anjian: Liu Deng Peng Luo Shixing Zichanjieji Zhuanzheng de Yangban* (*All Types of Cases: Model Examples of the Bourgeois Dictatorship Exercised by Liu, Deng, Peng and Luo*), June 1968, pp.18-33.

Du Jinxiang & Wang Xiaoyan — *Yixue Lunlixue Jiaocheng* (A Training Course in Medical Ethics), Ci Xue Publishing House, May 1998.

Du Zhizheng — *Yixue Lunlixue Tanxin* (New Explorations in Medical Ethics), *Henan Yike Daxue* Publishing House, October 2000.

Dui Hua Foundation — "Statistics on Political Crime in the People's Republic of China" (Volumes 1 & 2), San Francisco, April 2001 and May 2004.

Eckholm, Erik — Silk Workers in Standoff with Beijing Over Union," *New York Times*, 15December 2000.

— "China is Said to Abuse Promoter of Factory Union," *New York Times*, 9February 2001.

— "China's Crackdown on Sect Stirs Alarm over Psychiatric Abuse: Rights Groups Cite Rise in Medical Detentions," *New York Times*, 19 February 2001, p.1.

— "'Psychiatric' Solution to Dissent is on the Rise in China," *International Herald Tribune*, 19 February 2001, p.1.

Employees from the Hongshan State Farm — "*Shei Boduole Nongchang Zhigong de Minzhu Quanli? Hangzhou Shi Xiaoshan Qu Hongshan Nongchang de Zhigong Qianming*" (Who is Stripping the State Farm Employees of their Democratic Rights? List of Signatories to Petition from Employees of the Hongshan State Farm, Xiaoshan District, Hangzhou Municipality), 11 April 2004, available at: www.yuluncn.com/Article_Show.asp?ArticleID=210.

European Falun Gong Information Centre — "48 Falun Gong Deaths Reported in June and July" (press statement), 20 August 2004.

Evans. Harriet & Donald, Stephanie (eds.) — *Picturing Power in the People's Republic of China: Posters of the Cultural Revolution*, Rowman & Littlefield Publishers, Inc., 1999.

Faulk's Basic Forensic Psychiatry (Third Edition), revised by J.H. Stone, M. Roberts, J. O'Grady & A.V. Taylor with K. O'Shea, Blackwell Science (Oxford: 2000.)

Foot, Rosemary — *Rights Beyond Borders: The Global Community and the Struggle over Human Rights in China*, Oxford University Press, 2000.

Foshan Shi Fayuan Zhi (Annals of the Foshan Municipal Courts), compiled and published by the Foshan Municipal Intermediate Court (year of publication not known, but probably 1988 or 1989.)

Foucault, Michel — "About the Concept of the 'Dangerous Individual' in 19th Century Legal Psychiatry," in *Law and Psychiatry: Proceedings of an International Symposium Held at the Clark Institute of Psychiatry*, Toronto, Canada, February 1977, Pergamon Press (1978), pp.1-28.

Gallagher, Mary E. — "Use the Law as Your Weapon! The Rule of Law and Labor Conflict in China," in *Engaging Chinese Law*, Neil Diamant, Kevin O'Brien, Stanley Lubman (eds.), forthcoming, Stanford University Press, 2005.

Gan Yupei, (ed.) — *Xingfaxue Zhuanlun* (Essays on Criminal Law*)*, Beijing University Publishing House (volume marked: "for internal use only"), November 1989, p.512.

Geertz, Clifford — "Thick Description: Toward an Interpretive Theory of Culture," in Geertz, *The Interpretation of Cultures*, New York: Basic (1973), pp.1-30.

Geneva Initiative on Psychiatry — "Political Abuse of Psychiatry in China and the Response of the World Psychiatric Association," 27 August 2002.

Gittings, John — "China 'Sending Dissidents to Mental Hospitals'," *The Guardian*, 13 August 2002.

Gluzman, Semyon —"Law and Psychiatry: The Totalitarian Experience," *Journal of the American Academy of Psychiatry and the Law*, 2001, Vol. 29, p.332.

—*On Soviet Totalitarian Psychiatry*, International Association on the Political Use of Psychiatry (IAPUP) Amsterdam, 1989.

Goodenough, Patrick — "China's Denies Locking Up Opponents in Mental Asylums," *CNSNews.com*, 28 August 2002.

Greimel, Hans — "Top Psychiatric Group Plans Inspection of China over Alleged Abuse of Mental Patients," *Associated Press*, 26 August 2002.

Grudgings, Stuart — "China Faces Censure over 'Political Psychiatry'," *Reuters*, 23 August 2002.

Grudgings, Stuart — "Psychiatric Group Plans Investigation in China, *Washington Post*, 27 August 2002.

Gong'an Bu Fazhi Si — Gong'an Jiguan Banli Laodong Jiaoyang Anjian Fagui Huibian (A Compilation of Laws and Regulations for Use by Public Security Organs in Handling Cases of Re-education Through Labour), Jing Guan Jiaoyu Chubanshe (Police Officers Educational Publishing House), October 1992; volume marked "*neibu faxing*" (internal distribution only.)

Gong'an Bu Fubuzhang Luo Feng — "*Zai Quanguo Di Sanci Jingshen Weisheng Gongzuo Huiyishang de Jianghua*" (Speech by Deputy Minister of Public Security Luo Feng at the Third National Conference on Mental Health Work), 2003 (exact date not given), available at: http://www.cdpf.org.cn/.

Gostin, Larry — "Human Rights in Mental Health: A Proposal for Five International Standards Based upon the Japanese Experience," *International Journal of Law and Psychiatry*, Vol. 10, 1987, pp.353-368.

Gu Xiangdong et al — "*Shehui Jineng Xunlian Dui 32 Li Zhuyuan Manxing Jingshenfenliezheng Huanzhe de Liaoxiao Guancha* (An Examination of the Efficacy Deputy Minister of Public Security of Social Skills Training for 32 Chronic Schizophrenic Patients)," *Chinese Journal of Nervous and Mental Diseases*, Vol.20, No.2, pp.85-87.

Guan Xin — "How to Discern Mental Illness and Ascertain Legal Capacity," *"Renmin Sifa" Xuanbianben 1981 Nian* (*A Compilation of Articles from "People's Judiciary" 1981*) volume marked "for internal use only", Law Publishing House, 1983, p.590.

Gunn, John — "Dangerousness," in John Gunn & Pamela J. Taylor, eds., *Forensic Psychiatry: Clinical, Legal and Ethical Issues* (Butterworth & Heinemann, 1993), pp.624-645.

Gunn, John & Taylor, Pamela J. (eds.) — *Forensic Psychiatry: Clinical, Legal and Ethical Issues*, Butterworth & Heinemann, 1993.

Guo Daohui, Li Buyun & HaoTiechuan — *Zhongguo Dangdai Faxue Zhengming Lu* (A Record of Contention on the Science of Law in Contemporary China), *Hunan Renmin Chubanshe*, December 1998.

Guo Qun — "*Guanyu Fan'geming Zuizhang de Tiaozheng* (On Readjusting the Chapter on Crimes of Counterrevolution)," in Cui Qingsen (ed.), *Zhongguo Dangdai Xingfa Gaige* (*Reform in China's Contemporary Criminal Code*), Shehui Kexue Wenxian Press, November 1991.

Halpern, Abraham — "Abuses in China," *New York Times* (Letter to the Editor), 25 February 2001.

— "Lifers Take a Stand" (Letter to the Editor), *Psychiatric News*, 16 August 2002, Vol. 37, No. 16, p.26.

Harding, Luke — "In the Grip of the Ankang," *The Guardian*, December 20, 2005.

Haski, Pierre — "En Chine, des Asiles Très Politiques," *La Libération*, 23 August 2002.

Hentoff, Nat — "Torturers as Trading Partners," *Jewish World Review*, 20 March 2001.

Hewitt, Duncan — "China 'Detaining Opponents in Mental Homes': Report Alleges a Secretive Network of 20 Police-Run Hospitals," *BBC News*, 19 February 2001.

Han Yanlong & Chang Zhaoru (eds.) — *Zhonghua Suweiai Gongheguo Chengzhi Fan'geming Tiaoli*,

(Regulations of the Chinese Soviet Republic on the Punishment of Counterrevolution), in "*Zhongguo Xin Minzhuzhuyi Geming Shiqi Genjudi Fazhi*" (Legal System of the Base Areas during the Revolutionary Period of New Democracy)," in *Wenxian Xuanbian* (Selected Documents), Vol. 3, *Zhongguo Shehui Kexue Chubanshe, Beijing*, 1981, pp. 5-11.

Harding, Timothy & Montandon, Cleopatre — "Does Dangerousness Travel Well? A Cross-National Perspective on Medico-Legal Applications," in John R. Hamilton & Hugh Freeman, eds., *Dangerousness: Psychiatric Assessment and Management*, Gaskell, 1982, pp.46-52.

Hausman, Ken — "WPA, Chinese Psychiatrists Agree on Psychiatry Abuse Charges," P*sychiatric News*, August 6, 2004, Vol. 39, No. 15, p.2.

He Haibo — "*Quru de Sifa – Ping Han Zhenxi An Yishen Panjue*" (An Insult to the Judiciary – Assessing the Judgment of First Instance in the Case of Han Zhenxi), *Bei-Da Falü Xinxi Wang* (Beijing University Law Information Network), undated, available at: 211.100.18.62/research/lgyd/details.asp?lid=1955.

He Jiali et al — "*Butong Shiduan Qigong Suo Zhi Jingshen Zhang'ai Linchuang Duizhao Yanjiu Ji Zhenduan Biaozhun Tantao* (A Clinical Comparative Study of, and Diagnostic Criteria for, Qigong-induced Mental Disorders Over Various Periods)," *Chinese Journal of Nervous and Mental Diseases*, 2000, Vol.26, No.2, pp.116-117.

Heilongjiang Provincial People's Procuracy — *Heilongjiang Jiancha Zhi* (Annals of the Heilongjiang Procuracy), Heilongjiang Renmin Chubanshe, 1988.

Hickling, Frederick W. — "The Political Misuse of Psychiatry: An African-Caribbean Perspective," *Journal of the American Academy of Psychiatry and the Law*, 2002, Vol. 30, No. 1, pp.112-9.

Hilton, Isabel — "The China Scandal," *The Guardian*, 22 February 2001.

Hintzen, Geor H. — "The Place of Law in the PRC's Culture," *Cultural Dynamics*, 1999, Vol. 11, No. 2, pp.167-192.

Hong, Veron Mei-Ying — "Improving Human Rights in China: Should Re-Education Through Labor Be Abolished?" *Columbia Journal of Transnational Law*, 2003, Vol.42, pp.303-326.

Hou Jie — "*Wang Wanxing de 'Liu Hao Bingfang'*" (Wang Wanxing's "Sick Room No.6"), in *Beijing Zhi Chun* (Beijing Spring), November 2002, No. 14.

Hsia Yu-fen, M.D., & Tsai Neng — "Transcultural Investigation of Recent Symptomatology of Schizophrenia in China," *American Journal of Psychiatry*, November 1981, Vol.138, No.11, pp.1484-6.

Hsu, Francis L.K. — "A Brief Report on the Police Co-operation in Connection with Mental Cases in Peiping," in R. Lyman et al (ed.), *Social and Psychological Studies in Neuro-Psychiatry* (Beijing: Henri Vetch, 1939), pp.202-230.

Human Rights in China — *Detained at Official Pleasure: Arbitrary Detention in the People's Republic of China*, June 1993.

— *Empty Promises: Human Rights Protections and China's Criminal Procedure Law in Practice*, New York, February 2001.

— *Not Welcome at the Party: Behind the "Clean-Up" of China's Cities — A Report on Administrative Detention under "Custody and Repatriation"*, HRIC Arbitrary Detention Series, No. 2, September 1999.

— *Reeducation Through Labor (RTL): A Summary of Regulatory Issues and Concerns*, New York, February 2001, p.4.

Human Rights Watch — "China: End Political Abuse of Psychiatry: World Psychiatric Association Should Act in Yokohama," 12 August 2002.

— "China: No Medical Reason to Hold Dissident - Expert Team Finds Wang Wanxing Wrongly Sent to Asylum for 13 Years" [co-published by Global Initiative on Psychiatry), March 17, 2006.

— "China: Political Prisoner Exposes Brutality in Police-Run Mental Hospital – Eyewitness Testimonies from Notorious Ankang Asylum," November 2, 2005.

— "China: WPA Action on Psychiatric Abuse Falls Short," 27 August 2002.

— *Dangerous Meditation: China's Campaign Against Falungong*, January 2002.

— *Death by Default: A Policy of Fatal Neglect in China's State Orphanages*, 1996.

— *Democracy Wall Prisoners: Xu Wenli, Wei Jingsheng and Other Jailed Pioneers of the Chinese Pro-Democracy Movement*, Vol.5, No. 6, March 1993.

— *Detained in China and Tibet: A Directory of Political and Religious Prisoners*, 1994.

— *Organ Procurement and Judicial Execution in China*, New York, 1994.

— "Uzbekistan: Dissident in Psychiatric Detention," 12 April 2001.

Human Rights Watch/Asia and Human Rights in China — "Whose Security? An Analysis of 'State Security' in China's New Criminal Code," *A Human Rights Watch Report*, Vol. 9, No. 4 (c), April 1997.

Hung, Veron Mei-Ying — "Reassessing Reeducation through Labour," *China Rights Forum* (New York), No. 2, 2003, pp.35-41.

Huo Kediao & Liu Xiehe — "*Sifa Jingshenbing Jianding 1755 Li Fenxi*" (An Analysis of 1,755 Cases of Forensic Psychiatric Appraisal), in Fayixue Jinzhan Yu Shijian (Advances and Practices in Forensic Medicine), Hou Yiping & Liu Shicang (eds.), *Chengdu Keji Daxue Chubanshe* (Chengdu Science and Technology University Press), October 1999, pp.337-41.

Huo Kediao, Liu Xiehe, Hu Zeqing & Zhang Wei — "210 Li Sifa Jingshenbingxue Jianding Anli Fenxi" (An Analysis of 210 Cases of Forensic Psychiatric Appraisal), *Zhongguo Fayixue Zazhi* (China Journal of Forensic Medicine), 1987, Vol.2, No.4, pp.198-202.

International Confederation of Free Trades Unions — "China: ICFTU Complaint to ILO: Additional information - Cases No. 1930 & 2031 (Appeals and Protests, 2/6/2002)," and "People's Republic of China: Annual Survey of Violations of Trade Union Rights (2002) (Country Reports: Annual Survey of Trade Union Rights, 6/1/2002.)"

Jacoby, Robin & Munro, Robin — "Abuse of Psychiatry: Beijing Needs to Get a Stern Message," *International Herald Tribune*, 26 August 2002.

Ji Shi — *Li Hongzhi and His "Falun Gong" – Deceiving the Public and Ruining Lives* (New Star Publishers, Beijing 1999.)

Jia Rubao — "More on the Essential Nature of Mental Illness," (Employees' Hospital of the Huashan Metallurgy and Vehicle Repair Plant, Huayin, Shaanxi Province), *Xin Yixue – Shenjing Xitong Jibing Fukan (New Medicine – Supplementary Series on Diseases of the Nervous System)*, 1977, Vol.3, No.2, pp.142-143; article dated April 1977.

Jia Yicheng et al — "On Several Basic Concepts in Forensic Psychiatry," *Chinese Journal of Nervous and Mental Diseases*, 1983, Vol. 9, No. 2, p.119.

Jia Yicheng — "Summary and Analysis of Papers Submitted to the First National Academic Conference on Forensic Psychiatry," (Psychiatric Teaching and Research Group of the Shanghai Railways Medical College), September 1987, *Shanghai Archives of Psychiatry* (*Shanghai Jingshen Yixue*), 1987, No.3, pp.118-24.

Jia Yicheng (ed.) — *Shiyong Sifa Jingshenbingxue (Applied Forensic Psychiatry)*, Anhui Renmin Chubanshe, September 1988.

Jia Yicheng — "A Discussion of Certain Legal Issues Concerning the Hospitalization of the Mentally Ill," *Shanghai Archives of Psychiatry*, 1998, No.1, pp.6-10.

Jian Lushi — "*Jiuzhu Jigou, Jiu Zheyang Chengquan le Ren Zhi*" (Here's How the Relief Agencies Prop up Rule by Man), *Jiancha Ribao*, June 19, 2002.

Jin Juanjuan et al — "*Dui Xingshi Anjian Zhong Sifa Jingshen Yixue Jianding de Jidian Sikao*" (Various Thoughts on Judicial Psychiatric-Medical Appraisal in Criminal Cases), *21 Jiankang Wang* (21st Century Health Net), 8 February 2004.

Johnson, Ian — "Death Trap: How One Chinese City Resorted to Atrocities to Control Falun Dafa," *Wall Street Journal*, 25 December 2000, p.1; "Falun Dafa Fight Stifles Others, Too: Beijing's Blitz Squelches Unorthodox Views," *Wall Street Journal*, 6 February 2001; and "Burden of Belief: As Crackdown Grows, Falun Gong's Faithful Face a New Pressure," *Wall Street Journal*, 28 March 2001.

Kahn, Joseph— "Sane Chinese Put in Asylum, Doctors Find," *New York Times*, 17 March 2006.

Kang Ming — "*Ankang Yiyuan de Xingzhi, Renwu, Zuoyong*" (The Nature, Tasks and Function of the Ankang Hospitals), available at the website of the Hangzhou PSB Ankang Hospital: www.ak-hospital.com/lwsx.htm.

Kent, Ann — *China, the United Nations, and Human Rights: The Limits of Compliance*, University of Pennsylvania Press (Philadelphia), 1999.

Kiev, Ari — *Transcultural Psychiatry* (Free Press, 1982).

Kleinman, Arthur — *Social Origins of Distress and Disease: Depression, Neurasthenia and Pain in Modern China*, Yale University Press, 1986.

Kleinman, Arthur & Lee, Sing — "Psychiatry in its Political and Professional Contexts: A Response to Robin Munro," *Journal of the American Academy of Psychiatry and the Law*, Vol.30, No.1 (2002), pp.120-125.

Kosachev, A.L. — "Clinical and Forensic Evaluation of Psychopathy of a Paranoid Type," Moscow 1973 (publisher unknown); cited in Gluzman (op cit), p.40.

Kremb, Jurgen — "Wie ein Tier am Pfahl," *Der Spiegel*, No.32 (August 1992), pp.140-146.

Kristof, Nicholas D. & WuDunn, Sheryl — *China Wakes: The Struggle for the Soul of a Rising Power*, Random House, 1994.

Kwok, Kristine — "Dissident Held in Mental Hospital 13 Years is Sane, Rights Group Says," *South China Morning Post*, 18 March 2006.

Lamson, H.D. — *Social Pathology in China*, Shanghai: The Commercial Press, 1935.

Lan Tongren — *"Xi'an Shi Xincheng Gong'an Fen Ju Ba Yi Wugu Funü Meng Xiaoxia Baibai Guanzai Jingshenbing Yuan Changda Shi Nian!"* (Xi'an City's Xincheng PSB Sub-Bureau Incarcerates Innocent Woman Meng Xiaoxia in Mental Hospital for as Long as Ten Years!), *Boxun Xinwen Wang*, 27 July 2004, available at: peacehall.com/news/gb/yuanqing/2004/07/200407272240.shtml.

Langer, Annette — "Psychoknast in China: Irre ist, wer aufbegehrt," *Der Spiegel*, November 21, 2005.

Langfitt, Frank — "Chinese Activist Released after 6-month Detention," The Baltimore Sun, July 19, 2001.

Lao Yan — *"Qiangzhi Jiedu Suo Shi Zenmoyang Jinxing Wenming Guanlide?"* (What are the "Civilized Management Methods" Used in Drug Rehabilitation Centres?), 7 June 2003; available at: members.lycos.co.uk/sixiang002/Shame/ShouRong/ShouRong015.txt.

Lee, Klaudia & Wiest, Nailene Chou — "Democrat's Punishment is Unusual, Says Scholar," *South China Morning Post*, 21 August 2004.

Lee, Sing — "Who is Politicising Psychiatry in China?" *British Journal of Psychiatry*, 2001, No.179, pp.178-179.

Lee, Sing & Kleinman, Arthur — "Psychiatry in its Political and Professional Contexts: A Response to Robin Munro," *Journal of the American Academy of Psychiatry and the Law*, 2002, Vol. 30, No. 1, pp.120-5.

Levenson, Lev — "Psychiatrists and Officers in Defense of Traditional Values," *Ekspress Khronika*, January 31, 1997.

Li Congpei, Li Yongzhi, Liu Jinsheng & Fang Mingzhao — *"Jingshen Fenliezheng Sifa Jingshenbing Jianding An Li Fenxi* (An Analysis of Cases Involving the Forensic-Psychiatric Evaluation of Schizophrenia)," *Chinese Journal of Nervous and Mental Diseases*, 1987, Vol. 20, No.3, pp.135-138.

Li Congpei (ed.) — *"Zai Sifa Jingshen Jianding Zhong Kefou Yong Jingmai Mazui Fenxi?"* (When Carrying Out a Judicial Psychiatric Appraisal, Is it Permissible to Use Intravenous Drug Interrogation?), *Linchuang Jingshen Yixue Zazhi* (Journal of Clinical Psychological Medicine), 1999, No.1.

Li Congpei (ed.) — *Sifa Jingshenbingxue* (*Forensic Psychiatry*), Renmin Weisheng Chubanshe, February 1992.

Li Li & Li Shaoping — *"Lun Fan'geming Xuanchuan Shandong Zui de Rending* (On the Determination of Crimes of Counterrevolutionary Propaganda and Incitement)," *Xiandai Faxue* (*Contemporary Jurisprudence*), 1990, No.1.

Li Tianfu et al — *Fanzui Tongjixue* (Criminal Statistics), Qunzhong Chubanshe, 1988.

Li Wenyan — *"Fan'geming Zui Gaiwei Weihai Guojia Anquan Zui Qianyi* (My Humble Views on the Changeover from Counterrevolutionary Crimes to Crimes of Endangering State Security)," *Fazhi Ribao* (*Legal Daily*), 14 March 1991.

Li Xinde — *"Ta Huanyou 'Pianzhixing Jingshenbing' ma?"* (Was He Really Suffering from "Paranoid Psychosis"?), *Gong-Shang Daobao* (Business Director), 25 March 2003.

— *"Ta Shi Zenmeyang Chengle 'Jingshenbing' de?"* (How Did He End Up as "Mentally Ill"?), *Gong-Shang Daobao*, 26 March 2004.

— "*Shei Boduole Nongchang Zhigong de Minzhu Quanli? – Laizi Hangzhou Shi Xiaoshan Qu Hongshan Nongchang de Diaocha*" (Who is Stripping the State Farm Employees of their Democratic Rights? – An Investigation Report from Hongshan State Farm, Xiaoshan District, Hangzhou City), Zhongguo Yulun Jiandu Wang (China Public Opinion Monitoring Network), 17 April 2004; available at: www.yuluncn.com.

Li Xintian — "One Decade of the Clinical Application of Artificial Hibernation Therapy in China," *Zhonghua Shenjing Jingshenke Zazhi (Chinese Journal of Nervous and Mental Diseases)*, 1959, No. 6.

Li Yan — "*Zhi'an Chufa Youwang Quxiao Laojiao*" (Administrative Punishments: The Prospect for Abolition of Labour Re-education), *Nanfang Dushi Bao* (Southern Metropolis Daily), 28 July 2004.

Liao Jiangsen — *Jingshenbing Beiwanglu* (A Memorandum of Mental Illness), *Jingguan Jiaoyu Chubanshe*, Police Officers Publishing House, Beijing, December 1994; volume marked: *neibu faxing* (restricted circulation.)

Lin Hong et al — "*1979-1998 Nian Sifa Jingshenbing Jianding Anli de Fenxi* (An Analysis of Cases of Forensic Psychiatric Evaluation, 1979-98)," Chinese Journal of Psychiatry, 2000, Vol.33 No. 4.

Lin Huai (ed.) — *Jingshen Jibing Huanzhe Xingshi Zeren Nengli He Yiliao Jianhu Cuoshi* (Capacity of Mental Illness Sufferers for Criminal Responsibility and Measures for Their Medical Guardianship), Renmin Fayuan Chubanshe, 1996.

Lin Tongren — "*Wei Gong Zao Da Zhi Can, Tao Gongdao Bei Qiangsong Jingshenbing Yuan Shi Nian*" (Beaten and Crippled for Upholding Truth, and Forcibly Sent to A Mental Hospital for Ten Years for Seeking Justice), *Da Ji Yuan* (Epoch Times), 27 July 2004.

Lingle, Christopher — "China Part of Psychiatric Axis of Evil," *Taipei Times*, 18 September 2002.

Liu Anqiu (ed.) — *Sifa Jingshenbingxue Jichu Zhishi* (*Basic Knowledge in Forensic Psychiatry*), Qunzhong Chubanshe, 1983.

Liu Baiju, *Jingshen Zhang'ai Yu Fanzui* (Mental Disorders and Crime), Vols. 1 & 2, Beijing: *Shehui Kexue Wenxian Chubanshe*, Social Sciences Documentary Publishing House, August 2000.

Liu Bin (ed.) — "*Henan Tongbai: Jia Fuyuan 'Jingshenbing' Sharen An*" (A Case of Murder by "Mentally Ill" Jia Fuyuan in Tongbai, Henan Province), in *Ershi Shiji Mo Pingfan Yuan-Jia-Cuo An Anli Jishi* (A True Record of Rectifying Wrong and Unjust Criminal Cases in the Late 20th Century), available at: www.shuku.net.

Liu Binyan — *A Higher Kind of Loyalty*, Pantheon Books (New York), 1990.

Liu Dechao — "*Dui Weihai Shehui Zhi'an de Jingshenbingren de Chuli* (On the Handling of Mentally Ill People Who Endanger the Public Order of Society)," *Xiandai Faxue* (*Modern Jurisprudence*), 1990, No. 2, pp.69-71.

Liu Guangren (ed.) — *Hukou Guanlixue* (*The Administration of Household Residence*), (Beijing: Zhongguo Jiancha Chubanshe (volume marked "for distribution within the public security organs only"), 1992.

Liu Jianguo (ed.) — *Laodong Jiaoyang – Shiyong Duixiang, Ban'an Chengxu, Wenshuo Zhizuo* (Re-education Through Labour – Targets of Use, Procedures for Case Handling, and Completion of Documents), *Zhongguo Jiancha Chubanshe* China Procuracy Publishing House, July 2002; volume marked: "*neibu faxing*" (internal distribution only.)

Liu Yan et al — "*Yi-Huan Shuangfang Dui Zhuyuan Jingshen Jibing Huanzhe Quanyi de Taidu Bijiao*" (A Two-Way Comparison of the Hospital's and the Patient's Attitudes Concerning the Rights and Interests of Hospitalized Mentally Ill Persons), Shanghai Jingshen Yixue (*Shanghai Archives of Psychiatry*), 12 January 2004.

Liu Zhenqing & Chen Jingyi, "*Zhongguo Gong'an Xitong de Jingshen Weisheng Fuwu*" (China's Public Security System of Mental Health Services), *Shanghai Jingshen Yixue* (Shanghai Archives of Psychiatry), 16 February 2004

Long Qingchun (ed.) — *Sifa Jingshen Yixue Jianding Zixun Jieda* (Consultative Questions and Answers for Forensic-Psychiatric Medical Evaluations), Chinese University of Politics and Law Publishing House, 1994.

Long Qingchun et al — "*Qiangzhi Yiliao Qianjian*" (Some Undeveloped Thoughts on Coercive Medical Treatment), a paper presented at the Fifth National Academic Conference on Psychiatry, October 2003.

López-Ibor, Prof. Juan J. — "Circular Letter to All Presidents of WPA Member Societies," 24 January 2002; copy on file with the author.

Lü Chengrong et al — "*Jujinxing Jingshen Zhang'ai 30 Li*" (Thirty Cases of Prison Psychosis), Shanghai Jingshen Yixue (Shanghai Archives of Psychiatry), 1996, Vol. 8, No. 2, p.101.

Lü Shilun — "Several Theoretical Questions Relating to the Construction of the Legal System," *Gao-Xiao Lilun Zhanxian* (Colleges' Theoretical Front), 1996, No. 4

Lu Shulian & Liu Keli — "*Sifa Jingshen Jianding Zhong Shaoshu Minzu Huanzhe Xiongsha An 84 Li Fenxi*" (An Analysis of 84 Forensic Psychiatric Appraisals in Cases Involving Violent Crimes by Members of Minority Nationalities), *Shanghai Jingshen Yixue* (Shanghai Archives of Psychiatry), 1988, Vol.6, No.3, pp.124-6.

Lü Xianrong (ed.) — *Sifa Jingshen Yixue Anli Ji* (*A Compilation of Forensic Psychiatric Medical Cases*), Ankang Hospital of the Wuhan Municipal Public Security Bureau, 1992.

Lu, Sunny Y. & Galli, Viviana B. — "Psychiatric Abuse of Falun Gong Practitioners in China," *Journal of the American Academy of Psychiatry and the Law*, 2002, Vol. 30, No. 1, pp.126-130.

Lubman, Stanley B. — *Bird in a Cage: Legal Reform in China After Mao*, Stanford University Press, 1999, p.297.

Luo Dahua (ed.) — *Fanzui Xinlixue* (*Psychology of Crime*), Qunzhong Chubanshe (volume marked "for internal distribution only", 1984 p.216.

Luo Jiming, Li Shenlu & Tang Xiaofeng — "An Analysis of Forty-One Mentally Ill People Involved in Cases of a Political Nature," (Hangzhou Ankang Municipal Hospital), December 1996, *Journal of Clinical Psychological Medicine* (*Linchuang Jingshen Yixue Zazhi*), 1996, Vol.6, No. 6, pp.356-357.

Declan, Lyons & Munro, Robin — "Dissent as a Symptom: Why China has Questions to Answer," *British Journal of Psychiatry*, June 2002, No.180, pp.551-2.

Ma Shaohua — "*Bu Shi Jingshenbing, Xuyao Shenme Zhengju*" (Why Should Evidence be Required to Show that Someone is Not Mentally Ill?), *Zhongguo Qingnian Bao* (China Youth Daily Online), 18 January 2002.

Magnier, Mark — "Chinese Dissident Tells of Abuse in Asylum," *Los Angeles Times*, November 9, 2005.

Mao Shulin et al — "Chapter Seven: Psychopathology and Crime," *Fanzui Xinlixue* (*Psychology of Crime*), Beijing: Qunzhong Chubanshe, 1985, p.222.

McDonald, Hamish — "China Abolishes Vagrancy Law after Death," Sydney Morning Herald, June 20 2003.

McElroy, Damien — "Psychiatrists' Move to Expel China over Political Abuse Fails," *Daily Telegraph*, 27 August 2002.

McGregor, Richard — "Attack on China's Use of 'Political' Psychiatry," *Financial Times*, 13 August 2002.

Miller, Robert — "The Ethics of Involuntary Commitment to Mental Health Treatment," in Sidney Bloch & Paul Chodoff (eds.), *Psychiatric Ethics*, Oxford University Press, 1991.

Miller, Robert D — "*Hendricks v. People*: Forcing the Insanity Defense on an Unwilling Defendant," *Journal of the American Academy of Psychiatry and the Law*, 2002, Vol.30, No.2, pp.295-7.

Ministry of Health — *Jingshen Jibing Sifa Jianding Guanli Banfa* (Administration Methods for Psychiatric Judicial Appraisal), issued informally sometime in early 2000. Full Chinese text available at: http://www.fmedsci.com/sfjs/sfjs11.htm.

Ministry of Public Security — "Detailed Rules on the Disciplinary Administration of Prisons and Labor-Reform Detachments (Trial Draft)," February 1982, *A Compilation of Standard Interpretations of the Laws of the People's Republic of China: Supplementary Volume* (Jilin People's Publishing House, 1991), p.798.

— "*Quanguo Gong'an Jiguan Di'yi Ci Jingshenbing Guan-Zhi Gongzuo Huiyi Jiyao*" (Key-Point Summary of the First National Public Security Conference on Custody and Treatment of the Mentally Ill), issued on 13 December 1987.

Mirsky, Jonathan — "Chinese Mental Hospitals," *Apple Daily*, 20 February 2001.

— "China's Psychiatric Terror," *The New York Review of Books*, Vol. L, No.3, 27 February 2003, pp.38-42.

Morozov, G.V. & Kalashnik, Ia.M. (eds.) — *Forensic Psychiatry*, International Arts and Sciences Press, Inc., White Plains: New York, 1970.

Mu Xin — "Inmate No. 6813 in Qincheng Prison," *Mao's Great Inquisition: The Central Case Examination Group, 1966-1979*; *Chinese Law and Government*, Vol.29, No.3 (May-June 1996), pp.74-75.

Muminovic, Mirza — "Psychiatric Association to Investigate Abuse in China," *British Medical Journal*, 2002, No.325, p.513.

Munro, Robin — "China's Democracy Movement: A Midwinter Spring," *Survey: Journal of East-West Studies*, No.121 (Summer 1984), pp.70-98.

— "China's Ultra-left on Trial: The Purge of the Gang of Four," 1988, unpublished research paper for Amnesty International.

— *Dangerous Minds: Political Psychiatry in China Today and its Origins in the Mao Era*, Human Rights Watch & Geneva Initiative on Psychiatry (New York and Hilversum), August 2002.

— "Judicial Psychiatry in China and its Political Abuses," *Columbia Journal of Asian Law*, 2000, Vol. 14, No.1, pp.1-128.

— "On the Psychiatric Abuse of Falun Gong and Other Dissenters in China: A Reply to Stone, Hickling, Kleinman and Lee," *Journal of the American Academy of Psychiatry and the Law*, 2002, Vol.30, No.2, pp.266-274.

— "Political Bedlam: China's Judicial Psychiatry," *Asian Wall Street Journal* (Editorial Page), 19 February 2001.

— "Political Psychiatry in Post-Mao China and its Origins in the Cultural Revolution," *Journal of the American Academy of Psychiatry and the Law*, 2002, Vol. 30, No. 1, pp.97-106.

— "Syncretic Sects and Secret Societies: Revival in the 1980s," *Chinese Sociology and Anthropology*, Summer 1989, Vol.21, No. 4.

— "The Ankang: China's Special Psychiatric Hospitals," *The Journal of Comparative Law*, Vol. 1, Issue 1, 2006, pp.41-87.

Ng, Vivien W. — "Ch'ing Law Concerning the Insane: An Historical Survey," *Ch'ing Shi Wen-t'i (Problems in Ch'ing History)*, December 1980, Vol.4, No.4.

NPC Standing Committee — "Decision on Strictly Prohibiting Drugs," 28 December 1990.

— "Decision on Strictly Prohibiting Prostitution," 4 September 1991; and PRC State Council, "Measures for Detention for Re-Education of Prostitutes," 4 September 1993.

— "Resolution on Approving the Decision of the State Council on the Issue of Reeducation through Labor" (*Quanguo Renmin Daibiao Dahui Changwu Weiyuanhui Pizhun Guowuyuan Guanyu Laodong Jiaoyang Wenti De Jueding De Jueyi*), August 1, 1957.

— "Resolution on Approving the Supplementary Decision of the State Council on the Issue of Re-education through Labor" (*Quanguo Renmin Daibiao Dahui Changwu Weiyuanhui Pizhun Guowuyuan Guanyu Laodong Jiaoyang De Buchong Guiding*), November 29, 1979.

Office of the Commissioner for Human Rights — "The Protection and Promotion of the Human Rights of Persons with Mental Disabilities," CommDH (2003)1, Seminar organized by the Commissioner for Human Rights and hosted by the WHO Regional Office for Europe, 5-7 February 2003, in Copenhagen.

Okasha, Ahmed — "Memo on the Issue of Alleged Political Abuse of Psychiatry in China," September 2003; available at: www.wpanet.org/generalinfo/china619.html.

— "Message from WPA President on the Visit to China," February 2004; available at: http://www.wpanet.org/generalinfo/letter0204.html.)

O'Neill, Mark — "Dissidents Tortured at Ankang," *South China Morning Post*, November 5, 2005.

— "Exile Plea for Threatened Dissident: Wife Fears for Life of Political Prisoner Transferred to Mental Ward Housing Murderers," South China Morning Post, 3 August 2002.

— "Psych Retort," *South China Morning Post*, December 5, 2005.

Pan, Philip P. — "Torture is Breaking Falun Gong: China Systematically Eradicating Group," The Washington Post, 5 August 2001.

— "Falun Gong Sees Abuse in Hospitals," *International Herald Tribune*, 27 August 2002.

— "The Silent Treatment from Beijing: Mental Hospitals Allegedly Used to Quiet Dissidents, Falun Gong," *The Washington Post*, 26 August 2002, p.A01.

Pearson, Veronica — "Law, Rights, and Psychiatry in the People's Republic of China," *International Journal of Law and Psychiatry*, 1992, Vol.15, pp.409-423.

— *Mental Illness in the People's Republic: An Exploratory Study of Chinese Experience*, Ph.D. thesis, University of York, 1991.

— *Mental Health Care in China: State Policies, Professional Services and Family Responsibilities*, (Gaskell, 1995.)

— "The Chinese Equation in Mental Health Policy and Practice: Order Plus Control Equal Stability," International Journal of Law and Psychiatry, 1996, Vol.19, pp.437-58.

Peerenboom, Randall — *China's Long March toward Rule of Law*, Cambridge University Press, 2002.

— "Out of the Pan and into the Fire: Well-Intentioned but Misguided Recommendations to Eliminate All Forms of Administrative Detention in China," *Northwestern University Law Review*, 2004, Vol. 98, No.3, pp.991-1104.

Phillips, Michael R. — "The Transformation of China's Mental Health Services," *The China Journal*, January 1998, No.39.

Phillips, Michael R. & Pearson, Veronica & Ruiwen Wang (eds.) — "Psychiatric Rehabilitation in China: Models for Change in a Changing Society," *British Journal of Psychiatry*, August 1994, Vol.165, Supplement 24.

Pomfret, John — "Chinese Rape Case Highlights Arbitrary Detention Policies," The Washington Post, 2 August 2000, p.A24.

— "Leaders of Independent Chinese Labor Union Fear Crackdown," *Washington Post*, December 15, 2000.

PRC State Council — State Council Document No. 91, 1983, *Guowuyuan Pizhuan Minzhengbu Guanyu Dui Di'erci Guonei Geming Zhanzheng Shiqi Sufanzhong Bei Cuosha Renyuan de Chuli Yijian de Tongzhi* (Notification of the Ministry of Civil Affairs, As Approved and Circulated by the State Council, Concerning the [Ministry's] Opinion on How to Handle the Cases of Persons Wrongly Killed in the Course of Campaigns to Suppress Counterrevolution During the Period of the Second Revolutionary Civil War), in *Xinfang Gongzuo Shiyong Zhengce Fagui Shouce, Zhonggong Zhongyang Bangongting* (A Handbook of Policies, Laws and Regulations for Use in Petitions and Visits Work), issued by the Office of the CPC Central Committee (document marked "for internal distribution only"), Falü Chubanshe, July 1992.

Qin Xudong — "*Cong Yi Fen Qiqiao de Xingzheng Panjueshu Shuoqi*" (Reflections on a Suspiciously Strange Administrative Case Judgment), *Xingzheng Yu Fazhi* (Administration and the Legal System), 2003, No.6.

Qinghua University Military Corps — "*'Kuangren' Ri Ji – Zalan Liu-Deng Fan'geming Zhuanzheng*" (Diary of a "Madman" – Smash the Counterrevolutionary Dictatorship of Liu and Deng), compiled and edited by *Qinghua Daxue Jinggangshan Bingtuan*, Beijing: 1967.

Qiu Jinyou — "*Shei Boduole Nongchang Zhigong de Minzhu Quanli? (Fu Tu) – Wode Shensu Zhuang*" (Who is Stripping the State Farm Employees of their Democratic Rights (illustrated with photos) – My Petition), 11 April 2004, available at: www.yuluncn.com.

— "*Shei Yao Jubao, Jiu Ba Shei Guanjin Kanshousuo – Du 'Guanya Li Yuchun Shi Weile Baohu Haishi*

Weile Fengkou' Yiwen Yougan" (Whoever Tries to Expose Us, We'll Lock Up in the Detention Centre – Some Thoughts After Reading "Was Taking Li Yuchun into Custody a Way of Protecting Her or Silencing Her?"), *Zhongguo Weiquan Fuwu Wang* (China Rights Protection Services Network), 4 July 2004; available at: www.weiquancn.com.

Qiu Renzong et al — *Bingrende Quanli* (Patients' Rights), published jointly by *Beijing Yike Daxue* and *Zhongguo Xiehe Yike Daxue*, August 1996.

Reich, Walter — "Diagnosing Soviet Dissidents," *Harper's*, August 1978, pp.31-37.

Ren Lijun & Liu Yongsheng — "*40 Nian Shouwang Feichang Shijie*" (Forty Years of Standing Guard Over an Extraordinary World), *Fazhi Wanbao*, 21 July 2004.

Rodley, Nigel S. — United Nations, Economic and Social Council, *Report of the Special Rapporteur on Torture, Submitted Pursuant to Commission on Human Rights Resolution 1992/32*, (New York: United Nations, January 12, 1995), General E/CN.4/1995/34.

Rosenthal, Elisabeth — "China is Said to Hold Devotees of Sect in a Psychiatric Hospital," *New York Times*, January 21, 2000.

— "In Rural China, Mental Hospitals Await Some Who Rock the Boat," *New York Times*, February 15, 2002

— "Psychiatric Group to Investigate China, but Resists Penalties," *New York Times*, 27 August 2002; and *International Herald Tribune*, 28 August 2002.

Rosenthal, Eric & Rubenstein, Leonard S. — "International Human Rights Advocacy under the 'Principles for the Protection of Persons with Mental Illness,'" *International Journal of Law and Psychiatry,* 1993, Vol.16, p.257.

Rubenstein, Leonard S. — "Shine a Light on China," *New York Times* (Letter to the Editor), 22 February 2001.

Rothman, David J. — Director of the Center for the Study of Society and Medicine at the Columbia College of Physicians and Surgeons, New York; personal communication to the author, July 11, 2002.

Sabbatini, Renato M.E. — "The History of Shock Therapy in Psychiatry," *Brain and Mind*, No. 4, Dec. 1997–March 1998.

Salzberg, Stephan M. — "Japan's New Mental Health Law: More Light Shed on Dark Places?" *International Journal of Law and Psychiatry*, 1991, Vol. 14, pp.137-169.

— "Taiwan's Mental Health Law," *International Journal of Law and Psychiatry*, 1992, Vol. 15, pp.43-75.

Sarkar, Sameer P., MD — "A British Psychiatrist Objects to the Dangerous and Severe Personality Disorder Proposals," *The Journal of the American Academy of Psychiatry and the Law*, 2002, Vol. 30, No. 1, p.6-9.

Schechter, Danny — "Is Falun Gong Going Crazy?" Index on Censorship, 2001, No.4.

Schram, Stuart R. — *The Political Thought of Mao Tse-tung*, Harmondsworth: Pelican Books, 1971.

Seymour, James D. — *The Fifth Modernization: China's Human Rights Movement, 1978-1979*, Earl M. Coleman Enterprises, 1980.

Shan Huaihai et al — "A Study of the Comparison Between Hysteric-like Episodes Caused by Chinese

Qigong (Deep Meditation) and Hysteria with Psychosocial Stress," *Chinese Journal of Nervous and Mental Diseases*, 1992, Vol.18, No.3, pp.156-158.

— "Clinical Phenomenology of Mental Disorders Caused by Qigong Exercise," *Chinese Medical Journal* (in English), 1989, Vol.102, No.6, pp.445-448.

— "*Falun Gong Wei Shenme Hui Youfa Jingshen Zhang'ai*" (Why Does Falun Gong Induce Mental Disorder?), *Xinli Jiankang Tongxun* (Bulletin of Psychological Health), 2002, No.1.

— "*Qigong Suo Zhi Jingshen Zhang'ai de Linchuang Ziliao yu Zhenduan* (Clinical Material and Diagnosis on Mental Disorders Induced by Qigong)," *Chinese Journal of Nervous and Mental Diseases*, 1999, No.3.

Shao Zongwei — "Re-education Law Revamp Due Soon," *China Daily*, February 5, 2001.

Shapiro, Hugh L. — *The View from a Chinese Asylum: Defining Madness in 1930s Peking*, unpublished doctoral dissertation: Harvard University, Graduate School of Arts and Sciences, January 1995.

She Jianguo et al — "*Meng Xiaoxia Anjian: Kaowen Jingshenbingren Shouzhi Zhi*" (The Meng Xiaoxia Case: An Interrogation into the System of Custody for the Mentally Ill), *Hua Shang Bao* (China Business View), 6 July 2004.

Shen Jun & Gong Yantao — "*Falun Gong Anjian Sifa Jingshenbing Jianding Chutan*" (A First Look at the Forensic Psychiatric Evaluation of Falun Gong Cases), *Linchuang Jingshen Yixue Zazhi* (Journal of Clinical Psychological Medicine), 2000, Vol. 10, No. 5, pp.313-314.

Shen Muci, Jin Wei, Cai Jianhua, & Han Baojin — "*Sifa Jingshen Yixue Jianding 654 Li Fenxi* (An Analysis of 654 Cases of Forensic-Psychiatric Medical Evaluation)," *Chinese Journal of Nervous and Mental Diseases*, 1988, Vol.21, No.3, pp.166-168.

Shen Yucun (ed.) — *Jingshenbingxue* (Psychiatry) 3rd *Edition*, People's Health Publishing House, May 1997.

Shen Zheng (ed.) — *Falü Jingshenbingxue* (Legal Psychiatry) China Politics and Law University Press, 1989.

Shooter, Mike (President of the Royal College of Psychiatrists) — Speech to the WPA General Assembly, Yokohama, 26 August 2002; copy on file with the author.

Si Wen — "Cong *Suowei 'Sharen Zhizhao' Kan Falü Zhidu de Zhubu Wanshan Guocheng*" (A Case of the So-called "Murderer's License" Shows How the Legal System is Being Gradually Perfected), *Renmin Wang*, 9 July 2002.

Smith, Theresa C. & Oleszczuk, Thomas A. — *No Asylum: State Psychiatric Repression in the Former USSR*, New York University Press, 1996.

Spencer, Richard — "Tiananmen Protester's 13 Years of Torment in Psychiatric Prison," *The Telegraph*, November 4, 2005.

Stalin, J.V. — *Marxism and Problems of Linguistics*, first published in the June 20, July 4, and August 2, 1950 issues of *Pravda*.

Stone, Alan A. — "Investigating Psychiatric Abuses," *Psychiatric Times*, November 2002, Vol. XIX, Issue 11.

— "Psychiatrists on the Side of the Angels," *Journal of the American Academy of Psychiatry and the Law*, 2002, Vol. 30, No. 1, pp.107-11.

— "Response to Munro" (Letter to the Editor), *The Journal of the American Academy of Psychiatry and the Law*, 2002, Vol. 30, No. 4, pp.589-90.

— "The China Psychiatry Crisis: Following Up on the Plight of the Falun Gong," *Psychiatric Times*, May 2005, Vol. XXII, Issue 6.

— "The Plight of the Falun Gong," Psychiatric Times, November 2004, Vol. XXIII, Issue 13.

Sullivan, Michael — "Psychiatric Abuse in China: A Symptom of Disease," *Association for Asian Research* (www.asianresearch.org), 19 September 2002.

Sun Dongdong — *Jingshenbingren de Falü Nengli* (Legal Capacity of the Mentally Ill), Xiandai Chubanshe, 1992.

Supreme People's Procuratorate — *Xingshi Fanzui Anli Congshu — Fan'geming Zui*, (Criminal Case-Studies Series: Vol.1: Crimes of Counterrevolution), Beijing: Zhongguo Jiancha Chubanshe, November 1992, p.238.

Svensson, Marina — *The Chinese Conception of Human Rights: The Debate on Human Rights in China*, 1898–1949, Department of East Asian Languages, Lund University, 1996

Tang Xiaofeng et al — "A Survey of the Current State of China's Ankang Hospitals," *Shanghai Archives of Psychiatry*, 1996, Vol. 8, No.1, pp.24-5.

Tanner, Murray Scot — "Shackling the Coercive State: China's Ambivalent Struggle Against Torture", *Problems of Post-Communism*, Sept-Oct, 2000.

Tao Dejian — "*Jingshenbing? Zhengzhifan?*" (Mentally Ill Person? Or Political Prisoner?), undated, available at: www.taosl.net/fy024.htm.

Tao Guotai et al — "Clinical Observations on 2,663 Cases of Insulin Shock Treatment," *Chinese Journal of Nervous and Mental Diseases*, No.1, 1960, pp.19-24

The World Medical Association, Inc. — "Discussion Document on the Political Abuse of Psychiatry," DD 1/Psych/2001, submitted to the WMA Medical Ethics Committee at the 159th WMA Council Session at Divonne-les-Bains, France, 3-6 May 2001.

Tian Zu'en, Yu Qingbo, Qi Wei, Wang Ping, Chen Lifeng & Yu Tian — "*Jingshenbingren de Xingshi Falü Nengli* (Criminal Legal Capacity of the Mentally Ill)," *Chinese Journal of Nervous and Mental Diseases*, 1988, Vol.21, No.3, pp.169-171.

U.N. Committee Against Torture — "Consideration of the Initial Report of the Union of Soviet Socialist Republics (CAT/C/5/Add.11), 15 November 1989," CAT A/45/44 (1990.)

— "Consideration of Reports Submitted by States Parties Under Article 19 of the Convention – Third Periodic Report of States Parties Due in 1997 (Addendum): China," Paragraphs 168-179, 4 May 1999.

— "Second Periodic Report of States Parties Due in 1992: Russian Federation, 07/02/96.

U.N. General Assembly, report of the Third Committee — *Principles for the Protection of Persons with Mental Illness and for the Improvement of Mental Health Care* (New York: United Nations, December 17, 1991), A/46/721.

U.N. Working Group on Arbitrary Detention — "Civil and Political Rights, Including the Question of Torture and Detention. Opinion No. 20/2001 (China): Communication addressed to the [Chinese] Government on 14 June 2001 Concerning Wang Wanxing," 59th Session of the Commission on Human

Rights, Item 11 (b) of the provisional agenda, E/CN.4/2003/8/Add.1, pp. 4-7.

— "Civil and Political Rights, Including the Question of Torture and Detention. Opinion No. 20/2001 (China): Communication addressed to the [Chinese] Government on 26 June 2001 Concerning Cao Maobing," 59th Session of the Commission on Human Rights, Item 11 (b) of the provisional agenda, E/CN.4/2003/8/Add.1, pp. 47-49.

— "Report on the Visit to the People's Republic of China," E/CN.4/1998/44/ADD.2.

Valenstein, Elliot S. — *Great and Desperate Cures: The Rise and Decline of Psychosurgery and Other Radical Treatments* (Basic Books, February 1986).

van Voren, Robert (ed.) — "Comparing Soviet and Chinese Political Psychiatry," *Journal of the American Academy of Psychiatry and the Law*, 2002, Vol. 30, No. 1, pp.131-5.

— *Soviet Psychiatric Abuse in the Gorbachev Era*, Amsterdam: International Association on the Political Use of Psychiatry (IAPUP), 1989, p.10.

— "The WPA World Congress in Yokohama and the Issue of Political Abuse of Psychiatry in China," report to Geneva Initiative on Psychiatry, September 1, 2002; copy on file with the author.

Vidaillet, Tamora — "UN's Robinson Sees Small Rights Progress," *Reuters*, 20 August 2002.

Volpin, A.S. — "Let Pyotr Grigorenki Have a Fountain Pen," *samizdat* manuscript dated 20 July 1970; cited in Bloch and Reddaway, *Russia's Political Hospitals* (op cit), p.72.

Walker, N. — *Crime and Insanity in England*, Edinburgh University Press, 1979, p.193.

Walsh, Nick Paton — "Russia Bans Brain Surgery on Drug Addicts," *The Guardian*, 9 August 2002

Wan Yanhai — "*Zhonghua Jingshen Kexue Hui Renwei Tongxinglian Xingwei Shi Zhengchangde*" (The Chinese Society of Psychiatry Views Homosexual Behaviour as Normal), *Aizhi*, 3 March 2001, available at: http://www.aizhi.org/xljk/ccmd-3.htm.

Wang Hanbin — Speech to the Fifth Session of the Eighth National People's Congress, March 6, 1997.

Wang Jingxiang — "China's Achievements Over the Past Decade in Insulin Shock Therapy Work," *Chinese Journal of Nervous and Mental Diseases*, No.6, 1959, pp.349-351.

Wang Li — "Wang Li's Testament," *Chinese Studies in Philosophy*, Vol.26, nos. 1-2 (Fall-Winter 1994-95), p.5.

Wang Qian — "*Jingshenbingyuan Qiangzhi Shouzhi Zhengchangren Beipan Peichang*" (Court Orders Mental Hospital to Pay Compensation for Forcibly Hospitalizing a Normal Person), *Xinhua Wang* (Xinhua Net), 10 March 2004, available at: www.fmedsci.com.

Wang Zenghui — "An Analysis of 116 Cases of Forensic Psychiatric Appraisal of the Mentally Retarded," *Linchuang Jingshen Yixue Zazhi* (Journal of Clinical Psychological Medicine), 1996, No.6.

Waterlow, Mark — "Political Psychiatry in China," *eMental-health.com*, 2 August 2001.

Wei Jingsheng — "A Twentieth-Century Bastille," in James D. Seymour (ed.), *The Fifth Modernization: China's Human Rights Movement*, New York: Human Rights Publishing Group, 1980, p.217.

Wei Qingping et al — "An Analysis of Expert Psychiatric Testimony on Epileptic Patients' Illegal Actions," *Chinese Journal of Nervous and Mental Diseases*, 2000, Vol.26, No.2, pp.65-67.

Wei Qingping et al — "*Dianxian Huanzhe Weifa de Sifa Jingshen Yixue Jianding Fenxi*" (An Analysis of Expert Psychiatric Testimony on Epileptic Patients' Illegal Actions, *Chinese Journal of Nervous and Mental Diseases*, 2000, Vol.26, No.2, pp.65-67.

Wing, J.K. — "Psychiatry in the Soviet Union," *British Medical Journal*, No.1 (March 9, 1974), pp.433-436.

Woods, Andrew H. — "A Memorandum to Chinese Medical Students on the Medico-Legal Aspects of Insanity," *Journal of the National Medical Association of China*, Vol.9 (September 1923), pp.203-212.

World Health Organization — *Mental Health Care Law: Ten Basic Principles*, 1996 (WHO/MNH/MND/96.9).

Wu Jiasheng — "*Qiantan Jingshenbingren Weifa Zhaohuo Xingwei de Zeren Nengli* (A Brief Discussion of the Legal Capacity of Mentally Ill Persons Who Behave Unlawfully and Create Disastrous Incidents)," *Faxue (Jurisprudence)*, 1985, No.40, pp.43-45.

Wu Lieming — "*Nao Liti Dingxiang Shoushu Zhiliao Manxing Jingshenbing Suoban Chongdong Xingwei de Qinian Suifang*" (A Clinical Review of the Use of Stereotactic Brain Surgery to Treat Chronic Mental Illness Accompanied by Impulsive Behaviour), *Shanghai Jingshen Yixue* (Shanghai Archives of Psychiatry), 1993, Vol. 5, No. 2, pp.134-5.

Wu Wei & Qin Juan — "*Xi'an Shi Ankang Yiyuan Fu-Yuanzhang Shexian Lanyong Zhiquan Bei Tiqi Susong*" (Deputy Director of Xi'an Ankang Hospital to be Prosecuted on Suspicion of Abuse of Official Power), *Xinhua Wang* (Xinhua News Net), 18 March 2003; available at: www.xinhuanet.com.

Wu Xianguang — "*WPA Jue Diaocha Zhong-Gong Liyong Jingshenbingyuan Duifu Yiyi Renshi*" (WPA Decides to Investigate CCP's Use of Psychiatric Hospitals to Deal with Dissidents), *Zhongyang She* (China News Agency, Taiwan), 28 August 2002.

Wu Xinchen, "An Exploration of the Hallmarks of Criminal Behavior among Schizophrenics," *Chinese Journal of Nervous and Mental Diseases*, 1983, Vol.16, No.6, pp.338-339.

Xia Yufen, Zheng Zhanpei et al — "*Woguo Wangxiangxing Jingshen Fenliezheng de Zhengzhuang Bianqian*" (The Changing Symptomatology of Delusional Schizophrenia in China), *Shanghai Jingshen Yixue* (Shanghai Archives of Psychiatry), 1990, Vol.2, No.3, pp.133-6.

Xi'an Municipal Public Security Bureau — "Various Regulations on Implementing the *Xi'an Municipal Methods for the Compulsory Shelter of Mentally Ill Persons Who Seriously Endanger Social Safety*," 1 March 2006; see: http://www.39.net/focus/jkshxw/161669.html.

Xie Bin — "*Sifa Jingshenbing Xuejia Zheng Zhanpei Jiaoshou*," in *Falü Yu Yixue Zazhi* (Journal of Law and Medicine), 1999, Vol.6, No.3, p.99.

Xie Bin & Zhang Mingyuan — "*Shanghai Shi 'Jingshen Weisheng Tiaoli' Jianjie*" (An Introduction the "Shanghai Municipal Mental Health Regulations"), *Zhonghua Jingshenke Zazhi*, November 2002, Vol.35, No.4.

Xie Bin, Wang Shiqing & Zheng Zhanpei — "*Jingshenke Linchuang Gongzuo Zhong de Yixie Falü Wenti*" (Several Legal Questions in Psychiatric Clinical Work), *Xinli Jiankang Tongxun* (Bulletin of Psychological Health), 2001, No.3.

Xu Bing & Min Sheng — "Reminiscences on the Article '*Speech is No Crime* and *Making Speech a Crime*'," in Guo Daohui et al., eds., *Zhongguo Dangdai Faxue Zhengming Shilu* (A Record of the

Contention on the Science of Law in Contemporary China), Hunan Renmin Chubanshe, 1998, pp.183-189.

Xu Chengxun — "*Sifa Jingshenbingxue Jianding 195 Li Fenxi*" (An Analysis of 195 Cases of Forensic Psychiatric Appraisal), *Shandong Jingshen Yixue* (Shandong Psychiatric Medicine), 1989, No.1, pp.50-54.

Xu Peijiang et al — "*Nao Liti Dingxiang Shu Zhiliao 6 Li Manxing Jingshen Fenliezheng 7 Nian Suifang*" (Seven-year Clinical Follow-up on the Use of Stereotactic Brain Surgery in Six Cases of Chronic Schizophrenia), *Zhongguo Minzheng Yixue Zazhi* (China Civil Affairs Medical Journal), 1996, Vol.8, No.3, pp.145-6.

Xu Shenghan — "Psychophysiological Reactions Associated with Qigong Therapy," *Chinese Medical Journal*, Vol.107, 1994, No.3, pp.230-233.

Xu Shoubin — "The Legal Protection and Restriction of Rights of the Mentally Ill," *Fazhi Shijie (World of Legality)*, 1994, No.6, p.26.

Xu Sisun & Xie Liya — "*27 Li Sifa Jingshenbing Chongxin Jianding Anli de Fenxi*" (An Analysis of 27 Forensic Psychiatric Reappraisal Cases), Shanghai Jingshen Yixue (Shanghai Archives of Psychiatry), 1991, Vol.3, No.4, pp.194-6.

Xu Taoyuan — "*Zhongguo Jingshenbingxue Sishi Nian*" (Forty Years of Psychiatry in China), *Shanghai Jingshen Yixue*, 1989, Vol.1, No.1, pp.7-9.

Yan Shanming — "*Guanyu Jingshenbing Benzhi Wenti de Tantao*" (An Inquiry into the Essential Nature of Mental Illness), *Xin Yixue Fukan – Shenjing Xitong Jibing (New Medicine Review – Series on Diseases of the Nervous System)*, 1978, No.4, pp.109-10.

Yang Desen — "Mental Disease Cannot be Regarded as an Ideological Defect: An Opinion on the Essential Nature of Mental Illness," *Xin Yixue–Jingshen Xitong Jibing Fukan* (New Medicine–Supplementary Series on Diseases of the Nervous System), 1976, Vol. 2, No. 3, pp.187-189.

— "On the Legal Responsibility of Mentally Ill Persons for Their Illegal Conduct," *Chinese Journal of Nervous and Mental Diseases*, 1985, Vol.11, No. 5, pp.310–312.

— "*Qigong Neng Zhiliao Shenjingzheng yu Jingshen Jibing ma?* (Can Qigong Cure Neurosis and Mental Illness?)," *Chinese Journal of Nervous and Mental Diseases*, 2000, Vol.26, No.1, pp.52-53.

— "Subjective Conjecture is No Substitute for Scientific Research," *Xin Yixue–Shenjing Xitong Jibing Fukan* (New Medicine–Supplementary Series on Diseases of the Nervous System), 1978, Vol.4, Nos.5-6, pp.329-332.

Yang Qu — "*You Bing*" (Sick), *Zhongguo Qingnian Bao*, 2 December 2001.

Yang Xingmei & Ge Meifang — "*Yanzhong Yingxiang Shehui Zhi'an de Jingshen Jibing Huanzhe 81 Li Chubu Diaocha Fenxi*" (Analysis of a Preliminary Investigation into 81 Cases of Mentally Ill Persons Who Seriously Affected Public Order), *Shanghai Jingshen Yixue* (Shanghai Archives of Psychiatry), 1987, Vol.1, No.1, pp.32-4.

Yang Yonggang — "*Cong 'Youbing Wuzui Lun' Dao Jingshen Weisheng Lifa*" (From the "Innocent-Because-Ill Theory" to Mental Health Legislation), *Zhong Fa Wang* website, 23 September 2002; at: www.china1laws.com.

Yao Peng & Zhu Qian — "*Guanyu Jingshenbing Jianding de 'Jianding'*" (An 'Evaluation' of Judicial Evaluation), *Nüxing Wang*, 4 August 2004, available at:

www.china-women.com/gb/2004/08/04/zgfnb/zhxw/6.htm.

— "*Yige Nüren de Shiba Nian Shanghen*" (A Woman's 18-Year-Long Wounds), *Nüxing Wang* (Women's Network), 2 August 2004, available at: www.china-women.com/gb/2004/08/02/zgfnb/zhxw/2.htm.

Yao Zuhua et al — "*Jin 40 Nian Sifa Jingshenbingxue Jianding Anli de Bijiao* (A Comparative Study on the Case Expertise of Forensic Psychiatrics Over the Past 40 Years)," *Chinese Journal of Psychiatry*, 2000, Vol.33, No.1, pp.47-49.

Yevgeny Pashukanis — *The General Theory of Law and Marxism*. See John N. Hazard (ed.), *Soviet Legal Philosophy* (1951), Harvard University Press, Cambridge, pp. 111-225.

York, Geoffrey — "Chinese Dissident Diagnosed with 'Litigation Mania'," *Globe and Mail*, November 3, 2005.

Yuan Shangxian — "*105 Li Fayi Jingshenbingxue Jianding Baogao*" (A Report on 105 Cases of Legal-Medical Psychiatric Appraisal), *Zhongguo Fayixue Zazhi* (China Journal of Forensic Medicine), 1988, Vol.3, No.1, pp.44-5.

Zeng Wenyou et al (ed.) — *Jing Guan Bi Du* (*Essential Reading for Police Officials*), (Police Officials Publishing House, Beijing, October 1992); volume marked "for internal circulation only".

Zhai Jian'an (ed.) — *Shiyong Fayixue Cidian (A Dictionary of Applied Forensic Science)*, People's Health Publishing House, September 1994.

Zhang Jun — *Xingshi Cuo'An Yanjiu (Research on Miscarriages of Criminal Justice)*, Qunzhong Chubanshe, 1990, pp.110-111.

Zhang Junxian — "An Analysis of the Forensic Evaluation of 83 Cases of Schizophrenia," *Fayixue Zazhi* (*Journal of Forensic Medicine*), 1986, Vol.1, No.2, pp.33-36.

Zhang Lizi — "*Baohu Jingshenbingren Quanyi – Lifa Zhengzai Jinxing Shi*" (Protect the Rights and Interests of the Mentally Ill – Legislation Currently Underway), Jiankang Bao (Health News), 31 March 2004.

Zhang Mingyuan et al — "An Inventory for the Assessment of Life Events: Some Common-Pattern Outcomes," *Chinese Journal of Nervous and Mental Diseases*, 1987, No.2.

Zhang Wei, Huo Kediao & Liu Xiehe — "*Fayi Jingshenbingxue Jianding de Siwei Fangshi* (Modes of Thought in Forensic Psychiatric Appraisals)," in *Fayixue Jinzhan yu Shijian* (*Advances and Practices in Forensic Medicine*), Chengdu Science and Technology University Press, 1999.

Zhang Weiguo — "*Ba Zhengchang Ren Biancheng Jingshenbing Huanzhe de Zhong-Gong Jiquan Zhuanzhi*" (CCP Totalitarian System Labels Normal People as Mentally Ill), 22 August 2002; in *Da Ji Yuan* (Epoch Times), 31 August 2002.

Zhang Xiaoshan — "A Fragmentary Reminiscence: In Commemoration of the Fifth Anniversary of the Death of My Father, Hu Feng (*Pianduan de Huiyi: Jinian Fuqin Hu Feng Shishi Wu Zhounian*)," in *Historical Materials on the New Literature (Xin Wenxue Shiliao)*, 1990, No.4.

Zhang Xinkai — "*Zhuanti Taolun – Jingshen Weisheng Yu Fa*" (Special Discussion – Mental Health and the Law), 9 January 2003, *Zhongguo Jingshen Weisheng Wang* (China Mental Health Net.)

Zhang Xinzhi — "A Preliminary Analysis of 50 Cases of Crime by the Mentally Ill," in Zhou Yingde (ed.), *Fanzui Zhenchaxue Gailun: Cankao Ziliao* (General Theory of Criminal Investigation: Reference Materials), Beijing 1987, pp.417-422; volume marked: "Internal teaching materials: keep confidential."

— "A Preliminary Analysis of 111 Cases of Crimes by the Mentally Ill," in Zhai Jian'an (ed.), *Zhongguo Fayi Shijian* (*Forensic Medical Practice in China*), Police Officers' Educational Publishing House, August 1993, pp.556–561.

Zhao Haibo — "On the Fundamental Principles and Methods of Forensic Medical Investigation," in Cui Jian'an (ed.), *Zhongguo Fayi Shijian* (China's Forensic Medical Practice), Police Officers' Educational Press, August 1993, pp.47-48.

Zhao Jiancong et al — "*Woguo Sifa Jingshenbingxue Xianzhuang de Yanjiu* (A Study on the Current Data of Judicial Psychiatry in China)," *Chinese Journal of Psychiatry*, 1999, No.1, pp.53-54.

Zhao Ling — "*Zhongguo 'Zheng-Fa Xi' Lichi 'Renquan' Huayu*" (China's "Politics and Law Network" Strives to Uphold "Human Rights" Language), *Nanfang Zhoumo* (Southern Weekend), 2 July 2004.

Zheng Chengshou et al — "*80 Niandai yu 90 Niandai Sifa Jingshenbingxue Jianding Anli de Duizhao Yanjiu*" (A Comparative Study on the Case Expertise of Forensic Psychiatrics Between the 1980s and 1990s), *Zhonghua Jingshenke Zazhi* (Chinese Journal of Psychiatry), 1998, No.4, pp.228-230.

Zheng Guosheng — "What Kind of Society is the Society under the Socialist market Economy?" *Yifa Zhiguo, Jianshe Shehuizhuyi Fazhi Guojia,* Liu Hainian et al (eds.), 1996, p.440.

Zheng Hongbo et al — "*Lian 'Falun Gong' Yinzhi Jingshen Zhang'ai 4 Li Baogao* (A Report on Four Cases of Mental Disorders Induced by 'Falun Gong')," *Chinese Journal of Nervous and Mental Diseases*, 2000, Vol.26, No.3, p.142.

Zheng Rong — "*'Feng' Zhangfu Zhuanggao 'Pan Jinlian' – Quan Zhangfu Bingtui, 'Chu Xin Ji Lü'*" (A "Mad" Husband Sues "Pan Jinlian" – Wife Concocts Weird Scheme to Make Husband Take Disability Retirement), *Fazhi Kuaibao* (Legal System Express), 7 June 2004.

Zheng Yanping & Yang Desen — "Life Events, Mental Anxiety and Neurosis," *Chinese Journal of Nervous and Mental Diseases*, 1983, No.2.

Zheng Zhanpei — *Sifa Jingshen Jianding de Yinan Wenti Ji Anli* (Thorny Problems and Case Examples in Judicial Psychiatric Appraisal), Shanghai Medical University Press, 1996, pp.275-309.

— "*Zhanwang Woguo Sifa Jingshen Yixue*" (Prospects for China's Judicial Psychiatric Medicine), *Shanghai Jingshen Yixue* (Shanghai Archives of Psychiatry), 1990, Vol.2, No.3, pp.53-6.

Zheng Zhanpei et al — "*Woguo Sifa Jingshenbingxue Jianding Gongzuo de Xianzhuang ji Zhanwang* (Present Situation and Future Prospects of China's Judicial Psychiatric Appraisals Work)," *Chinese Journal of Psychiatry*, 1999, Vol.32, No.4, p.201.

Zhong Xingsheng & Shi Yaqin — "A Preliminary Analysis of 210 Cases of Forensic Psychiatric Medical Assessment," *Chinese Journal of Nervous and Mental Diseases*, 1987, Vol.20, No.3, pp.139-141.

Zhong Youbin — "*Dui Woguo Jingshenbingxue Xianzhuang de Jidian Yijian Ji Dui Zhuanye Kanwu de Xiwang*" (Several Viewpoints on the Current State of Psychiatry in China and Some Hopes for Our Specialist Journals and Periodicals), *Shenjing Jingshen Jibing Zazhi* (Journal of Nervous and Mental Diseases), 1979, Vol.5, No.4, pp.220-1.

Zhou, Dr. Shiyu et al. (eds.) — *A Report on Extensive and Severe Human Rights Violations in the Suppression of Falun Gong in the People's Republic of China — August 2000 Update* (Chapter 3: Detention and Abuse in Mental Hospitals), Golden Lotus Press, August 2000.

Zhu Hengqing — *Lu Ling: Wei Wancheng de Tiancai* (Lu Ling: A Talent Unfulfilled), Shandong Wenyi Chubanshe, April 1997, pp.112-113.

Zhu Qihua et al (eds.) — *Tianjin Quanshu* (An Encyclopaedia of Tianjin), Tianjin People's Publishing House, December 1991, p.630.

Zhu Xiaoyang & Benjamin Penny (eds.) — "The Qigong Boom," *Chinese Sociology and Anthropology*, Fall 1994, vol.27, No.1.

II: By Title

— "A Follow-up Review of Stereotactic Brain Surgery in Cases of Chronic Schizophrenia," *Zhonghua Shenjing Waike Zazhi* (*Chinese Journal of Neurosurgery*), 1992, Vol.8, No.4, pp.263-265.

— "A Position Paper on Psychiatric Abuses in the People's Republic of China, Submitted by the [APsaA's] Committee on Social Issues," 20 October 2001; copy on file with the author.

— "Accusation about Psychotherapy for 'Dissidents', Falun Gong Practitioners Refuted," *Xinhua* reports of 4 and 5 October 2002.

— "AFP Reports 2,000 protest Against Failed Investment Firm," *FBIS Daily Report*, November 16, 1998.

— "Analysis of a Survey of 250 Cases of Mental Illness," *Xin Yixue – Shenjing Xitong Jibing Fukan* (*New Medicine – Supplementary Series on Diseases of the Nervous System*), 1972, No.8, pp.12-16.

— "'*Ankang Yiyuan' Xia Yue Choujian*" ('Ankang Hospital' to be Built Next Month), Nanfang Ribao, 20 October 2000.

— "APA Committee Calls for Investigation of Chinese Psychiatric Abuses," *Psychiatric News*, June 16, 2000.

— "Assistance for Jailed Labour Activist Still Needed," *China Labour Watch* press release, January 7, 2001.

— "Bad Medicine in China" (editorial), *The Washington Post*, June 23, 2000.

— *Banning of the Falun Gong and Subsequent Arrests of Practitioners*, Report of the United Nations Sub-Commission on Prevention of Discrimination and Protection of Minorities, August 4, 1999.

— "*Beijing Jiang Dui Ben Shi Aicibing Ren Shixing Mianfei Kangbingdu Yaowu Zhiliao*" (Beijing Set to Supply Free Antiviral Medical Treatment to the City's HIV-AIDS Sufferers), *Beijing Wanbao*, 14 July 2003.

— "Brain Surgery 'Cure' for Heroin Addicts," *The Australian*, 29 May 2004

— *Breach of Trust: Physician Participation in Executions in the United States*, a joint report by the American College of Physicians, Human Rights Watch, the National Coalition to Abolish the Death Penalty, and Physicians for Human Rights (New York, March 1994.)

— "'Caged Man' Set Free," *Yangcheng Wanbao*, March 29, 1998; also in BBC Summary of World Broadcasts, April 13, 1998.

— "China: Country Reports on Human Rights Practices – 2003," Bureau of Democracy, Human Rights, and Labor, February 25, 2004.

— "China Denies Mental Patient 'Abuse'," *BBC News*, 27 August 2002.

— "China Locks Up Dissidents in Mental Hospitals," *The Vanguard* (Nigeria), 17 August 2002.

— "China Misusing Psychiatry for Political Ends," *The Hindu*, 14 August 2002.

— "China's Psychiatric Abuse" (interview with Robert van Voren), *Radio Netherlands*, 14 August 2002.

— "China Rejects Mental Hospital Charge," *Associated Press*, 27 August 2002.

— "China Slams Study Alleging Psychiatric Abuse," *Reuters*, 20 February 2001.

— "China Urged to Throw Open the Doors to Its Mental Asylums," *CNN*, 23 August 2002.

— "China vs America," *The Spectator* (Editorial), 7 April 2001.

— "Chinese Asylums a Political Minefield," *The Australian*, 14 August 2002.

— "Conclusions and Recommendations of the Committee against Torture: China," (Concluding Observations/Comments, A/55/44), 9 May 2000, Paragraph 127.

— "Conference Briefing Papers: International Conference on Mental Health Law, Taipei, Taiwan, June 1-3, 1992"; place and date of publication unknown.

— "*Cong Chen Lining Anjian Kan Bianse Long Qi Benyu zhi Liu de Fan'geming Zuilian (The Case of Chen Lining Shows Us the Counterrevolutionary Features of the Chameleon-like Qi Benyu and His Ilk)*," published in the Red Guard journal *Xin Bei-Da — Changcheng* (New Beijing University — Great Wall, March 20, 1968), pp.1-4.

— "Contortions of Psychiatry in China," Editorial, *New York Times*, 25 March 2001.

— "Court Reaches Final Decision on Sun Zhigang Case," Xinhua News Agency June 28, 2003.

— "*Dalian Shi Jianhu Zhiliao Guanli Zhaoshi Zhaohuo Jingshenbingren Tiaoli*" (Dalian Municipal Regulations on the Guardianship, Treatment and Management of Mentally Ill People Who Create Disasters or Incidents), passed by the Standing Committee of the Dalian Municipal People's Congress on 4 November 1992 and effective as of 17 December 1992, available at: www.dl.gov.cn/togov/law/local/688_15942.htm.

— *Dangdai Zhongguo de Shenpan Gongzuo* (Judicial Work in Contemporary China), Vol.1, Contemporary China Publishing House, 1993.

— Decision of the Standing Committee of the National People's Congress on Banning Heretical Cult Organizations and Preventing and Punishing Cult Activities, adopted at the 12th Session of the Standing Committee of the Ninth NPC on October 20, 1999; English translation in *Beijing Review*, 1999, No.45.

— "Dissidents Stage Fast to Protest Reincarceration," Agence France Presse, February 27, 1998

— "Detained in Psychiatric Institution for Petitioning Authorities About Abuse," Zhang Gonglai, *Ren Yu Renquan* (Chinese-language website affiliated with Human Rights in China), January 2003, available at www.hrichina.org.

— "Dissidents Reportedly Subject to Mental Abuse," *St Petersburg Times*, 27 August 2002.

— "Duma Appeal on Dangerous Religious Sects," *Moscow Rossiyskaya Gazeta*, December 28, 1996; translated in FBIS, same date.

— "Ethical Guidelines for the Practice of Forensic Psychiatry," adopted by the American Academy of Psychiatry and the Law in May 1987 (and revised in October 1989.)

— "Evidence Comes from Official Public Sources," *Saarbruecker Zeitung*, 24 August 2001.

— *Explanation of the Supreme People's Court and Supreme People's Procuracy Concerning Laws Applicable to Handling Cases of Organizing and Employing Heretical Cult Organizations to Commit Crimes*, adopted at the 1079th Meeting of the SPC on October 9, 1999 and at the 47th Meeting of the Ninth Procuratorial Committee of the SPC on October 9, 1999; English translation in *Beijing Review*, 1999, No.45.

— *Falun Gong Health Effect Survey of Ten Thousand Cases in Beijing*, available at: www.falundafa-pa.net/survey/survey98-1_e.html.

— "*Fangtan: Zhongguo Lanyong Jingshenbingyuan Guanya Yiyi Renshi*" (Interview: China Misuses Mental Hospitals to Detain Dissidents), *BBC News*; in *Da Ji Yuan* (Epoch Times), 14 August 2002.

— "Falun Gong Practitioners Suffer Mental Trauma and Death As A Result of the Jiang Group's Abuse of Psychiatry," Falun Dafa Clear Wisdom.net, 23 July 2004.

— "Fifty Years of Progress in China's Human Rights," Xinhua News Agency, February 17, 2000, p.1.

— "Give Full Prominence to Politics and Revolutionize the Clinical Management of Mental Illness," ("*Tuchu Zhengzhi, Cujin Jingshenbing Linchuang Guanli Gongzuo Geminghua*,"), by psychiatrists from Tianshui Mental Hospital, Gansu Province, *Chinese Journal of Neurology and Psychiatry*, 1966, Vol.10, No.2, pp.107-108.

— "Giving Help to Those Who Need It," *China Daily*, 2 August 2004.

— "*Gong'an Bu Fubuzhang Tian Qiyu zai Quanguo Jingshenbing Fangzhi Kangfu Gongzuo Huiyi Kaimushi-shang de Jianghua*" (Deputy Minister of Public Security Tian Qiyu's Speech at the National Work Conference on Mental Illness Prevention, Cure and Recovery), 13 May 1993, available at: www.cdpf.org.cn/nj/ala071/.

— "*Gong'an Juzhang Weifu Sifang 'Jingshenbing Shashou' Yuan Shi Hei Laoda*" (PSB Bureau Chief Privately Intercedes on Behalf of a "Mentally Ill Murderer" Who Turns Out to be a Major Gang Leader), *Wuhan Wanbao*, 11 November 2001.

— "*Gong'an Xitong Jingshenbing Guan-Zhi Gongzuo Chengxiao Xianzhu* (Public Security System's Work of Custody and Treatment of the Mentally Ill Achieves Conspicuous Results)," *Renmin Gong'an Bao* (People's Public Security News), May 18, 1990, p.1.

— "*Guangdong Sheng Shourong Anzhi Zhaohuo Zhaoshi Jingshenbingren Zanxing Banfa* (Guangdong Provincial Temporary Methods for the Shelter and Settlement of Mentally Ill People Who Create Disasters or Incidents)," issued by the Guangdong Provincial People's Government on January 17, 1990, in *Guangdong Sheng Fagui Guizhang Huibian* (A Compilation of Guangdong Provincial Laws, Regulations and Rules [January 1989-December 1990]), edited and published by the Office of the Guangdong Provincial People's Government, pp.275-276.

— "*Guangzhou Shi Shouzhi Shubai Zhong An Jingshenbingren – Bingren Ruyuan Yi, Chuyuan Nan*" (Guangzhou City Takes into Custody for Treatment Hundreds of Mentally Ill People Who Commit Serious Crimes – Going in is Easy, But Getting Out is Hard), *Xinxi Shibao* (Information Times), 28 April 2004.

— *Guanyu Jingshen Jibing Sifa Jianding Zanxing Guiding* (Temporary Regulations for Judicial Appraisal of the Mentally Ill), issued jointly by the Supreme People's Court, Supreme People's Procuracy, Ministry of Public Security, Ministry of Justice and Ministry of Civil Affairs, July 11,

1989.

— *"Guanyu Xingshi Anjian Ban'an Qixian de Buchong Guiding"* (Supplementary Provisions of the Standing Committee of the National People's Congress Regarding the Time Limits for Handling Criminal Cases), passed by the NPC Standing Committee on July 7, 1984; in Wang Huai'an et al (eds.), *Zhonghua Renmin Gongheguo Falü Quanshu*, Changchun: Jilin Renmin Chubanshe, 1989, p.223.

— "Harbin Woman Allegedly Persecuted for Exercising Her Right to Petition," Human Rights in China (press release), January 7, 2003.

— "Hazardous and Irreversible Treatments in Psychiatry: Who Decides?" SK&F Publications (London), 1980, Vol. 3, No. 6.

— *"Heilongjiang Sheng Jianhu Zhiliao Guanli Weihai Shehui Zhi'an Jingshenbingren Tiaoli"* (Heilongjiang Provincial Regulations on the Guardianship, Treatment and Management of Mentally Ill People Who Endanger Public Order), passed on 9 February 1996 and effective as of 1 March 1996.

— *"Jianchi Xiulian Bei Guan Jingshenbingyuan Ji Shiyong Jingshen Yaowu de Anli Huibian"* (A Collection of Cases of Falun Gong Practitioners Sent to Mental Hospitals or Given Psychotropic Drugs for Persisting in Their Practice), Minghui.net, 6 October 2003.

— *Jianshen Qigong Guanli Zanxing Banfa* (Temporary Methods for Administering Bodybuilding and Qigong), State Administration for Sports, 8 September 2000; available at http://www.china.org.cn/chinese/zhuanti/tyzcfg/890184.htm.

— *"Jiedu Suoli Duguo 100 Xiaoshi Nü Jizhe Tiyan 'Jiedu'"* (A Female Reporter Experiences "Drug Detox" during a 100-hour Visit to a Drug Rehabilitation Centre), *Mei Ri Xin Bao*, 6 April 2002

— *"Jingshenbing Jianding Zenme Chengle 'Sharen Zhizhao'"* (How Psychiatric Evaluation Has Become a "Murderer's License"), *Beijing Qingnian Bao*, 16 July 2002.

— *Jingshenbing Rending Zhengju – Changyong Zhengju Falü Shouce*, China Law Publishing House (Zhongguo Fazhi Chubanshe), Beijing, January 2004.

— *"Jingshenbingren Side Qi 'Suo'"* (A Mentally Ill Man Dies from his "Shackles"), *Nanfang Zhou Mo* (Southern Weekend), 13 March 2003.

— "Johannesburg Principles on National Security, Freedom of Expression and Access to Information," in *The New World Order and Human Rights in the Post-Cold War Era: National Security vs. Human Security*, papers from the International Conference on National Security Law in the Asia Pacific, November 1995 (Korea Human Rights Network, 1996.)

— "Joint Directive of the Supreme People's Court, Supreme People's Procuratorate and Ministry of Public Security Concerning the Clearing Out of Aged, Weak, Sick and Disabled or Mentally Ill Prisoners," April 16, 1979, *Jiancha Gongzuo Shouce* (*A Handbook of Procuratorial Work*), Vol.1, Yunnan Sheng Renmin Jianchayuan, December 1980, pp.281-283.

— "Longtime Chinese Dissident Released," Associated Press, in *Taipei Times*, November 3, 2005.

— "Man Detained in Iron Cage for Ten Years in Guangdong," *Yangcheng Wanbao*, March 28, 1998.

— "Many 'Unjust, False and Erroneous' Verdicts Also Found Among Cases Tried Between 1977 and 1978," *Renmin Sifa Xuanbian* (A Compilation of Articles from "People's Justice" Magazine), Law Publishing House, February 1983, pp.116-8; volume marked "for internal use only."

— "Material on the Hu Feng Counterrevolutionary Clique" (May 1955), *Quotations from Chairman*

Mao Tse-tung, Peking Foreign Languages Press, 1966.

— "Medical Scientists Reveal Falun Gong Fallacies," *Xinhua News Reports*, July 24, 1999; reproduced in FBIS, same date.

— "*Meng Xiaoxia Beiju Xia-Pian (Tu): Zhuitao Gongdao de Lu Hai Yao Zou Duo Jiu*" (Meng Xiaoxia's Tragedy, Part Two [With Photos]: How Much Farther Must She Journey in Search of Justice?), *Hua Shang Bao* (China Business View), 8 March 2004.

— "Nation's Mentally Ill Need More Care," *China Daily*, November 27, 2000.

— "Notice of the State Council on Circulating the Trial Practices of the Ministry of Public Security on Re-education through Labor" (*Guowuyuan Guanyu Zhuanfa Gonganbu Zhiding De Laodong Jiaoyang Shixing Banfa De Tongzhi*), January 21, 1982.

— "Notification of Bureau No. 11 of the Ministry of Public Security on Strengthening and Reorganizing the Management of Solitary Confinement Cells (July 12, 1983)," *Zhonghua Renmin Gongheguo Falü Guifanxing Jieshi Jicheng* (A Compilation of Standard Interpretations of the Laws of the People's Republic of China), Jilin People's Publishing House, October 1990, pp.1591-1593.

— "Observations on the Effectiveness of Stereotactic Brain Surgery in Cases of Schizophrenia with Aggressive Behaviour," *Chinese Journal of Nervous and Mental Diseases*, 1992, Vol.18, No.3, pp.153-155.

— "On Khrushchev's Phoney Communism and its World Historical Lessons (Ninth Letter to the Soviets)," *Renmin Ribao (People's Daily),* July 14, 1964.

— "Penal-System Medical and Health Work Has Been Greatly Strengthened and Developed in Recent Years," *Fanzui Yu Gaizao Yanjiu* (Research in Crime and Reform), 1994, No.4, pp.53-55.

— "Practice Guideline: Forensic Psychiatric Evaluation of Defendants Raising the Insanity Defense," Supplement to *Journal of the American Academy of Psychiatry and the Law*, Vol. 30, No. 2, 2002, p.3.

— PRC Regulations on Reform through Labour (*Laodong Gaizao Tiaoli*) 26 August 1954; in *Gong'an Fagui Huibian* (1950-1979), Beijing: Qunzhong Chubanshe, 1980, pp. 397-409.

— "Probe Set for Dissident 'Abuse'," *Associated Press*, 27 August 2002.

— "Psychiatric Abuse in China," *The Japan Times* (Editorial), 5 September 2002.

— "Psychiatric Abuse in the Soviet Union," Helsinki Watch, May 1990.

— "Psychiatric Abuse of Dissidents 'Rampant'," *Agence France Presse*, 13 August 2002.

— "*Quanguo Sifa Jingshenbing Jianding Danwei Mingce*" (National Register of Judicial Psychiatric Appraisal Units), issued on 21 January 2003 by the Judicial Psychiatric Appraisals Specialist Committee of the Chinese Society of Psychiatry.

— "Red Guard Publications: Part III — Special Issues," Vol.16, Center for Chinese Research Materials, Association of Research Libraries, Washington D.C. (1975), pp.5186-5187.

— "*Kao Mao Zedong Sixiang Zhihao Jingshenbing*" (Rely on Mao Zedong Thought to Cure Mental Illness), *Renmin Ribao* (People's Daily), August 10, 1971.

— "Reply of the Supreme People's Court on the Question of the Handling of Crimes Committed by Mentally Ill Persons," June 2, 1956.

— "Rights Group Says China Sent Labour Activist to Mental Hospital," *Agence France Presse*, April 11, 2000.

— "*Ruci zheban 'wei zhengfu paiyou jienan*'," SinoLaw (*Zhongguo Fazhi Wang*: available at www.sinolaw.net.cn), June 11, 2002.

— Security Administration Punishments Law of the PRC (*Zhonghua Renmin Gongheguo Zhi'an Guanli Chufa Fa*), effective 1 March 2006.

— "Shanghai Detention Center for the Mentally Disordered: An Interview with Mr. C," *Human Rights Tribune* (journal of the New York-based monitoring group Human Rights in China), Vol.1, No.5 (October 1990), p.16.

— *Shanghai Jingshen Weisheng Tiaoli* (Shanghai Municipal Mental Health Regulations), passed by the Standing Committee of the Shanghai Municipal People's Congress on 28 December 2001 and effective as of 7 April 2002.

— "*Shanghai Shi Gaoji Renmin Fayuan, Shanghai Shi Renmin Jianchayuan, Shanghai Shi Gong'an Ju Guanyu Banli Fanzui Xianyiren, Beigaoren zai Xingshi Susong Qijian Huan Jingshenbing de Anjian de Guiding*" (Provisions of the Shanghai High People's Court, Shanghai Municipal People's Procuracy and Shanghai Municipal Public Security Bureau on the Handling of Cases Where Criminal Suspects or Defendants Become Mentally Ill During the Criminal Process), Document *Hu-Jian-Fa* [2003] No.272 (month and day of issue not available); available on the Internet at *Dongfang Lüshi Wang* (Eastern Lawyers Network): www.lawyers.org.cn.

— "*Shanghai Shi Jianhu Zhiliao Guanli Zhaoshi Zhaohuo Jingshenbingren Tiaoli*" (Shanghai Municipal Regulations on the Guardianship, Treatment and Management of Mentally Ill People Who Create Incidents or Disasters), promulgated on August 29, 1986, in *Shanghai Gong'an Nianjian, 1988* (Shanghai Public Security Yearbook, 1988), Shanghai Social Sciences Publishing House (volume marked: "for internal distribution only"), December 1988), pp.343-346.

— *Shanghai Shi Sifa Jiandingren Zhiye Daode Guifan* (Shanghai Municipal Code of Professional Ethics for Forensic Evaluators) 15 October 2003.

— "*Shei You Quan Ba Zhengchang Ren Songjin Jingshenbingyuan?*" (Who Has the Right to Have a Normal Person Confined in a Mental Hospital?), Zhongguo Qingnian Bao (China Youth Daily), 4 June 2001.

— "*Shenyang Ankang Yiyuan Jiang Yi Falun Gong Xueyuan Guanshi Zhi Si*" (Falun Gong Practitioner Killed by Being Force-Fed in Shenyang Ankang Hospital), 14 October 2002, available at: yuanming.net/articles/200210/13152.html.

— "*Shenyang Shi Shouzhi Weihai Shehui Zhi'an Jingshenbingren Banfa*" (Shenyang Municipality's Methods for the Custody and Treatment of Mentally Ill People Who Endanger Public Order), promulgated by the Shenyang Municipal People's Government, 4 January 1996, available at: http://www.law999.net/law/doc/d007/1996/01/04/00042801.html.

— "*Shijie Jingshenbingxue Dahui Jiemu: Zhong-Gong Beize Lanyong Jingshenbingxue*" (WPA Congress Opens: CCP Accused of Misusing Psychiatry), *Da Ji Yuan* (Epoch Times), 25 August 2002.

— "*Shijie Jingshenbing Xuehui 12 Jie Nianhui Jueyi: Zhuanjia Jiang Fu Zhongguo Diaocha*" (WPA's 12th Congress Resolves to Send Experts to Investigate China Situation), *Da Ji Yuan* (Epoch Times), 29 August 2002.

— "*Shijie Jingshenbingxue Xiehui Jiang Diaocha Dalu Jingshenbing Jingcha Neimu*" (World Psychiatric Association to Investigate Police Background to Mainland Psychiatric Cases), *Da Ji Yuan* (Epoch Times), 31 August 2002.

— "*Shijie Jingshenbingxuejia Huiyi Jue Pai Daibiaotuan Fu Zhongguo Shicha*" (WPA Conference Decides to Send Inspection Mission to China), *Da Ji Yuan* (Epoch Times), 26 August 2002.

— *Sichuan Shengqing* (A General Account of Sichuan Province), published "for internal use only" by Sichuan People's Press, December 1987, p.548.

— "Soviet Abuse of Psychiatry for Political Purposes," Helsinki Watch, (New York: Human Rights Watch), January 1988.

— "Statistics of Mentally Disordered Offenders 1999 — England and Wales," U.K Government, available at http://www.homeoffice.gov.uk/rds/pdfs/hosb2100.pdf.

— "Study and Discussion Notes on 'Analysis of a Survey of 250 Cases of Mental Illness'," by unnamed authors from Yichun District Mental Hospital, Jiangxi Province, *Xin Yixue (New Medicine)*, 1973, Vol.4, No.3, pp.176-178; cover date March 15, 1973.

— "*Tebie de Guanhuai – Anhui Sheng Hefei Shi Gong'an Ju Ankang Yiyuan Jianwen*" (A Special Kind of Care – Record of a Visit to the Ankang Hospital of Hefei City PSB, Anhui Province) *Fazhi Ribao*, 10 November 2000.

— *The Effect of Falun Gong on Healing Illnesses and Keeping Fit: A Survey Among Practitioners in Beijing Zizhuyuan Assistance Center, October 18, 1998* (February 2000), available at: www.falundafa-pa.net/survey/survey98-2_e.html.

— "The World Medical Association Resolution on the Abuse of Psychiatry," initiated in the WMA Medical Ethics Committee on 20 May 2001 and adopted by the WMA General Assembly on 10 June 2002 in Washington DC; available at: http://www.wma.net/e/policy/a3.htm.

— "Thoughts on Reforming the Labour Reform System's Administrative Structure," *Laogai Laojiao Lilun Yanjiu* (Theoretical Studies in Labour Reform and Labour Re-education), 1990, No.2, p.43.

— "*Tianjin Shi Shouzhi Guanli Weihai Shehui Zhi'an Jingshenbingren Banfa*" (Tianjin Municipal Methods for the Shelter and Management of Mentally Ill People Who Endanger Public Order), 8 December 1991; available at: http://www.fl5.cn/fagui/difang/fg3/200603/57785.html.

— "*Tuchu Zhengzhi, Zou Woguo Jingshenbing Fangzhi Gongzuo Ziji de Lu*," Chinese Journal of Neurology and Psychiatry, 1966, Vol.10, No.2, pp.95-97.

— "Various Regulations by the Ministry of Public Security and the Ministry of Justice Concerning the Detailed Implementation of the Central Committee's Transferral of the Work of Labour Reform and Labour Re-education Over to the Judicial Administrative Departments," 9 June 1983, in *Zhonghua Renmin Gongheguo Falü Guifanxing Jieshi Jicheng* (A Collection of Standard Interpretations of the Laws of the PRC – Supplementary Volume), Jilin People's Press, December 1991, p.813.

— "*Weisheng Bu, Minzheng Bu, Gong'an Bu Guanyu Jiaqiang Jingshen Weisheng Gongzuo de Yijian*" (Opinion of the Ministries of Health, Civil Affairs and Public Security on the Strengthening of Mental Health Work), April 20, 1987, in *Zhonghua Renmin Gongheguo Weisheng Fagui Huibian 1986-1988* (PRC Compilation of Laws and Regulations on Health, 1986-1988), Law Publishing House, June 1990, pp.366-369.

— "Will Operations Root Out Desire for Drugs?" People's Daily Online, 4 July 2004; available at:

www.xinhuanet.com.

— "Worker Demand Release of Chinese Unionist from Mental Asylum," *Agence France Presse*, December 17, 2000.

— "World Psychiatric Association: Madrid Declaration on Ethical Standards for Psychiatric Practice," approved by the WPA General Assembly on 25 August 1996.

— "World Psychiatric Association to Investigate Abuses in China's Mental Hospitals," *Falun Dafa Information Center*, 28 August 2002.

— "WPA Executive Committee Plan of Action on Falun Gong, August 25, 2002"; and "Update on the World Psychiatric Investigation on the Case of Falun Gong Practitioners Admitted to Chinese Psychiatric Hospitals," dated August 2002; copies on file with the author.

— "WPA Statements and Viewpoints on the Rights and Legal Safeguards of the Mentally Ill," adopted by the WPA General Assembly in Athens, October 17, 1989; in Geneva Initiative on Psychiatry, *Human Rights and Professional Responsibilities of Physicians in Documents of International Organizations*, Amsterdam and Sofia, 1998, pp.70-71.

— "Xue Jifeng: Detained in a Psychiatric Hospital for Championing Worker Rights," *China Rights Forum*, Summer 2000, pp.28-29.

— "*Yi Nü Cuo Dang Jingshenbing, E Yun Tian Lun Jian*" (A Woman Wrongly Taken to be Mentally Ill Tragically Ends up Being Gang Raped), *People's Daily Online*, 2 August 2000.

— *Zanxing Fan'geming Zhizui Fa* (Temporary Law on the Punishment of Crimes of Counterrevolution), Nanjing, 9 March 1928.

— "*Zhaoshi Zhaohuo Jingshenbingren de Shouzhi Guiding*" (Regulations on the Admission and Treatment of Mentally Ill People Who Create Incidents or Disasters), undated copy available at: http://police.shqp.gov.cn/gb/content/2003-07/09/content_324.htm.

— "*Zhewei Jingcha You Mei You Jingshenbing?*" (Was This Policeman Mentally Ill?), *Beijing Qingnian Bao* (Beijing Youth News), 22 January 2002, p.23.

— "*Zhiji Dongbei Shouli Jiedu Kai'eshu 2 Xiaoshi 45 Fen Shoushu Chenggong Wancheng*" (An Eye-witness Account of Northeast China's First Successful Frontal-Lobe Brain Operation, Lasting 2 Hours and 45 Minutes, to Cure Drug Addiction), *Dongbei Xinwen Wang* (Northeast News Net), 5 July 2004; available at: www.fx120.net/news/news-map/200407050950238801.htm.

— "*Zhong-Gong Guo Mei Chu Shuo-li: Shangfang Funü Jing Bei Xin-Fang Xitong Youxiu Jiti Guanjin Jingshenbingyuan*" (Nowhere in the Chinese Communist Party's Nation to Seek Redress: A Female Petitioner is Locked Up in a Mental Hospital by a "Superior Collective Unit" of the Visits and Complaints Network), *Nanfang Zhoumo* (Southern Weekend), June 6, 2002.

— "*Zhong-Gong Jingshenbing Qiufan Kewang Jieshou Guoji Jiandu*" (CCP's Psychiatric Prisoners Can Now Expect International Scrutiny), *Zhongguo Shibao* (China Times), 24 August 2002.

— *Zhongguo Gong'an Baike Quanshu* (China Encyclopaedia of Public Security), Jilin People's Publishing House, February 1990.

— "*Zhongguo Shang Bai Suo Jingshenbingyuan Jieshou Zhengzhi Renwu*" (Over 100 Chinese Mental Hospitals Accepting Political Tasks), *Da Ji Yuan* (Epoch Times), 14 June 2004.

— "*Zhongguo Shuqian Yiyi Renshi Bei Guanru Jingshenbingyuan*" (Several Thousand Dissidents Sent to Mental Hospitals), *Meiguo Zhi Yin* (Voice of America), 14 August 2002.

— *Zhonghua Suweiai Gongheguo Chengzhi Fange'ming Tiaoli* (Regulations of the Chinese Soviet Republic on the Punishment of Counterrevolution), Central Executive Committee of the Chinese Soviet Republic, 8 April 1934; available at: http://www1.openedu.com.cn/yth/248/file_info.php?file_id=9127&sura_id=14&topic_code=C5010D

— "*Zuigao Renmin Fayuan, Zuigao Renmin Jianchayuan Guanyu Banli Fan'geming Baoluan he Zhengzhi Dongluan Zhong Fanzui Anjian Juti Yingyong Falü de Ruogan Wenti de Yijian* (Opinion of the Supreme People's Court and Supreme People's Procuracy on Several Questions Concerning the Specific Application of Law in the Handling of Criminal Cases Committed During the Counterrevolutionary Rebellion and Political Turmoil)," August 1, 1989, in *Sifa Shouce* (Judicial Handbook), Vol.6, People's Court Publishing House, Dec. 1990, pp.100-105.

INDEX

Administrative law
  administrative detention
    forensic psychiatric committal, 57-59
    "re-education through labour, 54-57
    reform, "better the devil one knows"?
      59-61
    security regulations, 52
    "shelter for deportation", 52-53
    "shelter for investigation", 52
    "shelter for re-education", 53-54
  detention, legal context, 35
  legal reforms
    challenging government agencies, 42-43
    limitations on claims against government agencies, 43, 47-49

American Psychiatric Association
  resolutions for action on China, 282, 285–286

American Psychoanalytic Association
  resolution for action on China (2001), 283

Analysis of Forty-one Mentally Ill People, Hangzou Ankang Hospital, article
  dissidents, political case increase, 160
  dissidents, psychiatric committals, 160
  psychiatric diagnoses, table, 160–161
  "reactionary" documents, 161–162
  summaries of several cases, 161

"Analysis of a Survey of 250 Cases of Mental Illness", article, 123–127

Ankang case notes 2000-2005, victims go to court
  developments, possible new questioning, 280
  Han Zhenxi, wrongful psychiatric incarceration
    Ankang internal affair ruling, 266–268
    court ruling, 265
    judges' pre-judgment announcement, 265–266
    psychiatric appraisal, 263–265
  legal legerdemain, 279–280
  legal-psychiatric documents, non use in civil matters, 279
  Meng Xiaoxia, reprimand and criminal assault
    administrative lawsuit, 273
    assault background, 270–271
    legal debate on Meng's case, 274–276
    legal issues, 274–275
    psychiatric committal, 271–272
    "specific administrative action", 275–276
  non administrative action, custody and treatment policy, 279
  political dissidents as prime targets, 260
  Qiu Jinyou, administrative corruption
    exposure initial campaign, 260–261
    psychiatric appraisal and committal, 261–262
    wrongful psychiatric incarceration claim, 262–263
  statistical interpretation difficulties, 259–260
  Wang Fenglai, conspiracy for committal
    background details, 276–277
    psychiatric appraisal and committal, 277–278
    wrongful psychiatric incarceration claim, 278
  Wang Henglei, death during committal
    administrative lawsuit, 268–269
    court ruling, 269
    death and response, 269–270

Ankang institutes for the criminally insane
  admissions criteria and procedure
    categories of and special criteria, 256–257, 260
    judiciary, lack of role, 254–255
    operational criteria, 256–257
    political dissidents, mentally ill, 255–256, 260
    regulations, 254–255
    Shanghai Ankang as institutional model, 253–255
    Wang Chaoru, case of, 258–259

Beijing Ankang
  regime at, 11
  Wang Wanxing
    detention of, 6-8
    diagnosis, 10-11
    interviews, 9, 10-11
    release of, 8-9, 12
    reports on, 7-8, 12-13

custody and treatment system
   admissions, 248–249
   background and origins, 245–247
   guiding documents, Ministry of Public
      Security, 247–248
   psychosurgery, involuntary, 249–253
defence of by Kang Ming, 281–282
developments from 1990s, 14-15
Falun Gong dissent and "Ankang Wards",
   236–237
guiding documents, Ministry of Public
   Security, 247–248
objective of, 255
origins and background, 245–247
psychosurgery, involuntary
   caution, need for, 251–253
   experimental psychosurgery, current, 253
   growing use of, 249–250
   results, assessment of, 250–251
regime
   Die Zeit interviews, Qiu Jinyou and Meng
      Xiaoxia, 13-14
   generally, 11
   origins, 1983 textbook, 188
Shanghai Ankang
   description, 242
   fear and discipline in, 242–244
   political dissidents, 244
   punishments, 243–244
   Wang Miaogen, case of, 244–245
Special Psychiatric Hospitals
   China, change of name to Ankang, 242,
      246–247
   Soviet Union, of, 241–242
U.N. Working Group on Arbitrary Detention
   Report, 7-8
victims go to court *see* **Ankang case notes
2000-2005, victims go to court**
World Psychiatric Association, request for
   inspection, 253

Beijing Ankang *See also* **Wang Wanxing**
regime at, 11
Wang Wanxing
   detention of, 6-8
   diagnosis, 10-11
   interviews, 9, 10-11
   release of, 8-9, 12
   reports on, 7-8, 12-13
**Bukovsky, Vladimir and Dr. Gluzman,
Semyon**
A Manual on Psychiatry for Dissenters, 5

**C, Case of Mr., Cultural Revolution and
political cases,** 116–117
**Cao Maobing, case of, workers rights
activists,** 212–215
**Chen Lining, case of, Cultural Revolution and
forensic psychiatric detention** 106–108
Chenzhou experience, the
   "Analysis of a Survey of 250 Cases of Mental
      Illness", article, 123–127
   challenge to findings, 127–128
   Mao Zedong Thought and, 124–128
   treatment outcome statistics, 126
China *see also* **Psychiatric abuse in China,
conclusions**
changes, international influence and pressure,
   304–305
changes within China
   change, possible? xiii–xiv, 280
   legal and psychiatric reform movement,
      303
   political psychiatric repression, cracks
      appearing, 302–303
judicial psychiatry and political dissent
   agnostic approach to, 21
   background, 3-4, 6
   individual case-based approach, 20
   psychiatric theory, dialogue, 20
   publications and sources, study of, 20-21
   reason for, 5, 21-22, 35
political abuse of psychiatry
   change, possible? xiii–xiv, 280
   Falun Gong, x, 159, 224–237
   forensic practice, xi–xii, 237–240
   psychiatric punishment, reasons for, xii–
      xiii
   research into, x–xi
   Royal College of Psychiatrists
      investigative mission call, 288–289
   Soviet transplant of forensic psychiatry, xi

World Psychiatric Association,
    investigation by, xiii, 290–293
political psychiatry, official statistics, 22-34
China's forensic psychiatric inquisition
    A, example of Mr. A, 109–110
    forensic practice, xi–xii, 237–240
    mentally ill people, evaluation, 110–111
    misuse of psychiatric techniques, 112–113
    psychiatric profession, effect on, 111–112
    Qi Benyu, "directives", 106–107, 108–109
Chinese Communist Party
    dissidents seen as threat, 3, 21-23
    law and Marxist doctrines, 36-37
Chinese Society of Psychiatry
    joint statement with WPA, 2004
        condemnation of, 294–296
        content and effect, 294
"Clinical mode of thought", 180–181
"Compulsive antithetical thought disorder", 203
Compulsory committals see also **Mentally ill offenders, legal context**
    British system, 75–77
    Falun Gong dissenters, 225–227, 230, 236–237
    forensic psychiatric committal, 57-59, 97
    international standards, 173
    legislation lack, effect, 168-169
    legislation, need for, 166
    legislation, preparation and reluctance, 166–168, 169
Council of Europe
    Rules protecting involuntary patients, 79, 82–84
"Counterrevolution"
    changing composition of cases, 65–67
    "crimes of endangering state security", 66–67
    dangerousness criterion, the, 173–176
    historical background, 62–63
    political cases, high rate of, 178–182
    political dissidents, apparent decline in numbers of, 61, 63–65
Counterrevolutionary behaviour, authentic and borderlines cases
    delusional schizophrenia

"compulsive antithetical thought disorder", 203
        generally, 200–201, 203
        indirect suicide/self-punishment, 203
        Liu Baiju and, 201–203
        research on, 201
    "folie politique", 200
    Gluzman, Dr. Semyon, 200
    L, Mr, case study, delusional schizophrenia, 203–205
    Li, Ms, case study, delusional schizophrenia, 205–206
    "pseudo-counterrevolutionaries"
        cases of, 203–206
        Liu Baiju, 207–209
        meaning, 22, 67, 203
Counterrevolutionary behaviour by the mentally ill
    Identifying Counterrevolutionary Behaviour by the Mentally Ill, 189–190
    Liu, case of, counterrevolutionary behaviour, 190–192
    Manifestations of Counterrevolutionary Behaviour by the Mentally Ill, 188–189
    "political cases", defining, 188–190
    Wang Fumian, case of, counterrevolutionary behaviour
        background facts, 192–193
        Liu Binyan and Cao Changqing investigations, 193–195
"Crimes of endangering state security" introduction of, 66–67
Criminal insanity concept
    comparative overview, 67–78
    compulsory committals, British system, 75–77
    defence of insanity, 71–72
    "forensic" definition, *Faulk's Basic Forensic Psychiatry,* 67–68
    forensic psychiatrist's role, 77–78
    "forensic psychiatry", 68–69
    insanity as defence, 71–72, 78
    insanity prosecution, 73–74
    legal responsibility, historical origins, 70–72
    legal responsibility (*mens rea*), 69–70
    "M'Naghten rule", 71–72
    psychiatric evaluation, British system, 75

safeguards, role of due process, comparison with British system, 74–78
Criminal Procedure Law reforms, 45-46
Cultural Revolution, the
  effect on psychiatry, 105–106, 131–133
  forensic psychiatry in crisis
    C, case of Mr., 116–117
    Chen Lining, case of, 106–108
    China's forensic psychiatric inquisition, 108–113
    Yan Weibing, case of, 113–116
  general psychiatry in crisis
    Chenzhou experience, the, 123–128
    China's mental patients in the dock, 122–123
    Chinese psychiatry awakes from the nightmare, 138–149
    "ideological defect theory", refuting, 134–138
    Mao Zedong Thought to re-educate the mentally ill, 124–128, 129
    mental illness as "political sickness", 117–122
    observations on, some preliminary, 131–133
    post Cultural Revolution, "a nuanced reversal", 158
    post-Mao counterattack, 133–134
    thought reform for the mentally ill, "lancing the boil", 128–131
  medical neglect and prison psychosis, 149–153
  reduced abuse following, 157–158, 159
Custody and treatment system, Ankang institutes
  admissions, 248–249
  background and origins, 245–247
  guiding documents, Ministry of Public Security, 247–248
  psychosurgery, involuntary, 249–253

Delusional schizophrenia
  "compulsive antithetical thought disorder", 203
  generally, 200–201, 203
  indirect suicide/self-punishment, 203
  L, Mr, case study, delusional schizophrenia, 203–205
  Li, Ms, case study, delusional schizophrenia, 205–206
  Liu Baiju and, 201–203
  research on, 201
Deng Xiaoping
  "socialist democracy" policies, 38-39

"Evil cult-induced mental disorder", 237

Falun Gong dissent
  "Ankang Wards", 236–237
  background to protests, 224–225
  compulsory hospital committals
    large numbers of, 225–227, 230, 236–237
    legal process, lack of due, 236
  crackdown, justifications for
    legal justifications, 231–232, 233–234, 236
    medical justifications, 232–233, 234–235
    national security threat, no plausible evidence, 233–234
  deaths in mental hospitals, 229–230
  forensic assessment of detainees
    case studies, 237–240
    "evil cult-induced mental disorder", 237
  "ideological defect" theory, reappearance of, compulsory committals, large numbers of, 225–227, 230, 236–237
    deaths in mental hospitals, 229–230
    "psychiatrize", attempts to, 230–231
    Zhou Caixia, case of, 227–229
  national security threat, no plausible evidence, 233–234
  political abuse, research, x
  psychiatric abuse, increase of, 159
  "psychiatrize", attempts to, 230–231
  United Nations, response of, 234
  World Psychiatric Association, limitation on investigation, 287, 290, 293–294
"Folie politique", 200
Forensic psychiatrist
  difficult position of, 297–298
  role of, 77–78
Forensic psychiatry *See also* **Criminal insanity concept; Forensic psychiatry in crisis,**

the Cultural Revolution; Political psychiatry
Analysis of Forty-one Mentally Ill People, Hangzhou Ankang Hospital, article, 160–162
Falun Gong dissent, forensic assessment case studies, 237–240
"evil cult-induced mental disorder", 237
forensic practice, xi–xii, 237–240
forensic psychiatric 1987 survey, Jia Yicheng, 158–159
Forensic Psychiatric Appraisals, Journals 1976-95, Table 2, 29
Forensic Psychiatric Appraisals, Yunnan Hospital, Table 1, 28
forensic psychiatric committal, 57-59
meanings, 4, 67–70
paranoid psychosis, 177–178
official statistics
  assessment, 30-34
  cases, decline in number of, 23–30
survey, 1987, 158–159

Forensic psychiatry in crisis, the Cultural Revolution
C, Case of Mr., 116–117
Chen Lining, case of, 106–108
China's forensic psychiatric inquisition
  A, example of Mr. A, 109–110
  mentally ill people, evaluation, 110–111
  misuse of psychiatric techniques, 112–113
  psychiatric profession, effect on, 111–112
  Qi Benyu, "directives", 106–107, 108–109
effect on psychiatry, 105–106
post Cultural Revolution, "a nuanced reversal", 158
Qi Benyu, Anding Hospital "directives", 106–107, 108–109
Yan Weibing, case of, 113–116

General psychiatry in crisis, the Cultural Revolution
Chenzhou experience, the
  "Analysis of a Survey of 250 Cases of Mental Illness", article, 123–127
  challenge to findings, 127–128
  Mao Zedong Thought and, 124–128

treatment outcome statistics, 126
China's mental patients in the dock, 122–123
Chinese psychiatry awakes from the nightmare,
  post-Mao reaction to Cultural Revolution, 138–138, 149
  Yang Desen, subjective conjecture and scientific research article, 139–149
effect on psychiatry, 131–133
"ideological defect theory", refuting, 134–138
Jia Rubao on thought reform, 128–131
Mao Zedong Thought to re-educate the mentally ill, 119–121, 124–128, 129
mental illness as "political sickness", 117–118
mental illness is political
  Anti-Rightist Movement, 121–122
  genesis of school of thought, 118–119
  Mao Zedong Thought, 119–121
  psychotherapy, 120
observations on, some preliminary, 131–133
post-Mao counterattack, 133–134
psychotherapy, 120
thought reform for the mentally ill, "lancing the boil"
  mental illness, political causation, 128–129
  mental patients, culprits or victims? 129–130
  thought reform as therapeutic process, 130–131
ultra-Marxist ideology and mental illness, 132–133, 303–304
Yang Desen
  "hyperdiagnosis", 135-136
  initial counterattack by, 133–134
  mental illness as "ideological defect", insufficiency of, 137–138
  mental illness, pathological thoughts before and after, 136–
  mentally ill people, political responsibility of, 134–135
  "ideological defect" theory, article refuting, 134–138
Geneva Initiative on Psychiatry, 281, 289–290
Gluzman, Semyon, Dr.
  Bukovsky, Vladimir with *A Manual on Psychiatry for Dissenters*, 5

counterrevolutionary behaviour, 200
methodology of
   individual case-based approach, 19
   psychiatric theory, dialogue, 19-20
   publications and sources, examination of, 20

Han Zhenxi, case of, wrongful psychiatric incarceration
Ankang internal affair ruling, 266–268
court ruling, 265
judges' pre-judgment announcement, 265–266
psychiatric appraisal, 263–265
Hangzhou Ankang Hospital *see* **Analysis of Forty-one Mentally Ill People, Hangzhou Ankang Hospital, article**
Hospitalisation *see also* **Mentally ill offenders, legal context**
compulsory forensic, 97
international standards, 173
Hu Feng, case of, dissident writer, 101, 103
Huang Shurong, case of, political insanity
background facts, 218–219
Nanfang Zhoumo, investigative journalism, 219–221
press response elsewhere, 222–223
Human rights
dialogue with Western governments, 40
involvement with, gradual, 39-40
low level of consciousness of, 41
protection for, pressures for greater, 40-41
"hyperdiagnosis", 100, 158
"hypodiagnosis", 100, 135–136

"ideological defect" theory
Falun Gong dissent
   compulsory committals, large numbers of, 225–227, 230, 236–237
   deaths in mental hospitals, 229–230
   "psychiatrize", attempts to, 230–231
   Zhou Caixia, case of, 227–229
refuting, 134–138
Insanity *see also* **Criminal insanity concept; Mental illness**
judicial treatment
   early treatment, 91

hospitalisation, compulsory forensic, 97
"latent schizophrenia", 96–97
"paranoid psychosis", 95–96, 97
People's Republic, early years, 93–104
prior to 1949, 91–93
"psychopathic hospitals", 91–93
psychosurgery, 99
schizophrenia, 94–96, 97
Serbski School of Forensic Psychiatry, 94–99
"sluggish schizophrenia", 94–95, 96, 97
Soviet Union, early influence, 93–94
therapeutic regime, 98–99
legal-psychiatric abuse, patterns of,
forms of, 103–104
Hu Feng, case of, 101, 103
"hyperdiagnosis", 100, 158
"hypodiagnosis", 100
Lu Ling, case of, 101–102
severe medical neglect, 100
presumption of and lack of instinct for self-preservation, 177–182, 300
International campaign, the
American Psychiatric Association resolutions for action, 282, 285–286
American Psychoanalytic Association resolution for action (2001), 283
Ankang system, defence by Kang Ming, 281–282
changes, international influence and pressure, 304–305
China, different approaches to question of, 287–288
Geneva Initiative on Psychiatry, 281, 289–290
initial concerns over psychiatric abuse and Chinese response, 281–282
present situation, 296
Royal College of Psychiatrists
investigative mission call at WPA Yokohama meeting, 288–289
resolution for action (2001), 282–283
World Medical Association (WMA)
psychiatric abuse debate (2001), 284
psychiatric abuse resolution (2002), 284–285
World Psychiatric Association (WPA)

Ankang facilities, request for inspection, xiii, 253, 283, 286–287
Chinese Society of Psychiatry, joint statement with, 2004, 294
Chinese Society of Psychiatry, joint statement, condemnation, 294–296
Falun Gong cases, limitation on investigation, 287, 290, 291, 293–294
present situation, 296
Yokohama meeting, appeal to vice Premier Mrs. Wu Yi, 291–292
Yokohama meeting, Chinese responses to, 290–29, 292–293
Yokohama meeting, investigative mission call, 288–289, 290
Yokohama meeting, summary of outcome by Robert van Voren, 289–290

International legal and ethical standards on psychiatric custody
Council of Europe Rules protecting patients involuntary patients, 79, 82–84
cruel and unusual punishment
Russian Federation, response, 86–87
UN Convention against Torture, 86, 87
United Nations
Convention against Torture, 86, 87
International Covenant on Civil and Political Rights, 79
Principles for Protection of Persons with Mental Illness and Health Care, 22, 80–82
Universal Declaration of Human Rights, 79
World Psychiatric Association
Declaration of Hawaii, 84–85, 86
Declaration of Madrid, 85–86

Involuntary psychosurgery *see* **Psychosurgery, involuntary**

Jia Rubao
thought reform
mental illness, political causation, 128–129
mental patients, culprits or victims? 129–130
refutation of by Yang Desen, 144–146
thought reform as therapeutic process, 130–131

Jia Yicheng
forensic psychiatric 1987 survey and, 158–159
Soviet Union and "special psychiatric hospitals", 3

Jiang Zemin
rule of law and development of, 46

"Judicial appraisal mode of thought", 180–181

Judicial psychiatry and political dissent *see also* **Beijing Ankang; Legal norms and procedures for psychotic offenders; Political psychiatry; Wang Wanxing, case of**
Bukovsky, Vladimir and Dr. Gluzman, Semyon and *A Manual on Psychiatry for Dissenters*, 5
China
agnostic approach to, 21
background, 3-4, 6
extent of use, overview 17-19
individual case-based approach, 20
psychiatric theory, dialogue, 20
publications and sources, study of, 20-21
developments from 1990s, 14-15
domestic and international legal framework, overview, 16
overview of book's structure, 15-16, 19-22
psychiatry law and politics interrelationship, 16-17
reasons for, 5, 21-22, 35
Soviet Union, application in, 3, 4-6, 19
Law and psychiatry, 1949 to 1960s
cases of Lu Ling and Hu Feng, 101–104
judicial treatment of insanity prior to 1949, 91–93
legal-psychiatric abuse, patterns of, 100, 158
People's Republic, early years, 93–104
Serbski School of Forensic Psychiatry, 94–99
rule of law and development of, 46

Kang Ming, defence of Ankang system, 281–282

L, Mr, case study, delusional schizophrenia, 203–205
Law and psychiatry, 1949 to 1960s
  cases of Lu Ling and Hu Feng, 101–104
  judicial treatment of insanity prior to 1949, 91–93
  legal-psychiatric abuse, patterns of, 100, 158
  People's Republic, early years, 93–104
  Serbski School of Forensic Psychiatry, 94–99
Legal norms and procedures for psychotic offenders
  appraisal committees, setting up of, 169–170
  compulsory custodial treatment
    legislation lack, effect, 168–169
    legislation, need for, 166
    legislation, preparation and reluctance, 166–168, 169
  criminal law revisions, 163–166
  expert evaluations, 165
  judicial appraisal
    draft regulations, 2000, 170–171
    lack of discretion on those to be examined, 171–172
    psychiatric assessors, pressures on, 172
    regulations, 1989, 169–170
    Shanghai Municipal Regulations, 171
  "legal responsibility", problem of, 163
  police powers, 165–166
  Supreme People's Court, 1956 directive, 163–164
  Yang Yiyong, case of, 168–169
Legal-medical issues
  civil incompetence, assumption of, 183–184
  civil-style appraisals, political cases, 182–184, 185–187
  "clinical mode of thought", 180–181
    compulsory forensic, 97
  dangerousness criterion, the, 173–176
  dissidence equated with violence, 176
  evaluation questions, political offenders, 174
  feigning or "malingering", 181
  hospitalisation and detention, international, standards, 173
  "judicial appraisal mode of thought", 180–181
  Li Mou, case of, 184–187
  "litigious mania", 177, 178
  paranoid psychosis, 95–96, 97, 177–178
  political cases, high rate of, 178–182
  "political mania", 177, 178
  presumption of insanity and lack of instinct for self-preservation, 177–182, 300
  "presumption of sanity", call for, 179–180
  self-preservation, lack of instinct for, 177–182, 300
  serious crimes by mentally ill, 174–176
Legal-psychiatric abuse, patterns of
  "hyperdiagnosis", 100, 158
  "hypodiagnosis", 100
  severe medical neglect, 100
Legal-psychiatric encounters
  authentic and borderline cases, 200–206
  counterrevolutionary behaviour by the mentally ill, 188–198
  distinguishing a paranoiac from a political dissident, 195–200
  "political insanity", a theory for the new millennium, 206–223
Legal reforms *See also* **Administrative law; Human rights; Rule of law**
  administrative detention reform, 59-61
  administrative law
    challenging government agencies, 42-43
    limitations on claims against government agencies, 43, 47-49
  Criminal Procedure Law reforms, 45-46
  Cultural Revolution and effects, 37-38
  Deng Xiaoping, "socialist democracy" policies, 38-39
  historical background, 35-37
  limitations on, 43, 47-49
  overview, 35-37
Li, Ms, case study, delusional schizophrenia, 205–206
Li Mou, case of, legal medical issues, 184–187
"**Litigious mania**", 177, 178
Liu Baiju
  "compulsive antithetical thought disorder", 203
  delusional schizophrenia, 201–203
  indirect suicide/self-punishment, 203
  "political crimes"

compulsory detention, frequency, 207–208
compulsory detention, reasons for, 208–210
initial analysis, 206–207
"negative political speech and action", 206, 209–210
"pseudo-counterrevolutionaries", 207–210

Liu, case of, counterrevolutionary behaviour, 190–192

Lu Ling, case of, dissident writer, 101–102

Lubman, Stanley
rule of law
current position, 48-49, 50-51
low level of rights consciousness, 41
pressures for reform, 44-45

Mao Zedong
Chenzhou experience and, 124–128
Mao Zedong Thought, guide not substitute, 145–147
Mao Zedong Thought to re-educate the mentally ill, 119–121, 124–128, 129

Medical neglect
criminal offenders, extent and quality of care, 149–151
prison, nature of and changes, 150–151
prison psychosis, 151–153
severe medical neglect, legal-psychiatric abuse, 100

Meng Xiaoxia, case of, reprimand and criminal assault
administrative lawsuit, 273
assault background, 270–271
legal debate on Meng's case, 274–276
legal issues, 274–275
psychiatric committal, 271–272
"specific administrative action", 275–276

Mental illness
"Analysis of a Survey of 250 Cases of Mental Illness", article, 123–127
common disease, as, 141–142
essential nature of, 139–140
evaluation, 110–111
"ideological defect", insufficiency of, 137–138
pathological thoughts before and after, 136–137

political causation, as, 128–129
political, is
Anti-Rightist Movement, 121–122
genesis of school of thought, 118–119
Mao Zedong Thought, 119–121
psychotherapy, 120
political responsibility of persons having, 134–135
"political sickness", as, 117–118
thought reform for the mentally ill, 128–131
ultra-Marxist ideology and mental illness, 132–133, 303–304
United Nations:Principles for the Protection of Persons with Mental Illness, 22, 80–82

Mentally ill offenders, legal context
Analysis of Forty-one Mentally Ill People, Hangzhou Ankang Hospital, article
dissidents, political case increase, 160
dissidents, psychiatric committals, 160
psychiatric diagnoses, table, 160–161
"reactionary" documents, 161–162
summaries of several cases, 161
categories of and special criteria, 256–257
China's mental patients in the dock, 122–123
compulsory forensic, 97
Cultural Revolution, reduced abuse following, 157–158, 159
forensic-psychiatric 1987 survey, 158–159
forensic psychiatry, survival of Maoist orthodoxy, 158, 159
hyperdiagnosis, survival of, 158
Jia Yicheng, forensic psychiatric 1987 survey, 158–159
legal norms and procedures for psychotic offenders
appraisal committees, setting up, 169–170
compulsory custodial treatment, 166–169
criminal law revisions, 163–166
expert evaluations, 165
judicial appraisal
draft regulations, 2000, 170–171
lack of discretion on those to be examined, 171–172
regulations, 1989, 169–170
Shanghai Municipal Regulations, 171

"legal responsibility", problem of, 163
operational criteria, 256–257
police powers, 165–166
political abuse, a nuanced reversal of policy, 157–162
psychiatric assessors, pressures on, 172
security authorities general view, 162
Supreme People's Court, 1956 directive, 163–164
Yang Yiyong, case of, 168–169
legal-medical issues, some thorny
civil incompetence, assumption of, 183–184
civil-style appraisals, political cases, 182–184, 185–187
"clinical mode of thought", 180–181
compulsory forensic, 97
dangerousness criterion, the, 173–176
dissidence equated with violence, 176
evaluation questions, political offenders, 174
feigning or "malingering", 181
hospitalisation and detention, international, standards, 173
"judicial appraisal mode of thought", 180–181
Li Mou, case of, 184–187
"litigious mania", 177, 178
paranoid psychosis, 177–178
political cases, high rate of, 178–182
"political mania", 177, 178
presumption of insanity and lack of instinct for self-preservation, 177–182
"presumption of sanity", call for, 179–180
self-preservation, lack of instinct for, 177–182, 300
serious crimes by mentally ill, 174–176
Methodology *See* **Research and methodology**
"M'Naghten rule", 71–72
Munro, Robin
articles on Chinese psychiatric abuse, 281
conclusions on China's psychiatric inquisition, 297–305
Wang Wanxing interview, 9, 10-11

Overview
book's structure, 19-20

Paranoiac, distinguishing from a political dissident
Long Qingchun and the difference, 195–196
Zhu, case of Mr
case study of, 196–198
commentary on, 198–200
"Paranoid psychosis", 95–96, 97, 177–178
Peerenboom, Randall
administrative detention reform, 59-61
legal reforms to 1998, 38
rule of law, current position, 48, 49-50
Petitioners and complainants persecuted by corrupt officials, 215–216
Political abuse of psychiatry, Soviet and Chinese experience
complexities, iii–iv
dangerousness criterion, the, 173–176
forms of, 103–104
legal norms and procedures for psychotic offenders, 163–172
policy, a nuanced reversal
Analysis of Forty-one Mentally Ill People, Hangzhou Ankang Hospital, article, 160–162
Cultural Revolution, reduced abuse following, 157–158, 159
forensic-psychiatric 1987 survey, 158–159
forensic psychiatry, survival of Maoist orthodoxy, 158, 159
Soviet psychiatry
early reports, iv–v
reasons for abuse, vi–viii
United States investigation and report, v–vi
Political crimes, legal handling of
"counterrevolution"
changing composition of cases, 65–67
"crimes of endangering state security", 66–67
historical background, 62–63
dangerousness criterion, the, 173–176
political cases, high rate of, 178–182
political dissidents, apparent decline in numbers of, 61, 63-65
Political dissident, distinguishing from a paranoiac *see* **Paranoiac, distinguishing from a political dissident**

Political dissidents
    Ankang institutes and, 255–256
    apparent decline in numbers of, 61, 63-65
    deterrence against dissident activity, 298
    dissidents, lack of self-preservation, 300
    Shanghai Ankang, and, 244
"Political insanity", a theory for the new millennium
    Huang Shurong, case of, political insanity
        background facts, 218– 219
        Nanfang Zhoumo, investigative journalism, 219– 221
        press response elsewhere, 222– 223
    Liu Baiju and "political crimes"
        compulsory detention, frequency, 207–208
        compulsory detention, reasons for, 208–210
        initial analysis, 206–207
        "negative political speech and action", 206, 209–210
        "pseudo-counterrevolutionaries", 207–210
    petitioners and complainants persecuted by corrupt officials, 215–216
    workers rights activists
        Cao Maobing, case of, 212–214
        Cao Maobing, Working Group on Arbitrary Detention and, 214–215
        Xue Jifeng, case of, 210–212
    Zhang Gonglai, case of, 216–218
"Political mania", 177, 178
Political psychiatry
    official statistics
        assessment, 30-34
        cases, decline in number of, 23–30
        nature and range of, 22-23
    official statistics, research
        examples, 24-26
        Forensic Psychiatric Appraisals, Journals 1976-95, Table 2, 29
        Forensic Psychiatric Appraisals, Yunnan Hospital, Table 1, 28
        mental hospitals, numbers of, 31-32
        "political cases", numbers, 31-34
        Shen Muci, Jin Wei, 26-27
        Shen Zheng, 23
        Yao Zuhua *et al*, 27-29
        Zhang Xinzhi, 23–24
        Zhao Jiancong *et al*, 29-30
Prison
    nature of and changes, 150–151
    prison psychosis, 151–153
    psychiatric care, extent and quality, 149–151
"Pseudo-counterrevolutionaries" *see* **Counterrevolutionary behaviour, authentic and borderlines cases**
Psychiatric abuse in China, conclusions
    authorities' use of, reasons for
        corruption, increased potential, 302
        deterrence against dissident activity, 298
        dissidents, lack of self-preservation, 300
        ideological emphasis of Chinese Marxism, 300 –301
        international image and prestige, 299
        political changes post Mao, 298
        post Mao limitations on political manifestations, 301–302
        repressive regime self-justification, 298–299
        Soviet Union influence, 299–300, 301
        ultra-Marxist ideology and mental illness, 132–133, 303–304
    changes, international influence and pressure, 304–305
    changes within China
        legal and psychiatric reform movement, 303
        political psychiatric repression, cracks appearing, 302–303
    forensic psychiatrists, difficult position of, 297–298
Psychiatric evaluation
    British system, 75
    expert evaluations, 165
    judicial appraisal
        draft regulations, 2000, 170–171
        lack of discretion on those to be examined, 171–172
        psychiatric assessors, pressures on, 172
        regulations, 1989, 169–170
        Shanghai Municipal Regulations, 171
Psychiatry *see* **Forensic psychiatry, the Cultural Revolution; General psychiatry in crisis, the Cultural Revolution;**

Political abuse of psychiatry, Soviet and Chinese experience
"Psychopathic hospitals", 91–93
Psychosurgery, involuntary
  caution, need for, 251–253
  experimental psychosurgery, current, 253
  growing use of, 99, 249–250
  results, assessment of, 250–251
Psychotherapy during the Cultural Revolution, 120

Qi Benyu, Anding Hospital "directives", 106–107, 108–109
Qiu Jinyou, case of, administrative corruption exposure
  initial campaign, 260–261
  psychiatric appraisal and committal, 261–262, 282
  wrongful psychiatric incarceration claim, 262–263

Research and methodology
  book's approach to, 15-16, 19
  Gluzman, Dr. Semyon, methodology of, 19-20
Royal College of Psychiatrists
  investigative mission call at WPA Yokohama meeting, 288–289
  resolution for action on China (2001), 282–283
  support for resolution for action on China, 283, 290
Rule of law *See also* Administrative law
  assessing reforms, 43-44, 47-51
  Criminal Procedure Law reforms, 45-46
  development of
    current progress, 46-47
    Jiang Zemin and, 46
    limitations on, 43, 47-49
    low level of consciousness and, 41-42
    minimal level ("thin" rule of law) assessment, 49-50
    normative conceptions ("thick description"), 50-51
  pressures for reform, 44-45
  punishment without crime
    administrative detention, 52-57

arbitrary detention yardstick, 51-52
Russian Federation
  political abuse, impact of reform
  international development of ethics, ix–x
  mistake and abuse, risk of, viii–ix
  reform and rule of law, viii
  UN Convention Against Torture, implementation, 86–87
Russian Society of Psychiatrists, China resolution support, 283

Schizophrenia
  delusional schizophrenia, 201–206
  judicial treatment of, 94–96, 97
  "latent schizophrenia", 96–97
  "sluggish schizophrenia", 94–95, 96, 97
  Yang Desen and, 143–144
Serbski School of Forensic Psychiatry, judicial treatment of insanity, 94–99
Severe medical neglect, 100 *see also* Medical neglect
Shanghai Ankang
  description, 242
  fear and discipline in, 242–244
  institutional model, as, 253–255
  political dissidents, 244
  punishments, 243–244
  Wang Miaogen, case of, 244–245
"Sluggish schizophrenia", 94–95, 96, 97
Soviet Union *see also* Russian Federation
  China, early influence, 93–94
  Gluzman, Semyon Dr., methodology of, 19-20
  influence of, 299–300, 301
  judicial psychiatry and political dissent
    Bukovsky, Vladimir and Dr. Gluzman, Semyon and *A Manual on Psychiatry for Dissenters*, 5
    dissent, 3, 4-6
    individual case-based approach, 19
    reason for, vi–viii, 5
  paranoid psychosis, 177–178
  political abuse of psychiatry
    early reports, iv–v
    inappropriate treatment, realisation of, vii
    reasons for abuse, vi–viii, 5
    United States, impact on, viii–x

United States investigation and report, v–vi
Special Psychiatric Hospitals, description, 241–242
Special Psychiatric Hospitals *see also* **Ankang**
China, change of name to Ankang, 242, 246–247
Soviet Union, of, 241–242

Thought reform, Jia Rubao
mental illness, political causation, 128–129
mental patients, culprits or victims? 129–130
refutation of by Yang Desen, 144–146
thought reform as therapeutic process, 130–131

Ultra-Marxist ideology and mental illness, 132–133, 303–304
United Nations
Convention against Torture, 86, 87
Falun Gong dissent, response to, 234
International Covenant on Civil and Political Rights, 79
Principles for the Protection of Persons with Mental Illness and for Improvement of Mental Health Care, 1991, 22, 80–82
Universal Declaration of Human Rights, 79
Working Group on Arbitrary Detention, Wang Wanxing, Report on, 7-8
United States of America
Russian reform, impact of
international development of ethics, ix–x
mistake and abuse, risk of, viii–ix
reform and rule of law, viii
Soviet Union, investigation and report, v–vi
U.S.S.R. *See* **Soviet Union**

Victims go to court *see* **Ankang case notes 2000-2005, victims go to court**

Wang Chaoru, case of, police custody criteria, 258–259
Wang Fenglai, case of, conspiracy for committal
background details, 276–277
psychiatric appraisal and committal, 277–278
wrongful psychiatric incarceration claim, 278

Wang Fumian, case of, counterrevolutionary behaviour, 192–195
Wang Henglei, case of, death during committal
administrative lawsuit, 268–269
court ruling, 269
death and response, 269–270
Wang Miaogen, case of, self-harm protest, 244–245
Wang Wanxing, case of, political dissident and psychiatric committal
background, 6-7
Beijing Ankang
regime at, 11
summary medical report, 10
Global Initiative on Psychiatry, examination report, 12-13
Human Rights Watch summary of Frankfurt interview, 9, 10–11
"political monomania" and drugs diagnosis, 10-11
release of, 8-9, 12
U.N. Working Group on Arbitrary Detention Report, 7-8
Workers rights activists
Cao Maobing, case of, 212–215
Xue Jifeng, case of, 210–212
World Medical Association (WMA)
psychiatric abuse debate (2001), 284
psychiatric abuse resolution (2002), 284–285
World Psychiatric Association (WPA)
Ankang facilities, request for inspection, xiii, 253, 283, 286–287
China and psychiatric abuse, present situation, 296
Chinese Society of Psychiatry
joint statement, 2004, 294
joint statement, condemnation, 294–296
Declaration of Hawaii, 84–85, 86
Declaration of Madrid, 1996, 22, 85–86, 283, 290
Yokohama meeting (2002)
appeal to vice Premier Mrs. Wu Yi, 291–292
Chinese responses to, 290–291, 292–293

Falun Gong cases, limitation on investigation, 287, 290, 291, 293–294
Royal College of Psychiatrists investigative mission call, 288–289
summary of outcome, Robert van Voren, 289–290

Xue Jifeng, case of, workers rights activists, 210–212

Yan Weibing, case of, Cultural Revolution and feigning mental illness, 113–116

Yang Desen
"hyperdiagnosis", 135-136
"ideological defect" theory, article refuting, 134–138
initial counterattack on ultra-leftist psychiatry, 133–134
mental illness as "ideological defect", insufficiency of, 137–138
mental illness, pathological thoughts before and after, 136

mentally ill people, political responsibility of, 134–135
subjective conjecture and scientific research article
bourgeois worldview not fundamental factor, 142–144
defining real scope of debate, 140
Jia Rubao, refutations of, 144–147
Marxism-Leninism and Mao Zedong Thought, guide not substitute, 145–147
mental illness as common disease, 141–142
mental illness, essential nature of, 139–140
Yang Desen's postscript, 147–149

Zhang Gonglai, case of, political insanity, 216–218
Zhou Caixia, case of, Falun Gong dissent, 227–229
Zhu, Mr, distinguishing a paranoiac from a political dissident
case study of, 196–198
commentary on, 198–200